PHILIP'S

STREET ATLAS

UNRIVALLED DETAIL FROM THE BEST-SELLING ATLAS RANGE*

NAVIGATOR® OXFORDSHIRE

www.philips-maps.co.uk
Published by Philip's, a division of
Octopus Publishing Group Ltd
www.octopusbooks.co.uk
Carmelite House,
50 Victoria Embankment
London EC4Y 0DZ
An Hachette UK Company
www.hachette.co.uk

First edition 2023
First impression 2023
OXFFA

ISBN 978-1-84907-631-9

© Philip's 2023

**Ordnance Survey
Licensed Data**

This product
includes
mapping data
licensed from
Ordnance
Survey® with the permission of the
Controller of His Majesty's Stationery
Office. © Crown copyright 2023.
All rights reserved. Licence number
100011710.

CONTENTS

T0301105

III Key to map symbols

IV Key to map pages

VI Route planning

VIII Major administrative and Postcode boundaries

1 Street maps at 3½ inches to 1 mile

261 Street map of Oxford city centre
at 7 inches to 1 mile

262 Index of towns, villages, streets, hospitals, industrial estates, railway stations, schools, shopping centres, universities and places of interest

NAVIGATOR
OXFORDSHIRE

STREET ATLAS

UNRIVALLED DETAIL FROM THE BEST-SELLING ATLAS RANGE

PHILIP'S

CONTENTS

Key to map symbols

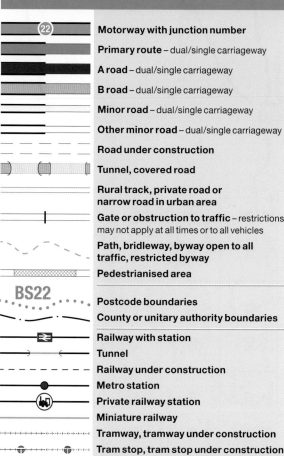

	Motorway with junction number
	Primary route – dual/single carriageway
	A road – dual/single carriageway
	B road – dual/single carriageway
	Minor road – dual/single carriageway
	Other minor road – dual/single carriageway
	Road under construction
	Tunnel, covered road
	Rural track, private road or narrow road in urban area
	Gate or obstruction to traffic – restrictions may not apply at all times or to all vehicles
	Path, bridleway, byway open to all traffic, restricted byway
	Pedestrianised area
BS22	Postcode boundaries
	County or unitary authority boundaries
	Railway with station
	Tunnel
	Railway under construction
	Metro station
	Private railway station
	Miniature railway
	Tramway, tramway under construction
	Tram stop, tram stop under construction
	Bus, coach station

	Ambulance station		
	Coastguard station		
	Fire station		
	Police station		
	Accident and Emergency entrance to hospital		
H	Hospital		
+	Place of worship		
i	Information centre – open all year		
	Shopping centre, parking		
P&R / PO	Park and Ride, Post Office		
	Camping site, caravan site		
	Golf course, picnic site		
ROMAN FORT	Non-Roman antiquity, Roman antiquity		
Univ	Important buildings, schools, colleges, universities and hospitals		
	Woods, built-up area		
River Medway	Water name		
	River, weir		
	Stream		
	Canal, lock, tunnel		
	Water		
	Tidal water		

58 / 87 / 246 **Adjoining page indicators and overlap bands** – the colour of the arrow and band indicates the scale of the adjoining or overlapping page (see scales below)

The dark grey border on the inside edge of some pages indicates that the mapping does not continue onto the adjacent page

The small numbers around the edges of the maps identify the 1-kilometre National Grid lines

Abbreviations

Acad	Academy	Meml	Memorial
Allot Gdns	Allotments	Mon	Monument
Cemy	Cemetery	Mus	Museum
C Ctr	Civic centre	Obsy	Observatory
CH	Club house	Pal	Royal palace
Coll	College	PH	Public house
Crem	Crematorium	Recn Gd	Recreation ground
Ent	Enterprise	Resr	Reservoir
Ex H	Exhibition hall	Ret Pk	Retail park
Ind Est	Industrial Estate	Sch	School
IRB Sta	Inshore rescue boat station	Sh Ctr	Shopping centre
Inst	Institute	TH	Town hall / house
Ct	Law court	Trad Est	Trading estate
L Ctr	Leisure centre	Univ	University
LC	Level crossing	W Twr	Water tower
Liby	Library	Wks	Works
Mkt	Market	YH	Youth hostel

Enlarged maps only

	Railway or bus station building
	Place of interest
	Parkland

The map scale on the pages numbered in blue is 3½ inches to 1 mile
5.52 cm to 1 km • 1:18 103

0 ¼ mile ½ mile ¾ mile 1 mile
0 250m 500m 750m 1km

The map scale on the pages numbered in red is 7 inches to 1 mile
11.04 cm to 1 km • 1:9051

0 220yds 440yds 660yds ½ mile
0 125m 250m 375m 500m

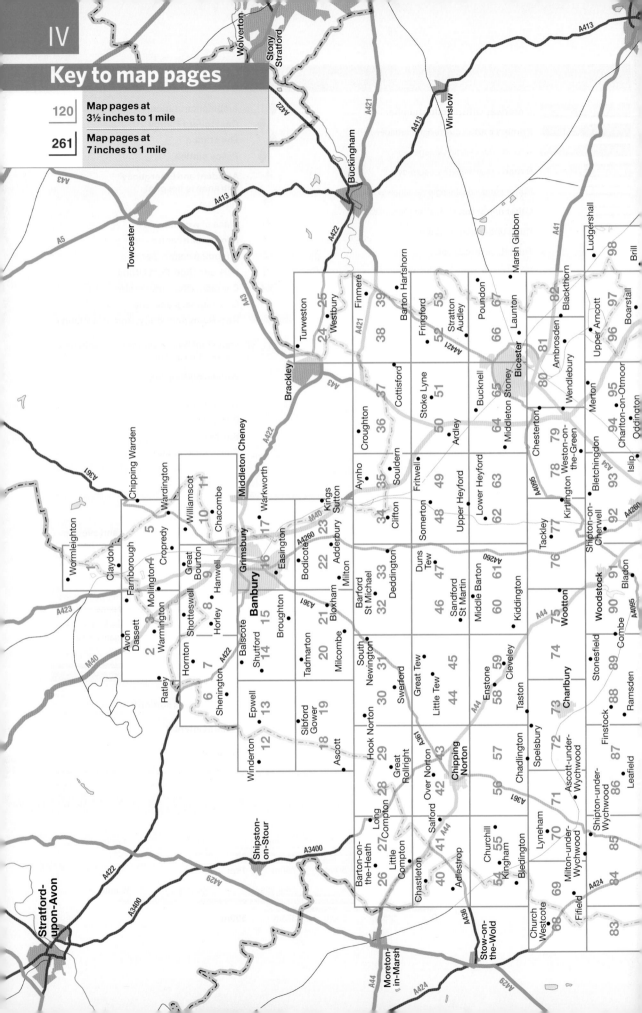

Key to map pages

120	Map pages at 3½ inches to 1 mile
261	Map pages at 7 inches to 1 mile

Aylesbury

Haddenham

Princes Risborough

Chinnor

Henley-on-Thames

Twyford
Wargrave
Sonning
Caversham
Reading

Thame
Towersey 148 149
Henton
130

Long Crendon 128 129
Shabbington
Chinnor 168 169
Kingston Blount
Bledlow Ridge
Stokenchurch 188 189
Beacon's Bottom
Fawley 226
Lower Assendon 244
Shiplake
Wargrave 255

Tiddington 146 147
Wheatley 144 145
Cuddesdon
Sydenham 166 167
Aston Rowant
Lewknor
Watlington 186 187
Greenfield 206 207
Middle Assendon
Shepherd's Green 242 243
Sonning Common 252 253
Tokers Green
238 259 260

Long Crendon
Wormingall 126 127
Holton
Horspath 142 143
Garsington
Tetsworth
Great Haseley 164 165
Stoke Talmage
Brightwell Baldwin 184 185
Ewelme 204 205
Crowmarsh Gifford
Nettlebed 224 225
Stoke Row
Nuffield 222 223
Woodcote 240 241
Whitchurch Hill 250 251
Pangbourne
Whitchurch 256 257

Beckley 110 111
Stanton St John 124 125
Headington
Cowley
Little Milton 162 163
Stadhampton
Chalgrove
Berinsfield 182 183
Dorchester
Long Wittenham
Warborough 202 203
Benson 222
Wallingford 220 221
Cholsey
Aston Tirrold
South Stoke 238 239
Moulsford
Goring 248 249

Noke
Marston 108 109
Oxford 261
Botley
North Hinksey
Kennington 140 141
Sandford-on-Thames 160 161
Radley
Culham 180 181
Sutton Courtenay
Didcot 200 201
Brightwell-cum-Sotwell
Aston Upthorpe 218 219
Blewbury
Upton 236 237
Aldworth 247

Yarnton 106 107
Wolvercote
Cumnor 138 139
Northmoor
Wootton 158 159
Appleton
Marcham 178 179
Drayton
Milton 198 199
Steventon
Milton Hill
East Hendred 216 217
Harwell
Chilton 234 235
West Ilsley

Freeland
Cassington 120 121
Eynsham
Sutton 136 137
Stanton Harcourt
Standlake
Kingston Bagpuize 156 157
Longworth
Garford 176 177
East Hanney
West Hanney 196 197
Grove
Denchworth
Wantage
Ardington 214 215
Letcombe Regis
Childrey 232 233
Letcombe Bassett
246

South Leigh 104 105
Witney 118 119
Ducklington
Cote
Clanfield 154 155
Hinton Waldrist
Buckland
Charney Bassett 174 175
Stanford in the Vale 194 195
Baulking
Sparsholt 212 213
Letcombe Bassett 230 231

Minster Lovell 102 103
Curbridge
Brize Norton 116 117
Aston
Bampton 134 135
Littleworth 152 153
Faringdon
Great Coxwell 172 173
Longcot 192 193
Uffington
Woolstone 210 211
Ashbury 228 229
245
Baydon

Burford 100 101
Shilton
Carterton 114 115
Alvescot
Langford
Black Bourton 132 133
Kelmscott
Buscot 150 151
Lechlade-on-Thames
Watchfield 170 171
Shrivenham
Bourton 208 209
Bishopstone 227

Westwell 99
Eastleach Martin
Filkins
Southrop 113 131
Highworth 190 191
208

Swindon

Reading

Scale
0 5 10 miles
0 5 10 15 km

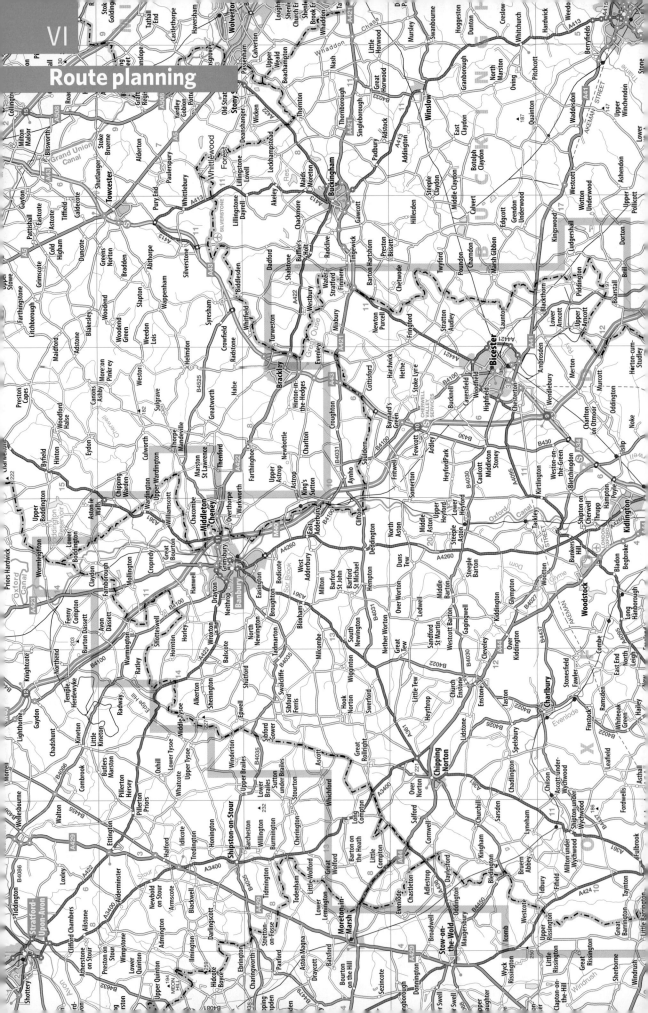

County and unitary authority boundaries
District boundaries
Postcode boundaries
Area covered by this atlas

Scale
0   5   10   15 km
0   5   10 miles

Warwickshire
Northamptonshire
Gloucester-shire
Buckinghamshire
Wiltshire
West Berkshire
Wokingham
Swindon
Reading

Oxfordshire
West Oxfordshire
Cherwell
Vale of White Horse
South Oxfordshire
Oxford

Mollington
OX17
OX16
Banbury
OX15
Bloxham
Hook Norton
CV36
Westbury
Aynho
NN13
GL56
Adlestrop
Chipping Norton
OX7
Fringford
OX27
OX25
Upper Heyford
OX26
Bicester
Tackley
Charlbury
OX20
Woodstock
Stonesfield
OX25
Ambrosden
Ludgershall
GL 54
OX5
Kidlington
HP18
Burford
OX29
Witney
Eynsham
OX28
OX18
Carterton
OX3
OX33
Shabbington
HP17
OX2
Wheatley
Thame
GL7
Bampton
Oxford
HP27
OX1
OX4
OX9
Chinnor
Lechlade-on-Thames
Garsington
OX44
OX39
Stadhampton
HP14
OX13
Abingdon-on-Thames
Stokenchurch
Marcham
Dorchester
Watlington
Faringdon
SN7
OX14
OX49
Highworth
Didcot
OX10
Wallingford
Nettlebed
SN6
Uffington
Wantage
Harwell
RG9
Shrivenham
OX12
Chilton
OX11
Henley-on-Thames
Bishopstone
RG17
RG20
Goring
Woodcote
Sonning Common
RG 10
SN4
RG8
RG4
SN8
Reading

SP
SU
200

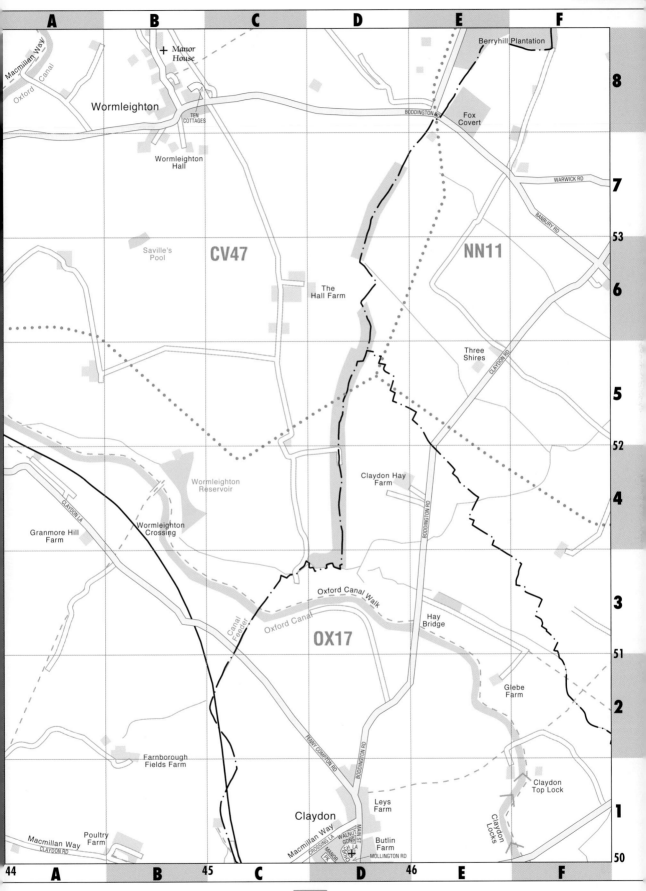

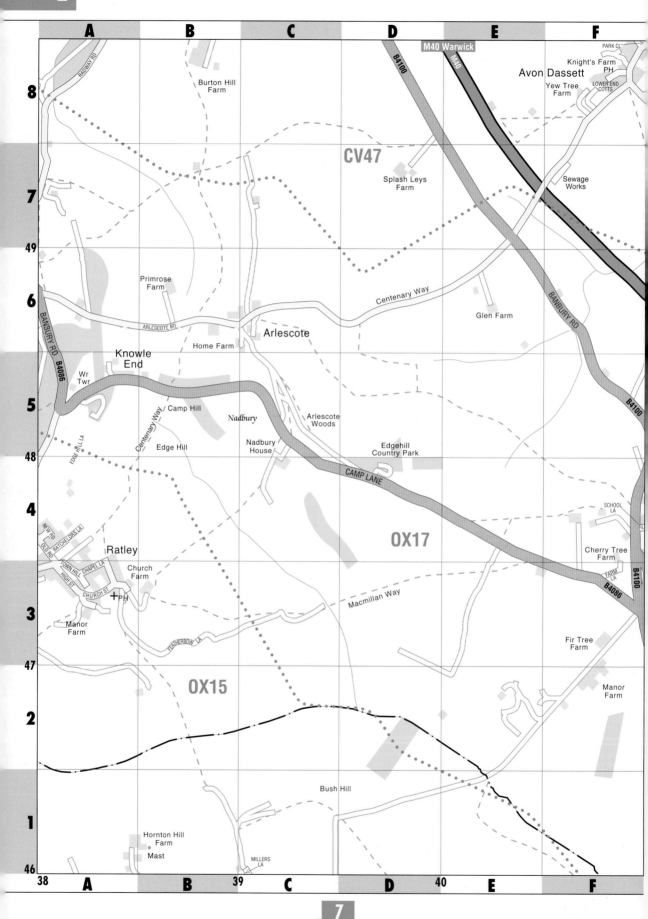

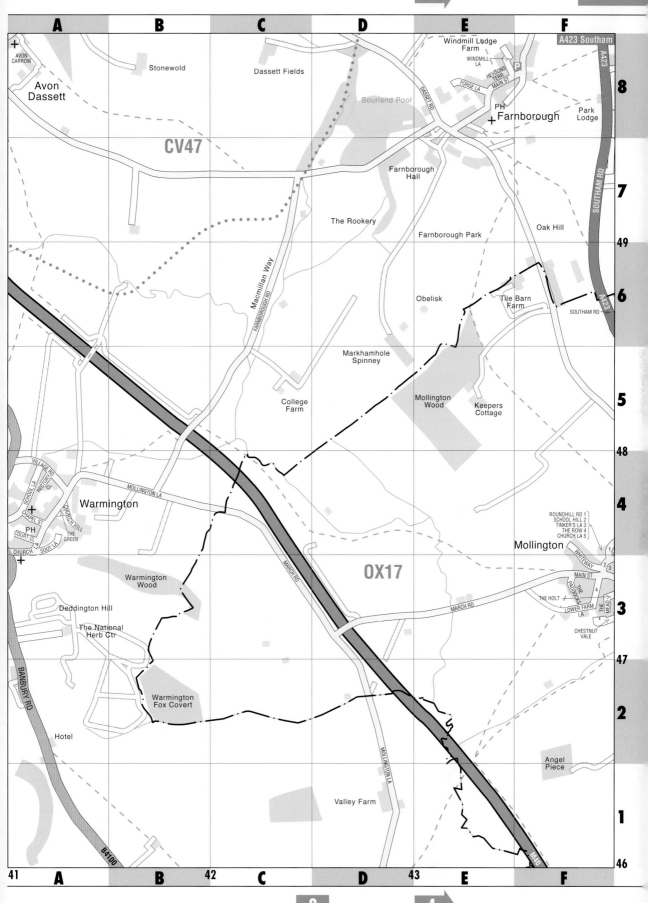

A B C D E F

AVON CARROW

Stonewold

Avon Dassett

Dassett Fields

Windmill Lodge Farm

WINDMILL LA

HEYDONS TERR

FORGE LA

MAIN ST

P

8

Sourland Pool

DASSETT RD

PH

Farnborough

Park Lodge

CV47

Farnborough Hall

A423

SOUTHAM RD

7

The Rookery

Farnborough Park

49

Oak Hill

Macmillan Way

FARNBOROUGH RD

Obelisk

Tile Barn Farm

A423

6

SOUTHAM RD

Markhamhole Spinney

Mollington Wood

Keepers Cottage

5

College Farm

48

VILLAGE RD

SCHOOL LA

RECTORY CL

MOLLINGTON LA

Warmington

CHURCH HILL

CHAPEL ST

PH

COURT CL

SOOT LA

THE GREEN

CHURCH LA

ROUNDHILL RD 1
SCHOOL HILL 2
TINKER'S LA 3
THE ROW 4
CHURCH LA 5

4

1,5

Mollington

WHITEWAY

2,3

MARCH RD

OX17

MAIN ST

THE PADDOCKS

4

THE HOLT

LOWER FARM LA

THE MEAD

A423

3

Warmington Wood

Deddington Hill

March Rd

CHESTNUT VALE

The National Herb Ctr

47

BANBURY RD

Warmington Fox Covert

Hotel

2

MOLLINGTON LA

Angel Piece

Valley Farm

1

A40

B4100

46

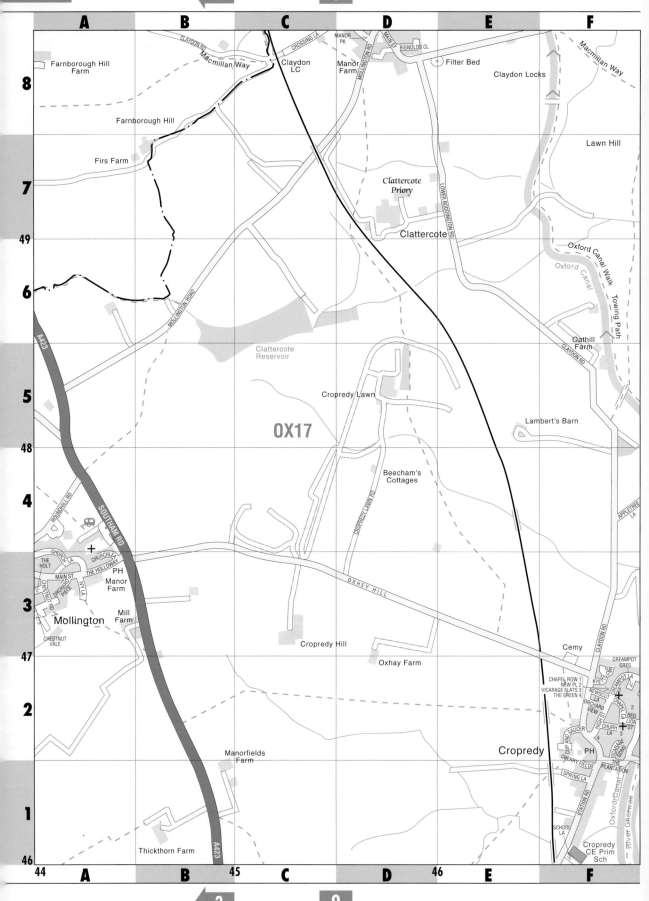

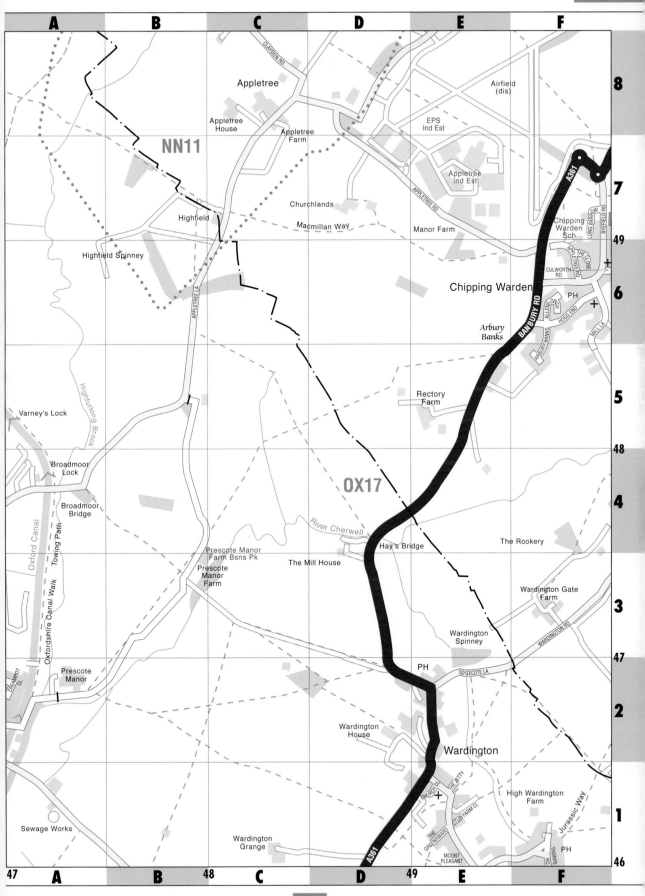

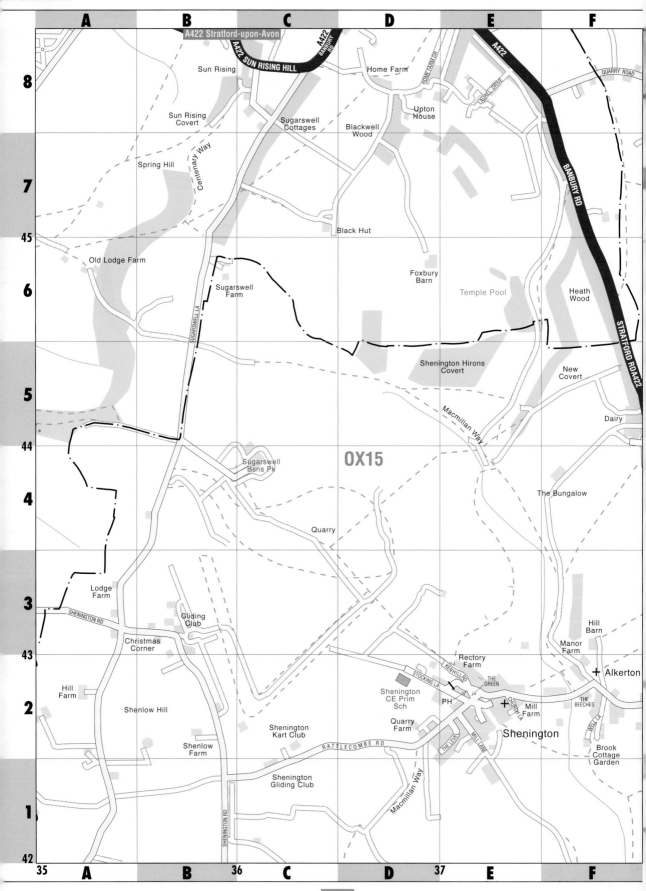

OX15

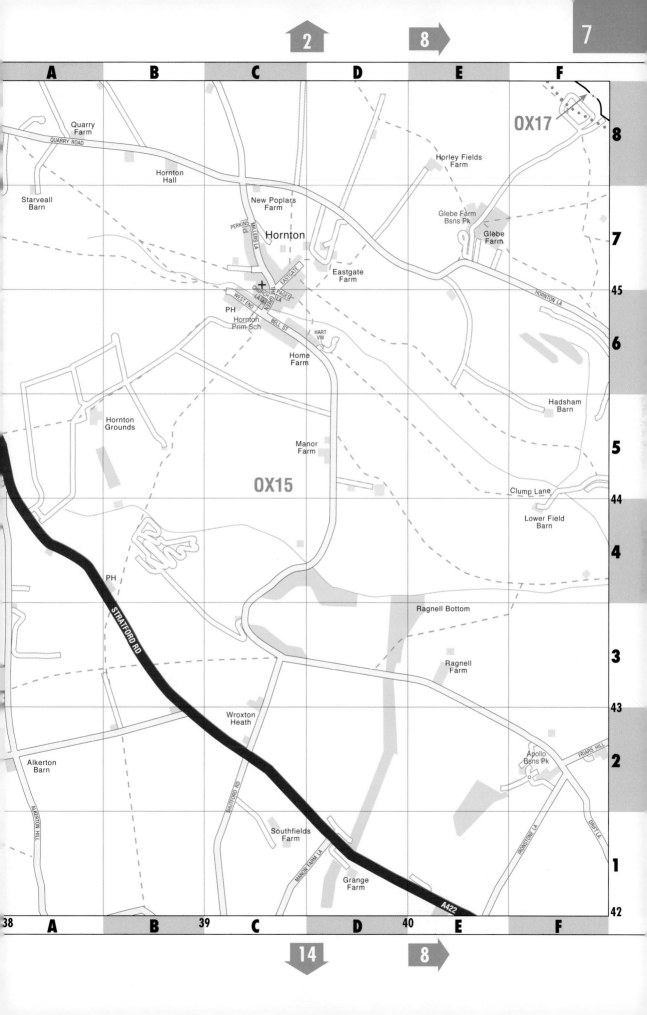

A B C D E F

8

7

45

6

5

44

4

OX15

3

43

2

1

42

41 A B 42 C D 43 E F

B4100

M40

Slated Barn

Slade Barn

Laurel Farm

MOLLINGTON RD

MOLLINGTON LA

BAKEHOUSE LA

BURY CT LA

Bury Court Farm

BANBURY RD

BACK HILL

SNIPE LA

NEW LA

MIDDLE LA

CORONATION LA

CHURCH LA

CHURCH LA

Shotteswell

Airstrip

OX17

Sor Brook

Hadsham House

Manor Farm

HORNTON LA

Clump Lane

Horley House

Water Tower

Hanwell

SPRINGFIELD

HANWELL CT

ROSE COTT

MAIN ST

PARK CL

PH

CHURCH LA

SACKVILLE CT

GULLICOTE LA

Hanwell Castle

Park Farm

LITTLE LA

MANOR ORCH

PH

LANE CL

OLD MANOR CT

Bramshill Barn

GULLIVER'S CL

WROXTON LA

Horley

THE OLD COUNCIL HOS

THE COUNCIL HOS

WARWICK RD

RIBSTON CL 1
PARSLEY PL 2
WINTER GDNS WY 3
BULLERS ST 4
ST VERNON WY 5

DE LA WARR RND

BISMORE RD

WATTS RD

NICKLING RD

HANA CL

DE LA WARR RND

NICKLING PL

JENKINSON RD

BAXTER DR

DUKES MEADOW DR

SAGE CL

FRIARS HILL

HORLEY PATH RD

Drayton Lodge

RIBSTONE PL

CH

KINGERLEE RD 1
JONES WY 2
GREVILLE RD 3
JARVIS CIRCLE 4
BUTTS FIELD 5
ACRES FIELD 6
TOWNS FIELD 7

WALKER RD

WINSTON DR

ELLISON DR

POULTER RD

Cemy

Lord's Spinney

QUEEN'S CRES

OX16

HERMON RD

WARWICK PK

FIRTREE CL

B4100

WINCHELSEA CL

CHEVIOT WAY

ROMNEY RD

HORSHAM CL

SUSSEX CL

HIGHLANDS

BARCOMBE

DRIFT LA

HORLEY PATH RD

SILVER ST

A422

F1
1 HEREFORD WAY
2 GUERNSEY WAY
3 JERSEY DR
4 SUSSEX DR

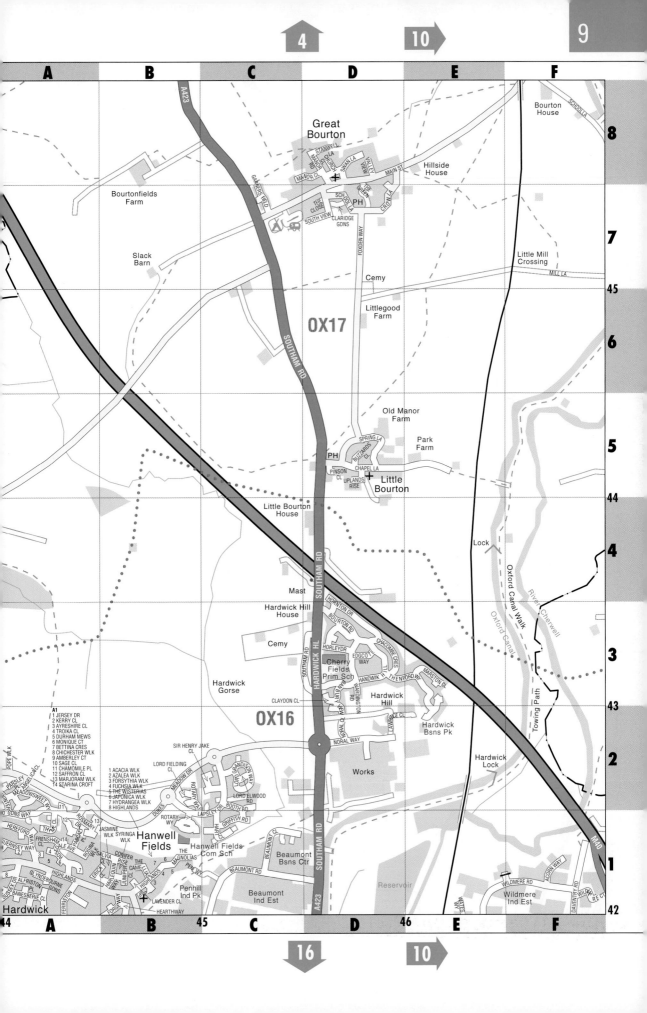

A B C D E F

8

Lower Lodge
CROPREDY LA
Williamscot
Williamscot House
Village Spinney
A361
Mount Pleasant
Chacombe RD
Barn Farm
Bennetts Farm
Trent Farm
CHELMSCOTE ROW
Upper Wardington
THE COUNCIL HOUSES
THORPE RD

Weir
THORPE RD

7
SCHOOL LA
Oxford Canal
Oxford Canal Wlk

WILLIAMSCOT HILL
Dawkins's Barn
Chacombe RD
Jurassic Way

45

6
Peewit Farm
MILL LA
River Cherwell
Williamscot Hill Farm
Bell Land

5
Redlunch Barn
Marsh Barn Farm
Coton Farm
Bridge Lake Fisheries
Works

44
OX17
The Priory
WARDINGTON RD
SILVER ST N
SILVER ST
BEAN FURLONG
POPLARS RD
Chacombe
Chacombe CE VA Primary Acad
CHURCH LA
PH
WESLEY RD
BENNETT CL
THORPE RD
BANBURY RD
THE RING
THORNHILL
MIDDLETON RD

4
BANBURY RD

3
DAVENTRY RD
Chacombe House
CH

43
Castle Farm

2
Seale's Farm
Jurassic Way

OX16
Yew Tree Cottage
THORPE RD
THE THINGS
CHACOMBE RD
CHENEY GDNS
MILLERS WAY
KINGS STILE
TANNERS CL
MICHAELMAS
STANWELL LEA 1
STANWELL DR 2
DRAYSONS CL
LEATHER LA
CHENEY CT
GLOVERS LA
CHURCH LA
RECTORY LA
HIGH ST
Windmill Farm
Huscote Farm

1
M40
A361
B4525

42
47 A 48 B C 49 D E F

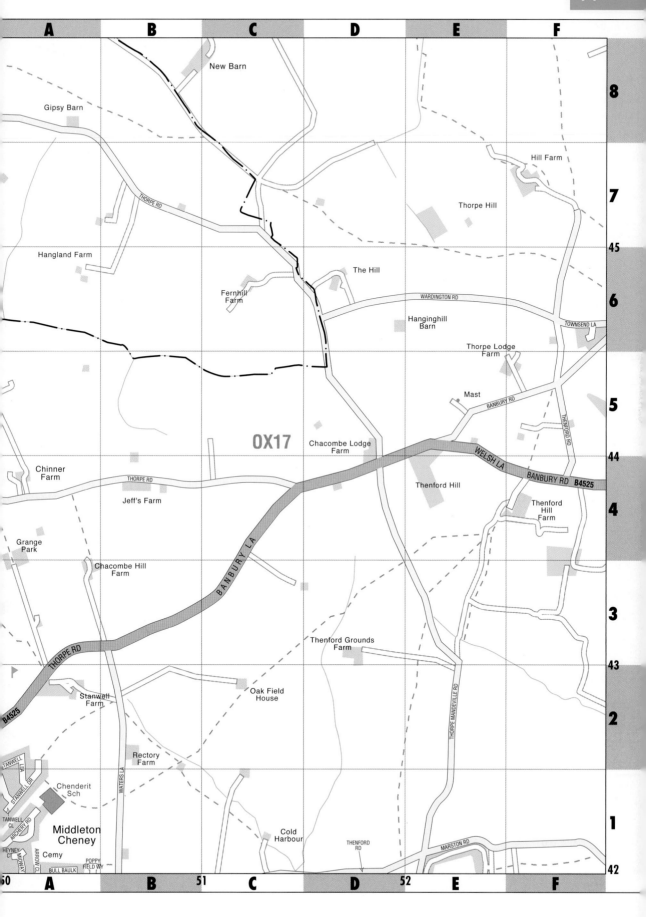

New Barn

Gipsy Barn

THORPE RD

Hangland Farm

Fernhill Farm

The Hill

Hill Farm

Thorpe Hill

WARDINGTON RD

Hanginghill Barn

Thorpe Lodge Farm

TOWNSEND LA

Mast

BANBURY RD

THENFORD RD

Chacombe Lodge Farm

OX17

Chinner Farm

THORPE RD

Jeff's Farm

Thenford Hill

WELSH LA

BANBURY RD B4525

Thenford Hill Farm

Grange Park

Chacombe Hill Farm

BANBURY LA

Thenford Grounds Farm

THORPE RD

B4525

Stanwell Farm

Oak Field House

WATERS LA

THORPE MANDEVILLE RD

Rectory Farm

TANWELL LEA

STANWELL DR

Chenderit Sch

TANWELL CL

Middleton Cheney

ARCHERY RD

HEYNEY CT

ARROW CL

MIDWAY

Cemy

BULL BAULK

POPPY FIELD WY

Cold Harbour

THENFORD RD

MARSTON RD

A B 51 C 52 D E F

50 A B C D E F

8 7 45 6 5 44 4 3 43 2 42 1

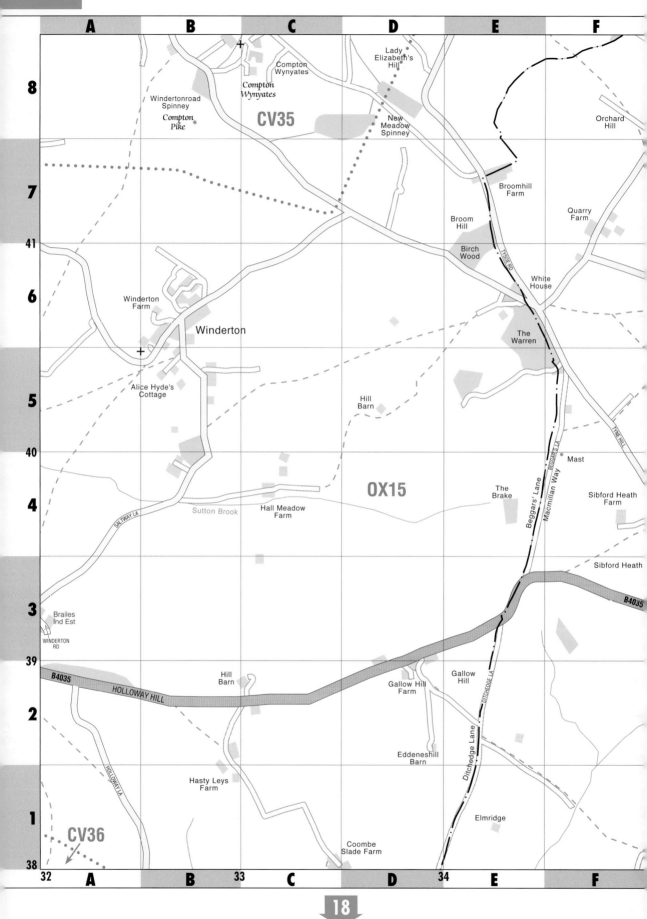

A B C D E F

8
Windertonroad
Spinney
Compton
Pike
Compton
Wynyates
Compton
Wynyates
CV35
Lady
Elizabeth's
Hill
New
Meadow
Spinney
Orchard
Hill

7
Broomhill
Farm
Broom
Hill
Birch
Wood
Quarry
Farm
White
House

41

6
Winderton
Farm
Winderton
The
Warren

5
Alice Hyde's
Cottage
Hill
Barn
TYSOE RD

40
Mast
The
Brake
OX15
Sibford Heath
Farm

4
SALTWAY LA
Sutton Brook
Hall Meadow
Farm
Beggars' Lane
BEGGAR'S LA
Macmillan Way
TYNE HILL

3
Brailes
Ind Est
WINDERTON
RD
Sibford Heath
B4035

39
B4035
HOLLOWAY HILL
Hill
Barn
Gallow Hill
Farm
Gallow
Hill
DITCHEDGE LA

2
Eddeneshill
Barn
Ditchedge Lane
HOLLOWAY LA

1
CV36
Hasty Leys
Farm
Elmridge
Coombe
Slade Farm

38
32 A B 33 C D 34 E F

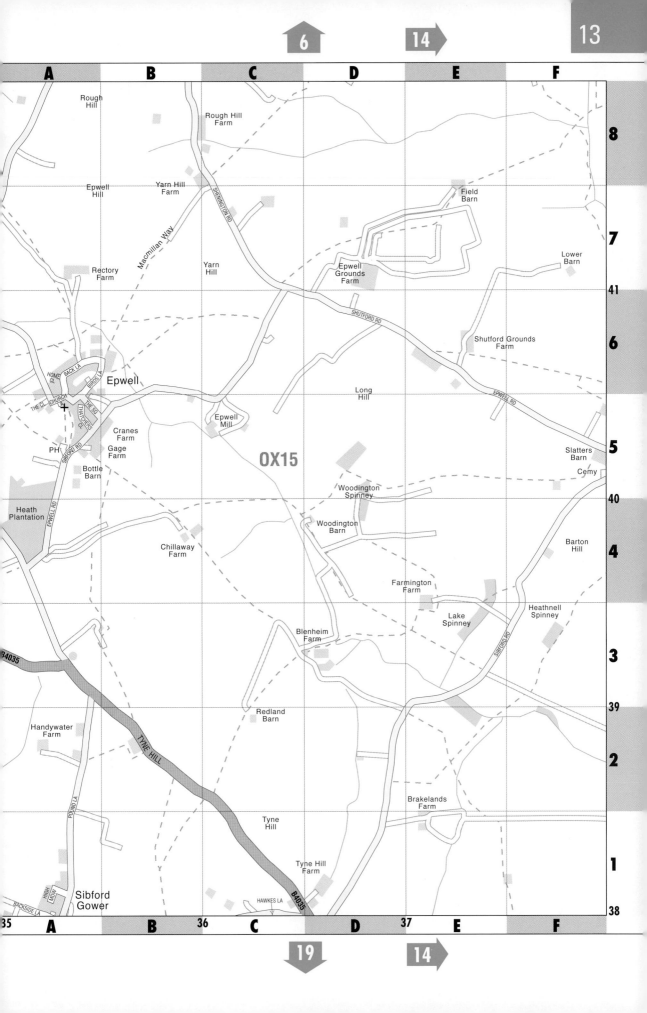

A · B · C · D · E · F

8

IRONSTONE LA
STRATFORD RD
A422

Ash Farm
PH
SHUTFORD RD
CHAPEL LA
MIDDLE LA
Balscote
THE HEDGES
Manor House
Priory Farm
MANOR FARM LA
Guide Post

Alkerton Grounds
ALKERTON HILL

7

41

Sewage Works

Maidenhill Cottage
Padsdon Bottom
Castle Bank

6

Balscote Mill
Shutford
PLCT RD
THE PLAIN RD
Beggars' Barn
Wroxton Mill
Claydonhill Covert

THE DAIRYGROUND
COOK'S HILL LA
LOWER END
THE MALT HOUSE
THE GREEN
WEST ST
THE DAIRYGROUND
IVY LA
BANBURY HILL
Claydon Hill

5

Cemy
Banbury Rd
Five Ways
BANBURY RD
Tythe Farm

EPWELL RD
SIBFORD RD
HIGH ST
THE RICKYARD
CHURCH LA
PH
Manor House

40

Barton Hill Farm
OX15
Shutford Bridge
Claydon Hill Bungalow
SHUTFORD RD
Welshcroft Hill

4

Round Hill
Jester's Barn
Jester's Hill
SHUTFORD ROAD
Broughton Grounds Farm

3

Madmarston Hill
Langley Hill

39

Castle Brow

2

Upper Lea Farm
Sandfine Wood
SANDFINE RD

Swalcliffe Mill (dis)
SWALCLIFFE LEA
Swalcliffe Lea
Fulling Mill Farm

1

GREEN LA
Preedys Farm

38

38 · A · 39 · B · C · D · 40 · E · F

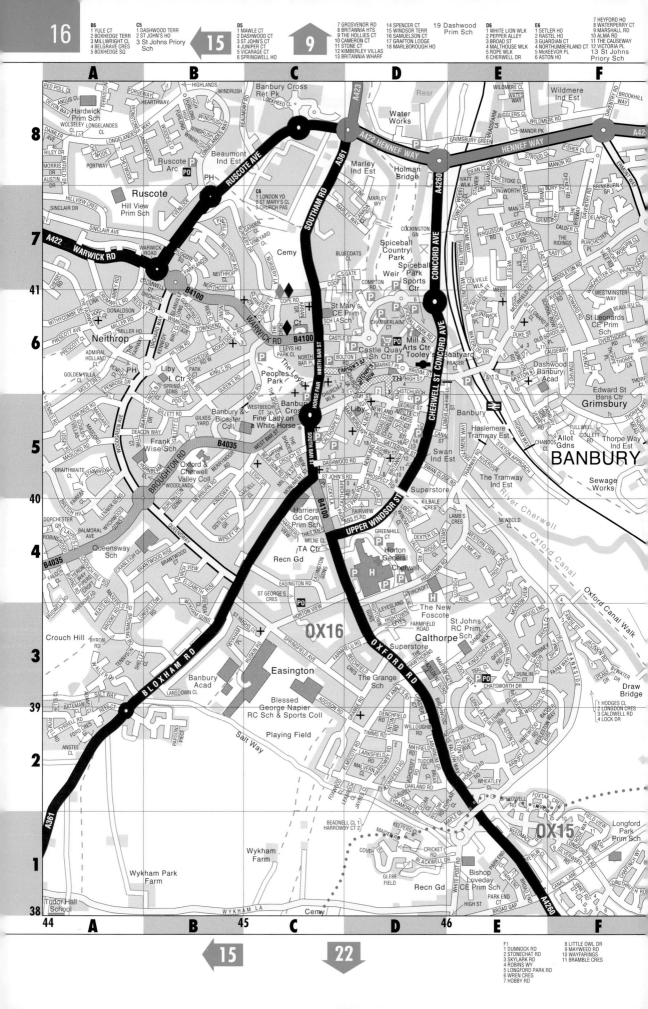

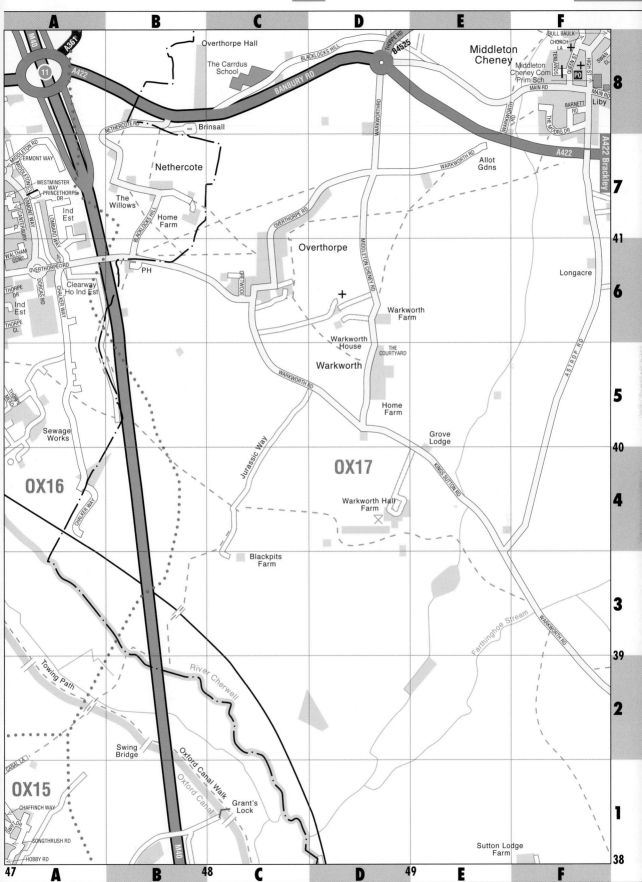

M40
A361
A422
11

Overthorpe Hall
The Carrdus School
Blacklocks Hill
BANBURY RD
THORPE RD
B4525
Middleton Cheney
BULL BAULK
CHURCH LA
QUEEN ST
HIGH ST
SWAN CL
Middleton Cheney Com Prim Sch
PO
MAIN RD
Liby
BARNETT RD
THE MAJORS DR

NETHERCOTE RD
Brinsall
WARKWORTH RD
WARKWORTH RD
Allot Gdns
A422
A422 Brackley

MIDDLETON RD
ERMONT WAY
WESTMINSTER WAY
PRINCETHORPE DR
The Willows
Home Farm
Nethercote
BLACKLOCKS HILL
OVERTHORPE RD
MIDDLETON CHENEY RD
Overthorpe
Longacre

EMONT WAY
CANTERBURY
Ind Est
LOMBARD WAY
WALTHAM GDNS
OVERTHORPE ORD
PH
CHETWODE
Warkworth Farm
Warkworth House
THE COURTYARD

ASTROP RD
THORPE DR
DORCAS RD
CHALKER WAY
Ind Est
THORPE CL
Clearway Ho Ind Est
WARKWORTH RD
Warkworth
Home Farm

Sewage Works
Grove Lodge

KINGS SUTTON RD

OX16
OX17

Jurassic Way
CHALKER WAY

Warkworth Hall Farm

Blackpits Farm

WARKWORTH RD
Farthinghoe Stream

Towing Path
River Cherwell

Swing Bridge
Oxford Canal Walk
Oxford Canal
OX15
CHAFFINCH WAY
SWIFT DR
Grant's Lock
SONGTHRUSH RD
HOBBY RD
Sutton Lodge Farm

CANAL LA

8
7
41
6
5
40
4
3
39
2
1
38

47 48 49

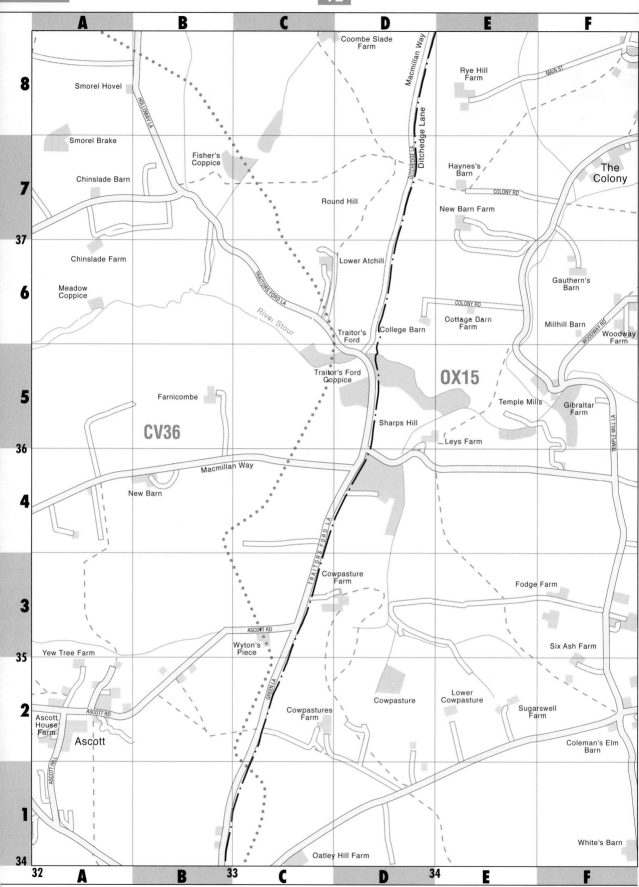

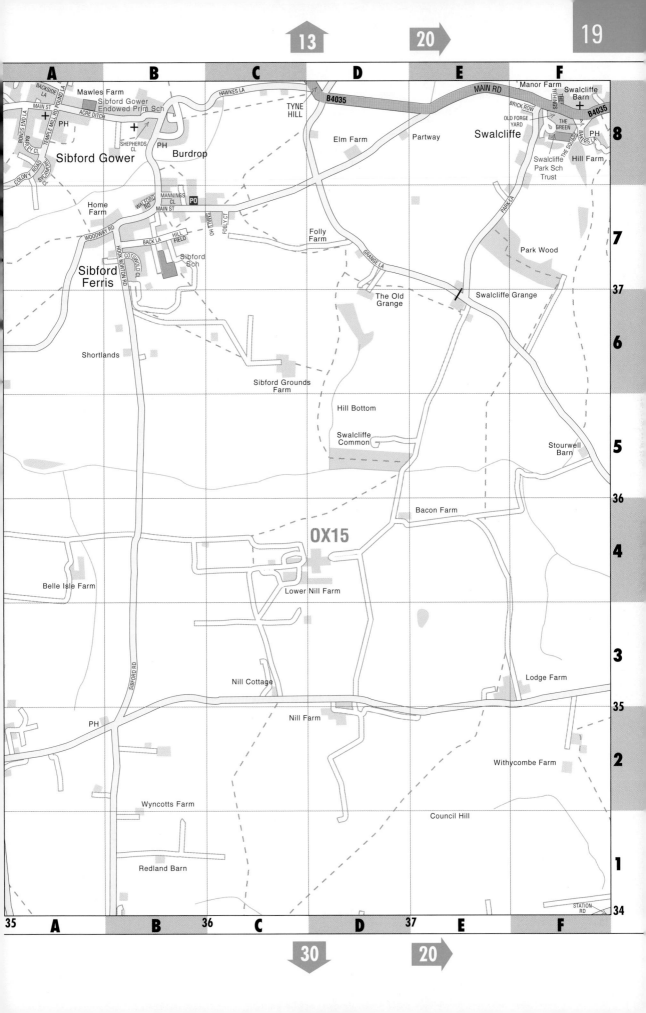

A   **B**   **C**   **D**   **E**   **F**

B4035 MAIN RD SWALCLIFFE RD

GREEN LA

USHERCOMBE VIEW

MAIN ST

OLD GLEBE

BAKERS LA

PH

8

Home Farm

Brick Farm

CHURCH FURLONG

Tadmarton

Austins Farm

BROOKFIELD RISE

M A I N R D

SHUTFORD RD

Five Acres Farm

HOLLOW RD

B4035

7

DRIFT ACRE

High Meadow Farm

Lower Tadmarton

TADMARTON RD

37

Ushercombe Barn

Lower Tadmarton Farm

Ushercoombe Copse

6

Tadmarton Heath

Ushercombe Farm

36

OX15

4

CH

Rye Hill

Highways Farm

Fern Hill

3

Wigginton Heath

CH

35

Ryehill Barn

Cedar Bungalow

2

OAK FARM DR

OAK FARM CL

THE OLD COUNCIL HOS

MAIN RD

HEATH CL

PH

THE GREEN

Resr

Lessor Farm

STATION RD

1

The Waterfowl Sanctuary & Children's Farm

Brickfield Farm

34

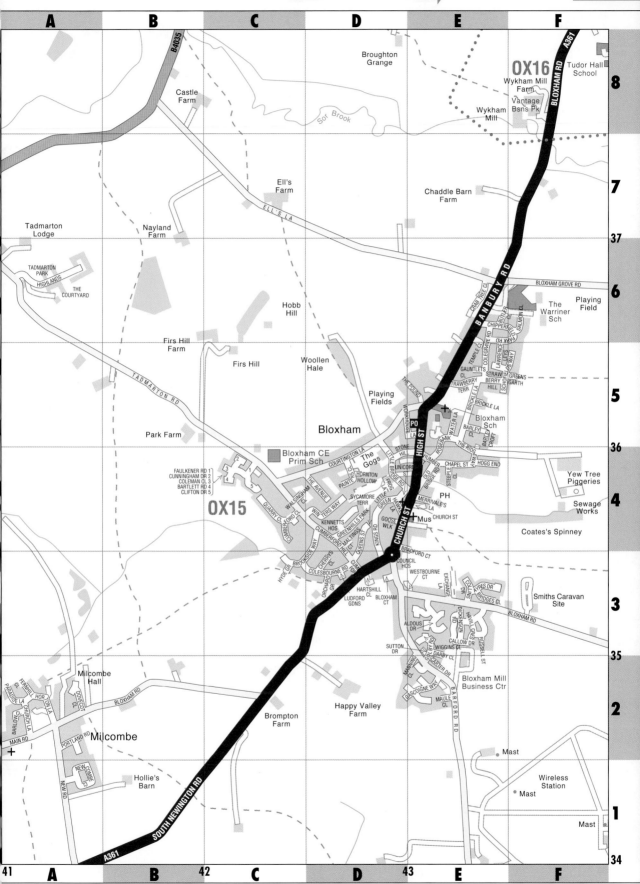

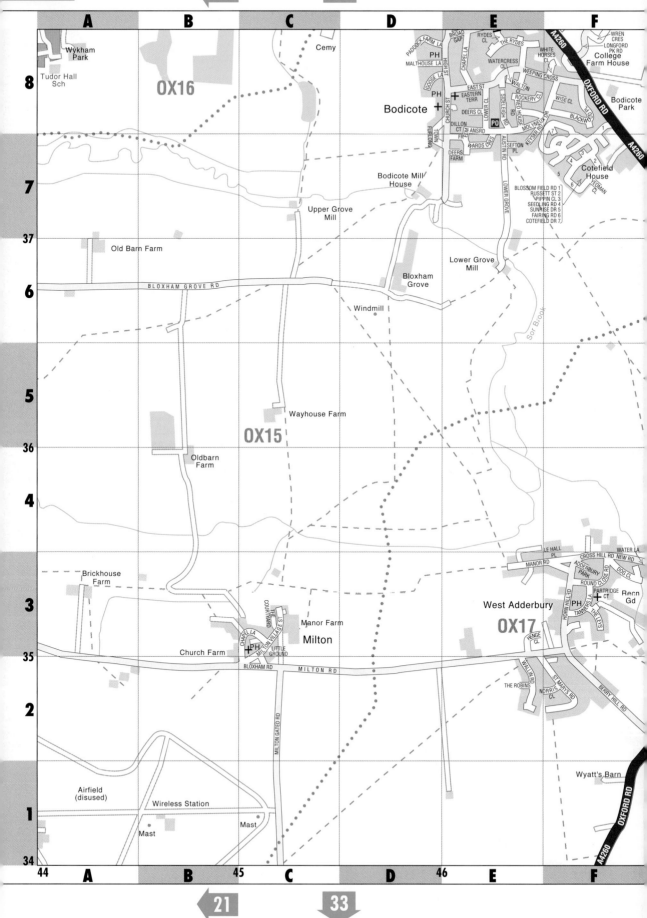

OX16

Wykham Park

Tudor Hall Sch

8

Cemy

7

Bodicote Mill House

Upper Grove Mill

37

Old Barn Farm

6

BLOXHAM GROVE RD

Bloxham Grove

Windmill

Lower Grove Mill

Sor Brook

5

Wayhouse Farm

OX15

36

Oldbarn Farm

4

Brickhouse Farm

3

West Adderbury

OX17

Manor Farm

Milton

35

Church Farm

2

Bloxham Rd

Milton Rd

The Robins

1

Airfield (disused)

Wireless Station

Mast

Mast

Wyatt's Barn

34

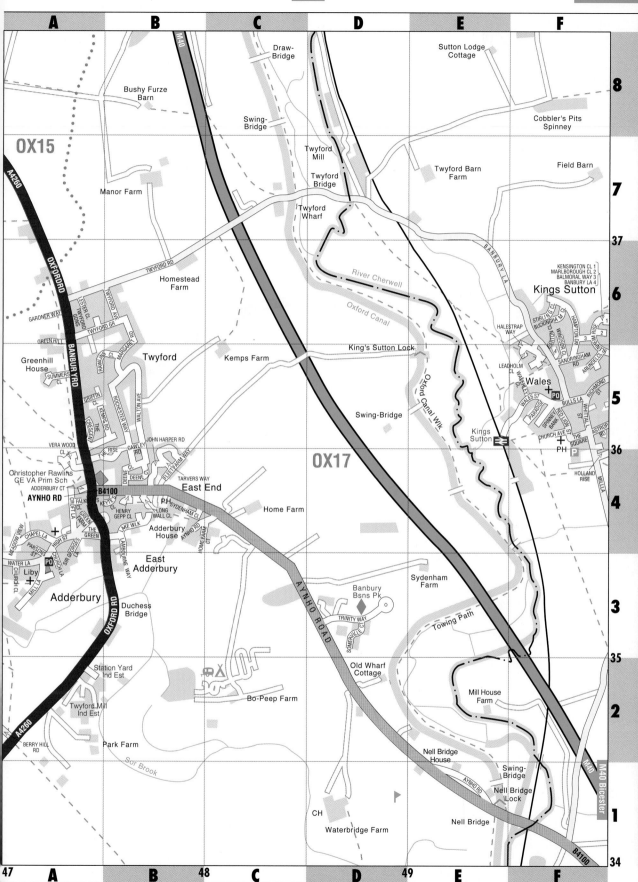

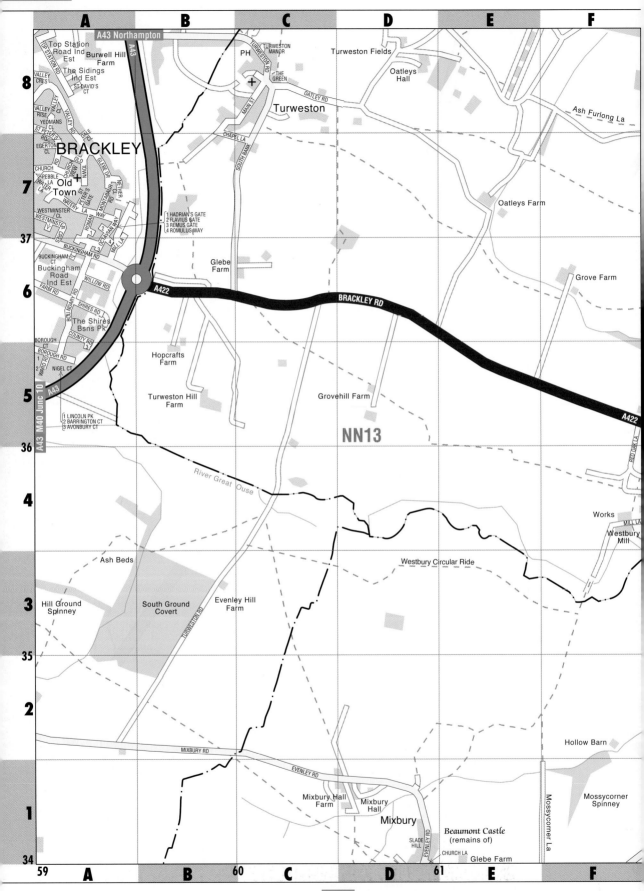

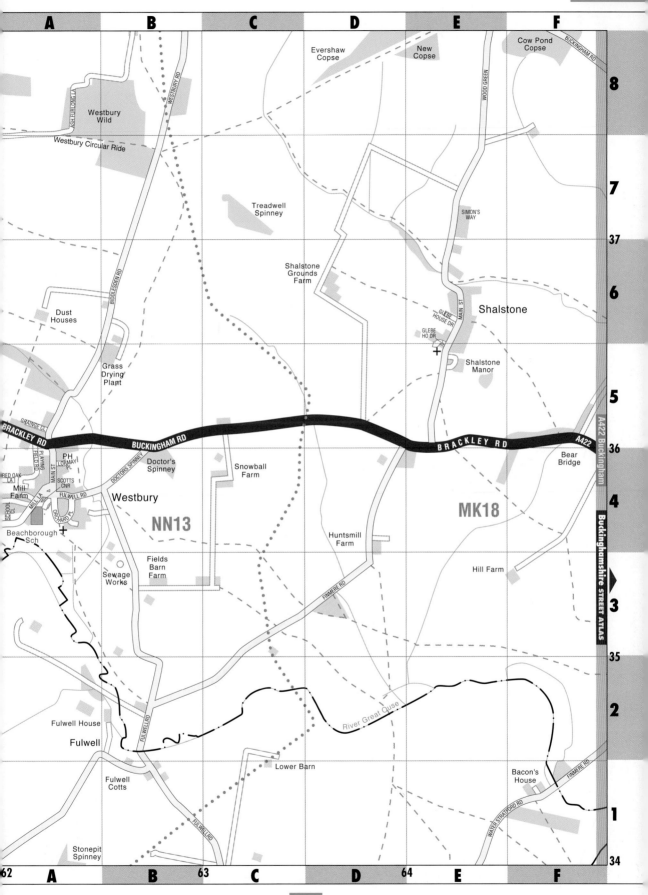

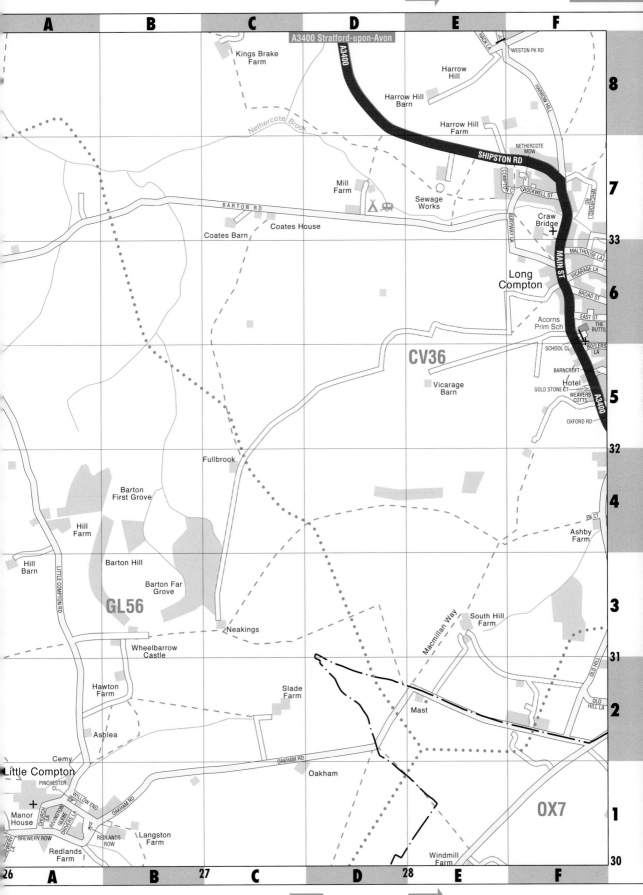

A B C D E F

8

7

33

6

5

32

4

3

31

2

1

30

A3400 Stratford-upon-Avon

Kings Brake Farm

Nethercote Brook

Harrow Hill

Harrow Hill Barn

Harrow Hill Farm

HACK LA

WESTON PK RD

HARROW HILL

SHIPSTON RD

NETHERCOTE MDW

WHICHFORD RD

Mill Farm

Sewage Works

COMPTON CT

CROCKWELL ST

BURWAY LA

Craw Bridge

MAIN ST

MALTHOUSE LA

VICARAGE LA

BARTON RD

Coates House

Coates Barn

Long Compton

BROAD ST

EAST ST

CV36

Acorns Prim Sch

THE BUTTS

SCHOOL CL

BUTLERS LA

BARNCROFT

Vicarage Barn

GOLD STONE CT

Hotel

WEAVERS COTTS

A3400

OXFORD RD

Fullbrook

Barton First Grove

Hill Farm

PK CT

Ashby Farm

Hill Barn

LITTLE COMPTON RD

Barton Hill

Barton Far Grove

GL56

Neakings

Macmillan Way

South Hill Farm

Wheelbarrow Castle

OLD HILL LA

OLD HILL LA

Hawton Farm

Slade Farm

Mast

Ashlea

Cemy

OAKHAM RD

Little Compton

PINCHESTER CL

WILLOW END

OAKHAM RD

Oakham

OX7

Manor House

CHURCH LA

RIVINGTON GLEBE

DRIVERS LA

BREWERY LA

BREWERY ROW

REDLANDS ROW

Langston Farm

Redlands Farm

Windmill Farm

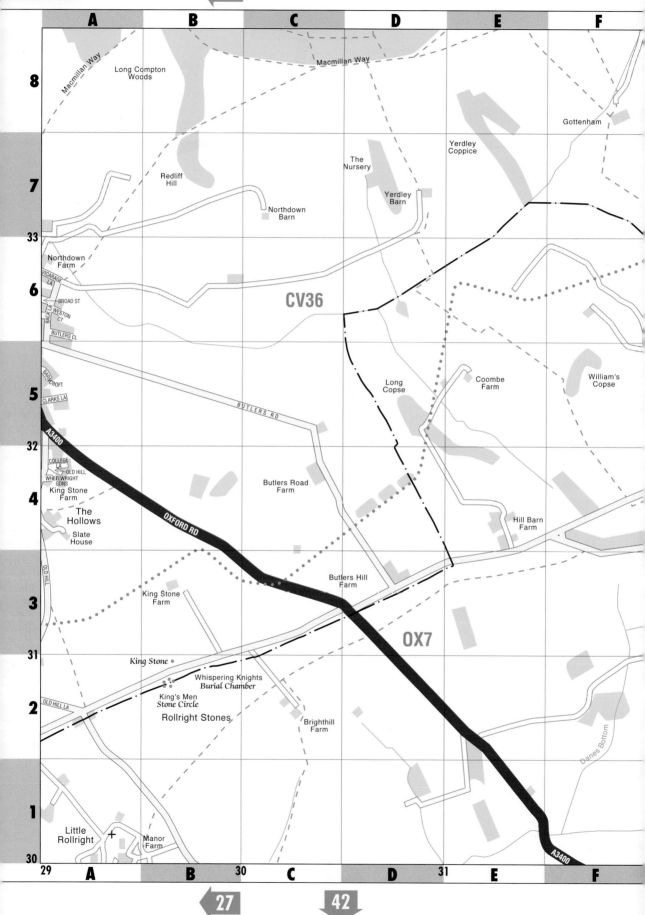

A   B   C   D   E   F

8

Macmillan Way
Long Compton Woods
Macmillan Way

Gottenham

7

Redliff Hill

Yerdley Coppice

The Nursery

Northdown Barn

Yerdley Barn

33

Northdown Farm

CV36

VICARAGE LA

6

BROAD ST

WESTON CT

BACK LA

BUTLERS CL

BARNCROFT

Long Copse

Coombe Farm

William's Copse

5

CLARKS LA

BUTLERS RD

A3400

32

COLLEGE LA

OLD HILL

WHEELWRIGHT GDNS

King Stone Farm

Butlers Road Farm

Hill Barn Farm

4

The Hollows

OXFORD RD

Slate House

OLD HILL

Butlers Hill Farm

3

King Stone Farm

OX7

31

King Stone •

Whispering Knights
Burial Chamber

2

Old Hill La

King's Men Stone Circle

Rollright Stones

Brighthill Farm

Danes Bottom

1

Little Rollright

Manor Farm

30

29   A   B   30   C   D   31   E   F

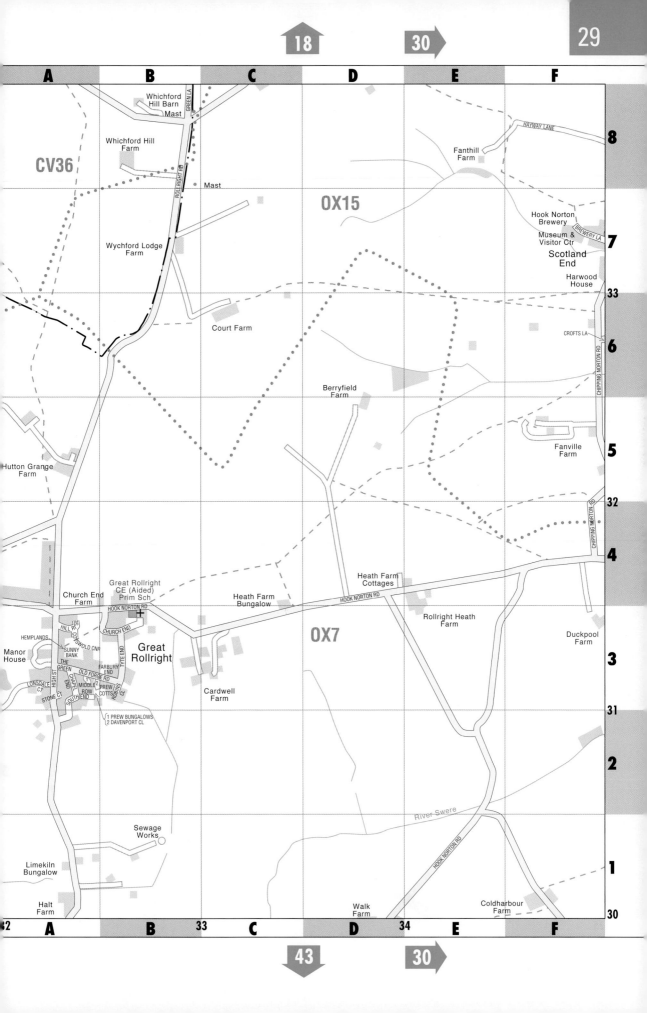

A B C D E F

8
7
33
6
5
32
4
3
31
2
1
30

CV36

Whichford
Hill Barn
Mast

Whichford Hill
Farm

GREEN LA

ROLLRIGHT RD

Mast

OX15

Fanthill
Farm

HAYWAY LANE

Hook Norton
Brewery

BREWERY LA

Museum &
Visitor Ctr

Scotland
End

Harwood
House

CROFTS LA

CHIPPING NORTON RD

Wychford Lodge
Farm

Court Farm

Berryfield
Farm

Fanville
Farm

CHIPPING NORTON RD

Hutton Grange
Farm

Heath Farm
Cottages

Great Rollright
CE (Aided)
Prim Sch

Church End
Farm

HOOK NORTON RD

Heath Farm
Bungalow

Rollright Heath
Farm

Duckpool
Farm

OX7

HEMPLANDS
Manor
House

HILL RD
COTSWOLD CNR
SUNNY
BANK
THE
GREEN
FARBURY
END
OLD FORGE RD
MIDDLE
ROW
PREW
COTTS
ROBBINS
CL
TYTE END
CHURCH END

**Great
Rollright**

LONSDALE
CT
STONE CT
CHAPEL
END
SOUTH END
HIGH ST

Cardwell
Farm

1 PREW BUNGALOWS
2 DAVENPORT CL

Sewage
Works

River Swere

HOOK NORTON RD

Limekiln
Bungalow

Halt
Farm

Walk
Farm

Coldharbour
Farm

A   B   C   D   E   F

8

Round Hill
HAYWAY LA
Hook Norton
CASCADE RD

Redlands Farm
SIMMONS WY
1 BEAVINGTON RD
2 PINFOLD CL
3 HERITAGE CL
GOLDINGS RD
BOURNE LA
WHITTONS CL
RECTORY RD
SIBFORD RD
THE CLEER
Hook Norton CE Prim Sch
ORCHARD RD
HOLLYBUSH RD
CHAPEL ST
East End
THE GREEN
TITE LA
EAST END
IRONSTONE HOLLOW
STATION RD
AUSTIN'S WAY
THE GRANGE
THE SIDINGS
Wks

Crushill Farm
Wks
BRYMBO COTTS
Sewage Works

Railway Farm

Butter Hill

7

Round Close Rd
CLAY BANK
BREWERY LA
THE BOURNE
GLEND
OLD SCHO
WATERLA
OSNEY
THE SHEARINGS
MOBBS CL
HEATH CT
HIGH ST
BELL'S LA
DOWN END
WELL BANK
PARK HILL
QUEEN'S LA
PO
Down End
Cemy
Manor Farm

33

Scotland End
SCOTLAND END
NETTING ST
CHIPPING NORTON RD
BROOKSIDE RD
Liby
PH
MIDDLE HILL
BRIDGE HILL
BRICK HILL
ROPE WAY
PARK RD
BEANACRE RD
PARK CL
NORTHROP
Park Farm

OX15

6

CROFT'S LA
BURY CROFT
SWERFORD RD
SOUTHROP RD
Southrop
Gilden Farm
Grounds Farm
Cradle Farm

5

CHIPPING NORTON RD

Cradle House Farm

32

South Hill

Highwood Farm

Cradle Barn

4

South Hill Farm
Archell Farm
COW LA

3

Swerford Park Farm
Swerford Park
Swerford Park
HOOK NORTON RD
Church End
Between Towns
East End
CHAPEL END
Ash Hill Farm
CHAPEL HILL
ST MARY'S LA

31

OX7
River Swere
Swerford
Grange Farm

2

COW LA

A36

1

Coltscombe
BANBURY RD
Pomfret Castle

30

Hayes's Barn
A361
Spring Farm

35   A   36   B   37   C   D   E   F

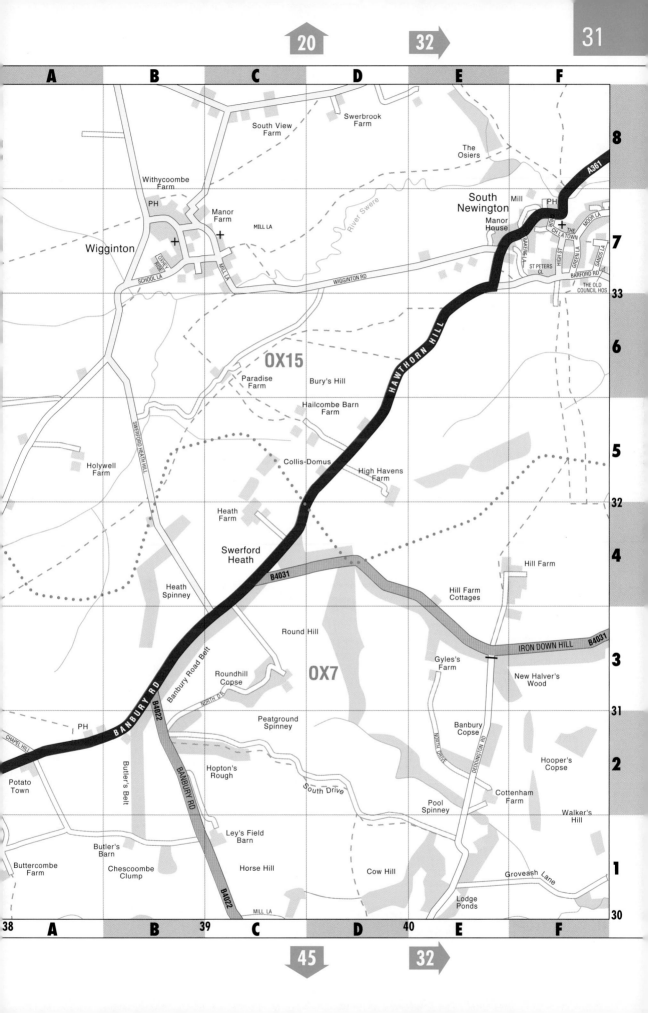

A   B   C   D   E   F

8

A361 SOUTH NEWINGTON RD

The Baulk

MOOR LA

River Swere

Barford St John

7

MEAD RD   CHURCH LA

33

BARFORD RD

Mead Farm

Manor Farm

Rignell Farm

The Manor House

PO

PH

Lower St

SHILTON RD

BURTON'S

SUMMER LEY

6

Rignell Hall

SOUTH NEWINGTON RD

CHURCH ST

THE ROCK

ROCK CL

HORN HILL

Buttermilk Farm

THE GREEN

Barford St Michael

Brasenose College Farm

Barford Lodge

BROAD CL

ROBB'S CL

HIGH ST

TOWNSEND

5

OX15

Spring Hill Farm

NETHER WORTON RD

32

HEMPTON ROAD

4

STEEPNESS HILL   B4031

Irondown Farm

Iron Down

IRON DOWN HILL

B4031

IRON DOWN HILL

Norton Grounds Farm

NETHER WORTON RD

3

Upper Grove Ash Farm

Ilbury Farm

Irondown Spinney

31

Lower Grove Ash Farm

2

Raven Hill

Hawk Hill

OX7

GROVEASH LA

Nether Worton

1

The Boltons

Manor Farm

Ford

Nether Worton House

FLIGHT HILL

30

41   A   B   42   C   D   43   E   F

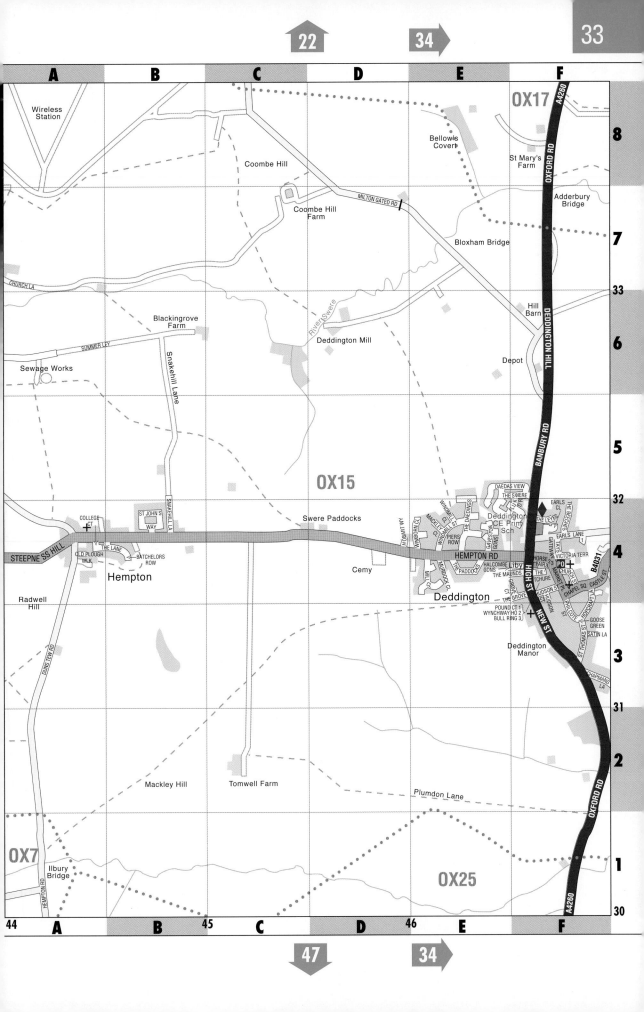

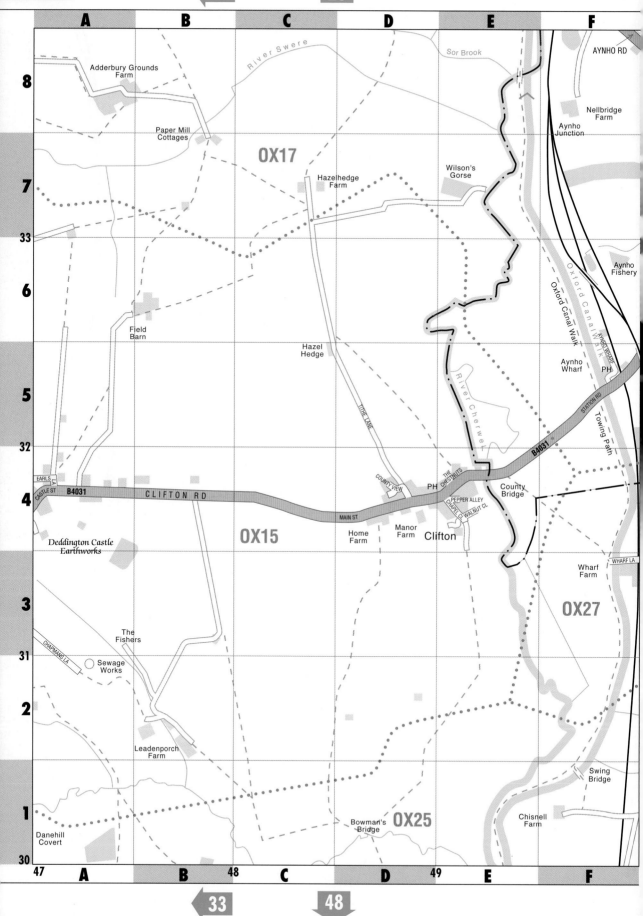

A B C D E F

8

7

33

6

32

5

32

4

3

31

2

1

30

47 A B 48 C D 49 E F

River Swere

Sor Brook

AYNHO RD

Adderbury Grounds Farm

Paper Mill Cottages

OX17

Hazelhedge Farm

Wilson's Gorse

Nellbridge Farm

Aynho Junction

Aynho Fishery

Field Barn

Oxford Canal Walk

Oxford Canal Walk

AYNHO WHARF

Aynho Wharf

PH

Hazel Hedge

River Cherwell

STATION RD

Towing Path

EARLS LA

CASTLE ST

B4031   CLIFTON RD

MAIN ST

TITHE LANE

COUNTY VIEW

THE CHESTNUTS

PH

PEPPER ALLEY

CHAPEL CL   WALNUT CL

Clifton

County Bridge

B4031

County Bridge

WHARF LA

Deddington Castle Earthworks

OX15

Home Farm

Manor Farm

Wharf Farm

OX27

CHAPMANS LA

The Fishers

Sewage Works

Leadenporch Farm

Swing Bridge

Danehill Covert

Bowman's Bridge

OX25

Chisnell Farm

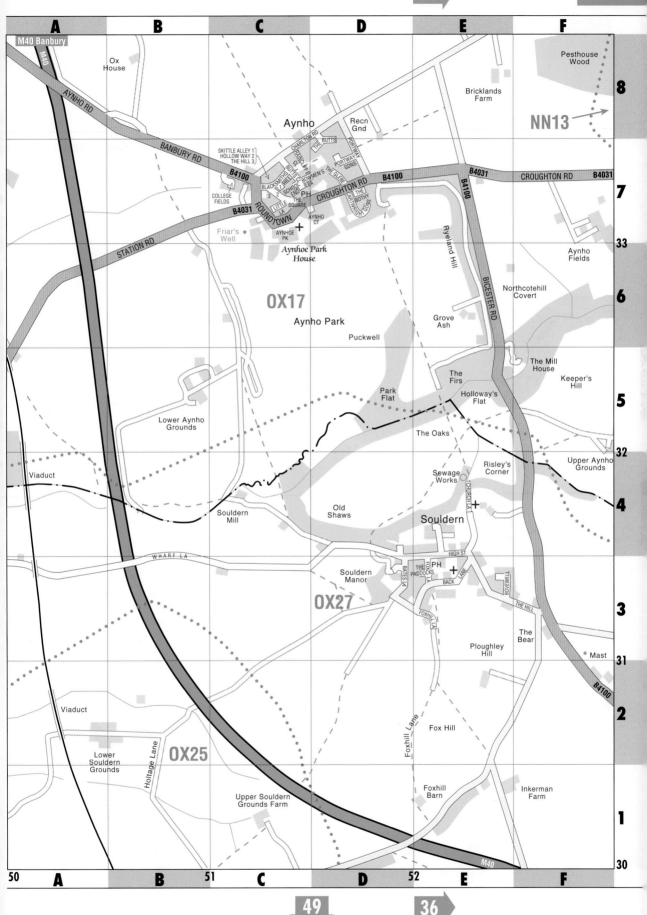

A B C D E F

M40 Banbury

Ox House

Aynho

Pesthouse Wood

8

Bricklands Farm

NN13

SKITTLE ALLEY 1
HOLLOW WAY 2
THE HILL 3

Recn Gnd

CHARLTON RD

THE BUTTS

GRANGE CL

BLACKSMITHS

BUTTS CL

PORTWAY

PORTWAY GDNS

COLLEGE FIELDS

BOWMEN'S

SCHOOL END

THE GLEBE

CARTWRIGHT

THE BOTHY

CROUGHTON RD

B4100

B4031

CROUGHTON RD

B4031

7

B4100

ROUNDTOWN

LITTLE LA

THE SQUARE

AYNHO CT

AYNHO PK

BANBURY RD

Friar's Well

Aynhoe Park House

33

STATION RD

B4031

Aynho Fields

OX17

Ryeland Hill

6

Northcotehill Covert

Aynho Park

BICESTER RD

Puckwell

Grove Ash

The Mill House

Keeper's Hill

Lower Aynho Grounds

Park Flat

The Firs

Holloway's Flat

5

The Oaks

32

Viaduct

Souldern Mill

Old Shaws

Sewage Works

Risley's Corner

Upper Aynho Grounds

Souldern

CHURCH LA

4

WHARF LA

Souldern Manor

THE PADDOCKS

BATES LA

HIGH ST

FOOT LA

PH

BACK LANE

BOVEWELL

OX27

FOXHILL LA

THE HILL

The Bear

3

Ploughley Hill

Mast

31

B4100

Viaduct

OX25

Lower Souldern Grounds

Holtage Lane

Foxhill Lane

Fox Hill

2

Upper Souldern Grounds Farm

Foxhill Barn

Inkerman Farm

1

M40

30

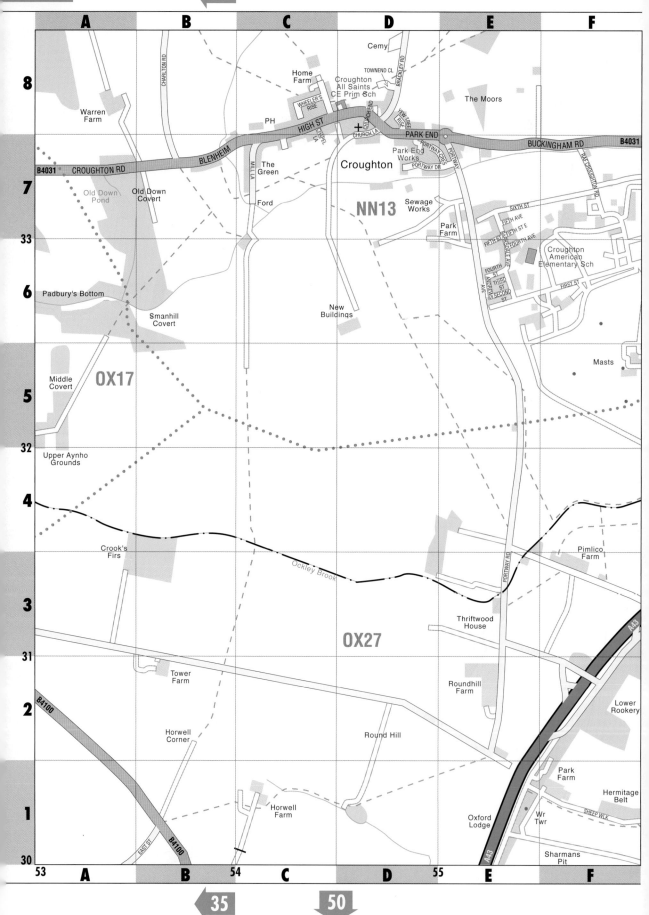

Warren Farm

CHARLTON RD

Cemy

TOWNEND CL

Home Farm

Croughton All Saints CE Prim Sch

BRACKLEY RD

The Moors

WHEELER'S RISE

PH

HIGH ST

CHAPEL LA

CHURCH END

CHURCH LA

YEW TREE RISE

PARK END

PORTWAY CRES

PORTWAY

BUCKINGHAM RD

B4031

B4031 CROUGHTON RD

BLENHEIM

MILL LA

The Green

Ford

Croughton

Park End Works

PORTWAY DR

NN13

Sewage Works

Old Down Pond

Old Down Covert

Park Farm

SIXTH ST

FIFTH AVE

FIFTH ST E

FIFTH ST

LONSDALE AVE

FOURTH AVE

FOURTH ST

ST ANDREWS AVE

THIRD ST

SECOND ST

FIRST ST

Croughton American Elementary Sch

Padbury's Bottom

Smanhill Covert

New Buildings

Masts

Middle Covert

OX17

Upper Aynho Grounds

Crook's Firs

Ockley Brook

Pimlico Farm

PORTWAY RD

OX27

Thriftwood House

B4100

Tower Farm

Roundhill Farm

Lower Rookery

Horwell Corner

Round Hill

Park Farm

Hermitage Belt

SHEEP WLK

Horwell Farm

Oxford Lodge

Wr Twr

EAST ST

B4100

A43

A43

Sharmans Pit

53 54 55

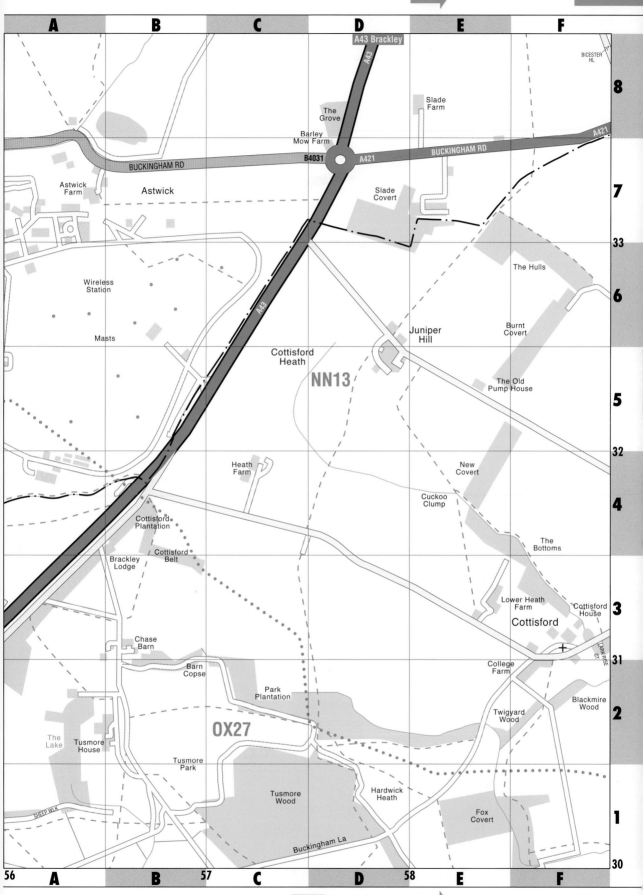

A B C D E F

8

A43 Brackley

BICESTER HL

Slade Farm

The Grove

Barley Mow Farm

A421

7

BUCKINGHAM RD

B4031 A421 BUCKINGHAM RD

Astwick Farm

Astwick

33

Slade Covert

The Hulls

Wireless Station

6

Burnt Covert

A43

Cottisford Heath

Juniper Hill

Masts

NN13

The Old Pump House

5

Heath Farm

32

New Covert

Cuckoo Clump

4

Cottisford Plantation

The Bottoms

Brackley Lodge

Cottisford Belt

Lower Heath Farm

Cottisford House

3

Cottisford

Chase Barn

31

Barn Copse

College Farm

DARK RISE CT

Park Plantation

Twigyard Wood

Blackmire Wood

2

OX27

The Lake

Tusmore House

Tusmore Park

Hardwick Heath

Fox Covert

1

SHEEP WLK

Tusmore Wood

Buckingham La

30

56 A B 57 C D 58 E F

	A	B	C	D	E	F

Barrow Hill

Mixbury

CHURCH LA

MOSSYCORNER LA

The Bowling Green

8

BICESTER HILL

BUCKINGHAM RD

A421

COTTESFORD RD

Monk's House

MAIN ST

Mixbury Lodge Farm

7

Monk's House Barn

BANBURY RD

A421

33

Mixbury Plantation

6

The Pits

Middle Farm

NN13

FEATHERBED LA

5

Park Thorns

Diggings Wood

32

Coldharbour Farm

MK18

4

Wr Twr

LAKE VIEW

KENNEL COTTAGES

HETHE RD

Cottisford Pond

Shelswell Plantation

Pondhead

3

31

The View

The Belt

Shelswell Park

Home Farm

2

The Cut

Spilsmere Wood

Windmill Hook

Shelswell

OX27

1

Hethe Spinney

30

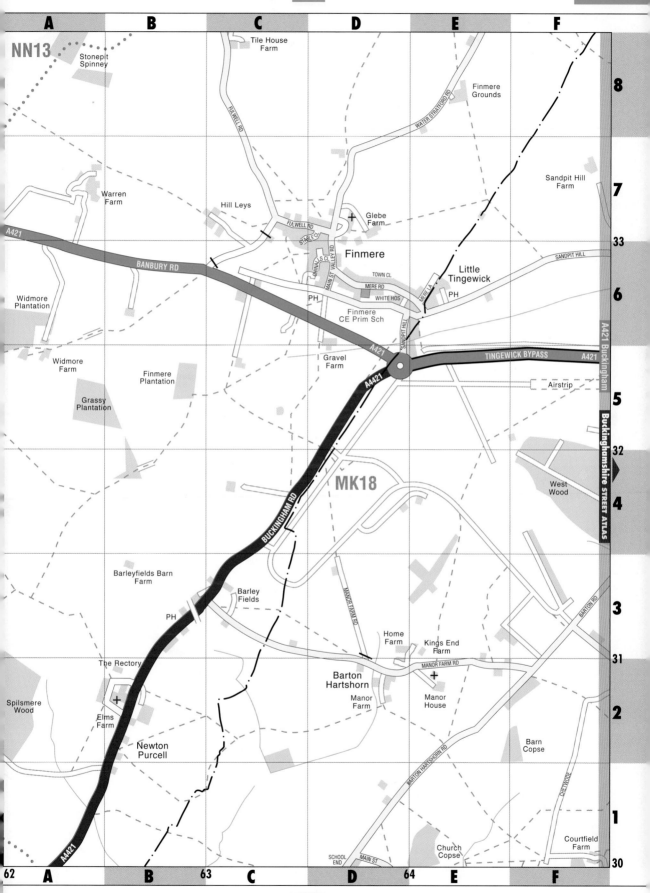

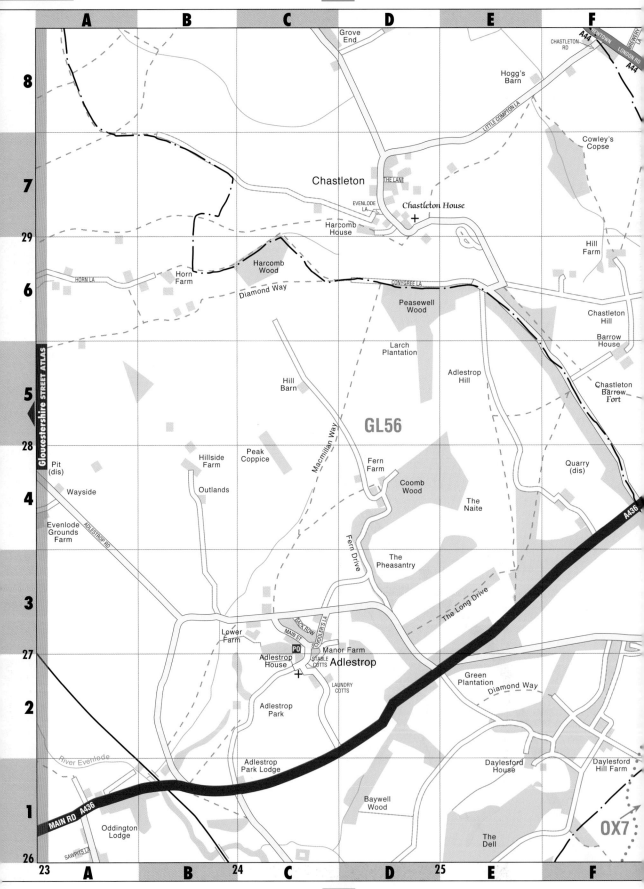

A B C D E F

8

7

29

6

5

28

4

3

27

2

1

26

23 24 25

GL56

OX7

Grove End

CHASTLETON RD
A44
KIGHTOWN
BREWERY RD
LONDON RD
A44

Hogg's Barn

LITTLE COMPTON LA

Cowley's Copse

Chastleton

THE LANE

EVENLODE LA

Chastleton House

Harcomb House

Hill Farm

Horn LA

Horn Farm

Harcomb Wood

CONYGREE LA

Diamond Way

Peasewell Wood

Chastleton Hill

Barrow House

Larch Plantation

Adlestrop Hill

Chastleton Barrow Fort

Hill Barn

Peak Coppice

Macmillan Way

Fern Farm

Coomb Wood

The Naite

Quarry (dis)

Pit (dis)

Wayside

Hillside Farm

Outlands

Evenlode Grounds Farm

ADLESTROP RD

Fern Drive

The Pheasantry

The Long Drive

A436

Lower Farm

BRACK ROW
MAIN ST
SCHOOLER'S LA
PO

Manor Farm

STABLE COTTS

Adlestrop

Green Plantation

Diamond Way

Adlestrop House

LAUNDRY COTTS

Adlestrop Park

River Evenlode

Adlestrop Park Lodge

Daylesford House

Daylesford Hill Farm

MAIN RD A436

Oddington Lodge

Baywell Wood

The Dell

SAWPITS LA

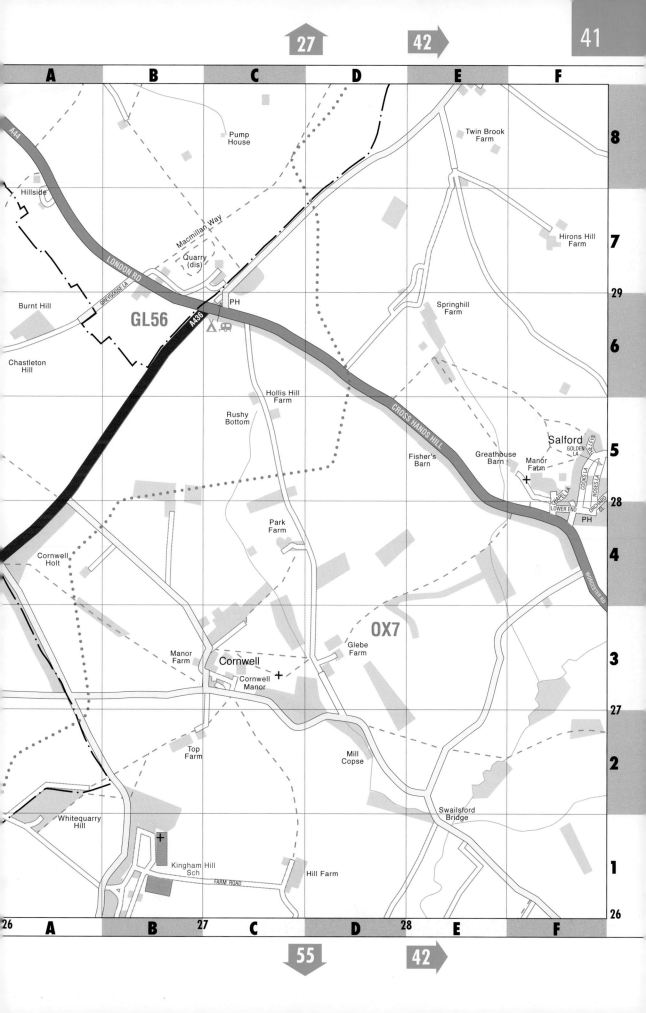

A B C D E F

A3400

8

Manor Farm

Choicehill Farm

Little Meadows

7

29

6

Over Norton House

Witts Farm

Over Norton Park

Choicehill Rd

Rectory Farm

Salford

Over Norton

THE PENN

PENFIELD

Home Farm

Main St

Firs Farm

THE GREEN

5

Larches Farm

GOLDEN LANE

NEW HOUSE YD

UPPER END

Quarhill Cl

CLEEVES CNR

BLUE ROW

THE CLOSE

ORCHARD CL

28

OX7

Chipping Norton War Memorial Com Hospl

Cromwell Pk

4

The Cleeves

Over Norton Rd

Wilcox Rd

NICALL RD

COTSHILL GDNS

ACKERMAN RD

FOLLAND CT

MARLBOROUGH RD

BANBURY RD

A44

CHALFORD

BANBURY ROAD CROSSING

NORTON PK

WESTCOTE PL

PARK RD

Worcester Rd

Elmsfield Farm Ind Est

CHURCH LA

SPRING ST

B4026

LONDON RD

A44

SUMMERTON

ROCK HILL

ROCKHILL FARM CT

WORCESTER RD

Salford Mill

A44

WHITEHOUSE LA 1
VICTORIA PL 2
GODDARDS LA 3
MIDDLE ROW 4
KINGS HEAD CT 5
HILL LAWN CT 6
WITHERS CT 7
CONYGREE TERR 8
MARKET PL 9
PENHURST GDNS 10
REGENT CT 11
STANLEY CL 12

ELMSFIELD RD WEST

Liby

CHURCH ST

DUSTON'S LA

Holy Trinity RC Sch

PORTLAND PL

DICKENSON CT

ROCK HILL

COOK BRASSEY CL

SHEPARD WAY

ROWELL WAY

ALBION PL

LODGE TERR

Wr Twr

3

Bridge Field

Worcester Cemy

Worcester Road Ind Est

GLOVERS

WARDS RD

FOXFIELD CT

Tank Farm

Nuholme

Primsdown Ind Est

NEW ST A44

THE MKT

P PO

FOX CL

FOXEL CL

HITCHMAN DR

27

WORCESTER RD

KENNEL LA

COX LA

TOY LA

COMMON LA

Station Yard Ind Est

WALTER CRAFT CT

LEWIS RD

STANTON RD

DUNSTAN AVE

WITHERS WAY

CROSS LEYS

GROSS LEYS

WEST ST

B4450

BURFORD RD

A361

HITCHMAN DR

L Ctr

Chipping Norton Sch

2

Cornwell Hill Farm

Sewage Works

Chipping Norton Common

CRAFTS MILL TERR

WEBB CRES

ARUNDEL VW

THE LEYS

WARPING HOUSE

MILL RD COTTS

BLISS MILL

WILLIAM CL

SPRING

WESTEND RD

THE GREEN

CHIPPING NORTON

1 ALFRED TERRS
2 JOHNSTON WAY
3 NORTON GREEN CT
4 VERNON HO
5 BRASENOSE VILLAS
6 CHURCHILL PL
7 MARKET PL
8 HITCHMANS MWS

PARADISE TERR

ALEXANDRA SQ

St Mary's CE(Aided) Prim Sch

ALBION ROW

Allot Gdns

1

Meads Farm

Westend Farm

LORDS PIECE RD

TILSLEY RD

EDWARD STONE RISE

CHURCHILL RD

HAILEY VIEW

MARSHALL

HILL CL

WALTERBUSH RD

BURROWS CLOSE

COTSWOLD CRES

COTSWOLD TERR

CHARLBURY RD

HOWES LA

B4026

Westfield Farm

B4450

CORNISH RD

HANNIS RD

HAILEY CRES

STARES CY

EVANS WAY

STOPFORD PL

A361

1 BRASSEY HO
2 WILKINS HO
3 BLISS HO
4 COTSWOLD CRES BGLWS

26

29 A B 30 C D 31 E F

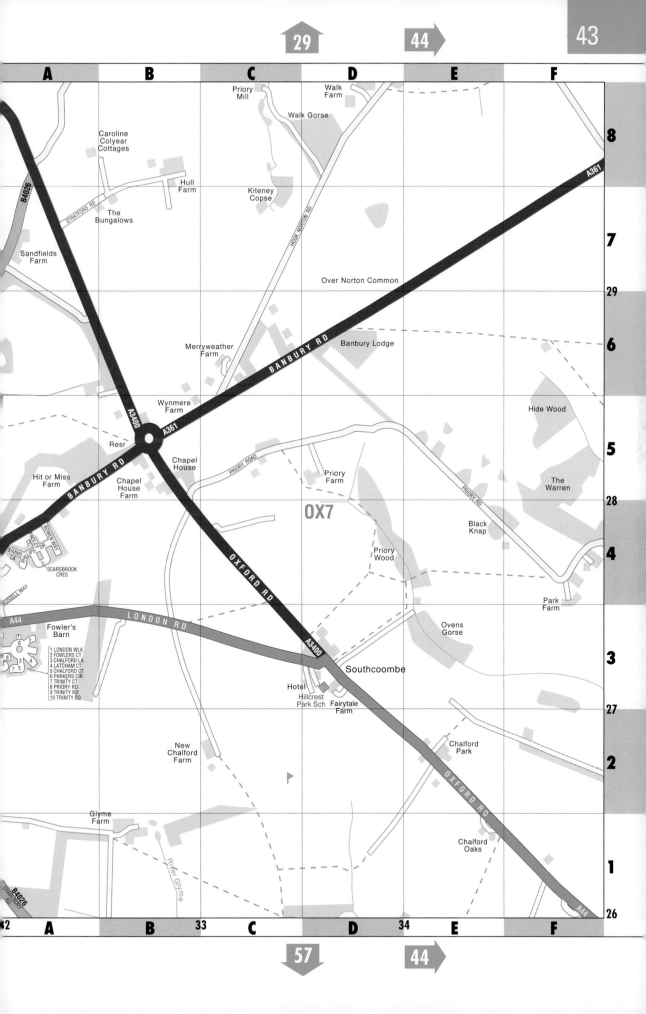

A   B   C   D   E   F

8
7
29
6
5
28
4
3
27
2
1
26

Priory Mill
Walk Farm
Walk Gorse
Caroline Colyear Cottages
Hull Farm
Kiteney Copse
B4026
STRATFORD RD
The Bungalows
A361
Sandfields Farm
HOOK NORTON RD
Over Norton Common
Banbury Lodge
Merryweather Farm
BANBURY RD
Hide Wood
Wynmere Farm
A3400
A361
Resr
Chapel House
Priory Farm
The Warren
Hit or Miss Farm
Chapel House Farm
PRIORY ROAD
PRIORY RD
Black Knap
OX7
BOWER WAY
CHALFORD DR
PHILLIPS LA
SIMMS LA
OXFORD RD
Priory Wood
SCARSBROOK CRES
Park Farm
RUSSELL WAY
Fowler's Barn
A44
LONDON RD
Ovens Gorse
A3400
Southcoombe
1 LONDON WLK
2 FOWLERS CT
3 CHALFORD LA
4 LATCHAM CT
5 CHALFORD CT
6 PARKERS CIR
7 TRINITY CT
8 PRIORY RD
9 TRINITY RD
10 TRINITY SQ
Hotel
Hillcrest Park Sch
Fairytale Farm
New Chalford Farm
Chalford Park
OXFORD RD
Glyme Farm
Chalford Oaks
River Glyme
B4026
A44

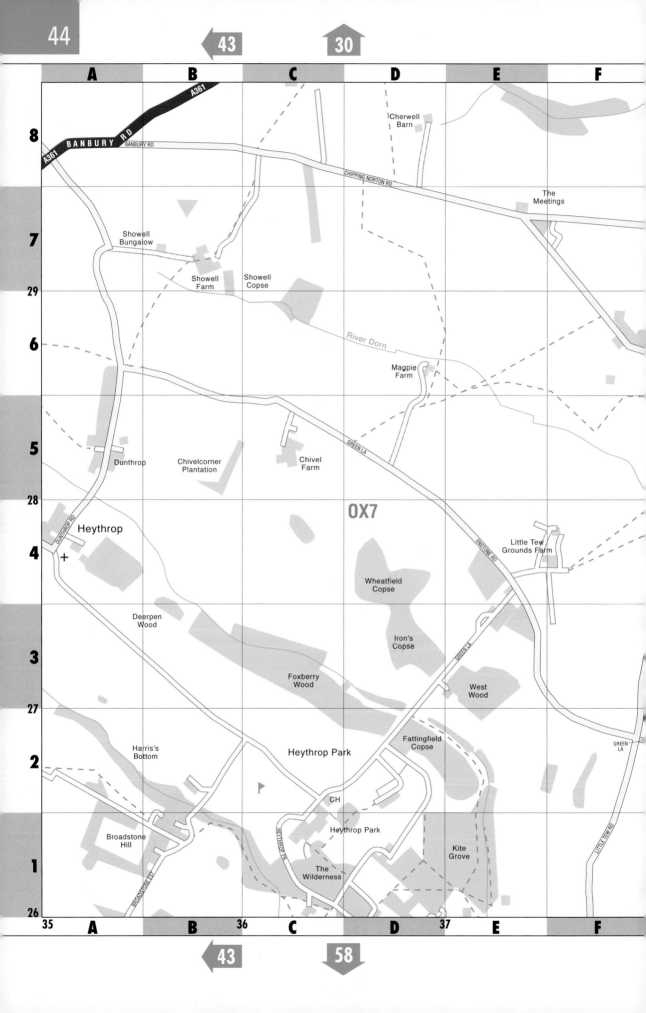

A   B   C   D   E   F

8   BANBURY RD   A361
A361   BANBURY RD
CHIPPING NORTON RD

Cherwell Barn

The Meetings

7   Showell Bungalow

29   Showell Farm   Showell Copse

River Dorn

6   Magpie Farm

5   Dunthrop   Chivelcorner Plantation   Chivel Farm   GREEN LA

OX7

28

Heythrop   Little Tew Grounds Farm

4   +   ENSTONE RD

Wheatfield Copse

Deerpen Wood

Iron's Copse   GREEN LA

3   Foxberry Wood   West Wood

27   GREEN LA

Harris's Bottom   Fattingfield Copse

2   Heythrop Park

CH   Kite Grove

Broadstone Hill   HEYTHROP PK   Heythrop Park   LITTLE TEW RD

1   The Wilderness

BROADSTONE EST

26

35   A   B   36   C   D   37   E   F

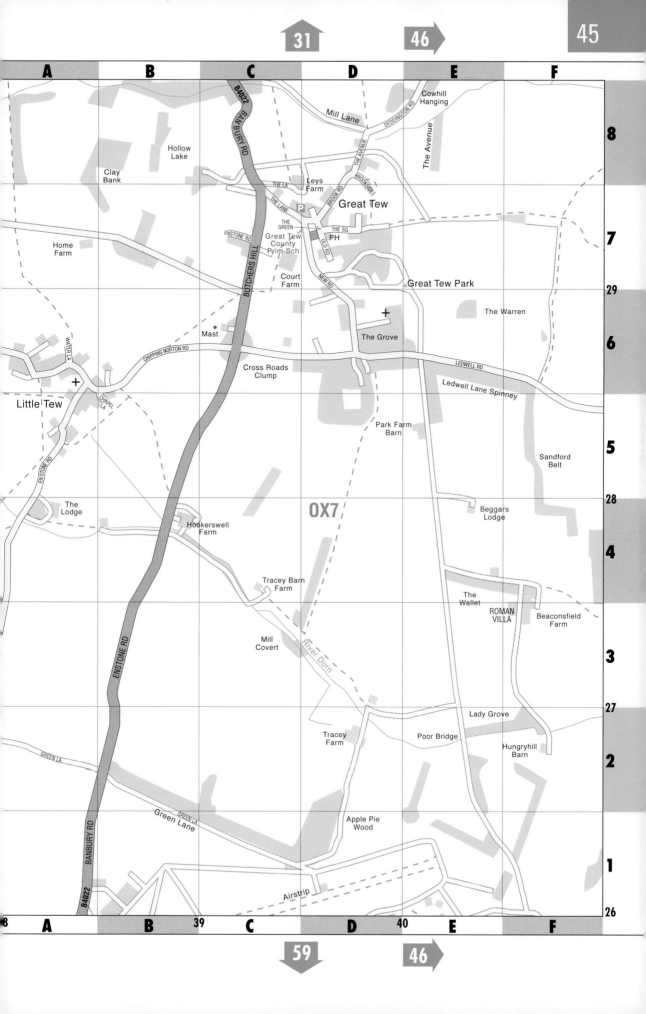

31
46
46

A **B** **C** **D** **E** **F**

8

B4022
BANBURY RD
Mill Lane
Cowhill Hanging
DEDDINGTON RD
THE AVENUE
The Avenue

Hollow Lake
Clay Bank
THE LA
Leys Farm
BROOKSIDE
Great Tew
P
THE LANE
THE GREEN

7

Home Farm
ENSTONE RD
Great Tew County Prim Sch
THE SQ
PH
OLD RD
BUTCHERS HILL

29

Court Farm
NEW RD
Great Tew Park

6

WATER LA
CHIPPING NORTON RD
Mast
The Grove
The Warren
LEDWELL RD

Cross Roads Clump
Ledwell Lane Spinney

Little Tew
CHAPEL LA

5

Park Farm Barn
Sandford Belt

28

ENSTONE RD
The Lodge
OX7
Beggars Lodge

4

Hookerswell Farm
The Wallet
ROMAN VILLA
Beaconsfield Farm

Tracey Barn Farm

3

Mill Covert
River Dorn

Lady Grove

27

GREEN LA
Tracey Farm
Poor Bridge
Hungryhill Barn

2

B4022
BANBURY RD
Green Lane
GREEN LA
Apple Pie Wood

1

Airstrip

26

A 39 **B** **C** **D** 40 **E** **F**

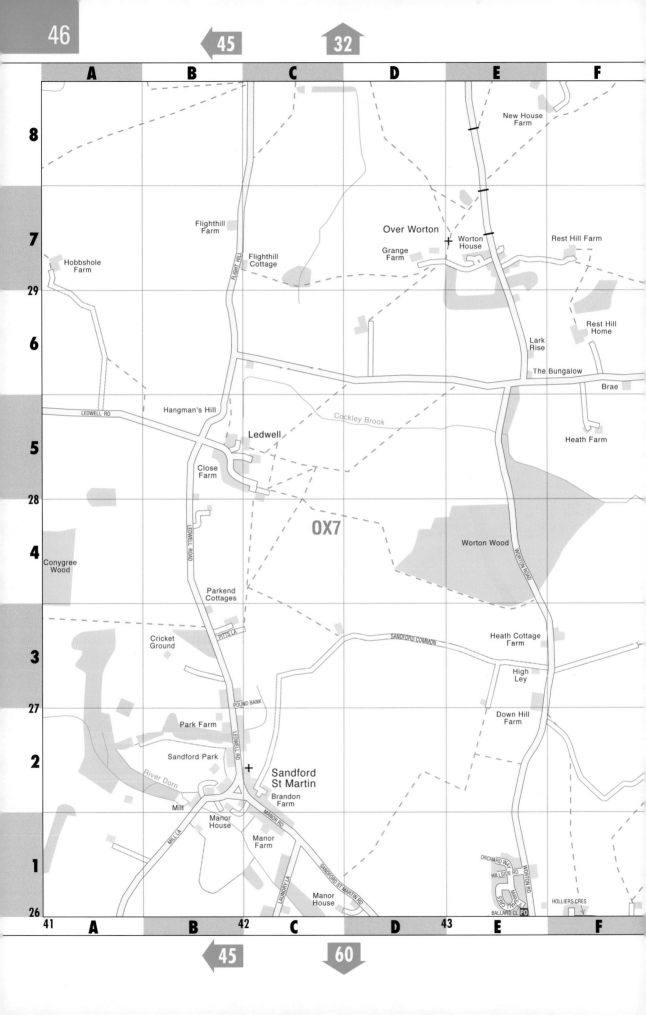

8

7

29

6

New House Farm

Over Worton

Flighthill Farm

Worton House

Rest Hill Farm

FLIGHT HILL

Flighthill Cottage

Grange Farm

Hobbshole Farm

Lark Rise

Rest Hill Home

The Bungalow

Brae

LEDWELL RD

Hangman's Hill

Cockley Brook

Ledwell

Heath Farm

5

Close Farm

28

OX7

LEDWELL ROAD

Worton Wood

WORTON ROAD

4

Conygree Wood

Parkend Cottages

PITTS LA

Sandford Common

Heath Cottage Farm

3

Cricket Ground

High Ley

27

POUND BANK

Park Farm

Down Hill Farm

LEDWELL RD

2

Sandford Park

River Dorn

Sandford St Martin

MANOR RD

Mill

Brandon Farm

MILL LA

Manor House

Manor Farm

SANDFORD ST MARTIN RD

ORCHARD WAY

HILLSIDE RD

WORTON RD

1

LAUNDRY LA

Manor House

MARSHALL CRES

HOLLIERS CRES

BALLARD CL

PO

26

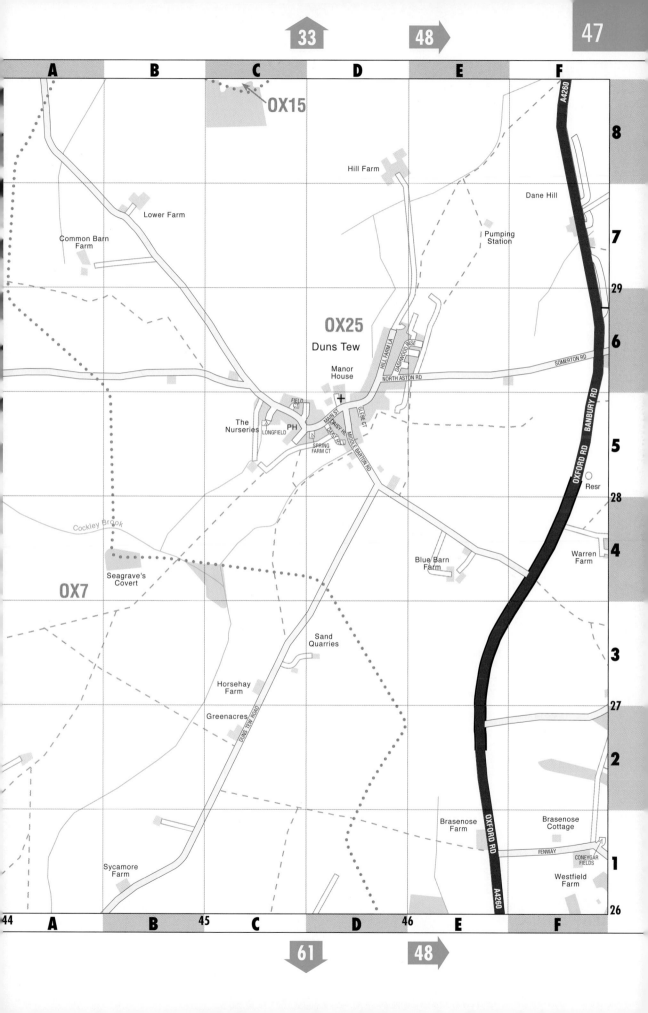

OX15

OX25
Duns Tew

Hill Farm

Dane Hill

Pumping
Station

Lower Farm

Common Barn
Farm

Manor
House

Somerton Rd

HILL FARM LA
DASHWOOD RISE
NORTH ASTON RD

FIELD
The
Nurseries
LONGFIELD
PH
MAIN ST
DAISY HL
GLEBE CT
MIDDLE BARTON RD
SPRING
FARM CT

OXFORD RD
BANBURY RD
A4260

Resr

Cockley Brook

Seagrave's
Covert

OX7

Blue Barn
Farm

Warren
Farm

Sand
Quarries

Horsehay
Farm

DUNS TEW ROAD

Greenacres

Brasenose
Farm

Brasenose
Cottage

OXFORD RD
FENWAY
CONEYGAR
FIELDS

Sycamore
Farm

Westfield
Farm

A4260

47 34

A B C D E F

8

Coldharbour
Farm

Dane Hill
Farm

Ram
Spinney

Manor House
Farm

Somerton
Lock

7

Mill
Cottage

SOMERTON RD

29

The
Green

THE GREEN

HALL CL

THE GREEN

North Aston
Hall

North Aston
Farm

ST MARYS WLK

Millhouse

Rectory
Farm

CANAL WHARF

6

SOMERTON RD

North
Aston

The
Folly

Towing Path

Somerton

CHURCH ST

WATER ST

DOVECOTE LA

ARDLEY RD

THE SLOCK

WALNUT RISE

HEYFORD
RD

FRITWELL
RD

Jersey Manor
Farm

MIDDLE ASTON RD

River Cherwell

Oxford Canal Walk

Oxford Canal

ASTON VIEW

5

28

Hendon
Farm

HEYFORD RD

LC

Somerton
Crossing

OX25

Warren
Copse

Warren
Lodge

Grange
Farm

4

MIDDLE ASTON LA

3

Pig
Unit

Middle
Aston

CLOCK CT

OAKRIDGE

HOMEFARM LA

Heyford Common
Lock

27

Middle Aston
House

2

Lakeside
Farm

Hatch End
Ind Est

The
Brambles

Upper
Heyford

SOMERTON RD

1

Steeple Aston

Dr Radcliffe's
CE Sch

SHEPHERDS HL

GRANGE PK

FENWAY

FIR LA

Allen's
Lock

ALLENS LA

RISING HILL

OLD RECTORY 1
NEW COLLEGE SQ 2
RECTORY CL 3

MILL LA

PH

26

WESTFIELD
FARM MWS

WATER LA

NORTH SIDE

COW LA

HIGH ST

47 62

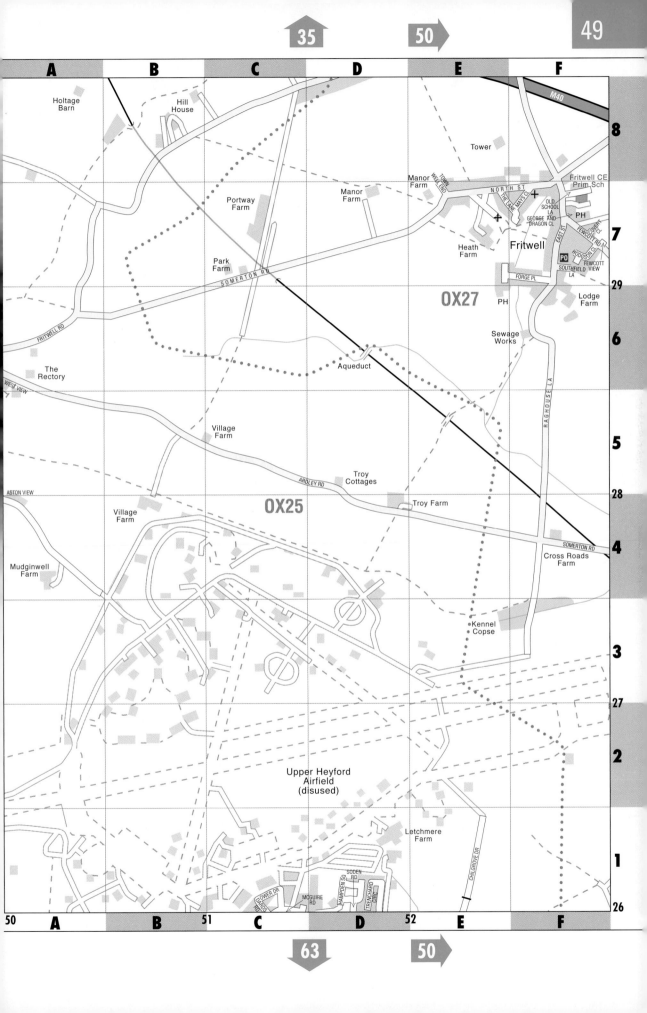

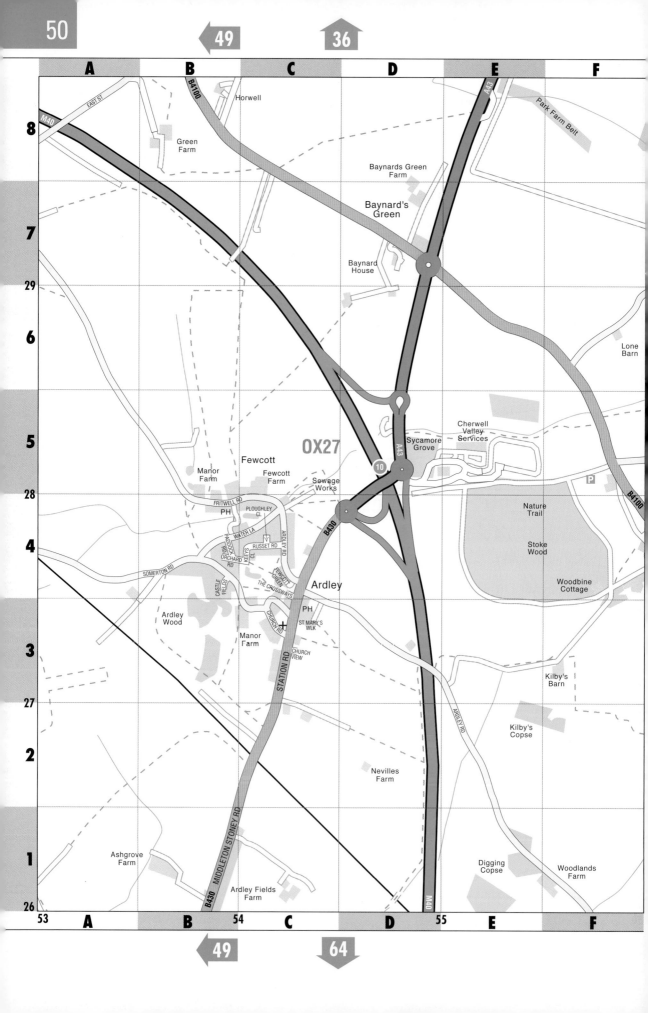

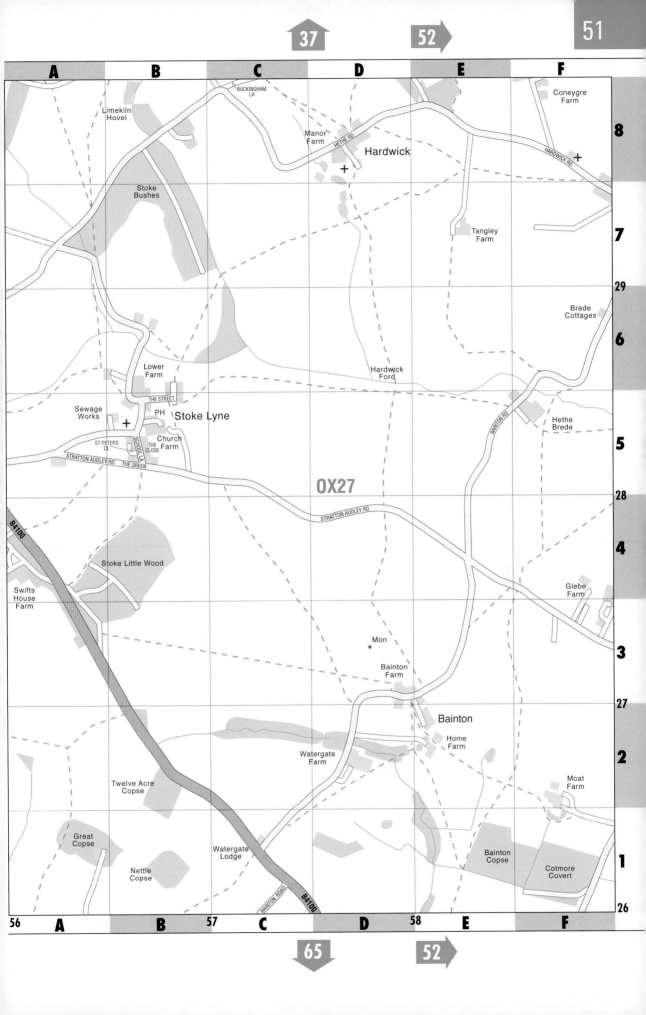

A B C D E F

8
7
29
6
5
28
4
27
3
2
1
26

Buckingham La
Limekiln Hovel
Manor Farm
Coneygre Farm
Hardwick
HETHE RD
HARDWICK RD
Stoke Bushes
Tangley Farm
Brede Cottages
Lower Farm
Hardwick Ford
THE STREET
PH
Stoke Lyne
BAINTON RD
Hethe Brede
Sewage Works
ST PETERS CL
SCHOOL LA
Church Farm
THE CLOSE
STRATTON AUDLEY RD
THE GREEN
OX27
STRATTON AUDLEY RD
28
Stoke Little Wood
Glebe Farm
B4100
Swifts House Farm
Mon
Bainton Farm
Bainton
Home Farm
Watergate Farm
Moat Farm
Twelve Acre Copse
Great Copse
Watergate Lodge
Bainton Copse
Nettle Copse
Cotmore Covert
BAINTON ROAD
B4100

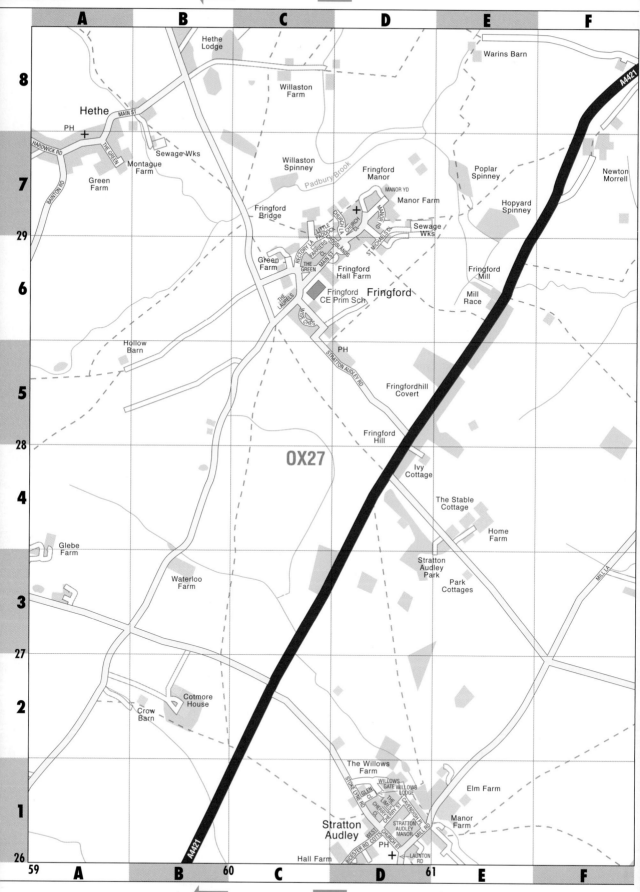

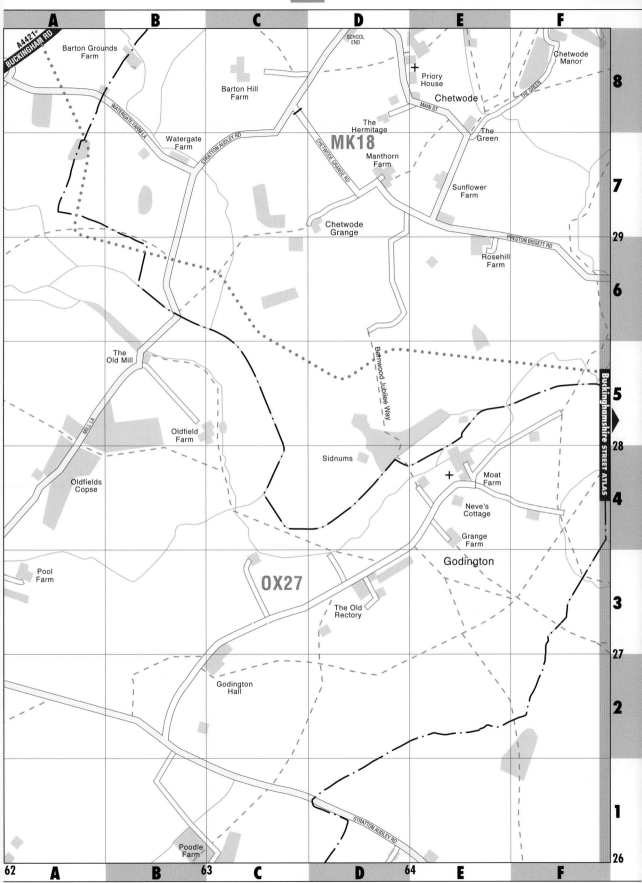

A4421

BUCKINGHAM RD

Barton Grounds
Farm

WATERGATE FARM LA

Watergate
Farm

STRATTON AUDLEY RD

Barton Hill
Farm

SCHOOL
END

Priory
House

Chetwode
Manor

THE GREEN

Chetwode

MAIN ST

The Green

The
Hermitage

MK18

CHETWODE GRANGE RD

Manthorn
Farm

Sunflower
Farm

Chetwode
Grange

PRESTON BISSETT RD

Rosehill
Farm

The
Old Mill

Bernwood Jubilee Way

Buckinghamshire STREET ATLAS

MILL LA

Oldfield
Farm

Sidnums

Moat
Farm

Oldfields
Copse

Neve's
Cottage

Grange
Farm

Godington

OX27

Pool
Farm

The Old
Rectory

Godington
Hall

STRATTON AUDLEY RD

Poodle
Farm

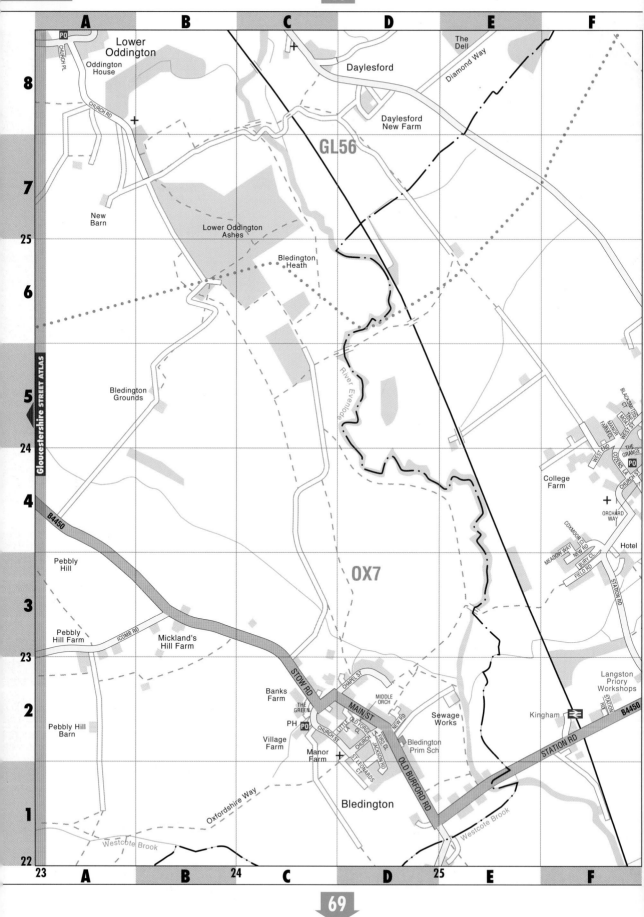

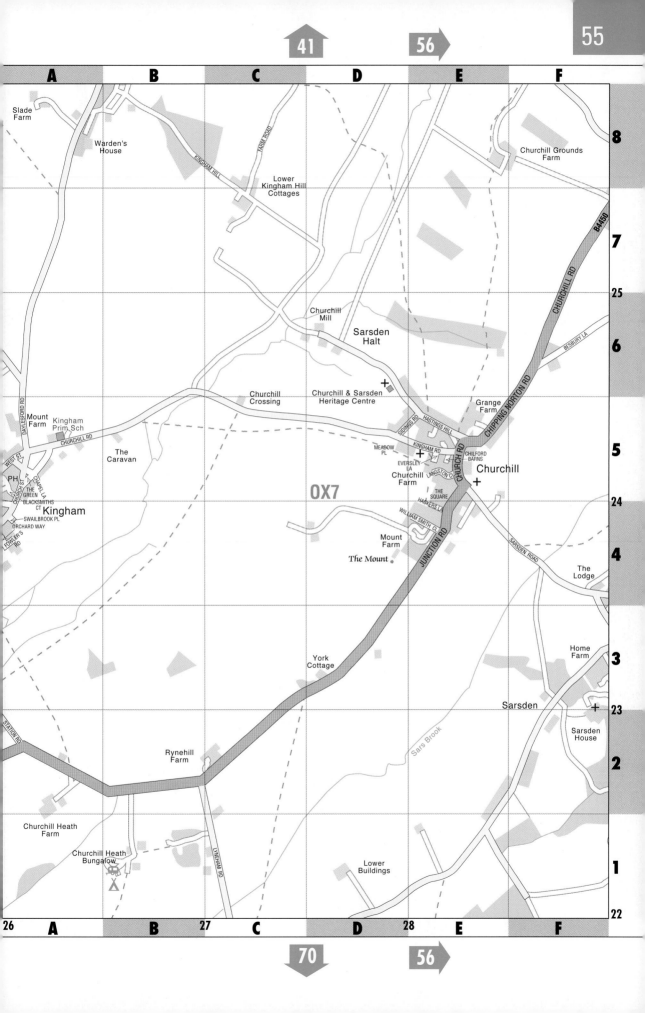

A B C D E F

8

Slade
Farm

Warden's
House

Churchill Grounds
Farm

KINGHAM HILL

FARM ROAD

Lower
Kingham Hill
Cottages

B4450

7

25

CHURCHILL RD

Churchill
Mill

Sarsden
Halt

6

BESBURY LA

CHIPPING NORTON RD

Churchill
Crossing

Churchill & Sarsden
Heritage Centre

Grange
Farm

DAYLESFORD RD

Mount
Farm

Kingham
Prim Sch

CHURCHILL RD

The Caravan

SIDINGS RD

HASTINGS HILL

KINGHAM RD

CHURCH RD

Chilford
Barns

Churchill

5

WEST ST

MEADOW
PL

EVERSLEY
LA

LANGSTON CL

24

PH

CHURCH ST

CHAPEL LA

THE
GREEN

BLACKSMITHS
CT

Churchill
Farm

Kingham

SWAILBROOK PL

ORCHARD WAY

FOWLER'S
RD

OX7

THE
SQUARE

HACKERS LA

WILLIAM SMITH CL

JUNCTION RD

Mount
Farm

SARSDEN ROAD

The
Lodge

4

The Mount

York
Cottage

Home
Farm

3

STATION RD

Rynehill
Farm

Sars Brook

Sarsden

23

Sarsden
House

2

Churchill Heath
Farm

LYNEHAM RD

Churchill Heath
Bungalow

Lower
Buildings

1

22

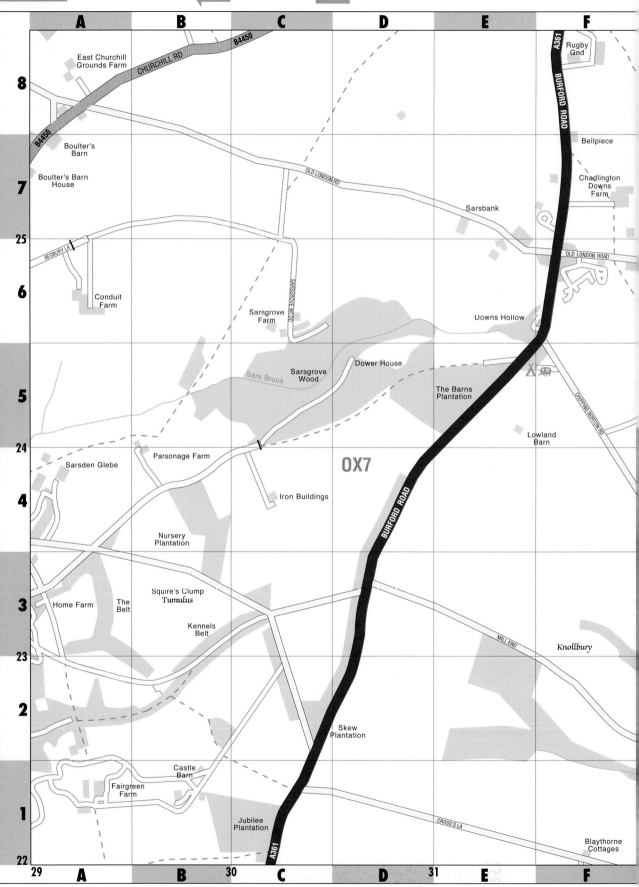

East Churchill
Grounds Farm

CHURCHILL RD B4450

8

B4450

Boulter's
Barn

Boulter's Barn
House

7

Old London Rd

Sarsbank

25

BESBURY LA

6

Conduit
Farm

Sarsgrove
Farm

SARSGROVE WOOD

Dower House

Sars Brook

Sarsgrove
Wood

The Barns
Plantation

5

Sarsden Glebe

Parsonage Farm

24

OX7

Iron Buildings

Burford Road

4

Nursery
Plantation

Squire's Clump
Tumulus

3

Home Farm

The
Belt

Kennels
Belt

23

A369

Rugby
Gnd

BURFORD ROAD

Bellpiece

Chadlington
Downs
Farm

Old London Road

Downs Hollow

Lowland
Barn

CHIPPING NORTON RD

MILL END

Knollbury

Skew
Plantation

2

Castle
Barn

Fairgreen
Farm

1

Jubilee
Plantation

A361

Cross's La

Blaythorne
Cottages

22

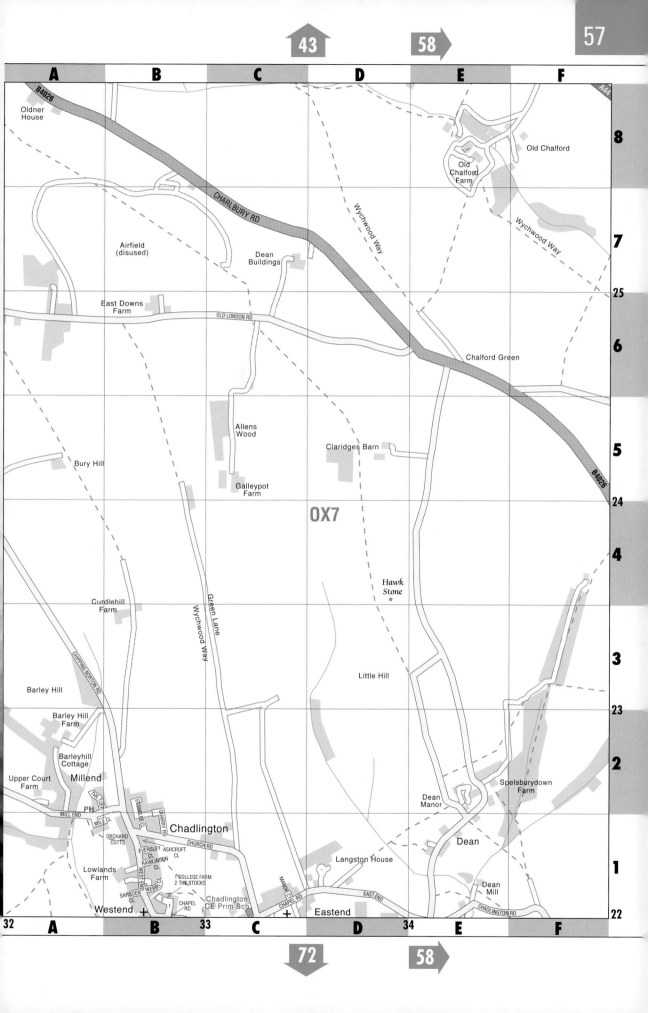

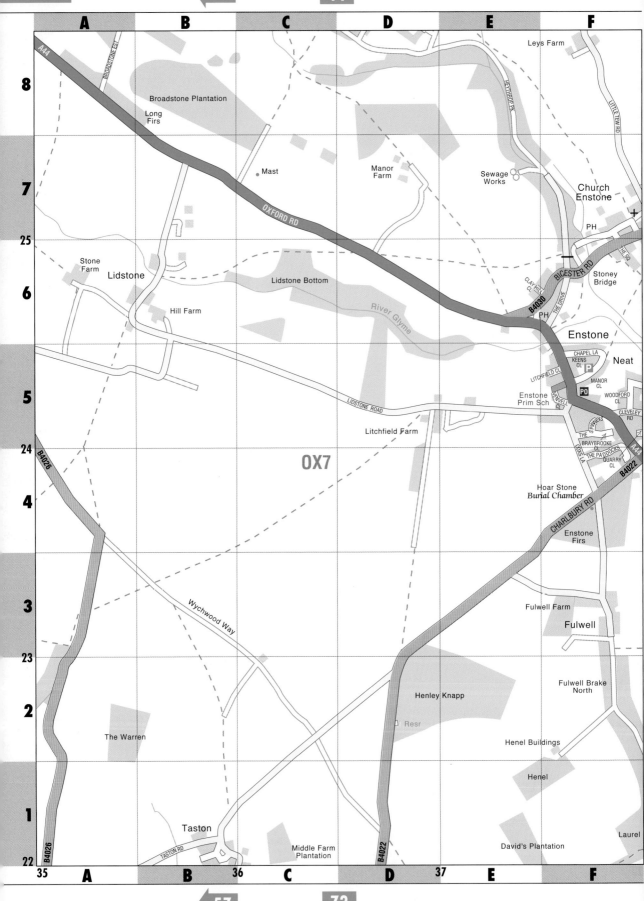

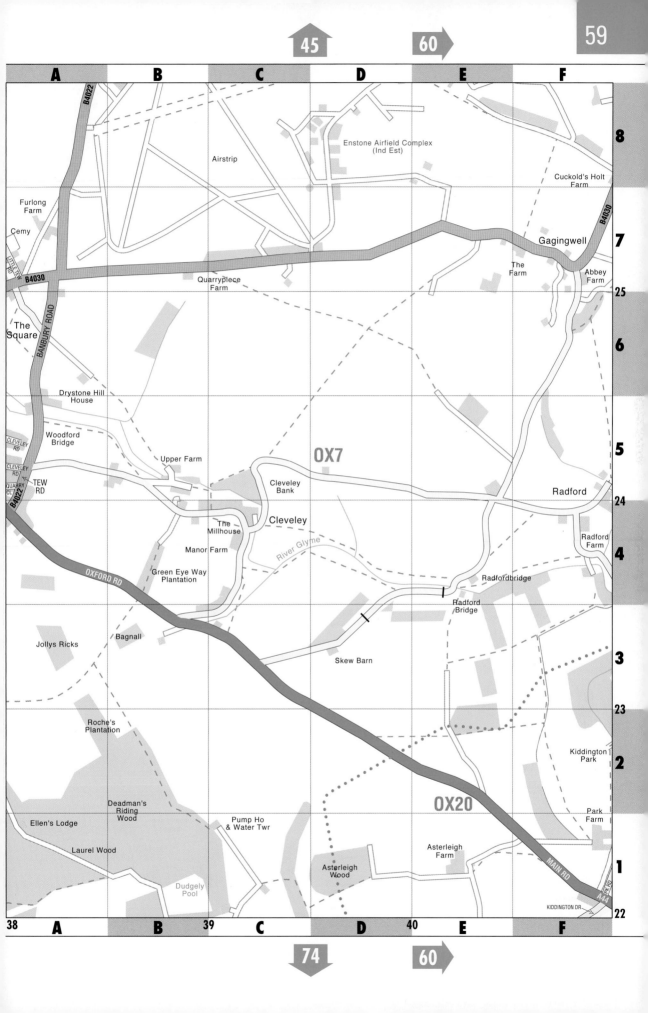

45   60

A   B   C   D   E   F

8

7

25

6

5

24

4

3

23

2

1

22

B4022

Furlong Farm

Cemy

LITTLE TEW RD

B4030

The Square

BANBURY ROAD

Drystone Hill House

CLEVELEY RD

Woodford Bridge

CLEVELEY RD

QUARRY CL

TEW RD

B4022

Jollys Ricks

OXFORD RD

Roche's Plantation

Ellen's Lodge

Deadman's Riding Wood

Laurel Wood

Dudgely Pool

Airstrip

Enstone Airfield Complex (Ind Est)

Quarryplece Farm

Upper Farm

Cleveley Bank

The Millhouse

Cleveley

Manor Farm

Green Eye Way Plantation

Bagnall

River Glyme

Skew Barn

Pump Ho & Water Twr

Asterleigh Wood

Cuckold's Holt Farm

B4030

Gagingwell

The Farm

Abbey Farm

OX7

Radford

Radford Farm

Radfordbridge

Radford Bridge

Kiddington Park

OX20

Park Farm

Asterleigh Farm

MAIN RD

A44

PK RD

KIDDINGTON DR

38   A   B   39   C   D   40   E   F

74   60

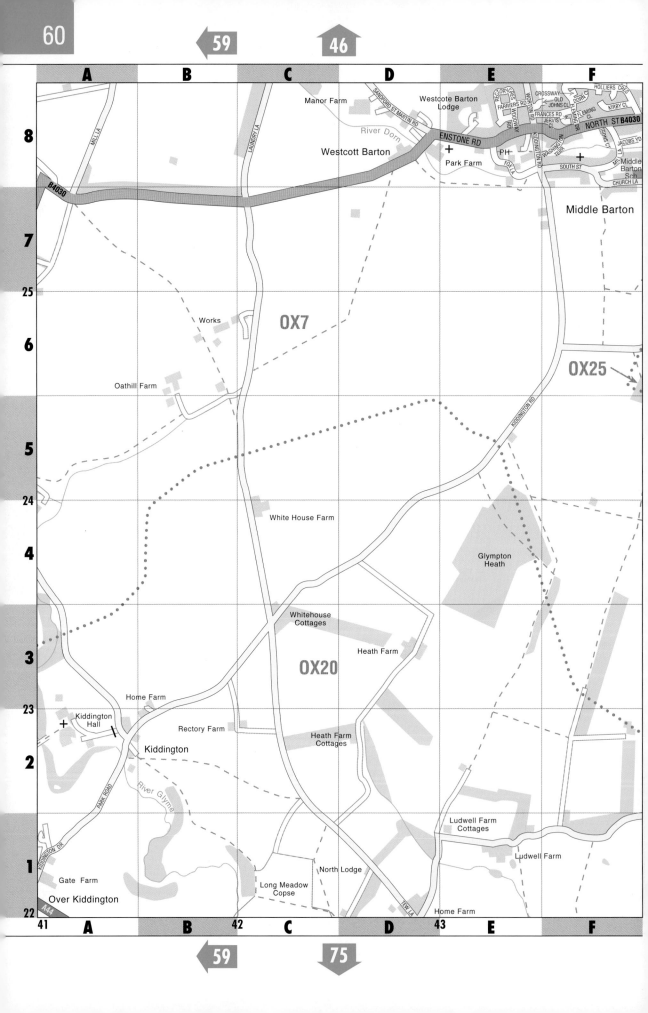

8

Manor Farm

Sandford St Martin Rd

Laundry La

Westcote Barton Lodge

River Dorn

ENSTONE RD

Westcott Barton

Park Farm

PH

RECTORY CRES
FARRIERS RD
FRANCES RD
OLD JOHNS CL
WOODWAY
WORTON RD
CROSSWAY
FLEMING RD
JERVIS CL
DORN CL
HOLLIERS CRES
KIRBY CL
NORTH ST **B4030**

B4030

FOX LA

KIDDINGTON RD

SOUTH ST

WASHINGTON TERR

FLEMING DR

TYDNES CT

JACOBS YD

MILL LA

Middle Barton Sch

CHURCH LA

Middle Barton

7

25

Works

OX7

6

Oathill Farm

OX25

5

24

White House Farm

KIDDINGTON RD

4

Glympton Heath

Whitehouse Cottages

OX20

3

Heath Farm

Home Farm

23

Kiddington Hall

Rectory Farm

Heath Farm Cottages

Kiddington

2

PARK ROAD

River Glyme

Ludwell Farm Cottages

Ludwell Farm

1

KIDDINGTON DR

Gate Farm

Over Kiddington

A44

North Lodge

Long Meadow Copse

TEW LA

Home Farm

22

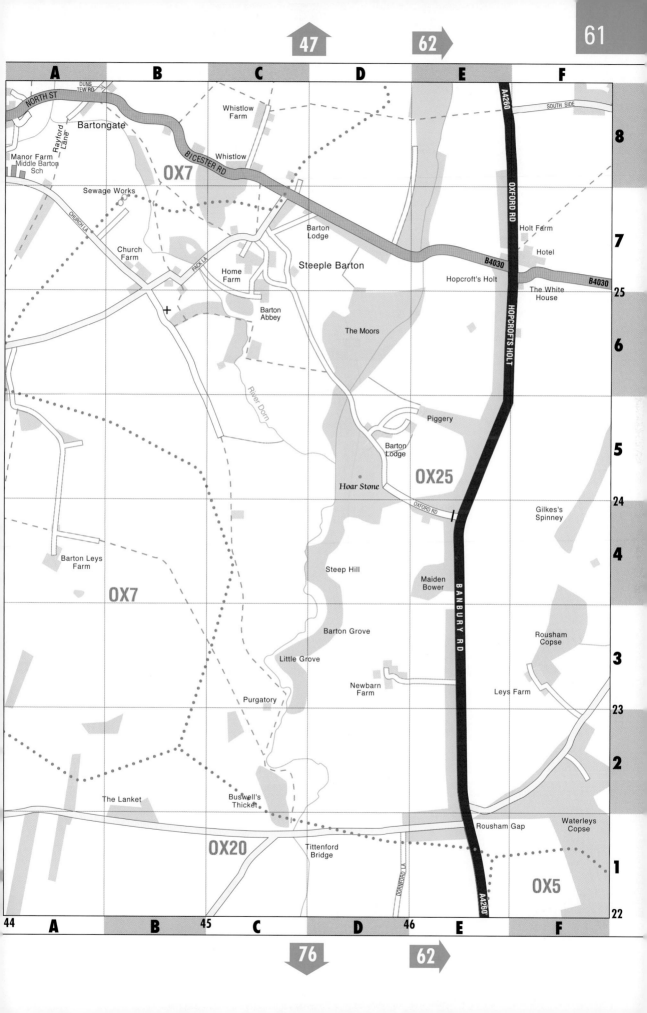

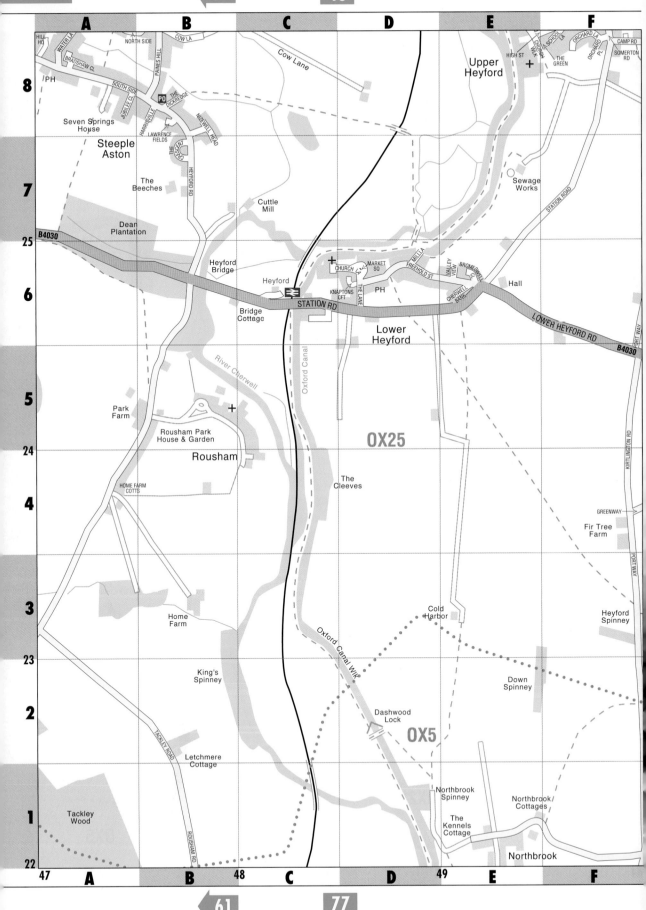

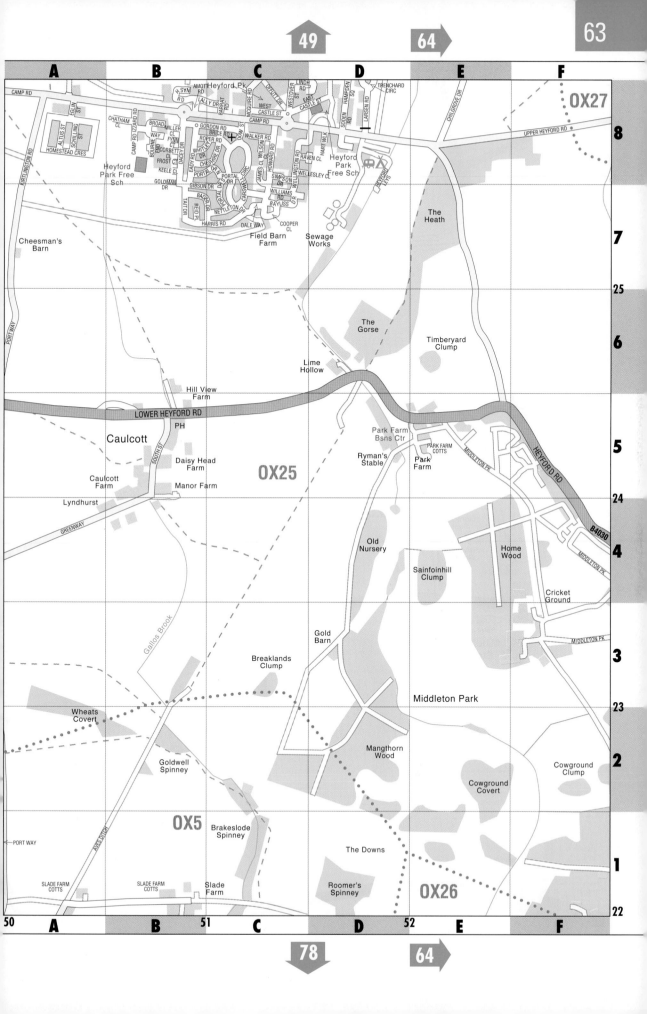

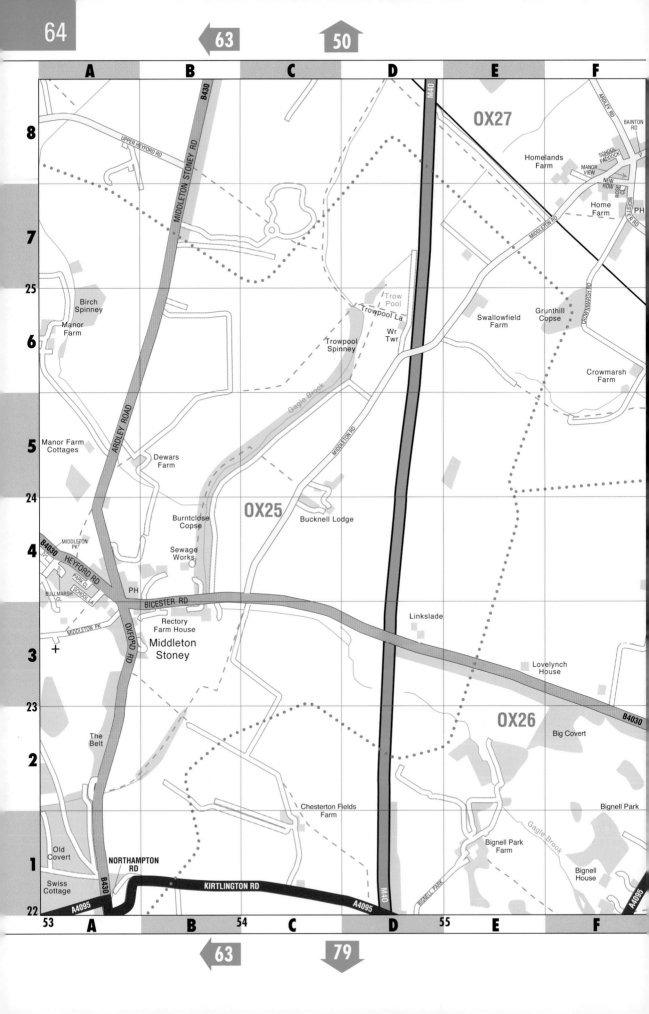

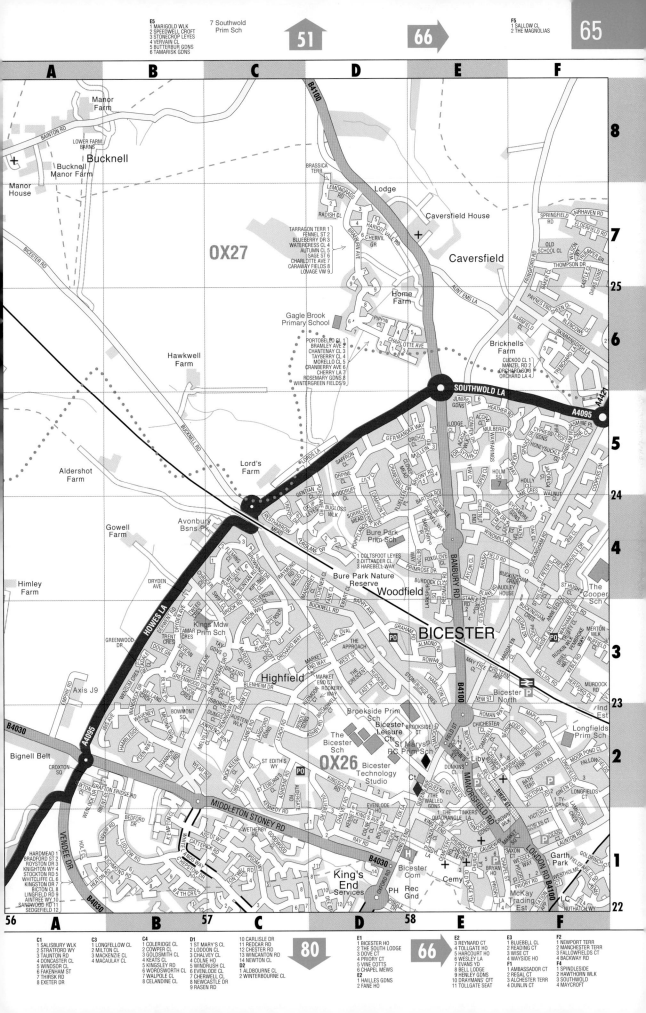

A B C D E F

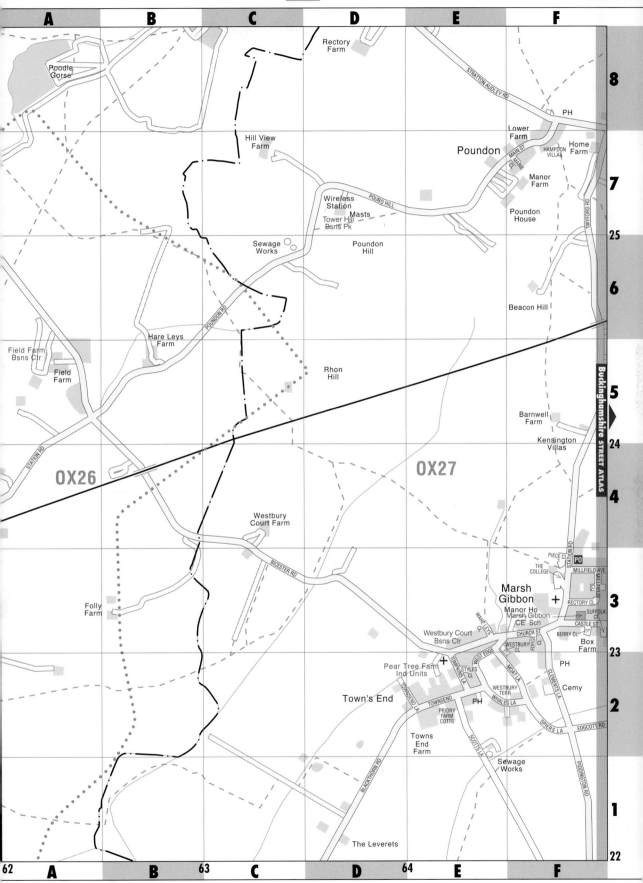

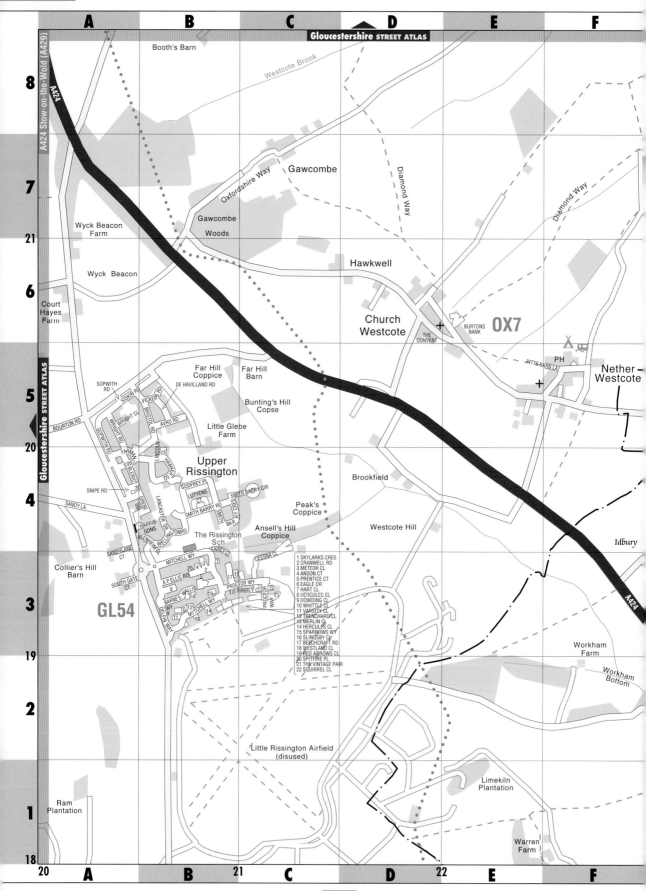

A424 Stow-on-the-Wold (A429)

Booth's Barn

Westcote Brook

Gloucestershire STREET ATLAS

8

7

21

6

5

20

4

3

19

2

1

18

Oxfordshire Way

Gawcombe

Gawcombe
Woods

Diamond Way

Diamond Way

Hawkwell

Wyck Beacon
Farm

Wyck Beacon

Church
Westcote

THE
CONVENT

BURTONS
BANK

OX7

PITTS BARN LA

PH

Court
Hayes
Farm

Far Hill
Coppice

Far Hill
Barn

Nether-
Westcote

Sopwith
Rd

DE HAVILLAND RD

Bunting's Hill
Copse

VICKERS RD

BRISTOL RD

AVRO RD

Little Glebe
Farm

BOURTON RD

SISKIN RD

WRIGHT CL

WRIGHT RD

SOPWITH RD

WINGURN CL

HAWKER CL

Upper
Rissington

Brookfield

SNIPE RD

SANDY LA

S3G

BLENOT RD

GODFREY PL

LUTYENS

LANCASTER DR

SMITH BARRY RD

SMITH BARRY CIR

RY CRES

SMITH
BAR

Peak's
Coppice

Westcote Hill

Idbury

Collier's Hill
Barn

HARRIS
GDNS

BLENHEIM CL

WELLINGTON RD

The Rissington
Sch

FAIREY CL

Ansell's Hill
Coppice

CESSNA CL

SANDYLANE
CT

SOUTH GATE
CT

MITCHELL WY

A P ELLIS RD

PROCTOR WY

FIREFLY CL

PROCTOR
WAY

GL54

BARNES
WY

WALLIS

MITCHELL WY

DELFIN WY

1 SKYLARKS CRES
2 CRANWELL RD
3 METEOR CL
4 ANSON CT
5 PRENTICE CT
6 EAGLE DR
7 HART CL
8 HERCULES CL
9 DOWDING CL
10 WHITTLE CL
11 VARSITY CL
12 TRENCHARD CL
13 MERLIN CL
14 HERCULES CL
15 SPARROWS WY
16 SLINGSBY CL
17 BEECHCRAFT RD
18 WESTLAND CL
19 RED ARROWS CL
20 SPITFIRE PL
21 THE VINTAGE PAIR
22 SQUIRREL CL

Workham
Farm

Workham
Bottom

Little Rissington Airfield
(disused)

Limekiln
Plantation

Ram
Plantation

Warren
Farm

20 A **21** B C **22** D E F

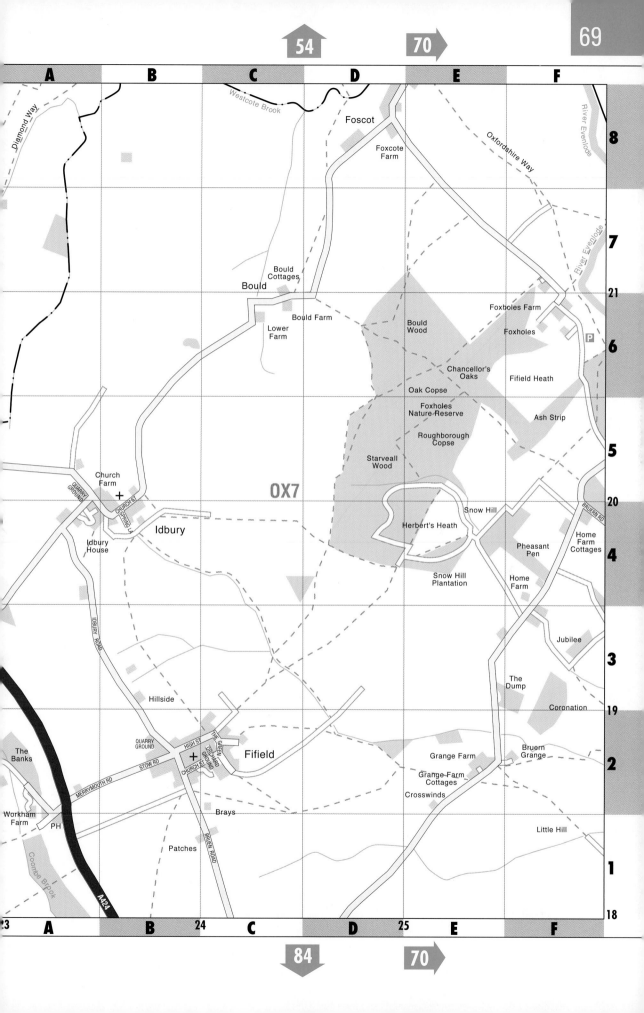

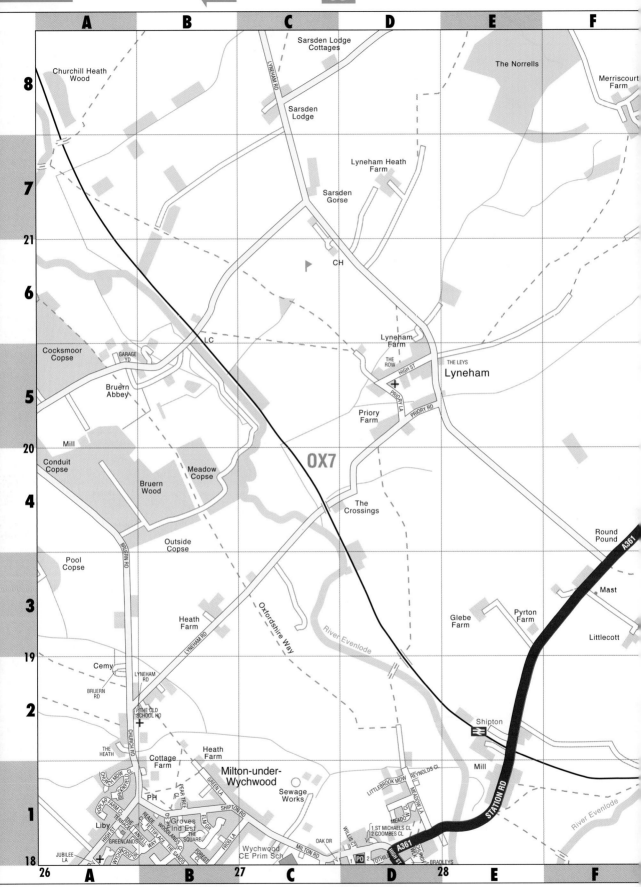

	A	B	C	D	E	F

8

Churchill Heath Wood

The Norrells

Merriscourt Farm

Sarsden Lodge Cottages

LYNEHAM RD

Sarsden Lodge

7

Lyneham Heath Farm

Sarsden Gorse

21

CH

6

LC

Cocksmoor Copse

GARAGE YD

Lyneham Farm

THE ROW

HIGH ST

THE LEYS

Lyneham

Bruern Abbey

5

PRIORY LA

PRIORY RD

Priory Farm

20

Mill

OX7

Conduit Copse

Meadow Copse

Bruern Wood

4

The Crossings

Round Pound

A361

Outside Copse

Mast

3

Pool Copse

BRUERN RD

Heath Farm

LYNEHAM RD

Oxfordshire Way

River Evenlode

Glebe Farm

Pyrton Farm

Littlecott

19

Cemy

LYNEHAM RD

BRUERN RD

2

THE OLD SCHOOL RD

Shipton

1

THE HEATH

CHURCH RD

Cottage Farm

PH

Heath Farm

GREEN LA

Milton-under-Wychwood

Sewage Works

Mill

STATION RD

River Evenlode

POPLAR FARM CL

BROCKHILL CL

THE TERRACE

PEAR TREE CL

SHIPTON RD

ELM GR

FROG LA

LITTLEBROOK MDW

REYNOLDS CL

MEADOW LA

MEADO

Liby

HIGH ST

READE

WOODLANDS CL

FETTIPLACE

ANGEL

THE SANDS

GROVES IND EST

THE SQUARE

FORESH

OAK DR

WILLIS CL

1 ST MICHAELS CL
2 COOMBES CL

A361

18

JUBILEE LA

WYCHWOOD

GREENLANDS

WYCHWOOD CL

WAY

MILTON RD

Wychwood CE Prim Sch

PO

2

HIGH ST

OTHILL

CHURCH WLK

BRADLEYS

26	A	**27**	B		C	**28**	D		E		F

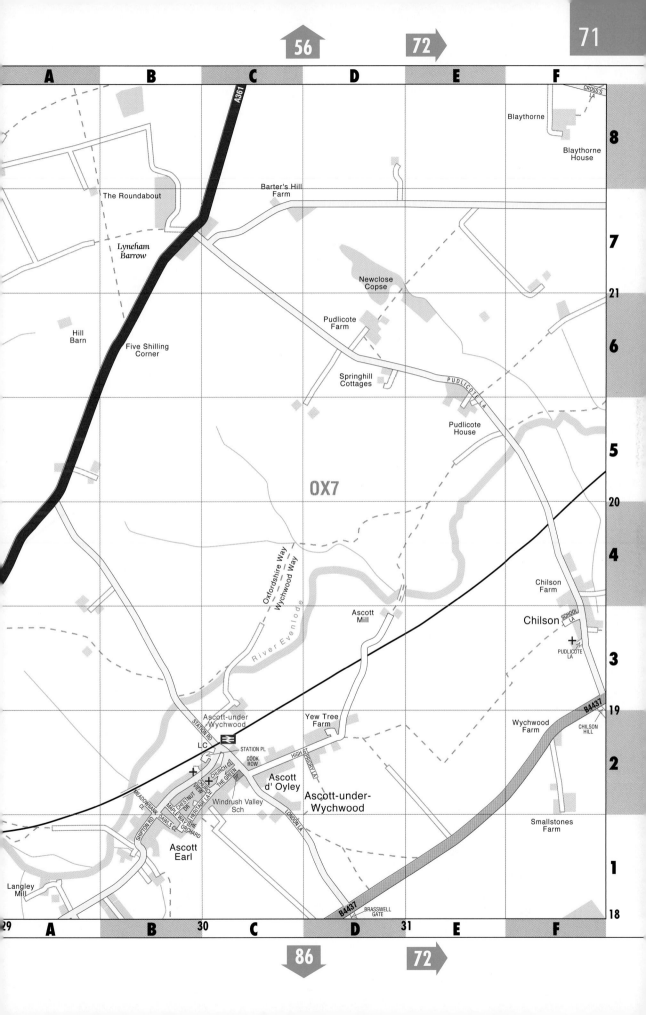

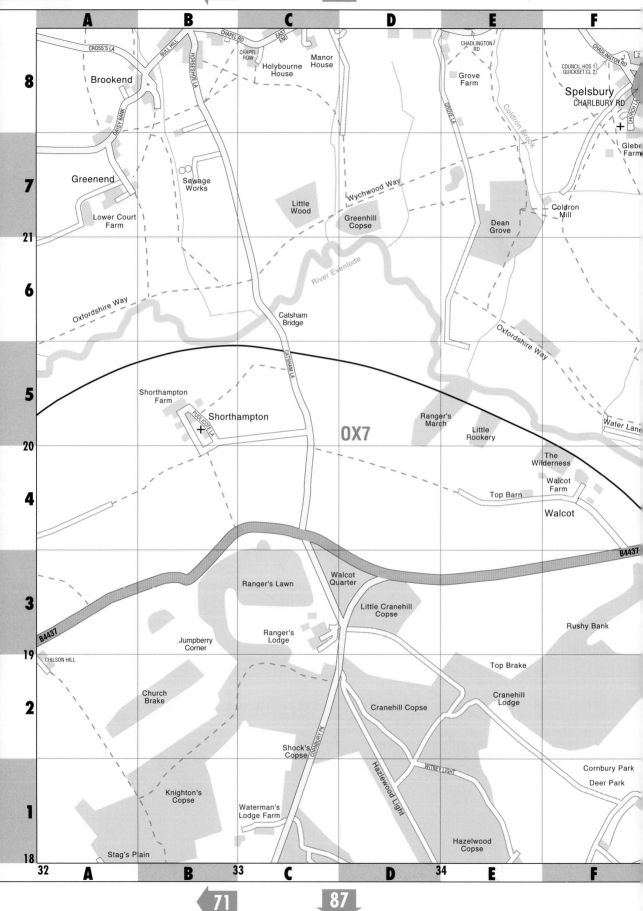

A **B** **C** **D** **E** **F**

8

CROSS'S LA

Brookend

BULL HILL

HORSESHOE LA

CHAPEL RD

EAST END

CHAPEL ROW

Holybourne House

Manor House

CHADLINGTON RD

Grove Farm

Coldron Brook

COUNCIL HOS 1
QUICKSET CL 2

CHADLINGTON RD

2

Spelsbury
CHARLBURY RD

CHURCH LA

DAISY BANK

Glebe Farm

7

Greenend

Sewage Works

Little Wood

Wychwood Way

Greenhill Copse

GROVE LA

Dean Grove

Coldron Mill

Lower Court Farm

21

River Evenlode

6

Oxfordshire Way

Catsham Bridge

Oxfordshire Way

Water Lane

CATSHAM LA

5

Shorthampton Farm

PUDLICOTE LA

Shorthampton

OX7

Ranger's March

Little Rookery

The Wilderness

Walcot Farm

20

Walcot

4

Top Barn

B4437

B4437

3

Ranger's Lawn

Walcot Quarter

Little Cranehill Copse

Rushy Bank

19

CHILSON HILL

Jumpberry Corner

Ranger's Lodge

Top Brake

Cranehill Lodge

2

Church Brake

CORNBURY PK

Cranehill Copse

Shock's Copse

WITNEY LIGHT

HAZELWOOD LIGHT

Cornbury Park
Deer Park

1

Knighton's Copse

Waterman's Lodge Farm

Hazelwood Copse

18

Stag's Plain

32 **A** 33 **B** **C** 34 **D** **E** **F**

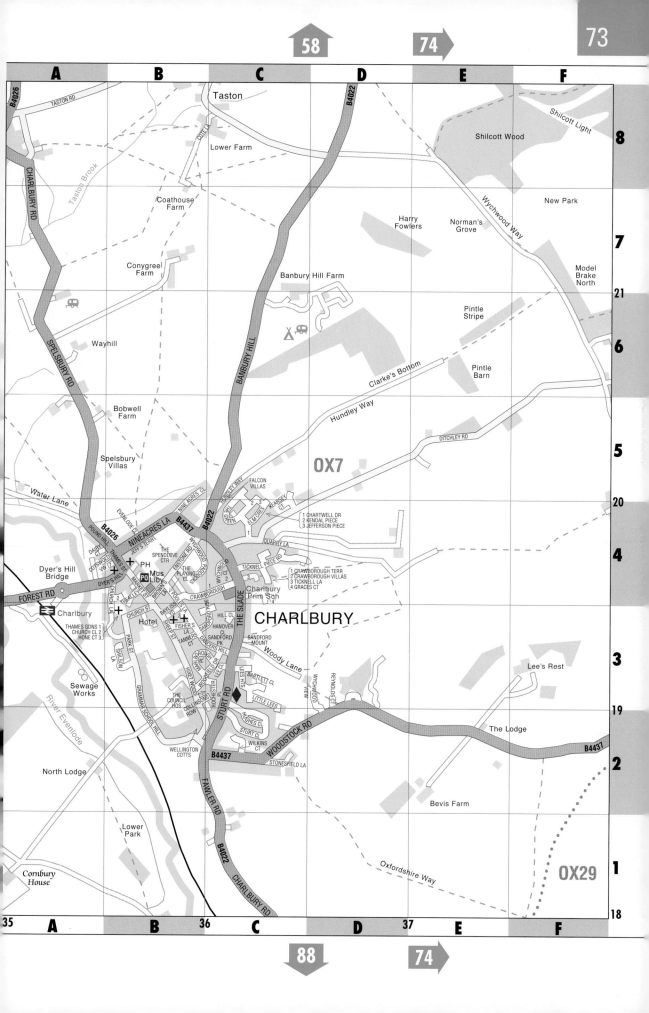

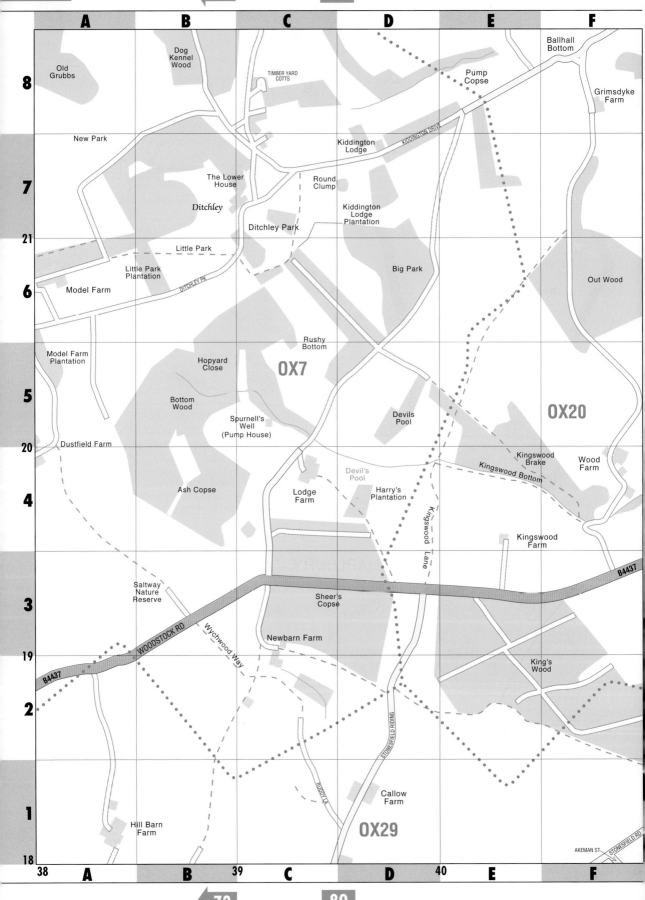

A | B | C | D | E | F

8

Old Grubbs

Dog Kennel Wood

TIMBER YARD COTTS

Pump Copse

Ballhall Bottom

Grimsdyke Farm

New Park

KIDDINGTON DRIVE

Kiddington Lodge

7

The Lower House

Round Clump

Kiddington Lodge Plantation

21

Ditchley

Ditchley Park

Little Park

Big Park

Out Wood

6

Little Park Plantation

DITCHLEY PK.

Model Farm

Rushy Bottom

Model Farm Plantation

Hopyard Close

OX7

5

Bottom Wood

Devils Pool

OX20

20

Dustfield Farm

Spurnell's Well (Pump House)

Devil's Pool

Kingswood Brake

Kingswood Bottom

Wood Farm

4

Ash Copse

Lodge Farm

Harry's Plantation

Kingswood Lane

Kingswood Farm

B4437

Saltway Nature Reserve

Sheer's Copse

3

WOODSTOCK RD

Wychwood Way

Newbarn Farm

King's Wood

19

B4437

2

STONESFIELD RIDING

BUCKY LA

Callow Farm

1

Hill Barn Farm

OX29

AKEMAN ST

STONESFIELD RD

18

38 | A | B | 39 | C | D | 40 | E | F

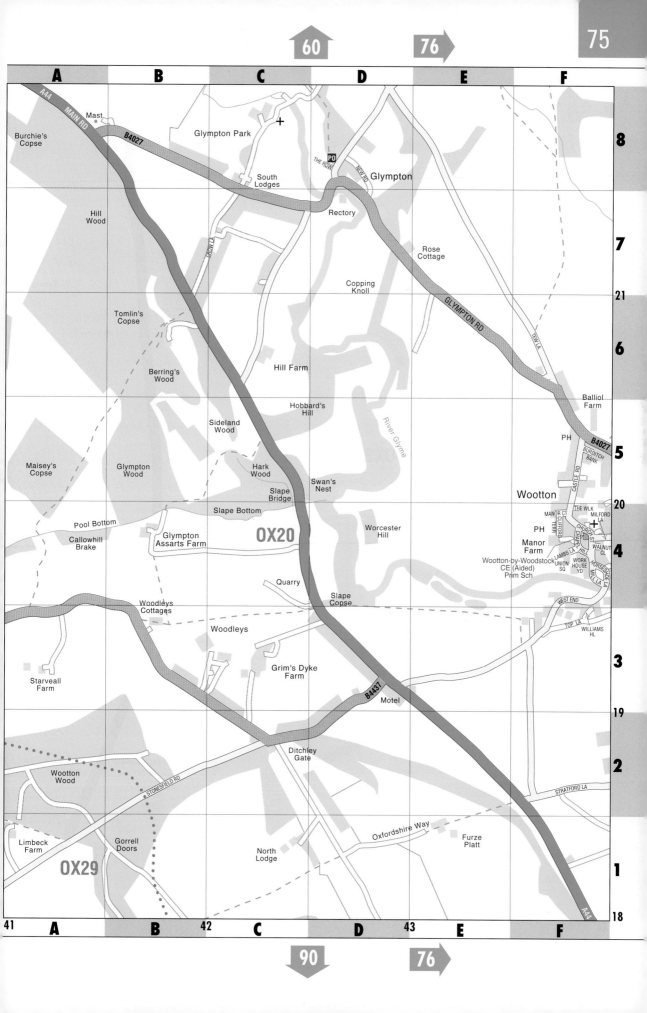

A   B   C   D   E   F

8

Burchie's
Copse

Mast

Glympton Park

A44

MAIN RD

B4027

South
Lodges

PO
THE ROW

NEW RD

Glympton

7

Hill
Wood

Rectory

Rose
Cottage

GLYMPTON RD

TEW LA

21

6

Tomlin's
Copse

CROW LA

Copping
Knoll

Berring's
Wood

Hill Farm

Balliol
Farm

B4027

5

Maisey's
Copse

Glympton
Wood

Sideland
Wood

Hobbard's
Hill

River Glyme

PH

BURDITCH
BANK

CASTLE RD

Wootton

Hark
Wood

Slape
Bridge

Swan's
Nest

THE WLK

MILFORD
LA

20

Pool Bottom

Callowhill
Brake

Glympton
Assarts Farm

Slape Bottom

OX20

Worcester
Hill

MANOR CT
CLIFFORD
TERR

CHAPEL HILL

PH

Manor
Farm

CHURCH ST

LAMBS LA

WALNUT
CL

4

Woodleys
Cottages

Quarry

Slape
Copse

Wootton-by-Woodstock
CE (Aided)
Prim Sch

UNION
SQ

WORK
HOUSE
YD

HORSESHOE LA

MILL LA

Woodleys

WEST END

TOP LA

WILLIAMS
HL

3

Starveall
Farm

Grim's Dyke
Farm

B4437

Motel

19

Wootton
Wood

STONESFIELD RD

Ditchley
Gate

2

STRATFORD LA

Limbeck
Farm

OX29

Gorrell
Doors

North
Lodge

Oxfordshire Way

Furze
Platt

1

A44

18

41   A   B   42   C   D   43   E   F

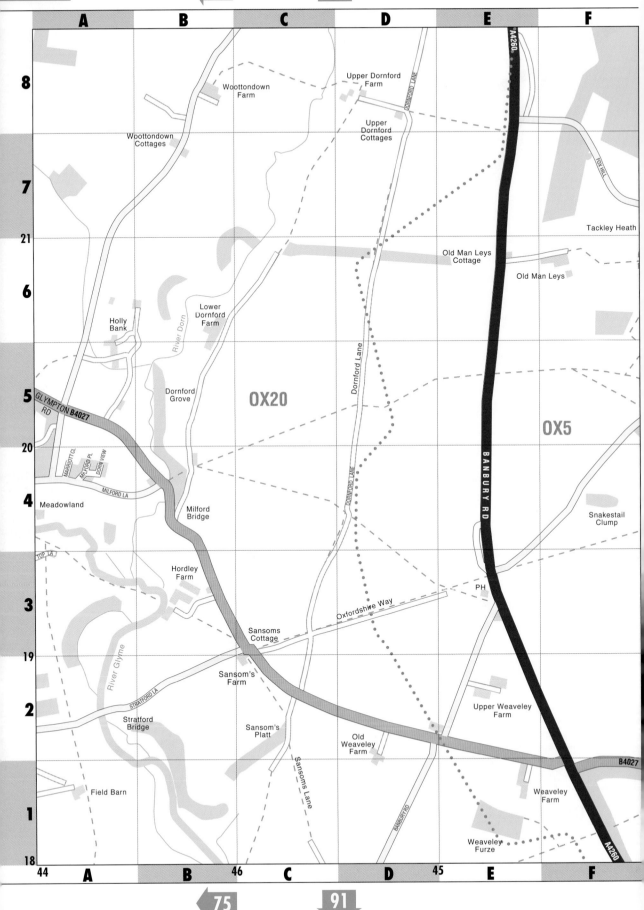

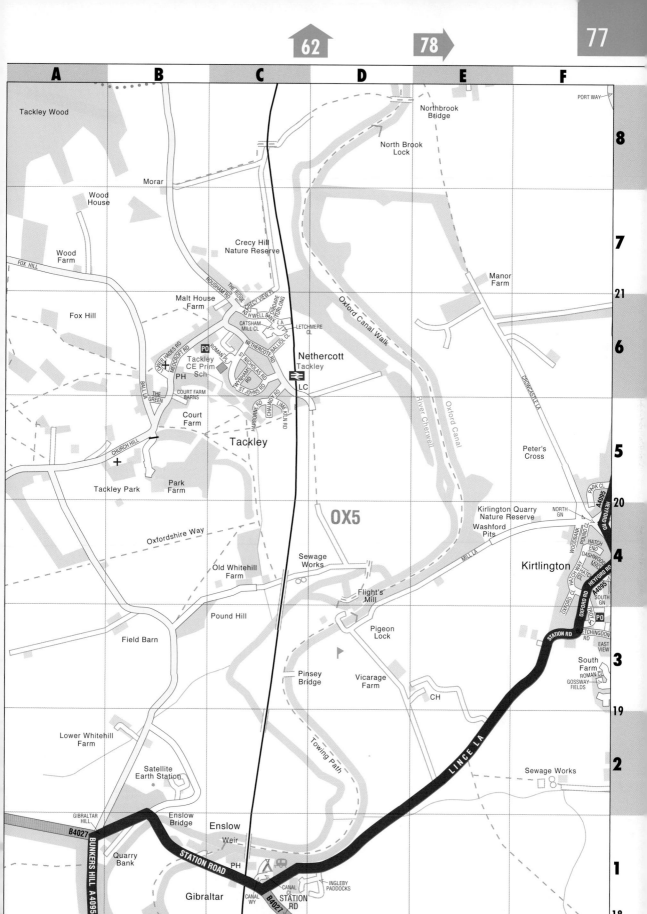

Tackley Wood

Morar

Wood House

Wood Farm

FOX HILL

Fox Hill

Crecy Hill Nature Reserve

ROUSHAM RD
THE RIDGE
CRECY VIEW PL
ASH WELL BANK
TIDMARSH FURLONG

Malt House Farm

CATSHAM MILL CL
LETCHMERE CL

NETHERCOTE RD
BALLIOL CL

PO
ROMAN PL

ST NICHOLAS RD

SWEET HADES RD
METCROFT RD

+

PH

THE GREEN

Tackley CE Prim Sch

TWYNHAMS RD
ST JOHNS RD

HARBORNE RD
CHAUNDY RD
LIME KILN RD

Nethercott
Tackley

LC

BALL LA

COURT FARM BARNS

Court Farm

CHURCH HILL

+

Tackley

Oxford Canal Walk

River Cherwell

Oxford Canal

Manor Farm

CROWCASTLE LA

Peter's Cross

Tackley Park

Park Farm

Oxfordshire Way

OX5

Kirlington Quarry Nature Reserve
Washford Pits

PARK CL

A4095 HEYFORD RD

NORTH GN

Old Whitehill Farm

Sewage Works

MILL LA

Kirtlington

WOODBANK
POUND CL
HATCH END
DASHWOOD MEWS
HATCH WAY
OXFORD CL
OXFORD RD

SOUTH GN

PO

Pound Hill

Flight's Mill

BLETCHINGDON RD
EAST VIEW

STATION RD

Field Barn

Pigeon Lock

South Farm
ROMAN CL
GOSSWAY FIELDS

Lower Whitehill Farm

Pinsey Bridge

Vicarage Farm

CH

LINCE LA

Satellite Earth Station

Towing Path

Sewage Works

GIBRALTAR HILL
B4027

BUNKERS HILL A4095

Quarry Bank

Enslow Bridge

Enslow

Weir

STATION ROAD

PH

Gibraltar

CANAL WY
STATION RD
CANAL CL

INGLEBY PADDOCKS

B4027

PORT WAY

Northbrook Bridge

North Brook Lock

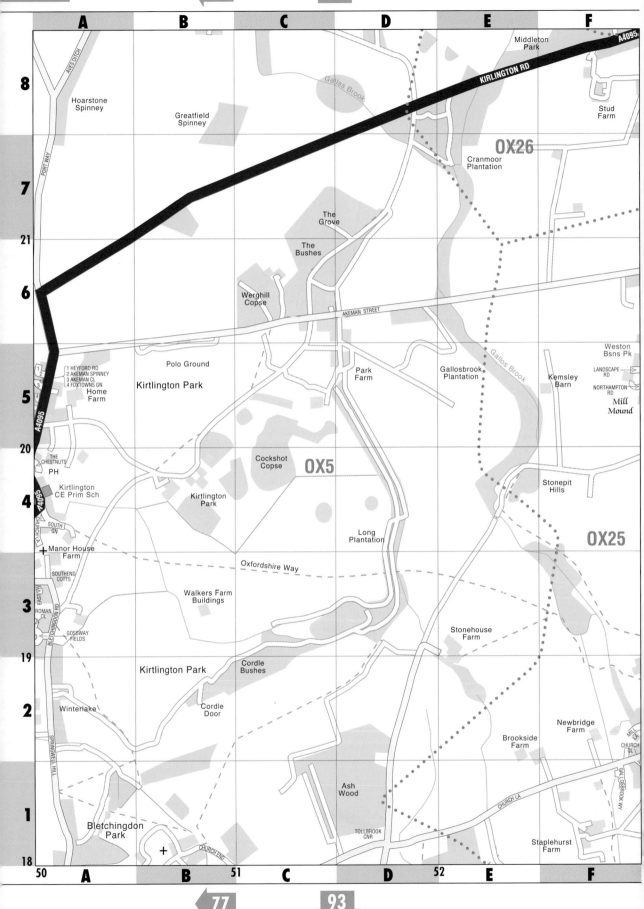

A B C D E F

8

Hoarstone
Spinney

Greatfield
Spinney

Middleton
Park

KIRLINGTON RD

A4095

Stud
Farm

OX26

7

Gallos Brook

Cranmoor
Plantation

21

The
Grove

The
Bushes

6

Werghill
Copse

AKEMAN STREET

Gallos Brook

Weston
Bsns Pk

LANDSCAPE
RD

NORTHAMPTON
RD

Polo Ground

Park
Farm

Gallosbrook
Plantation

Kemsley
Barn

Mill
Mound

5

1 HEYFORD RD
2 AKEMAN SPINNEY
3 AKEMAN CL
4 FOXTOWNS GN

Home
Farm

Kirtlington Park

A4095

20

THE
CHESTNUTS

PH

Cockshot
Copse

OX5

Stonepit
Hills

4

A4095

CHURCH LA

Kirtlington
CE Prim Sch

Kirtlington
Park

Long
Plantation

OX25

SOUTH
GN

Manor House
Farm

Oxfordshire Way

Stonehouse
Farm

SOUTHEND
COTTS

EAST WY

ROMAN CL

BLETCHINGDON RD

3

GOSSWAY
FIELDS

Walkers Farm
Buildings

19

Kirtlington Park

Cordle
Bushes

Newbridge
Farm

MILL LA

CHURCH CL

2

Winterlake

Cordle
Door

Brookside
Farm

SPRINGWELL HILL

Ash
Wood

CHURCH LA

GALLOSBROOK WY

1

Bletchingdon
Park

CHURCH END

TOLLBROOK
CNR

Staplehurst
Farm

18

50 A B 51 C D 52 E F

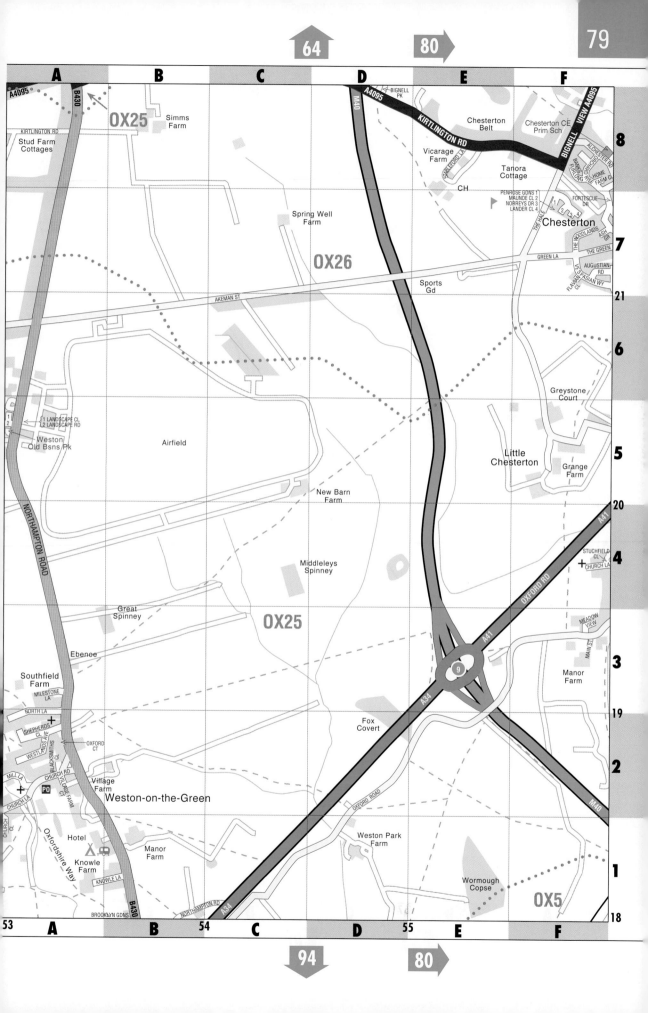

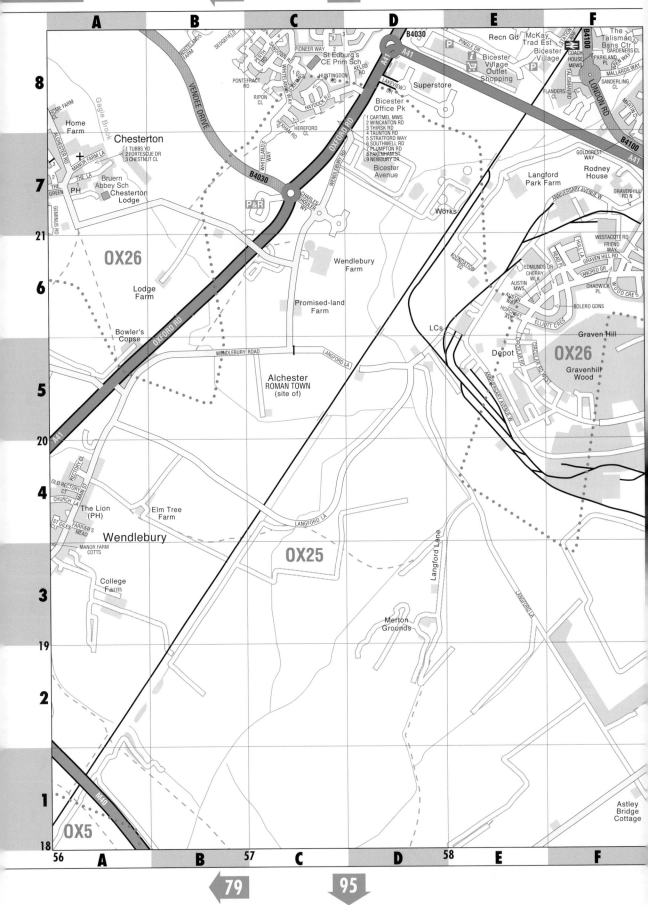

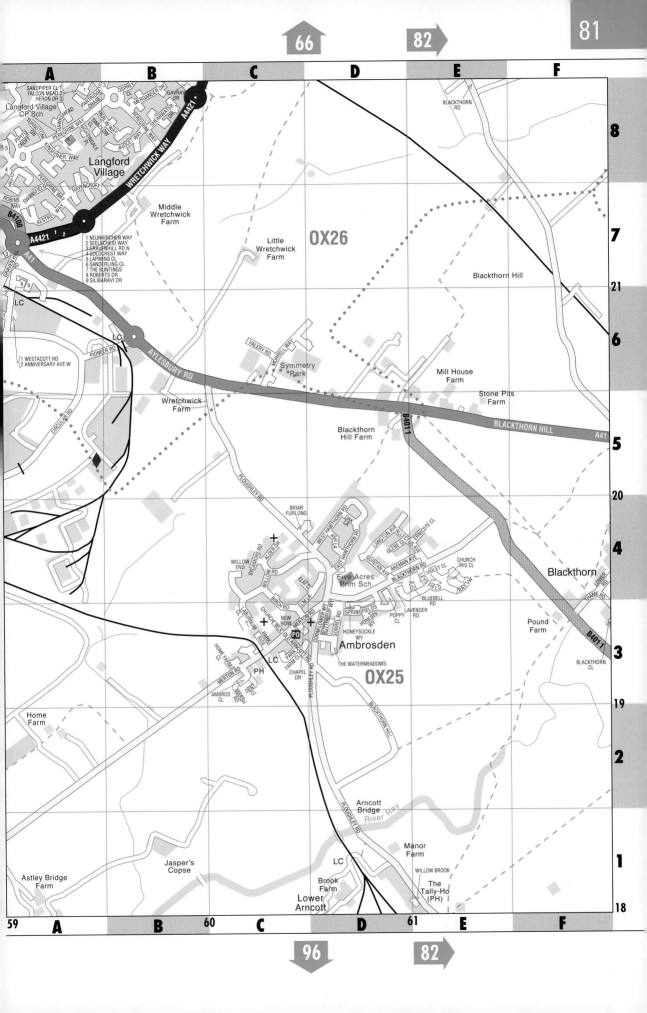

A **B** **C** **D** **E** **F**

OX26

8

Marsh-Field Farm

SCOTTS LANE

Yew Elm Farm

Furze Ground

OX27

7

Berrnwood Jubilee Way

Essex Farm

21

MARSH GIBBON RD

Oakapple Farm

BLACKTHORN RD

PIDDINGTON RD

6

Grange Farm

HEET RD

A41

5

BICESTER RD

Heath Bridge

River Ray

Weir Farm

WEIR LA FARM CL

20

AYLESBURY RD

BICESTER RD A41 A41 AYLESBURY

Westbury Farm

LOWER RD

Leaches Farm

4

Blackthorn

STATION RD

ELM TREE FARM

ELM TREE CL

BLACKTHORN CL

EAST VIEW

SWAN CL

Shaw's Farm

Lower Cow Leys Farm

CHAPEL CL

THAME RD

HP18

3

B4011

OX25

Piddington Cow Leys

MARSH GIBBON RD

Middle Cow Leys Farm

19

Blackthorn Bridge

2

Bridge Farm

Upper Cow Leys Farm

Treadwell's Barn

New Farm

1

HP18

18

B4011

62 **A** **B** **63** **C** **D** **64** **E** **F**

Buckinghamshire Street Atlas

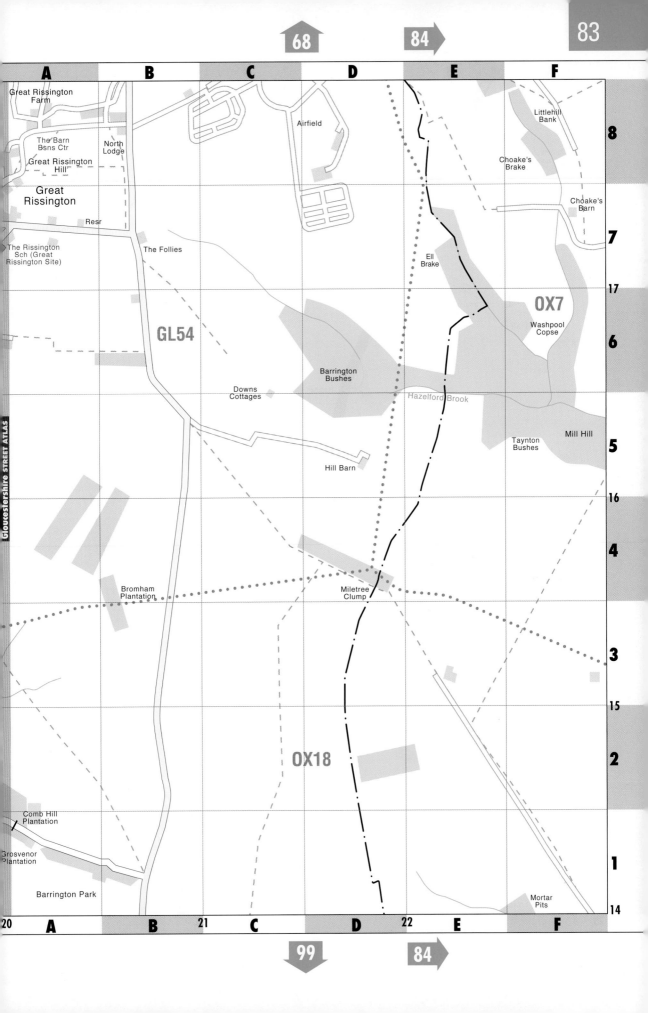

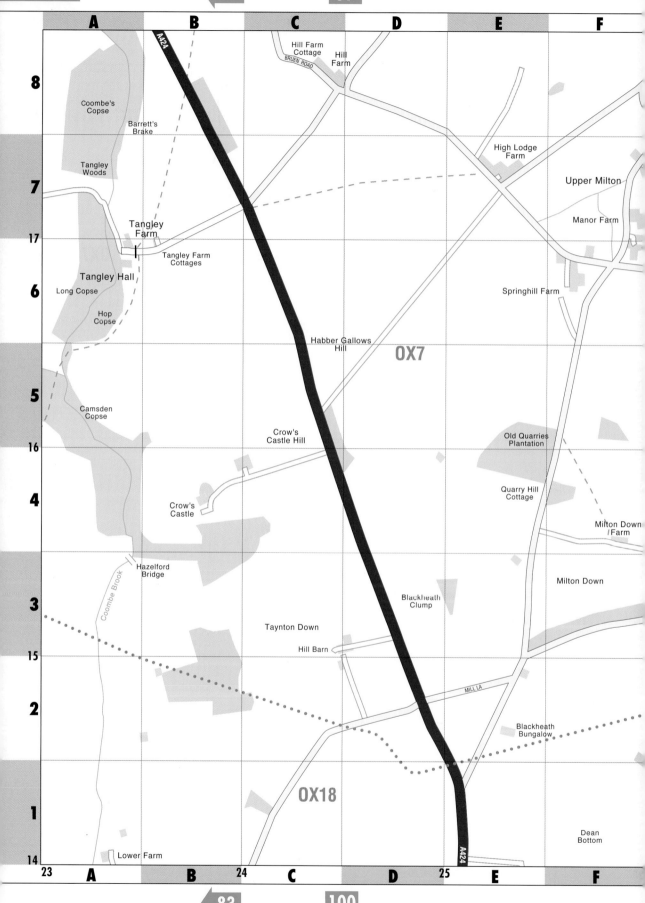

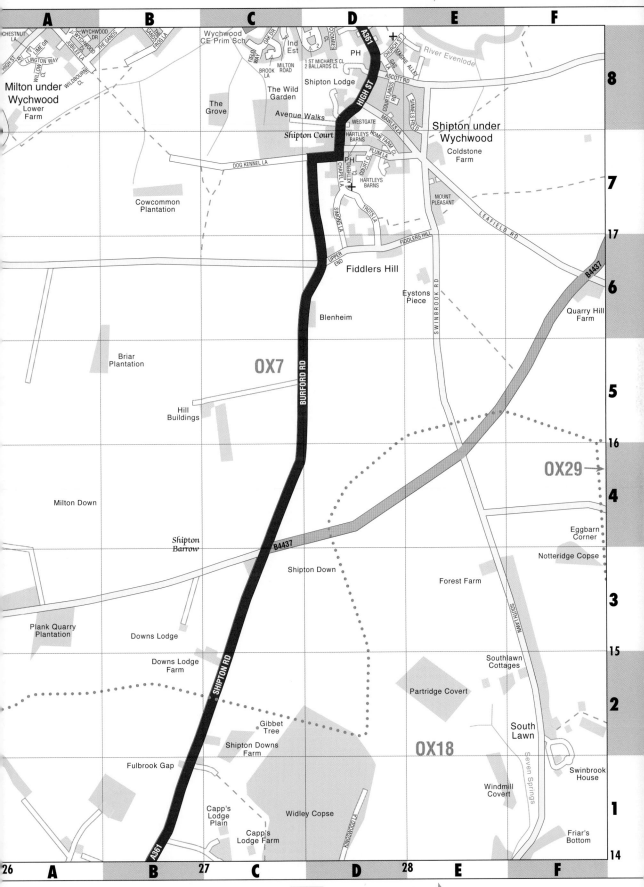

A B C D E F

8

Wychwood Manor

Fernhill Farm

Coldwell Brook

B4437

OX7

Brasswell Gate

Wychwood Way

7

Coldwell Bridge

Boynal Copse

Kingstandin Farm

17

B4437

Brasswell Corner

6

Priest Grove

Woefield Green

Kingswood Clump

Fairspear Farm

LEAFIELD RD

Fairspear Farm

5

Langley Holding Cottage

The Grove

Fairspear House

Farfield Corner

Limekiln Spinney

16

Homefield Spinney

4

Mast

FAIRSPEAR RD

Langley

Chimney-end

Bramington Farm

Langley Farm

Leafield Tech Ctr

Mast

LOWER END

PO

PH

THE GREEN

3

CHAPEL CL

Leafield

RIDINGS BGLWS

PH

Leafield CE (Controlled) Prim Sch

Church Farm

WITNEY LA

15

The Ridings Farm

Potter's Hill Farm

Potter's Hill

THE RIDINGS

2

Buttermilk Farm

OX18

Lowbarrow Farm

Leafield Pig Farm

Hill Farm

BUTTERMILK LA

1

Wastidge Spinney

Fordwells Farm Barns

PURRANTS LA

14

29

A B 30 C D 31 E F

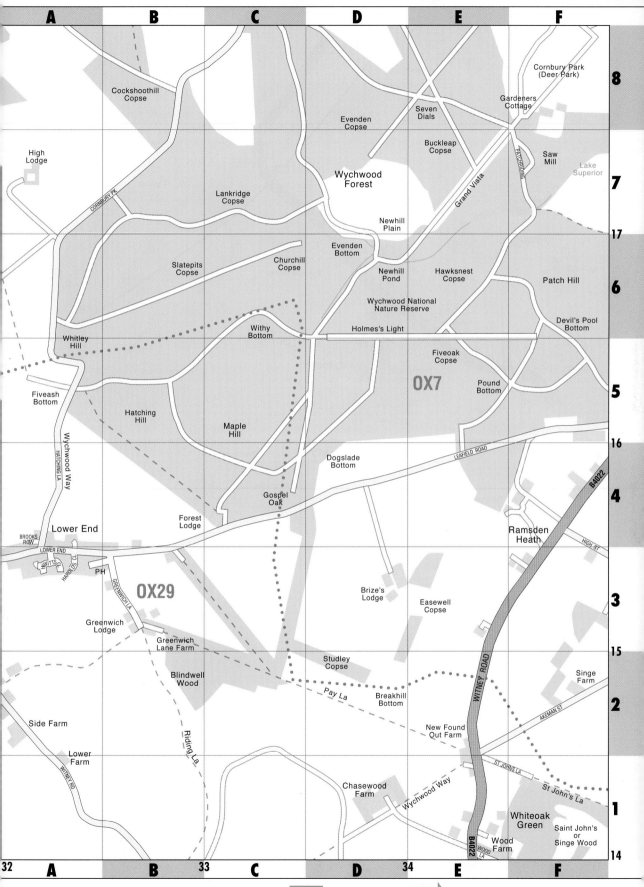

87
73

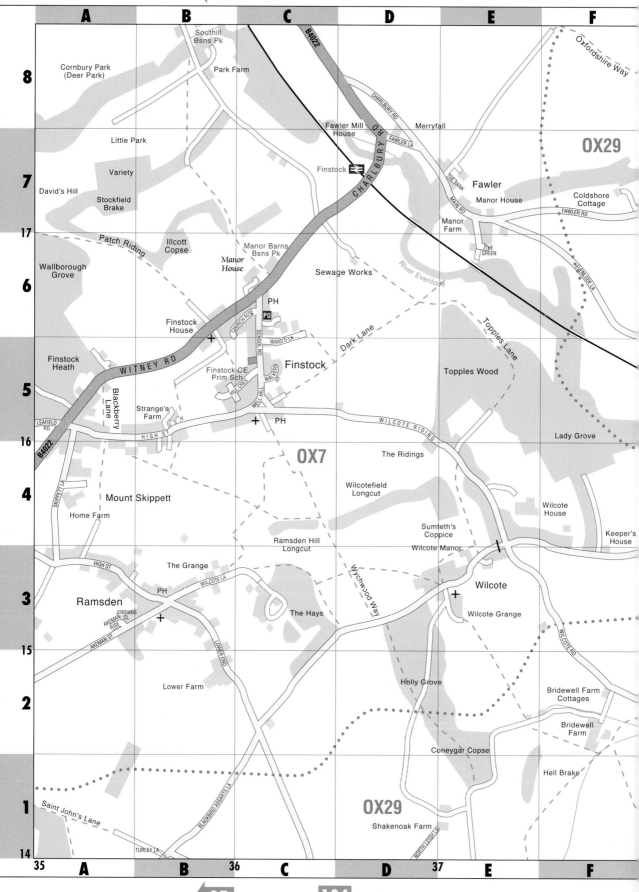

87
104

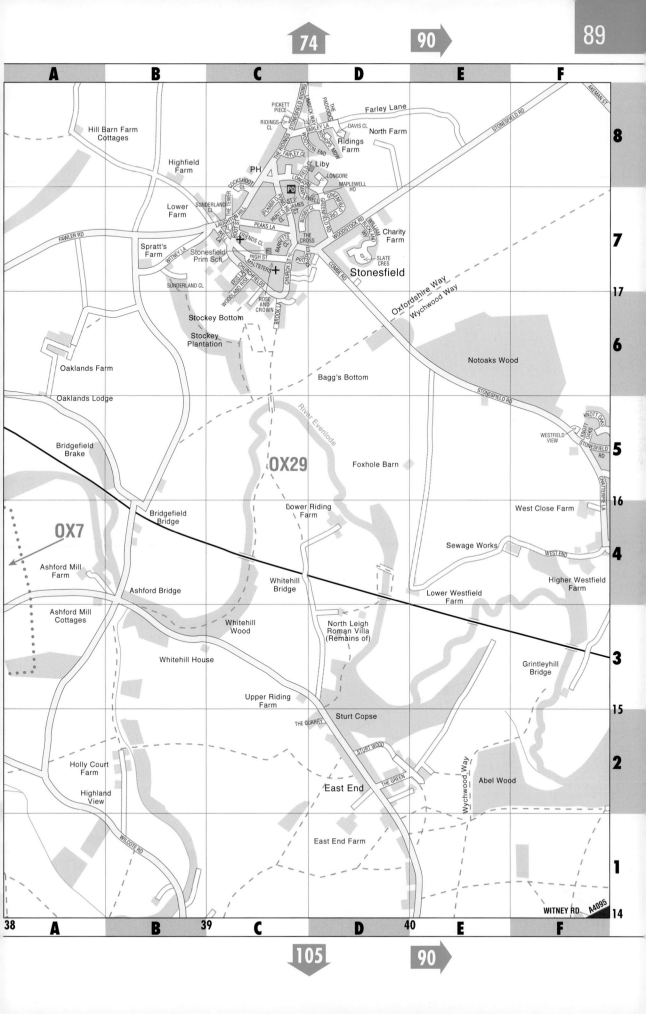

A B C D E F

8

Littleworth Farm

Oxfordshire Way
Wychwood Way

The Big Clump

Stonefield Steps

Mapleton Pond

7

Akeman Street Farm

Park Farm

Great Park

OX20

Column of Victory

17

Fourteen Acre Clump

6

Square Firs

Long Firs

Blenheim Park

Fair Rosamund's Well

Queen Pool

Grand Bridge

SQUARE FIRS

KNOTT OAKS

STONESFIELD RD

New Park

Wychwood Way

The Lake

5

Combe

CHATTERPIE LA

Foxhole Farm

PARK RD

ORCHARD CL

Manor Farm

16

PH

CHURCH WLK

COMBE GATE

ROBIN HILL

WEST END

Combe CE Prim Sch

MARLBOROUGH TERR

Combe Lodge

EAST END

High Park

4

Resr

Peagle Wood

Wedgehook Wood

BOLTON'S LA

Boltons Farm

EAST END

High Lodge

HORNS LA

OX29

Combe Cliff

Dog Kennel Hill

3

Combe

River Evenlode

Combe Mill

15

2

MILLWOOD END

MILLWOOD FARM BARNS

BOLSOVER CL

BROOK WAY

BELWOOD DR

Millwood Farm

EVENLODE VALE

MILLWOOD VALE

SWAN LA

CORN ST

PH

BAKER'S CT

MYRTLE CL

Long Hanborough

Myrtle Farm

WASTIE'S ORCH

PH

Park La

Long House

Long Hanborough Bridge

A4095

1

WITNEY RD

SLATTERS CT

HURDESWELL

BECKETTS CL

NEW RD

CHURCHILL WAY

GLYME WAY

CHURCH RD

ROOSEVELT RD

RILEY CL

PO

Hanborough Manor CE Sch

MAIN RD

BURLEIGH CT

Mast

REGENTOR

REAR RELIANCE WAY

OLYMPIAN CL

Hanborough

Hanborough Bsns Pk
Oxford Bus Mus

LODGE RD

BARK SIDE

FENLOCK RD

FERN FOX RD

LOWER RD

Fenlock Ct

A4095

14

A4095

41 42 43

A B C D E F

A1
1 LANGFORD WAY
2 GESSEY CL
3 GREENWAY LA
4 PITTICK CL
5 WILLIS CT

E1
1 BEDFORD MWS
2 RENOWN CT

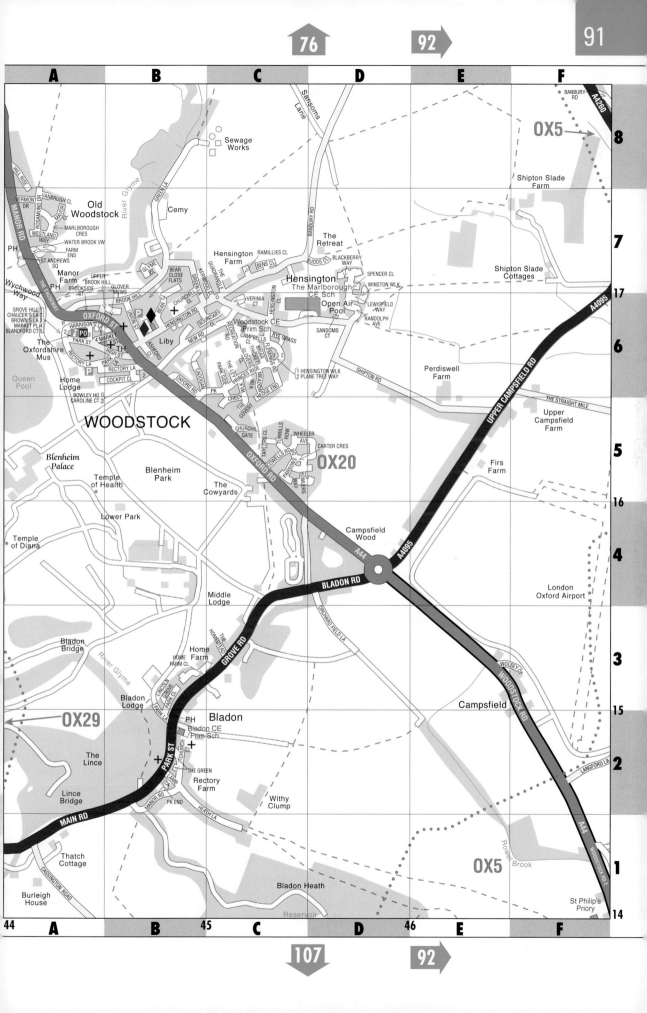

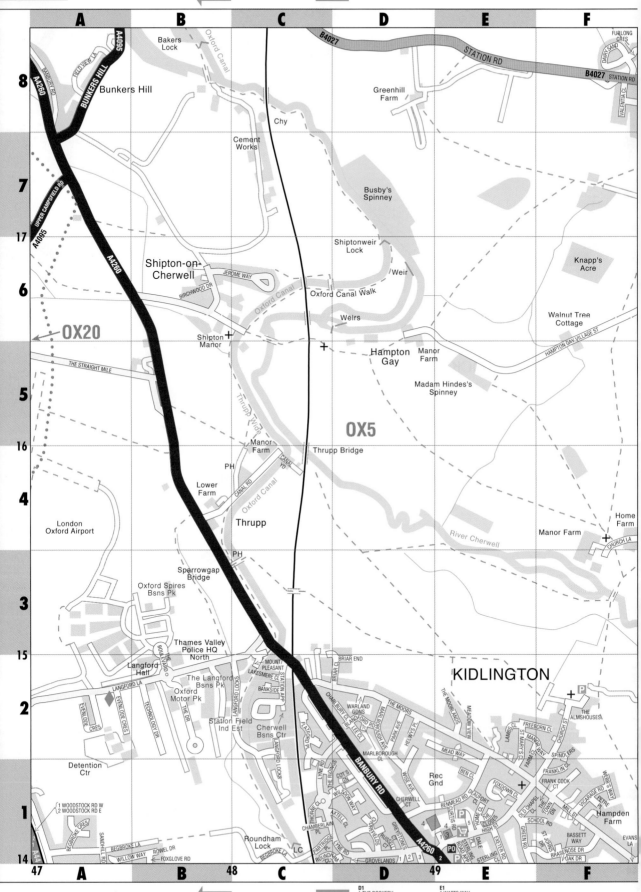

91 108

D1
1 THE ROOKERY
2 HEYFORD MEAD
3 CROWN RD
4 North Kidlington
Prim Sch

E1
1 WATTS WAY
2 OXFORD RD
3 North Kidlington Prim Sch
4 Oxford English Acad
5 FORESTERS WAY

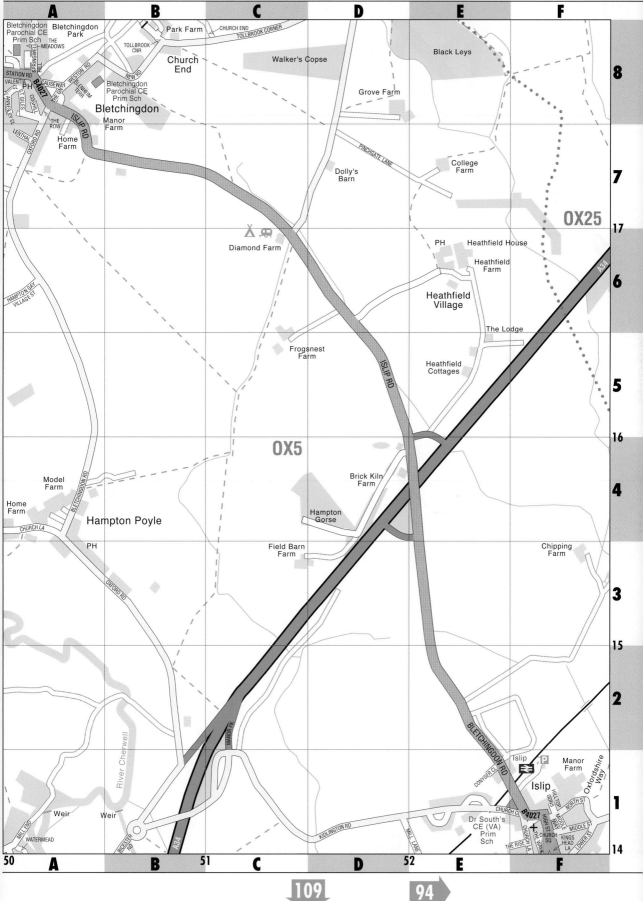

A   B   C   D   E   F

8

NORTHAMPTON
RD
PH
B430
NORTHAMPTON RD
NORTHAMPTON
RD
OXFORD
RD
A34

Weston Wood

LC
Holts Farm

7

Gallos Brook

OX25

MANSADOR RD

17

A34   Family Farm

Oddington
Wood

6

Rowles Farm

Oddington
Grange

5

Barndon
Farm

New House
Farm

16

Oxfordshire Way

4

OX5

RAY VIEW

HIGH ST

Brookfurlong
Farm

Hillcroft Farm

3

Otter House

COLLEGE
FARM CL

15

MAIN ST

Oddington

2

Rectory Farm

New River Ray

Logg Farm

1

River Ray

OX3

14

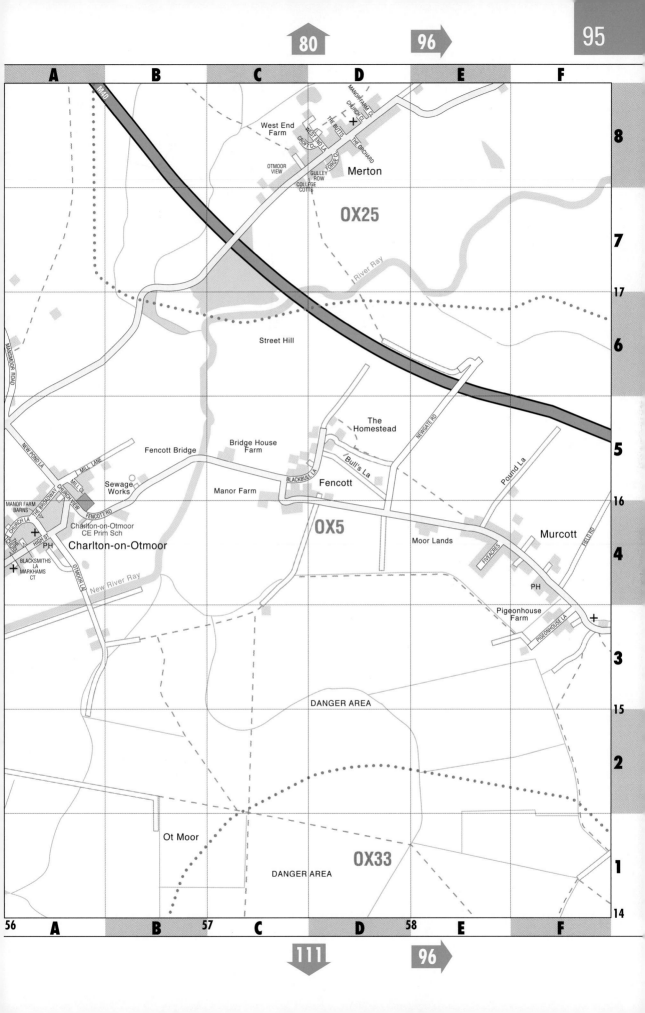

A   B   C   D   E   F

8

Astley Bridge Farm

PALMER AVE

LC

LC

LC

River Ray

OX25

MEADOW VW

PATRICK HAUGH RD

7

Depot

Upper Arncott

LC

Arncott Hill

17

NORRIS RD

PLOUGHLEY RD

GREEN LA

PEALE CL

HOPCRAFT CL

MILL LA

L SIDE CL

CL STABLES

CROFT

BUCHANAN RD

HARPER CL DS

GREENFIELD

WOODPIECE RD

BUCHANAN CT

Arncott Wood

6

LCs

THE VILLAGE CL

ORCHARD CL

MURCOTT RD

Arncott Hill Farm

LC

LC

Depot

ARNCOTT WOOD RD

5

FIELD RD

LC

LC

LC

Boarstall Lane

16

New Park Farm

Red House Farm

4

OX5

ARNCOTT RD

Oldhouse Spinney

Marlake House

Latchmeads

Four Winds Farm

3

Whitecross Green Farmhouse

Lower Panshill Farm

Pans Hill

15

MURCOTT RD

Manor Farm

Upper Panshill Farm

HP18

2

Whitecross Green Wood

Nature Reserve

PANSHILL

1

M40

OX33

STUDLEY RD

14

Upper Wood

Oriel Wood

59   A   B   60   C   D   61   E   F

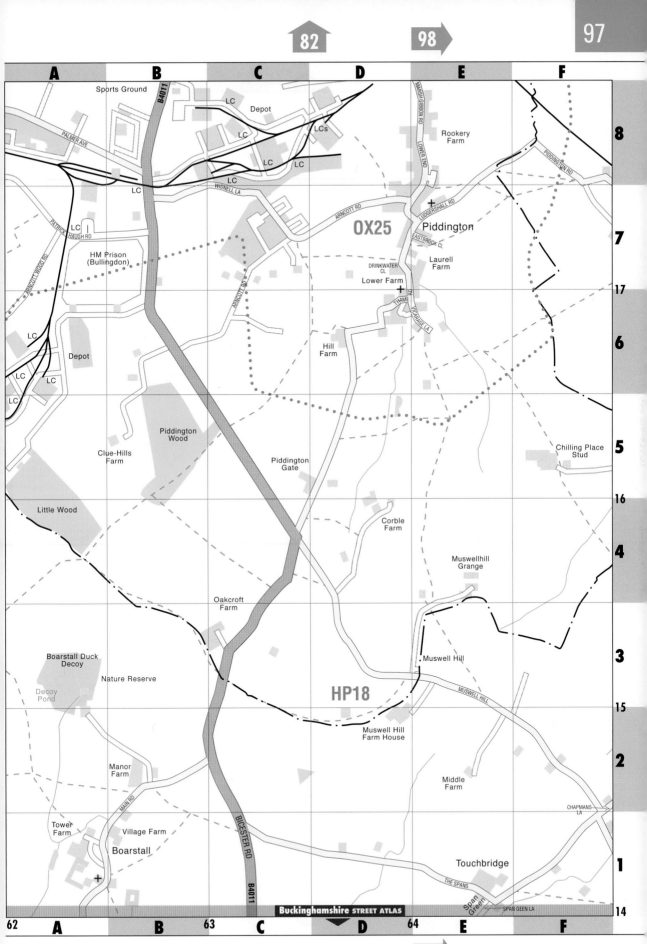

A   B   C   D   E   F

8

Sports Ground

PALMER AVE

B4011

LC

Depot

LC

LCs

LC

LC

LC

WIDNELL LA

LC

MARSH GIBBON RD

LOWER END

Rookery
Farm

PIDDINGTON RD

ARNCOTT RD

OX25

LUDGERSHALL RD

Piddington

7

PATRICK HAUGH RD

LC

HM Prison
(Bullingdon)

ARNCOTT WOOD RD

EASTBROOK CL

Laurell
Farm

DRINKWATER
CL

Lower Farm

17

ARNCOTT RD

THAME RD

VICARAGE LA

LC

LC

LC

Depot

LC

LC

Hill
Farm

6

Piddington
Wood

Clue-Hills
Farm

Piddington
Gate

Chilling Place
Stud

5

Little Wood

16

Corble
Farm

Muswellhill
Grange

4

Oakcroft
Farm

Boarstall Duck
Decoy

Decoy
Pond

Nature Reserve

Muswell Hill

HP18

MUSWELL HILL

3

Muswell Hill
Farm House

15

Manor
Farm

MAIN RD

Middle
Farm

2

CHAPMANS
LA

Tower
Farm

Village Farm

BICESTER RD

B4011

Boarstall

Touchbridge

THE SPANS

1

Span Green

SPAN GEEN LA

14

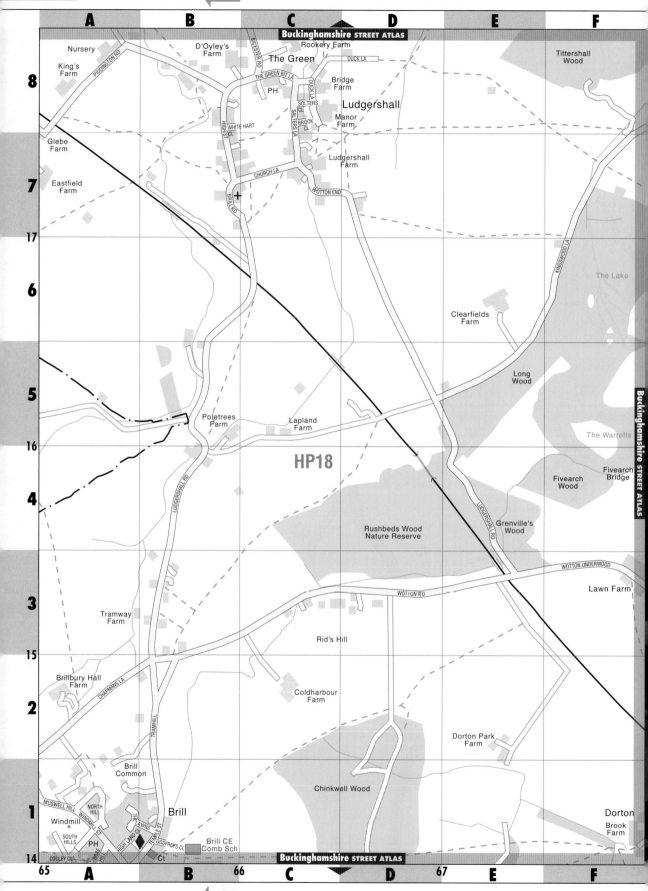

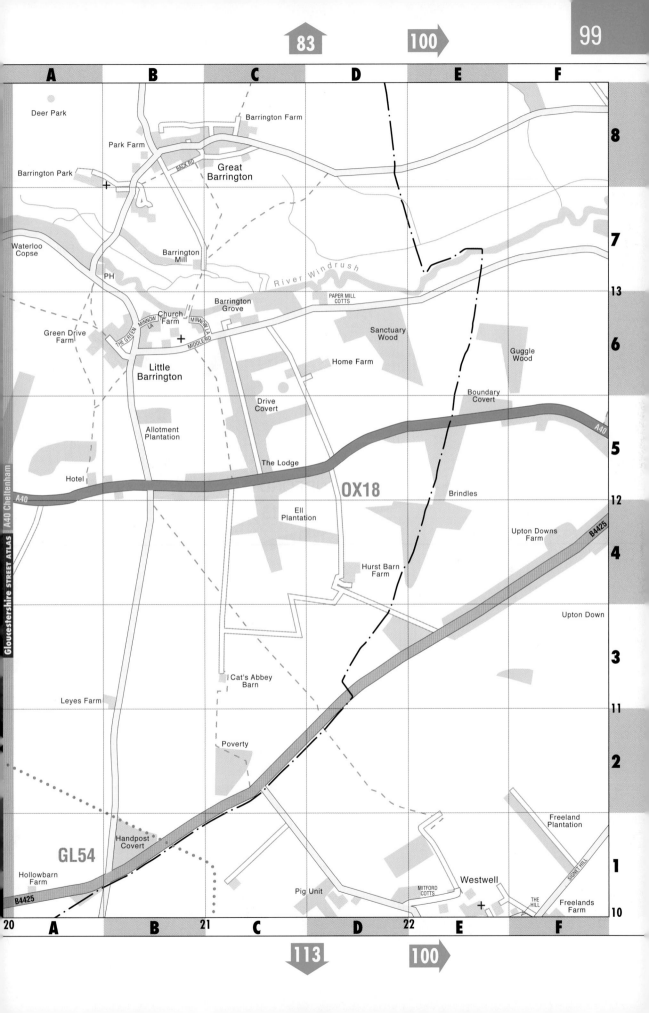

Deer Park

Barrington Farm

Park Farm

BACK RD

Great
Barrington

Barrington Park

Waterloo
Copse

Barrington
Mill

River Windrush

PH

PAPER MILL
COTTS

Green Drive
Farm

THE GREEN

MINNOW LA

Church
Farm

MINNOW LA

MIDDLE RD

Barrington
Grove

Sanctuary
Wood

Guggle
Wood

Little
Barrington

Home Farm

Drive
Covert

Boundary
Covert

A40

Allotment
Plantation

The Lodge

OX18

Brindles

Upton Downs
Farm

B4425

Hotel

A40

Ell
Plantation

Upton Down

Hurst Barn
Farm

Leyes Farm

Cat's Abbey
Barn

Poverty

Freeland
Plantation

Handpost
Covert

GL54

Hollowbarn
Farm

B4425

Pig Unit

MITFORD
COTTS

Westwell

SIGNET HILL

THE
HILL

Freelands
Farm

Gloucestershire STREET ATLAS   A40 Cheltenham   A40 Cheltenham

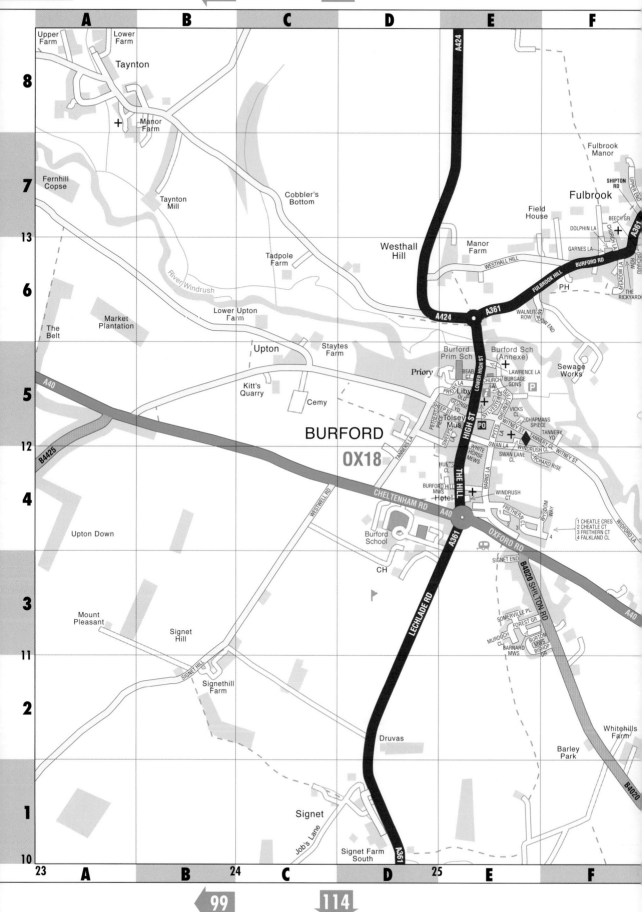

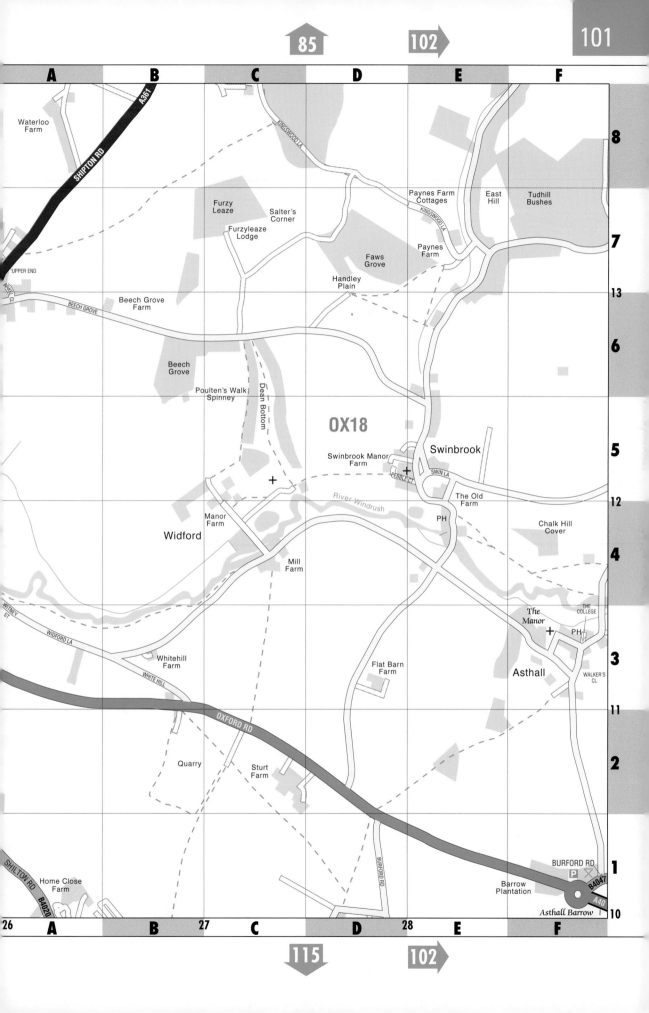

A B C D E F

8

Waterloo
Farm

SHIPTON RD
A361

KINGSWOOD LA

Paynes Farm
Cottages

East
Hill

Tudhill
Bushes

Furzy
Leaze

Salter's
Corner

KINGSWOOD LA

7

Furzyleaze
Lodge

Faws
Grove

Paynes
Farm

UPPER END

ARKEL CL

Handley
Plain

13

BEECH GROVE

Beech Grove
Farm

6

Beech
Grove

Poulten's Walk
Spinney

Dean Bottom

OX18

Swinbrook

5

Swinbrook Manor
Farm

PEBBLE CT

SWIN LA

The Old
Farm

Chalk Hill
Cover

12

River Windrush

PH

Manor
Farm

Widford

4

Mill
Farm

THE
COLLEGE

WITNEY ST

The
Manor

PH

WIDFORD LA

Whitehill
Farm

Asthall

3

WHITE HILL

Flat Barn
Farm

WALKER'S
CL

OXFORD RD

11

Quarry

Sturt
Farm

2

BURFORD RD

BURFORD RD

SHILTON RD

B4020

Home Close
Farm

Barrow
Plantation

P

B4047

1

A40

Asthall Barrow

10

A   B   C   D   E   F

8

Field
Assarts

Hens Grove

Roustage

Fordwells

Fordwells
Farm House

NORTON
TERR

Home
Farm

HOME FARM
COTTS

BUTTERMILK LA

7

BOCKETT'S
CNR

Stockley
Copse

MINSTER RIDINGS

13

Wisdom's Bottom

College Farm

Asthall Leigh

Wisdom's
Copse

BOCKETT'S CORNER

6

The
Olde Farm

PH

Pool's
Bottom

The Grove

Postern
Bottom

Holywell
Barn

Pinnocks
Farm

Standridge
Copse

5

NINETY CUT HILL

Worsham Turn
Cottage

WORSHAM
TURN

Shorthazel
Bottom

OX29

Bangry
Bottom

12

OX18

Kitesbridge
Farm

Foxhole
Bottom

MINSTER RIDINGS

4

Stonefold

Cot
Farm

The
Grove

Asthall Farm

Little
Minster

Minster
Lovell
Mill

SCHOOL LA

PH

3

The
Bungalow

River Windrush

Lower Field
Farm

LOWER CRES

SCHOOL HILL

11

Folly
Farm

WYCHWOOD VIEW

UPPER CRES

PH

MITRE LANES

B4047

Minster
Lovell

B4047

2

Factory

Worsham

BURFORD RD

Works

HOLLOWAY LA

GREEN LA

AYMS
BOWLES
AVE

BLAKE
CRES

STRATFORD
ROW

BUSBY DR

O'CONNORS
RD

WHITEHALL CL

WEHRISC

LOVELL
CL

CHARTERVILLE CL

DRYLANDS RD

RIPLEY AVE

COTSWOLD CL

DR

St Kenelm's
CE Sch

PO

BRIZE NORTON RD

1

Barrow
Farm

B4047

A40

Charterville
Allotments

B4477

10

29   A   30   B   C   D   31   E   F

◀ 103

▲ 118

A1
1 NEW MILL MS
2 CARPENTERS SQ
3 HYDE MD VW
4 STENTER RI
5 MEADOW LA
6 LOOM LA
7 BURFORD RD
8 WINCHESTER CT
9 COLLIER CRES
10 WENMAN CL
11 MARRIOTT'S CL

A2
1 BLANKET WAY
2 POINT PL
3 EMPSON CRES

B1
1 PRIOR MILL LA
2 Oxford Int Coll of Beauty
3 Zedcor Bsns Pk
4 BRIDGE ST
5 WOODGREEN HILL
6 INDUSTRIAL EST

C1
1 NEWLAND

D1
1 NORTHFIELD ROW
2 OXFORD HILL
3 WOODBANK

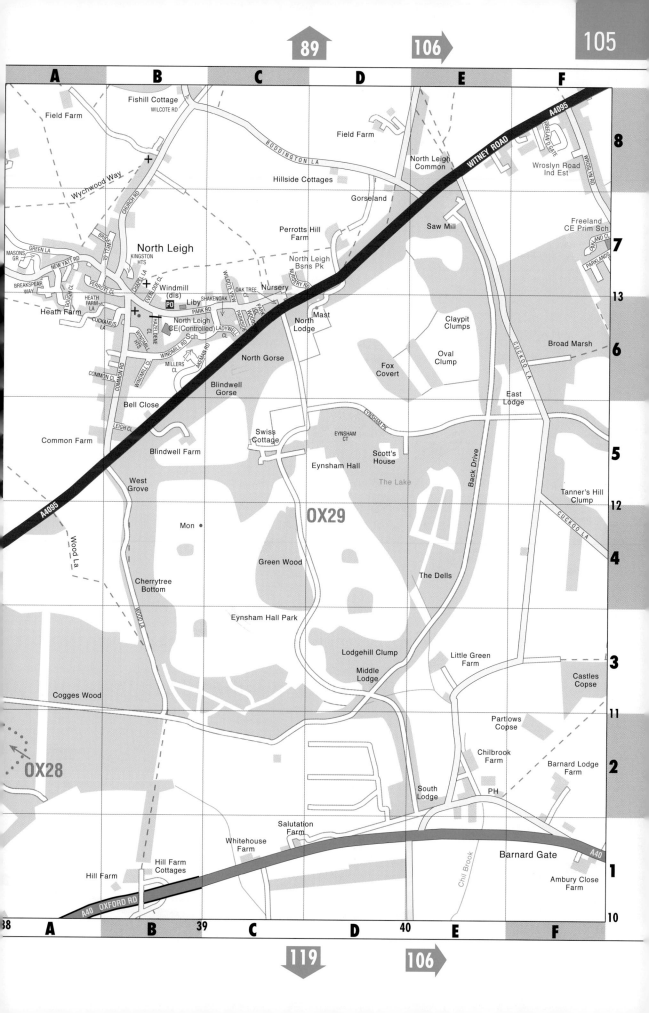

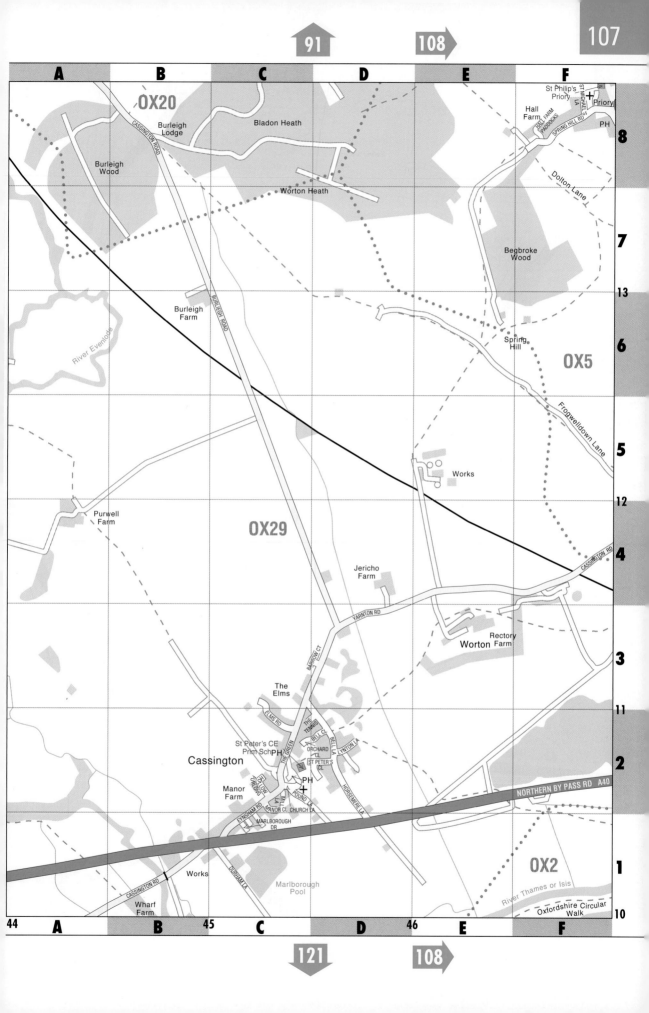

OX20

Burleigh Lodge

Bladon Heath

St Philip's Priory
Priory
PH
Hall Farm
HALL FARM PADDOCKS
ST MICHAEL'S LA
SPRING HILL RD

Burleigh Wood

CASSINGTON ROAD

Worton Heath

Dolton Lane

Begbroke Wood

Burleigh Farm
BURLEIGH ROAD

River Evenlode

Spring Hill

OX5

Frogwelldown Lane

Works

Purwell Farm

OX29

Jericho Farm

YARNTON RD

CASSINGTON RD

Worton Farm
Rectory

The Elms

ELMS RD
THE TENNIS
BELL CL
BELL LA
LYNTON LA

St Peter's CE Prim Sch
PH
THE GREEN
ORCHARD CL
ST PETER'S CL

Cassington

Manor Farm
PH
POUND LA
MANOR CL
CHURCH LA
HORSEMERE LA

EYNSHAM RD
MARLBOROUGH DR

NORTHERN BY PASS RD A40

OX2

Works

DURHAM LA

Marlborough Pool

River Thames or Isis

Oxfordshire Circular Walk

Wharf Farm
CASSINGTON RD

E7
1 St Thomas More
  RC Prim Sch
2 West Kidlington
  Prim Sch

F8
1 ANDOVER CT
2 BLENHEIM CT
3 CLEVEDON CT
4 DORCHESTER CT
5 EXETER CT
6 FARNHAM CT

7 GUILDFORD CT
8 HERTFORD CT

A   B   C   D   E   F

8

Begbroke

Parker's Farm

Begbroke Hill

Begbroke
Science Park

SANDHILL RD   FOXGLOVE
FERNHILL RD   RD   QUARRY END

1 WOODSTOCK RD E
2 WOODSTOCK RD W
3 WOODSTOCK RD

Rowel Brook

Oxfordshire
Fire & Rescue
Service HQ

Gosford

FERNHILL CL 1
MORRELL CL 2
BELGROVE CL 3
GROVE LANDS 4

Gosford Hill
Sch

7

13

POPPY
CL

Yarnton

SANDY LA

Sandy Lane
Crossing

KIDLINGTON

Edward
Field Prim
Sch

Kidlington &
Gosford Mast
Sports Ctr
TV Police
HQ South

6

Yarnton

College
Farm

Kidlington Green
Lock

Sewage
Works

OX5

Garden City

Stratfield
Farm

Superstore

5

Yarnton
House
William Fletcher
Prim Sch

Little Blenheim

PH

LC

Stratfield Brake
Sports Gd

12

Frogwelldown
Lane

Hill
Farm

The Red Lion
(PH)

Oxford
Ind Pk

Ickworth

Stratfield
Brake

4

Manor
House

Stonehouse
Farm

WOODSTOCK RD

Frieze Farm

FRIEZE WAY

3

OX29

Mead
Farm

Loop Farm

Peartree Hill

Motel

11

Oxey Mead

OX2

Duke's Lock

PEARTREE
INTERCHANGE

Service
Area

Mast

2

A40

NORTHERN BY-PASS RD

Red Barn
Farm
Cottage

P&R
Pear Tree

SOLLERSHOTT

King's Weir

Pixey Mead

Hotel

North Way A40

1

Yarnton or West Mead

King's
Lock

WESTERN BY-PASS RD

NORTHERN BY-PASS RD

Manor
Farm

Weir

Thames Path

River Thames or Isis

10

47   A   48   B   C   48   D   49   E   F

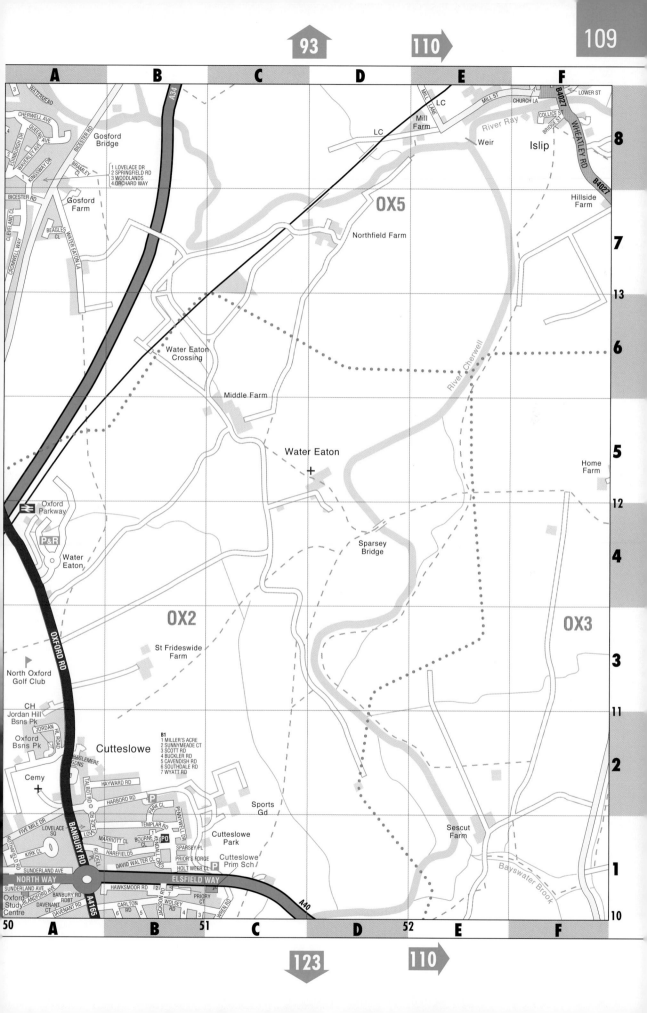

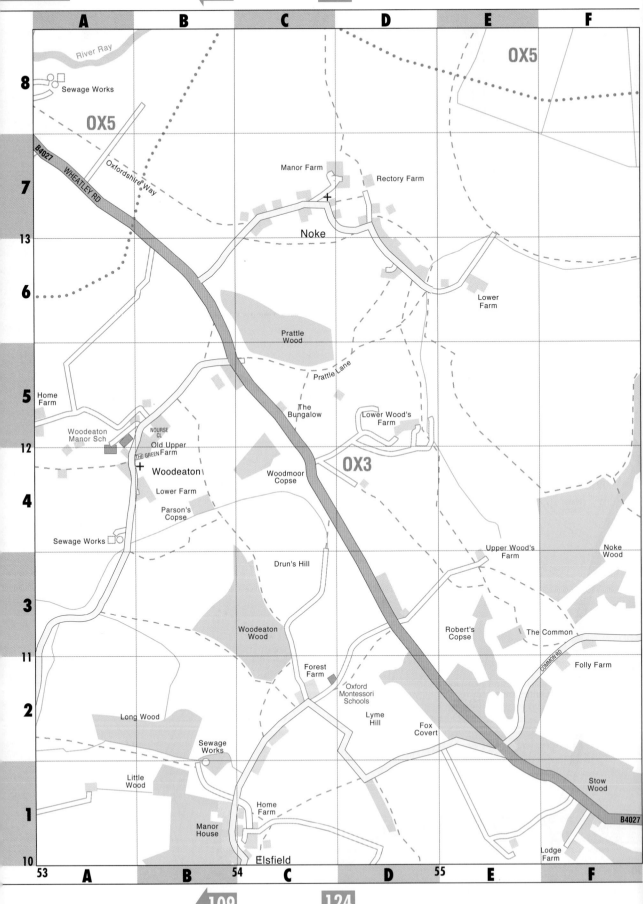

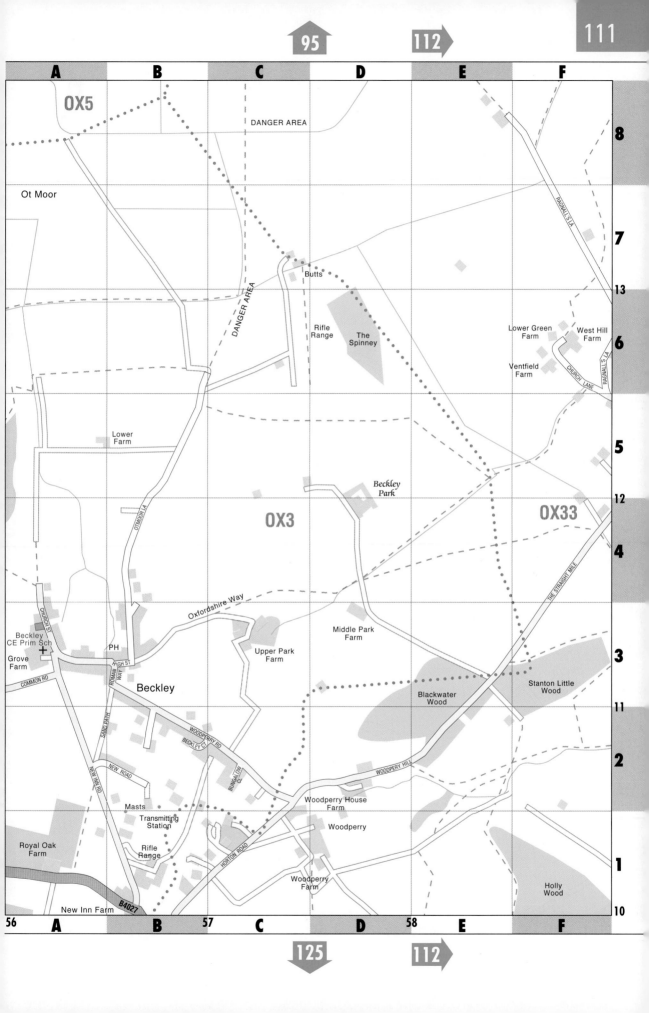

A B C D E F

OX5

DANGER AREA

8

Ot Moor

7

RAGNALL'S LA

13

DANGER AREA

Butts

Rifle
Range

The
Spinney

Lower Green
Farm

West Hill
Farm

6

Ventfield
Farm

CHURCH LANE

RAGNALL'S LA

Lower
Farm

5

Beckley
Park

OTMOOR LA

12

OX3

OX33

4

THE STRAIGHT MILE

Oxfordshire Way

Middle Park
Farm

CHURCH ST

Beckley
CE Prim Sch

PH

Upper Park
Farm

Grove
Farm

HIGH ST

ROMAN WAY

Blackwater
Wood

Stanton Little
Wood

3

COMMON RD

Beckley

11

WOODPERRY RD

BECKLEY ST

SAND PATH

NEW ROAD

BUNGALOW CL

WOODPERRY HILL

2

NEW INN RD

Masts

Woodperry House
Farm

Woodperry

Transmitting
Station

HORTON ROAD

Royal Oak
Farm

Rifle
Range

Woodperry
Farm

Holly
Wood

1

B4027

New Inn Farm

10

A　B　C　D　E　F

8

7

13

6

5

12

4

3

11

2

1

10

M40

M40 Thame (A418)

Old Arngrove Farm

New Arngrove Farm

Gardner's Barn

Warren Farm

Tippens Copse

Nursery

Sermin's Copse

Pasture Farm

Danes Brock

Studley Farm

THE ORCHARD

BRILL RD

Horton-cum-Studley

MILL LA

THE OLD GN

CHURCH LA

VENTFIELD CL

THE GREEN

Hotel

FORGE CL

Manor Farm

PRIORY CL

New Farm

STANTON ST JOHN RD

Bernwood Jubilee Way

RAGNALL'S LA

Studley Priory

Moors Farm

OAKLEY RD

Sewage Works

HP18

THE STRAIGHT MILE ROAD

CH

OX33

Studley Wood

Corner Farm

P

Oakley Wood

Bernwood Butterfly Trail

Forest Nature Reserve

Shabbington Wood

The Moat

Bernwood Forest

York's Wood

Danesbrook Farm

Danes Brook

Moorbirge Brook

Oxfordshire Way

Menmarsh Guide Post

Hell Coppice

MILL ST

Moorbirge Bridge

MENMARSH RD

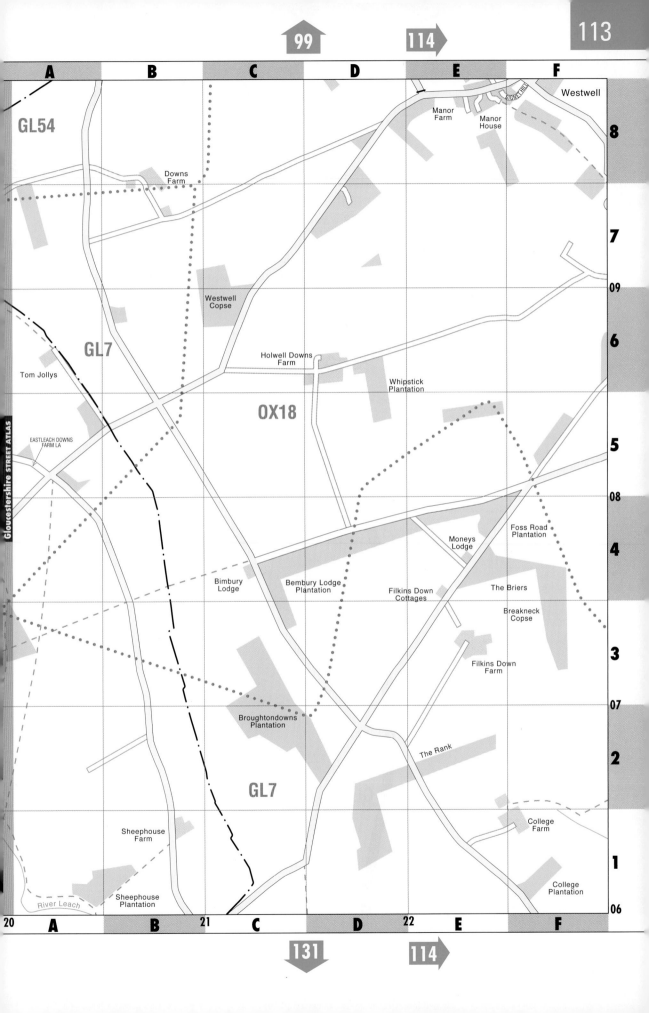

A   B   C   D   E   F

8

7

09

6

5

08

4

3

07

2

1

06

GL54

Westwell

Manor Farm

Manor House

Downs Farm

Westwell Copse

GL7

Holwell Downs Farm

OX18

Whipstick Plantation

Tom Jollys

EASTLEACH DOWNS FARM LA

Foss Road Plantation

Moneys Lodge

Bimbury Lodge

Bembury Lodge Plantation

Filkins Down Cottages

The Briers

Breakneck Copse

Filkins Down Farm

Broughtondowns Plantation

The Rank

GL7

College Farm

Sheephouse Farm

Sheephouse Plantation

River Leach

College Plantation

20   A   B   21   C   D   22   E   F   06

	A	B	C	D	E	F

8

Job's Lane

Tansley's Buildings

Shill Brook

Sturt Copse

Mount Zion Bottom

Upper Glissard's Plantation

7

Manor Farm

Holwell Plantation

OAK VIEW SYCAMORE PL

HAWTHORN DR

BIRCH DR

BEECH DR

Porters Buildings

Shilton Downs Farm

LADBURN LA

Holwell

+

Old Pits Plantation

09

GLISSARD WAY

WOODSIDE DR

RHINO ROW

FOXWOOD LA

Groveground Plantation

Glissard's Wood

Lower Glissard's Plantation

6

Bradwell Grove

Hen and Chicken Wood

Woodside Farm

HEN N CHICK LA

THE COTTAGES

Cotswold Wildlife Park & Gardens

5

Aston Copse

Fishpond Copse

OX18

Westfield Farm

The Kennels

08

Home Farm

Bradwell Grove Wood

4

South Lodge

Bradwell Grove Park

Manor Dairy Farm

Works

Scrubs Farm

3

Furze Ground

07

Pumphouse Plantation

2

GL7

Hill Plantation

Kencot Hill Farm

1

Furzey Hall Farm

A361

06

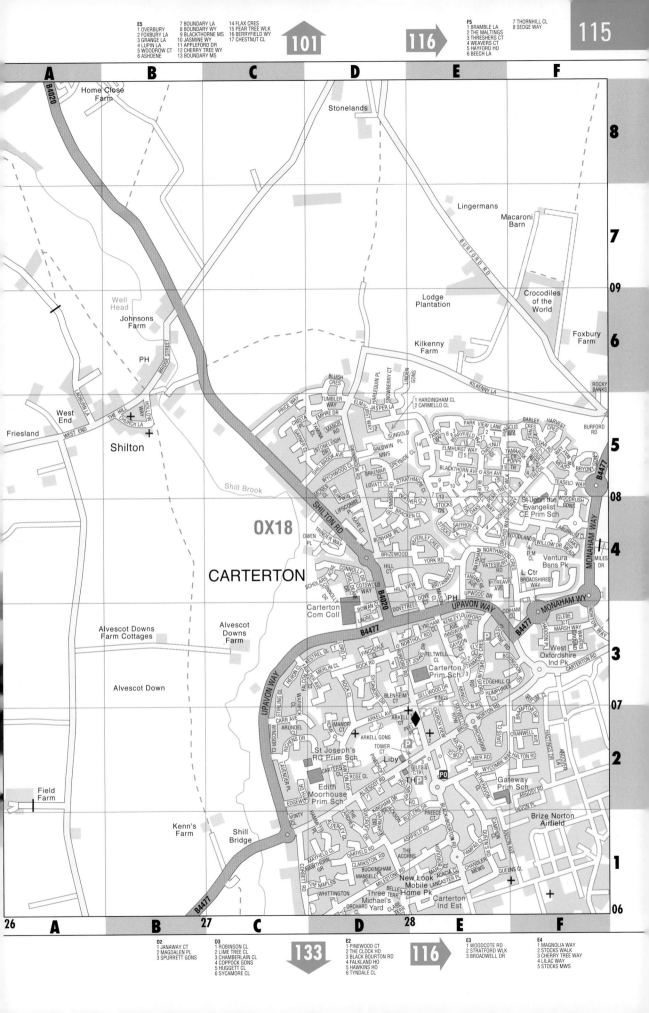

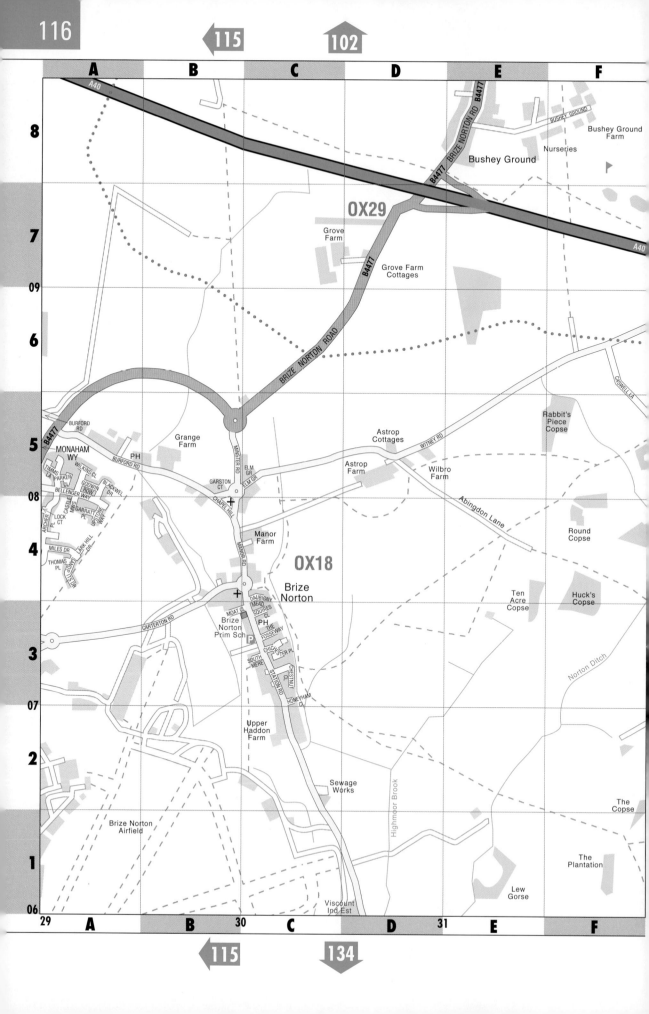

A40

OX29

Bushey Ground

BUSHEY GROUND

Bushey Ground Farm

Nurseries

B4477 BRIZE NORTON RD B4477

Grove Farm

B4477

Grove Farm Cottages

A40

BRIZE NORTON ROAD

Rabbit's Piece Copse

CASWELL LA

Astrop Cottages

WITNEY RD

B4477

BURFORD RD

MONAHAM WY

PH

BURFORD RD

Grange Farm

MINSTER RD

ELM GR

GARSTON CT

ELM GR

Astrop Farm

Astrop Cottages

Wilbro Farm

Abingdon Lane

Round Copse

TIMMS LA

PARKER CL

WILKINS CL

GODWIN DROW

BLACKWEL DR

BELLENGER WAY

CASTLE MWS

GARRATT PL

UPSTONE

ARCHER

LOCK CT

CHAPEL HILL

OX18

MANOR RD

Manor Farm

Brize Norton

Ten Acre Copse

Huck's Copse

MILES DR

LARK HILL DR

THOMAS PL

SMIPSTUR

DAUBIGNY MEAD

SQUIRES CL

PH

THE FOSSEWAY

CARTERTON RD

MOAT CL

Brize Norton Prim Sch

P

SOUTH MERE

CHIC

CHESTER PL

STATION RD

CHESTNUT CL

HONEYHAM CL

Norton Ditch

Upper Haddon Farm

Highmoor Brook

Sewage Works

The Copse

Brize Norton Airfield

The Plantation

Lew Gorse

Viscount Ind Est

118

A8
1 CORN BAR
2 WELCH WY
3 WOODFORD WY
4 CORNDELL GDNS
5 COOPER MS
6 CROFTERS MS

7 SWAN CT
8 Thames International
9 Abingdon & Witney Coll

10 Wychwood Brewery
11 The Batt Church of England (VA) Prim Sch

12 APPLEGARTH CT
13 CROFTERS CT

117

104

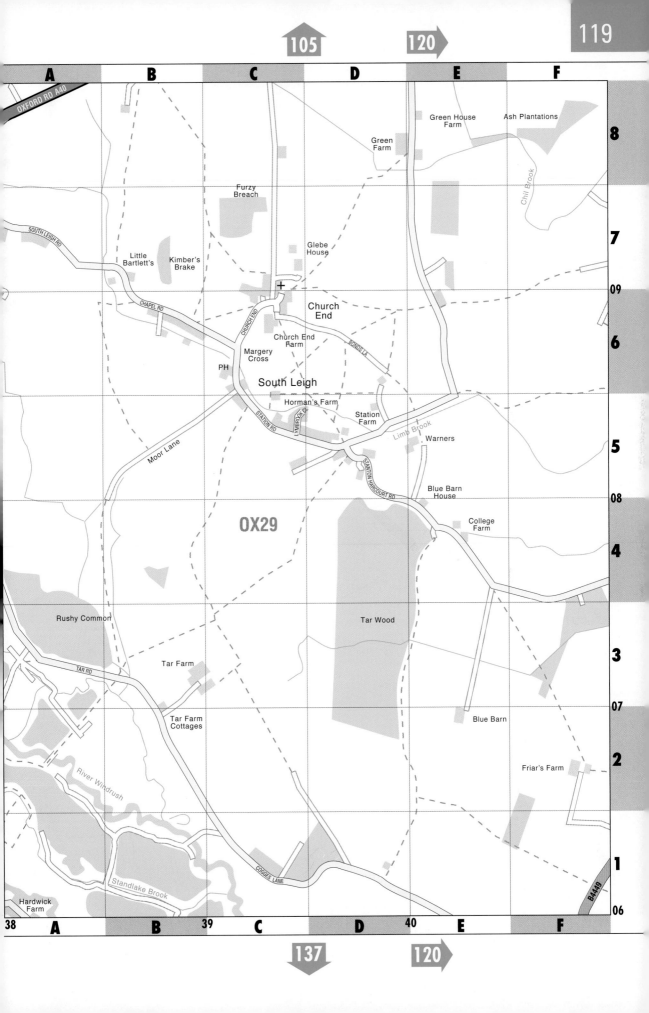

119 106

A B C D E F

8

7

09

6

5

08

4

3

07

2

1

06

Chil Brook

Twelve Acre Farm

Paddock Close

Lower Barn

A40

PH

ELM PL

OLD WITNEY RD

FRUITLANDS

TILGARSLEY RD

WITNEY RD

SHAKESPEARE RD

STRATFORD DR

FALSTAFF CL

DUNCAN CL

SPARECROFT

GREEN'S RD

MARLBOROUGH PL

MARLBOROUGH

PELICAN PL

HANBOROUGH CL

HANBOROUGH RD

WITHAM RD

WITHAM VIEW

MILLMOOR

BEECH RD

DOVEHOUSE CL

B4449

1 COBBETTS CL
2 LITTLE LA
3 WRIGHTS LA

Eynsham Com Prim Sch

CASSINGTON RD

MEAL LA

Bartholomew Sch

Bartholomew CL

STAR CL

SAYWELL CRES

WILLOWS EDGE

THORNBURY RD

QUARTERMAN WAY

BLAKEMAN LA

BERRY CL

CASTELL

CHILBRIDGE ROAD

CHILBRIDGE RD

MERTON CT

MERTON CL

MERTON CT

STANTON RD

CLOVER PL

BLANKSTONE CL

Chil Brook

WOODLANDS

EVANS CL

EVANS RD

JOHN LOPES RD

BACK LA

MILL ST MEWS

NEWLAND

HAWTHORN

Sp Ctr

CLOVER PL

GRANGE MILL CT

SWAN ST

ACRE END ST

THAMES ST

HEY CROFT

ABBEY ST

LOMBARD ST

HIGH ST

MILL ST

QUEENS LA

QUEEN'S

NEWLAND ST

TANNERS LA

ORCHARD CL

BITTERELL

HAZELDENE CL

Liby

PO

P

ABBEY PL

1 THE SQUARE
2 SWANLANDS RD
3 ACRE END CL

Abbey Farm

Eynsham

OXFORD RD

WHARF RD PI

B4044

B4449

Old Station Way

SWAN BATH

Oasis Pk

Southfield Cottages

STANTON HARCOURT RD

SOUTHFIELD RD

Oakfield Ind Est

PINK HILL LA

Southfield Barn

OX29

Foxley Farm

Limb Brook

STANTON HARCOURT RD

Bell Bridge

The Bungalow

Pinkhill Farm

Weir

Thames Path

University Cottages

EYNSHAM RD

Nicholls' Farm

Sutton Farm

Sutton Green

BEAUMONT GREEN

Beaumont House

Sutton

B4449

MAIN ROAD

NEW RD

FOXBURROW

SUTTON LA

BURR CL

Cox's Farm

DUCK END LANE

Lower Farm

Sewage Works

PH

River Thames or Isis

Towing Path

OX2

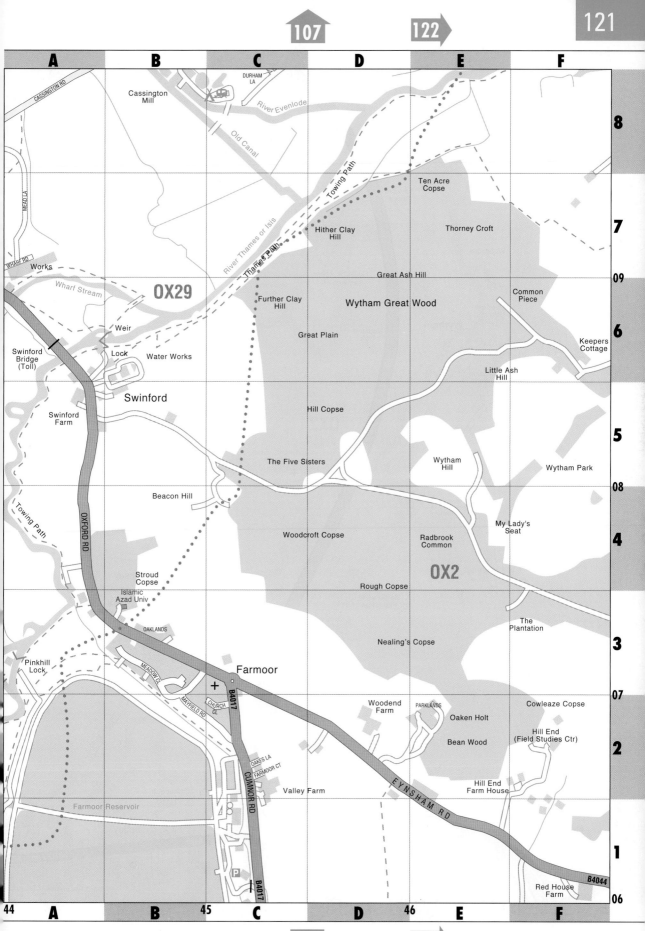

A B C D E F

8

7

09

6

5

08

4

07

3

2

06

1

CASSINGTON RD

Cassington Mill

DURHAM LA

River Evenlode

Old Canal

MEAD LA

WHARF RD

Works

Wharf Stream

OX29

Weir

Lock

Water Works

Swinford Bridge (Toll)

Swinford

Swinford Farm

Towing Path

OXFORD RD

Beacon Hill

Stroud Copse

Islamic Azad Univ

OAKLANDS

Pinkhill Lock

MEADOW CL

MAYFIELD RD

CHURCH CL

Farmoor

+

B4017

OAKES LA

FARMOOR CT

CUMNOR RD

Valley Farm

Farmoor Reservoir

B4017

Towing Path

Thames Path

River Thames or Isis

Hither Clay Hill

Ten Acre Copse

Thorney Croft

Great Ash Hill

Further Clay Hill

Wytham Great Wood

Common Piece

Great Plain

Keepers Cottage

Little Ash Hill

Hill Copse

Wytham Hill

Wytham Park

The Five Sisters

Woodcroft Copse

Radbrook Common

My Lady's Seat

OX2

Rough Copse

The Plantation

Nealing's Copse

Woodend Farm

PARKLANDS

Oaken Holt

Cowleaze Copse

Bean Wood

Hill End (Field Studies Ctr)

Hill End Farm House

EYNSHAM RD

Red House Farm

B4044

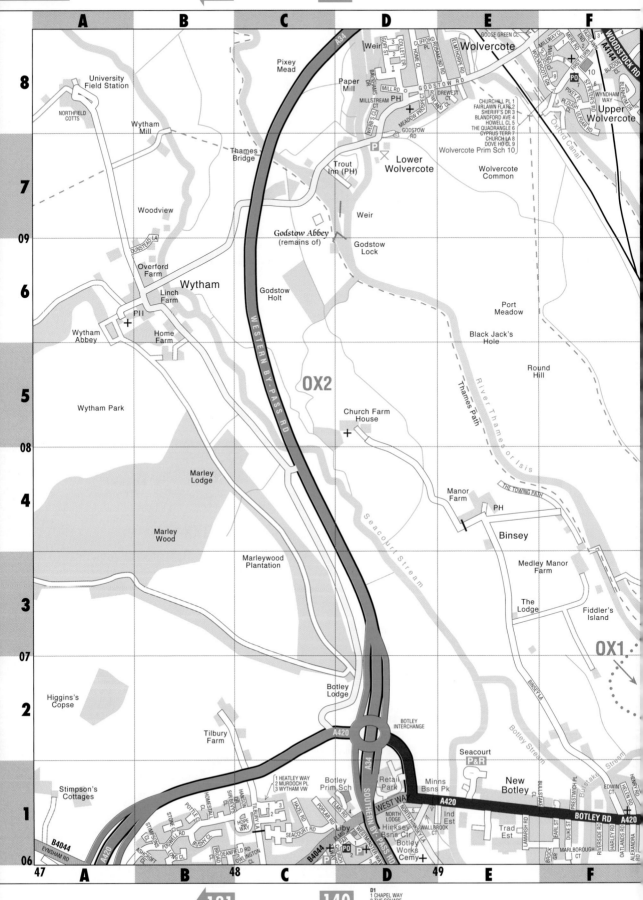

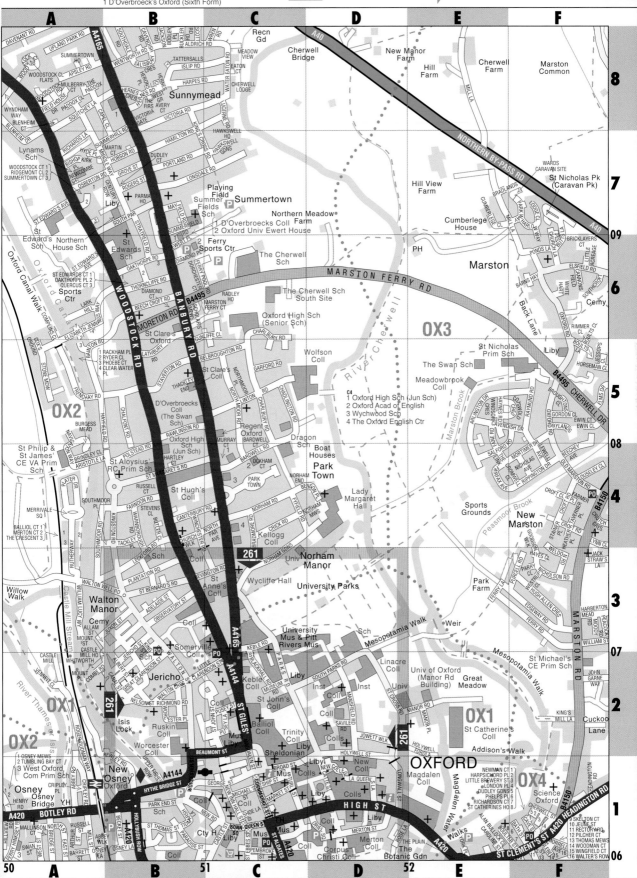

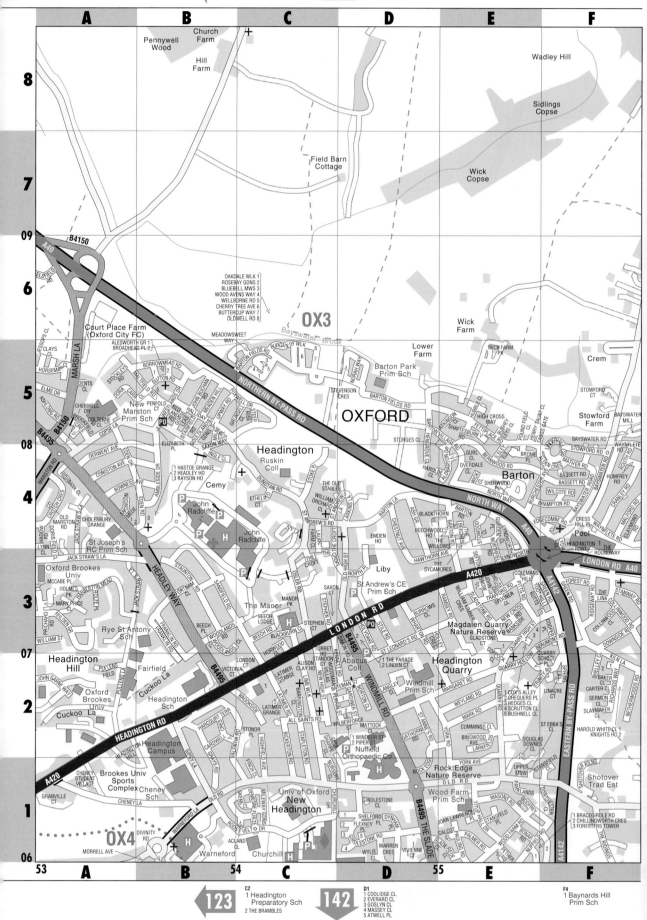

← 123
1 Headington
Preparatory Sch
2 THE BRAMBLES

142
D1
1 COOLIDGE CL
2 EVERARD CL
3 GOSLYN CL
4 MASSEY CL
5 ATWELL PL

F4
1 Baynards Hill
Prim Sch

A   B   C   D   E   F

8

B4027
New Inn
Farm

BECKLEY RD
HORTON RD

Stanton
House

SNOWS LA
ROUND LA
Mill
Farm

MILL ST
SILVER
BIRCHES

Kennels

Sewage
Works

FREELANDS
COTTS
CHURCH CL

7

Stanton
St John

COX LANE
MIDDLE RD

SIMMNS
CL

HILLCRAFT RD
COURTFIELD
RD

Stanton
Great Wood

BAYSWATER RD

Shepherd's
Pit

CHEQUERS
CL
STANTON
COTTS
PH

09

PH

Recn
Gd

WHEATLEY RD

OX33

6

Ashen
Copse

Breach
Farm

5

Bayswater
Mill

BAYSWATER MILL RD
BAYSWATER
RD

1 HUMFREY RD
2 MALFORD RD
3 CLAYMOND RD
4 Endeavour Acad
5 TURNER VIEW

Minchin
Court Farm

STANTON RD

08

WAYNFLETE WAY
WATERMAN
BAYSWATER
FARM

BAYSWATER
FARM
HAWKES
CL

MICKLE WAY

Sewage
Works

ROBERTS
CL
HILL VIEW

Sandhills

BADGER

PH

Vent
Farm

THE DALE
COLWELL
DR

BELBUSH LA
ELTON CL
ELTONETT AVE

Sandhills
Com
Prim Sch

POLECAT END LA

MILTON
CRES
POWELL
CL

WHEATLEY RD

4

MEREWOOD AVE
HOOPER CL
BURDELL AVE
BURSILL
CL
SWEETGREEN CL

Manor
Farm

MAIN STREET

BANK
COTTS

Cemy

Forest
Hill

B4027

SPRING LA
BARTON
CRES

LONDON RD

OX3

Thornhill
Farm

CHURCH HILL

Red Hill
Farm

Red
Hill

3

THE
LARCHES
DOWNSIDE END
Swilly

P

P&R

Thornhill

07

DOWNSIDE RD
POND CL
RINGWOOD RD
STANWAY RD

Risinghurst

PO

Pointed
Covert

Lodge

Shotover
House

A40

2

KILN LA
WYCHWOOD LA
LEWIS RD
COLLINWOOD RD
GROVELANDS RD

Monk's
Wood

Thorn
Hill

Obelisk

SHOTOVER EST

SHOTOVER RD
BAYSWATER RD

Monk's
Farm

Shotover
Hill

Forest
Farm

The
Spinney

Home
Farm

1

OLD RD

P

Shotover Plain

Shotover
Country Park

Ochre
Pits

06

125
112

A **B** **C** **D** **E** **F**

8

MILL ST

Moorbirge Brook

Clearsale

Hursthill

HP18

Wood Farm

MENMARSH RD

Waterperry Common

7

Bernwood Forest

Commonleys Farm

SMITH'S LA

09

Polecat End

Waterperry Wood

Park Farm House

Park Farm

6

Drunkard's Corner

WATERPERRY COMMON

Oxfordshire Way

Parson's Farm

5

Polecat End Hollows

POLECAT END LA

Marsh Copse

Ledall Cottage

08

Holton Wood

OX33

4

Buryhook Barn

Holton Brook

M40

3

B4027

Keeper's Cottage

WHEATLEY RD

Warren Farm

Pond Farm

Old Park Farm

Cottage Copse

Warren Wood

07

Lyehill Quarries (dis)

BURYHOOK CNR

SHOTOVER EST

B4027

Warwick Close Farm

2

A40

HOME CL

Wheatley Park Sch

BARNS CL

The Rectory

Holton Place

LONDON RD

Recn Gd

Holton

Church Farm

+

The Park Sports Ctr

PARK HILL

John Watson Sch

1

Wheatley

Oxford Brookes Univ (Wheatley Campus)

Garden Copse

WATERPERRY RD

M40

06

WESTFIELD RD

WESTFIELD RD

LONDON RD

A40

COLLEGE CL

59 **A** **B** 60 **C** **D** 61 **E** **F**

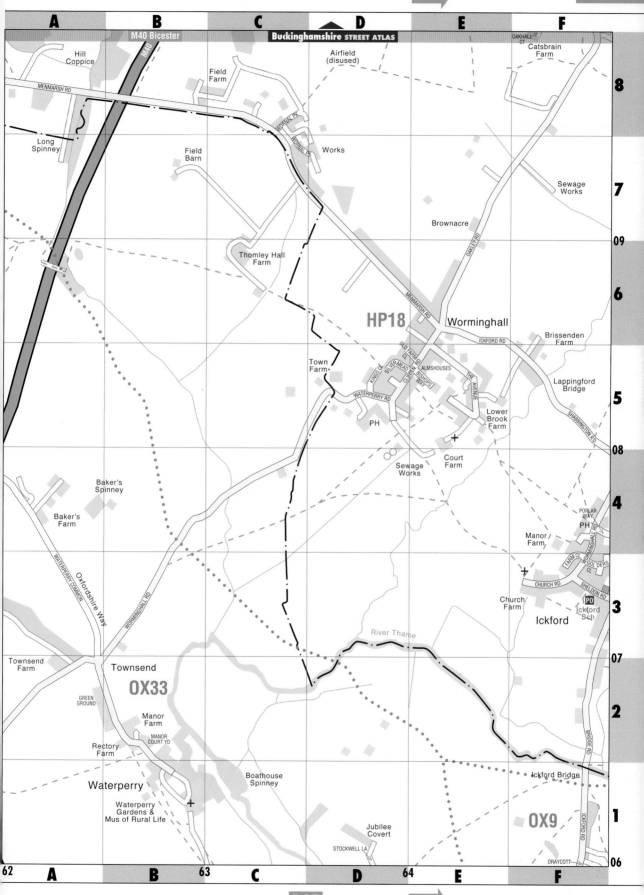

Buckinghamshire **STREET ATLAS**

M40 Bicester

Hill Coppice

MENMARSH RD

Long Spinney

Field Farm

Field Barn

Airfield (disused)

WORNAL PK

WORNAL CL

Works

Catsbrain Farm

OAKHALL CT

Sewage Works

Thomley Hall Farm

Brownacre

OAKLEY RD

MENMARSH RD

HP18

Worminghall

ICKFORD RD

Brissenden Farm

Town Farm

OLD FARM CL

SILVER MEAD

KING'S CL

BISHOPS WAY

ALMSHOUSES

THE AVENUE

SHABBINGTON RD

Lappingford Bridge

WATERPERRY RD

PH

Lower Brook Farm

Baker's Spinney

Sewage Works

Court Farm

Baker's Farm

POPLAR WAY

PH

Manor Farm

GOLDERS

Oxfordshire Way

WORMINGHALL RD

WATERPERRY COMMON

FARM CL

CHURCH RD

SHELDON RD

Church Farm

Ickford

Ickford Sch

PO

River Thame

Townsend Farm

Townsend

OX33

GREEN GROUND

Manor Farm

MANOR COURT YD

Rectory Farm

Boathouse Spinney

Ickford Bridge

BRIDGE RD

OX9

ICKFORD RD

Waterperry

Waterperry Gardens & Mus of Rural Life

Jubilee Covert

STOCKWELL LA

DRAYCOTT

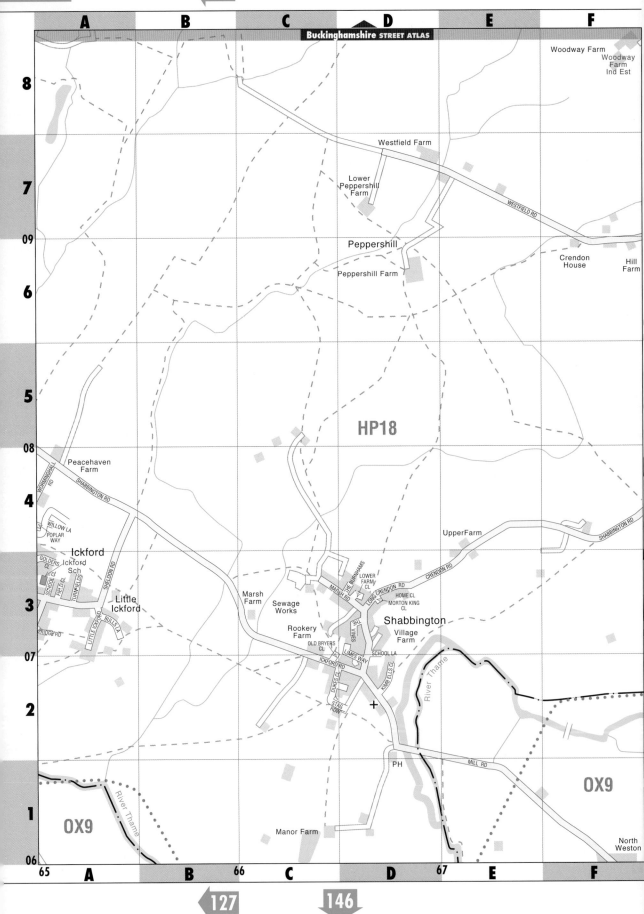

Buckinghamshire STREET ATLAS

A B C D E F

8

7

09

6

5

08

4

3

07

2

1

06

65 66 67

Woodway Farm
Woodway Farm Ind Est

Westfield Farm

Lower Peppershill Farm

WESTFIELD RD

Peppershill

Crendon House

Hill Farm

Peppershill Farm

HP18

Peacehaven Farm

WORMINGHALL RD

SHABBINGTON RD

WILLOW LA

POPLAR WAY

Ickford

GOLDERS CL

Ickford Sch

SCHOOL CL

FIELD CL

TURNFIELDS

SHELDON RD

Little Ickford

Marsh Farm

Sewage Works

LITTLE ICKFORD

BULLS LA

BRIDGE RD

Rookery Farm

OLD BRYERS CL

ICKFORD RD

DUKES CL

STAG ROW

LIMES WAY

THE VINES

KING ELLS CL

SCHOOL LA

MARSH RD

LONG CRENDON RD

THE BURNHAMS

LOWER FARM CL

HOME CL

MORTON KING CL

Shabbington

Village Farm

UpperFarm

CRENDON RD

SHABBINGTON RD

River Thame

OX9

PH

MILL RD

OX9

Manor Farm

North Weston

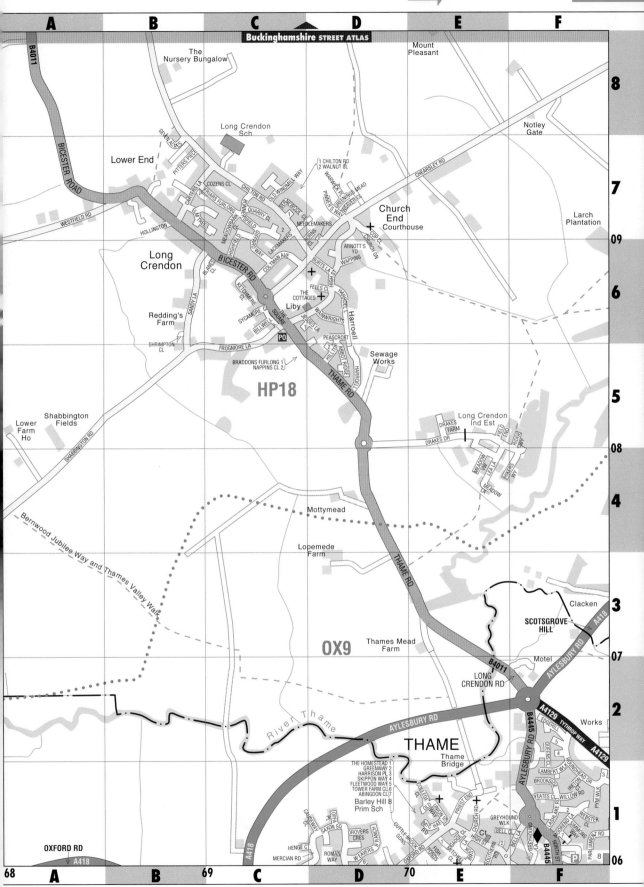

129

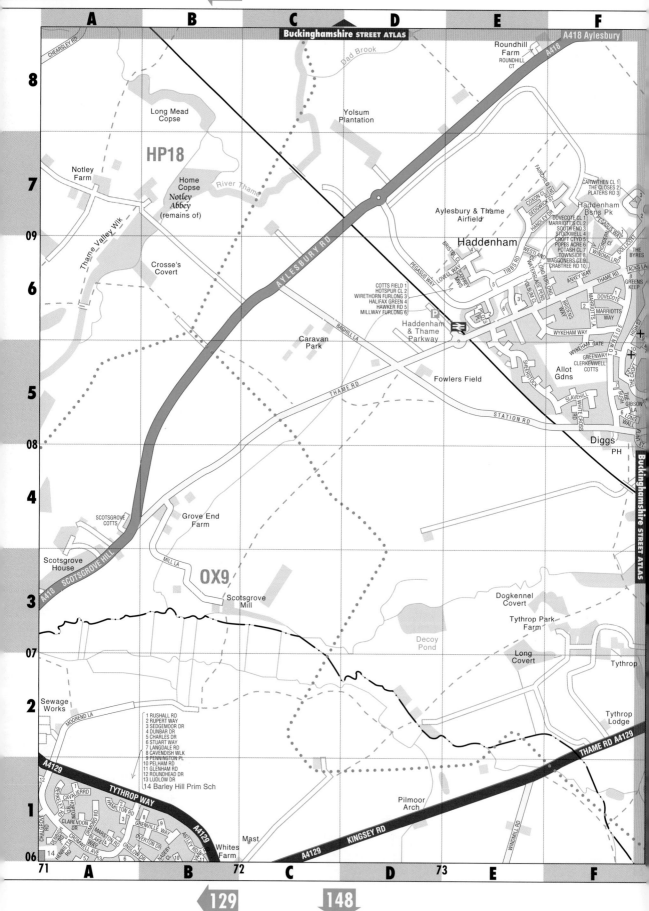

A418 Aylesbury

Roundhill
Farm
ROUNDHILL
CT

A418

Dad Brook

Long Mead
Copse

Yolsum
Plantation

HP18

Notley
Farm

Home
Copse
Notley
Abbey
(remains of)

River Thame

Thame Valley Wlk

Aylesbury & Thame
Airfield

Haddenham

Crosse's
Covert

CARWITHEN CL 1
THE CLOSES 2
PLATERS RD 3

Haddenham
Bsns Pk

COXON CL 1
SEDGWICK ST

FAIRCHILD RD

DOVECOTE CL 1
MARRIOTTS CL 2
SOUTH END 3
STOCKWELL 4
CROFT CTYD 5
POPES ACRE 6
POTASH CL 7
TOWNSIDE 8
WAGGONERS CT 9
CRABTREE RD 10

PEGASUS WAY

WINDMILL RD

THE
BYRES

DOLLICOT

GREENS
KEEP

BRISTOL CL
PEGASUS WAY

LOWELL WAY
JEFFREY
MWS

LONG PK

TIBBS CT
BANKS RD

VOLSUM CL

PHDS
PH

ANKEY WAY

THAME RD

DOVECOTE

MARRIOTTS LA

MARRIOTTS
WAY

HIGH ST

TACKS
KEEP

COTTS FIELD 1
HOTSPUR CL 2
WIRETHORN FURLONG 3
HALIFAX GREEN 4
HAWKER RD 5
MILLWAY FURLONG 6

P

Haddenham
& Thame
Parkway

Caravan
Park

BAGHILL LA

THAME RD

Fowlers Field

WYKEHAM WAY

BROTHERS
WAY

WYKEHAM GATE

GREENWAY
CLERKENWELL
COTTS

Allot
Gdns

SHEERSTICK

STATION RD

SLAVEHILL

WHITE CROSS RD

THE CROFT

LONG
WALL

BUSH
LA

GIBSON

Diggs
PH

Buckinghamshire STREET ATLAS

Scotsgrove
COTTS

Grove End
Farm

Scotsgrove
House

SCOTSGROVE HILL

A418

MILL LA

OX9

Scotsgrove
Mill

Dogkennel
Covert

Tythrop Park
Farm

Decoy
Pond

Long
Covert

Tythrop

Tythrop
Lodge

Sewage
Works

MOOREND LA

1 RUSHALL RD
2 RUPERT WAY
3 SEDGEMOOR DR
4 DUNBAR DR
5 CHARLES WAY
6 STUART WAY
7 LANGDALE RD
8 CAVENDISH WLK
9 PENNINGTON PL
10 PELHAM RD
11 GLENHAM RD
12 ROUNDHEAD DR
13 LUDLOW DR
14 Barley Hill Prim Sch

A4129

THAME RD A4129

TYTHROP WAY

A4129

Pilmoor
Arch

CHALGROVE
RD

BERKELEY RD

HOPTON RD

CAVALIER RD

CLARENDON
DR

ORMOND RD

DERWENT
AVE

HENRIETTA
RD

CROMWELL
WAY

BLAKE
WAY

HAMILTON RD

MARSTON RD

GRENVILLE WAY

OVERTON DR

ONSLOW DR

MASERY CL

ASTLEY RD

A4129

Whites
Farm

Mast

A4129 KINGSEY RD

WINDMILL RD

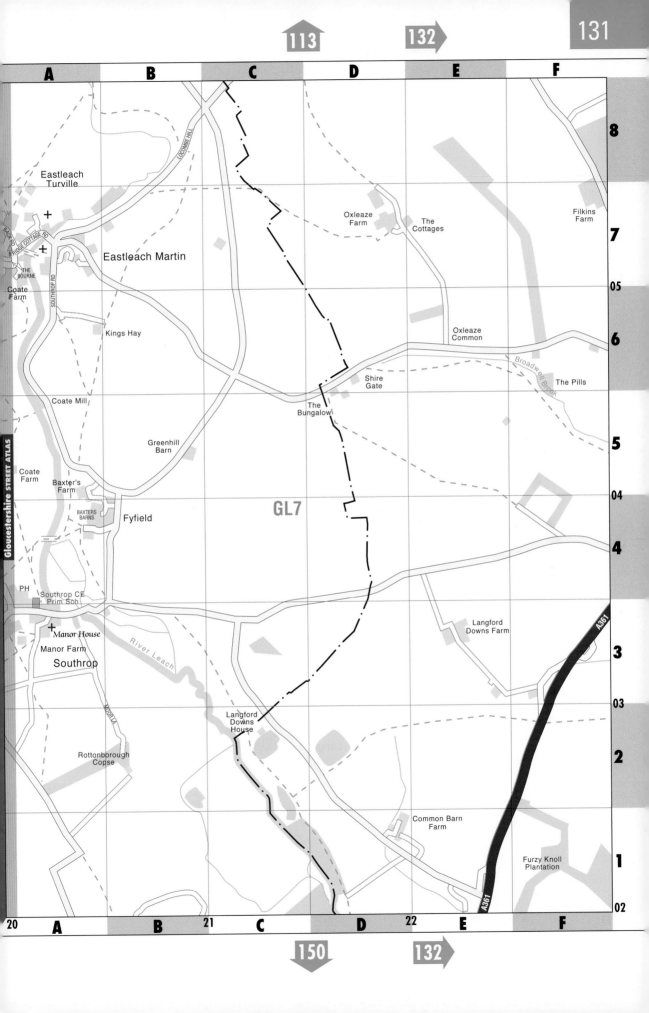

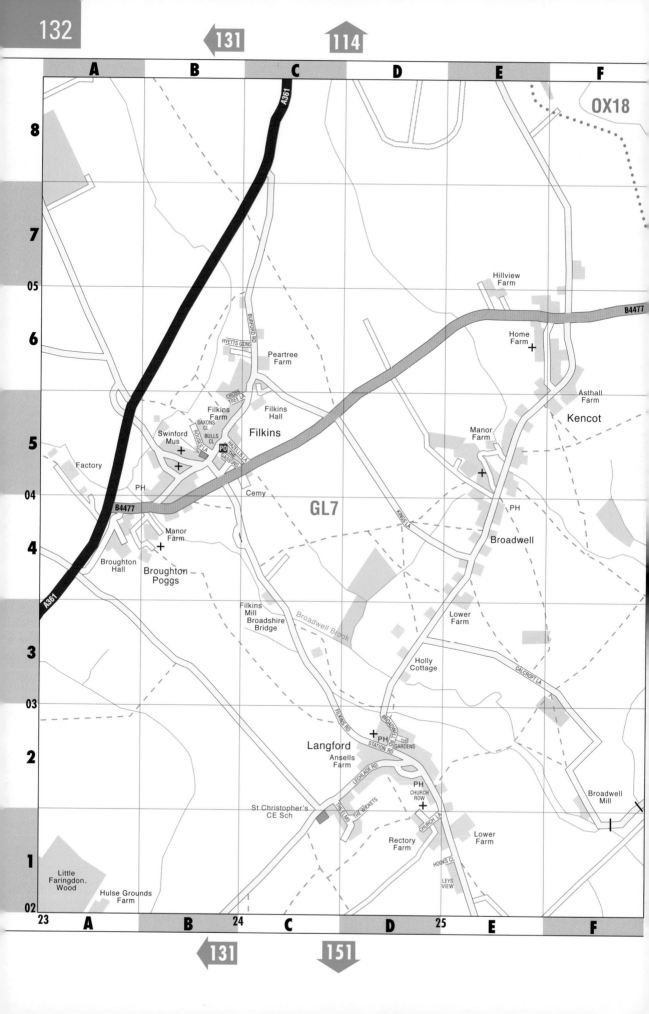

OX18

B4477

8

05

7

6

BURFORD RD

HYETTS GDNS

Peartree
Farm

Hillview
Farm

Home
Farm

Asthall
Farm

Kencot

CROSS
TREE LA

Filkins
Farm

Filkins
Hall

SAXONS
CL

BULLS
CL

Swinford
Mus

ROUSES LA

HAZELLS LA

Filkins

THE
BASSONS

PO

Manor
Farm

5

Factory

PH

Cemy

GL7

KINGS LA

PH

Broadwell

04

B4477

Manor
Farm

4

Broughton
Hall

Broughton
Poggs

Filkins
Mill
Broadshire
Bridge

Broadwell Brook

Lower
Farm

CALCROFT LA

A361

Holly
Cottage

03

3

FILKINS RD

Langford

Ansells
Farm

BROADWELL RD

STATION RD

PH

THE
GARDENS

2

LECHLADE RD

PH
CHURCH
ROW

Broadwell
Mill

St Christopher's
CE Sch

THE ELMS

THE WICKETS

CHURCH LA

Rectory
Farm

Lower
Farm

HOOKS CL

LEYS
VIEW

1

Little
Faringdon
Wood

Hulse Grounds
Farm

02

23 A 24 B C 25 D E F

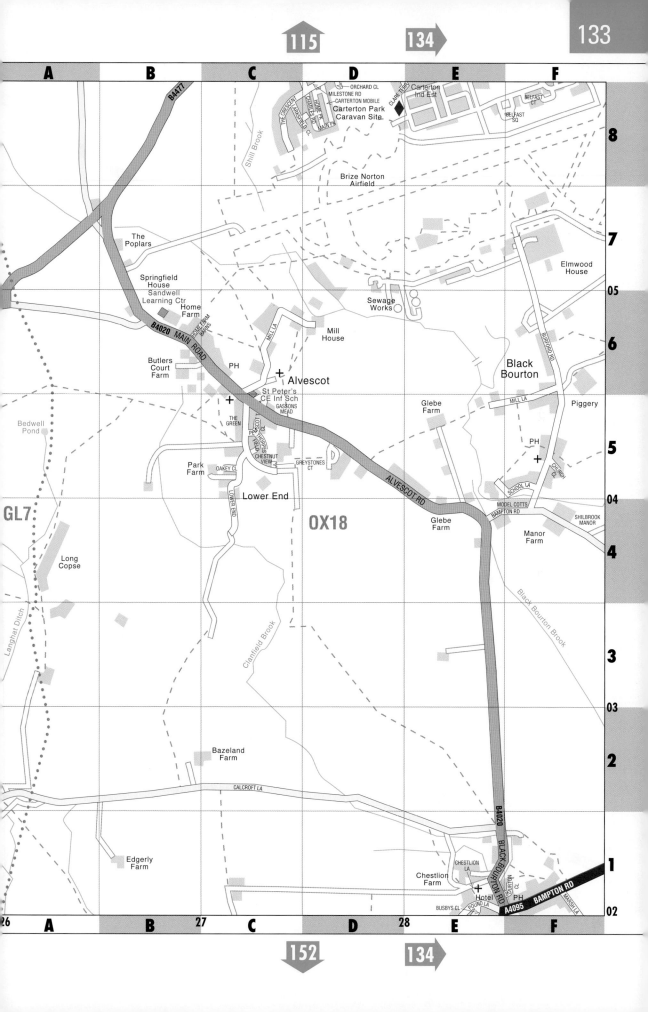

A B C D E F

8

7

05

6

5

04

4

03

3

02

2

1

02

26 A B 27 C D 28 E F

B4477

ORCHARD CL
MILESTONE RD
CARTERTON MOBILE
Carterton Park
Caravan Site
THE CRESCENT
HOME PK
CHARLES RD
LARKSFIELD CL
MAIN PK

CLARE TERR
Carterton
Ind Est
BELFAST
CT
BELFAST
SQ

Shill Brook

Brize Norton
Airfield

The Poplars

Elmwood
House

Springfield
House
Sandwell
Learning Ctr
Home
Farm
HOME FARM
BARNS

MILL LA

Mill
House

Sewage
Works

Black
Bourton

BURFORD RD

B4020 MAIN ROAD

Butlers
Court
Farm

PH

Alvescot

St Peter's
CE Inf Sch
GASSONS
MEAD

Glebe
Farm

MILL LA

Piggery

PH

CHURCH CL

THE
GREEN

LOCOST
THORPES
FIELD

CHESTNUT
VIEW

GREYSTONES
CT

P

SCHOOL LA

MODEL COTTS
BAMPTON RD

SHILBROOK
MANOR

Bedwell
Pond

Park
Farm

OAKEY CL

LOWER END

Lower End

ALVESCOT RD

Glebe
Farm

Manor
Farm

GL7

OX18

Long
Copse

Clanfield Brook

Black Bourton Brook

Langhat Ditch

Bazeland
Farm

CALCROFT LA

B4020

BLACK BOURTON RD

Edgerly
Farm

Chestlion
Farm

CHESTLION
LA

Hotel

BUSBYS CL

POUND LA

BOLTON CL

PH

A4095

BAMPTON RD

MARSH LA

	A	B	C	D	E	F

8

Brize Norton
Airfield

Lower
Haddon
Farm

Viscount
Ind Est
STATION RD

Ven
Bridge

Piggery

7

Lew Heath
House

A4095

05

STATION RD

6

Deanery
Farm

Hobbs
Buildings

Garson's
Copse

Highmoor Brook

5

Mill
Farm

The
Windmill

SHINGLETON WAY 1
QUICK ROW 2
VESEY CT 3
FOWLER CL 4
WHITAKER LA 5
SHERGOLD RD 6
WHEATSHEAF CRES 7

04

The
Plantation

OX18

Bampton
CE Prim Sch

WOODLEY DR

Bampton

4

Field
Cottage

BAMPTON RD

Shill Brook

Cemy

MANOR
VIEW

Bampton

GLEBELANDS

LANDELL'S

TANNERY

NEW RD

CALAIS DENE

3

WINDSOR COTTS 1
VICTORIA COTTS 2
BELL LA 3
CHURCH CL 4

Liby

CHURCH ST

CHURCH VIEW

CHEAPSIDE

BROAD ST

THE LANES

THE PIECES

MERCUR

BOURTON
COTTS

SHREWSBURY
PL

TH

ROSEMARY
LA

MOONRAKER
LA

HIGH ST

ASTON RD

B4449

MERCUR

03

PH

Ham
Court

CLANFIELD RD

BRIDGE ST

PH

ALBION
PL

MARKET
SQ

PO

The
Grange

CHAPEL
CL

Shill Brook

2

COWLEAZE
CNR

Weald
Manor

BARN END

MILL

MT GREEN

PRIMROSE LA

ST MARY'S
CT

WEALD ST

Backhouse
Farm

Weald Manor
Farm

THE PADDOCKS

1

A4095 BAMPTON RD

Black Bourton
Brook

Weald
Farm

Weald

Masts

HARWAY LA

Masts

02

Glebe
Farm

Masts

29	A	B	30	C	D	31	E	F

135
118

| A | B | C | D | E | F |

8

Boys Wood

Long Train

Cokethorpe Park

Home Wood

A415

B4449 FAIRFIELD

STANDLAKE RD

Hardwick

A415

7

Claywell Farm

Rickless Hill

Breach Farm Cottage

ASTON RD

05

Manor Farm

Westfield Farm

Hawthorn Farm

6

Yelford

College Farm

CALAIS LA

5

OX29

04

4

Cote Lodge Farm

Brighthampton Cut

3

COTE RD

B4449

Green Acres

New Shifford Farm

New Shifford Cottages

ASTON RD

B4449

03

South Farm

2

Cote

OX18

Chicken Hatchery

New Cottages

1

Cote House

Cote Bungalow

Cote House Farm

Shifford

02

| 35 | A | B | 36 | C | D | 37 | E | F |

135
155

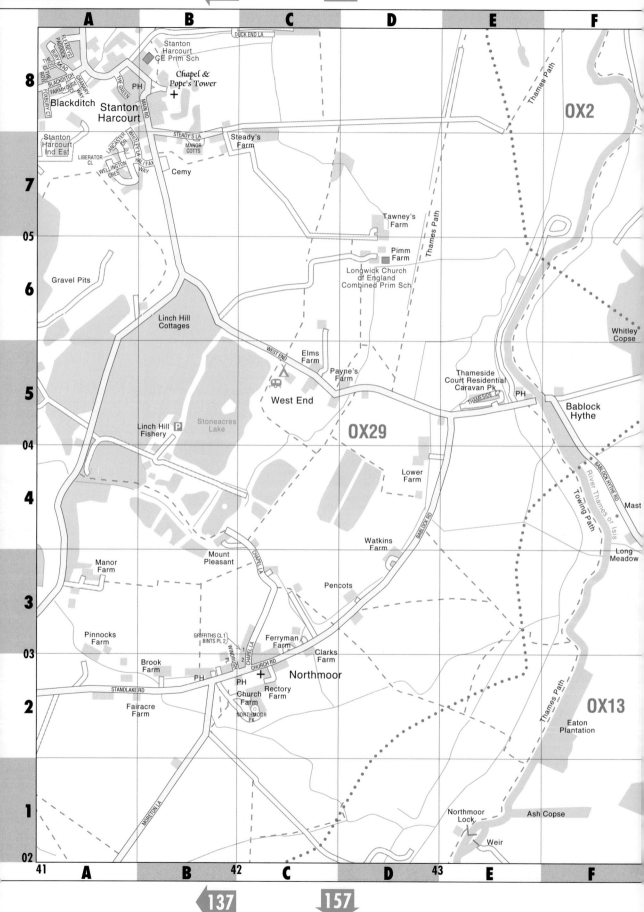

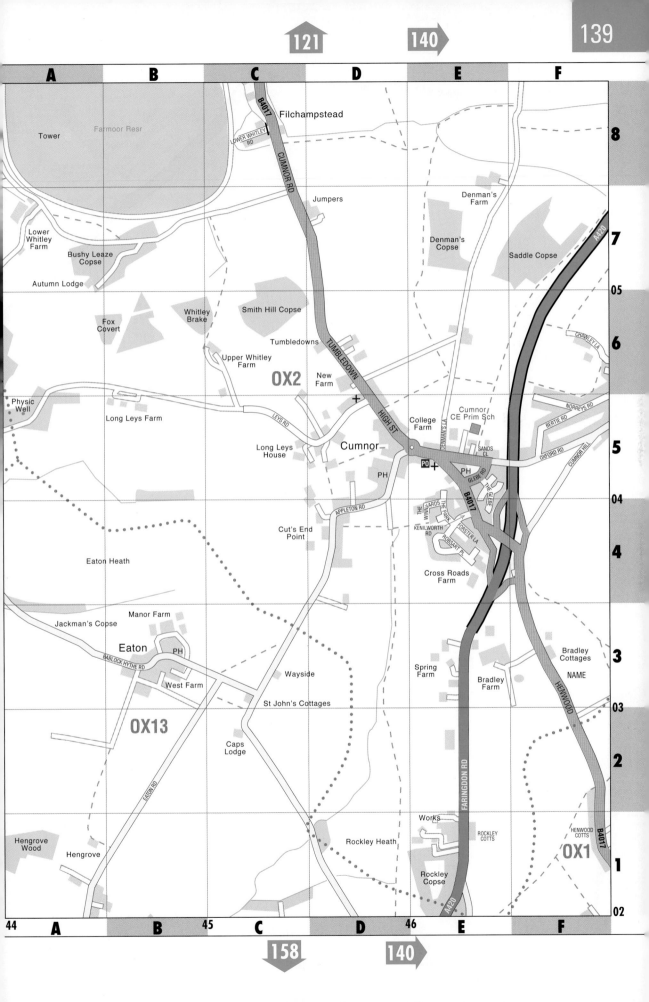

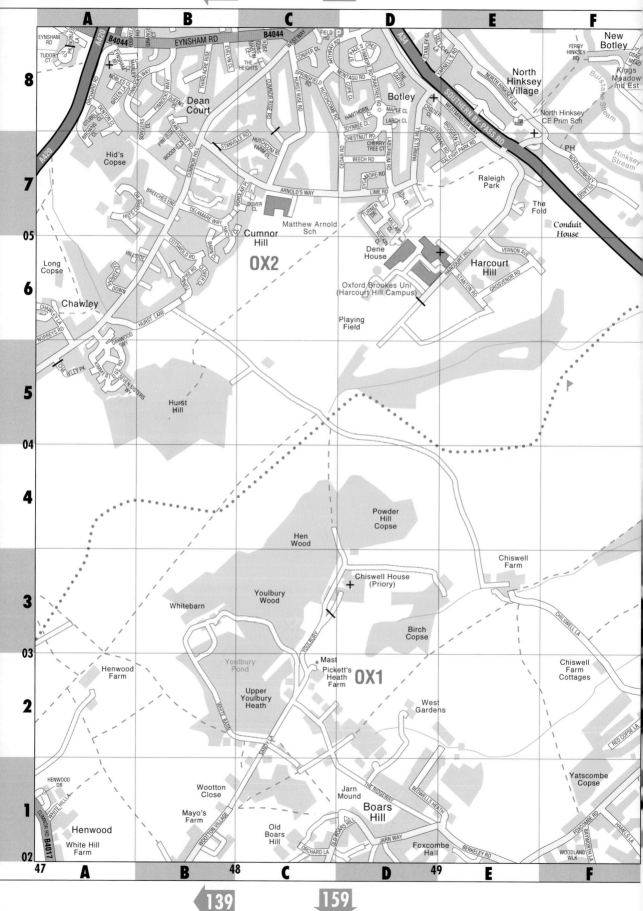

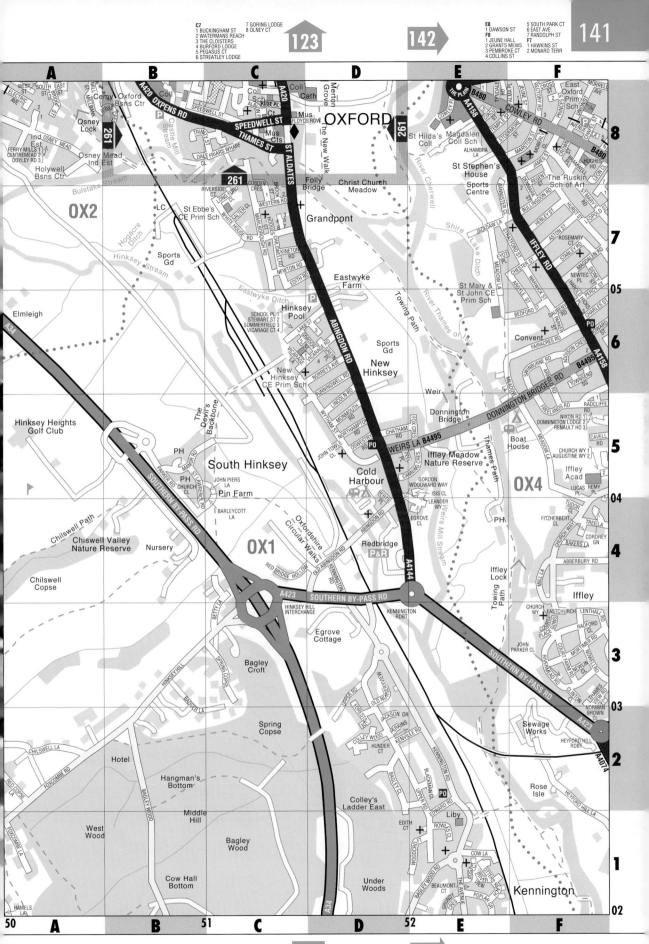

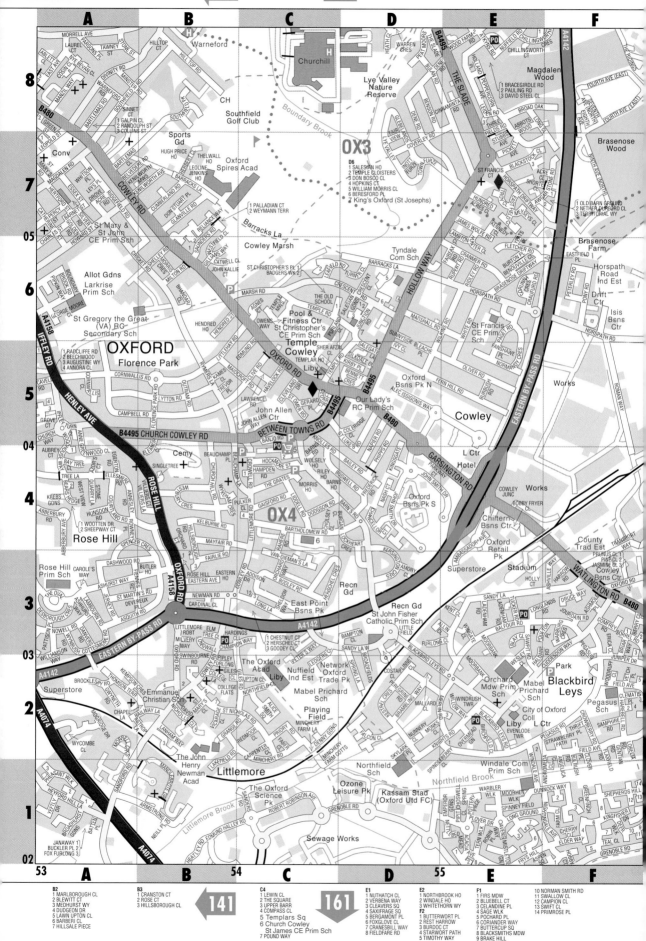

B2
1 MARLBOROUGH CL
2 BLEWITT CT
3 MEDHURST WY
4 DUDGEON DR
5 LAWN UPTON CL
6 BARBERI CL
7 HILLSALE PIECE

B3
1 CRANSTON CT
2 ROSE CT
3 HILLSBOROUGH CL

C4
1 LEWIN CL
2 THE SQUARE
3 UPPER BARR
4 COMPASS CL
5 TEMPLARS SQ
6 Church Cowley
  St James CE Prim Sch
7 POUND WAY

E1
1 NUTHATCH CL
2 VERBENA WAY
3 CLEAVERS SQ
4 SAXIFRAGE SQ
5 BERGAMONT PL
6 FOXGLOVE CL
7 CRANESBILL WAY
8 FIELDFARE RD

E2
1 NORTHBROOK HO
2 WINDALE HO
3 WHITETHORN WY

F2
1 BUTTERWORT PL
2 REST HARROW
3 BURDOC CT
4 STARWORT PATH
5 TIMOTHY WAY

F1
1 FIRS MDW
2 BLUEBELL CT
3 CELANDINE PL
4 SAGE WLK
5 POCHARD PL
6 CORIANDER WAY
7 BUTTERCUP SQ
8 BLACKSMITHS MDW
9 BRAKE HILL

10 NORMAN SMITH RD
11 SWALLOW CL
12 CAMPION CL
13 SWIFT CL
14 PRIMROSE PL

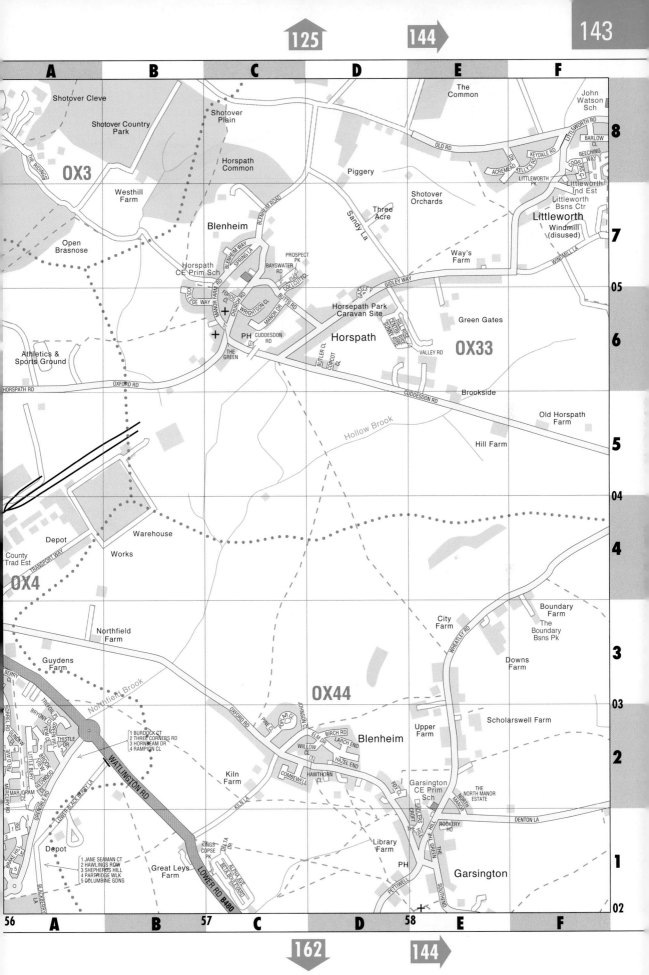

Shotover Cleve

Shotover Country Park

OX3

Westhill Farm

Open Brasnose

The RIDINGS

Shotover Plain

Shotover Common

Horspath Common

BLENHEIM ROAD

Blenheim

Horspath CE Prim Sch

BLENHEIM WAY

SPRING LA

COLLEGE WAY

HANNAH FARM RD

CHURCH RD

WRIGHTSON CL

MANOR DR

FORDS RD

BUTTS RD

PROSPECT PK

BAYSWATER RD

COLLCUTT CL

PH

CUDDESDON RD

THE GREEN

Athletics & Sports Ground

HORSPATH RD

OXFORD RD

The Common

Piggery

Sandy La

Three Acre

Shotover Orchards

Way's Farm

GIDLEY WAY

KSLEY

Horspath Park Caravan Site

FULL PITCHER

CENTRE DRIVE

SUNNY RISE

Horspath

VALLEY RD

BUTLER CL

COPCOT CL

CUDDESDON RD

Green Gates

OX33

Brookside

Old Horspath Farm

Hill Farm

Hollow Brook

John Watson Sch

LITTLEWORTH RD

OLD RD

ACREMEAD

KELLY'S RD

KEYDALE RD

LITTLEWORTH PK

BARLOW CL

BEECHING WAY

COOP

Littleworth Ind Est

Littleworth Bsns Ctr

Littleworth

Windmill (disused)

WINDMILL LA

OX4

County Trad Est

Depot

Warehouse

Works

TRANSPORT WAY

Northfield Farm

Guydens Farm

Northfield Brook

BERRY

SORREL RD

SAXON WAY

TREE GUILD GREEN HILL

BRYONY RD

YEW CL

BROOK VIEW

LITTLE BURY

REDWOOD

THISTLE DR

MARJORAM CL

GRENFELL RD

LOWER BLACKBERRY LA

MERCURY RD

BRAMBLE HILL

BLACKBERRY LA

Depot

WATLINGTON RD

1 JANE SEAMAN CT
2 HAWLINGS ROW
3 SHEPHERDS HILL
4 PARTRIDGE WLK
5 COLUMBINE GDNS

Great Leys Farm

KINGS COPSE PK

LOWER RD B480

DELTA DR

ALPHA AVE

BETA RD

1 BURDOCK CT
2 THREE CORNERS RD
3 HORNBEAM DR
4 RAMPION CL

OX44

OXFORD RD

PINE CL

Kiln Farm

KILN LA

COMBEWELL

JOHNSON CL

POPLAR CL

ELM DR

WILLOW CL

BIRCH RD

LARCH END

HAZEL END

HAWTHORN CL

Blenheim

FOX CL

City Farm

WHEATLEY RD

Upper Farm

Garsington CE Prim Sch

CROFT

CARTERS HILL

THE GREEN

PETTIWELL

Library Farm

PH

SOUTHEND

ROOKERY HO

DENTON LA

Garsington

Downs Farm

Boundary Farm

The Boundary Bsns Pk

Scholarswell Farm

NORTH MANOR

THE NORTH MANOR ESTATE

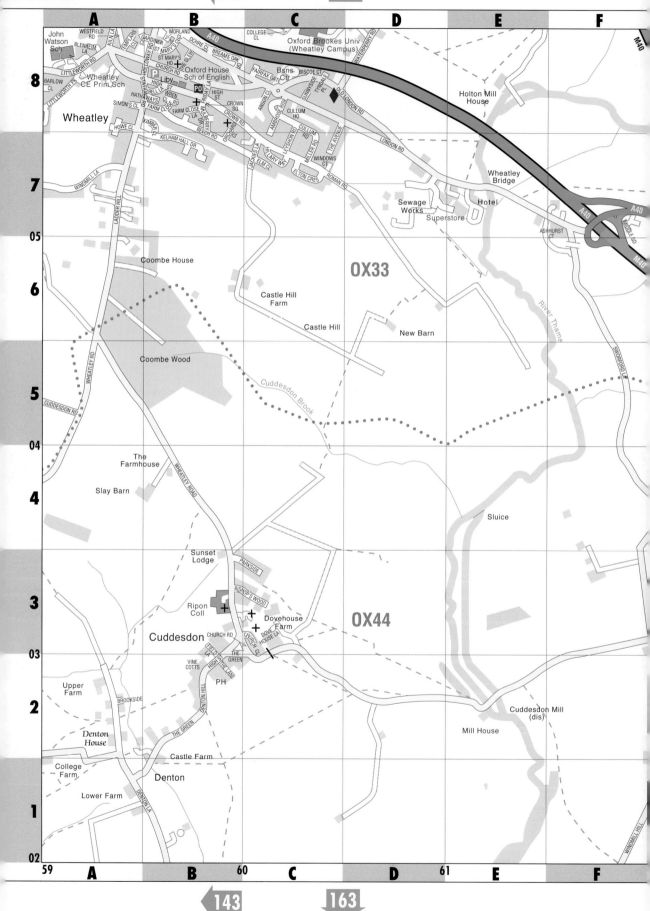

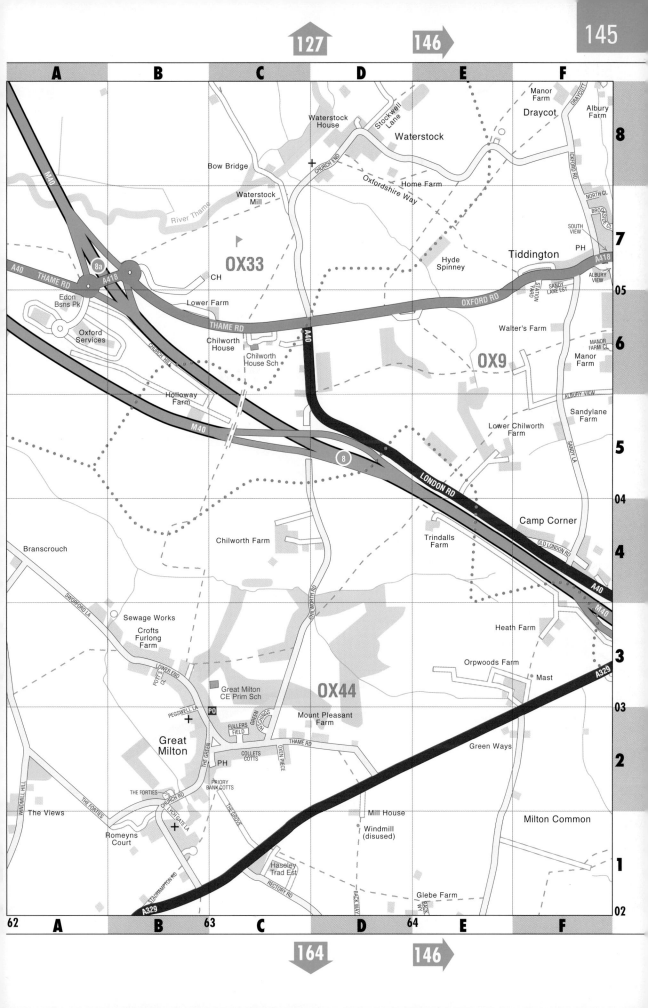

127
146
164
146

A B C D E F

8
7
05
6
5
04
4
M40
03
3
2
03
1
02

62 A B 63 C D 64 E F

Manor Farm
Draycot
Albury Farm
DRAYCOTT
OXFORD RD
NORTH CL
BROOKSIDE CL
SOUTH VIEW
PH
ALBURY VIEW
A418

Waterstock House
Stockwell Lane
Waterstock
Home Farm
Oxfordshire Way
Tiddington
STATION YARD
SANDY LANE EST

Bow Bridge
CHURCH END
Hyde Spinney
Oxford Rd
Walter's Farm
MANOR FARM CL

River Thame
Waterstock Mill
OX33
CH
Lower Farm
THAME RD
Chilworth House
Chilworth House Sch
OX9
Manor Farm
ALBURY VIEW
Sandylane Farm
SANDY LA

M40
A40
THAME RD
A418
8a
Edon Bsns Pk
Oxford Services
CHURCH HILL
Holloway Farm
M40
Lower Chilworth Farm

A40
THAME RD
8
LONDON RD
Camp Corner
OLD LONDON RD

Branscrouch
Chilworth Farm
Trindalls Farm
A40
M40

SWORFORD LA
Sewage Works
Crofts Furlong Farm
CHILWORTH RD
Heath Farm
Orpwoods Farm
Mast
A329

LOWER END
POTTS CL
OX44
Great Milton CE Prim Sch
Mount Pleasant Farm
Green Ways

PEGSWELL LA
PO
GREEN
FLETCHINGS
THAME RD

Great Milton
FULLERS FIELD
COLLETS COTTS
OXEN PIECE
PH
THE GREEN
Milton Common

THE FORTIES
PRIORY BANK COTTS
Mill House
Windmill (disused)

WINDMILL HILL
The Views
CHURCH RD
LYCH GATE LA
THE GROVE
Romeyns Court
Haseley Trad Est
RECTORY RD
BACK WAY
BACK WAY
Glebe Farm

STADHAMPTON RD
A329

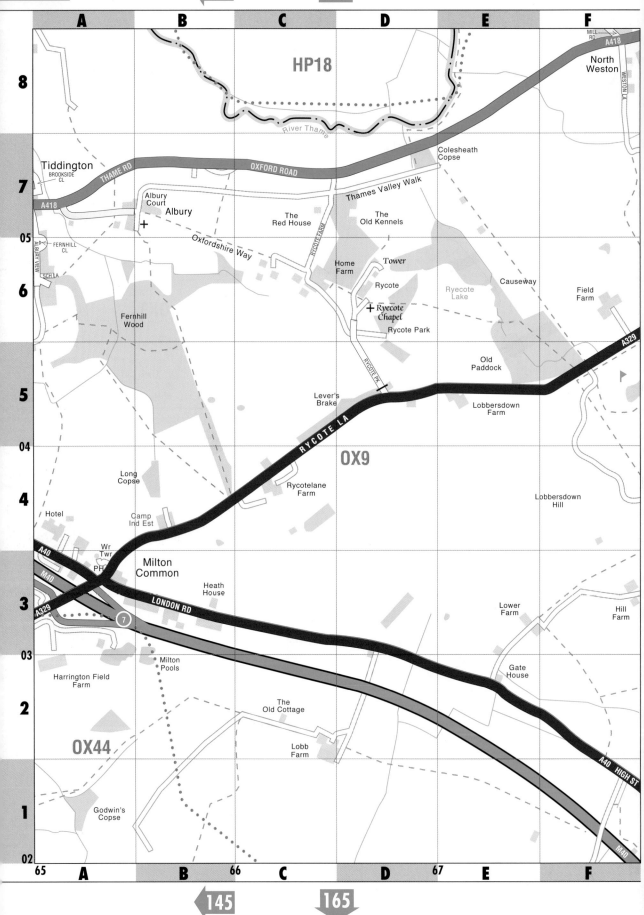

145
128

HP18

North Weston

Tiddington

BROOKSIDE CL

THAME RD

OXFORD ROAD

Colesheath Copse

A418

Thames Valley Walk

Albury Court

Albury

The Red House

The Old Kennels

FERNHILL CL

ALBURY VIEW

SCH LA

Oxfordshire Way

RYCOTE FARM

Home Farm

Tower

Rycote

Causeway

Field Farm

Fernhill Wood

Ryecote Lake

Ryecote Chapel

Rycote Park

RYCOTE PK

Old Paddock

A329

Lever's Brake

RYCOTE LA

OX9

Lobbersdown Farm

Long Copse

Rycotelane Farm

Lobbersdown Hill

Hotel

Camp Ind Est

Wr Twr

PH

Milton Common

Heath House

LONDON RD

Lower Farm

Hill Farm

A40

M40

A329

7

Milton Pools

Gate House

Harrington Field Farm

The Old Cottage

OX44

Lobb Farm

A40 HIGH ST

Godwin's Copse

M40

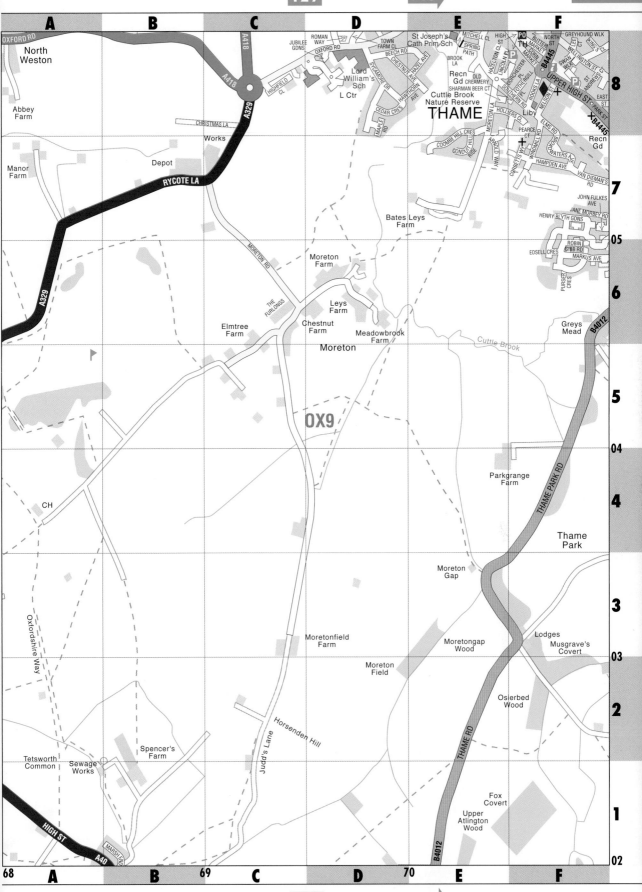

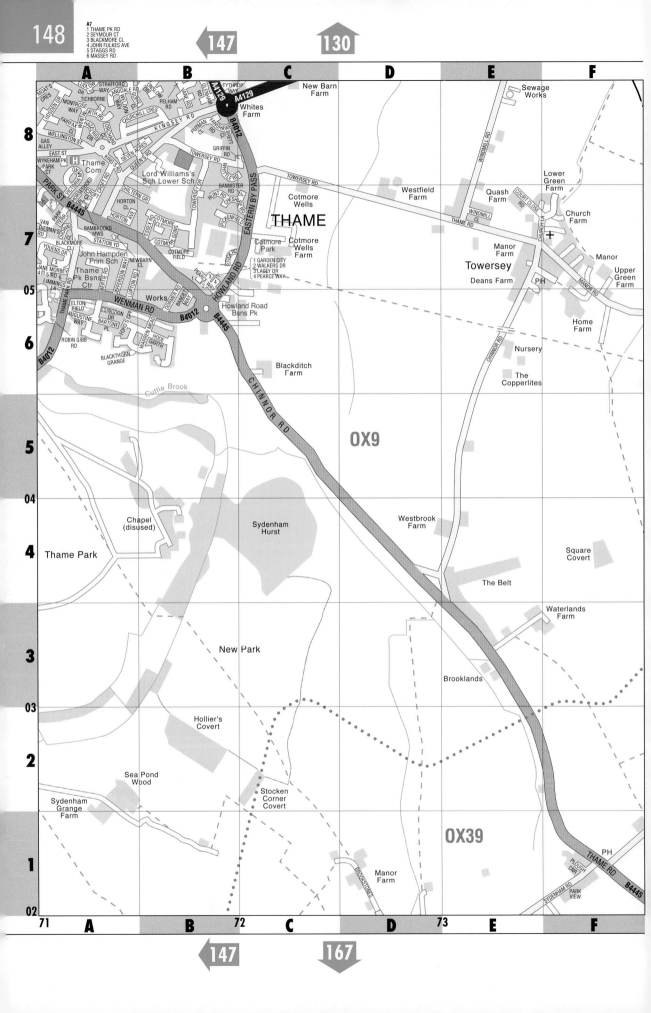

148

A7
1 THAME PK RD
2 SEYMOUR CT
3 BLACKMORE CL
4 JOHN FULKES AVE
5 STAGGS RD
6 MASSEY RD

147 130

New Barn Farm
Whites Farm
Sewage Works
Lower Green Farm

Westfield Farm
Church Farm

Cotmore Wells
THAME
Quash Farm
Manor

Cotmore Park
Cotmore Wells Farm
Manor Farm
Towersey
Upper Green Farm

1 GARDEN CITY
2 WALKERS DR
3 LAGEY DR
4 PEARCE WAY

Deans Farm
PH
Home Farm

Howland Road Bsns Pk
Nursery
The Copperlites

Blackditch Farm

Cuttle Brook

OX9

Westbrook Farm
Square Covert

Chapel (disused)
Sydenham Hurst

Thame Park
The Belt

Waterlands Farm

New Park

Brooklands

Hollier's Covert

Sea Pond Wood

Stocken Corner Covert

OX39

Sydenham Grange Farm

PH
THAME RD
PLOUGH CNR
Manor Farm
PARK VIEW
SYDENHAM RD
B4445

Thame Com
Lord Williams's Sch Lower Sch
John Hampden Prim Sch
Thame Pk Bsns Ctr
WENMAN RD
Works

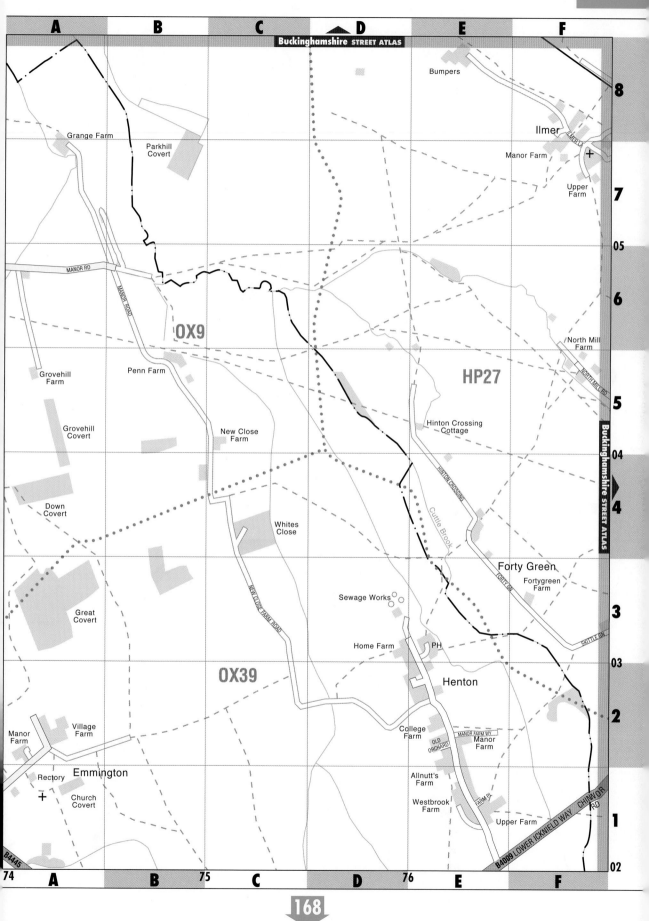

A B C D E F

8
7
05
6
5
04
4
3
03
2
1
02

Bumpers

Ilmer

Manor Farm

Upper Farm

LIMES LA

North Mill Farm

NORTH MILL RD

Grange Farm

Parkhill Covert

MANOR RD

MANOR ROAD

OX9

Penn Farm

Grovehill Farm

Grovehill Covert

New Close Farm

Down Covert

HP27

Hinton Crossing Cottage

HINTON CROSSING

Cuttle Brook

Whites Close

Forty Green

Fortygreen Farm

FORTY GN

SKITTLE GN

Great Covert

NEW CLOSE FARM ROAD

Sewage Works

OX39

Home Farm

PH

Henton

Manor Farm

Village Farm

College Farm

OLD ORCHARD

MANOR FARM WY

Manor Farm

Emmington

Rectory

Church Covert

Allnutt's Farm

Westbrook Farm

FARM PL

Upper Farm

CHINNOR RD

B4009 LOWER ICKNIELD WAY

B4445

Buckinghamshire STREET ATLAS

74 A B 75 C D 76 E F

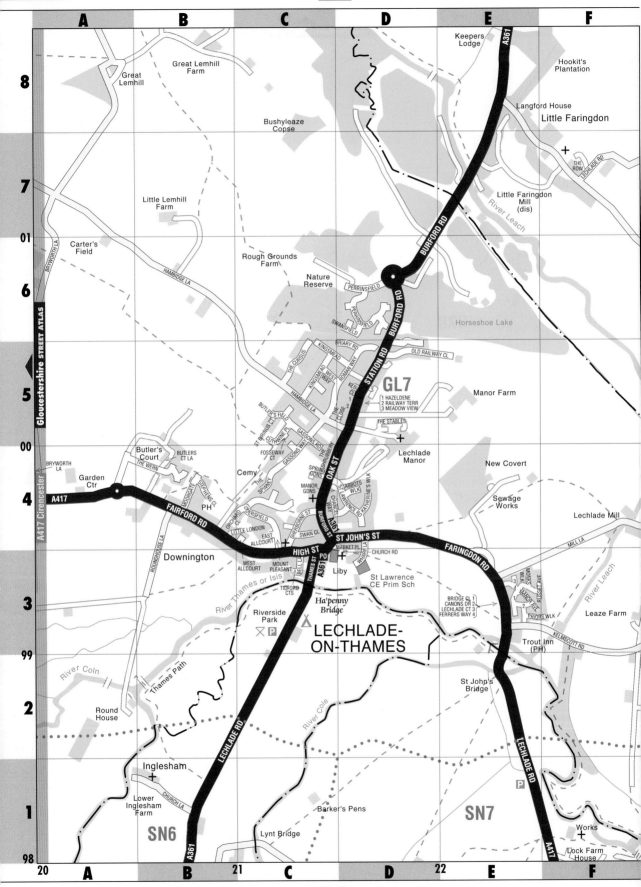

Gloucestershire STREET ATLAS

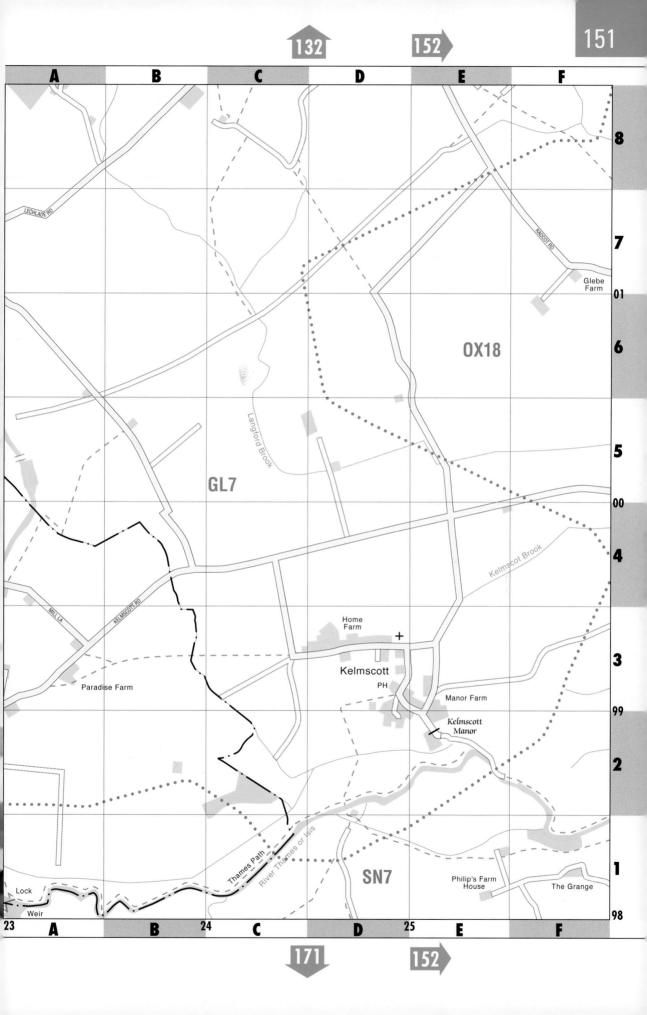

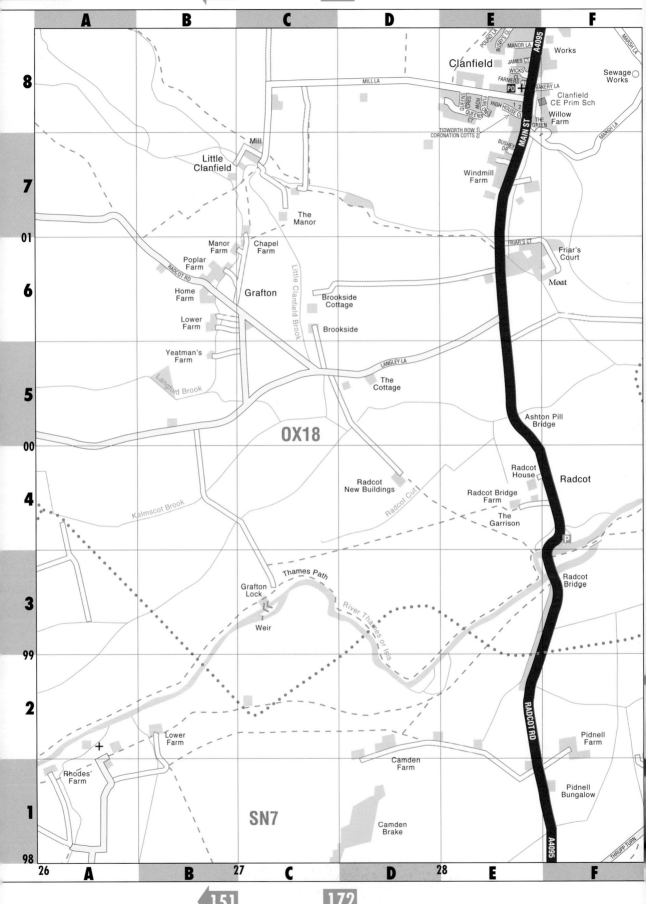

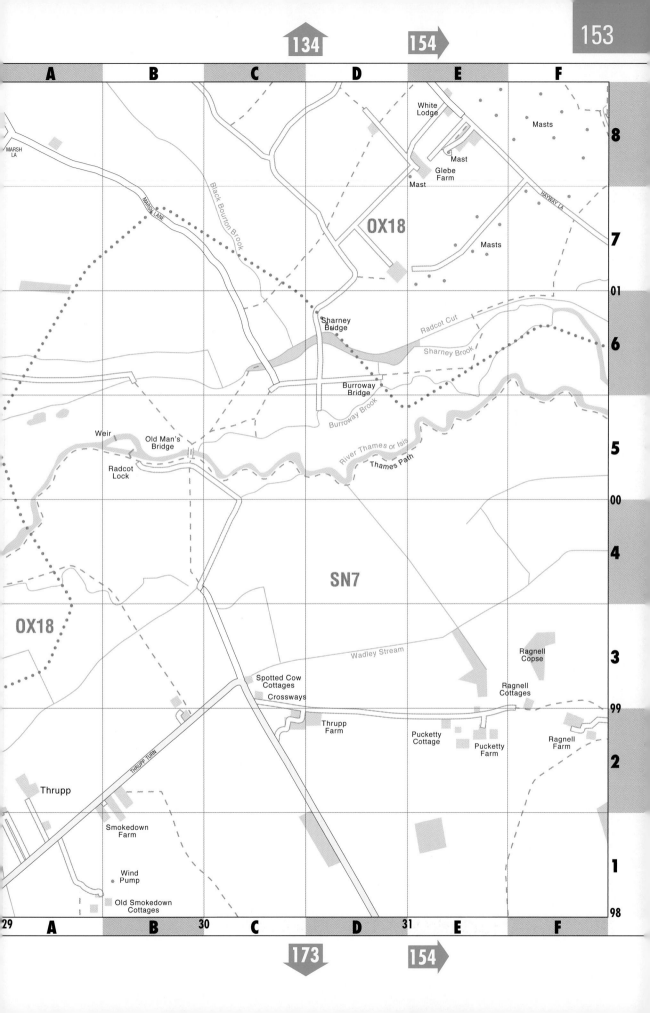

153
135

| | A | B | C | D | E | F |

8

Meadow
Arch Bridge

Meadow Farm
Cottages

Meadow Brook

BUCKLAND RD

Shill Brook

HAM LA

OX18

7

Meadow
Farm

Great Brook

01

Hoskins
Barn

Isle of Wight
Bridge

6

River Thames or Isis

Thames Path

Tadpole
Bridge

Tadpole

PH

5

Rushey
Lock

Weir

00

4

Buckland
Marsh

Buckland Marsh
Farm

SN7

3

Carswell Marsh

Gore Farm

99

2

Vicar's
Copse

Marriage
Hill

The
Lakes

Weir

Deer Park

Manor
House

Sewage
Works

CARSWELL LA

Middle
Brake

Rivey
Brake

Buckland
House

Buckland

1

Rivey
Copse

Arch
Plantation

BUCKLAND
RD

ORCHARD
RD

ST GEORGE'S RD

98

| 32 | A | | B | 33 | C | | D | 34 | E | | F |

153
174

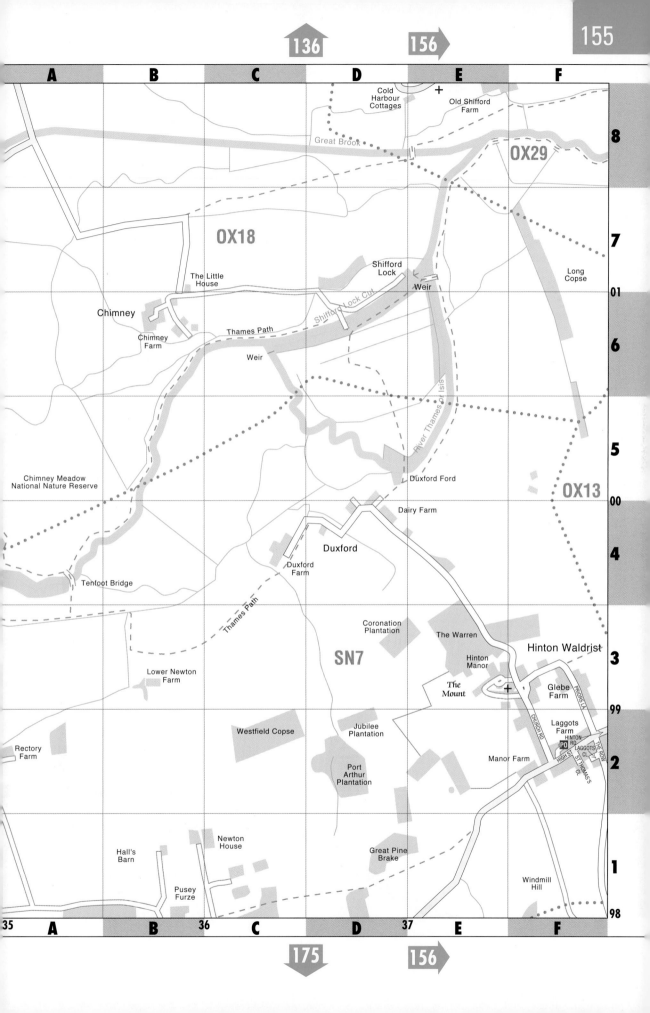

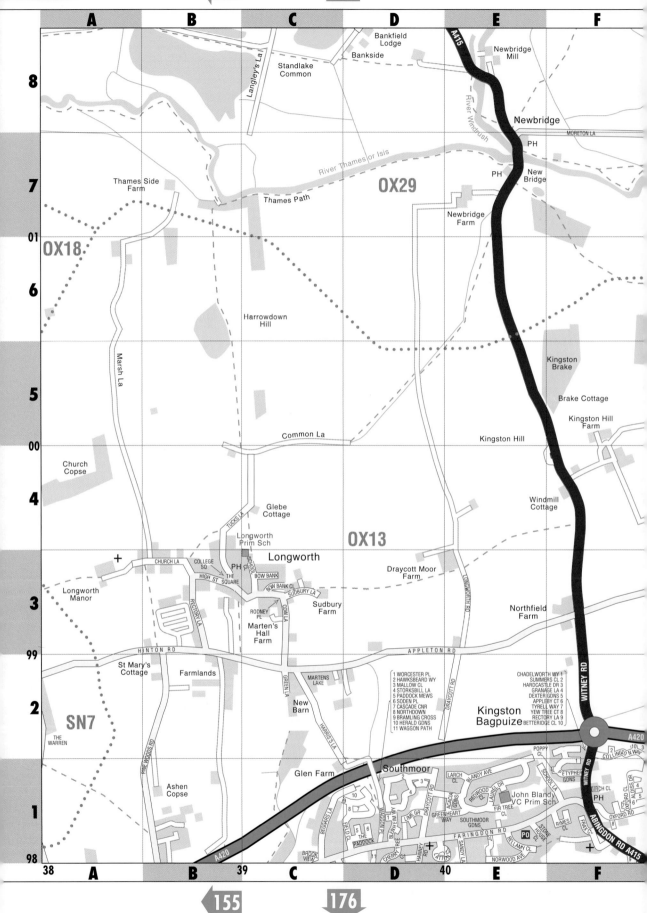

A B C D E F

8

7

01

OX18

6

5

00

4

3

99

2

1

98

38 A B 39 C D 40 E F

Bankfield Lodge
Bankside
Standlake Common
Langley's La
Newbridge Mill
Newbridge
PH
MORETON LA
River Windrush
A415
Thames Side Farm
River Thames or Isis
Thames Path
OX29
PH
New Bridge
Newbridge Farm
Harrowdown Hill
Kingston Brake
Brake Cottage
Marsh La
Kingston Hill Farm
Common La
Kingston Hill
Church Copse
Windmill Cottage
Glebe Cottage
TUCKS LA
Longworth Prim Sch
OX13
Longworth
CHURCH LA
COLLEGE SQ
PH
SCHOOL CL
Draycott Moor Farm
LONGWORTH RD
Northfield Farm
Longworth Manor
HIGH ST
THE SQUARE
BOW BANK
BOW BANK CL
SUDBURY LA
COW LA
Sudbury Farm
RODNEY PL
Marten's Hall Farm
RECTORY LA
HINTON RD
APPLETON RD
St Mary's Cottage
Farmlands
GREEN LA
MARTENS LAKE
1 WORCESTER PL
2 HAWKSBEARD WY
3 MALLOW CL
4 STORKSBILL LA
5 PADDOCK MEWS
6 SODEN PL
7 CASCADE CNR
8 NORTHDOWN
9 BRAMLING CROSS
10 HERALD GDNS
11 WAGGON PATH
DRAYCOTT RD
Kingston Bagpuize
CHADELWORTH WY 1
SUMMERS CL 2
HARDCASTLE DR 3
GRANAGE LA 4
DEXTER GDNS 5
APPLEBY CT 6
TYRELL WAY 7
YEW TREE CT 8
RECTORY LA 9
BETTERIDGE CL 10
WITNEY RD
A420
SN7
THE WARREN
New Barn
HARRIS LA
PINE WOODS RD
Ashen Copse
Glen Farm
BEGGARS LA
Southmoor
FRED CL
THE PADDOCK
BROOK VIEW
A420
CHERRY TREE
HANNEY RD
BLENHEIM WY
LIME GR
ACACIA GDNS
LARCH CL
DRAYCOTT RD
REDWOOD CL
BLANDY AVE
LAUREL DR
GREENHEART WAY
SOUTHMOOR GDNS
FIR TREE CL
John Blandy VC Prim Sch
SANDY LA
FARINGDON RD
NORWOOD AVE
BELLAMY CL
STONE HOUSE CL
RIMES CL
PO
POPPY CL
SCHOOL LA
PETYPHER GDNS
COLLINGWOOD WY
WITNEY RD
A420
BIRCH CL
OXFORD RD
ALDISS DR
FRAX CL
PH
ABINGDON RD A415

A B C D E F

8

MORETON LA

Stonehenge Farm

MORETON LA

Moreton

OX29

Water Furze

Thames Path

Cowslip Close

BADSWELL LA

The Fold

7

Woodlands

River Thames or Isis

Cheers Farm

01

MILLWAY LA

6

Appleton Lower Common

NETHERTON RD

Nurseries

The Lanket

North Audley Copse

Field Farm

Tubney Wood

North Audley Farm House

APPLETON COMM

Rose Hill

5

Marsh Farm

MARSH LA

Sandhill Cottage

00

OX13

Sewage Works

Appleton Upper Common

4

A420

Stone's Farm

Church Copse

Tubworth Barn

Tubney Lodge

3

Netherton

Bullock's Farm

Painton's Farm

NETHERTON LA

99

Manor Farm

Piling Hill

Tubney House

OLD COACH RD

Tubney

2

ISIS LONNS CL

MAIN RD

DIGGING LA

PH

MAIN RD

ABINGDON RD

Tubney Farm

HARDCASTLE DR

Fyfield

Tubney Farm

ALDISS DR

PARTRIDGE LA

Diginglane Cottages

Sandy Wood

OXFORD RD

EXETER GDNS

MORRIS DR

AELFRITH CT

The Spinney

DIGGING LA

1

Woodhouse Farm

98

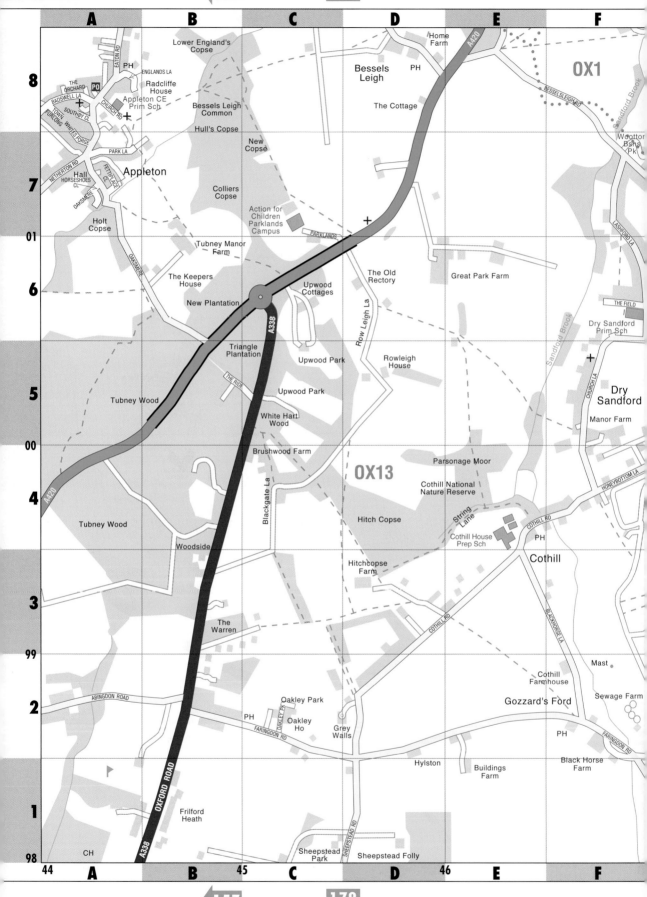

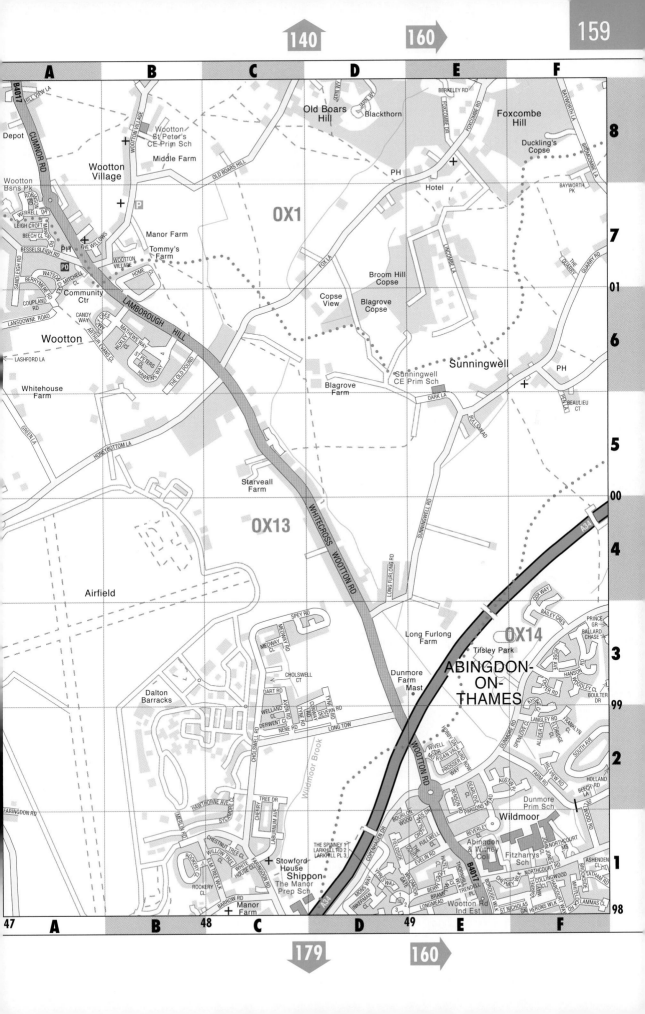

159
141

159
180

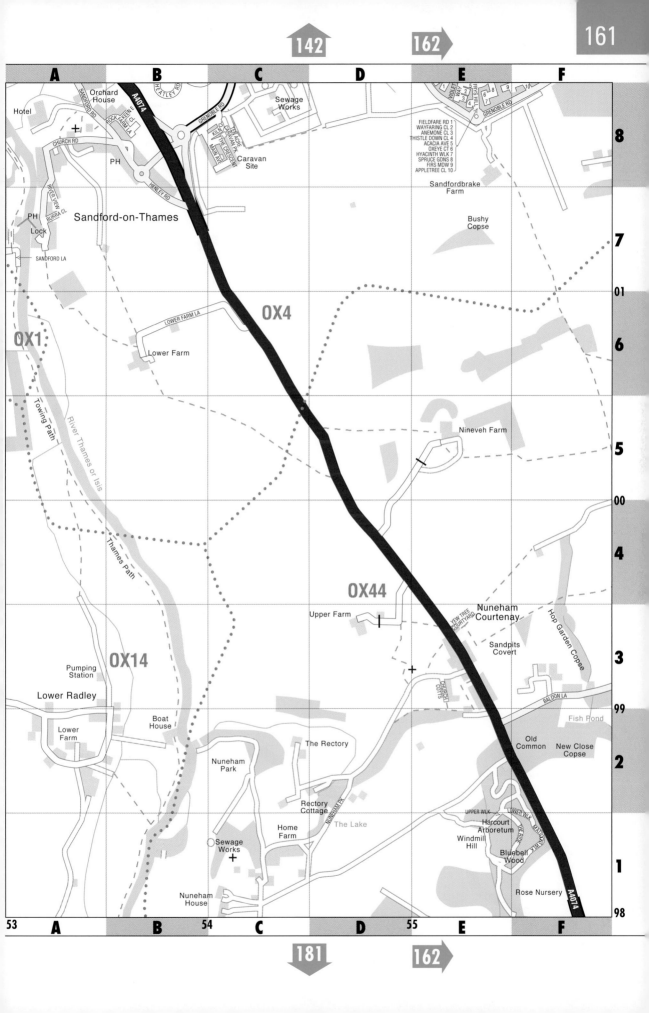

A B C D E F

8

OX4

LOWER BLACKBERRY LA

Hillsdown

WATLINGTON ROAD

B480

PETTIWELL

Manor House

Southend

Southend Farm

SOUTHEND

7

LOWER RD

01

The Manor House

Toot Baldon

PH

College Farm

LOWER ROAD

6

New Farm

WILMOTS

Manor Farm

Lower Farm

Court Leys

+

Baldon Brook

CHISEL HAMPTON HILL

5

Baldon Row

OX44

Gotham Farm

CUDDESDON RD

00

THE CROFT

PEBBLE HILL

4

Parsonage Farm

B480

Marsh Baldon CE Prim Sch

Marsh Baldon

Richmond Hill

THE GREEN

3

BALDON LA

PH

+

Durham Leys Farm

99

Baldon House

Marylands Farm

MARYLANDS GN

2

Little Baldon Farm

CLIFTON HAMTON ROAD

B4015

Sands Corner Copse

Baldon Brook

LITTLE BALDON FARM COTTS

1

Hanginglands Copse

B4015

98

56 A B 57 C D 58 E F

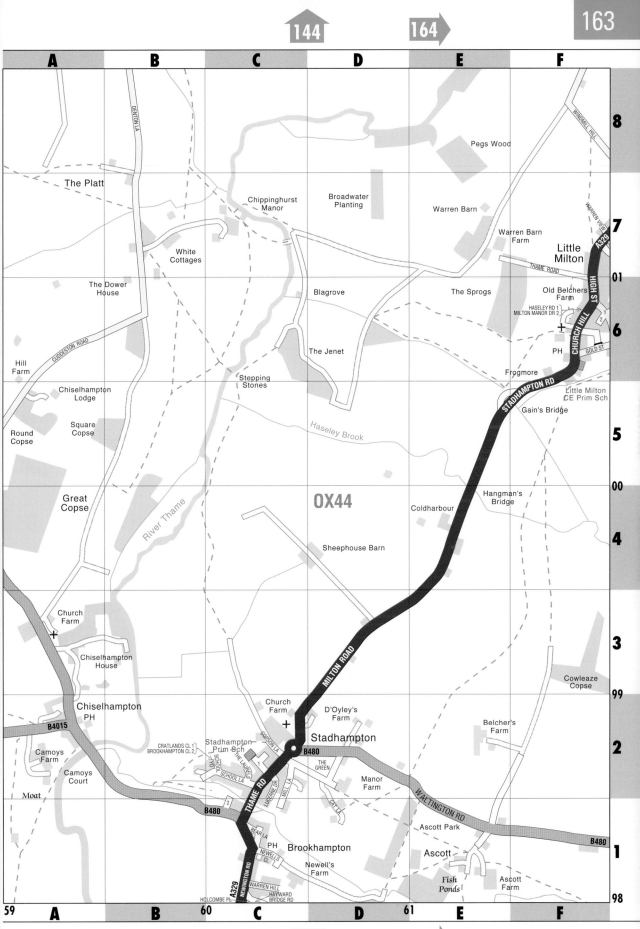

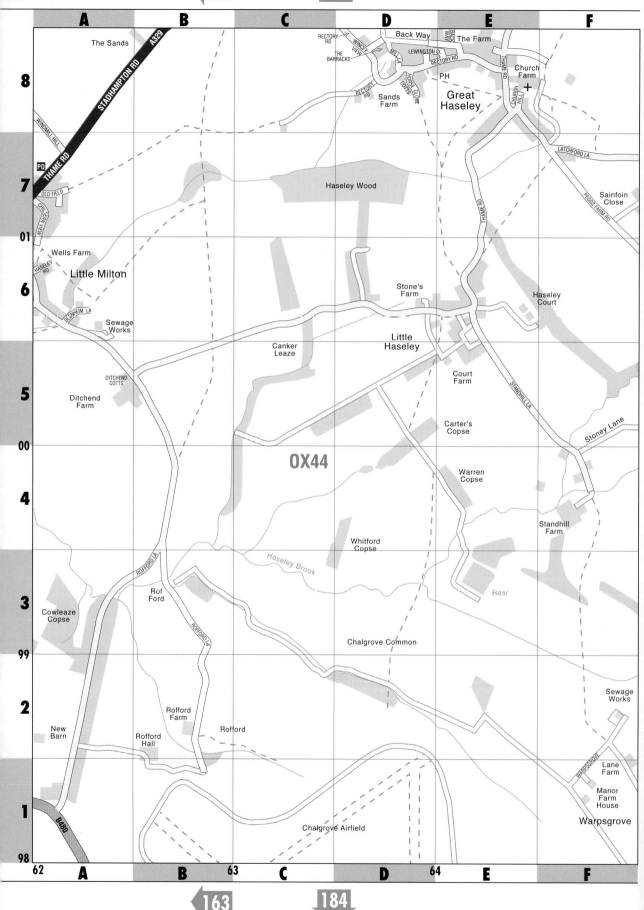

163
145

A   B   C   C   D   E   F

The Sands

STADHAMPTON RD

A329

RECTORY
RD

Back Way

BACK WAY

The Farm

WINGY
VIEW

MILL
LA

LEWINGTON CL

THE
BARRACKS

RECTORY RD

8

HORSE CLOSE

PH

Church
Farm

RECTORY
RD

Sands
Farm

Great
Haseley

THAME RD

CHURCH HILL

+

WINDMILL HILL

PO

THAME RD

Latchford La

OLD FIELD

7

CHILTERN VIEW

Haseley Wood

PEGGS FARM RD

Sainfoin
Close

01

HASELEY RD

Wells Farm

6

Little Milton

Stone's
Farm

Haseley
Court

BLENHEIM LA

Sewage
Works

Canker
Leaze

Little
Haseley

DITCHEND
COTTS

Court
Farm

STANDHILL LA

5

Ditchend
Farm

Carter's
Copse

Stoney Lane

00

OX44

Warren
Copse

4

Standhill
Farm

Whitford
Copse

Haseley Brook

ROFFORD LA

Hesr

3

Cowleaze
Copse

Rof
Ford

ROFFORD LA

Chalgrove Common

99

Sewage
Works

2

Rofford
Farm

Rofford

WARPSGROVE

Lane
Farm

New
Barn

Rofford
Hall

Manor
Farm
House

1

B480

Chalgrove Airfield

Warpsgrove

98

62   A   B   63   C   D   64   E   F

163
184

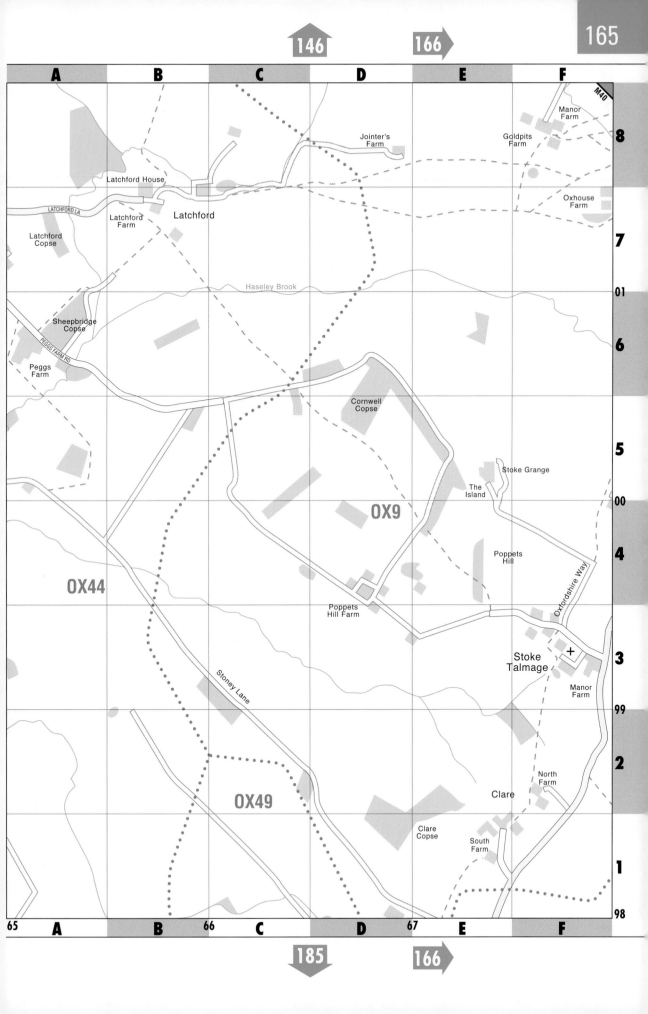

146 166

A B C D E F

8

Manor
Farm

Jointer's
Farm

Goldpits
Farm

Oxhouse
Farm

Latchford House

LATCHFORD LA

Latchford
Farm

Latchford

Latchford
Farm

Latchford
Copse

7

Haseley Brook

01

Sheepbridge
Copse

6

PEGGS FARM RD

Peggs
Farm

Cornwell
Copse

5

Stoke Grange

The
Island

00

OX9

Poppets
Hill

4

OX44

Oxfordshire Way

Poppets
Hill Farm

Stoke
Talmage

3

Manor
Farm

Stoney Lane

99

2

North
Farm

Clare

OX49

Clare
Copse

South
Farm

1

98

65 A B 66 C D 67 E F

185 166

165
147

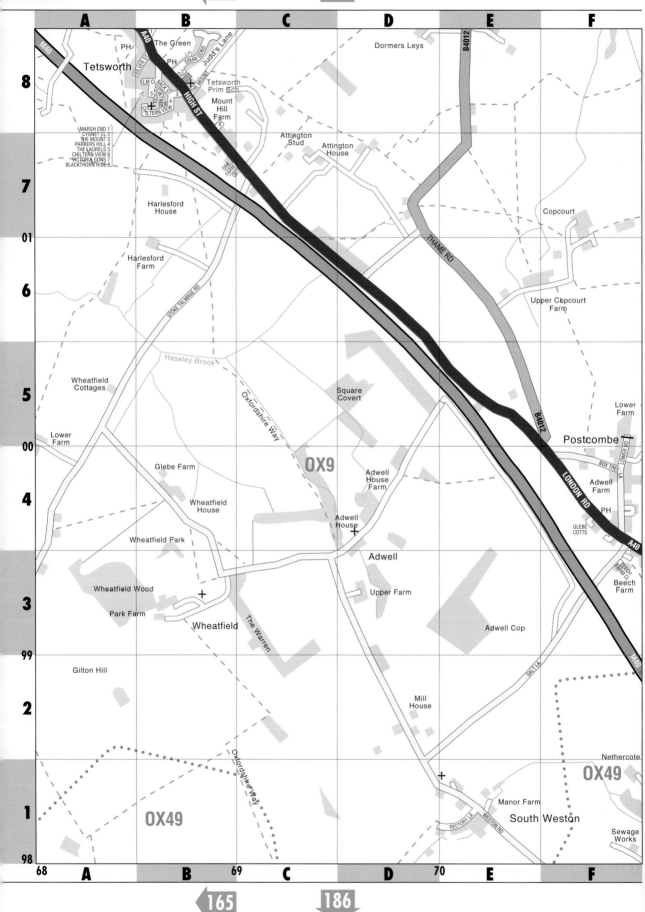

165
186

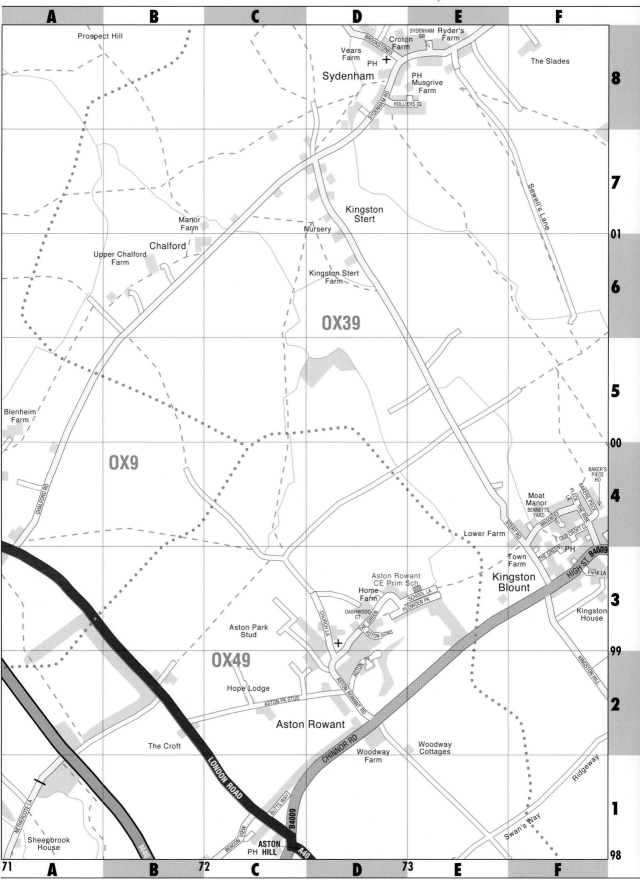

← 167
149

A   B   C   D   E   F

B4445

THAME RD

8

RUMPENNY
RUSHLAND FIELD
BRAKEN RD
THE PADDOCKS
WALNUT TREE CL
LOWER ICKNIELD WAY
WHEATFIELD
DENNES OAK
B4009

Lane Farm
ELDERDENE
HOLLAND
THE LA

WAINHILL

Lower Wainhill

LC

7

EMMINGTON VIEW
BURGIDGE WAY
NURSERY RD
DIMBLES ESTATE
SPRINGFIELD GDNS
MALYNS CL
LEYBURNE GDNS
B4009 LOWER RD
DOVELEAT
GRAFTON HO
BENTON DR
GRAFTON ORCH

New Farm
WINDMILL CL
OXFORD DOWN
EQUINE WY
Mill Lane Com Prim Sch

PH St Andrews CE Prim Sch
HIGH ST

Chinnor

The Icknield Line

Hempton Wainhill

Bledlow Cross

01

PILMORE NOW
HAWTHORN CL
MILL LA
FORESTERS RD
CHERRY TREE RD
WILLOW RD
BEECH RD
STATION RD
DUCK SQ
Liby
MASGRAVE RD
RECTORY MDW
CHURCH RD
LINE PIT
P PO
KEENS LA
LC

Middle Farm

6

CLEAVERS
MILLERS TURN
CONIGRE
ESTOVERS WAY
HAILEY CROFT
LACE MAKERS CT
RIDERS WAY
HI TWENCH
BENNETTS HI
RANNAL RD
St Andrews HO
FOX
COBLER
OAKLEY RD
TAINER WAY
ORCHARD WAY
DRUIDS WLK
RAVENSMEAD
GREENWOOD
WHEELERS END
MEADOW WAY
Saw Mill
STATION RD
HILL RD
GOLDEN HILLS

1 LEVERKUS CT
2 LEVERKUS HO
3 OLD SAWMILL PL
4 SEYMOUR PK RD
5 TREVERNE CTYD

Chinnor Hill Nature Reserve

ROBINS PLATT
ASHRIDGE
OAKLEY LA
STANLEY FLAT
HUNTERS
HOLLOW
ANDREWS RD
ELM DR
GLIMBERS GR
GREENWOOD AVE
FRITILLARY AVE
BARTZ AVE
OAK END WAY
BIRD
KILN RD
SUSSEX LA
WYCOMB RISE

1 WOODVILLE
2 WOODGREEN SQ
3 CORNFIELDS
4 GLIMBERS GR
5 UPPER FIELD
6 MIDDLE FARM CL

5

Oakley

CROWELL RD
LUMMAS MEAD
LINGWELL CL
NEWTON CL
LITTLEMOOR FIELD
SKIPPERS
MOOR
SIDE VW
CHAN PIT LA
KYTE RD
CHILTERN VW

Chinnor
Chinnor Hill

P

00

Crowell End Farm

OX39

Ridgeway

Crowell Farm

4

ICKNIELD CL
CHINNOR RD
Crowell
PH
CROWELL RD
HIGH ST
B4009

Oakley Hill

CHINNOR HILL
Manor Farm
CHINNOR RD
RED LANE
Woodlands Farm

3

Icknield Way

99

Sunley Wood

2

Swan's Way
Race Course

Venus Wood
Venus Wood

Crowellhill Wood
Crowell Hill
CROWELL HILL
SPRIGS HOLLY

Sprig's Alley

1

Grove Farm

Crowellhill Farm

SPRIGS HOLLY LA

Kingston Wood
KINGSTON HILL

HP14

98

74   A   B   75   C   D   76   E   F

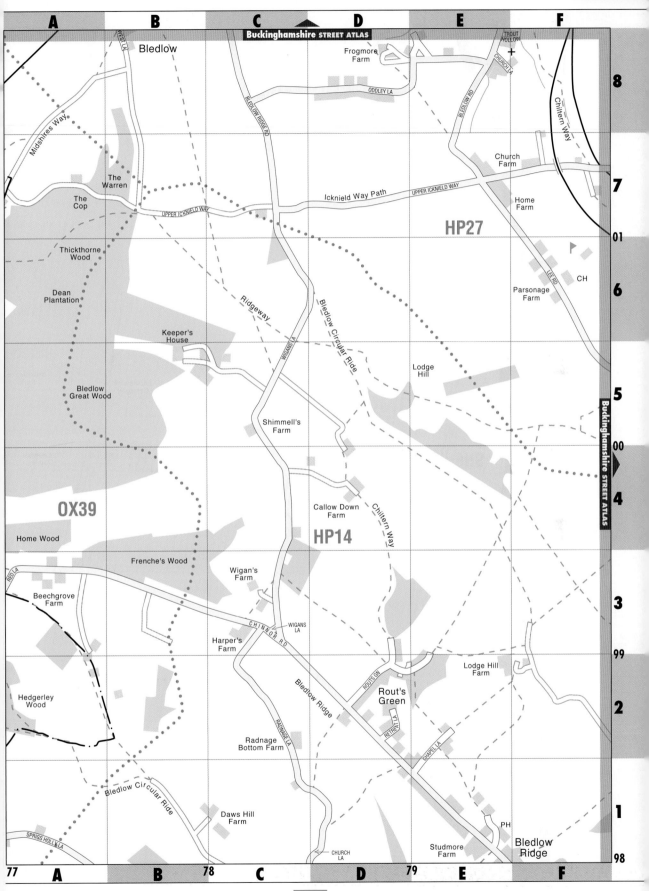

A B C D E F

8

7

01

6

HP27

Bledlow

Frogmore Farm

ODDLEY LA

BLEDLOW RIDGE RD

Trout Hollow

CHURCH LA

BLEDLOW RD

Chiltern Way

Church Farm

Home Farm

Midshires Way

WEST LA

The Warren

The Cop

Thickthorne Wood

Dean Plantation

UPPER ICKNIELD WAY

Icknield Way Path

UPPER ICKNIELD WAY

Ridgeway

Bledlow Circular Ride

WIGANS LA

Keeper's House

Bledlow Great Wood

Shimmell's Farm

Lodge Hill

Parsonage Farm

LEE RD

CH

5

00

4

OX39

Home Wood

Frenche's Wood

RED LA

Callow Down Farm

Chiltern Way

HP14

Wigan's Farm

Beechgrove Farm

CHINNOR RD

Harper's Farm

WIGANS LA

Hedgerley Wood

Bledlow Ridge

RADNAGE LA

Radnage Bottom Farm

Rout's Green

RETREAT LA

ROUTS GN

Lodge Hill Farm

3

99

2

SPRIGS HOLLY LA

Bledlow Circular Ride

Daws Hill Farm

CHURCH LA

CHAPEL LA

Studmore Farm

PH

Bledlow Ridge

1

98

77 A B 78 C D 79 E F

Buckinghamshire STREET ATLAS

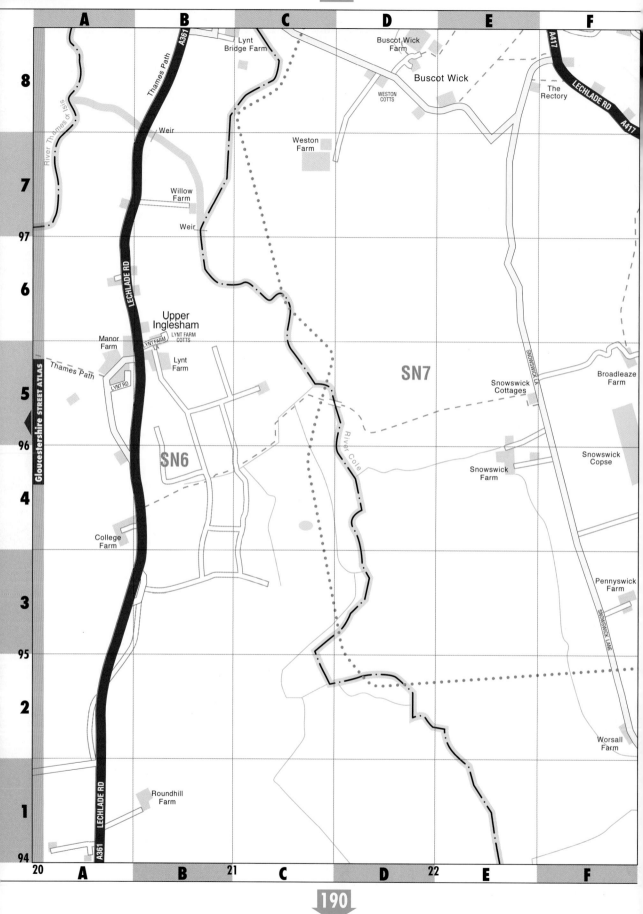

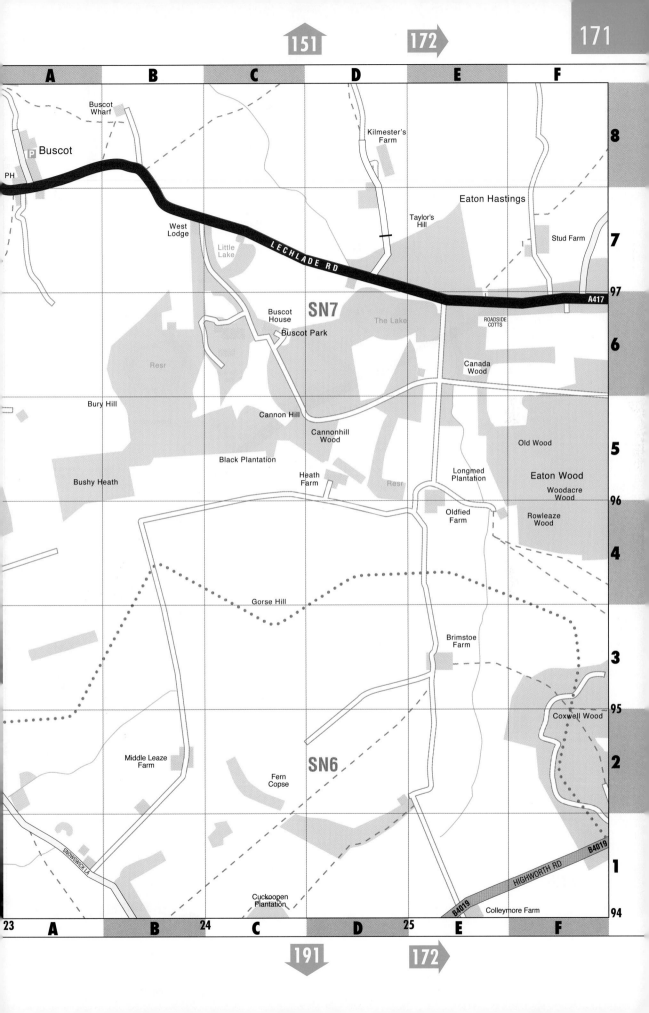

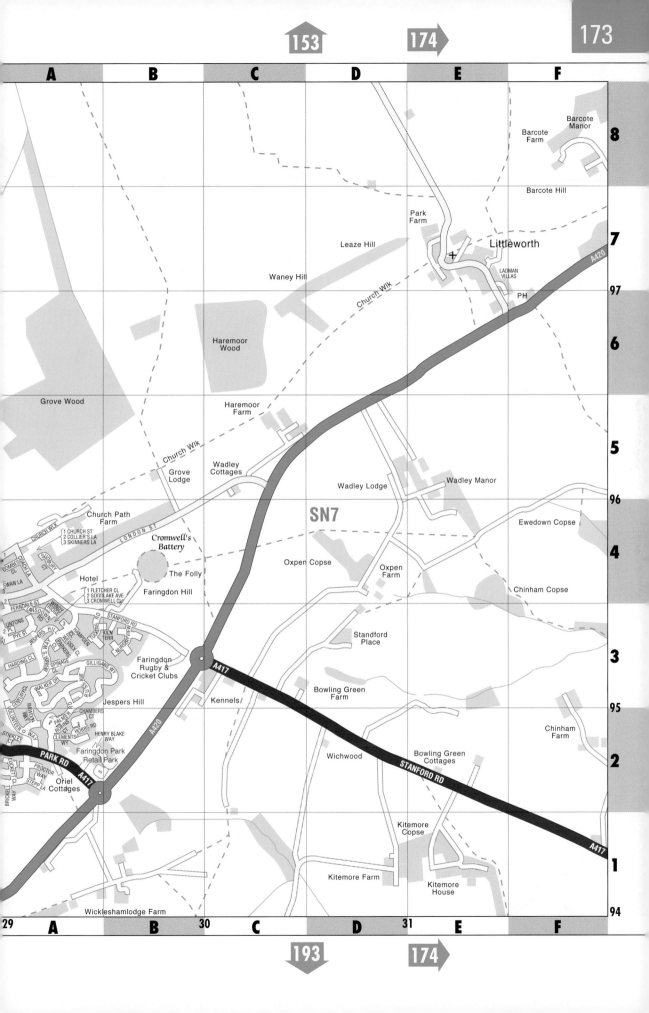

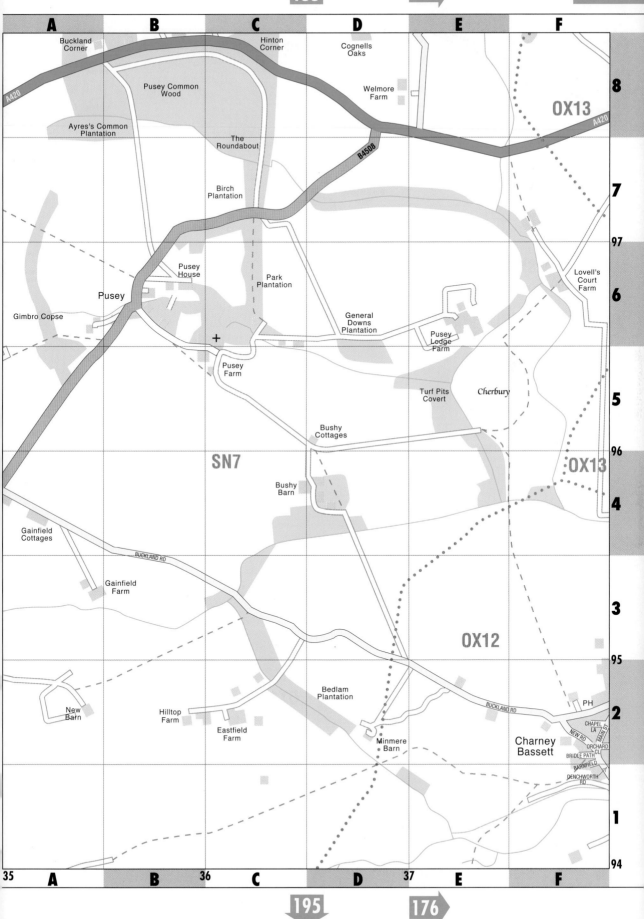

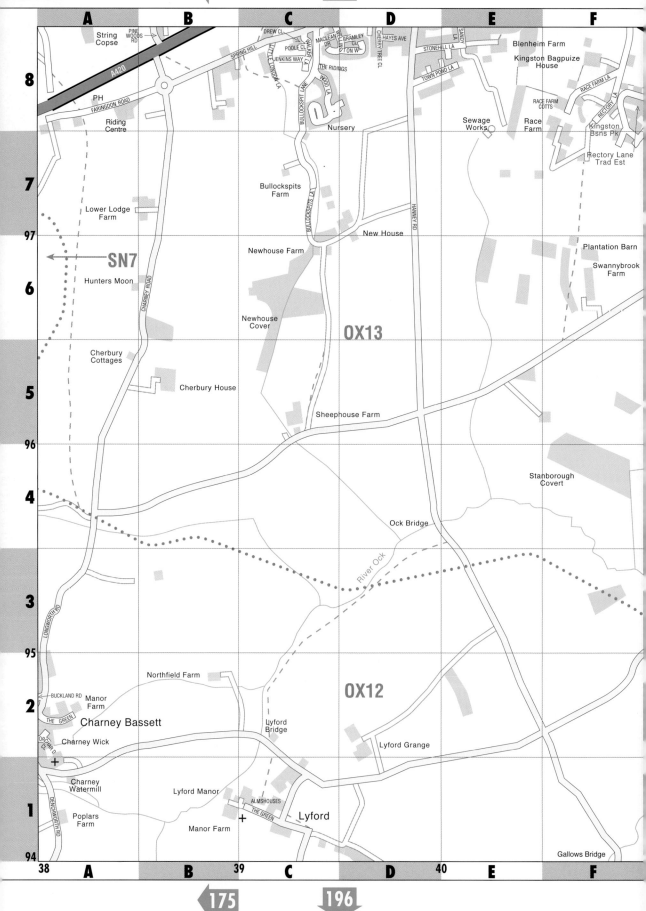

A415 ABINGDON RD

Sports Gnd

EDWARD STRAUSS PK

MARLE GDNS

BUCHAN PL

KINGSTON BUSINESS PK

OAKS CARAVAN

DIGGING LA

Pickwick Farm

Comberley

Fyfield Wick

Hamfield Barn

Dry Leys

KINGSTON ROAD

A415

Denys Farm

Resrs

Collin's Farm

Abingdon Prep Sch

Manor Farm

A338

River Ock

Millets Farm

MILLETS FARM COTTS

MANOR FARM COTTS

Garford

DAIRY MDW

College Farm

COLLEGE FARM COTTS

OX13

Garford Field

WANTAGE ROAD

OXFORD RD

Nor Brook

Venn Mill

Common Barn

Childrey Brook

OX12

Letcombe Brook

A338

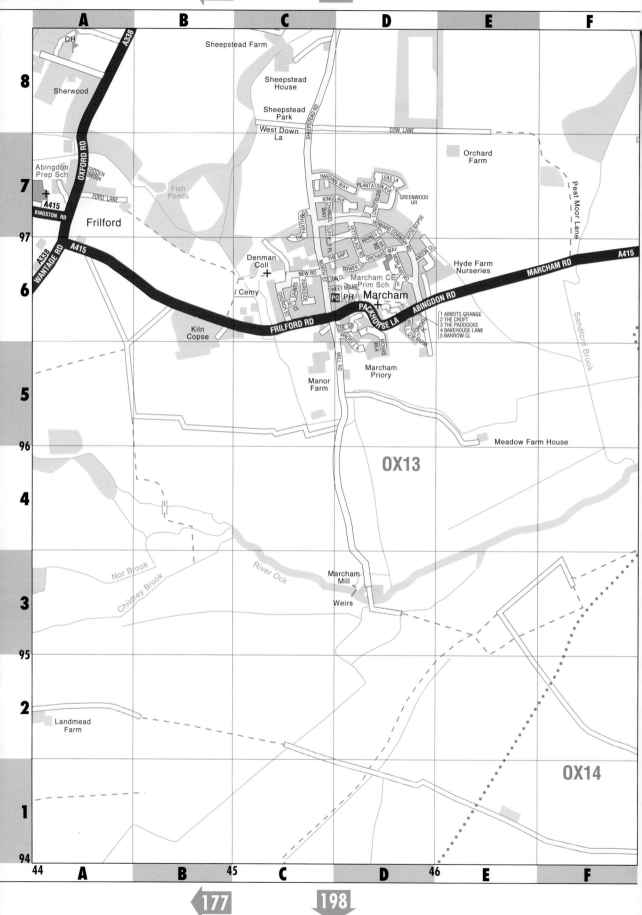

A   B   C   D   E   F

8

Sheepstead Farm

CH

Sherwood

Sheepstead
House

Sheepstead
Park

West Down
La

COW LANE

A338

OXFORD RD

Orchard
Farm

7

Abingdon Prep Sch

HIDDEN
BROOK

Fish
Ponds

HARDING WAY

LEAS LA

PLANTATION AVE

GREENWOOD
GR

Peat Moor Lane

A415
KINGSTON RD

Ford Lane

Frilford

97

A338 WANTAGE RD

A415

KINGS AVE

CHANCEL WAY

THE FAIRWAY

THE

LONGFIELDS

HOWARD CORNISH RD

DUFFIELD PL

HYDE COPSE

KAINES CT

SWEET BRIAR

ANSON CL

Hyde Farm
Nurseries

A415

MARCHAM RD

6

Denman
Coll

THE GAP

NORTH ST

NEW RD

ORCHARD WAY

MOPLAND RD

TOWER CL

Marcham CE
Prim Sch

PO PH 3

Marcham

ABINGDON RD

Sandford Brook

Cemy

PARKSIDE

SIMS CL

CHURCH ST

LION CL

PACKHORSE LA

OW FARM

TOWER PL

1 ABBOTS GRANGE
2 THE CROFT
3 THE PADDOCKS
4 BAKEHOUSE LANE
5 BARROW CL

Kiln
Copse

FRILFORD RD

THE GN

PRIORY LA

MONKS WLK

5

Manor
Farm

Marcham
Priory

MILL RD

Meadow Farm House

96

OX13

4

Nor Brook

Childrey Brook

River Ock

Marcham
Mill

Weirs

3

95

2

Landmead
Farm

OX14

1

94

44   A   B   45   C   D   46   E   F

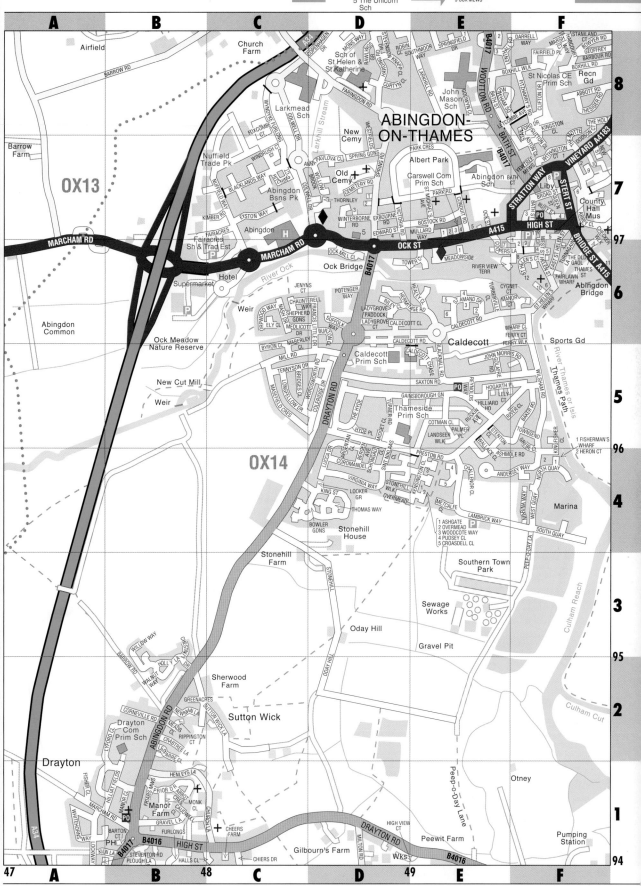

159
180

199
180

D7
1 BUCKLES CL
2 SPRING TERR
3 BUCKLAND MEWS
4 JUNIPER CT
5 The Unicorn Sch

E7
1 MAYOTT'S RD
2 CARSWELL CT
3 CROWN MEWS
4 TOMKIN'S ALMSHOUSES
5 OCK MEWS

E8
1 THORNHILL WLK
2 BOROUGH WLK
3 FINMORE CL

E6
1 MEADOWSIDE CT
2 BAILIE CL
3 MUSSON CL
4 THURSTON CL
5 SYMPSON CL
6 GODFREY CL
7 DRAYMANS WLK

F6
1 BREWERS CT
2 WINSMORE LA
3 HIVE MEWS
4 ST EDMUND'S LA
5 ST HELEN'S MEWS
6 BRICK ALLEY
7 MILL PADDOCK
8 GEORGE MORLAND HO
9 NEAVE MEWS

F6
10 LONG ALLEY ALMSHOUSES
11 MAUD HALE COTTS
12 ST HELEN'S MILL

F7
1 BANBURY CT
2 THE VINES
3 THE SQUARE
4 MARKET PL
5 LOMBARD ST

6 OLD STATION YD
7 BURGESS CL
8 THE CHARTER
9 MAGNETTE CT
10 QUAKERS CT
11 REGAL CL

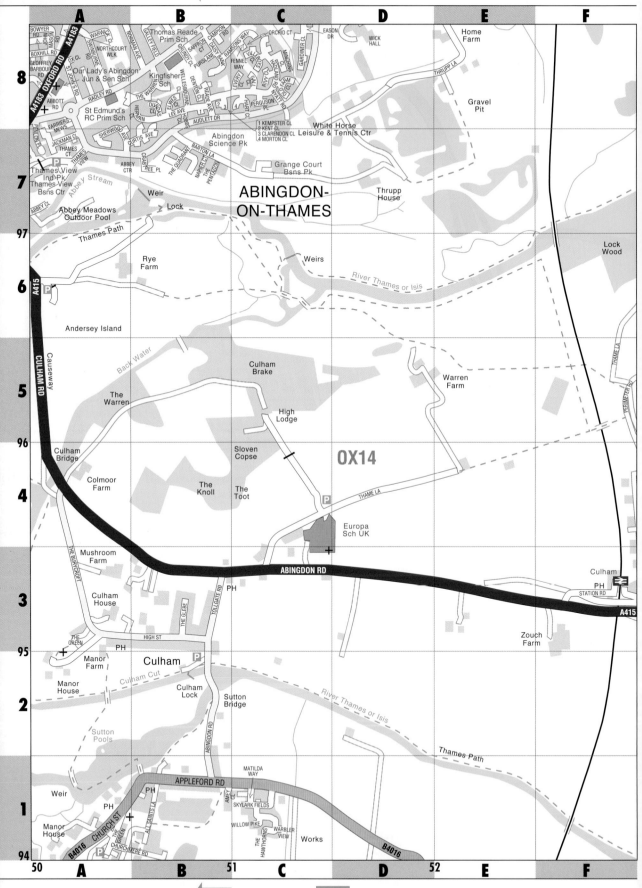

ABINGDON-ON-THAMES

OX14

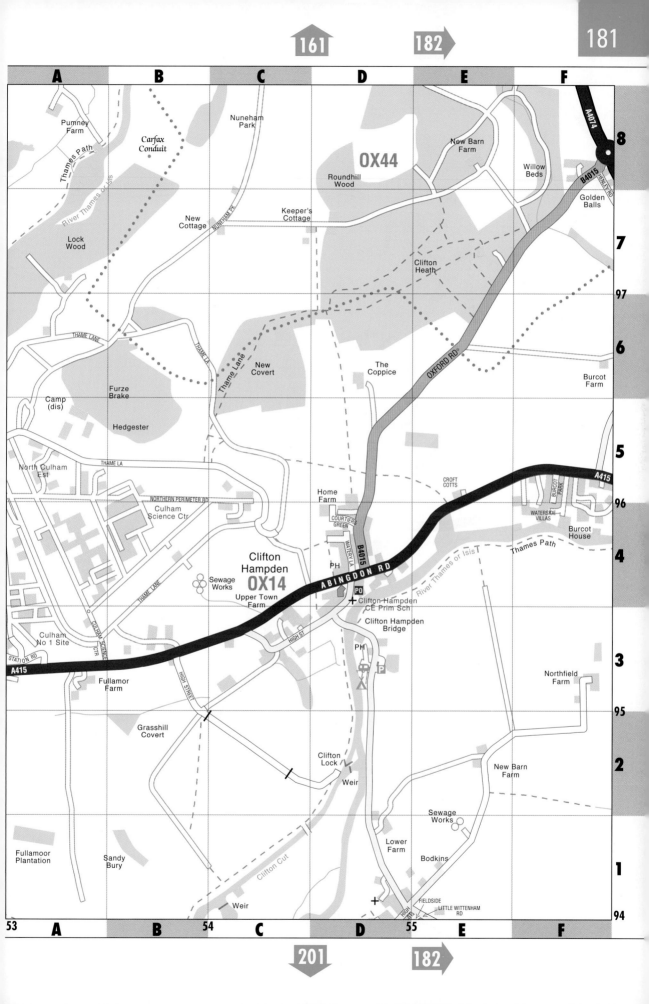

A B C D E F

8
7
97
6
5
96
4
3
95
2
1
94

Pumney Farm
Thames Path
Carfax Conduit
Nuneham Park
New Barn Farm
Willow Beds
OX44
A4074
B4015
HENLEY RD
Golden Balls
Roundhill Wood
New Cottage
Keeper's Cottage
NUNEHAM PK
Clifton Heath
Lock Wood
OXFORD RD
River Thames or Isis
Thame Lane
THAME LA
New Covert
The Coppice
Burcot Farm
Furze Brake
Camp (dis)
Hedgester
THAME LA
North Culham Est
Culham Science Ctr
A415
Croft Cotts
Burcot Park
Waterside Villas
Burcot House
96
NORTHERN PERIMETER RD
Home Farm
COURTIERS GREEN
Thames Path
B4015
River Thames of Isis
Clifton Hampden
OX14
PH
WATERY LA
ABINGDON RD
PO
Clifton Hampden CE Prim Sch
Sewage Works
Upper Town Farm
THAME LANE
Clifton Hampden Bridge
CULHAM SCIENCE CTR
HIGH ST
PH
P
Culham No 1 Site
STATION RD
A415
Fullamor Farm
Northfield Farm
HIGH STREET
Grasshill Covert
Clifton Lock
Weir
New Barn Farm
95
Fullamoor Plantation
Sandy Bury
Clifton Cut
Sewage Works
Lower Farm
Bodkins
Weir
HIGH ST
FIELDSIDE
LITTLE WITTENHAM RD

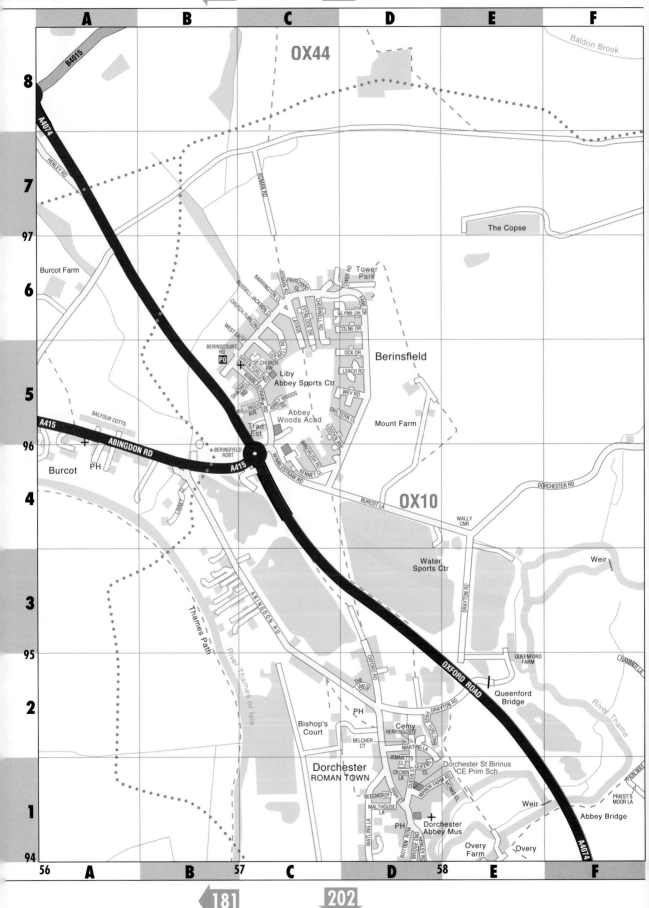

A B C D E F

OX44

Baldon Brook

B4015

A4074

Henley Rd

8

7

97

The Copse

Burcot Farm

6

Roman Rd

Russell Jackson Cl

Barrington Cl

Pritchard Cl

Roman Rd

Tower Rd

Tower Park

Crutch Furlong

West Croft

Evenlode Dr

Cherwell Rd

Lay Ave

Coe Way

Glyme Dr

Fane Dr

Colne Dr

Berinscourt Ho PO

Green Furlong

Church Vw

Liby

Abbey Sports Ctr

Ock Dr

Leach Rd

Berinsfield

Wimblestraw Rd

Shawell Rd

Bullingdon Ave

Abbey Cl

Abbey Woods

Wey Rd

Chiltern Cl

Dodds Ln

Mount Farm

5

96

A415

Balfour Cotts

Abingdon Rd

A415

Lodge Cl

Burcot

PH

Berinsfield RDBT

Trad Est

Abbey Woods Acad

Windrush Rd

Kennet Cl

Wimblestraw Rd

Burcot La

OX10

Dorchester Rd

Wally Cnr

4

Abingdon Rd

Thames Path

River Thames or Isis

Water Sports Ctr

Drayton Rd

Weir

3

95

Queenford Farm

Oxford Rd

The Limes

PH

Bishop's Court

Belcher Ct

Drayton Rd

Page Furlong

Oxford Road

Queenford Bridge

Hammer La

River Thame

2

Cemy

Herringcote

Martins La

Jemmetts Cl

Queens Cl

Crown La

Dorchester St Birinus CE Prim Sch

Dorchester

ROMAN TOWN

Beechcroft

Malthouse La

Watling La

High Rd

Manor Farm Rd

Queens Cl

Monks Cl

Weir

Priest's Moor La

Painswick

1

PH

Bridge End

Rotten Row

Henley Rd

Dorchester Abbey Mus

Abbey Bridge

A4074

Overy Farm

Overy

94

56 A B 57 C D 58 E F

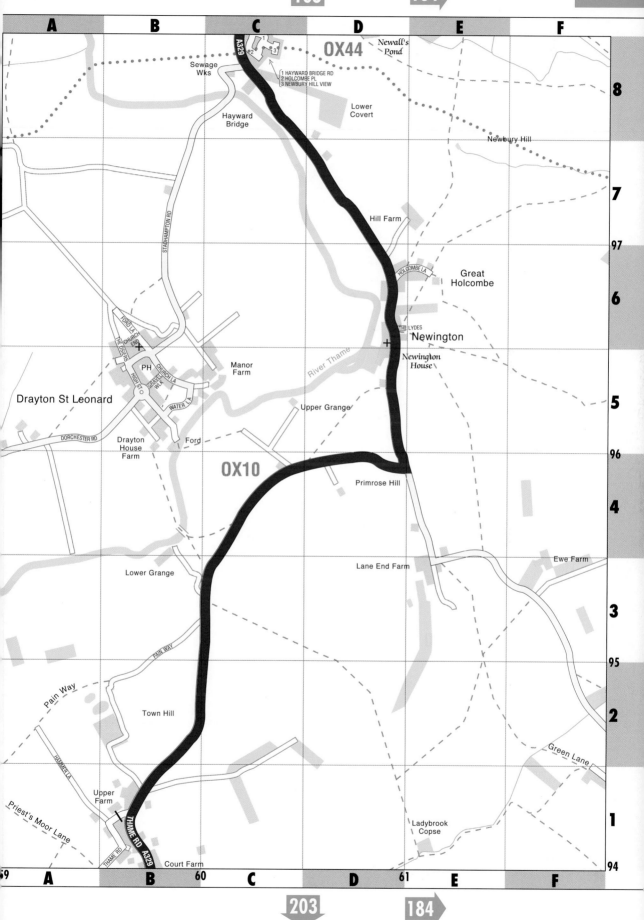

| A | B | C | D | E | F |

OX44

Newall's Pond

1 HAYWARD BRIDGE RD
2 HOLCOMBE PL
3 NEWBURY HILL VIEW

Sewage Wks

Hayward Bridge

Lower Covert

Newbury Hill

8

7

97

Hill Farm

HOLCOMBE LA

Great Holcombe

6

STADHAMPTON RD

River Thame

THE LYDES

Newington

Newington House

5

FORD LA
CHURCH END
THE OSIERS
PH
HIGH ST
CHURCH LA
GRAVEL WLK
WATER LA

Manor Farm

Drayton St Leonard

DORCHESTER RD

Drayton House Farm

Ford

Upper Grange

96

OX10

Primrose Hill

4

Lower Grange

Lane End Farm

Ewe Farm

PAIN WAY

3

95

Pain Way

Town Hill

Green Lane

2

HAMMER LA

Upper Farm

Priest's Moor Lane

THAME RD A329

THAME RD

Court Farm

Ladybrook Copse

1

94

| A | B | 60 | C | D | 61 | E | F |

59

183
164

A B C D E F

8

Chalgrove
Airfield

Newbury
Hill

Hitchcox
Poultry
Farm

Monument
Ind Pk

B480

OXFORD WAY

MARLEY LA

Chalgrove
Field

SIR JAMES MARTIN WAY

7

PH

Fox
Covert

BOWER END

BROOKSIDE EST

HIGH ST

SAW CL

GRASS

CINNAMON CL

ORCHARD
BRINKINFIELD RD

POPLAR FARM
RD

BAKERY
CL

Hampden's
Monument

Little Holcombe
Covert

97

Manor
Farm

FLEMMING AVE

ADEANE

MILLERS

CL

QUARTERMAIN
RD

LANGLEY RD

PADDOCK
CL

CARADEN LA

CHAPEL LA

FRENCH LAURENCE WAY

LIDDON RD

Chalgrove

MONUMENT RD

1 CHILTERN CL
2 CROMWELL CL
3 FRANCIS BROWN WAY
4 ATKINS RD
5 THE SPRINGS

RUSHY FURROW LA

Mill
House
THE RICKYARD

SWINSTEAD CT

THE GREEN

HARDINGS

PO

MANZEL

FAIRFAX RD

BC

BEDLEY

SIXPENNY LA

FARM CL

Langley
Hall

OX44

BROADWAY CL 1
HIGH ST 2

CHIBNALL

IRETON
CL

ARGOSY
CL

CLEMENTS RD

1

KING

HICKS CL

6

Langley Field
Farm

MILL LA

WILLOW MEAD

ST MARYS

RUPERT
CL

RUPERT
RD

FRANKLIN
CL

CHURCH LA

BERRICK RD

ACE CRES

B480

Church
Farm

96

Chalgrove
Farm

5

Southfield
Barn

CADWELL LA

Hares Leap

Hollandtide
House

Cadwell
Farm

4

Cadwell
Covert

Whitehouse
Farm

OX49

3

OX10

Lonesome
Farm

95

2

Manor
Farm

HOLLANDTIDE LA

Rumbolds La

Berrick
Prior

Green La

Hollandtide Bottom

1

PH

Ivyhouse
Farm

Rumbolds
Farm

Berrick
Salome

94

62 A 63 B C 63 D 64 E F

183
204

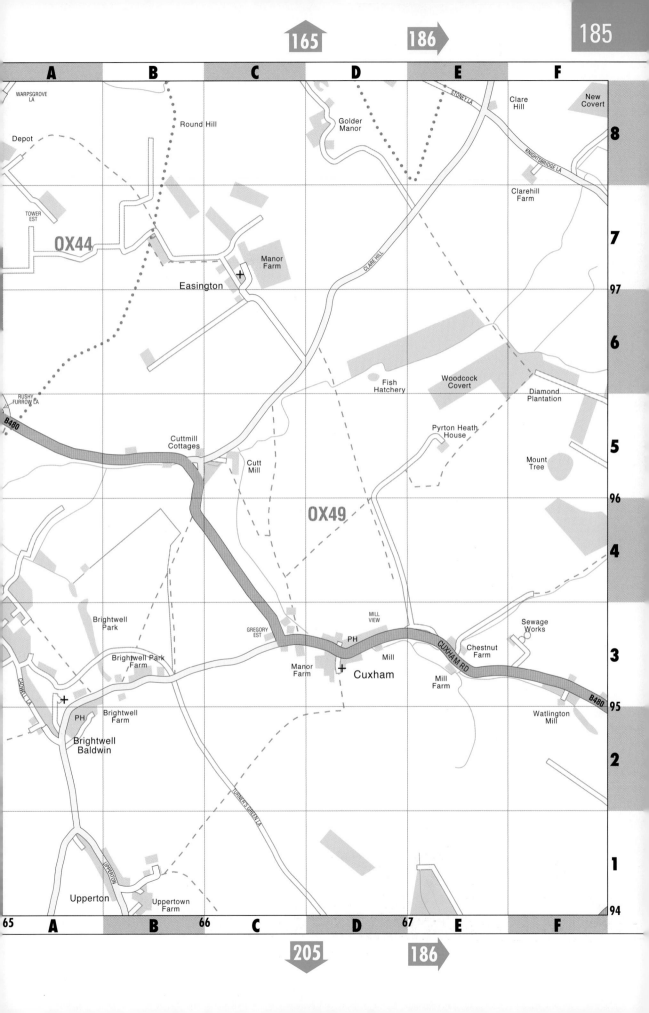

WARPSGROVE LA

Depot

Round Hill

Golder Manor

STONEY LA

Clare Hill

New Covert

KNIGHTSBRIDGE LA

8

TOWER EST

OX44

Clarehill Farm

7

Manor Farm

Easington

CLARE HILL

97

6

Fish Hatchery

Woodcock Covert

Diamond Plantation

RUSHY FURROW LA

B480

Cuttmill Cottages

Cutt Mill

Pyrton Heath House

Mount Tree

5

OX49

96

4

Brightwell Park

GREGORY EST

MILL VIEW

PH

Mill

CUXHAM RD

Chestnut Farm

Sewage Works

3

Brightwell Park Farm

Manor Farm

Cuxham

Mill Farm

B480

95

CADWELL LA

PH

Brightwell Farm

Watlington Mill

Brightwell Baldwin

2

TURNER'S GREEN LA

UPPERTON

1

Upperton

Uppertown Farm

94

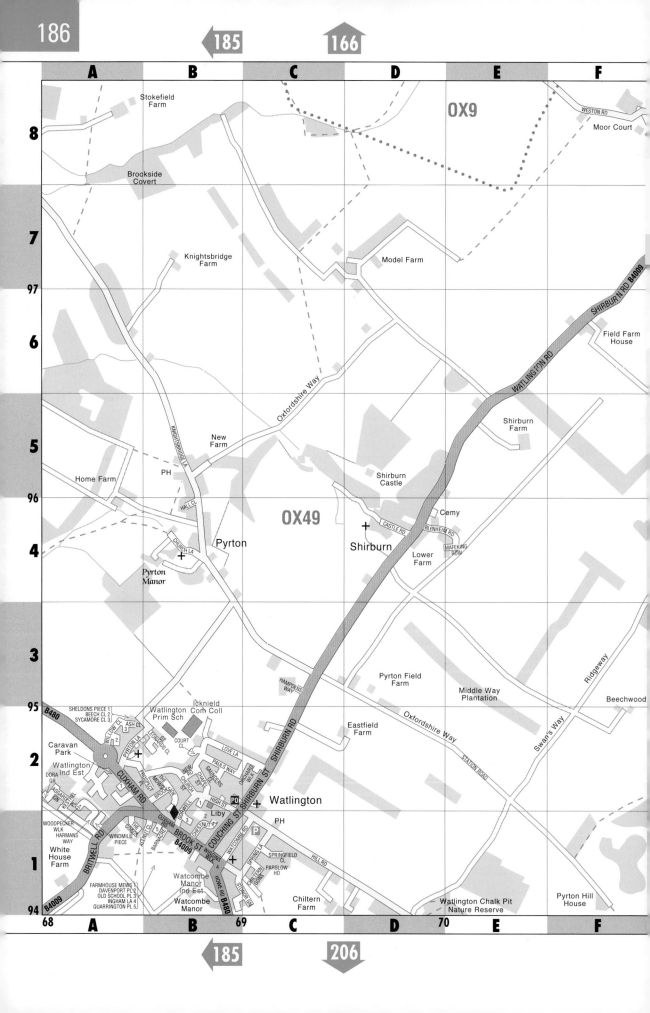

8

Stokefield Farm

OX9

WESTON RD

Moor Court

Brookside Covert

7

Knightsbridge Farm

Model Farm

SHIRBURN RD B4009

97

6

Field Farm House

WATLINGTON RD

Oxfordshire Way

Shirburn Farm

5

New Farm

KNIGHTSBRIDGE LA

Shirburn Castle

96

Home Farm

PH

OX49

Cemy

BLENHEIM RD

HALL CL

CASTLE RD

MAFEKING ROW

4

CHURCH LA

Pyrton

Shirburn

Lower Farm

Pyrton Manor

3

Pyrton Field Farm

HAMPDENS WAY

Middle Way Plantation

Ridgeway

Beechwood

95

SHELDONS PIECE 1
BEECH CL 2
SYCAMORE CL 3

B480

Icknield

Watlington Corn Coll

Watlington Prim Sch

Oxfordshire Way

Swan's Way

Eastfield Farm

STATION ROAD

WILLOW CL

ASH CL

Caravan Park

PYRTON LA

ST LEONARDS CL

COURT CL

LOVE LA

SHIRBURN RD

SHIRBURN ST

2

Watlington Ind Est

DORA GR

NEW CHURCH

PAULS WAY

ORCHARD WLK

SAUNDERS

THE SPUT

PROSPECT

BROOK ST

CHERRY

ASGARDBY GN

KESTON CL

HIGH ST

PO

Watlington

Liby

WOODPECKER WLK

HARMANS WAY

BRITWELL RD

CUXHAM RD

THE GOGGS

ACRE CL

CUXHAM RD

BARMORE

BROOK ST

WARDINS

COUCHING ST

CHESTNUT

PH

P

WATCOMBE WAY

HILL RD

1

White House Farm

WINDMILL PIECE

B4009

SPRING LA

SPRINGFIELD CL

CHILTERN GNS

STONOR GN

PARSLOW HO

Pyrton Hill House

FARMHOUSE MEWS 1
DAVENPORT PL 2
OLD SCHOOL PL 3
INGHAM LA 4
QUARRINGTON PL 5

Watcombe Manor Ind Est

HOWE RD

B480

Chiltern Farm

Watlington Chalk Pit Nature Reserve

Watcombe Manor

94

B4009

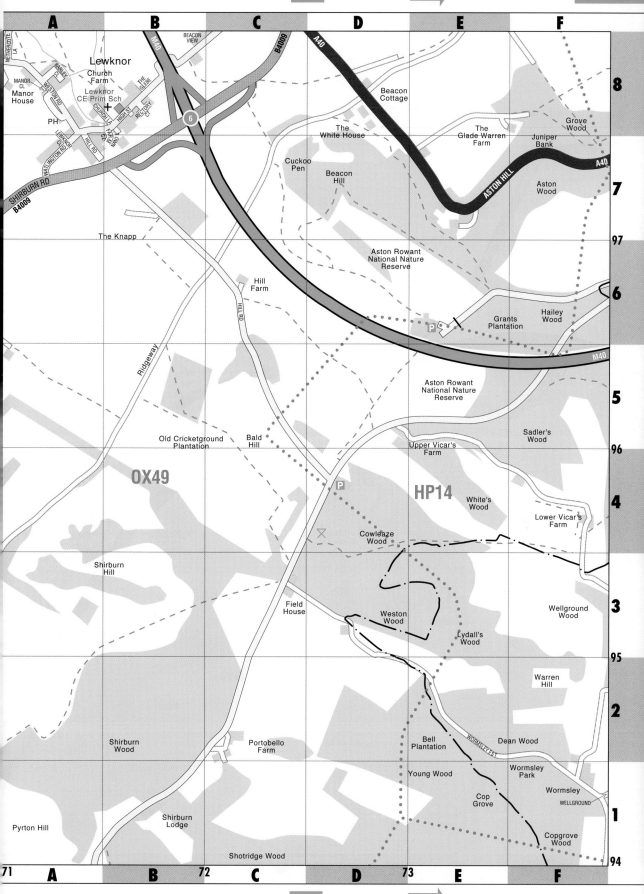

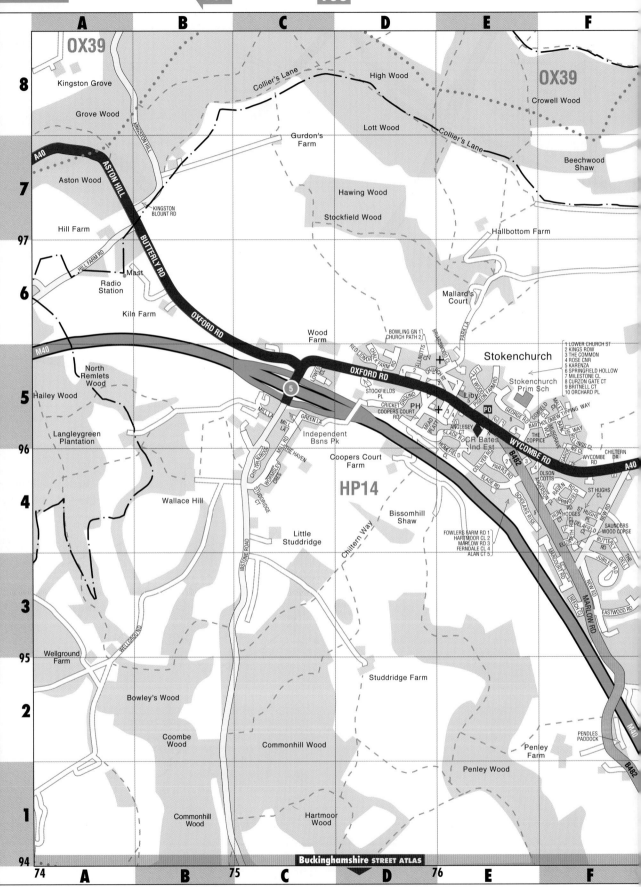

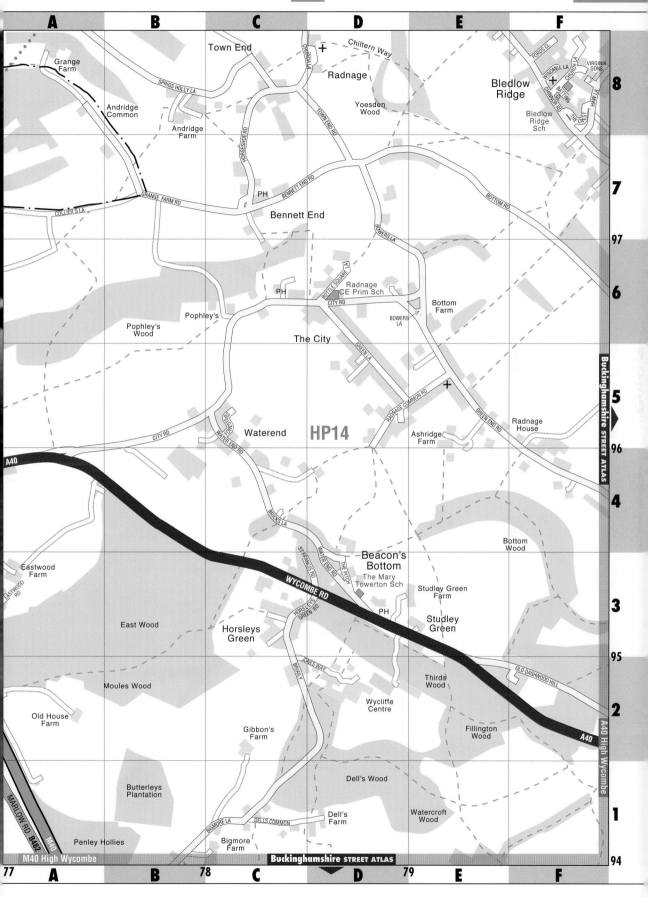

Town End

Chiltern Way

Radnage

Yoesden Wood

Grange Farm

SPRIGS HOLLY LA

Andridge Common

Andridge Farm

Bledlow Ridge

FORDS CL

WINDMILL LA

VIRGINIA GDNS

BALTING

HAW LA

CHINNOR RD

THE CREST

CHURCH LA

Bledlow Ridge Sch

COLLIER'S LA

GRANGE FARM RD

HORSESHOE RD

BENNETT END RD

PH

Bennett End

TOWN END RD

CHURCH LA

BOWERS LA

Bottom Rd

97

BOTTLE SQUARE LA

PH

Radnage CE Prim Sch

CITY RD

Bottom Farm

BOWERS LA

6

Pophley's

Pophley's Wood

The City

GREEN LA

RADNAGE COMMON RD

GREEN END RD

Radnage House

5

Waterend

CITY RD

WATER END RD

HP14

Ashridge Farm

96

Buckinghamshire STREET ATLAS

A40

M40

4

BRICKS LA

Bottom Wood

Eastwood Farm

EASTWOOD RD

WATER END RD

ST FRANCIS RD

THE PITCH

Beacon's Bottom

WYCOMBE RD

The Mary Towerton Sch

PH

Studley Green Farm

3

East Wood

Horsleys Green

HORSLEYS GREEN RD

Studley Green

Thirds Wood

OLD DASHWOOD HILL

95

Moules Wood

BRIALY

JONES WAY

Wycliffe Centre

Fillington Wood

A40

A40 High Wycombe

2

Old House Farm

Gibbon's Farm

Dell's Wood

Watercroft Wood

Butterleys Plantation

BIGMORE LA

DELLS COMMON

Dell's Farm

1

MARLOW RD B482

M40

Penley Hollies

Bigmore Farm

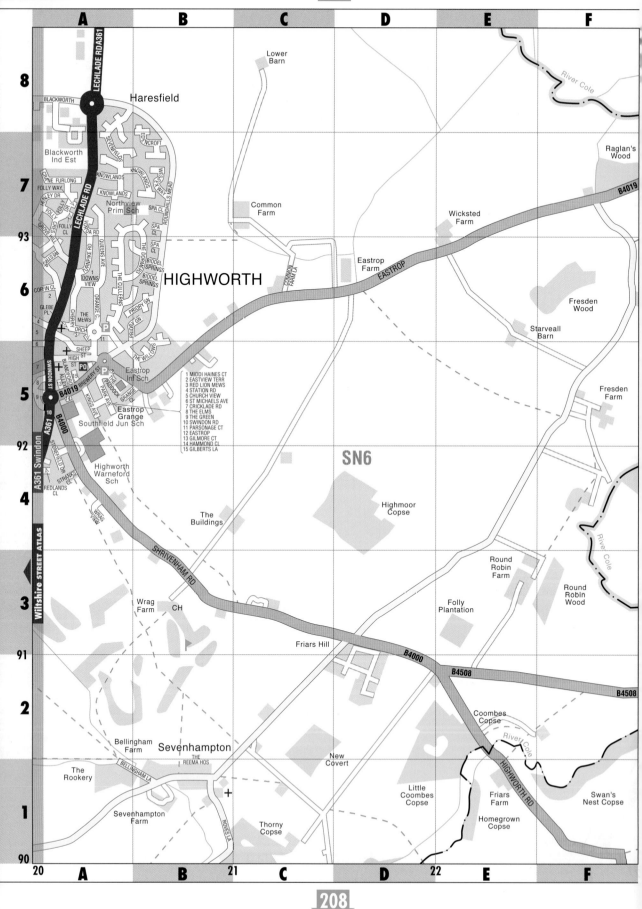

8

LECHLADE RD A361

BLACKWORTH

Haresfield

Lower
Barn

Blackworth
Ind Est

7

ONE FURLONG
FOLLY WAY
HONEY DR
FOLLY CRES
GROVE RD
CHELSEA

KNOWLANDS
SEVENFIELDS
EDENCROFT
WEST'S WAY
KNOWLANDS
ST LOUNGRY MEAD

KNOWLANDS

Common
Farm

Wicksted
Farm

B4019

Raglan's
Wood

River Cole

93

LECHLADE RD
SAMPHIRE RD
QUEENS AVE
DOWNS
VIEW
THE CULLERNS
SPA CL
SPA CL
SPA CL

Northview
Prim Sch

BIDDEL
SPRINGS
BIDDEL
SPRINGS

Eastrop
Farm

EASTROP

COMMON FARM LA

6

COFFIN CL
GLEBE PL
CHERRY
ORANGE CL
THE MEWS
ORCH
PRIORY GN
PRIORY GW

HIGHWORTH

Starveall
Barn

Fresden
Wood

5

LS NORMANS
A4019
BLANDFORD ALLEY
BREWERY ST
HIGH ST
SHEEP
ST
PO
P
THE
COMMON
GRANGE CL
THE WILLOWS

Eastrop
Inf Sch

Eastrop

Eastrop
Grange

Southfield Jun Sch

KINGS AVE
PARK AVE

1 MIDDI HAINES CT
2 EASTVIEW TERR
3 RED LION MEWS
4 STATION RD
5 CHURCH VIEW
6 ST MICHAELS AVE
7 CRICKLADE RD
8 THE ELMS
9 THE GREEN
10 SWINDON RD
11 PARSONAGE CT
12 EASTROP
13 GILMORE CT
14 HAMMOND CL
15 GILBERTS LA

Fresden
Farm

92

A361 Swindon
A4000
STONEFIELD DR
STRAINKS CL
REDLANDS CL

Highworth
Warneford
Sch

SN6

4

WRAG VIEW

The
Buildings

Highmoor
Copse

River Cole

3

Wiltshire STREET ATLAS

SHRIVENHAM RD

Wrag
Farm

CH

Friars Hill

Folly
Plantation

Round
Robin
Farm

Round
Robin
Wood

91

B4000

B4508

B4508

2

Bellingham
Farm

Sevenhampton
THE
REEMA HOS

New
Covert

Coombes
Copse

River Cole

HIGHWORTH RD

1

The
Rookery

BELLINGHAM LA

Sevenhampton
Farm

RIVES LA

Thorny
Copse

Little
Coombes
Copse

Friars
Farm

Homegrown
Copse

Swan's
Nest Copse

90

A **B** **C** **D** **E** **F**

Coleshill

Colleymore
Farm

8

Long
Shrubbery

Coleshill
Bridge

Home
Farm

Ashen
Copse
Farm

Coleshill Park

B4019

Ashen
Copse

7

Flamborough
Wood

93

Ashencopse
Cottage

Fresden
Barn

Waterloo
Copse

6

Vinthill
Withy
Bed

Waterloo
Lodge

Grove
Copse

Tellhard's
Copse

SN6

5

Strattenborough
Castle Farm

Watchfield Common
Wood
(Nature Reserve)

92

Pea Pits
Copse

SN7

Tithe
Farm

4

Westmill
Wind Farm

3

Southdown
Farm

91

Westmill
Bridge

B4508

Shrivenham Hundred
Bsns Pk

MAJORS RD

B4508

2

Westmill
Farm

Pennyhooks
Farm

LANCASTER GN 1
ARGOSY ST 2
HASTINGS RD 3
BEVERLEY RD 4

Watchfield
Prim Sch

Watchfield

1

Pennyhooks
Lane

Ratcoombe
Copse

Defence Acad
of the United
Kingdom

90

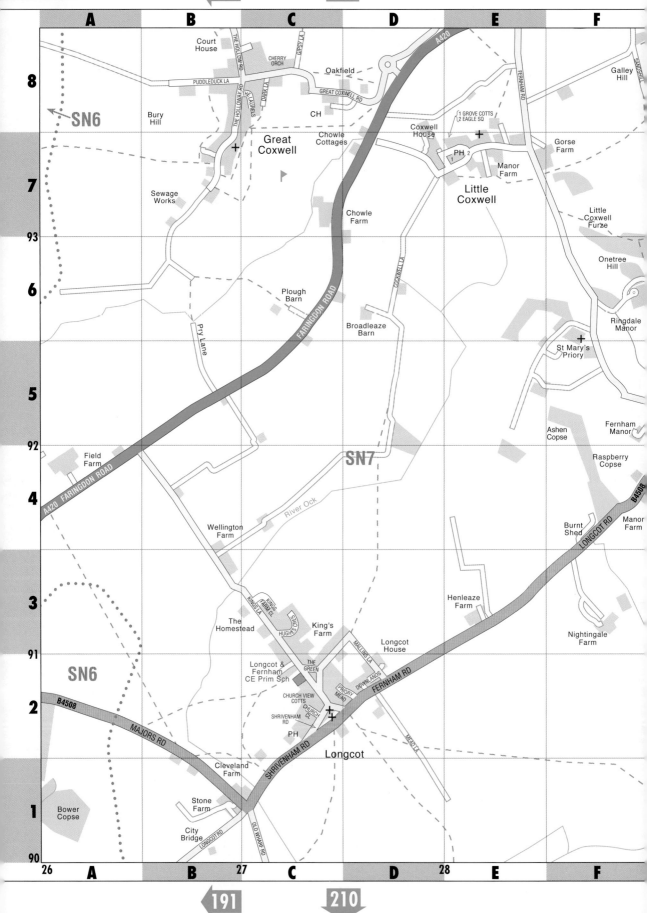

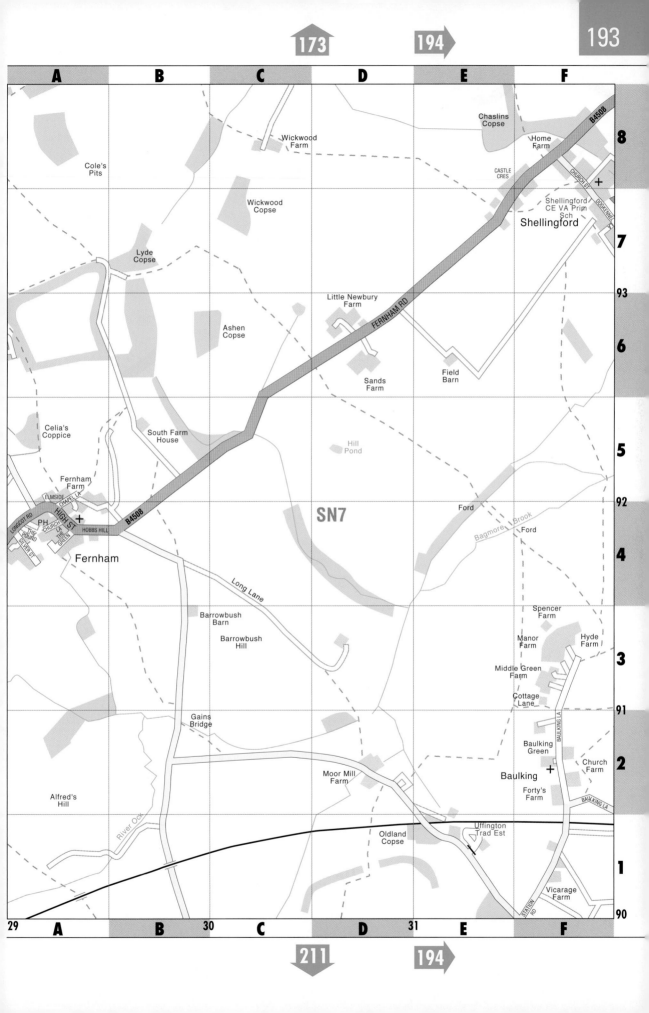

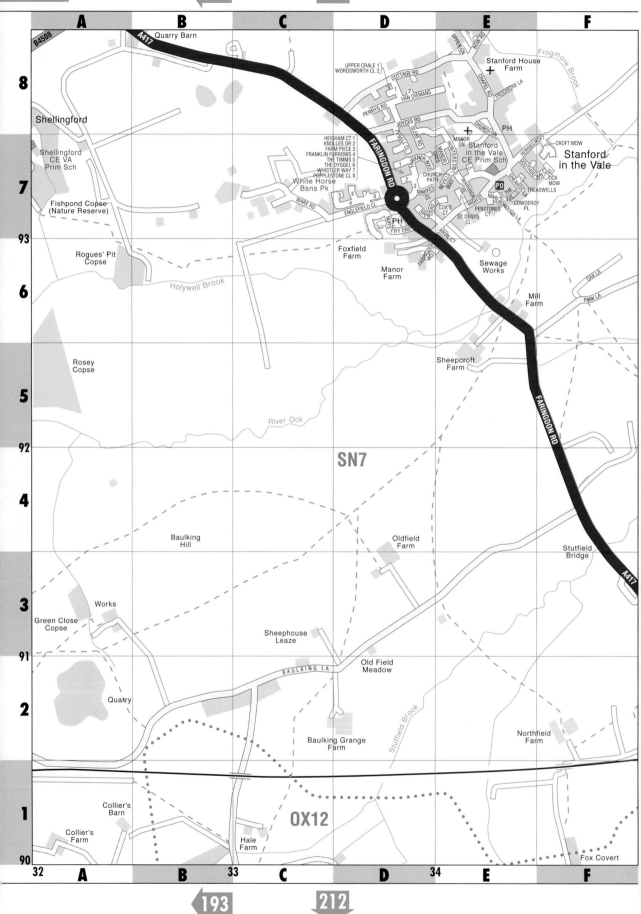

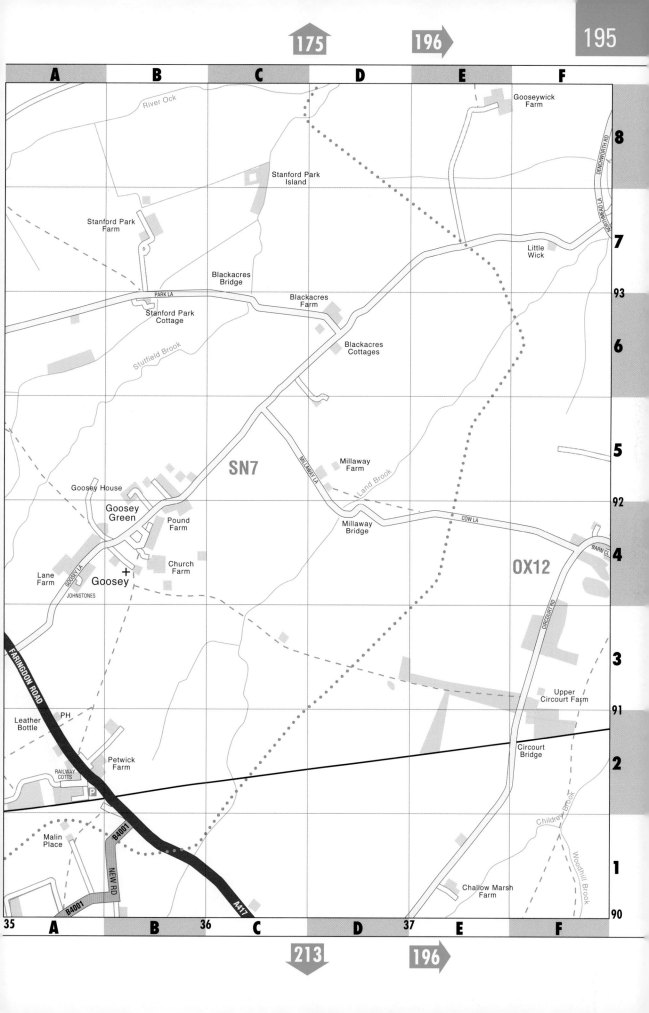

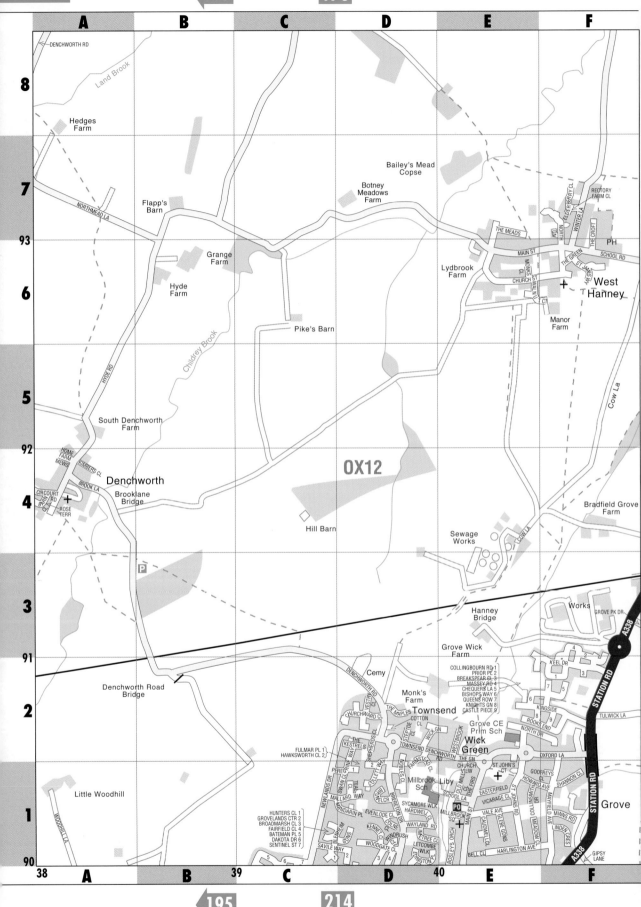

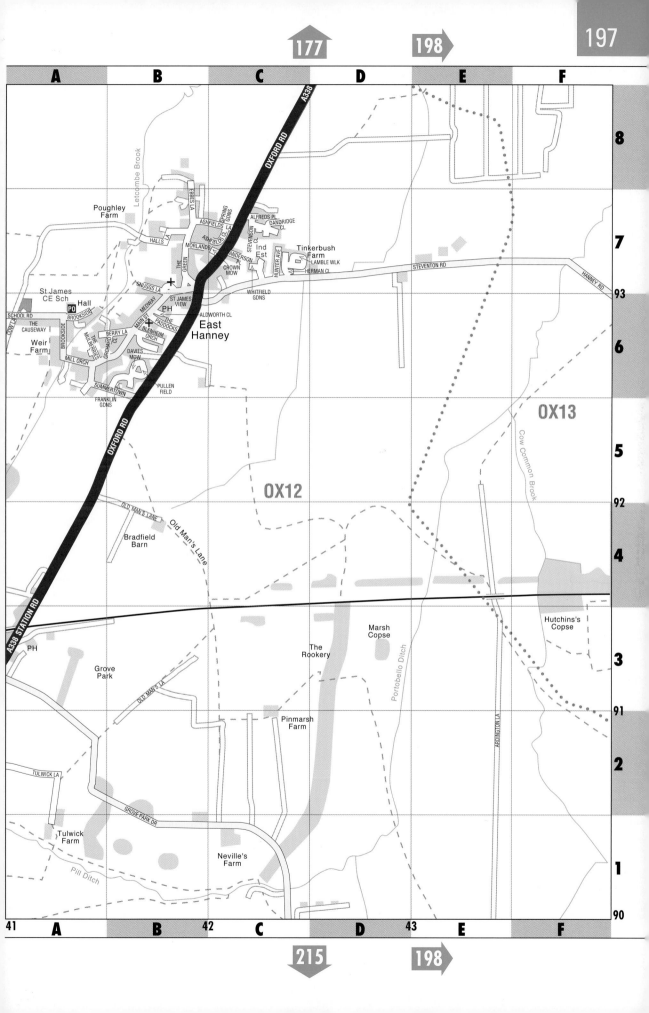

A B C D E F

8
7
93
6
5
92
4
3
91
2
1
90

A338
OXFORD RD

Letcombe Brook

Poughley
Farm

ASHFIELDS
EBBES LA
SPRING GDNS
ALFREDS PL
DANDRIDGE CL
ASHFIELDS CL LA
HALLS LA
MORLANDS
STEVENSON CL
Ind
Est
Tinkerbush
Farm
ANDERSON PL
LAMBLE WLK
HUNTER AVE
HERMAN CL

THE GREEN
SNUGGS LA
CROWN
MDW
WHITFIELD
GDNS
ST JAMES VIEW
ALDWORTH CL

St James
CE Sch
Hall
PO
SCHOOL RD
COW LA
THE
CAUSEWAY
BROOKSIDE
MEDWAY
PH
MAIN ST
THE
PADDOCKS
BLENHEIM
ORCH
East
Hanney

Weir
Farm
BROOKSIDE
THE
MULBERRIES
ORCHARD CL
BERRY LA
MILL ORCH
DAVIES
MDW
SUMMERTOWN
FRANKLIN
GDNS
PULLEN
FIELD

STEVENTON RD
HANNEY RD

OX13

Cow Common Brook

OX12

OLD MAN'S LANE
Old Man's Lane

Bradfield
Barn

A338 STATION RD

PH
Grove
Park
OLD MAN'S LA

The
Rookery

Marsh
Copse

Portobello Ditch

ARDINGTON LA

Hutchins's
Copse

Pinmarsh
Farm

TULWICK LA

GROVE PARK DR

Tulwick
Farm

Neville's
Farm

Pill Ditch

197
178

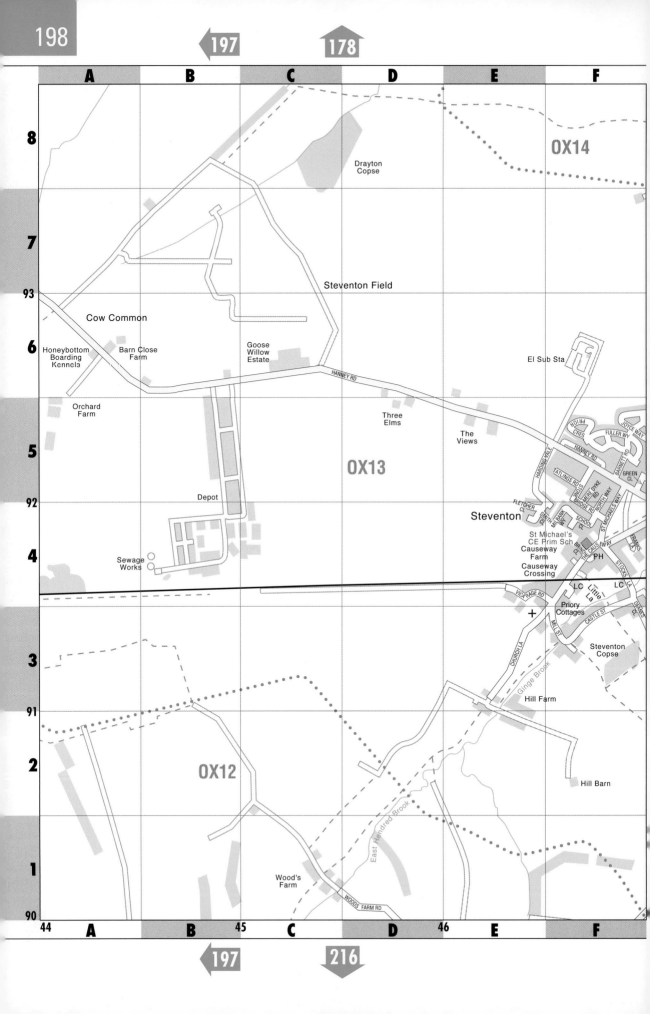

8

OX14

Drayton
Copse

7

Steventon Field

93

Cow Common

6

Honeybottom
Boarding
Kennels

Barn Close
Farm

Goose
Willow
Estate

El Sub Sta

HANNEY RD

Orchard
Farm

Three
Elms

The
Views

PRIOR
CRES

JOYCE WAY

FULLER WY

HANNEY RD

5

OX13

HARDINGVALE

TATLINGS RD CL

BARNETT RD

GREEN
CL

Depot

MERE DYKE
RD

NORTH WAY

ST MICHAELS WAY

FLETCHER
CL

BRIDGE RD

92

Steventon

SMITH
CL

MILBANK
WY

SCHOOL
CL

St Michael's
CE Prim Sch

EVANS

Sewage
Works

4

Causeway
Farm

Causeway
Crossing

BRAND
CL

THE CAUSEWAY

PH

STOCKS LA

DEANES
CL

LC

LC

Little
La

VICARAGE RD

Priory
Cottages

3

Steventon
Copse

CHURCH LA

Ginge Brook

91

Hill Farm

MILL ST

CASTLE ST

2

OX12

Hill Barn

East Hendred Brook

1

Wood's
Farm

WOODS FARM RD

90

197
216

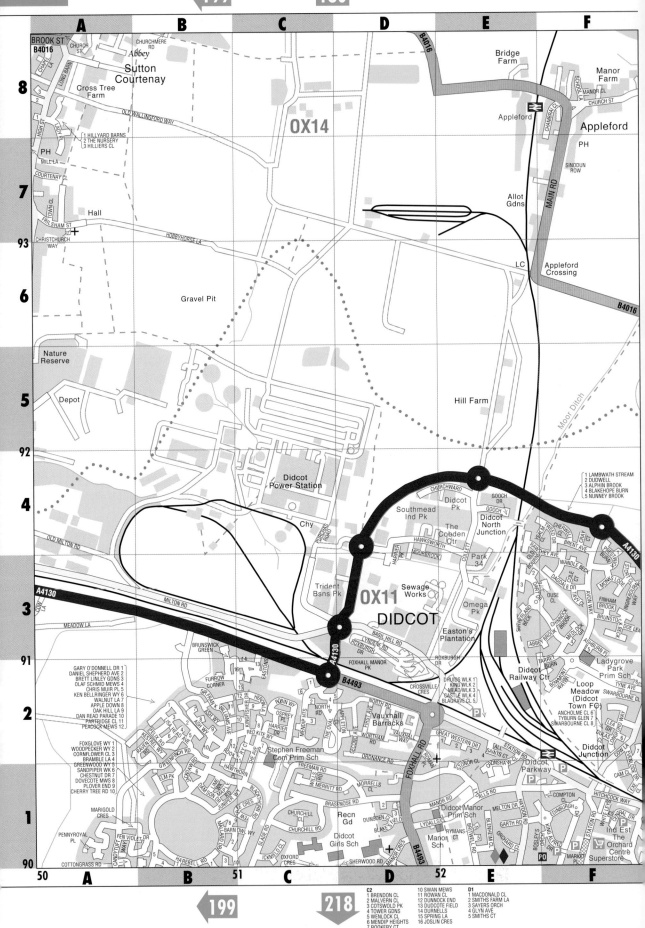

C2
1 BRENDON CL
2 MALVERN CL
3 COTSWOLD PK
4 TOWER GDNS
5 WENLOCK CL
6 MENDIP HEIGHTS
7 ROOKERY CT
8 SWALLOW MEWS
9 NIGHTINGALE WY
10 SWAN MEWS
11 ROWAN CL
12 DUNNOCK END
13 DUDCOTE FIELD
14 DURNELLS
15 SPRING LA
16 JOSLIN CRES

D1
1 MACDONALD CL
2 SMITHS FARM LA
3 SAYERS ORCH
4 GLYN AVE
5 SMITHS CT

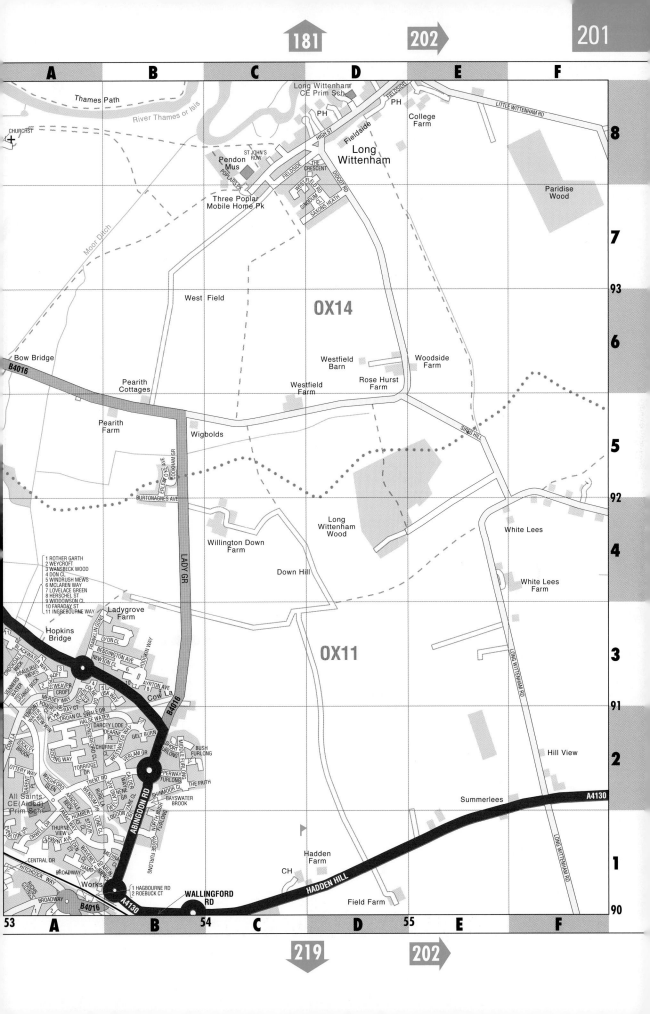

201
182

A B C D E F

8

| SAMIAN WAY | WATLING LA |
HAVEN CL
TENPENNY
ORCHARD HAVEN
BRIDGE END
WITTENHAM LA

Dorchester Bridge
Overy

Bridge End

Weir

Day's Lock

Dyke Hills

Little Wittenham Bridge

Sewage Works

HENLEY RD

MEADSIDE

A4074 OXFORD ROAD

GREEN LA

A4074

7

Little Wittenham

Thames Path

River Thame

River Thames or Isis

HENLEY RD

93

Little Wittenham Wood

OX14

Star Walk

Lowerhill Farm

6

Project Timescape

Wittenham Clumps

Hill Farm

HILLSIDE COTTS

HILLSIDE

Castle Hill

Felmore Copse

North Farm

5

Sinodun Hills

92

Brightwell Barrow **OX10**

4

SIRES HILL

Redgate Farm

Highlands Farm

Sinodun Hill

3

OX11

OLD DIDCOT RD

DIDCOT RD

Watermans Lane

LITTLE MARTINS

HIGH ROAD COTTS

OLD NURSERY LA

LITTLE LA

GREEN LANE FLATS

HIGH RD

GREENMERE

Style Acre

KING'S DITCH

91

GROVE COTTS

WEST END

THE SQUARE

CHURCH LA

Greenmere Path

WELLSPRINGS

Brightwell-cum-Sotwell CE (Controlled) Prim Sch

BRIGHTWELL ST

MONKS MEAD

BELL LA

DATCHET

BAKERS LA

BAKERS LA

SOTWELL ST

SLADE END

A4130

Brightwell-cum-Sotwell

2

A4130 HADDEN HILL

North Farm

WALLINGFORD RD

Kibble Ditch

Frog's Island Farm

Frogs' Island

Brightwell Manor

BRIGHTWELL ST

PH

PENNYGREEN LA

MACKNEY LA

Croft Path

Slade End

1

Park Farm

Mackney Court Farm

90

56 A 57 B C 58 D E F

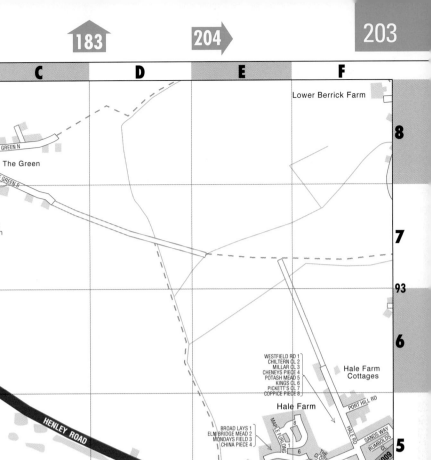
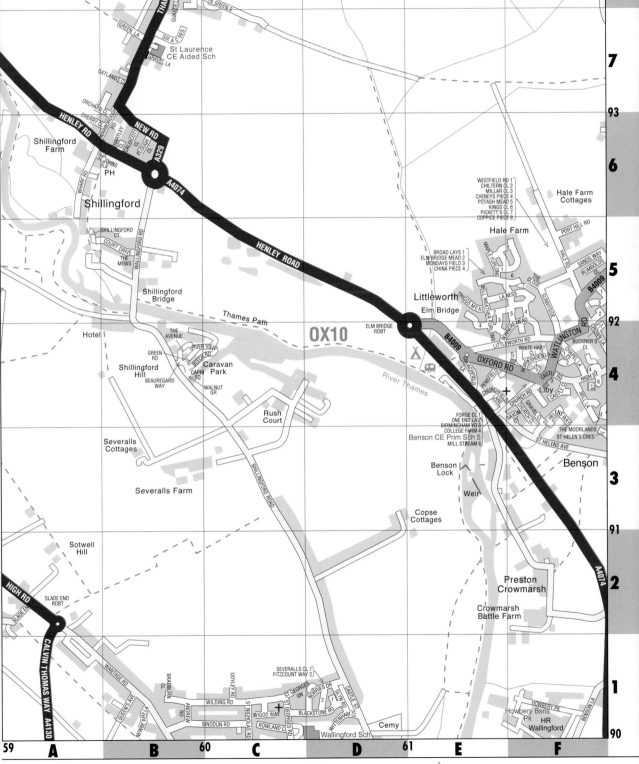

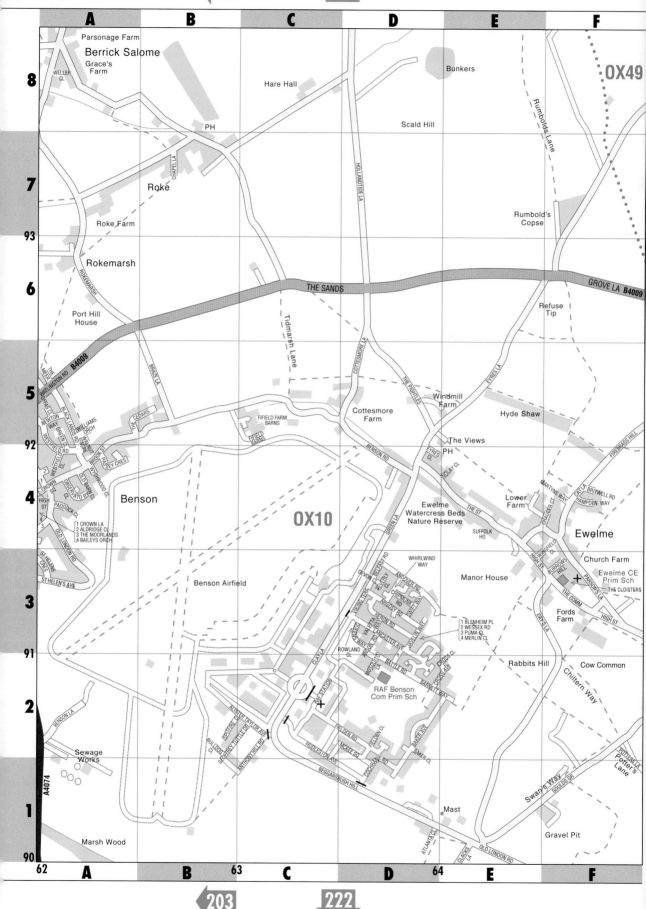

A **B** **C** **D** **E** **F**

8

Parsonage Farm
Berrick Salome
Grace's Farm
WELLER CL
Hare Hall
Bunkers
Scald Hill
OX49
Rumbolds Lane

PH
7
CHAPEL LA
Roke
HOLLANDTIDE LA
Rumbold's Copse

93
Roke Farm
Rokemarsh
ROKEMARSH
THE SANDS
GROVE LA B4009
Port Hill House
Refuse Tip

6

THE MEER
WALLINGTON RD B4009
BRACE LA
Tidmarsh Lane
THE PIGHTLE
COTTESMORE LA
Windmill Farm
EYRES LA
Hyde Shaw
FIREBRASS HILL

5
NEWTON WAY
GREEN CL
WESTFIELD RD
THE CEDARS
WILLIAMS ORCH
WALNUT
BROOK ST
WYCHWOOD CL
Fifield Farm Barns
IFIELD BARNS
Cottesmore Farm
BENSON RD
The Views
EYRES CL
PH
NIQLAY CL
THE ST
Lower Farm
MARTYNS WAY
BRITWELL RD
HAMPDEN WAY
CHAUCER CT

92
BLACKLANDS RIDE
PASSEY CRES
OLD BARN CL
DESERATO RYD
CROWN SQ
High St
PADDOCK CL
Benson
Ewelme Watercress Beds Nature Reserve
SUFFOLK HO
HIGH ST
BURROWS HILL
PARSONS LA
Ewelme
Church Farm
Ewelme CE Prim Sch
THE CLOISTERS

4
1 CROWN LA
2 ALDRIDGE CL
3 THE MOORLANDS
4 BAILEYS ORCH
OX10
GREEN LA
THE ST
WINGFIELD
DAYS LA
THE COMM
Fords Farm
HIGH ST

ST HELENS CRES
OLD LONDON RD
ST HELEN'S AVE
Benson Airfield
WHIRLWIND WAY
BELFAST RD
ANDOVER RD
CHIPMUNK RD
DERBY CL
Manor House
1 BLENHEIM PL
2 WESSEX RD
3 PUMA CL
4 MERLIN CL
Rabbits Hill
Cow Common
Chiltern Way

3
VIKING CL
DEVON RD
VALETTA RD
HERON RD
ARGOSY RD
JAVELIN WAY
ANSON RD
LANCASTER AVE
ROWLAND CL
BATTLE RD
CROSS CL
CROSS AVE
BARNETT WAY

91
BENSON LA
ALISTER TAYLOR AVE
GEOFFREY TUTTLE DR
ANTHONY HILL RD
CLARK LA
MOSQUITO LA
RAF Benson Com Prim Sch
BAKER AVE
BAKER CL

2
A4074
Sewage Works
BULLDOG CL
SPITFIRE CL
RAIL STATION
HUDDLESTON AVE
MCKEE SQ
COCHRANE RD
FELDEN CL
FELDEN RD
Mast
Swan's Way
GOULDS GR
POTTER'S LANE
Gravel Pit

1

90
Marsh Wood
BEGGARSBUSH HILL
ATLANTA CL
CLACKS LA
OLD LONDON RD

62 **A** 63 **B** **C** 64 **D** **E** **F**

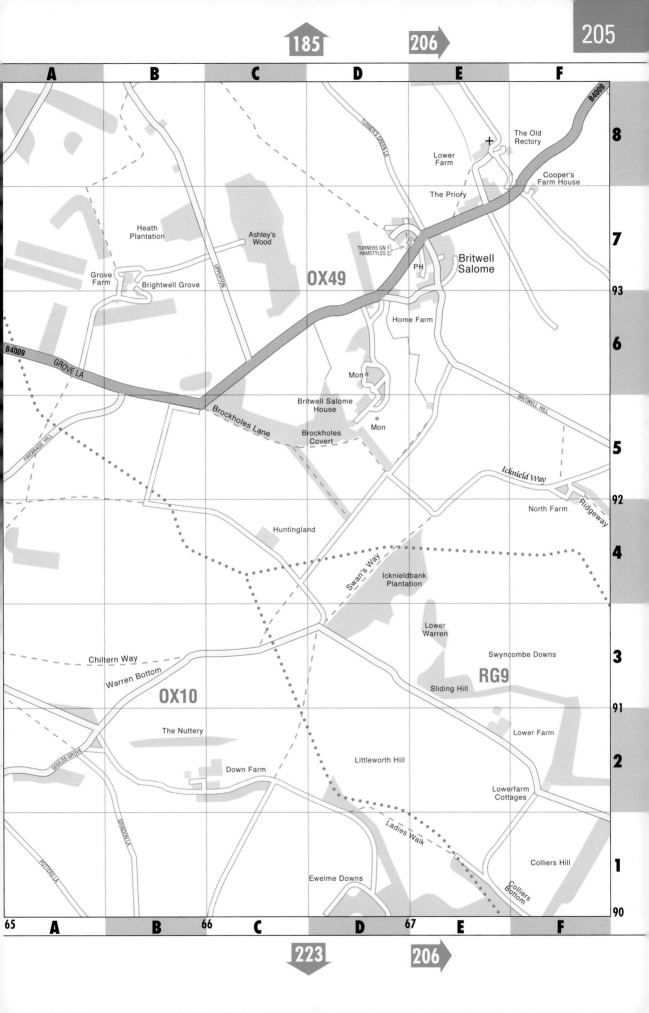

205
186

A B C D E F

8

Springfield Farm

White Mark Farm

White Mark

Cobditch Hill

HILL RD

Watlington Hill

P

7

HOWE RD

Icknield House

Swan's Way

Ridgeway

Piggery

Lys Farm House

Lower Dean

Lower Deans Wood

93

OX49

6

Dumbe Dore

Watlington Park

WATLINGTON PK

Dame Alice Farm

5

The Howe

Howe Combe

Greenfield Copse

Howe Farm

92

Britwell Hill

Ridgeway

Britwell Hill Farm

BRITWELL HILL

Woods Farm

HOWE HILL

Howe Wood

4

Dean Wood

Westernend Shaw

Mast

Ploughmans

Greenfield Manor

GREENFIELD

Lower Greenfield Farm

3

Coates Farm

91

COATES LANE

Coates Copse

RG9

B481

RED LA

PATEMORE LA

Grove Farm

2

Wr Twr

Cookley Green

B480

CHURCH LA

White Hill

RECTORY HILL

The Rectory

LADIES WALK

Church Wood

Reading La

Van Diemans

1

Colliers Hill

Swyncombe House

Cookley Farm

B481

90

68 A B 69 C D 70 E F

187

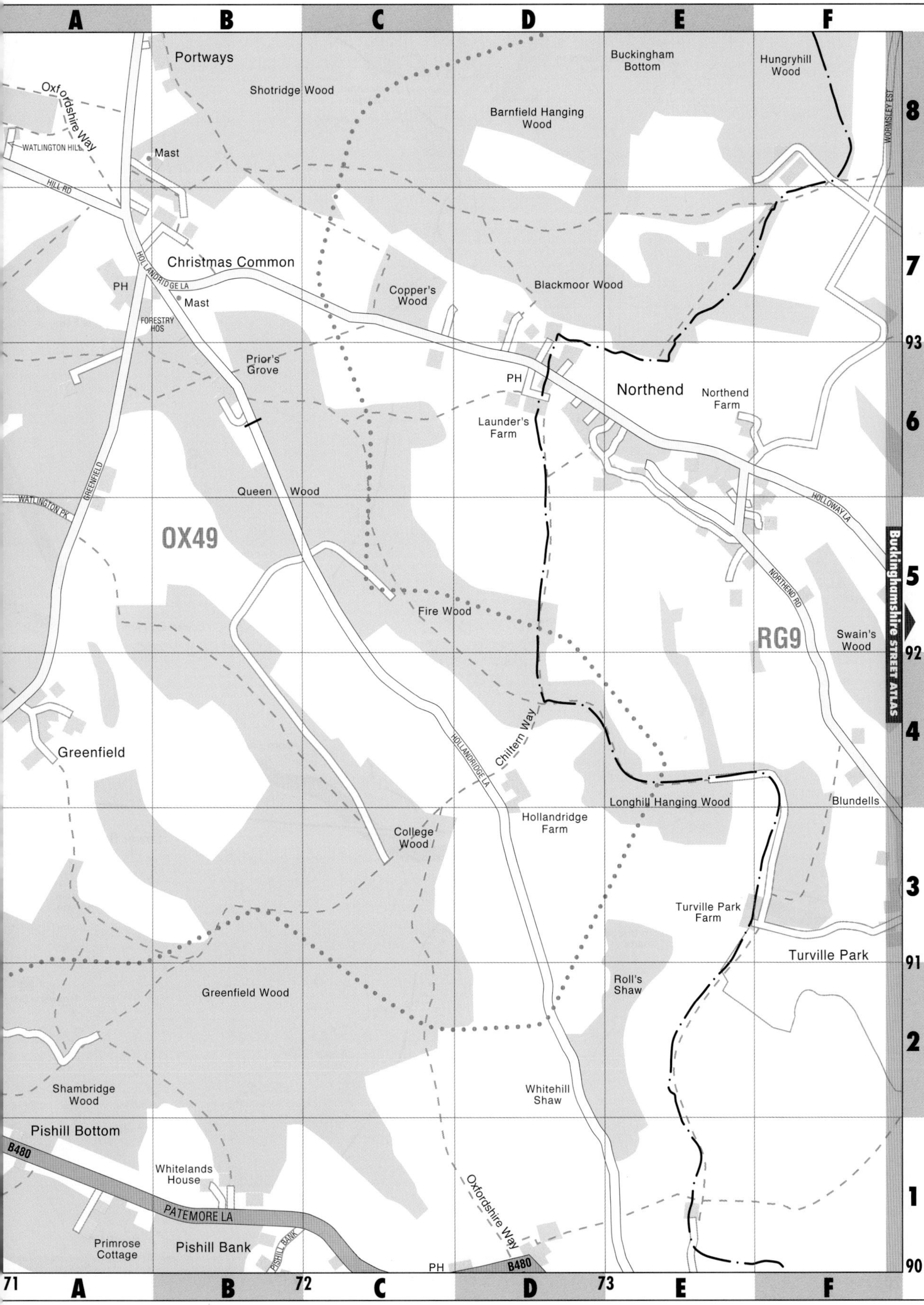
A
B
C
D
E
F
Portways
Shotridge Wood
Buckingham Bottom
Hungryhill Wood
Barnfield Hanging Wood
Oxfordshire Way
WATLINGTON HILL
Mast
HILL RD
WORMSLEY EST
8
Christmas Common
HOLLANDRIDGE LA
PH
Mast
FORESTRY HOS
Copper's Wood
Blackmoor Wood
7
93
Prior's Grove
PH
Northend
Northend Farm
Launder's Farm
6
Queen Wood
WATLINGTON PK
GREENFIELD
HOLLOWAY LA
OX49
NORTHEND RD
5
Fire Wood
RG9
Swain's Wood
92
Buckinghamshire STREET ATLAS
Chiltern Way
HOLLANDRIDGE LA
4
Greenfield
Longhill Hanging Wood
Blundells
Hollandridge Farm
College Wood
3
Turville Park Farm
Turville Park
91
Roll's Shaw
Greenfield Wood
2
Shambridge Wood
Whitehill Shaw
Pishill Bottom
B480
Whitelands House
Oxfordshire Way
1
PATEMORE LA
Primrose Cottage
Pishill Bank
PISHILL BANK
PH
B480
90
71
A
B
72
C
D
73
E
F

225

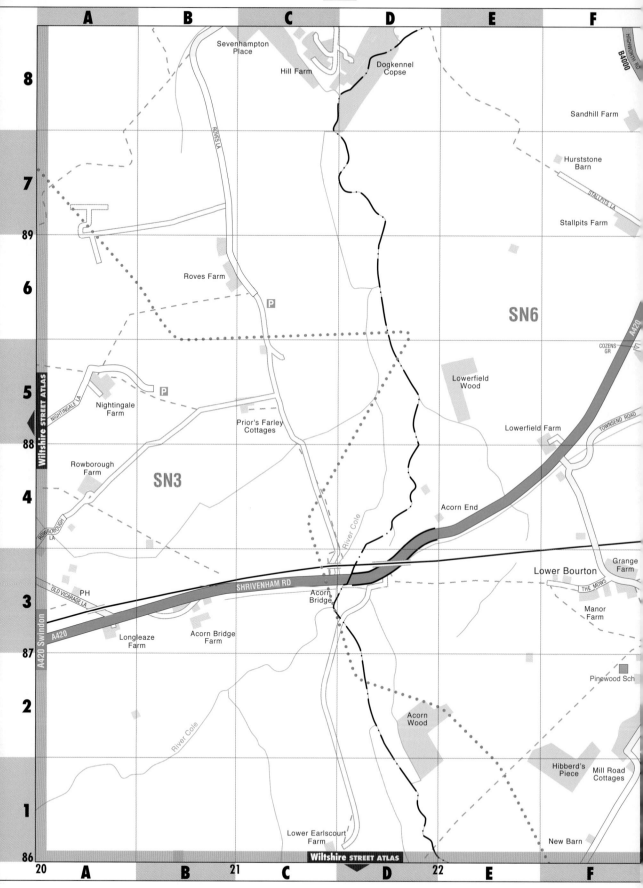

Sevenhampton Place

Hill Farm

Dogkennel Copse

Sandhill Farm

Hurststone Barn

B4000

HIGHWORTH RD

STALLPITS LA

Stallpits Farm

ROVES LA

Roves Farm

P

SN6

A420

COZENS GR

Lowerfield Wood

Lowerfield Farm

TOWNSEND ROAD

Wiltshire STREET ATLAS

NIGHTINGALE LA

P

Nightingale Farm

Prior's Farley Cottages

Rowborough Farm

SN3

Acorn End

River Cole

ROWBOROUGH LA

Lower Bourton

Grange Farm

THE MOWS

Manor Farm

OLD VICARAGE LA

PH

SHRIVENHAM RD

Acorn Bridge

A420 Swindon

A420

Longleaze Farm

Acorn Bridge Farm

Pinewood Sch

Acorn Wood

River Cole

Hibberd's Piece

Mill Road Cottages

Lower Earlscourt Farm

New Barn

20 · A · B · 21 · C · D · 22 · E · F

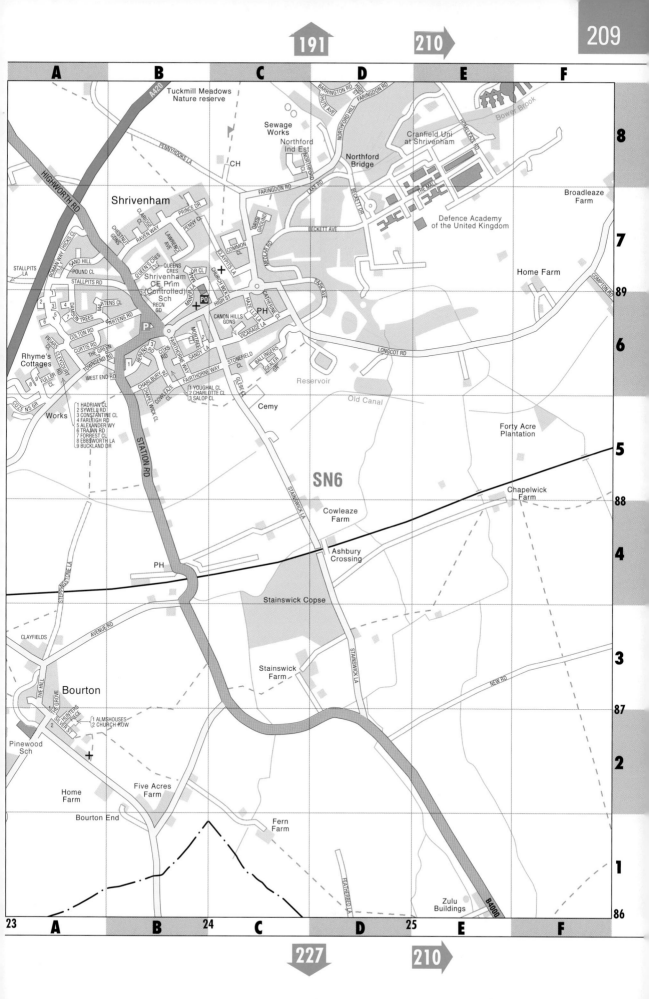

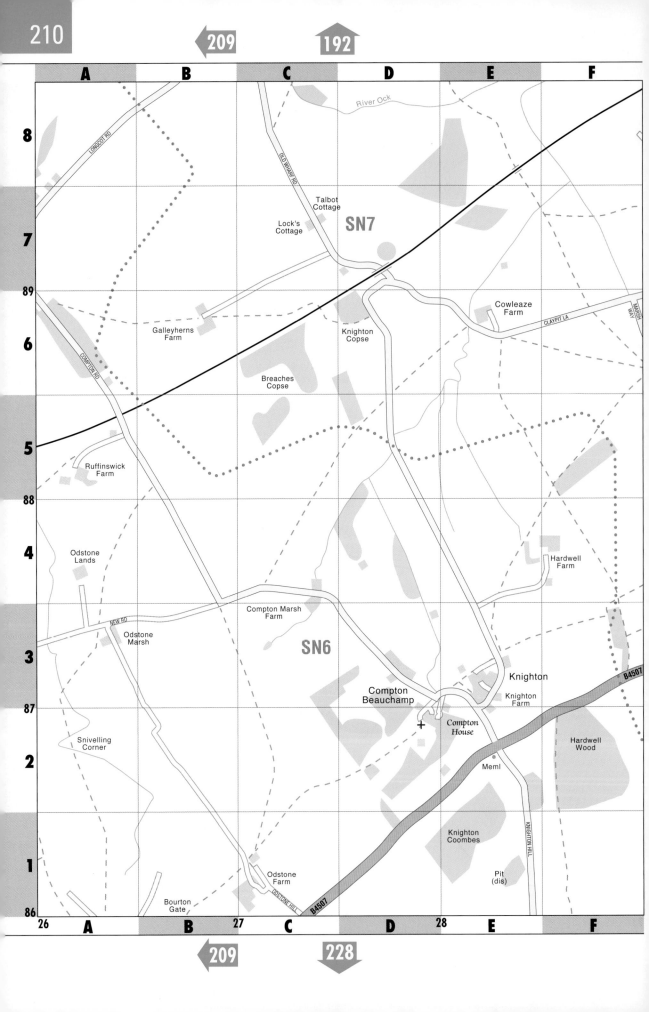

209
192

River Ock

LONGCOT RD

OLD WHARF RD

Talbot
Cottage

Lock's
Cottage

SN7

Cowleaze
Farm

CLAYPIT LA

MARSH WAY

Galleyherns
Farm

Knighton
Copse

COMPTON RD

Breaches
Copse

Ruffinswick
Farm

Odstone
Lands

Hardwell
Farm

NEW RD

Compton Marsh
Farm

Odstone
Marsh

SN6

Knighton

Compton
Beauchamp

Knighton
Farm

B4507

Snivelling
Corner

Compton
House

Hardwell
Wood

Meml

Knighton
Coombes

KNIGHTON HILL

Odstone
Farm

ODSTONE HILL

B4507

Pit
(dis)

Bourton
Gate

A B C D E F

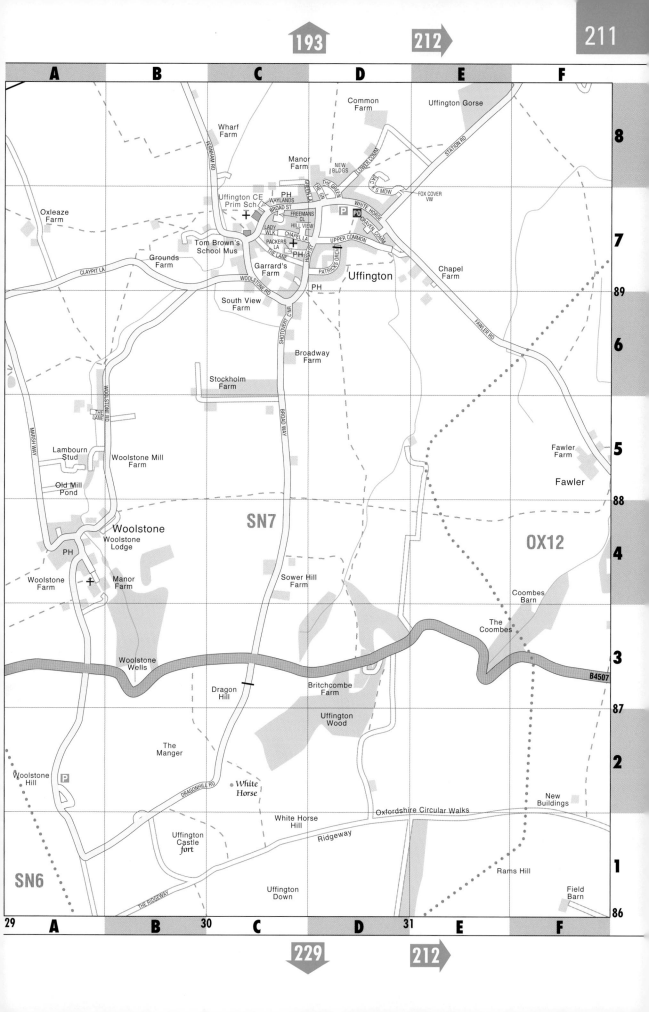

Uffington Gorse

Common Farm

Wharf Farm

Oxleaze Farm

Manor Farm

NEW BLDGS

STATION RD

Uffington CE Prim Sch

PH

WAYLANDS

BROAD ST

GREEN LA

THE GRN

THE GREEN

FREEMANS CL

HILL VIEW

WHITE HORSE

CRAVEN COMM

LOWER COMM

JAC'S MDW

FOX COVER VW

PO

P

CLAYPIT LA

Grounds Farm

Tom Brown's School Mus

LADY WLK

CHAPEL LA

PACKERS LA

THE LANE

HIGH ST

PH

PH

PATRICK'S ORCH

UPPER COMMON

Uffington

Chapel Farm

FERNHAM RD

Garrard's Farm

WOOLSTONE RD

South View Farm

PH

SHOTOVER CNR

FAWLER RD

Broadway Farm

Stockholm Farm

BROAD WAY

MARSH WAY

WOOLSTONE RD

THE LANE

Lambourn Stud

Woolstone Mill Farm

Old Mill Pond

SN7

Fawler Farm

Fawler

OX12

Woolstone

Woolstone Lodge

PH

Woolstone Farm

Manor Farm

Sower Hill Farm

Coombes Barn

The Coombes

Woolstone Wells

B4507

Dragon Hill

Britchcombe Farm

Uffington Wood

The Manger

Woolstone Hill

P

White Horse

Oxfordshire Circular Walks

New Buildings

Uffington Castle fort

White Horse Hill

Ridgeway

Rams Hill

Field Barn

SN6

THE RIDGEWAY

Uffington Down

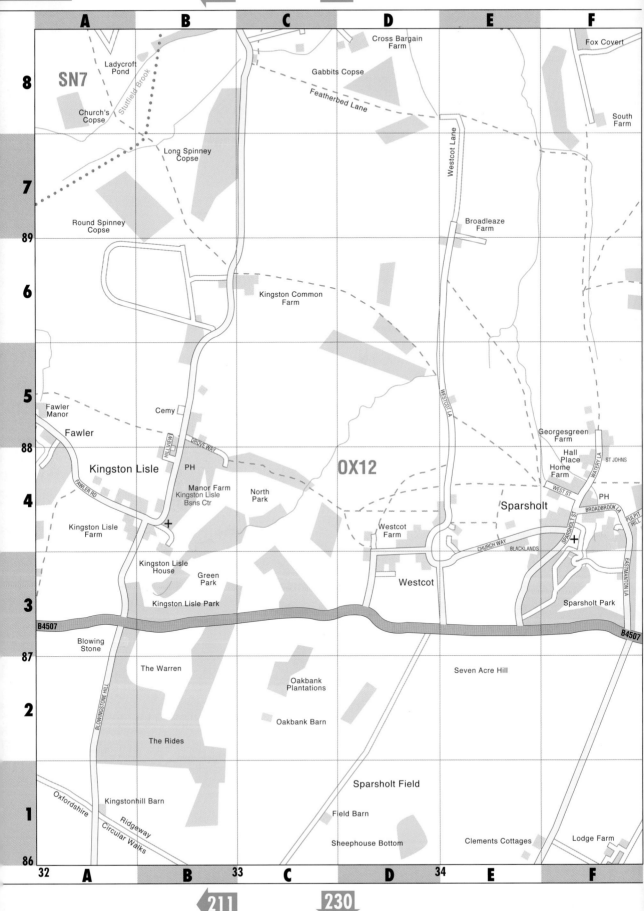

A B C D E F

8

SN7

Ladycroft
Pond

Church's
Copse

Stutfield Brook

Cross Bargain
Farm

Gabbits Copse

Featherbed Lane

Fox Covert

South
Farm

Long Spinney
Copse

7

Westcot Lane

Round Spinney
Copse

89

Broadleaze
Farm

6

Kingston Common
Farm

5

Fawler
Manor

Cemy

Fawler

WESTCOT LA

Georgesgreen
Farm

Hall
Place
Home
Farm

WATERY LA

St Johns

88

HILL VIEW

DROVE WAY

Kingston Lisle

PH

Manor Farm
Kingston Lisle
Bsns Ctr

North
Park

OX12

West Place

WEST ST

PH

BROADBROOK LA

PULPIT HILL

Sparsholt

4

FAWLER RD

Kingston Lisle
Farm

Westcot
Farm

SPARSHOLT ST

EASTMANTON LA

Kingston Lisle
House

Green
Park

Westcot

CHURCH WAY

BLACKLANDS

Sparsholt Park

3

Kingston Lisle Park

B4507

B4507

87

Blowing
Stone

The Warren

Seven Acre Hill

2

BLOWINGSTONE HILL

Oakbank
Plantations

Oakbank Barn

The Rides

Sparsholt Field

1

Oxfordshire

Kingstonhill Barn

Ridgeway

Circular Walks

Field Barn

Sheephouse Bottom

Clements Cottages

Lodge Farm

86

32 A B 33 C D 34 E F

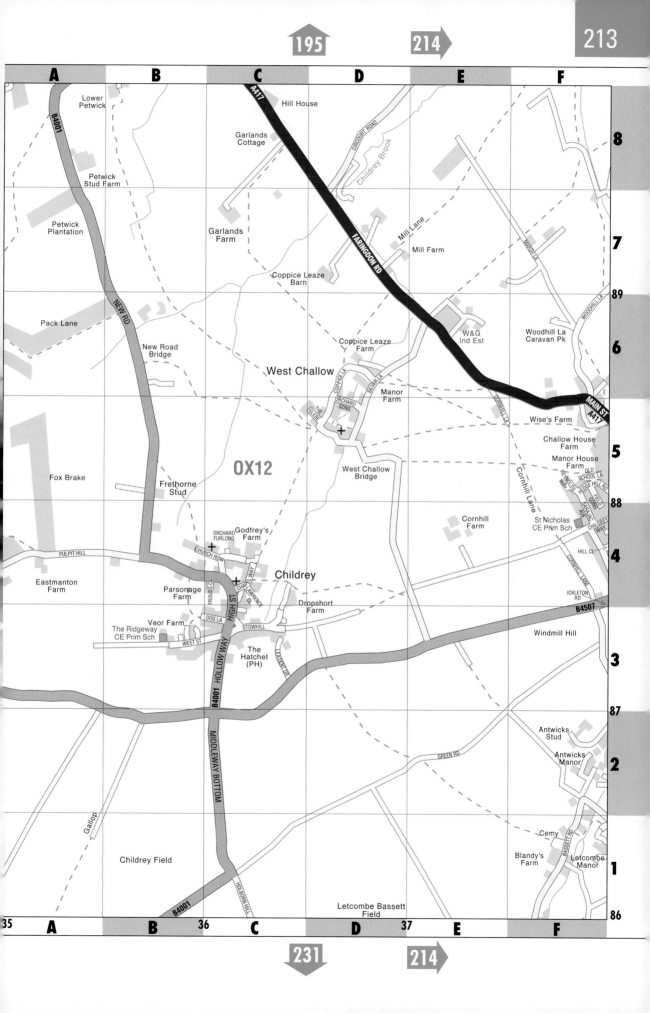

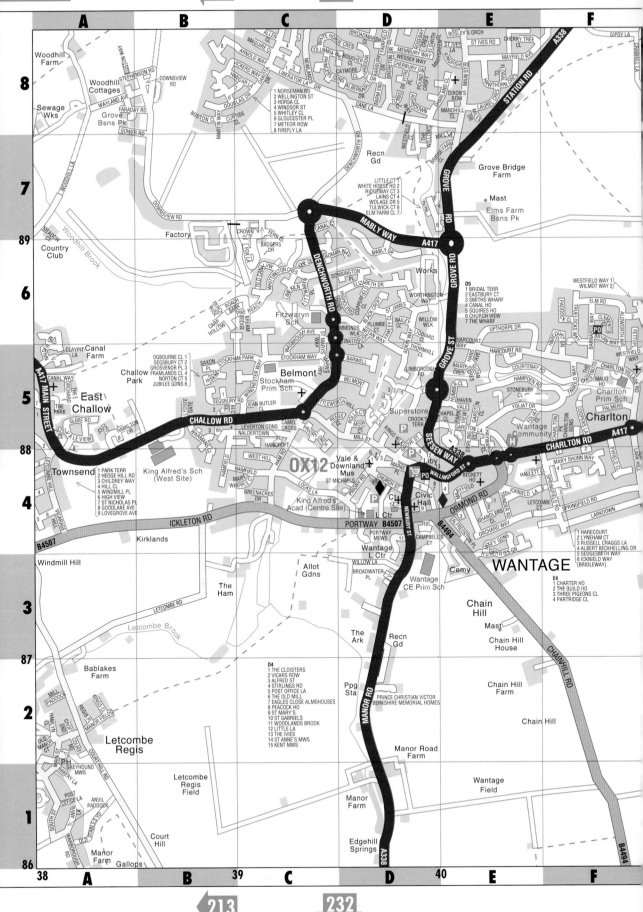

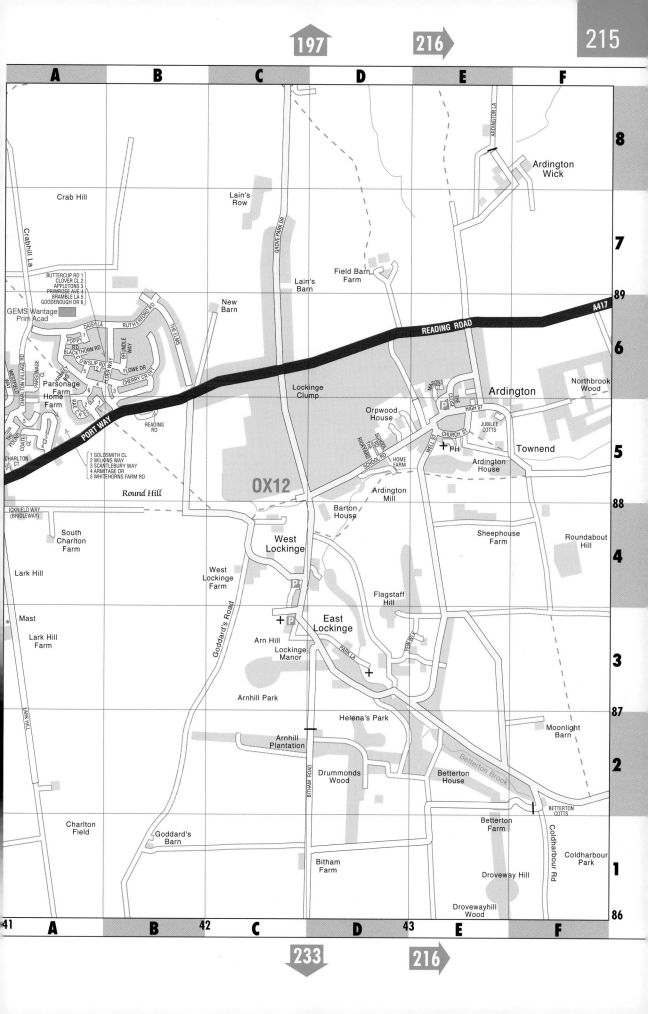

A B C D E F

8

Crab Hill

Lain's Row

7

Crabhill La

Field Barn Farm

89

Ardington Wick

Ardington La

BUTTERCUP RD 1
CLOVER CL 2
APPLETONS 3
PRIMROSE AVE 4
BRAMBLE LA 5
GOODENOUGH DR 6

GEMS Wantage Prim Acad

New Barn

Lain's Barn

Grove Park Dr

A417

READING ROAD

6

DAISY LA
POPPY RD
BLACKTHORN RD
COWSLIP RD
ELDER WAY
BRINDLE WAY
FLOWE DR
CHERRY CR
RUTHERFORD RD
THE ELMS

CHARLTON VILLAGE RD
WESTFIELD WAY
PARSONAGE RD

Parsonage Farm
Home Farm

Lockinge Clump

MASONS CL

Northbrook Wood

Ardington

HIGH ST

THE CLOSE

JUBILEE COTTS

P

Orpwood House

CHURCH ST

WELL ST

+ PH

Townend

5

THE POINT
HAMREY RD
RAE CRES
COATES CL 2
CHARLTON CT

READING RD

PORT WAY

1 GOLDSMITH CL
2 WILKINS WAY
3 SCANTLEBURY WAY
4 ARMITAGE DR
5 WHITEHORNS FARM RD

SCHOOL RD
THE RICKYARD

Home Farm

Ardington House

Ardington Mill

OX12

Barton House

Sheephouse Farm

88

ICKNIELD WAY (BRIDLEWAY)

Round Hill

South Charlton Farm

West Lockinge

Roundabout Hill

4

Lark Hill

West Lockinge Farm

P

Flagstaff Hill

Mast

Goddard's Road

+ P

East Lockinge

Arn Hill

PARK LA

TEW RICK

3

Lark Hill Farm

Lockinge Manor

+

Arnhill Park

87

LARK HILL

Helena's Park

Moonlight Barn

Arnhill Plantation

Betterton Brook

2

Drummonds Wood

Betterton House

Charlton Field

BITHAM ROAD

BETTERTON COTTS

Goddard's Barn

Betterton Farm

Coldharbour Rd

Coldharbour Park

1

Bitham Farm

Droveway Hill

Drovewayhill Wood

86

215
198

	A	B	C	D	E	F

8

Quab Hill

Quab Hill
Farm

FEATHERBED LA

Ludbridge Mill
(disused)

RIDGEWAY
CL

Greensands

New Barn

LUDBRIDGE
CL

7

WANTAGE RD

A417

PH

Lud Bridge

RAILWAY CL

East
Hendred

READING RD

Sheephouse
Barn

ALLINS LA

SMITHS
RICKYARD

HOME
FARM CL

COULINGS CL

ORCHARD CL

WHITE RD

OX11

89

A417

MILL LA

ORCHARD LA

OLD RD

THE GREENWAY

Recreation
Ground

Champs
Chapel Mus

BANKSIDE

CAT ST

Champel SQ

ST S HIGH

6

MILL LA

The Mill

The Hendreds
CE Prim Sch

FORD LA

PH

PO

West Hendred

THE SPINNEY

Hendred
House

THE MILLHAM

CHURCH ST

Lydebank
Plantation

Lockinge Brook

Hall

MANOR LA

GINGE
RD

MOUNT
PLEASANT
COTTS

ST MARY'S RD

St Amand's RC
Prim Sch

The Moors

HORN LA

COW Road

Red Barn

THE LYNCH

NEWBURY RD

Hill Farm

5

Park Hill

ST MARYS RD

88

Goldbury
Hill

Park Hill

OX12

Icknield

GINGE ROAD

GOLDBURY
COTTS

Park Hill
Row

Aldfield
Common

4

Pump
House

Shadwell's Row

Ginge Brook

Black Mills
Row

3

Parsonage
Barn

STILEWAY ROAD

87

Lower Farm

Ellaway's
Barn

TWENTIETH ST

West
Ginge

Ginge
House

East
Ginge

2

NINETEENTH
ST

RUTHERFORD LA

Upper Farm

Ginge
Manor

Deer Park

OX11

1

White Way

Downs
Cottage

Meashill
Plantation

86

44	A	45	B	C	46	D	E	F

215
234

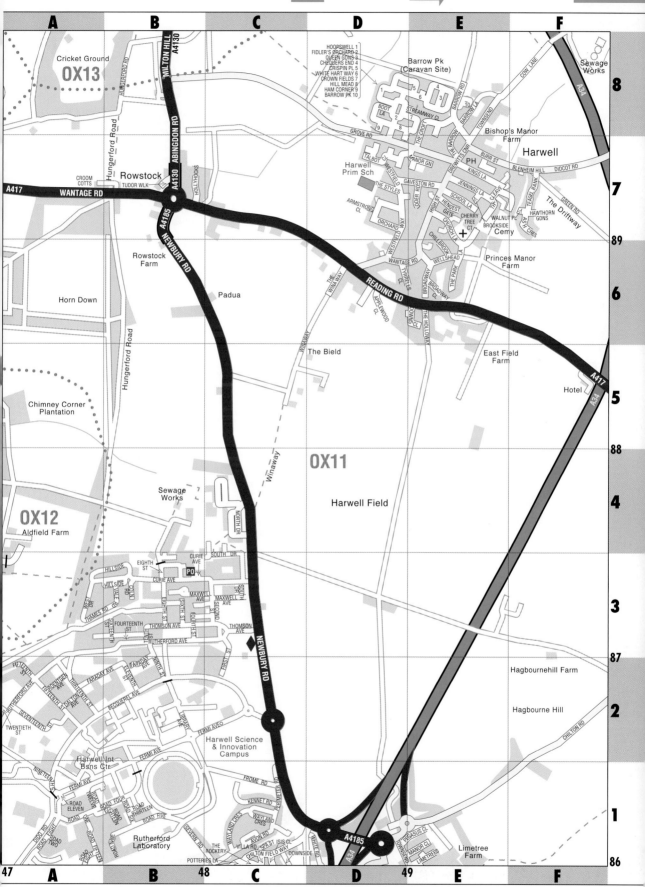

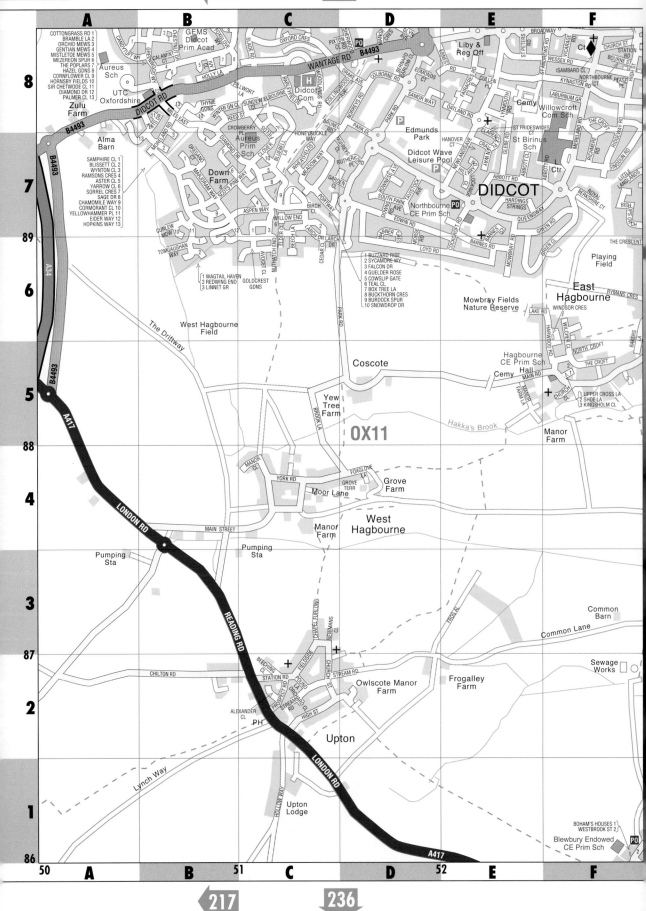

A8
1 SHANNON RD
2 SEVERN CRES
3 KENNETT PL
4 THAMES CT
5 MEDWAY GR
6 TYNE SQ
7 WESTERN AVE
8 QUEEN ELIZABETH CL
9 NUFFIELD CL
10 WESSEX RD
11 CAVENDISH CARAVAN PK
12 KYNASTON RD

A4130

Superstores

Fulscot Copse

Fulscot Bridge

HADDEN HILL

North Moreton

Alders Farm PH

QUEENS WAY

LONG WITTENHAM RD

Little Langlands

Cherry Tree Farm

GREAT MEAD

NEW RD

Fulscot Manor

Hakka's Brook

South Moreton Sch

DUNSOMER HILL

SANDS RD

KIRBY

South Moreton

HIGH CLEMENTS

PO

HIGGS CL

MAIN RD

PH

FIELDSIDE

Tadley

CHURCH LA

MILL LA

Mill Brook

OX11

Brookside

ANCHOR LA

Hagbourne Mill Farm

West Hagbourne Moor

BLEWBURY RD

Blewbury Mill

Sheencroft Farm

DIDCOT RD

HAGBOURNE RD

Aston Upthorpe

MORETON RD

Ham Cottages

Upthorpe Farm

Lower Ham Yard

Blewbury

The Old Mill

Bridus Way

CHAILEY GDNS

COSSICLE MEAD

WHITES CT

B4016

BESSELS WAY

Winterbrook Farm

Blewburton Hill

FRIMLEY YARD

THE CROFT

Thorpe Farm

THORPE ST

SPRING LA

FULLERS RD

PH

BAKER ST

Aston Tirrold

RECTORY LA

ASTON ST

Westbrook St

BERRY LA

LADYCROFT PK

BRIDUS MEAD

BRIDUS SOUTH

MILLBROOK CL

CHURCH ST

BESSELS LEA RD

53   A   B   54   C   D   55   E   F

86 87 88 89 8 7 6 5 4 3 2 1

	A	B	C	D	E	F

8

WALLINGFORD RD
ELM RD
LONG WITTENHAM RD
North Moreton
HIGH ST

Mackney
MACKNEY LA
Sherwood Farm

Kibble Ditch

Airstrip

7

PH
BEAR LA
DUNSOMER HILL

89

SANDS RD
Glebe Cottage

Mill Brook

6

Hithercroft Farm

HITHERCROFT RD

5

PH
CROWN LA
PAPER MILL LA
HIGH ST
LOYS LA
South Moreton
MILL LA
HITHERCROFT

OX11

88

ANCHOR LA
Cholsey Hill

OX10

4

MORETON RD
Hillgreen Farm

CHURCH RD

Poultry Farm

The Manor

3

Manor Farm

Cholsey and Wallingford Rly

Sewage Works

87

CHURCH RD

GOLDFINCH L

The Lees

2

Cholsey Prim Sch
PH
WALLINGFORD RD
MARYMEAD
CHURCH RD
CROSS RD
CHEQUERS PL
LITTLE LA
PO
ILGES LA
Caravan Park
THE FORTY
THE POUND

Lees Cottages

West End

HAWKSWORTH PL
WILLOW CL
DROVESIDE
POUND LA
AMWELL

1

STATION RD
SANDY LA
BRO
WEST END
PARFIT
FORD CL
THE ROWANS
KENTWOOD RD
ST GEORGES CL
CRESCENT WAY
LARKFIELD
HONEY LA
BEEHIVE CL
QUEENS
BUCKTHORN
CRES
DOWNSIDE
APIARY PL

Pancroft Farm

86

The Elms
HITHERCROFT
WESTFIELD RD
PAPIST WAY
Cholsey

56	A	57	B	C	58	D	E	F

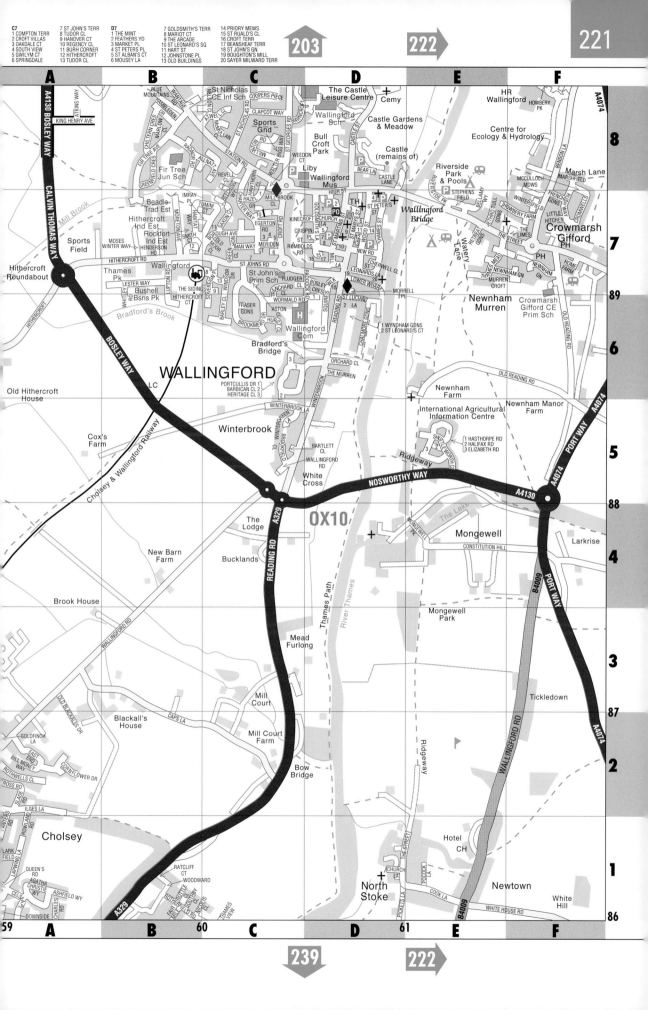

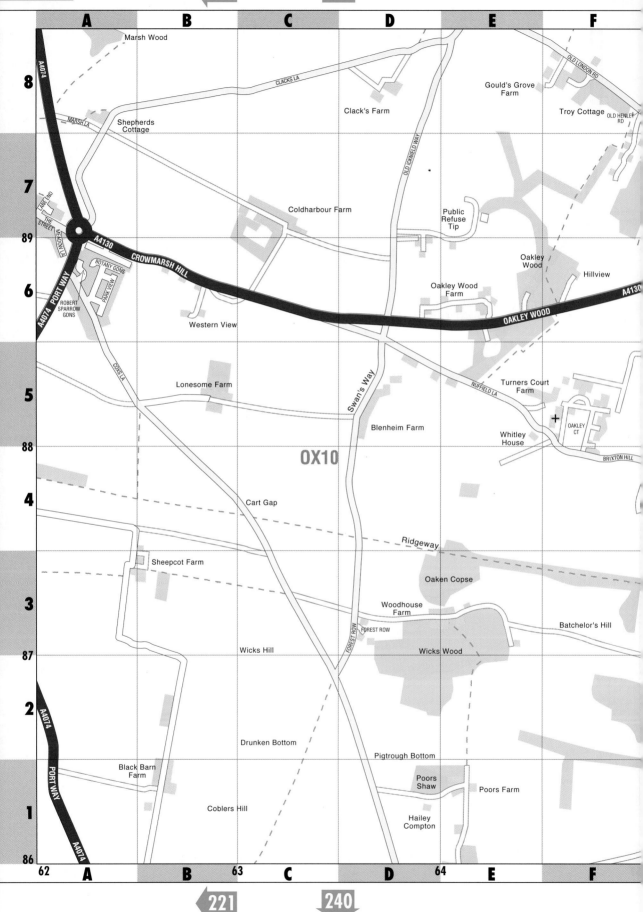

Marsh Wood

CLACKS LA

Clack's Farm

Gould's Grove
Farm

OLD LONDON RD

Troy Cottage

OLD HENLEY RD

MARSH LA

Shepherds
Cottage

A4074

Coldharbour Farm

OLD ICKNIELD WAY

Public
Refuse
Tip

Oakley
Wood

Hillview

LANE END

THE STREET

MEADOW LA

A4130

CROWMARSH HILL

Oakley Wood
Farm

A4130

PORT WAY

BOTANY GDNS

PARK VIEW

ROBERT
SPARROW
GDNS

A4074

Western View

OAKLEY WOOD

CONS LA

Lonesome Farm

Swan's Way

NUFFIELD LA

Turners Court
Farm

OAKLEY
CT

Blenheim Farm

Whitley
House

BRIXTON HILL

OX10

Cart Gap

Ridgeway

Oaken Copse

Sheepcot Farm

Woodhouse
Farm

Batchelor's Hill

FOREST ROW

FOREST ROW

Wicks Hill

Wicks Wood

A4074

Drunken Bottom

Pigtrough Bottom

PORT WAY

Black Barn
Farm

Poors
Shaw

Poors Farm

Coblers Hill

Hailey
Compton

A4074

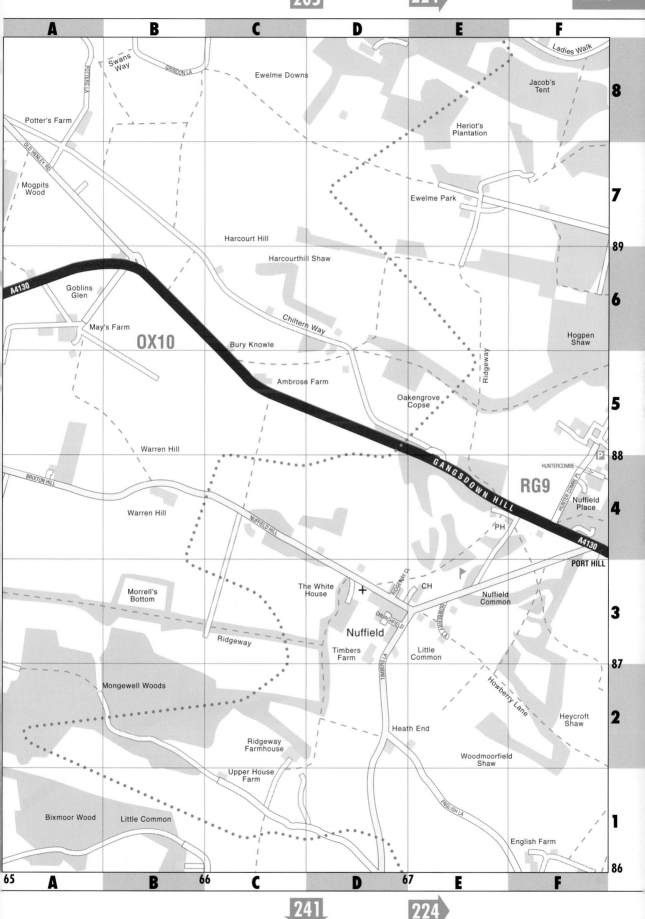

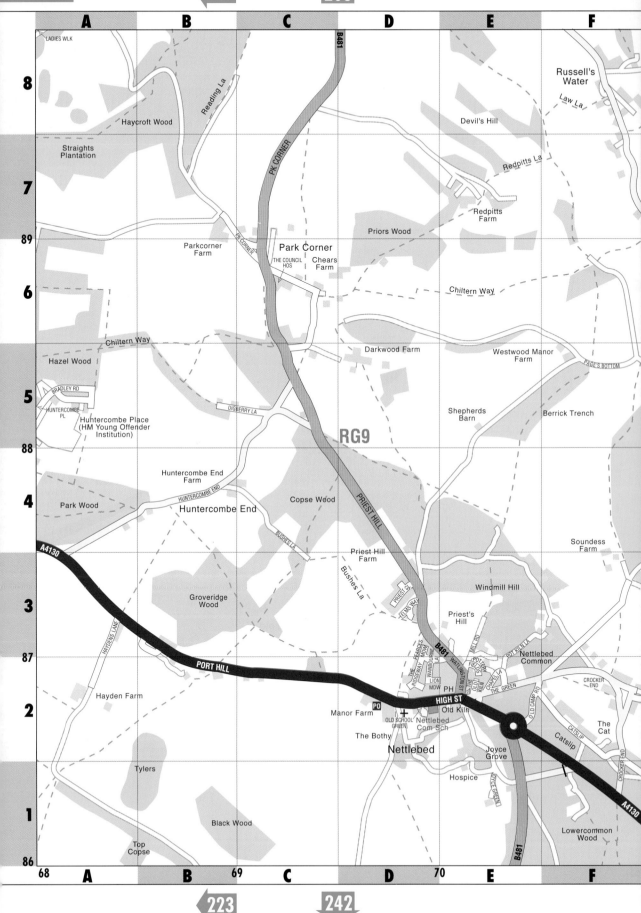

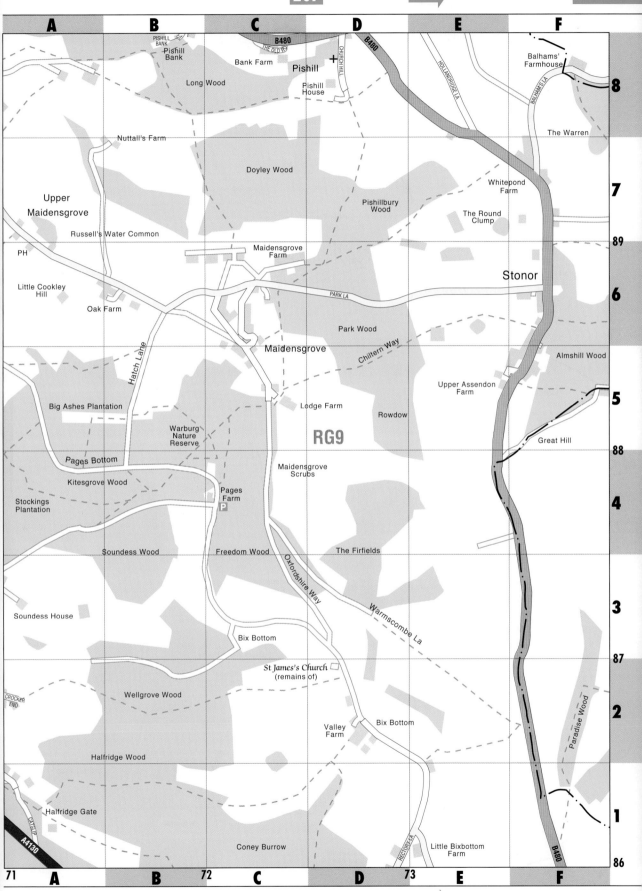

Buckinghamshire STREET ATLAS

Buckinghamshire STREET ATLAS

8

7

89

6

5

88

4

3

87

2

1

86

A   B   C   D   E   F

Southend

Southend Farm

Drovers

Balham's Wood

Chiltern Way

Stonor House

Kildridge Wood

Kimble Farm

Binfield Bottom

Great Wood

Old Luxters Farm Brewery

DUDLEY LA

Stonor Park (Deer Park)

Cockslease LA

Gussetts Wood

Jubilee Plantation

Henleyhill Wood

Coxlease

Coxlease Farm

Upper Woodend Farm

ROUNDHOUSE LA

Woodcocks Bill

Hanging Wood

Bosmore Farm

BOSMORE LA

RG9

Lower Woodend Farm

Jubilee Plantation

Roundhouse Farm

Highfield Plantation

Great Wood

Great Wood House

Jackson's Farm

Fawley Green

Fawley Green Farm

Red Hill

Fawley Bottom

CHURCH LA

Fawley

Fawley Bottom Farm House

BENHAMS LA

Kitchener's Firs

FAWLEY BOTTOM LA

DOBSON'S LA

Pallbach Hill

Eversdown

CROCKMORE LA

Brackenhill Stud Farm

Benhams

74   A   B   75   C   D   76   E   F

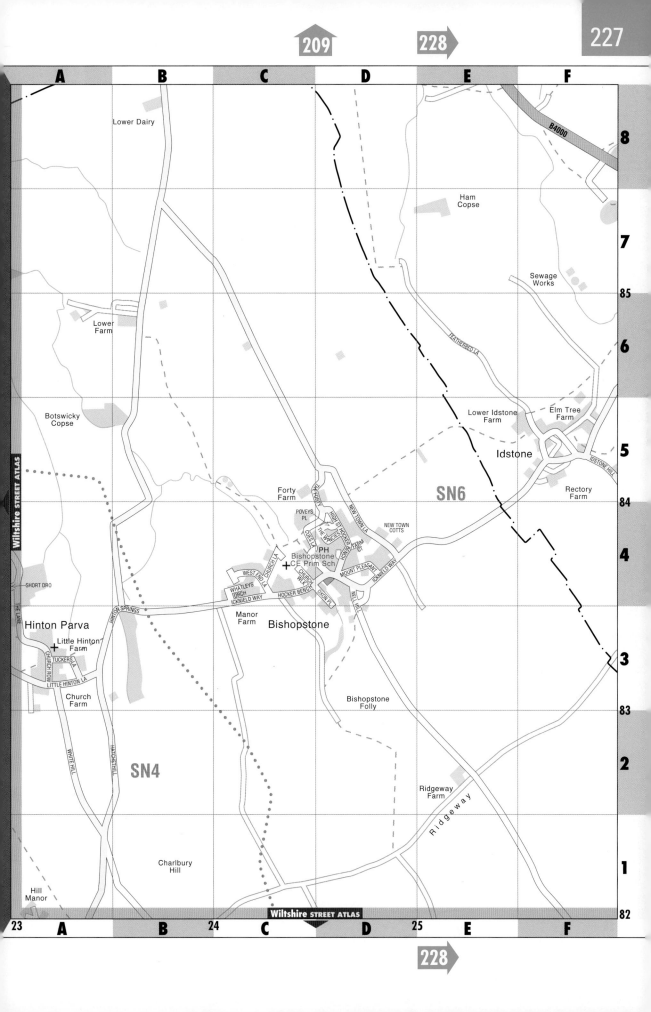

Wiltshire STREET ATLAS

Lower Dairy

B4000

Ham Copse

Sewage Works

Lower Farm

FEATHERBED LA

Lower Idstone Farm

Elm Tree Farm

Botswicky Copse

Idstone

SN6

Rectory Farm

IDSTONE HILL

Forty Farm

POVEYS PL

THE FORTY

HIGH ST

HOCKER BENCH

NEW TOWN LA

NEW TOWN COTTS

DITES LA

THE VINCIES

FARM CT

PH
Bishopstone
CE Prim Sch

WEST END LA

CHURCH LA

MOUNT PLEASANT

ICKNIELD WAY

WHATLEYS ORCH

CHURCH WLK

ICKNIELD WAY

HOCKER BENCH

DIXON PL

NELL HILL

SHORT DRO

Manor Farm

Bishopstone

THE LANE

Hinton Parva

Little Hinton Farm

HINTON SPRINGS

TUCKERS LA

CHURCH ROW

LITTLE HINTON LA

Church Farm

Bishopstone Folly

Ridgeway Farm

SN4

WHITE HILL

HATCHET HILL

Ridgeway

Charlbury Hill

Hill Manor

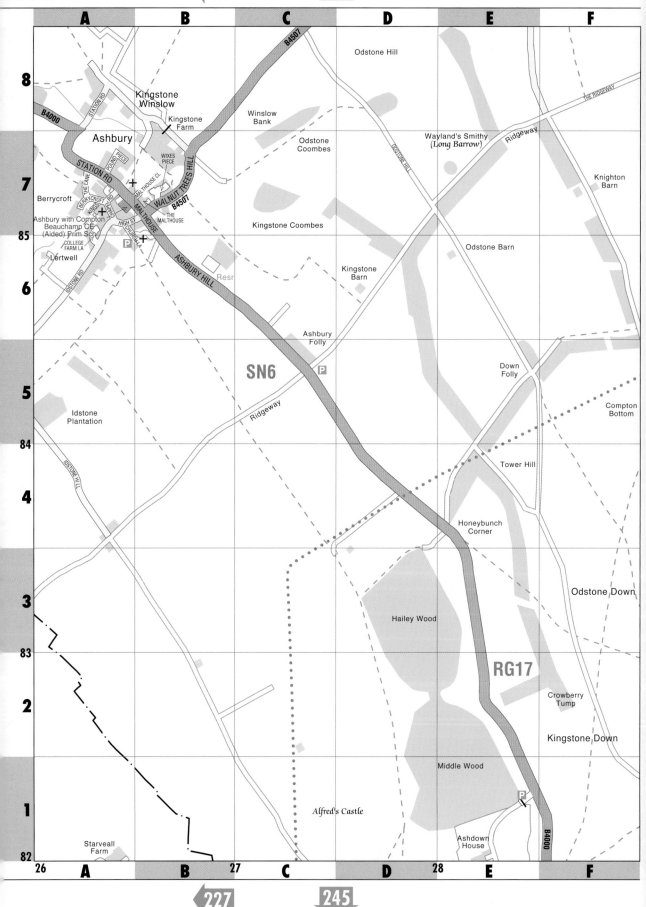

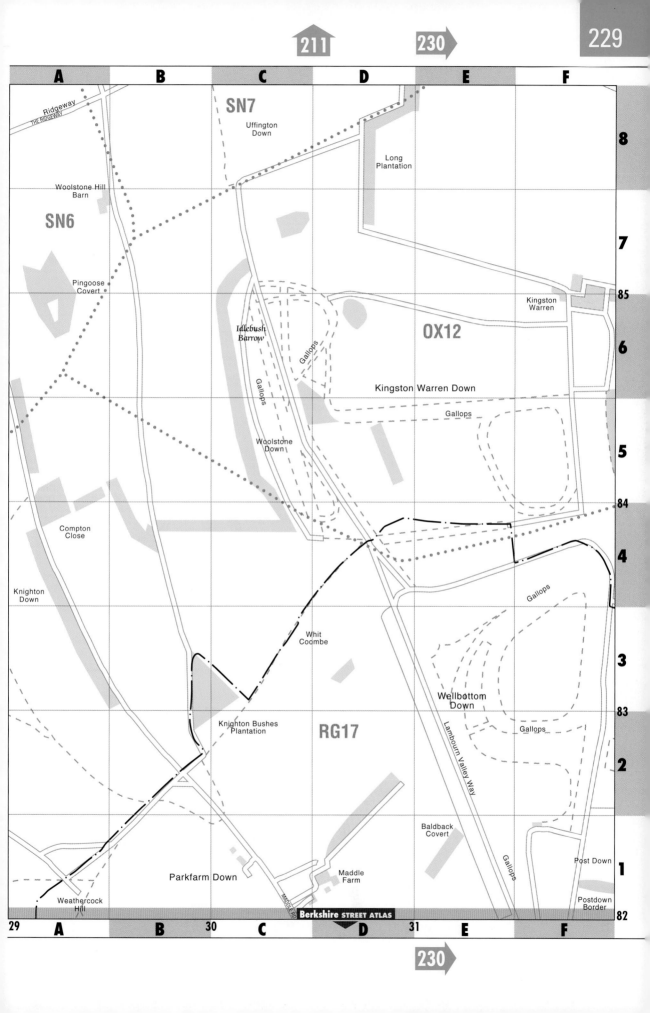

SN7

Uffington
Down

Long
Plantation

Ridgeway
THE RIDGEWAY

Woolstone Hill
Barn

SN6

8

Pingoose
Covert

7

Kingston
Warren

85

Idlebush
Barrow

OX12

6

Gallops

Gallops

Kingston Warren Down

Gallops

Woolstone
Down

5

84

Compton
Close

Gallops

4

Knighton
Down

Whit
Coombe

Gallops

Wellbottom
Down

3

83

Knighton Bushes
Plantation

RG17

Gallops

Lambourn Valley Way

2

Baldback
Covert

Gallops

Post Down

1

Parkfarm Down

MADDLE ROAD

Maddle
Farm

Postdown
Border

82

Weathercock
Hill

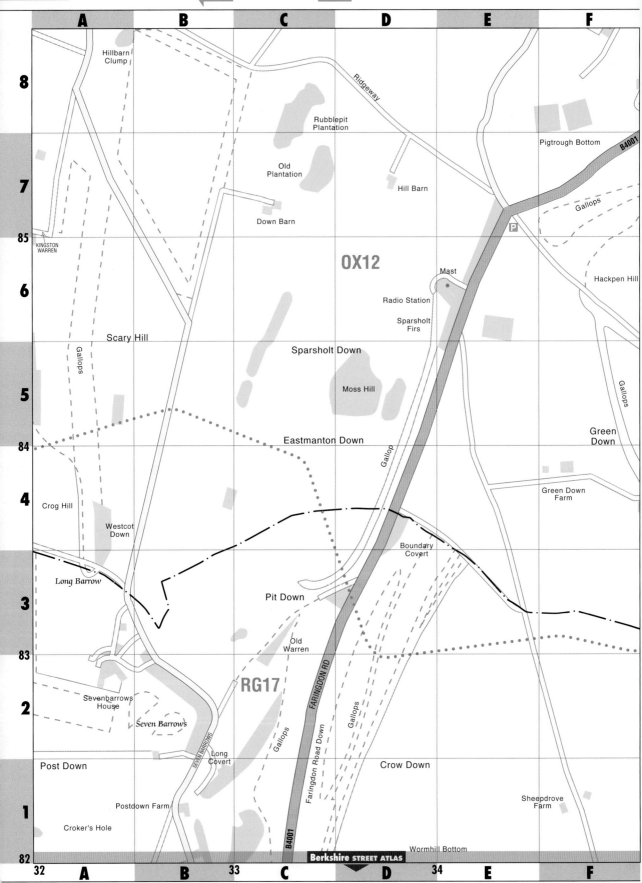

A   B   C   D   E   F

8

Hillbarn
Clump

Ridgeway

Rubblepit
Plantation

Pigtrough Bottom

B4001

7

Old
Plantation

Hill Barn

Gallops

Down Barn

85

KINGSTON
WARREN

OX12

P

Hackpen Hill

6

Mast

Radio Station

Sparsholt
Firs

Scary Hill

Sparsholt Down

5

Gallops

Moss Hill

Gallops

Green
Down

84

Eastmanton Down

Gallop

4

Crog Hill

Green Down
Farm

Westcot
Down

Boundary
Covert

3

Long Barrow

Pit Down

FARINGDON RD

RG17

Old
Warren

83

Sevenbarrows
House

Gallops

Gallops

2

Seven Barrows

SEVEN BARROWS

Long
Covert

Post Down

Crow Down

Sheepdrove
Farm

1

Postdown Farm

Croker's Hole

B4001

Wormhill Bottom

82

32   A   B   33   C   D   34   E   F

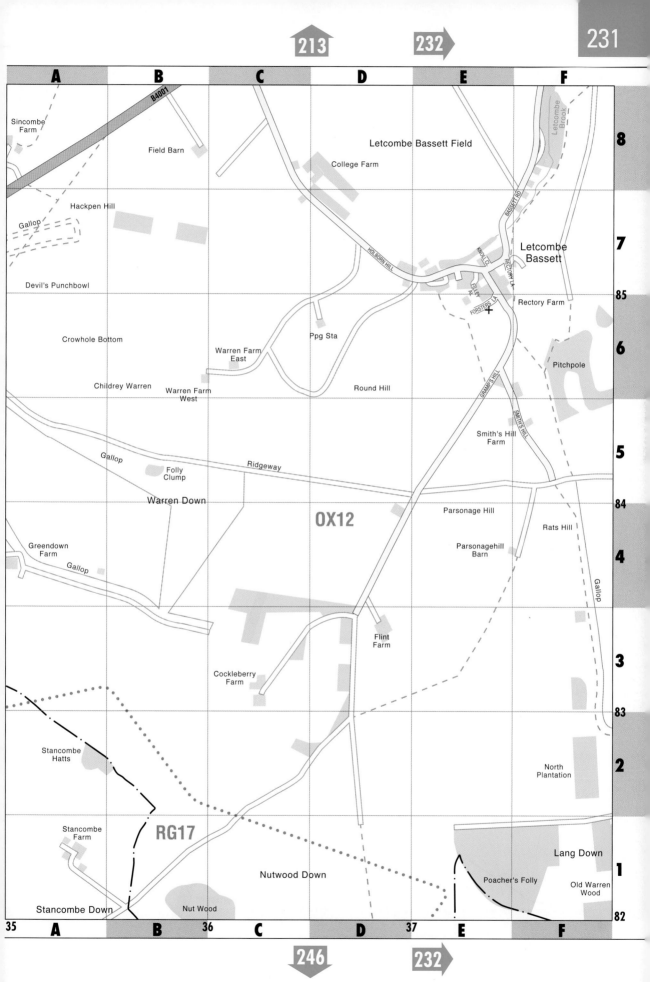

A B C D E F

35 36 37

8 7 85 6 5 84 4 3 83 2 1 82

B4001

Sincombe Farm

Field Barn

Letcombe Bassett Field

College Farm

BASSETT RD

Letcombe Bassett

Hackpen Hill

HOLBORN HILL

KNOLL CL.

RECTORY LA.

Gallop

Devil's Punchbowl

ABLEY

FORSTERS LA.

Rectory Farm

Crowhole Bottom

Ppg Sta

Pitchpole

Warren Farm East

GRAMP'S HILL

Childrey Warren

Warren Farm West

Round Hill

SMITH'S HILL

Smith's Hill Farm

Gallop

Ridgeway

Folly Clump

Warren Down

OX12

Parsonage Hill

Rats Hill

Greendown Farm

Gallop

Parsonagehill Barn

Gallop

Flint Farm

Cockleberry Farm

Stancombe Hatts

North Plantation

RG17

Stancombe Farm

Lang Down

Nutwood Down

Poacher's Folly

Old Warren Wood

Stancombe Down

Nut Wood

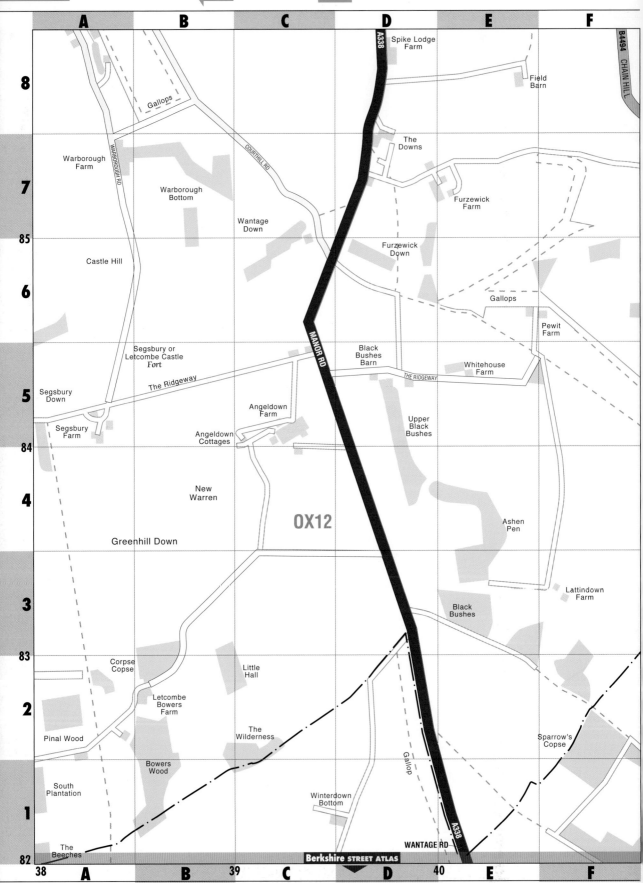

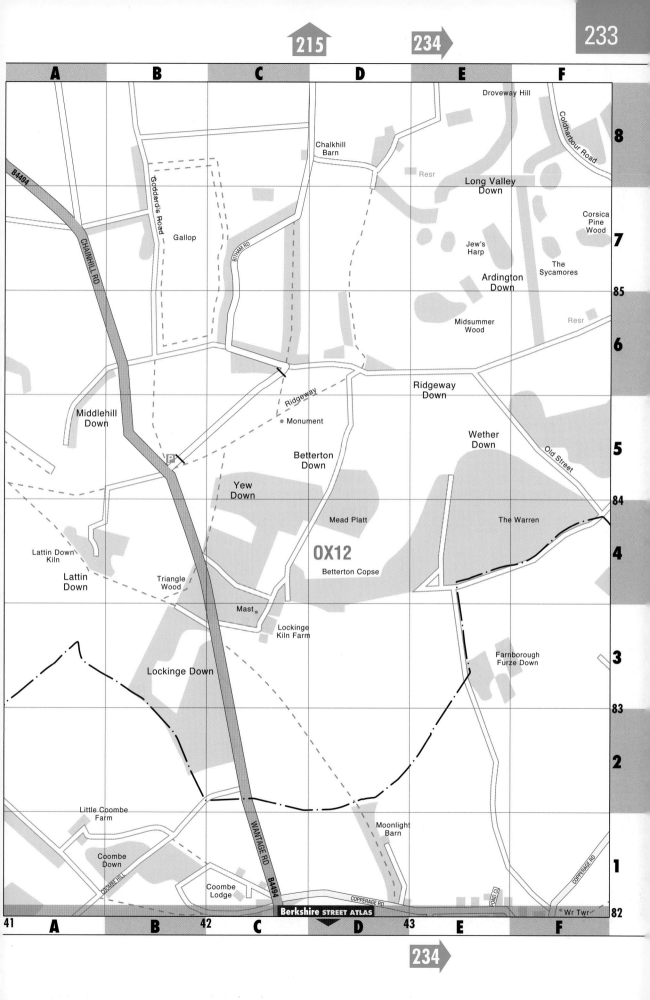

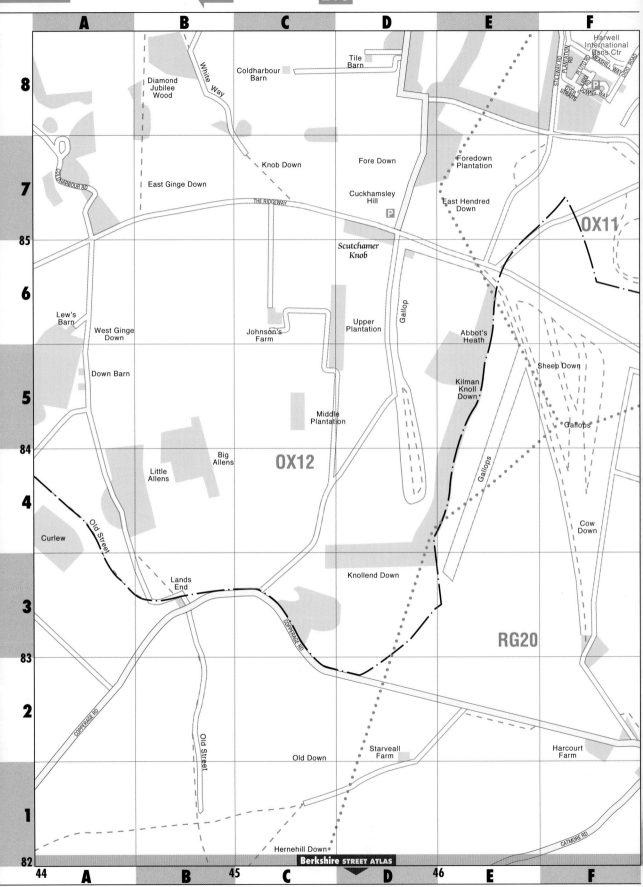

Harwell International Bsns Ctr

Coldharbour Barn

Tile Barn

Diamond Jubilee Wood

White Way

Knob Down

Fore Down

Foredown Plantation

COLDHARBOUR RD

East Ginge Down

THE RIDGEWAY

Cuckhamsley Hill

East Hendred Down

OX11

Scutchamer Knob

Lew's Barn

West Ginge Down

Johnson's Farm

Upper Plantation

Gallop

Abbot's Heath

Sheep Down

Down Barn

Kilman Knoll Down

Gallops

Middle Plantation

Big Allens

OX12

Little Allens

Gallops

Cow Down

Curlew

Old Street

Knollend Down

RG20

Lands End

COPPERAGE RD

Harcourt Farm

COPPERAGE RD

Old Street

Old Down

Starveall Farm

Catmore Rd

Hernehill Down

Berkshire STREET ATLAS

44   45   46
82   83   84   85

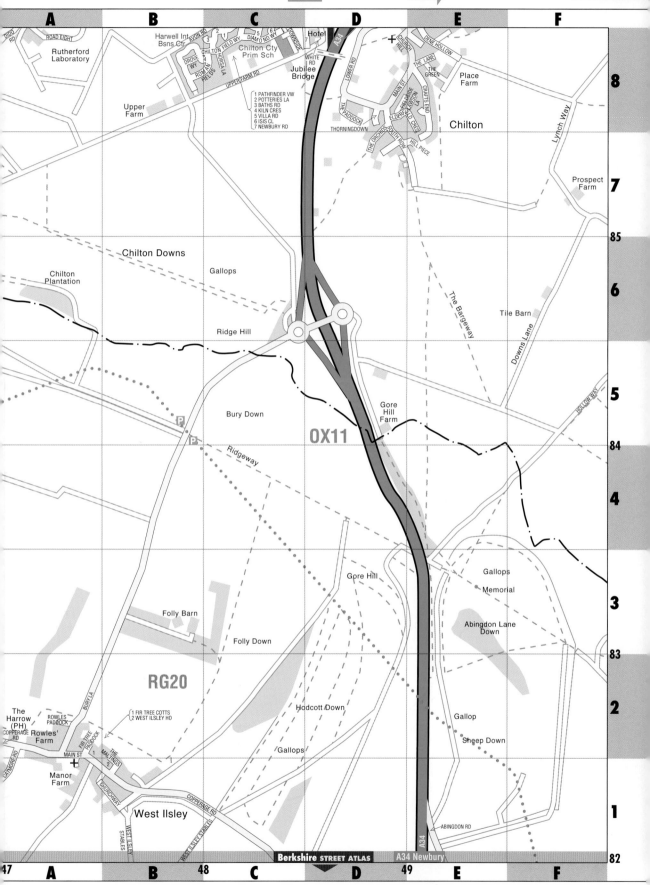

235
218

| | A | B | C | D | E | F |

8

LYNCH WAY

A417

LONDON RD

WESTBROOK ST

NOTTINGHAM

Watery La

A417

PH

HOLLOW WAY

New Buildings

7

CHURN EST

CHURN EST

85

Alden Farm

Churn Knob

The Kennels

Churn Knob

6

Tile Barn

Saltbox

BOHAMS RD

Rose Cottage

Churn Hill

5

OX11

Upper Chance Farm

84

Gallops

Old Butts

4

Churn Farm

The Firs

Gallops

3

83

Several Down

Gallops

Gallops

Gallops

2

Ridgeway

Compton Downs

Gallops

Gallops

Lower Chance Farm

Blewbury Down

1

Gallops

Ridgeway

SUNRISE HILL

CHURN RD

Ridgeway

82

| 50 | A | B | 51 | C | D | 52 | E | F |

235

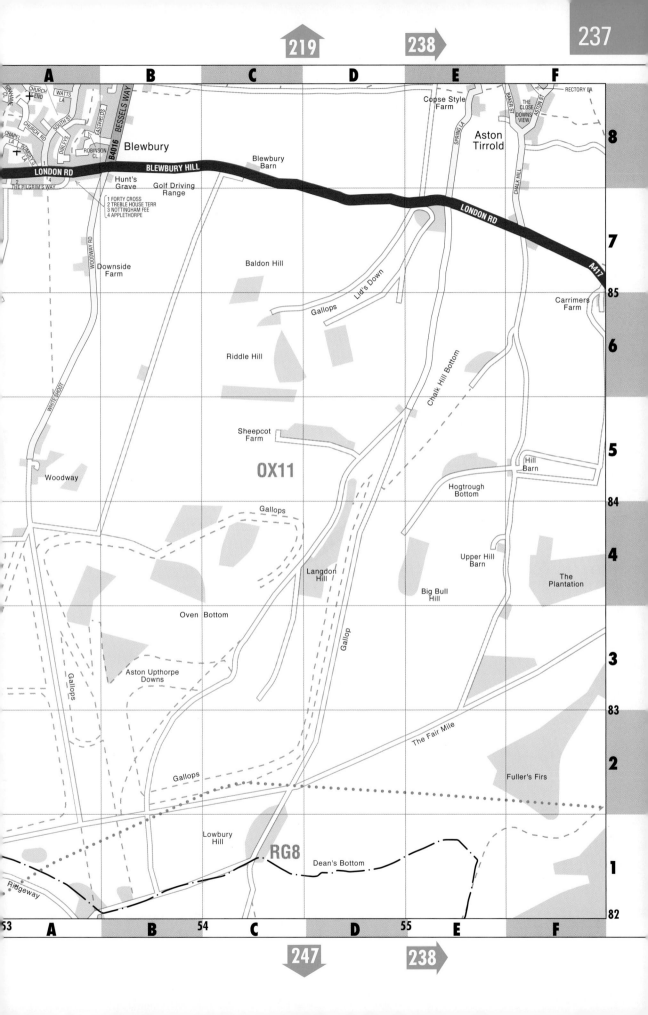

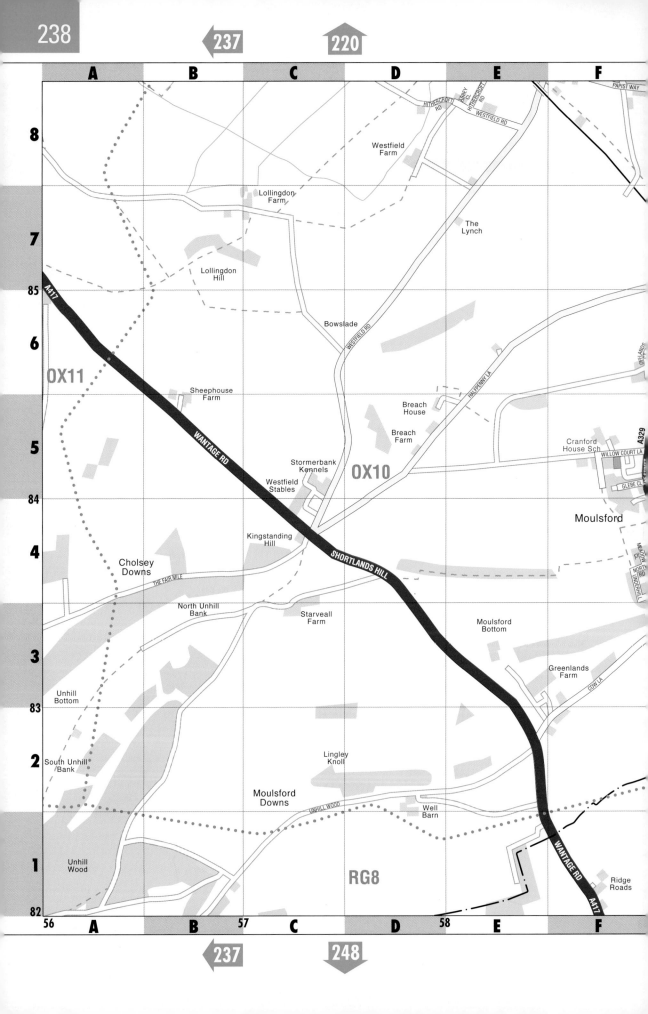

237
220

A B C D E F

8

7

85

6

OX11

5

84

4

3

83

2

1

82

56 57 58

237
248

A417

WANTAGE RD

PAPIST WAY

HITHERCROFT RD
ABBEY CL
HITHERCROFT RD
WESTFIELD RD

Westfield Farm

Lollingdon Farm

The Lynch

Lollingdon Hill

Bowslade

WESTFIELD RD

OFLANDS

A329

Sheephouse Farm

Breach House

HALFPENNY LA

Cranford House Sch

WILLOW COURT LA

Stormerbank Kennels

Breach Farm

OX10

GLEBE CL

Westfield Stables

Moulsford

Kingstanding Hill

SHORTLANDS HILL

MEADOW CL
NORTH CL
UNDERHILL

Cholsey Downs

THE FAIR MILE

North Unhill Bank

Starveall Farm

Moulsford Bottom

Greenlands Farm

COW LA

Unhill Bottom

Lingley Knoll

South Unhill Bank

Moulsford Downs

UNHILL WOOD

Well Barn

WANTAGE RD

Unhill Wood

RG8

Ridge Roads

A417

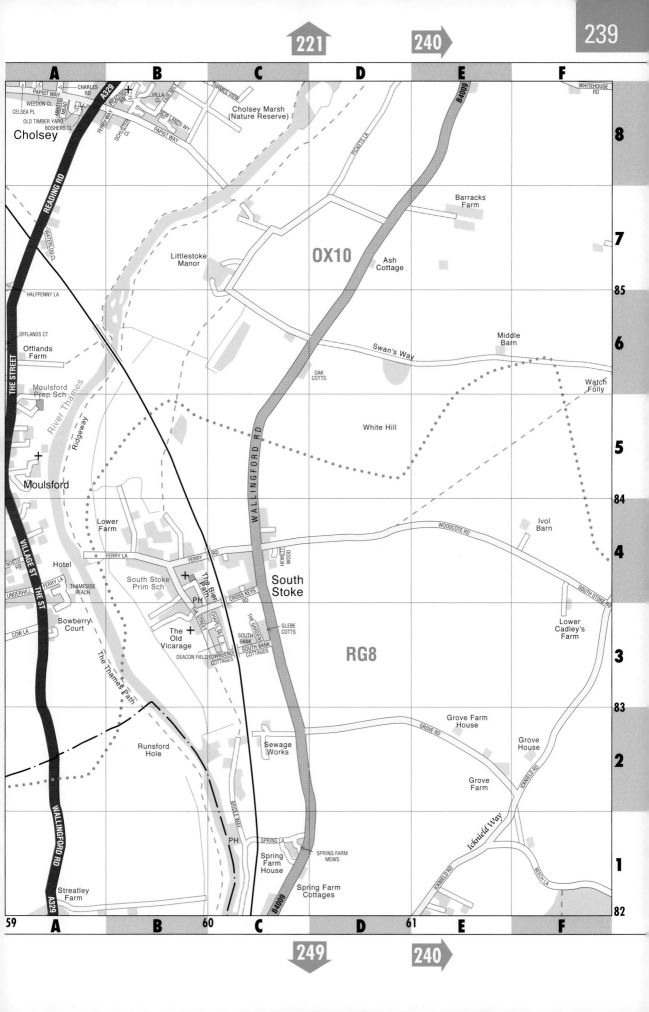

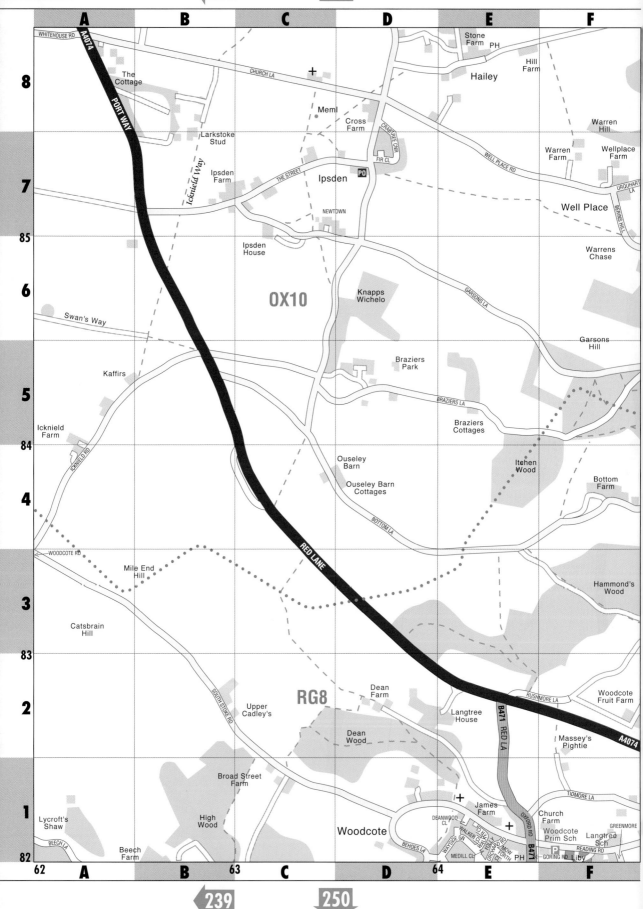

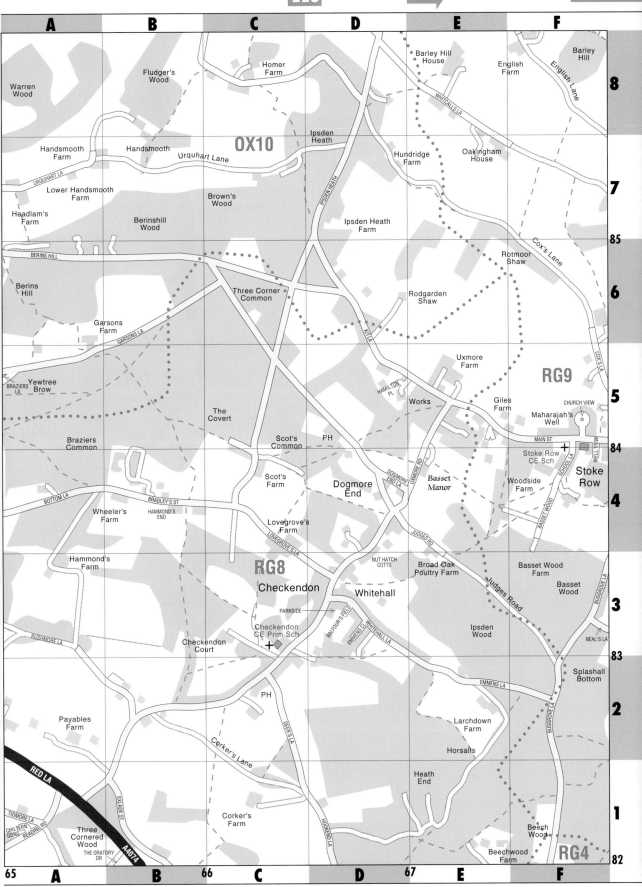

8

Warren Wood

Fludger's Wood

Homer Farm

Barley Hill House

English Farm

Barley Hill

English Lane

WHITCALLS LA

Handsmooth Farm

Handsmooth

Urquhart Lane

OX10

Ipsden Heath

Hundridge Farm

Oakingham House

7

URQUHART LA

Lower Handsmooth Farm

Brown's Wood

IPSDEN HEATH

Headlam's Farm

Berinshill Wood

Ipsden Heath Farm

85

Cox's Lane

BERINS HILL

Rotmoor Shaw

6

Berins Hill

Three Corner Common

Rodgarden Shaw

COX'S LA

Garsons Farm

GARSONS LA

KIT LA

Uxmore Farm

RG9

5

BRAZIERS LA

Yewtree Brow

The Covert

HAMILTON PL

Works

Giles Farm

Maharajah's Well

CHURCH VIEW

Braziers Common

Scot's Common

PH

MAIN ST

Stoke Row CE Sch

WELL VIEW

84

DOGMORE END LA

UXMORE RD

Basset Manor

SCHOOL LA

Stoke Row

Scot's Farm

Dogmore End

Woodside Farm

BASSET WOOD

4

BOTTOM LA

BRADLEY'S ST

HAMMOND'S END

Wheeler's Farm

Lovegrove's Farm

LOVEGROVE S LA

JUDGES RD

Hammond's Farm

RG8

Checkendon

Nut Hatch Cotts

Broad Oak Poultry Farm

Basset Wood Farm

Basset Wood

BUSGROVE LA

3

Whitehall

PARKSIDE

Judges Road

NEAL'S LA

RUSHMORE LA

BALFOUR'S FIELD

EMMENS CL

WHITEHALL LA

Checkendon Court

Checkendon CE Prim Sch

Ipsden Wood

83

EMMENS LA

Splashall Bottom

PH

DEER S LA

Payables Farm

Larchdown Farm

BUSGROVE LA

2

CORKER'S LANE

Horsalls

TIDMORE LA

EXLADE ST

Heath End

CHILTERN GDNS

READING RD

Corker's Farm

HOOKEND LA

Beech Wood

1

RED LA

Three Cornered Wood

THE ORATORY DR

A4074

Beechwood Farm

RG4

82

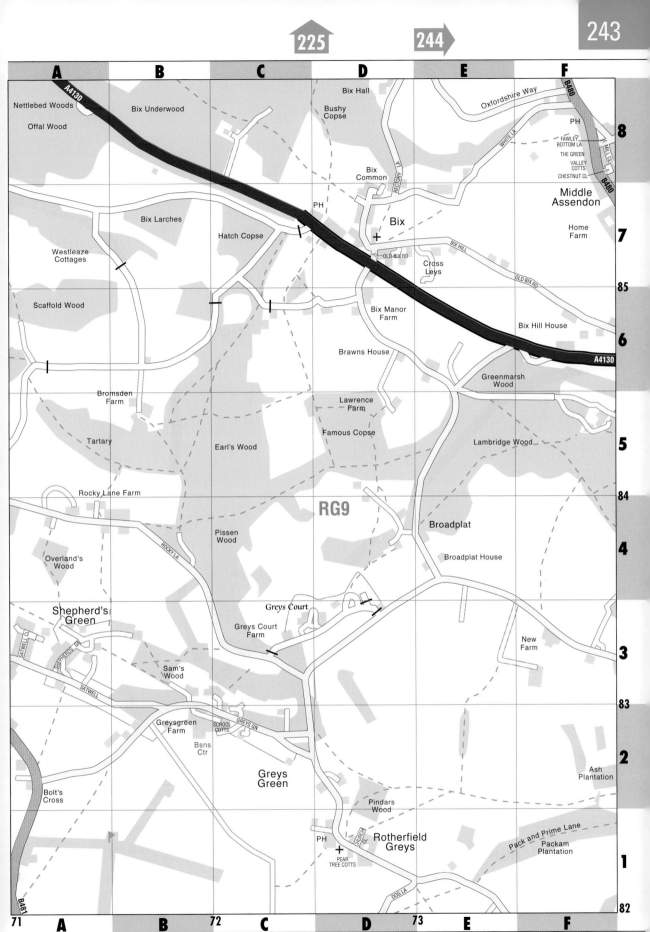

A
B
C
D
E
F

8

7

85

6

5

84

4

3

83

2

1

82

A4130

Nettlebed Woods

Offal Wood

Bix Underwood

Bix Hall

Bushy Copse

B480

Oxfordshire Way

PH

WHITE LA

FAWLEY BOTTOM LA

THE GREEN

VALLEY COTTS

CHESTNUT CL

MILL CL

B480

Middle Assendon

Bix Common

RECTORY LA

Bix Larches

Hatch Copse

PH

Bix

Cross Leys

BIX HILL

Home Farm

Westleaze Cottages

OLD BIX RD

OLD BIX RD

Scaffold Wood

Bix Manor Farm

Bix Hill House

A4130

Brawns House

Greenmarsh Wood

Bromsden Farm

Lawrence Farm

Tartary

Famous Copse

Earl's Wood

Lambridge Wood

RG9

Rocky Lane Farm

Broadplat

Pissen Wood

ROCKY LA

Broadplat House

Overland's Wood

Shepherd's Green

Greys Court

New Farm

SATWELL CL

SHEPHERDS GN

SATWELL

Sam's Wood

Greys Court Farm

Greysgreen Farm

SCHOOL COTTS

GREYS GN

Bsns Ctr

Greys Green

Ash Plantation

Bolt's Cross

Pindars Wood

Pack and Prime Lane

Packam Plantation

PH

CHURCH LA

Rotherfield Greys

PEAR TREE COTTS

DOG LA

B481

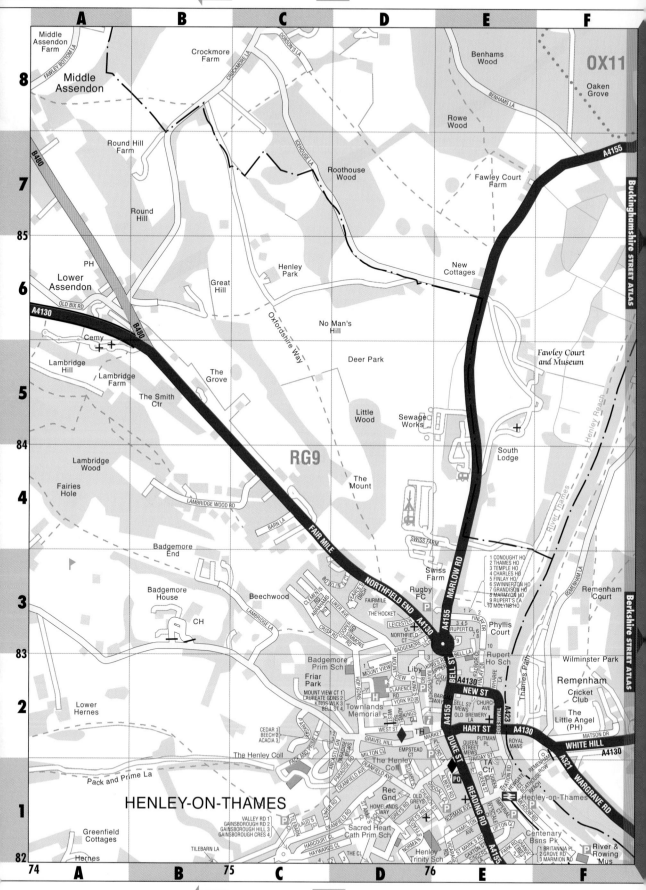

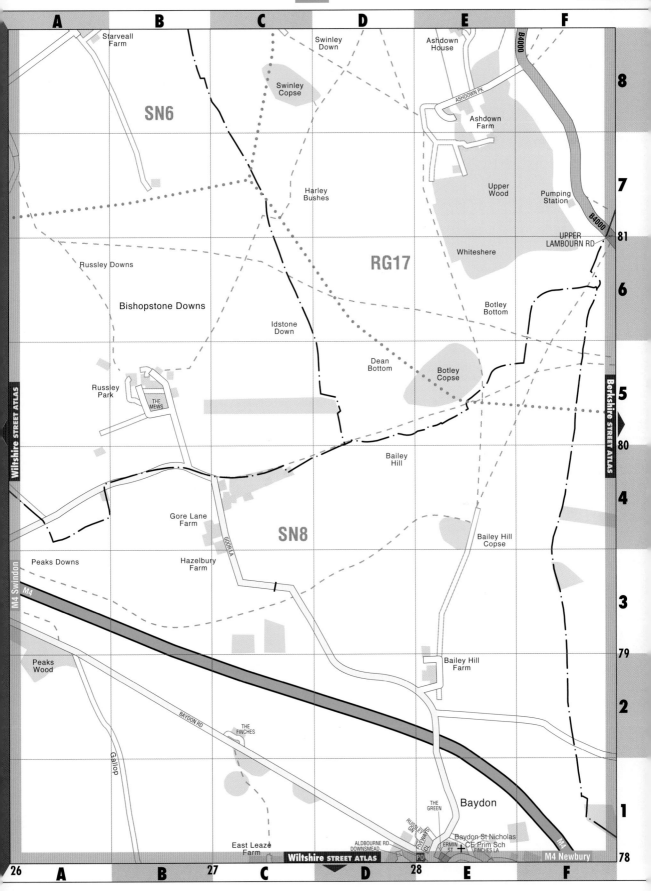

SN6

SN8

RG17

Starveall Farm

Swinley Down

Swinley Copse

Ashdown House

ASHDOWN PK

Ashdown Farm

B4000

Harley Bushes

Upper Wood

Pumping Station

B4000

Whiteshere

UPPER LAMBOURN RD

Russley Downs

Bishopstone Downs

Idstone Down

Botley Bottom

Dean Bottom

Botley Copse

Russley Park

THE MEWS

Bailey Hill

Gore Lane Farm

GORE LA

Bailey Hill Copse

Peaks Downs

Hazelbury Farm

M4 Swindon

M4

M4

Peaks Wood

Bailey Hill Farm

BAYDON RD

THE FINCHES

Gallop

THE GREEN

Baydon

RUSSLEY RD

FILEWAY CL

ERMIN ST

Baydon St Nicholas CE Prim Sch

FINCHES LA

East Leaze Farm

ALDBOURNE RD
DOWNSMEAD

PO

M4 Newbury

M4

81

8

7

6

5

80

4

3

79

2

1

78

26   A   B   27   C   D   28   E   F

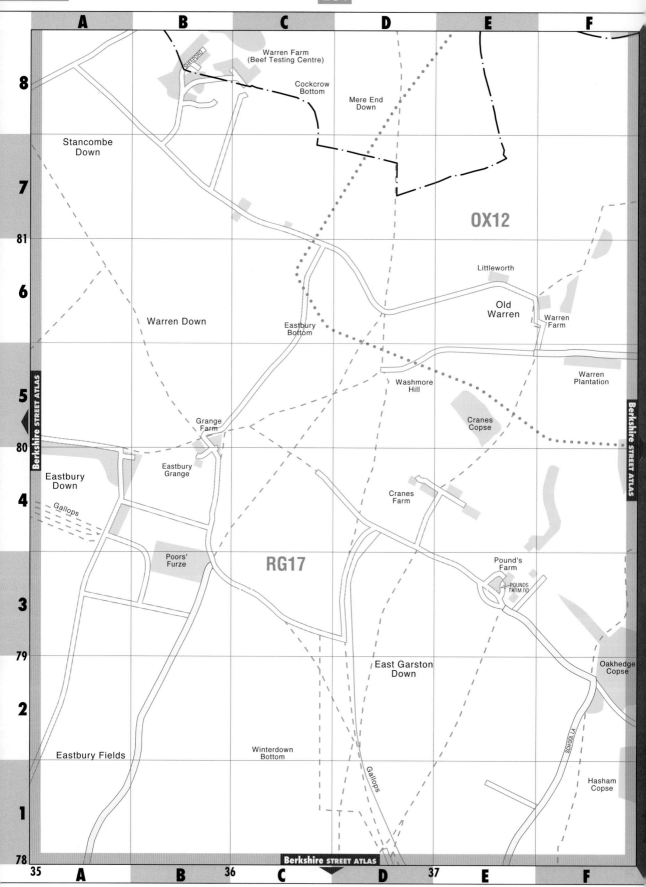

A　B　C　D　E　F

8

7

81

6

5

80

4

79

3

2

1

78

35　A　B　36　C　D　37　E　F

Stancombe
Down

Warren Farm
(Beef Testing Centre)

SHEPDRO.

Cockcrow
Bottom

Mere End
Down

OX12

Littleworth

Old
Warren

Warren
Farm

Warren Down

Eastbury
Bottom

Washmore
Hill

Warren
Plantation

Cranes
Copse

Grange
Farm

Eastbury
Grange

Eastbury
Down

Gallops

Cranes
Farm

Pound's
Farm

POUNDS
FARM RD

Poors'
Furze

RG17

Oakhedge
Copse

Eastbury Fields

Winterdown
Bottom

East Garston
Down

SCHOOL LA

Hasham
Copse

Gallops

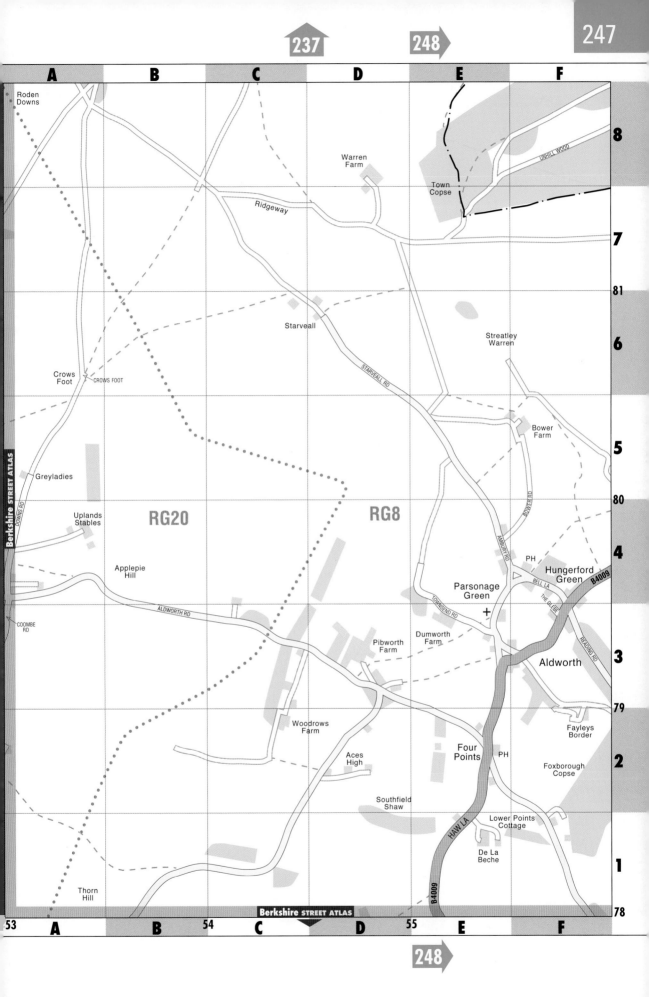

Roden Downs

Warren Farm

Ridgeway

Town Copse

UNHILL WOOD

Starveall

STARVEALL RD

Streatley Warren

Crows Foot
CROWS FOOT

Bower Farm

BOWKER RD

Greyladies

RG20

RG8

PH

Uplands Stables

Hungerford Green

Applepie Hill

AMBURY RD

BELL LA

B4009

Parsonage Green

THE GLEBE

READING RD

DOWNS RD

ALDWORTH RD

COOMBE RD

TOWNSEND RD

Dumworth Farm

Aldworth

Pibworth Farm

Woodrows Farm

Fayleys Border

Aces High

Four Points

PH

Foxborough Copse

Southfield Shaw

HAW LA

Lower Points Cottage

De La Beche

B4009

Thorn Hill

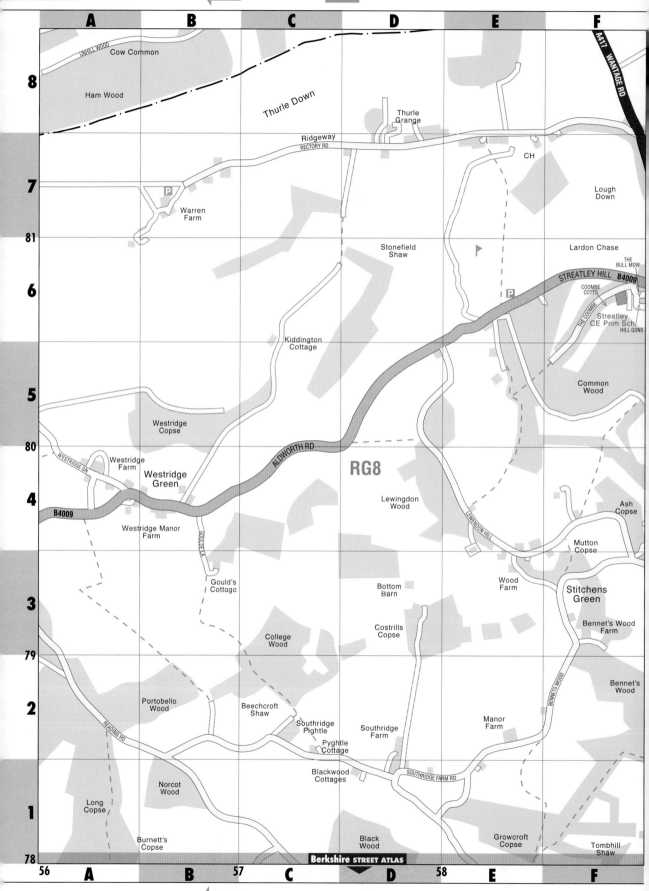

A | **B** | **C** | **D** | **E** | **F**

UNHILL WOOD

Cow Common

Ham Wood

Thurle Down

Thurle Grange

Ridgeway

RECTORY RD

CH

Lough Down

P

Warren Farm

Stonefield Shaw

Lardon Chase

THE BULL MDW

STREATLEY HILL **B4009**

COOMBE COTTS

Kiddington Cottage

P

Streatley CE Prim Sch

HILL GDNS

Common Wood

WESTRIDGE GN

Westridge Copse

ALDWORTH RD

RG8

Westridge Farm

Westridge Green

B4009

Lewingdon Wood

Ash Copse

Westridge Manor Farm

GOULD'S LA

LEWENDON HILL

Mutton Copse

Wood Farm

Stitchens Green

Gould's Cottage

Bottom Barn

Bennet's Wood Farm

College Wood

Costrills Copse

Bennet's Wood

BENNET'S WOOD

Portobello Wood

Beechcroft Shaw

Southridge Pightle

Southridge Farm

Manor Farm

READING RD

Pyghtle Cottage

Blackwood Cottages

SOUTHRIDGE FARM RD

Norcot Wood

Long Copse

Black Wood

Growcroft Copse

Tombhill Shaw

Burnett's Copse

56 | **A** | **B** | 57 | **C** | **D** | 58 | **E** | **F**

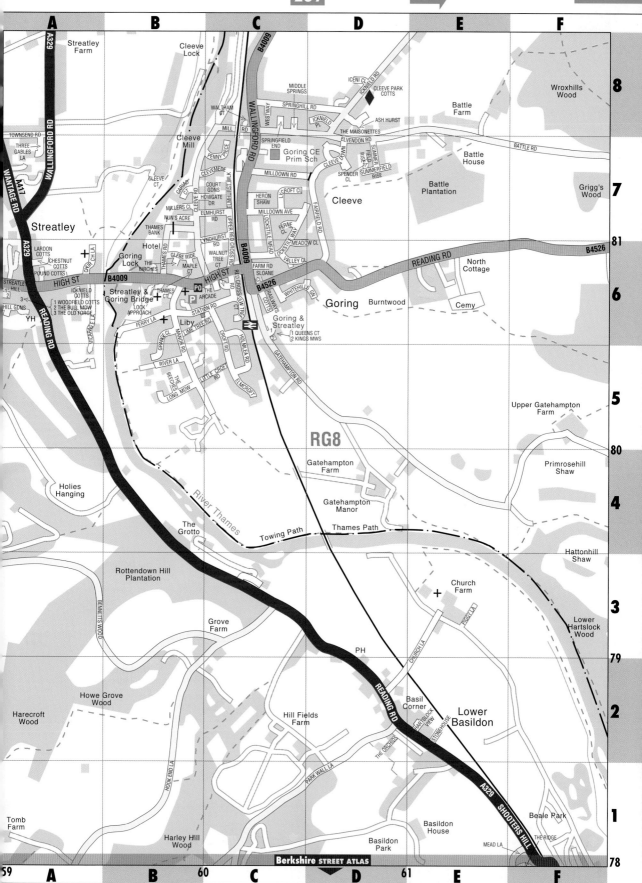

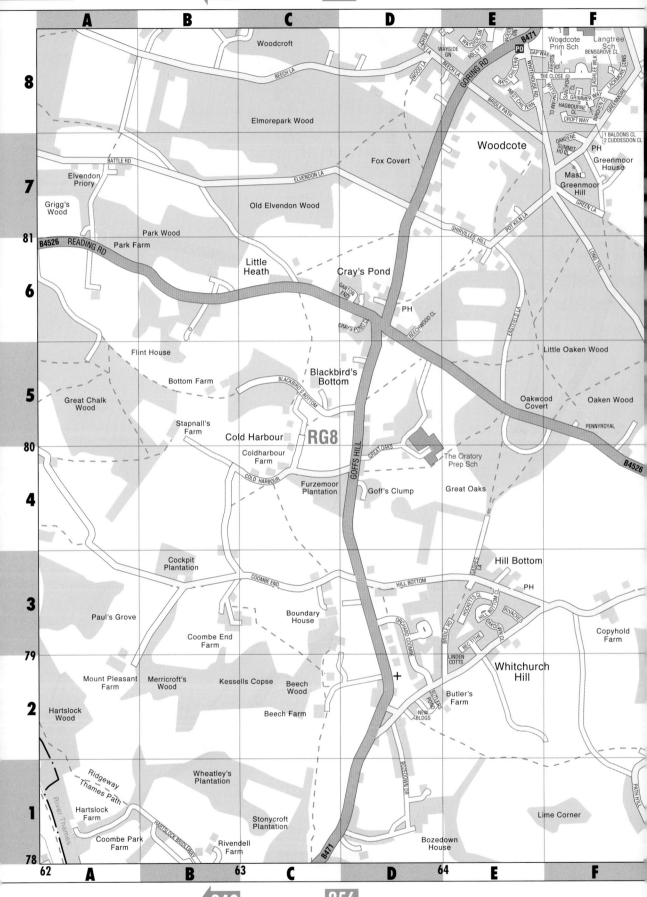

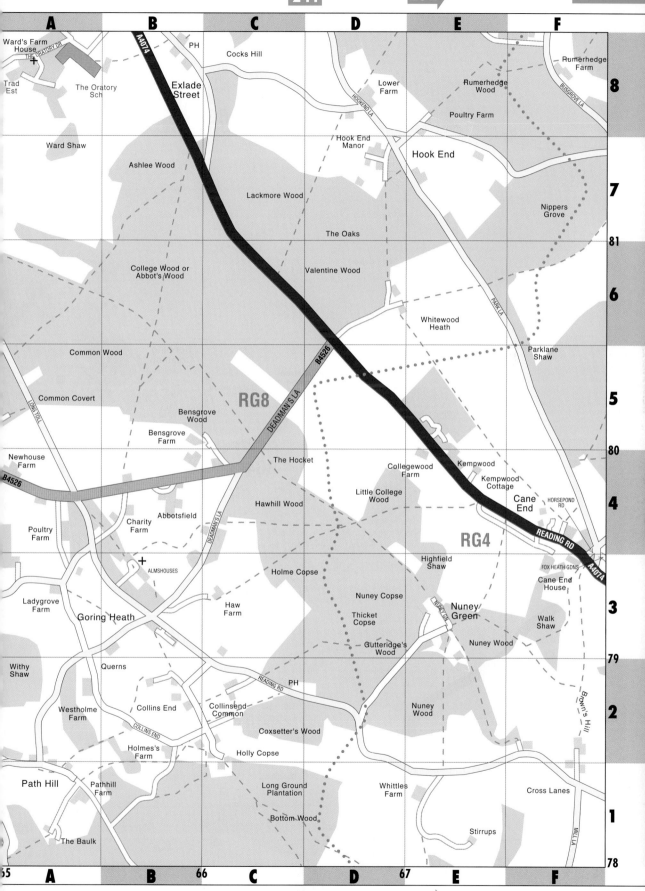

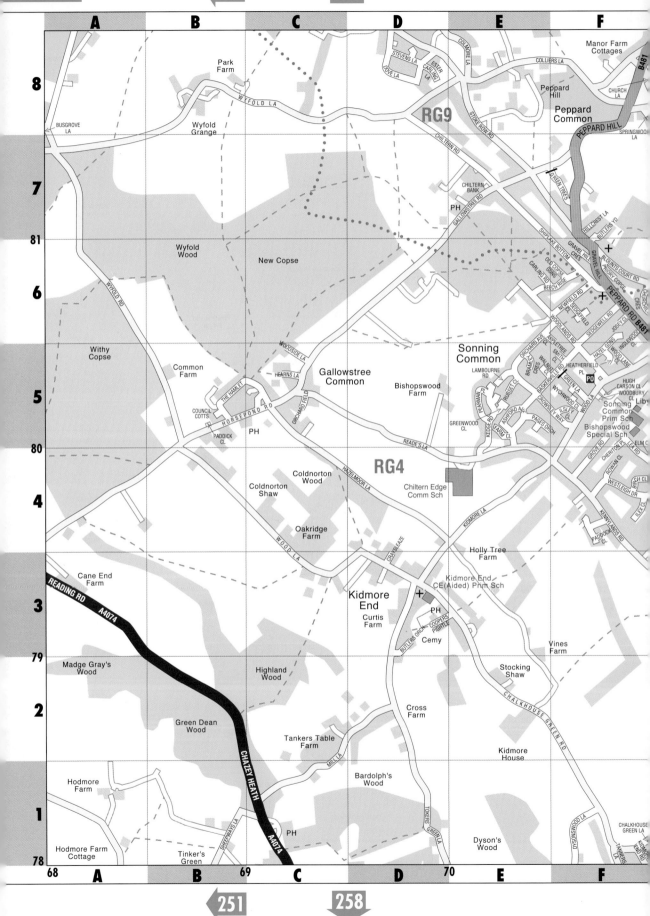

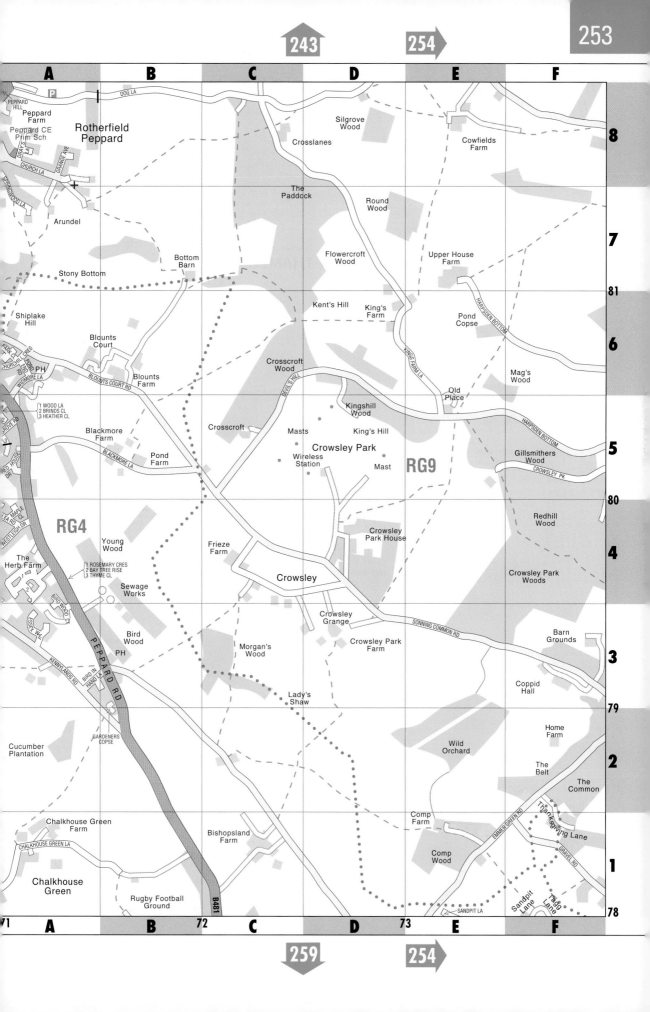

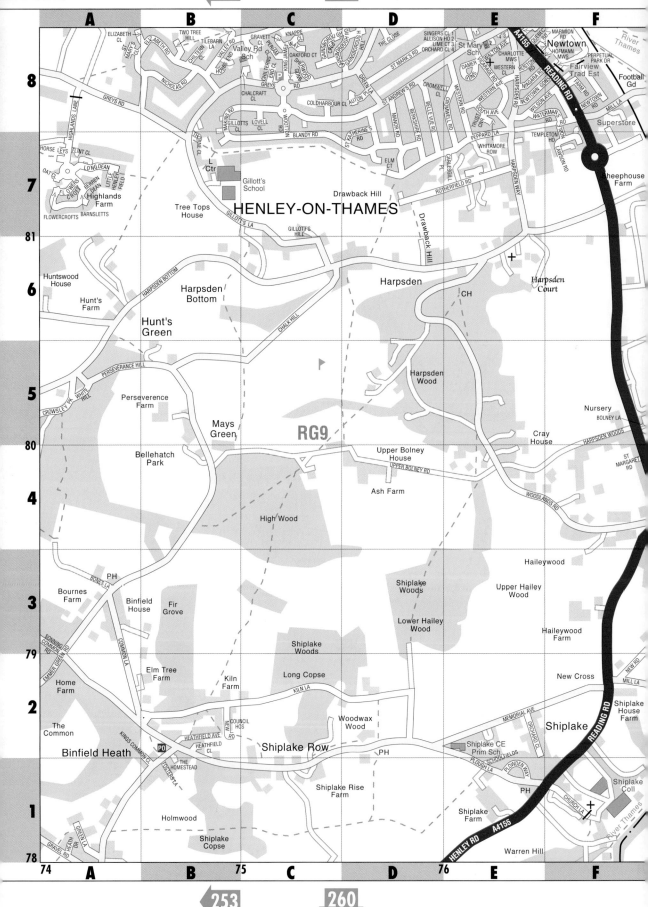

253
244
253
260

HENLEY-ON-THAMES

RG9

Newtown

Harpsden

Harpsden Bottom

Hunt's Green

Perseverence Farm

Mays Green

Bellehatch Park

High Wood

Shiplake Woods

Shiplake Row

Binfield Heath

Shiplake

Shiplake Coll

Warren Hill

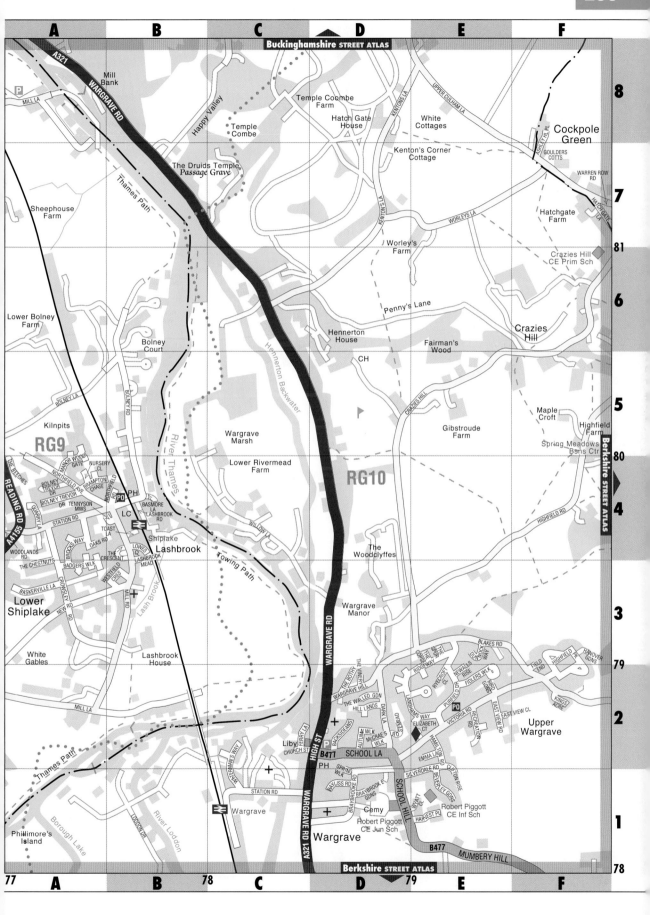

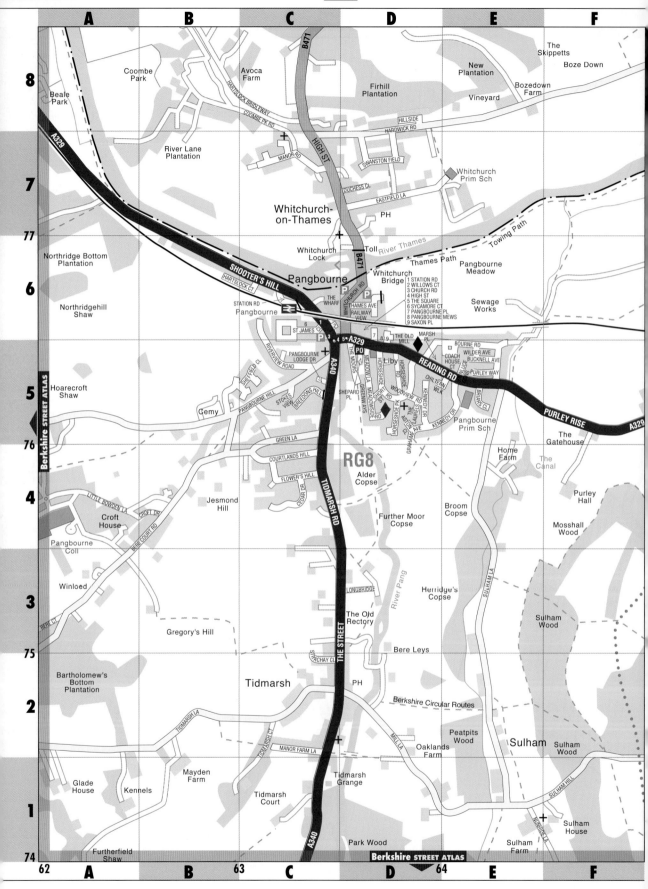

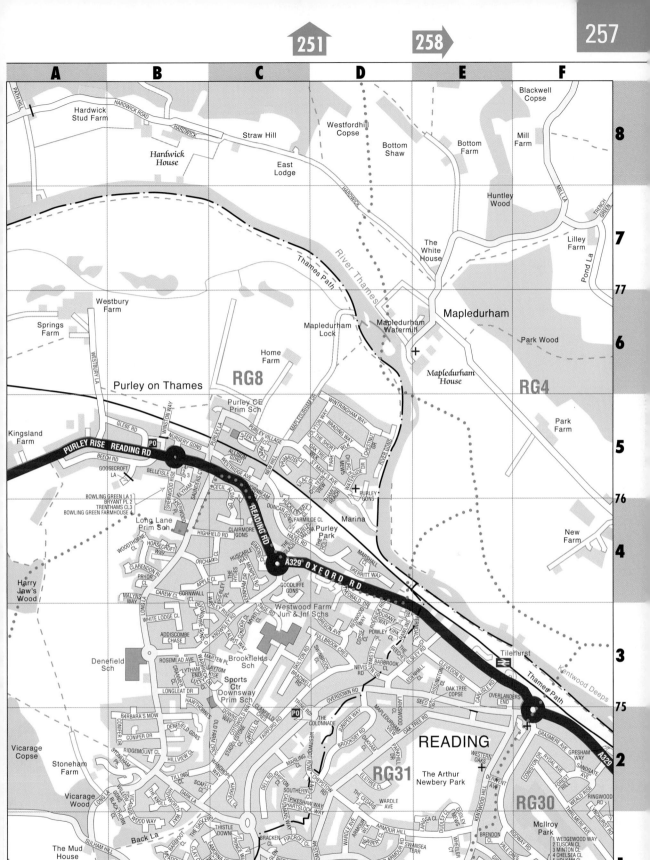

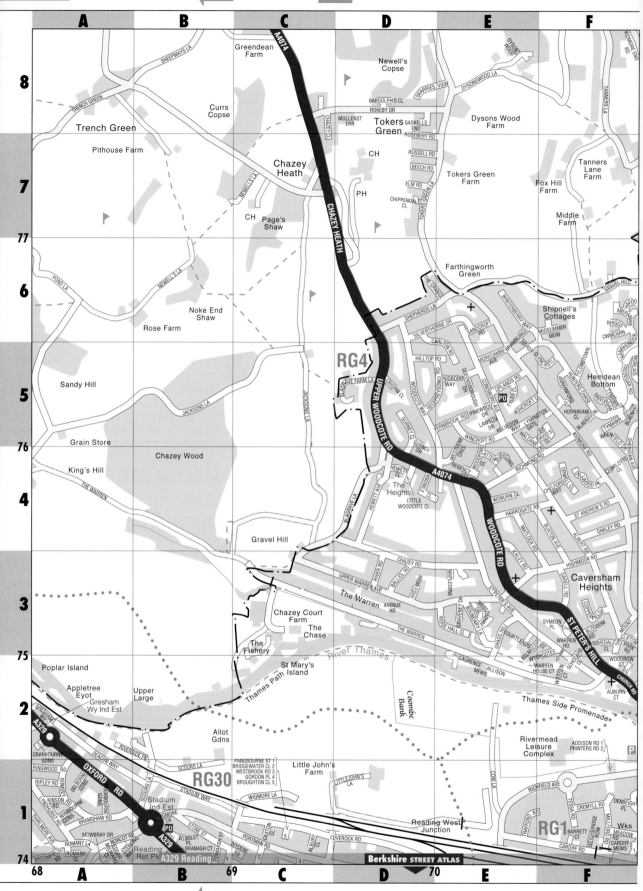

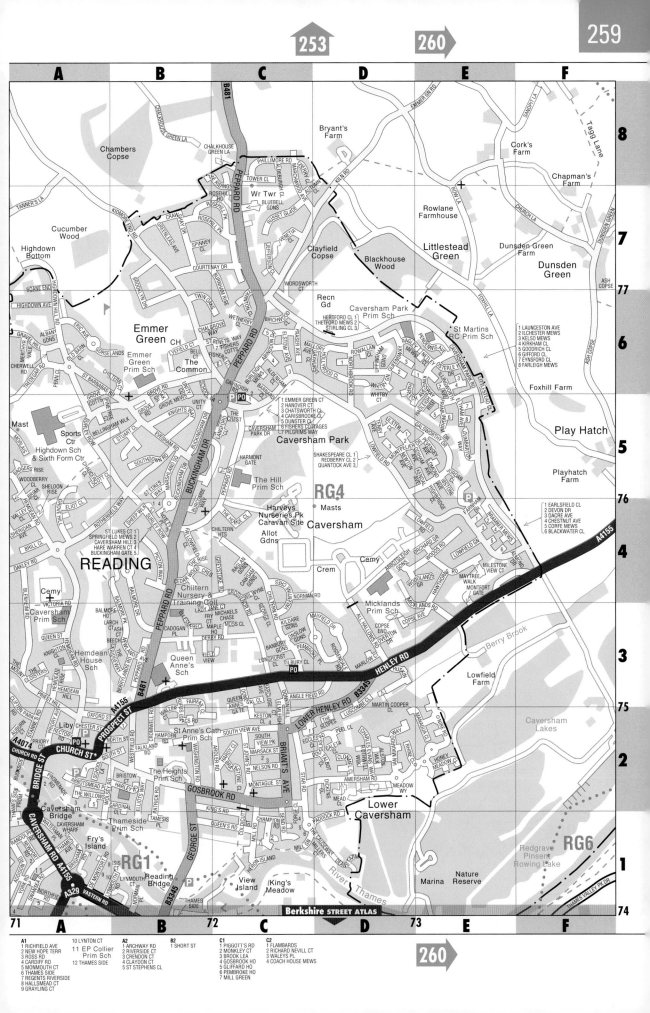

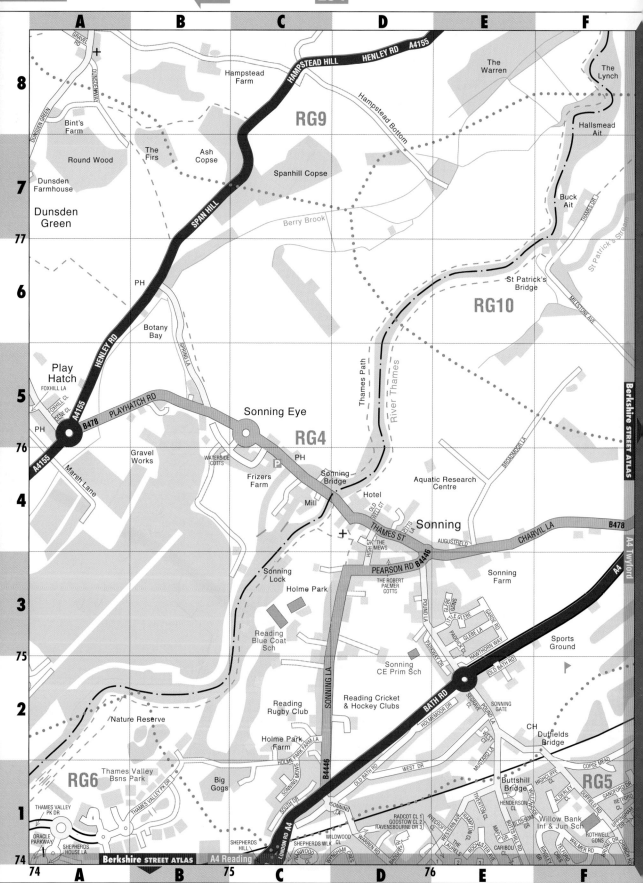

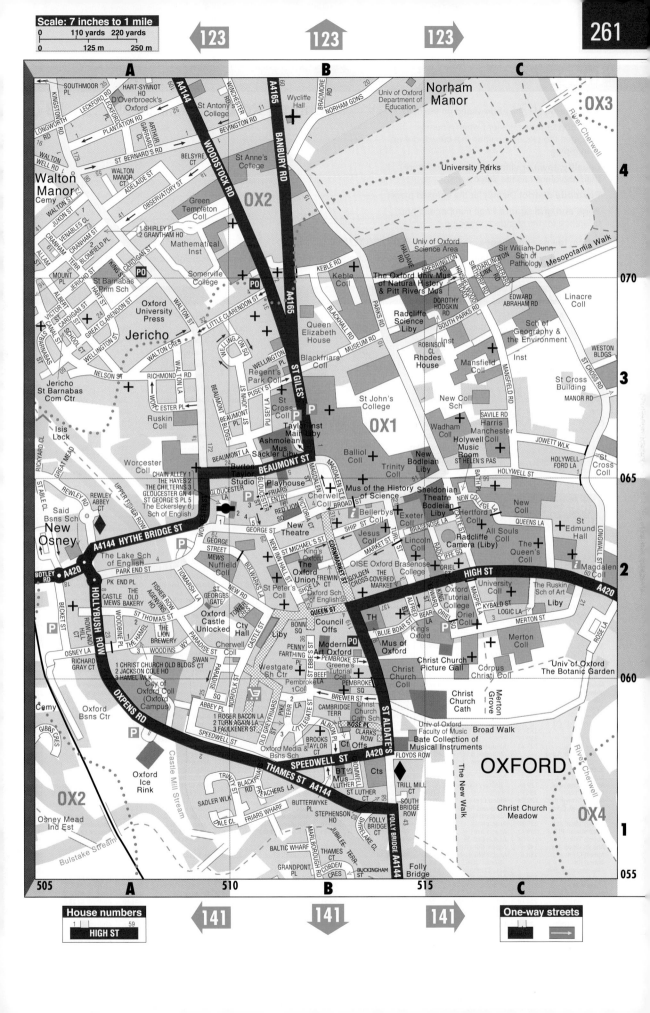

Index

Place name May be abbreviated on the map → **Church Rd** **6** Beckenham BR2..........**53** C6

Location number Present when a number indicates the place's position in a crowded area of mapping

Locality, town or village Shown when more than one place has the same name

Postcode district District for the indexed place

Page and grid square Page number and grid reference for the standard mapping

Cities, towns and villages are listed in CAPITAL LETTERS

Public and commercial buildings are highlighted in **magenta**   **Places of interest** are highlighted in blue with a star ★

Abbreviations used in the index

Acad	**Academy**	Comm	**Common**	Gd	**Ground**	L	**Leisure**	Prom	**Promenade**
App	**Approach**	Cott	**Cottage**	Gdn	**Garden**	La	**Lane**	Rd	**Road**
Arc	**Arcade**	Cres	**Crescent**	Gn	**Green**	Liby	**Library**	Recn	**Recreation**
Ave	**Avenue**	Cswy	**Causeway**	Gr	**Grove**	Mdw	**Meadow**	Ret	**Retail**
Bglw	**Bungalow**	Ct	**Court**	H	**Hall**	Meml	**Memorial**	Sh	**Shopping**
Bldg	**Building**	Ctr	**Centre**	Ho	**House**	Mkt	**Market**	Sq	**Square**
Bsns, Bus	**Business**	Ctry	**Country**	Hospl	**Hospital**	Mus	**Museum**	St	**Street**
Bvd	**Boulevard**	Cty	**County**	HQ	**Headquarters**	Orch	**Orchard**	Sta	**Station**
Cath	**Cathedral**	Dr	**Drive**	Hts	**Heights**	Pal	**Palace**	Terr	**Terrace**
Cir	**Circus**	Dro	**Drove**	Ind	**Industrial**	Par	**Parade**	TH	**Town Hall**
Cl	**Close**	Ed	**Education**	Inst	**Institute**	Pas	**Passage**	Univ	**University**
Cnr	**Corner**	Emb	**Embankment**	Int	**International**	Pk	**Park**	Wk, Wlk	**Walk**
Coll	**College**	Est	**Estate**	Intc	**Interchange**	Pl	**Place**	Wr	**Water**
Com	**Community**	Ex	**Exhibition**	Junc	**Junction**	Prec	**Precinct**	Yd	**Yard**

Index of towns, villages, streets, hospitals, industrial estates, railway stations, schools, shopping centres, universities and places of interest

Aba–Ane

A

Abacus Coll OX3. . . . . 124 D3
Abberbury Ave OX4. . . 142 A4
Abberbury Rd OX4. . . . 141 F4
Abbey Brook OX11. . . 200 E3
Abbey Cl OX14. . . . . . 179 F7
Abbey Ctr OX14. . . . . . 180 A7
Abbey Fishponds Nature
  Reserve★ OX14 . . . . 160 C1
Abbey Mdws Outdoor Pool
  OX14 . . . . 180 A7
Abbey Pl OX29. . . . . . 120 E7
Abbey Rd Banbury OX16. 16 A7
  Oxford OX2 . . . . 123 A1
  Watchfield SN6 . . . . . 191 F2
  Witney OX28 . . . . 117 F7
Abbey Sports Ctr
  OX10 . . . . 182 C5
Abbey St OX29. . . . . . 120 E7
Abbey Wlk OX1. . . . . . 123 A1
Abbey Woods Acad
  OX10 . . . . 182 C5
Abbey Woods Cl OX10 182 C5
Abbot Cres OX14 . . . . 179 B1
Abbot Ridge HP18 . . . 218 C8
Abbots Cl RG8. . . . . . 250 F8
Abbots Grange OX13. . 178 D6
Abbotsleigh Gdns
  RG4. . . . . 259 D4
Abbots Mead OX10 . . . 239 A8
Abbotsmead Pl RG4 . . 259 A2
Abbots Wlk GL7 . . . . . 150 D4
Abbots Wood OX3 . . . 142 E8
Abbott Cl OX11. . . . . . 218 E1
Abbott Rd
  Abingdon-on-Thames
  OX14. . . . . 179 F8
  Didcot OX11 . . . . 218 E7
Abelwood Rd OX29 . . . 90 A1
Aberaman RG4 . . . . . 258 F6
Abingdon Bsns Pk
  OX14 . . . . 179 C7
Abingdon Cl OX9 . . . . 129 F1
Abingdon County Hall
  Mus★ OX14 . . . . 179 F7
Abingdon Dr RG4. . . . 259 C6
Abingdon Hospl OX14 179 C7

Abingdon La OX29. . . . 117 A3
ABINGDON-ON-
  THAMES 179 E7
Abingdon Prep Sch
  OX13 . . . . 178 A7
Abingdon Rd
  Carterton OX18. . . . . . 115 E3
  Clifton Hampden OX14 . 181 D4
  Culham OX14. . . . . . . 180 C3
  Cumnor OX2 . . . . 139 E4
  Didcot OX11 . . . . 201 B1
  Dorchester OX10 . . . . 182 C3
  Drayton OX14 . . . . . . 179 B2
  Kingston Bagpuize
  OX13. . . . . 177 A8
  Marcham OX13 . . . . . 178 D6
  Rowstock OX11. . . . . . 217 B7
  Standlake OX29. . . . . . 137 C3
  Steventon OX13. . . . . . 199 A5
  Sutton Courtenay OX14 180 B2
  Tubney OX13. . . . . . . 157 E2
  West Ilsley RG20 . . . . 235 E1
Abingdon Sch OX14 . . 179 E7
Abingdon Science Pk
  OX14 . . . . 180 B7
Abingdon Terr OX11 . . 218 C8
Abingdon & Witney Coll
  (Abingdon Campus)
  OX14 . . . . 159 E1
Abingdon & Witney Coll
  (Witney Campus) **9**
  OX28 . . . . 118 A8
Ablett Cl OX4. . . . . . . 142 A8
Abrahams Rd RG9 . . . 244 C3
Abraham Way OX29. . . 102 D2
Acacia RG9. . . . . 244 D2
Acacia Ave OX4. . . . . . 142 E1
Acacia Cl OX18 . . . . . 115 E1
Acacia Gdns OX13 . . . 156 E1
Acacia Wlk Banbury OX16 9 B1
  Bicester OX26. . . . . . . 65 E5
Acer Cl OX18 . . . . 114 D7
Ackerman Rd OX7 . . . . 42 F3
Acland Cl OX3. . . . . . 124 C1
Acorn Cl OX26. . . . . . . 65 E5
Acorns Prim Sch CF36. . 27 F6
Acorn Way OX16. . . . . . . 9 F1
Acre Cl OX3 . . . . 142 F7
Acre Ditch OX15. . . . . . 19 A8
Acre End Cl OX29. . . . 120 E7
Acre End St OX29. . . . 120 E7
Acremead Rd OX33. . . 143 F8
Acres Field OX16 . . . . . 8 E1

Action for Children
  Parklands Campus
  OX13 . . . . 158 C7
Adam Ct RG9. . . . . . . 244 E2
Adams Cl OX16 . . . . . . 16 A2
ADDERBURY. 23 A3
Adderbury Ct OX17 . . . 23 A4
Adderbury Pk OX17. . . . 22 F3
Addiscombe Chase
  RG31. . . . . 257 B3
Addison Cres OX4 . . . 141 F6
Addison Dr OX4 . . . . . 142 C3
Addison Rd
  Banbury OX16. . . . . . . 16 C3
  Reading RG1 . . . . 259 A1
  1 Reading RG30 . . . . 258 F1
Adeane Rd OX44. . . . . 184 C7
Adelaide St OX2. . . . . 261 A4
Adkin Way OX12. . . . . 214 D6
ADLESTROP 40 D2
Adlestrop Rd GL56. . . . 40 A4
Admiral Holland Cl
  OX16. . . . . 16 A6
ADWELL. 166 D3
Adwell Sq RG9. . . . . . 244 D2
Aelfrith Ct OX13 . . . . 157 A1
Aerodrome La OX29 . . 117 B8
Agatha Christie Way
  OX10. . . . . 221 A1
Agenvins Ho OX1. . . . 261 A2
Agnes Ct OX4 . . . . . . 142 C6
Aintree Wy OX26. . . . . . 65 B1
Aird Row OX14 . . . . . 159 E2
Akeman Ave OX25. . . . 81 D4
Akeman Cl OX5. . . . . . 78 A5
Akeman Rd OX29 . . . . 105 B6
Akemanrise OX7. . . . . . 88 A3
Akeman
  Spinney OX5. . . . . 78 A5
Akeman St
  Chesterton OX26. . . . . 79 C6
  Combe OX29 . . . . 89 F8
  Combe OX29 . . . . 90 A6
  Kirtlington OX5 . . . . . . 78 D6
  Ramsden OX7 . . . . . . 88 A3
  Stonesfield OX29. . . . . 74 F1
  Whiteoak Green OX29 . . 87 F2
Alan Bullock Cl OX4 . . 123 E1
Alan Ct HP14 . . . . 188 E4
Albany Gdns RG4. . . . 259 A6
Albemarle Dr OX2 . . . 214 D8
Albert Beckhelling Dr
  OX12. . . . . 214 F4

Albert Rd
  Henley-on-Thames
  RG9. . . . . 244 E1
  Reading RG4 . . . . 258 F4
Albert St Banbury OX16 . 16 D5
  Oxford OX2 . . . . 261 A3
Albion Pl
  Bampton OX18 . . . . . . 134 E3
  Chipping Norton OX7 . . . 42 F3
  Oxford OX1 . . . . 261 B1
Albion Row OX7 . . . . . . 42 F1
Albion St OX7 . . . . 42 E3
ALBURY. 146 B7
Albury Cl RG30 . . . . . 258 C1
Albury View OX9 . . . . 146 A6
Alchester Rd OX26. . . . 80 A7
Alchester Terr **3** OX26 .65 F1
Aldbarton Dr OX3. . . . 124 E4
Aldbourne Cl **1** OX26. . 65 D2
Aldbourne Rd SN8. . . . 245 C1
Aldeburgh Cl RG4 . . . 259 C8
Alden Cres OX3. . . . . 124 F4
Aldenham Cl RG4. . . . 259 C6
Alder Dr OX25. . . . . . . 81 C4
Aldergate Rd OX26. . . . 65 C2
Alderley Cl
  Carterton OX18. . . . . . 115 D1
  Sonning RG5 . . . . 260 F1
Aldiss Dr
  Kingston Bagpuize
  OX13. . . . . 156 F1
  Kingston Bagpuize
  OX13. . . . . 157 A1
Aldous Dr OX15. . . . . . 21 E3
Aldrich Rd OX2 . . . . . 123 B8
Aldridge Cl OX10 . . . . 204 A4
Aldsworth Ct OX28. . . . 117 E8
Alder Cres OX3. . . . . . 124 F4
ALDWORTH. 247 F3
Aldworth Ave OX12. . . 214 F6
Aldworth Cl OX12. . . . 197 B6
Aldworth Rd
  Aldworth RG8 . . . . . . 247 B3
  Westridge Green RG8. . 248 C4
Alec Issigonis Way
  OX4. . . . . 142 D5
Alesworth Gr OX3 . . . 124 B5
Alexander Cl
  Abingdon-on-Thames
  OX14. . . . . 160 A3
  Kidlington OX5. . . . . . 108 F6
Alexander Way SN6. . . 209 A6
Alexandra Rd OX2 . . . 122 F1

Alexandra Sq OX7 . . . . 42 D1
Alfreds Pl
  East Hanney OX12 . . . 197 C7
  East Hanney OX12 . . . 197 C7
Alfred St Oxford OX1. . . 261 B2
  3 Wantage OX12. . . . 214 D4
Alfredston Pl OX12 . . . 214 E4
Alfred Terraces OX7. . . . 42 E2
Alfred Woods Ct **14**
  SN7 . . . . 172 F3
Alfriston Pl OX16 . . . . . . 9 A1
Alhambra La OX4. . . . 141 E8
Alice Batt Rd OX29. . . 117 C8
Alice Smith Sq OX4. . . 142 C2
Alison Clay Ho OX3 . . 124 C2
Alister Taylor Ave
  OX10. . . . . 204 C2
ALKERTON. 6 F2
Alkerton Hill
  Alkerton OX16. . . . . 7 A1
  Balscote OX15. . . . . . . 14 B7
Allam St Oxford OX1 . . 123 A3
  Oxford OX2 . . . . 261 A4
Allder Cl OX14. . . . . . 159 F2
Allectus Ave OX25 . . . . 81 D4
Allens La OX25 . . . . . . 48 E1
Allens Orch OX17. . . . . . 5 F6
Alley The OX7 . . . . 73 B4
All Hallows Rd RG4 . . 259 D3
Allin Cl OX4 . . . . 142 E3
Allins La OX12. . . . . . 216 D7
Allison Gdns RG8. . . . 257 C5
Allison Ho RG9 . . . . . 254 E8
Allnatt Ave OX10. . . . . 221 C8
Allnut Cl OX49. . . . . . 186 B1
Allnutts Cl HP14. . . . . 188 D5
All Saints CE Prim Sch
  OX11. . . . . 201 A2
All Saints Cl OX13 . . . 178 C6
All Saints Ct OX11 . . . 200 E2
All Saints La OX14 . . . 180 B1
All Saints Rd OX3. . . . 124 C2
All Soul's Coll OX1 . . . 261 C2
Alma Gn RG9. . . . . . . 242 A4
Alma Pl OX4 . . . . 141 F8
Alma Rd **10** OX16 . . . . 16 E6
Almhouses OX28 . . . . 104 C1
Almond Ave OX5 . . . . 108 E6
Almond Dr RG4. . . . . 259 F4
Almond Rd OX26 . . . . . 65 E3
Almshouses
  Bourton SN6 . . . . 209 A2

Almshouses continued
  Goring Heath RG8. . . . 251 B3
  Lyford OX12. . . . . 176 C1
  Worminghall HP18 . . . 127 E5
Almshouses The OX5 . . 92 F2
Alpha Ave OX44 . . . . . 143 C1
Alphin Brook OX11. . . 200 E3
Alston Wlk RG4. . . . . 259 D2
Altus St OX25. . . . . 63 A8
ALVESCOT. 133 C6
Alvescot Rd
  Alvescot OX18. . . . . . . 133 E5
  Carterton OX18. . . . . . 115 C2
Alvis Gate OX16 . . . . . 15 F8
Ambassador Ave OX4. 142 E4
Ambassador Ct **1**
  OX26. . . . . 65 F1
Amberley Ct **5** OX16 . . . 9 A1
Ambleside Dr OX3 . . . 124 B4
Ambros Cl OX25 . . . . . 81 C3
AMBROSDEN 81 D3
Ambrose Rise OX33. . . 144 C8
Ambury Rd RG8. . . . . 247 E4
Amersham Rd RG4 . . . 259 D2
Amey Cl OX14 . . . . . . 180 B1
Amey Cres OX13. . . . . 159 B6
Ammanford RG4. . . . . 258 F5
Amory Cl OX4 . . . . . . 142 D3
Amos Ct OX16 . . . . 16 D5
Ampney Orch OX18. . . 134 F3
Ampthill Way **4** SN7 . 172 E1
Amwell Pl OX10 . . . . . 220 F1
Amyce Cl OX14 . . . . . 160 B2
Ancastle Gn RG9 . . . . 244 D2
Ancholme Ct OX11. . . 200 F2
Anchor La OX11 . . . . . 220 A4
Ancil Ave OX26 . . . . . . 66 D2
Andersey Way OX14 . . 179 F4
Anderson Cl HP14 . . . 188 F4
Anderson Pl OX12 . . . 197 C7
Andersons Cl OX5 . . . 108 C8
Andover Cl
  Bicester OX26. . . . . . . 66 A4
  Reading RG31 . . . . . . 257 D1
Andover Ct **1** OX5. . . 108 F8
Andover La OX18 . . . . 115 F2
Andover Rd OX10. . . . 204 D3
Andrew Rd OX10 . . . . 203 B1
Andrews Ave NN13 . . . . 36 E6
Andrews Way OX18. . . 135 A3
Andromeda Cl OX4 . . . 142 F1
Anemone Cl OX4 . . . . 161 E8

Angelica Cl
Hardwick OX16 9 A2
Oxford OX4 142 F1
Angle Field Rd RG4 259 D3
Anglesey Ct HP14 188 E5
Angus Cl OX16 16 A8
Anna Pavlova Cl OX14 179 D7
Anne Greenwood Cl
OX4 142 A4
Annesley Cl OX5 93 A8
Annesley Rd OX4 142 A4
Anniversary Avenue W
OX26 80 F7
Anniversary Ave W OX25,
OX26 80 E5
Anniversary Ave West
OX26 81 A6
Annora Cl OX4 142 A5
Ansell Way OX7 70 B1
Anson Ave OX18 115 E1
Anson Cl
Marcham OX13 178 D6
Wheatley OX33 144 C8
Anson Ct GL54 68 B3
Anson Dr SN6 191 C2
Anson Rd OX10 204 D3
Anson Way OX26 66 A3
Anstee Cl OX16 16 A2
Anthony Hill Rd OX10 204 C1
Anvil Ct SN7 194 E7
Anvil La OX12 214 A1
Anvil Paddock OX12 214 A1
Anxey Way HP17 130 F6
AP Ellis Rd GL54 68 B3
Apiary Pl OX10 220 F1
Apley Way OX28 117 E8
Apollo Bsns Pk OX15 7 F2
Appleby Cl OX16 15 E7
Appleby Ct OX13 156 F1
Apple Cl RG31 257 B4
Apple Down OX11 200 B2
APPLEFORD 200 F8
Appleford Dr
Abingdon-on-Thames
OX14 160 B2
11 Carterton OX18 115 E5
Appleford Rd OX14 180 B1
Applegarth Ct 12
OX28 118 A8
APPLETON 158 A7
Appleton CE Prim Sch
OX13 158 A8
Appleton Cl OX11 200 D2
Appleton Common
OX13 157 C5
Appleton Rd
Cumnor OX2 139 D4
Longworth OX13 156 D3
APPLETREE 5 C8
Appletree Cl
Sandford-on-Thames
OX4 161 F8
Sonning Common RG4 252 E6
Appletree Ind Est OX17 5 E7
Appletree La
Chipping Warden OX17 5 B6
Cropredy OX17 4 F4
Appletree Rd
Chipping Warden OX17 5 E7
Chipping Warden OX17 5 F6
Applewood Cl OX11 217 D6
Approach The OX26 65 D3
Apsley Rd OX2 123 A8
Arbury Banks OX17 5 F5
Arbury Cl OX16 16 E2
Arcade The
Goring RG8 249 C6
9 Wallingford OX10 221 D7
Archer Place OX18 116 A4
Archery Rd OX17 11 A1
Archway Rd 1 RG4 259 A2
Arden Cl OX15 15 D8
ARDINGTON 215 E6
Ardington La OX12,
OX13 197 E2
ARDINGTON WICK 215 F8
Ardler Rd RG4 259 C2
ARDLEY 50 C4
Ardley Rd Ardley OX27 50 C4
Bucknell OX27 50 E2
Middleton Stoney OX25 64 A4
Somerton OX25 48 F6
Somerton OX25 49 C5
Argentan Cl OX14 179 D4
Argosy Cl OX44 184 E6
Argosy Rd
Benson OX10 204 D3
Carterton OX18 115 F2
Carterton OX18 115 F2
Argyle St OX4 141 F6
Aristotle La OX2 123 A4
Arkel Cl OX18 101 A6
Arkell Ave OX18 115 D2
Arkell Ct OX18 115 D2
Arkell Gdns
Carterton OX18 115 D2
Carterton OX18 115 D5
Arkwright Rd OX26 66 A3
ARLESCOTE 2 C6
Arlescote Rd OX17 2 B6
Arlington Cl OX18 115 E2
Arlington Dr OX3 123 E5
Armitage Dr OX12 215 A5
Armour Hill RG31 257 D1
Armour Rd RG31 257 D1
Armour Wlk RG31 257 D1
Armstrong Cl OX11 217 D7
Armstrong Rd OX4 142 B1
Arncott Rd
Piddington HP18 97 C6
Piddington OX25 97 D7
Arncott Rd *continued*
Upper Arncott OX5 96 D4
Arncott Wood Rd OX25 96 E6
Arndale Beck OX11 201 A2
Arnold Rd OX4 141 F6
Arnold's Way OX2 140 C7
Arnold Way OX9 147 E7
Arnott's Yd HP18 129 D6
Arran Gr OX16 16 C6
Arrow Cl OX17 11 A1
Arthray Rd OX2 140 D8
Arthur Evans Cl OX13 159 A6
Arthur Garrard Cl
OX2 261 A4
Arthur St OX2 123 A1
Arundel Cl
Carterton OX18 115 C2
Kings Sutton OX17 23 F5
Arundel Pl OX16 15 F5
Arundel View OX7 42 D2
Arun Mews OX11 201 A1
ASCOTT Hook Norton 18 A2
Stadhampton 163 E1
ASCOTT D'OYLEY 71 C2
ASCOTT EARL 71 B1
Ascott Hill CV36 18 A1
Ascott Rd Ascott CV36 18 A2
Shipton-under-Wychwood
OX7 85 D8
ASCOTT-UNDER-
WYCHWOOD 71 D2
Ascott-under-Wychwood
Sta OX7 71 C2
Ascot Way OX26 65 B1
Asgard Gn OX49 186 A2
Ash Ave OX18 115 E5
Ashburn Pl OX11 200 F3
Ashburton La OX15 30 B6
ASHBURY 228 A7
Ashbury Hill SN6 228 B6
Ashbury with Compton
Beauchamp CE Prim Sch
SN6 228 A7
Ashby Ct OX16 16 D5
Ashby Rd OX26 65 D2
Ash Cl Faringdon SN7 172 E3
Kidlington OX5 108 E7
Oxford OX2 140 D7
Watlington OX49 186 A2
Ashcombe Cl OX28 118 A8
Ash Copse
Reading RG4 259 F6
Reading RG4 259 F7
Ash Cres Harwell OX11 217 F7
Harwell OX11 217 F7
Ashcroft Cl
Chadlington OX7 57 B1
Oxford OX2 122 B1
Reading RG4 258 E5
Ashcroft Rd OX16 16 D2
Ash Ct RG4 259 B3
Ashdale Ave OX28 104 D3
Ashdene 6 OX18 115 E5
Ashdene Rd OX26 65 C2
Ashdown House★
RG17 245 E8
Ashdown Pk RG17 245 E8
Ashdown Way RG9 242 A1
Ash Dr OX15 16 F1
Ashenden Cl OX14 159 F1
Ashfield Rd OX18 115 E1
Ashfields Cl OX12 197 C7
Ashfields La OX12 197 C7
Ashfield Way OX10 221 A1
Ashford Ave RG4 252 E5
Ashford Cl OX20 91 B6
Ash Furlong La NN13 25 A7
Ashgate OX14 179 E4
Ash Gr Chesterton OX26 79 F7
Oxford OX3 124 D4
Ash Hurst RG8 249 D8
Ashhurst Ct OX33 144 F7
Ashhurst Way OX4 142 A3
Ash La OX25 81 D4
Ashlee Wlk RG8 250 F8
Ashley Hill Pl RG10 255 F7
Ashlong Rd OX3 124 A5
Ashmead Rd OX16 8 F1
Ashmolean Mus★
OX1 261 B3
Ashmole Pl OX4 142 F3
Ashmole Rd OX14 179 E4
Ashridge OX39 168 B6
Ashridge Cl OX16 16 E2
Ashsdown Way OX12 214 D8
Ashurst Way OX4 142 A3
Ashville Way OX4 142 F3
Ashwell Bank La OX5 77 C6
Ash Wy OX11 200 B2
Aspen Cl OX26 65 E5
Aspen Sq OX4 142 E1
Aspen Way OX11 218 C7
Asquith Pk OX14 199 F7
Asquith Rd OX4 142 A3
Aster Cl 5 OX11 218 B7
ASTHALL 101 F3
ASTHALL LEIGH 102 D6
Astley Ave OX5 108 F6
Astley Rd OX9 130 B1
ASTON 135 E3
Aston Cl
Abingdon-on-Thames
OX14 179 F7
Banbury OX16 16 E2
Pangbourne RG8 256 D5
Wallingford OX10 221 C7
Aston & Cote CE Prim Sch
OX18 135 E3
Aston Gdns OX49 167 D3
Aston Hill OX49 187 E7
Aston Ho 6 OX16 16 E6
Aston Pk OX49 167 D2
Aston Pk Stud OX49 167 C2
Aston Rd
Bampton OX18 134 F3
Ducklington OX29 118 A2
Ducklington OX29 118 B3
ASTON ROWANT 167 C2
Aston Rowant CE Prim Sch
OX49 167 E3
Aston Rowant National
Nature Reserve★
HP14 187 E5
Aston Rowant Rd
OX49 167 D2
Aston St
Aston Tirrold OX11 237 F8
Oxford OX4 141 F7
ASTON TIRROLD 237 E8
ASTON UPTHORPE 219 E2
Aston View
Somerton OX25 48 F5
Somerton OX25 49 A5
Aston Witney Rd
OX29 137 A3
Aston Works OX18 135 D3
Astrop La OX4 142 A8
Astrop Rd
Kings Sutton OX17 23 F5
Middleton Cheney OX17 17 F6
ASTWICK 37 B7
Atkinson Cl OX3 124 E5
Atkins Rd OX44 184 E6
Atkins Way OX10 221 A8
Atkyns Rd OX3 142 E8
Atlanta Cl OX10 204 D1
Atterbury Gdns RG4 258 E4
Atwell Cl OX10 221 C8
Atwell Pl 5 OX3 124 D1
Aubrey Ct OX4 142 A4
Auburn Ct Reading RG4 258 F2
Reading RG4 259 A2
Audlett Dr OX14 180 B8
Audley Ho OX26 65 F4
Augustfield RG4 260 E4
Augustian Rd OX26 79 F7
Augustine Way
Florence Park OX4 142 A5
Thame OX9 148 A6
Augustine Wy OX44 141 F5
Aunt Ems La OX27 65 E6
Austen Wlk OX26 65 C2
Austin Dr OX16 15 F8
Austin Mws OX26 80 E6
Austin Pl OX14 159 E2
Austin Rd OX15 22 E7
Austin's Way OX15 30 C8
Austin Way OX26 80 E6
Auton Pl RG9 254 D8
Autumn Cl
Caversfield OX27 65 D7
Reading RG4 259 C7
Autumn Wlk RG10 255 D2
Avens Way OX4 142 E1
Avenue Four OX28 118 B7
Avenue Ho RG4 258 D3
Avenue La OX4 141 F8
Avenue One OX28 118 A6
Avenue Rd
Banbury OX16 16 F6
Bourton SN6 209 A3
Avenue The
Bloxham OX15 21 D4
Chinnor OX39 168 D6
Didcot OX11 200 C2
Great Tew OX7 45 D8
Kennington OX1 160 E8
Shillingford OX10 203 B4
Wheatley OX33 144 C7
Worminghall HP18 127 E5
Avenue Three OX28 118 B6
Avenue Two OX28 118 B6
Avery Ct OX2 123 B8
Aves Ditch Caulcott OX5 63 A1
Kidlington OX5 78 A8
Avocet Way
Banbury OX16 16 E3
Bicester OX26 81 B8
Avonbury Bsns Pk
OX26 65 C4
Avonbury Ct NN13 24 A5
Avon Carrow OX17 3 A8
Avon Cres OX26 65 B3
AVON DASSETT 2 F8
Avon Rd
Abingdon-on-Thames
OX13 159 C2
Chilton OX11 235 B8
Harwell OX11 217 C1
Avon Way OX11 200 F3
Avro Rd GL54 68 B5
Awgar Stone Rd OX3 142 F7
Axis Rd SN6 191 E1
Axtell Cl OX5 92 D1
Ayers Dr Bloxham OX15 21 E3
Bloxham OX15 21 E3
Aylesbury Rd
Bicester OX25 81 B6
Blackthorn OX25 82 D4
Haddenham OX9 130 C6
Thame OX9 129 E2
Thame OX9 129 F3
Aylesbury & Thame
Airfield HP17 130 E7
AYNHO 35 C8
Aynho Ct OX17 35 D7
Aynhoe Pk OX17 35 C7
Aynho Fishery★ OX17 34 F6
Aynho Rd
Adderbury OX17 23 C3
Aynho OX17 35 A8
East Adderbury OX17 23 B4
Ayrshire Cl 3 OX16 9 A1
Ayrton Ave OX11 201 B3
Aysgarth Rd OX5 108 B6
Azalea Ave OX5 108 E6
Azalea Wlk OX16 9 B1
Azor's Ct OX4 142 A4

B

BABLOCK HYTHE 138 F5
Bablock Hythe Rd
OX13 139 B3
Bablock Rd OX29 138 D4
Back Hill OX17 8 C8
Back La Aston OX18 135 D3
Ducklington OX29 118 B4
Epwell OX15 13 A6
Eynsham OX29 120 E8
Long Compton CV36 28 A6
Sibford Ferris OX15 19 B7
Back Lane OX27 35 E3
Back Rd
Eastleach Martin GL7 131 A7
Great Barrington OX18 99 B8
Back Row GL56 40 C3
Backsideans RG10 255 D2
Backside La OX15 19 A8
Back St OX9 166 B8
Back Way OX44 145 D1
Backway Rd 4 OX26 65 F2
Badbury Cl SN7 172 E2
Bader Dr OX25 63 B7
Badgemore La RG9 244 D3
Badgemore Prim Sch
RG9 244 D2
Badger Cl OX33 125 E4
Badger La OX1 141 B3
Badger Mws OX28 103 F1
Badgers Copse OX14 160 E2
Badgers Dr OX12 214 C7
Badgers Rise
Reading RG4 259 A5
Reading RG5 260 D1
Badgers Wlk
Lower Shiplake RG9 255 A3
Temple Cowley OX4 142 C6
Badger Way OX16 16 F3
Badswell La
Appleton OX13 157 F8
Appleton OX13 158 A8
Baghill La HP17 130 C6
Bagley Cl OX1 141 D2
Bagley Wood OX1 141 B2
Bagley Wood Rd OX1 160 D7
Bailey Cl OX12 214 D6
Bailey Rd Banbury OX16 15 E6
Oxford OX4 142 D4
Baileys Orch OX10 204 E4
Bailie Cl 2 OX14 179 E6
BAINTON 51 E2
Bainton Cl OX26 66 C2
Bainton Rd
Bucknell OX27 65 A8
Hethe OX27 52 A7
Oxford OX2 123 A5
Stoke Lyne OX27 51 E5
Bakehouse La
Marcham OX13 178 D6
Shotteswell OX17 8 D8
Baker Ave OX10 204 D2
Baker Cl Benson OX10 204 D2
Bicester OX27 65 F7
Oxford OX3 124 F2
Baker Rd OX14 179 F5
Baker's Ct OX29 90 B1
Bakers La
Brightwell-cum-Sotwell
OX10 202 F2
Brightwell-cum-Sotwell
OX11 202 F2
East Hagbourne OX11 218 F6
Oxford OX4 141 F4
South Newington OX15 31 F7
Swalcliffe OX15 19 F8
Tadmarton OX15 20 C8
Bakers Piece
Kingston Blount OX39 167 F4
Witney OX28 104 B2
Baker's Piece Ho
OX39 167 F4
Baker St OX11 237 F8
Bakery Cl OX44 184 D7
Bakery La
Clanfield OX18 152 F8
Letcombe Regis OX12 214 A1
Baldon La OX44 161 F3
BALDON ROW 162 B5
Baldons Cl RG8 250 F8
Balfour Cotts OX14 182 A5
Balfour Rd OX4 142 E3
Balfour's Field RG8 241 D3
Balhams La RG9 225 F8
Ballard Chase OX14 160 A3
Ballard Cl OX7 46 E1
Ballards Cl OX7 85 D8
Ballingers SN6 209 C6
Balliol Cl OX5 77 C6
Balliol Coll OX1 261 B3
Balliol Ct OX2 123 A4
Balliol Dr OX11 219 B8
Balliol Rd Bicester OX26 65 F3
Reading RG4 258 D3
Ball La OX5 77 B5
Balmoral Ave OX16 15 F4
Balmoral Rd OX11 219 A8
Balmoral Way OX17 23 F6
Balmore Dr RG4 259 B4
Balmore Ho RG4 259 B3
Balmore Pk RG4 259 B3
BALSCOTE 14 C8
Baltic Wharf OX1 261 B1
Bambrooks Mws OX9 148 A7
BAMPTON 134 F4
Bampton CE Prim Sch
OX18 134 F4
Bampton Cl OX4 142 D3
Bampton Rd
Aston OX18 135 D2
Black Bourton OX18 133 E4
Black Bourton OX18 134 A4
Clanfield OX18 133 F1
Clanfield OX18 134 A1
Curbridge OX18, OX29 117 B4
Curbridge OX29 117 C5
BANBURY 16 F5
Banbury Acad OX16 16 B3
Banbury & Bicester
College OX26 66 B3
Banbury Bsns Pk OX17 23 D3
Banbury Cross Ret Pk
OX16 16 C8
Banbury Ct 1 OX14 179 F7
Banbury Gdns RG4 259 C3
Banbury Hill OX7 73 C5
Banbury La
Chacombe OX17 10 E4
Kings Sutton OX17 23 F5
Middleton Cheney OX17 11 C3
Wardington OX17 10 F8
Banbury Mus★ OX16 16 D6
Banbury Rd
Adderbury OX17 23 A6
Arlescote OX17 2 A6
Aynho OX17 35 B8
Bicester OX26 65 E4
Bloxham OX15 21 E6
Bunkers Hill OX5 92 A8
Chacombe OX17 10 D4
Chipping Norton OX7 42 F4
Chipping Norton OX7 43 A5
Chipping Norton OX7 44 A8
Chipping Warden OX17 5 F6
Cutteslowe OX2 109 A1
Deddington OX15 33 F5
Duns Tew OX7 47 F5
Enstone OX7 45 A1
Enstone OX7 59 A6
Finmere MK18 39 B6
Great Tew OX7 45 C8
Hornton OX15 6 C8
Hornton OX15 6 F7
Kidlington OX5 92 D1
Middleton Cheney OX17 17 C8
Mixbury NN13 38 E7
North Newington OX15 15 C3
Over Norton OX7 43 D6
Oxford OX2 123 B6
Shipton-on-Cherwell OX5 92 B5
Shotteswell OX17 8 B8
Shutford OX15 14 B5
Shutford OX15 14 D5
Swerford OX7 30 D1
Tackley OX5 76 E4
Thorpe Mandeville OX17 11 E5
Thorpe Mandeville OX17 11 F4
Upper Boddington NN11 1 F7
Warmington OX17 2 F6
Warmington OX17 3 A2
Woodstock OX20 91 D7
Banbury Road Crossing
OX7 42 F3
Banbury Road Rdbt
OX2 109 A1
Banbury Sta OX16 16 E5
Banbury View OX16 9 D3
Bandet Way OX9 148 B6
Banesberie Cl OX16 9 A1
Banister Dr OX17 8 E2
Banjo Rd OX4 142 C5
Bank Cotts OX33 125 E4
Banks Furlong OX26 79 F8
Bankside Banbury OX16 16 F3
Kidlington OX5 92 C2
Long Hanborough OX29 90 F1
Oxford OX3 124 E1
West Hendred OX12 216 B6
Bank The OX29 88 E7
Bannister Cl OX4 141 E7
Bannister Rd OX9 148 C7
Barbara's Mdw RG31 257 B2
Barberi Cl 6 OX4 142 B2
Barberry Pl OX26 65 E4
Barbican Cl OX10 221 D6
Barbrook Cl RG31 257 D3
Barbury Dr OX12 214 D8
Barclose Ave RG4 259 C3
Barcombe Cl OX16 8 F1
Barcote La SN7 174 A6
Bardolph's Cl RG4 258 D8
Bardwell Ct OX2 123 C4
Bardwell Rd OX2 123 C4
Bardwell Sch OX26 66 A4
Bardwell Terr OX26 65 F2
Barefoot Cl RG31 257 B1
Barfleur Cl OX14 160 B3
Barford Rd
Bloxham OX15 21 E2
South Newington OX15 32 A6
BARFORD ST JOHN 32 F7
BARFORD ST
MICHAEL 32 E5
Bargus Cl OX13 199 A4
Barksdale Ave NN13 36 E6
Barkus Way HP14 188 F5
Barley Cl Bloxham OX15 21 E5
Lewknor OX49 187 A8
Sibford Gower OX15 19 A8
Wallingford OX10 221 C6
Barleycott La OX1 141 C4
Barley Cres OX18 115 F5
Barley Croft OX15 21 E5
Barleyfields OX11 218 C8
Barleyfield Way OX28 104 E1
Barley Hill Prim Sch
OX9 130 A1
Barlin Cl OX29 137 F8
Barlow Cl
Milcombe OX15 21 A2
Wheatley OX33 143 F8
Barnacre OX49 186 B1
Barnard Cl RG4 259 C6
BARNARD GATE 105 F1
Barnard Mws OX18 100 E3
Barnards Way OX12 214 F6
Barn Bsns Ctr The
GL54 83 A8
Barn Cl
Denchworth OX12 196 A4
Kidlington OX5 108 D8
Oxford OX2 140 B6
Barncroft
Long Compton CV36 28 A5
Wallingford OX10 221 C8
Barn End OX18 134 E2
Barnes Cl OX11 218 E7
Barnes Rd OX11 218 E6
Barnet St OX4 142 A7
Barnett Rd
Middleton Cheney OX17 17 F8
Steventon OX13 198 F5
Barnett Way OX10 204 D2
Barnfield Cl OX27 65 F6
Barn La RG9 244 C4
Barn Owl Wy OX11 200 B1
Barns Cl OX33 126 B1
Barns Hay OX3 123 F6
Barns Ho OX4 142 C4
Barns La OX18 100 E4
Barnsletts RG9 254 A7
Barns Rd OX4 142 C4
Barn's Rd OX4 142 D4
Baroma Way RG9 244 E2
Baronshurst Dr OX44 184 D6
Baronsmead RG9 244 D2
Baron Way RG9 242 A2
Barracks La OX4 142 B7
Barracks The OX44 164 D8
Barrat Rd OX25 63 C8
Barrett Ct RG1 258 F1
Barretts Cl OX29 89 C7
Barrett St OX2 123 A1
Barrett's Way OX14 199 F6
Barrington Ave SN6 191 F1
Barrington Cl
Berinsfield OX10 182 C6
Oxford OX3 124 C2
Witney OX28 117 E7
Barrington Ct NN13 24 A5
Barrington Pk Rd OX18 83 A1
Barrington Rd SN6 209 D8
Barrow Cl OX13 178 D6
Barrow Ct OX29 107 D3
Barrow Hill Cl OX14 160 C2
BARROW HILLS 160 D1
Barrow La OX11 217 E8
Barrow Pk OX11 217 D8
Barrow Pk (Cvn Site)
OX11 217 E8
Barrow Rd
Abingdon-on-Thames
OX13 179 B8
Drayton OX14 179 B2
Harwell OX11 217 E8
Barrow The OX11 217 E7
Barry Ave OX26 65 D3
Bartholomew Ave
OX5 108 B5
Bartholomew Cl
Ducklington OX29 118 B4
Eynsham OX29 120 D8
Bartholomew Rd OX4 142 C4
Bartholomew Sch
OX29 120 D8
Bartholomew Sports Ctr
OX29 120 D7
Bartholomew Tipping Way
HP14 188 F5
Bartlemas Cl OX4 142 A7
Bartlemas Rd OX4 142 A8
Bartlett Cl
Charlbury OX7 73 C3
Wallingford OX10 221 C5
Witney OX28 118 A8
Bartlett Pl 1 OX13 199 C3
Bartlett Rd OX15 21 C4
BARTON 124 E4
Barton Cl OX17 23 F6
Barton Ct OX14 179 B1
Bartone Pl OX9 148 A6
Barton Fields Rd OX4 124 C5
BARTONGATE 61 A8
BARTON HARTSHORN 39 D2
Barton Hartshorn Rd
MK18 39 E1
Barton La
Abingdon-on-Thames
OX14 180 B7
Oxford OX3 124 D4
BARTON-ON-THE-
HEATH 26 E6
Barton Pool OX3 124 F4
Barton Rd
Barton Hartshorn MK18 39 F3
Long Compton CV36 27 C7
Oxford OX3 124 E4
Barton Village Rd OX3 124 E5
Bartsia Rd OX26 65 E4
Barwell OX12 214 D5
Basildon Park★ RG8 249 D1

Basil Hill Rd OX11 . . . 200 D3
Baskerville La RG9. . . 255 A3
Baskerville Rd RG4. . . 252 E5
Basmore La RG9. . . . . . 255 B4
Basset Ave OX26. . . . . . .65 F3
Bassett Rd
 Letcombe Bassett
 OX12. . . . . 231 F7
 Oxford OX3 . . . . . . 124 F4
Basset Way OX5 . . . . 108 F8
Batchelors La OX15. . . . .2 A4
Batchelors Row OX15. . .33 B4
Bate Collection of Musical
 Instruments★ OX1 . 261 B1
Bateman Cl OX16. . . . . 16 A3
Bateman Pl OX12. . . . 194 C1
Bateman St OX3. . . . . 124 D2
Bates La OX27. . . . . . . 35 D3
Bath Cres OX26. . . . . . .65 B1
Bath Ct OX14 . . . . 179 F7
Bathing Pl La OX28 . . . 104 A1
Bath Pl OX1 . . . . 261 C2
Bath Rd Banbury OX16 . . 16 C6
 Sonning RG4 . . . . 260 E2
Baths Rd OX11. . . . . . . 235 C8
Bath St
 Abingdon-on-Thames
 OX14. . . . . 179 E8
 Oxford OX4 . . . . 123 F1
Bath Terr OX26. . . . . . .65 F2
Batt Collection of England
 (Voluntary Aided) Prim
 Sch The [11] OX28. . . . . 118 A8
Batten Pl OX4 . . . . 142 A1
Batting Cl HP14. . . . . . 189 F8
Battle Cl OX26. . . . . . . 66 A3
Battle Rd Benson OX10. 204 D2
 Goring RG8 . . . . 249 F7
BAULKING 193 F2
Baulking La
 Baulking SN7. . . . . . 193 F2
 Kingston Lisle SN7 . . . 194 C2
Baxters Barns GL7. . . . 131 A4
Bayards Hill Prim Sch [1]
 OX3 . . . . 124 F4
BAYDON. 245 E1
Baydon Rd SN8. . . . . . 245 D1
Baydon St Nicholas CE
 Prim Sch SN8 . . . . . 245 E1
Bayliss Dr OX25 . . . . . 63 C7
Bayliss Rd RG10 . . . . . 255 D1
Bayliss Yd OX7 . . . . . . .73 B3
BAYNARD'S GREEN . . 50 D7
Baynhams Dr OX2 . . . . 122 D8
Bayswater Brook
 OX11. . . . . 201 B2
Bayswater Farm OX3 . 125 A4
Bayswater Farm Rd
 OX3 . . . . 125 A4
Bayswater Mill
 Oxford OX3 . . . . 125 A5
 Oxford OX4 . . . . 124 F5
Bayswater Mill Rd
 OX3 . . . . 125 A5
Bayswater Rd
 Blenheim OX33 . . . . . 143 C7
 Oxford OX3 . . . . 124 F4
 Oxford OX4 . . . . 124 F5
 Rissinghurst OX3. . . . 125 A1
Bay Tree Cl OX4 . . . . . 142 A4
Bay Tree Rise [2] RG4 . 253 A4
BAYWORTH. 160 A7
Bayworth La OX1. . . . . 159 F8
Bayworth Pk OX13. . . . 159 F7
Beachborough Sch
 NN13. . . . . 25 A4
BEACON'S BOTTOM . 189 D3
Beaconsfield Rd OX16 . 16 D2
Beacon View
 Aston Rowant OX49 . . 167 C1
 Lewknor OX49. . . . . . 187 B8
Beadle Trad Est OX10 . 221 B7
Beadnell Cl OX16. . . . . 16 D2
Beagle Cl OX14. . . . . . 160 C2
Beagles Cl OX5. . . . . . 109 A7
Beale Park★ RG8. . . . 249 F1
Beam Paddock OX18. . 135 A3
Beanacre Rd OX15. . . . .30 B6
Bean Furlong OX17. . . . 10 E4
Beanhill Cl OX29. . . . . 118 A5
Beanhill Rd OX29. . . . . 118 A5
Beansheaf Terr [17]
 OX10. . . . . 221 D7
Bear Cl OX20 . . . . .91 B6
Bear Close Flats OX20 . .91 B6
Bear Ct OX18 . . . . 100 E5
Bear Garden Rd OX16. . 16 C5
Bear La
 North Moreton OX11. . 220 A7
 Oxford OX1 . . . . 261 C2
 Stadhampton OX44. . . 163 C1
 Wallingford OX10 . . . 221 D8
Bears Hedge OX4. . . . . 142 A4
Beatrice Dr OX16. . . . . 16 A5
Beauchamp La OX4 . . . 142 B4
Beauchamp Pl OX4 . . . 142 B4
Beaufort Cl
 Bicester OX26. . . . . . 66 A3
 Didcot OX11 . . . . 219 B8
Beaulieu Cl OX16. . . . . .16 F6
Beaulieu Ct OX13 . . . . 159 F5
Beaulieu Mews OX11 . . 201 A3
Beaumaris Cl OX14 . . . .15 F7
Beaumont Bldgs OX1 . . 261 A3
Beaumont Bsns Ctr
 OX16 . . . . .9 C1
Beaumont Cl OX16. . . . . .9 C1
Beaumont Ct OX1 . . . . 141 E1

Beaumont Green
 OX29 . . . . 120 B2
Beaumont Ind Est OX16. . .9 C1
Beaumont La OX1 . . . . 261 B3
Beaumont Pl OX1. . . . . 261 B3
Beaumont Rd
 Banbury OX16. . . . . . . .9 C1
 Oxford OX3 . . . . 124 F4
Beaumont St OX1. . . . . 261 B3
Beauregard Way
 OX10. . . . . 203 B4
Beavington Rd OX15. . .30 B8
Bec Cl OX12 . . . . 214 B5
Beckdale Cl OX26. . . . . .65 B8
Becket St OX1 . . . . 261 A2
Beckett Ave SN6. . . . . 209 D7
Beckett Dr
 Radley OX14 . . . . . . 160 E3
 Shrivenham SN6 . . . . 209 D7
Beckett Ho OX12 . . . . 214 E4
Becketts Cl OX29. . . . . .90 B1
BECKLEY 111 B3
Beckley CE Prim Sch
 OX3 . . . . 111 A3
Beckley Ct OX3. . . . . . 111 B2
Beckley Rd OX33 . . . . 125 B8
Becquerel Ave OX11 . . 217 B2
Bec Tithe RG8. . . . . . . 250 E3
Beddington Ave OX11. 201 B3
Bedford Cl OX16. . . . . .15 F8
Bedford Dr OX26 . . . . . .65 B1
Bedford Mws [1] OX29 . .90 C1
Bedford St OX4. . . . . . 141 F6
Bedwells Heath OX1. . 140 D1
Beech Cl
 Faringdon SN7. . . . . 172 E3
 Stokenchurch HP14. . . 188 F3
 Watlington OX49. . . . 186 A4
 Wootton OX13. . . . . . 159 A7
Beechcraft Rd GL54. . . .68 B3
Beech Cres OX5 . . . . . 108 F6
Beechcroft OX10 . . . . 182 D1
Beech Croft Rd OX2 . . 123 B6
Beech Ct RG4 . . . . 259 B3
Beeches The
 Deddington OX15 . . . . .33 F4
 Goring RG8 . . . . 249 B5
 Lower Shiplake RG9 . . 255 A4
 Oxford OX3 . . . . 124 C4
 Reading RG31 . . . . . 257 D3
 Shenington OX15 . . . . . 6 F2
Beechey Ave OX3. . . . 123 F4
Beech Farm Cl OX9. . . 166 E3
Beechfield Cres OX16. . 16 D3
Beechgate OX28. . . . . 118 A6
Beech Gr
 Fulbrook OX18. . . . . . 100 F6
 Woodgreen OX28. . . . 104 C2
Beech Grove OX18. . . . 101 A6
Beeching Cl OX11 . . . . 218 C2
Beeching Way
 Wallingford OX10 . . . 221 C7
 Wheatley OX33 . . . . . 143 F8
Beech La
 Abingdon-on-Thames
 OX14. . . . . 159 F2
 [6] Carterton OX18 . . . 115 F5
 Didcot OX11 . . . . 218 C4
 Woodcote RG8. . . . . . 250 C8
Beech Lodge OX3 . . . . 124 C3
Beech Pl OX3. . . . . 124 B3
Beech Rd
 Chinnor OX39 . . . . . . 168 C6
 Eynsham OX29 . . . . . 120 E8
 Launton OX26. . . . . . 66 E2
 Oxford OX2 . . . . 140 D7
 Oxford OX3 . . . . 124 C3
 Purley on Thames RG8 . 257 B5
 Shillingford OX10 . . . 203 B4
 Thame OX9 . . . . 147 D8
 Tokers Green RG4. . . . 258 D7
 Wheatley OX33 . . . . . 144 B7
 Witney OX28. . . . . . . 117 F8
Beech Rise RG4 . . . . . 252 F6
Beechwood OX4. . . . . 142 A5
Beechwood Cl RG8 . . . 250 D6
Beechwood Ho OX3 . . 124 C4
Beef La OX1. . . . . 261 B2
Beehive Ct OX10. . . . . 220 F1
Beesley Rd OX16 . . . . . 16 A6
Beetham Ct OX13. . . . 199 C2
BEGBROKE 108 B8
Begbroke La
 Begbroke OX5. . . . . . .92 A1
 Kidlington OX5. . . . . . 92 C1
Begbroke Science Pk
 OX5 . . . . 108 B7
Beggarsbush Hill
 OX10. . . . . 204 D1
Beggars La OX13 . . . . . 156 C1
Beggar's La OX15. . . . . .12 F4
Behoes La RG8 . . . . . . 240 D1
Belbroughton Rd OX2 123 C5
Belcher Ct OX10. . . . . 182 D2
Belfast Cl OX18. . . . . . 133 F8
Belfast Rd OX10. . . . . 204 D3
Belfast Sq OX18 . . . . . 133 F8
Belgrave Cres [4] OX16. 116 B6
Belgrove Cl OX5. . . . . 108 D8
Bellamy Cl OX13 . . . . . 156 E1
Bellamy Wy OX10. . . . 221 E7
Bell Cl Cassington OX29 107 D2
 Grove OX12. . . . . . . 196 E1
 Thame OX9 . . . . 129 E1
Bell Ct RG4. . . . . 259 B6
Belleisle RG8. . . . . 257 B5
Bellenger Way
 Brize Norton OX18 . . . 116 A5
 Kidlington OX5. . . . . . 108 D8

Bellerbys Coll OX1 . . . 261 B2
Belle Terr OX18 . . . . . . 115 D1
Belle Vue Rd RG9. . . . . 254 D8
Bell Hill OX15 . . . . 30 B7
Bellingham La SN6 . . . 190 A1
Bellingham Wlk RG4. . 259 A5
Bell La Aldworth RG8. . 247 F4
 Bampton OX18 . . . . . 134 E3
 Bicester OX26. . . . . . 65 E2
 Brightwell-cum-Sotwell
 OX10. . . . . 202 E2
 Cassington OX29. . . . 107 D2
 Henley-on-Thames RG9. 244 E3
 Lechlade-on-Thames
 GL7. . . . . 150 C3
 Thame OX9 . . . . 129 F1
 Wheatley OX33. . . . . 144 B8
Bell Lodge [8] OX26 . . . .65 E2
Bell's La OX15 . . . . .30 B7
Bell St
 [4] Henley-on-Thames
 RG9. . . . . 244 D2
 Henley-on-Thames RG9. 244 E2
 Hornton OX15 . . . . 7 C6
Bell Street Mews RG9. 244 E2
Bell Weather Furlong
 OX10. . . . . 203 F5
BELMONT 214 C5
Belmont OX12. . . . . . . 214 D5
Belmont Mews OX9. . . 147 F8
Belsyre Ct OX2 . . . . . . 261 A4
Belvedere Rd OX4 . . . . 142 A7
Benares Gr RG9 . . . . . 242 A4
Ben Cl OX5. . . . . .92 E1
Benhams La RG9 . . . . 226 D2
Benmead Rd OX5. . . . . .92 E1
Bennett Wood RG8. . . 248 F2
Bennett Cl OX17. . . . . . 10 E4
Bennett Cres OX4 . . . . 142 D5
Bennett Dr OX16. . . . . .15 E6
BENNETT END 189 C7
Bennett End Rd HP14. . 189 D7
Bennett Rd SN7 . . . . . . 172 F3
Bennetts Yard OX39 . . 167 F4
Bennouville Cl OX4 . . . 142 E6
Bens Cl OX20. . . . . 91 C7
Bensgrove Cl RG8 . . . . 250 F8
BENSON 204 A4
Benson CE Prim Sch
 OX10 . . . . 203 E4
Benson Cl OX26 . . . . . .66 B3
Benson La
 Benson OX10. . . . . . 204 A2
 Crowmarsh Gifford
 OX10. . . . . 221 F8
Benson Pl OX2 . . . . . . 123 D4
Benson Rd
 Abingdon-on-Thames
 OX14. . . . . 159 E2
 Ewelme OX10. . . . . . 204 D8
 Oxford OX3 . . . . 142 D8
Bentley Cl OX16 . . . . . . 15 F8
Benton Dr OX9 . . . . . . 168 D7
Benwells OX39 . . . . . . 168 C6
Bere Court Rd RG8 . . . 256 B4
Bere Ct RG9. . . . . 256 A3
Berens Rd SN6 . . . . . . 209 B6
Beresford Pl [6] OX4 . . 142 D6
Bergamont Pl [5] OX4 . 142 E1
Bergen Ave OX14. . . . . 179 D4
BERINSFIELD 182 D5
Berinsfield Rdbt OX10 182 B4
Berins Hill
 Checkendon OX10. . . 241 A6
 Well Place OX10 . . . . 240 F7
Berkeley Cl OX16. . . . . .15 E7
Berkeley Rd
 Boars Hill OX1. . . . . . 140 E1
 Thame OX9 . . . . 130 A1
Berkshire Rd RG9. . . . 254 D8
Bernard Barlow Cl
 OX11. . . . . 218 D8
Bernard Cl OX5. . . . . . 108 C5
Berner's Way SN7 . . . . 173 A3
Bernewode Cl HP18 . . 129 C7
Bernwood Butterfly Trail★
 OX33 . . . . 112 E3
Bernwood Forest★
 OX33 . . . . 112 F2
Bernwood Rd
 Bicester OX26. . . . . . .65 F2
 Oxford OX3 . . . . 124 E4
Berren Dean RG9. . . . . 254 A7
BERRICK PRIOR 184 A2
Berrick Rd OX44. . . . . 184 B5
BERRICK SALOME . . 184 A1
Berry Cl Eynsham OX29 120 D7
 Marsh Gibbon OX27 . . .67 F3
 Oxford OX4 . . . . 142 F3
Berrycroft SN6 . . . . . . 228 A7
Berry Croft OX14 . . . . 159 E1
Berryfield Way
 Carterton OX18. . . . . 115 E5
 [16] Carterton OX18 . . 115 E5
Berryfield Wy [16]
 OX18. . . . . 115 D5
Berry Hill Rd OX17. . . . .22 F7
Berry La
 Blewbury OX11. . . . . 219 A1
 East Hanney OX12 . . . 197 B6
Berrylands Rd RG4 . . . 259 B3
Berrymere Rd OX13. . . 159 A7
Berrymoor Rd OX16 . . .16 B5
Bertie Pl OX1. . . . . 141 D5
Bertie Rd Cumnor OX2 . 139 F5
 Thame OX9 . . . . 148 A7
Besbury La OX7 . . . . . . .55 F6
Bessels Lea OX11 . . . . 219 A1
BESSELS LEIGH 158 D8
Besselsleigh Rd OX13. 158 F8

Bessels Way
 Blewbury OX11. . . . . . 219 B1
 Blewbury OX11. . . . . 237 B8
Bessemer Cl OX26. . . . 66 A2
Beta Bvd OX44. . . . . . 143 C1
Betony Way OX26. . . . . .65 E4
Betteridge Cl OX13 . . . 156 F2
Betterton Cotts OX12. 215 F2
Bettina Cres [7] OX16 . . .9 A1
Betts Cl OX16. . . . . 16 A2
Betty La OX1 . . . . 141 C3
Between Towns Rd
 OX4 . . . . 142 C5
Beverley Cl
 Abingdon-on-Thames
 OX14. . . . . 159 E1
 Chalgrove OX44. . . . . 184 E6
Beverley Cres OX4 . . . 115 E4
Beverley Gdns
 Bicester OX26. . . . . . 66 A4
 Wargrave RG10. . . . . 255 F5
Beverley Rd RG31. . . . 257 C1
Beverly Cl OX10 . . . . . 204 D3
Bevington Rd OX2 . . . 261 B4
Bhandari Cl OX4 . . . . . 142 B6
Bibury Cl OX28 . . . . . . 117 D8
BICESTER. 65 E3
Bicester Ave OX25 . . . .80 D7
Bicester Com Hospl
 OX26 . . . . 65 D1
Bicester Heritage★
 OX26 . . . . 66 A5
Bicester Hill NN13 . . . . 38 A8
Bicester Ho OX26 . . . . .65 E1
Bicester L Ctr OX26. . . 65 D2
Bicester North Sta
 OX26 . . . . .65 F3
Bicester Office Park
 OX26 . . . . 81 D8
Bicester Rd Aynho OX17 .35 E6
 Bicester OX26. . . . . . 66 B3
 Blackthorn OX25. . . . 82 B5
 Boarstall HP18 . . . . . 97 C1
 Bucknell OX27. . . . . . .64 F7
 Enstone OX7. . . . . . . .58 F6
 Kidlington OX5. . . . . . 108 F7
 Launton OX26. . . . . . 66 C2
 Long Crendon HP18 . . 129 C6
 Ludgershall HP18 . . . . 98 C8
 Marsh Gibbon OX27 . . 67 C3
 Middleton Stoney OX25. 64 B3
 Steeple Barton OX7 . . 61 B8
 Stratton Audley OX27. 66 C8
Bicester Technology
 Studio OX26 . . . . . . 65 D2
Bicester Village Outlet
 Shopping OX26. . . . . .80 E8
Bicester Village Sta
 OX26 . . . . .80 F8
Bickerton Rd OX3 . . . . 124 C2
Bicton Cl OX26 . . . . . . .65 B1
Biddel Springs SN6. . . 190 B6
Biddlesden Rd NN13. . .25 B6
Bidwell Rd OX16. . . . . .15 E2
Bigmore La HP14. . . . . 189 C1
Bignell Pk OX26 . . . . . 64 D1
Bignell View OX26. . . . .79 F8
Bignolds Cl OX17. . . . . . .4 D7
Bigwood Caravan
 Park OX14. . . . . 160 E6
Billings Cl HP14. . . . . . 188 F5
Bill Money Way OX10 . 221 A2
Billwell HP18. . . . . 129 C6
BINFIELD HEATH 254 A2
Bingley Gr RG5. . . . . . . 260 F1
Binning Cl OX14 . . . . . 199 B8
BINSEY. 122 F4
Binsey La OX2 . . . . 122 E2
Binswood Ave OX3 . . . 124 E2
Bints Pl OX29. . . . . 138 C3
Birch Cl
 Kingston Bagpuize
 OX13. . . . . 156 F1
 Sonning Common RG4. 252 F4
Birch Dr OX18 . . . . 114 C7
Birchen Cl RG8. . . . . . 250 F8
Birches The RG8. . . . . 249 B6
Birchfield Cl OX4. . . . . 142 E2
Birch Gr OX28 . . . . 104 E2
Birch Rd
 Ambrosden OX25 . . . . 81 C3
 Garsington OX44. . . . 143 D2
Birchwood
 Banbury OX16. . . . . . .16 D3
 Carterton OX18. . . . . 115 E2
Birchwood Cl RG4 . . . 259 C6
Birchwood Dr OX5. . . . .92 B6
Bird Cl OX16. . . . . 16 B6
Bird In Hand La RG4 . . 253 A4
Birdlip Cl OX28 . . . . . . 103 D1
Birds La OX15. . . . . 13 A6
Bird Wood Ct RG4 . . . 253 A3
Birmingham Yd OX10 . 203 F4
Biscoe Ct OX33 . . . . . . 144 C8
Bishop Carpenter CE Prim
 Sch OX15 . . . . 15 B4
Bishop Dr OX18. . . . . . 100 E3
Bishop Kirk Pl OX2 . . . 123 A7
Bishop Loveday CE Prim
 Sch OX15 . . . . 16 E1
Bishops Cl OX15. . . . . . 32 E6
Bishops Mdw OX29 . . .89 D8
Bishops Orch OX11 . . . 218 F7
BISHOPSTONE 227 C3
Bishopstone CE Prim Sch
 SN6. . . . . 227 D4
Bishops Way
 Townsend OX12 . . . . . 194 E2
 Worminghall HP18 . . . 127 E5
Bishop's Wood OX44. . 144 C3

Bishopswood Special Sch
 RG4 . . . . 252 F5
Bisley Cl OX26. . . . . . . 66 A3
Bismore Rd OX17. . . . . . .8 F2
Bitham Rd OX12 . . . . . 233 C7
Bitterell OX29. . . . . 120 F7
BIX. 243 D7
Bix Comm RG9 . . . . . . 243 D8
Bix Hill RG9 . . . . 243 E7
Blackberry La OX29. . . .88 A5
Blackberry Way OX20. .91 D7
Blackbird Assarts La
 OX29 . . . . .88 B1
BLACKBIRD LEYS . . . 142 F2
Blackbird Leys L Ctr
 OX4 . . . . 142 F2
Blackbird Leys Rd
 OX4 . . . . 142 D2
BLACKBIRD'S
 BOTTOM. 250 D5
Blackbird's Bottom
 RG8 . . . . 250 C5
BLACK BOURTON . . . 133 F6
Black Bourton Rd
 Carterton OX18. . . . . 115 E1
 [3] Carterton OX18 . . . 115 E2
 Clanfield OX18. . . . . . 133 E1
Blackbull La OX5 . . . . . 95 C5
Blackburn Cl OX4. . . . 124 C3
Blackburn Wlk OX3 . . . 66 A5
Black Croft OX12 . . . . 214 D6
BLACKDITCH 138 A8
Blackditch OX29. . . . . 138 A8
Blackfriars Coll OX1. . . 261 B3
Blackfriars Rd OX1 . . . 261 B1
Blackhall Rd OX1. . . . . 261 B3
Blackhorse La OX13 . . 158 F3
Blacklands OX12. . . . . 212 E4
Black Lands Rd
 Benson OX10. . . . . . 204 A4
 Benson OX10. . . . . . 204 A5
Blacklands Way OX14. 179 C7
Blacklocks Hill
 Banbury OX17. . . . . . 17 D8
 Nethercote OX17. . . . 17 B7
Blackman Cl OX1. . . . . 141 E2
Blackmore Cl
 Thame OX9 . . . . 148 A7
 [3] Thame OX9 . . . . . 148 A7
Blackmore La RG4. . . . 253 D5
Blacknall Rd OX14. . . . 179 E5
Blacksmiths Cl OX25. . 79 A2
Blacksmiths Ct
 Kingham OX7. . . . . . . .54 F5
 Kingham OX7. . . . . . . 55 A5
Blacksmiths Hill OX17 . 35 C7
Blacksmiths La OX5 . . 95 A4
Blacksmiths Mdw [8]
 OX4 . . . . 142 F1
Blackstock Cl OX3. . . . 142 E7
Blackstone Rd OX10 . . 203 D1
BLACKTHORN. 82 A4
Blackthorn Ave OX18 . 115 E5
Blackthorn Cl
 Blackthorn OX25. . . . .81 F3
 Blackthorn OX25. . . . .82 A3
 Oxford OX3 . . . . 124 E4
 Reading RG31 . . . . . 257 B1
Blackthorne Mews [9]
 OX18. . . . . 115 E5
Blackthorn Grange
 OX9 . . . . 148 A6
Blackthorn Hill OX25 . . 81 D2
Blackthorn Rd
 Ambrosden OX25 . . . . 81 D4
 Blackthorn OX27. . . . .82 C8
 Didcot OX11 . . . . 200 C1
 Launton OX26. . . . . . 66 E1
 Launton OX26. . . . . . 81 E8
 Marsh Gibbon OX26 . . 67 D1
 Wantage OX12 . . . . . 215 A6
Blackthorn Rise OX9. . 166 B8
Blackthorn Row SN7. . 172 E1
Blackwater Cl RG4. . . . 259 E4
Blackwater Way OX11 201 A3
Blackwell Dr
 Bodicote OX15. . . . . . 16 D1
 Brize Norton OX18 . . . 116 A5
Blackworth SN6. . . . . . 190 A8
Blackworth Ind Est
 SN6. . . . . 190 A7
BLADON 91 C2
Bladon CE Prim Sch
 OX20. . . . . .91 B2
Bladon Cl OX2 . . . . . . 122 F8
Bladon Rd OX20 . . . . . .91 D4
Blaenant RG4 . . . . 258 F5
Blaenavon RG4 . . . . . 258 F5
Blagrave Cl OX11 . . . . 200 E1
Blagrave Farm La
 RG4. . . . . 258 D5
Blagrave La RG4. . . . . 258 D4
Blake CE Aided Prim Sch
 The OX28 . . . . 118 C8
Blake Cres OX29. . . . . 102 D2
Blakehope Burn OX11 200 F3
Blakeman La OX29. . . 120 C7
Blake Rd OX26. . . . . . . .65 E4
Blakes Ave OX28. . . . . 118 D7
Blake's Field OX11. . . . 200 D1
Blakes Rd RG10. . . . . . 255 E3
Blake Way OX9 . . . . . . 130 A1
Blandford Alley SN6. . . 190 A5
Blandford Ave OX2 . . . 109 A1
Blandford Cl OX26 . . . .91 A6
Blandford Rd OX5 . . . . .92 D2
Blandy Ave OX13. . . . . 156 E1
Blandy Rd RG9 . . . . . . 254 C2
Blanes Cl HP18. . . . . . 129 C6
Blanket Way [1] OX28 . 104 A2

Blankstone Cl OX29. . . 120 D7
Blay Cl OX4 . . . . 142 E3
Bleache Pl OX4. . . . . . 142 D5
BLEDINGTON 54 D1
Bledington Prim Sch
 OX7 . . . . 54 D2
BLEDLOW 169 B8
Bledlow Rd HP27. . . . . 169 E8
BLEDLOW RIDGE 189 E8
Bledlow Ridge Rd
 HP27. . . . . 169 C8
Bledlow Ridge Sch
 HP14. . . . . 189 F8
Blencowe Cl OX27 . . . . .65 F6
BLENHEIM Garsington . 143 D2
 Horspath 143 C7
Blenheim Cl
 Didcot OX11 . . . . 200 F1
 Upper Rissington GL54. 68 B4
Blenheim Ct
 Carterton OX18. . . . . 115 D3
 [2] Kidlington OX5. . . . 108 F8
 Oxford OX2 . . . . 123 A8
Blenheim Dr
 Bicester OX26. . . . . . 65 C3
 Launton OX26 . . . . . . 66 E2
 Oxford OX2 . . . . 123 A7
 Witney OX28. . . . . . . 117 E7
 Wolvercote OX2 . . . . 122 F8
Blenheim Gdns OX12 . 196 C1
Blenheim Hill OX11. . . 217 F7
Blenheim La
 Freeland OX29 . . . . . 106 A6
 Little Milton OX44. . . 164 A6
 Wheatley OX33 . . . . . 144 A8
Blenheim Orch OX12. . 197 D6
Blenheim Palace★
 OX20 . . . . .91 A5
Blenheim Pl OX10 . . . . 204 D2
Blenheim Rd
 Banbury OX16 . . . . . . 16 E2
 Horspath OX33 . . . . . 143 C7
 Kidlington OX5. . . . . . 108 F8
 Reading RG4 . . . . . . 259 A3
 Shirburn OX49. . . . . . 186 D4
 Watchfield SN6. . . . . 191 C1
Blenheim Rise OX17. . . .23 F6
Blenheim Terr
 Bletchingdon OX5 . . . 93 A8
 Chipping Norton OX7 . 42 E1
Blenheim Way
 Horspath OX33 . . . . . 143 C7
 Kingston Bagpuize
 OX13. . . . . 156 D1
Bleriot Rd GL54. . . . . . .68 B4
Blessed George Napier RC
 Sch & Sports Coll
 OX16. . . . . 16 C3
BLETCHINGDON 93 B8
Bletchingdon Parochial CE
 Prim Sch OX5 . . . . . .93 A8
Bletchingdon Rd
 Bletchingdon OX5 . . . 78 A3
 Hampton Poyle OX5 . . 93 A4
 Islip OX5. . . . . 93 E2
 Islip OX5. . . . . 93 E4
BLEWBURY 237 B8
Blewbury Endowed CE
 Prim Sch OX11 . . . . 218 F1
Blewbury Hill OX11. . . 237 B8
Blewbury Rd OX11. . . . 219 B3
Blewitt Ct [2] OX4. . . . 142 B2
Blissett Cl [2] OX11. . . 218 B7
Blissett Terr [3] SN7 . . 172 E3
Bliss Ho OX7 . . . . .42 E1
Bliss Mill
 Chipping Norton OX7 . 42 C2
 Chipping Norton OX7 . 42 C2
Blomfield Pl OX2 . . . . 261 A4
Blossom Gr RG5. . . . . 260 E1
Blossom Rd RG4. . . . . 258 F3
Blossoms Glade OX14. 160 E6
Blounts Court Rd RG4,
 RG9. . . . . 253 B6
Blowings The OX29. . . 106 A7
Blowingstone Hill
 OX12. . . . . 212 A2
BLOXHAM 21 D5
Bloxham CE Prim Sch
 OX15 . . . . .21 C4
Bloxham Ct OX15. . . . . .21 E2
Bloxham Grove Rd
 OX15 . . . . .22 B6
Bloxham Mill Bsns Ctr
 OX15 . . . . .21 E2
Bloxham Rd
 Banbury OX16. . . . . . 16 B3
 Barford St Michael OX15 .32 F7
 Bloxham OX15. . . . . . 21 E3
 Milcombe OX15. . . . . 21 B2
 Milton OX17. . . . . . . 22 C3
Bloxham Sch OX15 . . . .21 E5
Bloxham Village Mus★
 OX15 . . . . 21 E4
Bluebell Cl [1] OX26. . . .65 E5
Bluebell Ct [2] OX4 . . . 142 F1
Bluebell Gdns RG4. . . 259 C7
Bluebell La OX11 . . . . 218 C2
Bluebell Mws [3] OX4 . 124 C5
Bluebell Ride OX14 . . . 160 E7
Bluebell Way OX14 . . . 115 F4
Blueberry Dr OX27. . . . 65 D7
Blue Boar St OX1. . . . . 261 B2
Bluecoats Cl OX10 . . . . 16 D6
Blue Mountains OX10. 221 B8
Blue Row OX7. . . . . . . .42 E5
Blush Cres OX18. . . . . . 115 D6
Blythe Pl OX26 . . . . . . .65 B3
BOARS HILL. 140 D1

BOARSTALL...........97 B1
Boarstall Duck Decoy★
 HP18..............97 A3
Boathouse Reach RG9 244 E1
Bobby Fryer Cl OX4... 142 E4
Bockett's Cnr OX18... 102 A7
Boddington La OX29.. 105 C8
Boddington Rd
 Claydon OX17...........1 D1
 Upper Boddington CV47...1 E8
BODICOTE..........22 D8
Bodleian Liby★ OX1.. 261 C2
Bodleian (New Liby)★
 OX1...............261 C1
Bodley Pl OX2..... 123 B8
Bodley Rd OX4..... 142 C3
Boham's Houses OX11 218 F1
Bohams Rd OX11... 236 D6
Bolero Gdns OX26....80 F6
Bolney La RG9......255 A5
Bolney Rd RG9......255 B5
Bolney Trevor Dr RG9. 255 A4
Bolsover Cl OX29.... 90 A1
Bolton Rd OX16....... 16 C6
Bolton's La OX29..... 90 C3
Bonar Rd OX3..... 124 E1
Bonds End La OX15... 19 A8
Bonds La OX29..... 119 D6
Bones La RG9......254 A3
Bonham Pl OX18.... 115 D4
Bonnersfield HP18... 129 C7
Bonners Mead OX12.. 203 F4
Bonn Sq Oxford OX1.. 261 B2
 Oxford OX4........ 123 C1
Book End OX29..... 103 C1
Booth Rd OX16.......9 C2
Boot La OX11....... 217 D8
Boot St OX8........ 89 C7
Boreford Rd OX14... 160 B2
Boroma Way RG9....244 E2
Borough Ave OX10... 221 C7
Borough Rd NN13.... 24 A5
Borough Wlk OX14... 159 E1
Borrowmead Rd OX3. 124 B5
Borwood Ct OX5.... 108 F6
Boshers Cl OX10.... 239 A8
Bosley Cres OX11... 221 D7
Bosleys Orch OX11.. 200 E1
Bosley's Orch OX11.. 200 E1
Bosmore La RG9.... 226 B4
Bostock Rd OX14... 179 E7
Boston Cl OX12.... 214 B8
Boston Rd Bicester OX26 66 A4
 Henley-on-Thames RG9. 254 E8
Boswell Rd OX4.... 142 D4
Botanic Garden The (Univ
 of Oxford)★ OX1.. 261 C2
Botany Gdns OX10... 222 A6
Bothy The Aynho OX17.. 35 D7
 Wargrave RG10......255 D2
BOTLEY............140 D8
Botley Intc OX2..... 122 D2
Botley Prim Sch OX2. 122 D1
Botley Rd OX2..... 122 F1
Botley Works OX2... 122 D1
Bottle Square La
 HP14..............189 D6
Bottom La
 Checkendon RG8.....241 A4
 Woodcote OX10......240 D1
Bottom Rd HP14.... 189 E7
Boucher Cl OX12... 214 D8
Boughton's Mill
 OX10..............221 D7
BOULD.............69 C7
Boulevard The OX5....92 B2
Boulter Dr OX14.... 160 A3
Boulter St OX4..... 123 F1
Boults Cl OX3..... 123 F5
Boults La OX3..... 123 F5
Boundary Brook Rd
 OX4..............142 A6
Boundary Cl OX20.... 91 C6
Boundary La
 Carterton OX18.... 115 E5
 Reading RG4...... 258 E3
Boundary Mews
 OX18..............115 E5
Boundary Rd NN13... 24 A6
Boundary Way
 OX18..............115 E5
Bourlon Wood OX14. 159 D1
 Cutteslowe OX2...... 109 B1
Bourne Cl Bicester OX26 65 D1
Bourne End OX25....63 B8
Bourne La OX15..... 30 A8
Bourne Rd RG8..... 256 E5
Bourne St OX11.... 218 F8
Bourne The
 Eastleach Martin GL7. 131 A7
 Hook Norton OX15.... 30 A7
BOURTON...........209 A3
Bourton Cl
 Clanfield OX18.... 133 F1
 Witney OX28...... 117 E8
Bourton Cotts OX18.. 134 E3
Bourton Rd
 Banbury OX16.......9 D3
 Upper Rissington OX7... 68 A5
Bovewell OX27.......35 E3
Bovingdon Rd OX18.. 115 F3
Bovington's Yd OX18. 115 D3
BOW..............174 E1
Bow Bank OX3..... 156 C3
Bow Bank Cl OX13.. 156 C3
Bower End OX44.... 184 C7
Bower Gn SN6...... 191 F2
Bowerman Cl OX5... 108 D8
Bower Rd RG8......247 F4

Bowers La
 Bledlow Ridge HP14.. 189 D7
 Bledlow Ridge HP14.. 189 E6
Bowfell Cl RG31.... 257 C2
Bowgrave Copse
 OX14..............160 C1
Bowlers Way OX20... 91 C5
Bowles Ave OX29... 102 D2
Bowley Ho OX20.....91 B6
Bowling Ct RG9.... 244 D3
Bowling Gn HP14... 188 D5
Bowling Green Cl
 OX18..............134 F4
Bowling Green Farmhouse
 RG8..............257 B5
Bowling Green La
 RG8..............257 B5
Bowmen's Lea OX17... 35 C7
Bowmont Sq OX26.... 15 E7
Bowmont Water OX11 200 F2
Bowness Ave
 Didcot OX11.......218 D7
 Oxford OX3....... 124 A4
Bow Rd SN7......174 E1
Bowsher Way OX18.. 135 F3
Bowyer Cl OX14.... 160 F2
Bowyer Rd OX14.... 179 F8
Boxhedge Rd OX16....16 B6
Boxhedge Sq OX16....16 B6
Boxhedge Terr OX16. 16 B6
Boxhill Rd OX14.... 179 F8
Boxhill Wlk OX14... 179 F8
Box Tree La
 Didcot OX11.......218 C7
 Postcombe OX9..... 166 F4
Boxwell Cl OX14.... 160 B2
Bozedown Dr RG8... 250 D1
Bracegirdle Rd OX3.. 124 C1
Bracken Cl
 Carterton OX18.... 115 D4
 Reading RG31..... 257 C1
BRACKLEY..........24 A7
Brackley Rd
 Brackley NN13....... 24 D6
 Croughton NN13..... 36 D8
 Shalstone MK18...... 25 C5
 Westbury NN13...... 25 A5
Brackstone Cl RG4... 259 C2
Bradburn Cl OX10... 203 B1
Bradburys The OX27... 66 D8
Braddens Furlong
 HP18..............129 C6
Bradfield Ct OX14... 199 D7
Bradford Cl OX15.... 21 D4
Bradford St OX26.... 65 A1
Brading Way RG8... 257 D5
Bradlands OX3.... 123 E7
Bradley Arc OX16....15 F6
Bradley's St RG8.... 241 B4
Bradmore Rd OX2... 123 C4
Bradshaw Cl OX25....62 A8
Bradstock's Way OX14 199 F6
BRADWELL GROVE.. 114 B6
Bradwell Rd RG31... 257 C3
Braeburn Ave OX27... 65 D7
Brae Hill HP18.......98 A1
Braemar Cl OX18.... 115 D5
Brailes Ind Est OX15..12 A3
Braithwaite Cl OX16. 16 A5
Brake Hill
 Oxford OX4...... 142 F1
 Oxford OX4...... 143 A1
Bramber Cl OX16.... 15 F7
Bramber Mews RG4.. 259 E4
Bramble Bank OX28. 104 D2
Bramble Cres OX15.. 16 F1
Bramble La
 Carterton OX18.... 115 F5
 Didcot OX11...... 200 B1
 Didcot OX11...... 218 B8
Brambles The OX3.. 124 C2
Bramblings OX18... 258 E6
Bramblings The OX26.. 66 A1
Brambling Way OX4.. 142 D2
Bramley Ave OX27... 65 D6
Bramley Cl
 Cutteslowe OX5..... 109 A8
 Southmoor OX13.... 176 D8
Bramley Cres RG4... 252 E5
Bramley Hts OX28... 117 F8
Bramling Cross OX13. 156 D1
Brampton Chase RG9. 255 A4
Brampton Cl OX14... 159 E1
Brampton Dr OX18.. 115 F2
Brampton Rd OX3... 124 A1
Bramshaw Rd RG30.. 258 A1
Bramwell Pl OX14... 141 F8
Branagh Ct RG30... 258 B1
Brandon Cl OX5.... 108 B8
Brantwood Cl OX16...16 B4
Brantwood Rise OX16..16 B4
Brasenose Coll OX1.. 261 C2
Brasenose Dr OX5.....92 F1
Brasenose Driftway
 OX4..............142 E6
Brasenose La OX1... 261 C2
Brasenose Rd OX11.. 200 D1
Brasenose Villas OX7.. 42 E2
Brashfield Rd OX26...65 E4
Brassey Cl OX7......42 F3
Brassey Ho OX7......42 E2
Brassica Terr OX27... 65 D8
BRASSWELL CORNER..86 F7
Brasswell Gate OX5...86 E8
Braybrooke Cl OX7....58 F5
Braybrooke Gdns
 RG10..............255 D1
Braybrooke Rd RG10.. 255 D1
Braze La OX10...... 204 A6

Braziers La
 Ipsden OX10........240 E5
 Ipsden OX10........241 A5
Breakspear Cl OX12.. 194 F2
Breakspear Way OX29 105 A7
Breame Oak Dr OX33. 144 B8
Bream Ridge OX12... 214 C6
Breeches End OX1... 140 B7
Breedons Hill RG8... 256 C5
Brenda OX11.......16 B4
Brendon Cl
 Didcot OX11...... 200 C2
 Reading RG30..... 257 E1
Brent Ave OX11..... 200 H4
Brent St OX11..... 200 H4
Brent Cl OX26....... 65 A2
Brentford Cl OX10... 220 E1
Brereton Dr OX12... 196 D1
Bretch Hill
 Banbury OX16....... 15 E7
 Banbury OX16....... 15 F6
Brett Cl OX9...... 148 B8
Brett Linley Gdns
 OX11..............200 B2
Brewer Cl OX13.... 199 A4
Brewers Ct OX14... 179 F6
Brewer St OX1..... 261 B1
Brewery La
 Chastleton GL56.....40 F8
 Hook Norton OX15....29 F7
Brewery Row
 Little Compton GL56...26 F1
 Little Compton GL56...27 A1
Brewery St SN6.... 190 A5
Briaily HP14....... 189 C2
Briants Ave RG4.... 259 C2
Briant's Ave RG4.... 259 C2
Briar Cl Banbury OX16. 16 D2
 Kidlington OX5...... 92 C2
 Reading RG4...... 259 A5
Briar End OX5....... 92 C2
Briar Furlong OX25... 81 C4
Briars Cl RG8...... 256 F5
Briarswood Cl HP14. 188 E5
Briar Thicket OX20... 91 C6
Briar Way OX4..... 142 F3
Briary Way GL7.... 150 D6
Briary Way OX18.... 115 F5
Brice Rd OX25...... 63 C8
Brick Alley RG8..... 179 F6
Brick Hill OX15......30 B6
Brick Kiln Rise SN7.. 172 F5
Bricklayers Ct OX3... 123 F6
Brickle La Bloxham OX15 21 E5
 Bloxham OX15...... 21 E5
Brick Row OX15......19 F8
Bricks La HP14.... 189 C4
Bridal Terr OX12... 214 D5
Bridens Way HP17... 130 F6
Bridewell Cl OX29... 105 B7
Bridge Cl Didcot OX11 219 A8
 Lechlade-on-Thames
 GL7..............150 E3
Bridge Cottage Rd
 GL7..............131 A7
BRIDGE END....... 202 D8
Bridge End OX18... 202 D8
Bridge Farm Cl OX12. 214 F7
Bridge Hill OX15.....30 B7
Bridge Rd HP18.... 127 F2
Bridges Cl
 Abingdon-on-Thames
 OX14..............179 C5
 Bloxham OX15...... 21 E3
Bridge St
 Abingdon-on-Thames
 OX14..............179 F6
 Bampton OX18.... 134 E3
 Banbury OX16....... 16 D6
 Islip OX5........ 109 F8
 Oxford OX1...... 123 A1
 Reading RG4...... 259 A2
 Shilton OX18.... 115 B6
 Witney OX28...... 104 B1
Bridgewater Ct RG30. 258 C1
Bridle Cl OX16..... 16 E3
Bridle Path
 Charney Bassett OX12. 175 F2
 Woodcote RG8...... 250 E8
Bridle Rd RG8..... 250 E3
Bridle Way The OX10. 239 C1
Bridus Mead OX11.. 219 B1
Bridus Way OX11... 219 A1
Brierley Pl RG31... 257 C4
Briggs Cl OX16.... 15 F4
Brigham Rd RG1.... 259 A1
BRIGHTHAMPTON... 137 B4
BRIGHTWELL
 BALDWIN........ 185 A4
BRIGHTWELL-CUM-
 SOTWELL........ 202 C2
Brightwell-cum-Sotwell
 CE (Controlled) Prim Sch
 OX10..............202 A2
Brightwell St OX10... 202 B2
BRILL.............98 B1
Brill CE Comb Sch
 HP18..............98 B1
Brill Cl RG4...... 259 A4
Brill Rd
 Horton-cum-Studley
 OX33..............112 C6
 Ludgershall HP18.... 98 B7
Brind Cl OX13.... 198 E4
Brindley La OX2... 123 A4
Brinds Cl RG4..... 253 A5
Brinkburn Gr OX16.. 16 F8
Brinkinfield Rd OX44. 184 D7
Bristol Cl HP17.... 128 E6
Bristol Rd Bicester OX26 66 A4

Bristol Rd continued
 Upper Rissington GL54.. 68 B5
Bristow Ct RG4.... 259 B2
Britannia Cl OX18.. 115 E4
Britannia Hts OX16.. 16 D5
Britannia Place
 RG9..............244 E1
Britannia St OX16.... 16 D5
Britannia Wharf
 OX16..............16 D5
Britnell Ct HP14.... 188 E5
Britwell Hill OX49... 206 B4
Britwell Rd
 Didcot OX11...... 200 E1
 Ewelme OX10.... 204 F4
 Watlington OX49.... 186 A1
BRITWELL SALOME.. 205 E7
Brixton Hill
 Nuffield OX10..... 223 A4
 Oakley Wood OX10.. 222 F4
BRIZE NORTON..... 116 C4
Brize Norton Airfield
 OX18..............116 A1
Brize Norton Prim Sch
 OX18..............116 C3
Brize Norton Rd
 Carterton OX18.... 115 E2
 Minster Lovell OX29.. 102 E2
Brizewood OX18.... 115 D4
Broadbrook La OX12. 212 F4
Broad Cl
 Barford St Michael
 OX15..............32 E5
 Kidlington OX5.... 108 D8
 Oxford OX2...... 122 B1
Broad End OX15......16 E1
Broad Field Rd OX5.. 108 B7
Broadfields OX4.... 142 D2
Broad Gap
 Bodicote OX15....... 16 E1
 Bodicote OX15....... 22 E8
Broadhead Pl OX3... 124 B5
Broad Hill OX28.... 104 C2
Broadhurst Gdns OX4. 142 A1
Broad Lays OX10... 203 E5
Broadmarsh Cl OX12. 214 D8
Broad Marsh La OX29 206 A6
Broadmoor La RG5.. 260 E4
Broad Oak OX3.... 142 E8
BROADPLAT........ 243 E4
Broadshires Way
 OX18..............115 F3
Broad St
 Abingdon-on-Thames
 OX14..............179 F7
 Bampton OX18.... 134 E3
 Banbury OX16....... 16 D6
 Long Compton CV36... 27 F6
 Long Compton CV36... 28 A6
 Oxford OX1...... 261 B2
 Uffington SN7.... 211 C7
Broadstone Est
 Enstone OX7....... 44 A1
 Enstone OX7....... 58 A8
Broadwater Pl OX12. 214 D3
Broadwaters Ave OX9. 147 F7
Broadway Didcot OX11 218 E8
 Harwell OX11.... 217 E6
 Witney OX28...... 103 D1
Broadway Cl
 Chalgrove OX44.... 184 D6
 Harwell OX11.... 217 E6
 Witney OX28...... 103 D1
Broadway The
 Charlton-on-Otmoor
 OX5..............95 A4
 Kidlington OX5.... 108 D8
BROADWELL....... 132 E4
Broadwell Cl OX26... 65 D2
Broadwell Dr OX18. 115 E3
Broadwell Rd GL7... 132 D2
Broad Wy OX25......63 B8
Brock Gr OX2...... 122 F1
Brocklesby Rd OX4.. 142 A2
Brocks Way RG9.... 255 A4
Brode Cl OX14.... 160 B2
Brogden Cl OX2.... 140 E7
Bromag Ind Est OX28. 103 B2
Brome Pl OX3.... 124 E4
Bromeswell Cl OX25... 62 E6
Bromsgrove SN7... 172 F3
Brook Cl HP18.......98 C8
Brook Cottage Gdn★
 OX15..............6 F2
Brook Dr OX14.... 199 F4
BROOKEND.........72 A8
Brooke Rd OX16.... 16 A3
Brookfield Cl
 Milton-under-Wychwood
 OX7..............70 A1
 Wallingford OX10.. 221 C5
Brookfield Cres OX3.. 124 A5
Brookfield Rise OX15.. 20 D7
Brookfields Sch RG31. 257 C3
BROOKHAMPTON... 163 C1
Brookhampton Cl
 OX44..............163 C1
Brook Hill OX20.....91 B6
Brookhill Way OX16...16 F8
Brook La
 Denchworth OX12... 196 A4
 Stonesfield OX29.... 89 C6
 Thame OX9...... 148 B8
 West Hagbourne OX11. 218 C5
 Woodgreen OX28... 104 E3
Brook Lea RG4.... 259 C1
Brooklyn Dr OX2.... 91 B6
Brooklyn Gdns OX25... 79 B1
Brookmead Dr OX10. 221 C6
Brook Rd Bicester OX26. 65 C3
 Great Tew OX7...... 45 D7

Brooksby Rd RG31... 257 D2
Brookside
 Abingdon-on-Thames
 OX14..............159 F1
 Cholsey OX10.... 220 F1
 Cuddesdon OX44... 144 A2
 East Hanney OX12.. 197 A6
 Great Tew OX7...... 45 D7
 Harwell OX11.... 217 E7
 Hook Norton OX15.... 30 A7
 Oxford OX3...... 124 C2
 Thame OX9...... 129 F1
 Watlington OX49.... 186 B2
Brookside Cl OX9... 145 F7
Brookside Ct
 Bicester OX26..... 65 E2
 Woodstock OX20.... 91 A6
Brookside Est OX44. 184 C7
Brookside Prim Sch
 OX26..............65 D2
Brookside Way OX15... 21 C4
Brooks Row OX29... 87 A4
Brook St Benson OX10 204 A4
 Kingston Blount OX39. 167 F4
 Oxford OX1...... 141 C7
 Sutton Courtenay OX14 200 A8
 Watlington OX49.... 186 B1
Brooks Taylor Ct OX1. 261 B1
Brookstones
 Sydenham OX39.... 167 D8
 Sydenham OX9.... 148 D1
Brook View
 Kingston Bagpuize
 OX13..............156 D1
 Oxford OX2...... 143 A2
Brook Way OX29.... 90 A1
Broome Way OX16... 16 F7
Broomfield Rd RG30.. 258 A1
BROUGHTON....... 15 C1
Broughton Castle★
 OX15..............15 B1
Broughton Cl RG30. 258 C1
BROUGHTON POGGS. 132 A4
Broughton Rd OX16... 15 E3
Broughtons Cl OX3... 123 F5
Browning Dr OX26... 65 C4
Browning Rd OX16... 16 A3
Browns Cl OX2.... 140 A8
Brown's La
 Charlbury OX7....... 73 B4
 Woodstock OX20.... 91 A6
Bruen Rd OX7...... 69 C1
Bruern Abbey Sch
 OX26..............80 A7
Bruern Rd
 Milton-under-Wychwood
 OX7..............69 F4
 Milton-under-Wychwood
 OX7..............70 A3
Brumcombe La OX1,
 OX13..............159 F8
Brundle Way OX12.. 215 B6
Brunel Cres OX12... 196 D1
Brunel Dr RG5.... 260 F1
Brunel Rd OX11... 218 C8
Brunstock Beck OX11. 200 F3
Brunswick Green
 OX11..............200 B3
Brunswick Pl OX16.. 16 E6
Bryan Ho OX26......6 E5
Bryan Way OX12... 214 F6
Bryant Pl RG8.... 257 B5
Bryant Way OX12... 214 F6
Brymbo Cotts OX15... 30 D8
Bryony Cl OX4.... 143 A2
Bryony Gdns OX18.. 115 F5
Bryony Rd OX26.....65 E5
Bryworth La GL7.... 150 A6
Buchanan Cl OX25....96 E7
Buchanan Rd OX25... 96 E7
Buchan Pl OX13.... 177 A8
Buchan Rd OX26.... 65 C4
Buckingham Cl
 Didcot OX11...... 219 B8
 Kings Sutton OX17... 23 F6
Buckingham Corner
 OX26..............65 F4
Buckingham Cres OX26 65 F3
Buckingham Ct NN13.. 24 A6
Buckingham Dr RG4.. 259 B5
Buckingham Gate
 RG4..............259 B4
Buckingham Pl OX18. 115 D1
Buckingham Rd
 Barton Hartshorn
 MK18..............39 C4
 Bicester OX26..... 65 F4
 Bicester OX27..... 66 A7
 Brackley NN13....... 24 A6
 Chetwode MK18.... 53 A8
 Croughton NN13.... 36 F7
 Croughton NN13.... 37 B7
 Croughton NN13.... 37 E7
 Mixbury NN13...... 38 A8
 Shalstone MK18.... 25 F8
 Westbury NN13...... 25 E8
Buckingham Road Ind Est
 NN13..............24 A6
Buckingham St
 Oxford OX1...... 141 C7
 Oxford OX1...... 261 B1
BUCKLAND........ 154 E1
Buckland CE Prim Sch
 SN7..............174 E8
Buckland Ct OX5.... 108 F7
Buckland Dr SN6.... 209 A6
BUCKLAND MARSH.. 154 D4
Buckland Mews
 OX14..............179 D7
Buckland Rd
 Bampton OX18.... 154 C7

Buckland Rd continued
 Buckland SN7..... 174 E8
 Charney Bassett OX12. 175 B4
 Charney Bassett OX12. 175 E2
 Charney Bassett OX13. 174 F4
 Gainfield SN7...... 174 F4
Buckler Pl OX4.... 142 A1
Buckler Rd OX2.... 123 B8
Bucklers Bury Rd
 OX14..............160 B3
Buckles Cl OX14... 179 D7
BUCKNELL..........65 A8
Bucknell Ave RG8... 256 E5
Bucknell Rd
 Bicester OX26..... 65 D3
 Bicester OX27..... 65 E5
Buckner's Cl OX10... 203 F4
Buckside Rd OX4... 259 A2
Buckthorn Cres OX11. 218 C5
Buckthorn La OX10.. 220 F1
Budds Cl OX20..... 91 D7
Bugloss Wlk OX26... 65 D4
Bulan Rd OX3.... 142 E8
Bulbush La OX17... 11 A1
Bulldog Cl OX10... 204 B2
Bullers St OX16......8 F2
Bull Hill OX7........72 B8
Bullingdon Ave OX10. 182 C5
Bullingdon Rd OX4.. 141 F7
Bull La OX18...... 135 E2
Bullmarsh Cl OX25... 64 A4
Bull Mdw The RG8... 248 F6
Bullockspit La OX13. 176 C7
Bullockspits La OX13. 176 C7
Bull Ring OX15......33 F4
Bulls Cl GL7...... 132 B5
Bulls La Ickford HP18. 128 A3
 Kings Sutton OX17.... 23 F5
Bull's La OX5...... 95 D5
Bullsmead OX13... 159 E5
Bull St OX18...... 135 E2
Bullstake Cl OX2... 122 F1
Bulrush Rd OX4.... 142 F1
Bulwarks La OX1... 261 B2
Bungalow Cl OX3... 111 C2
Bunkers Hill OX5.... 92 A8
BUNKERS HILL
 Bunkers Hill OX5.... 92 A8
 Shipton-on-Cherwell OX5 77 A1
Buntings The OX26... 81 A8
Bunyan Rd OX26.... 65 C4
Burbidge Cl OX7.... 42 E1
Burbush Rd OX4.... 142 E5
Burchester Ave OX3. 124 E4
Burchester Pl OX16..16 F7
Burcombe Way RG4.. 259 B4
BURCOT...........182 A4
Burcot La OX10.... 182 D4
Burcot Pk OX14.... 181 F5
Burdell Ave OX3.... 125 A4
Burditch Bank OX20.. 75 F5
Burdock Cl OX4.... 142 F2
Burdock Cl OX26.... 65 E4
Burdock Ct OX33... 143 A2
Burdock Spur OX11.. 218 C7
BURDROP..........19 B8
Bure La OX11..... 201 A2
Bure Park Nature
 Reserve★ OX26.... 65 D4
Bure Park Prim Sch
 OX26..............65 D4
Bure Pl OX26..... 65 D4
BURFORD..........100 D5
Burford Hill Mws
 OX18..............100 D4
Burford Lodge OX1 141 C7
Burford Prim Sch
 OX18..............100 E5
Burford Rd
 Black Bourton OX18. 133 F6
 Brize Norton OX18.. 116 A5
 Burford OX18.... 100 F6
 Carterton OX18.... 115 D3
 Carterton OX18.... 115 E7
 Chipping Norton OX7. 42 E2
 Filkins GL7...... 132 C6
 Lechlade-on-Thames
 GL7..............150 D6
 Minster Lovell OX18. 101 F1
 Minster Lovell OX29. 102 C2
 Shipton under Wychwood
 OX7..............85 C5
 Witney OX28...... 104 A1
 Witney OX29...... 103 D2
Burford Sch OX18.. 100 D4
Burford Sch (Annexe)
 OX18..............100 E5
Burgage Gdns OX18. 100 E5
Burgan Cl OX4.... 142 D4
Burgess Cl OX14... 179 F7
Burgess Mead OX2.. 123 A4
Burgidge Way OX3.. 168 B7
Burh Corner OX10. 221 C7
Burleigh Mews RG4.. 259 C6
Burleigh Rd OX20... 107 C6
Burleigh Rise OX3... 125 A3
Burlington Cres OX3. 125 A3
Burlington Gdns OX16. 16 A4
Burnham Rise RG4.. 259 C7
Burnhams The HP18. 128 D3
Burns Cl HP18.... 129 C7
Burns Cres OX26.... 65 C4
Burns Rd OX16..... 16 A4
Burra Cl OX4..... 161 A7
Burr Cl OX29...... 120 B1
Burrows Cl OX3.... 124 D3

Burrows Cres OX7 . . . . . .42 E1
Burrows Hill OX10 . . 204 F3
Burr St OX11 . . . . 217 E7
Bursill Cl OX3 . . . . 125 A3
Burswin Rd OX18 . . . . . 115 D5
Burtonagnes Ave
 OX14 . . . . 201 B5
Burton Cl OX14 . . . . . 179 D6
Burton Mws OX18 . . . 100 E3
Burton Pl OX4 . . . . . . 142 E6
Burtons Bank OX7 . . . .68 E6
Burton Taylor Studio★
 OX1 . . . . 261 B2
Burts La HP18 . . . . . 129 D6
Burwell Cl OX28 . . . . 117 E7
Burwell Ct OX28 . . . . 117 F7
Burwell Dr OX28 . . . . 117 F7
Burwell Mdw OX28 . . 117 F6
Bury Cl OX7 . . . . .54 F3
Bury Court La OX17 . . . .8 D8
Bury Croft Rd OX15 . . .30 B6
Burycroft The OX14 . . 180 A3
Buryhook Cnr OX33 . . 126 C2
Bury La RG20 . . . . . . 235 A2
Bury Mead OX29 . . . . 138 A8
Bury St OX14 . . . . . . 179 F7
Buryway La CV36 . . . . .27 F7
Busby Cl
 Freeland OX29 . . . . 106 A6
 Stonesfield OX29 . . . 89 D7
Busby Dr
 Banbury OX16 . . . . . . .15 E2
 Minster Lovell OX29 . . 102 D2
Busbys Cl
 Clanfield OX18 . . . . . 133 E1
 Clanfield OX18 . . . . . 152 E8
BUSCOT 171 A8
Buscot Dr OX14 . . . . 160 B2
Buscot Pk★ SN7 . . 171 C6
BUSCOT WICK 170 D8
Busgrove La
 Checkendon RG9 . . . 241 F2
 Sonning Common RG4 . 252 A8
 Stoke Row RG9 . . . . 242 A4
 Stoke Row RG9 . . . . 242 A4
 Woodcote RG8 . . . . . 251 F8
Bushell Bsns Pk
 OX10 . . . . 221 B7
Bushes La RG4 . . . . . 224 C4
Bushey Dr OX18 . . . . 152 E7
Bushey Gd OX29 . . . . 116 F8
BUSHEY GROUND . . . 116 E8
Bushey Leys Cl OX3. . 124 E5
Bushey Row OX18 . . . 134 F3
Bush Furlong OX11 . . 201 B2
Bushnell Cl OX3 . . . . 124 F3
Bush The HP17 . . . . . 130 F5
Bushy Cl OX2 . . . . . . 122 B1
Butchers Ct OX28 . . . 118 A8
Butchers Hill OX7 . . . 45 C7
Butcher's Row OX16 . . 16 D6
Butler Cl
 Bloxham OX15 . . . . . .21 E6
 Horspath OX33 . . . . . 143 E6
 Oxford OX2 . . . . 123 B4
Butler Ho OX4 . . . . . 142 B3
Butlers Cl CV36 . . . . . 28 A6
Butlers Ct La GL7 . . . 150 B4
Butlers Dr OX18 . . . . 115 E2
Butler's Field GL7 . . . 150 C5
Butlers La CV36 . . . . . 27 F5
Butlers Orch RG4 . . . 252 D3
Butlers Pond RG8 . . . 250 D2
Butlers Rd CV36 . . . . 28 C5
Butlers Yd RG9 . . . . . 252 F7
Butterbur Gdns 5
 OX26 . . . . .65 E5
Buttercross La 4
 OX28 . . . . 118 A7
Buttercross The★
 OX28 . . . . 118 B8
Buttercup Rd OX12 . . 215 A6
Buttercup Sq 6 OX4 . 142 F1
Buttercup Way 7
 OX4 . . . . 124 C5
Butterly Rd HP14 . . . 188 F4
Butter Market OX9 . . 147 F8
Buttermilk La OX29 . . .86 F1
Butterwort Pl 1 OX4 . 142 F2
Butterwyke Pl OX1 . . 261 B1
Butts Cl OX17 . . . . . . .35 C7
Butts Field
 Banbury OX16 . . . . .8 E1
 Banbury OX16 . . . . . . .15 E8
 Banbury OX16 . . . . . . .15 E8
Butts Hill Rd RG5 . . . 260 E1
Butts La OX3 . . . . . . 123 F7
Butts Rd
 Faringdon SN7 . . . . 172 F2
 Horspath OX33 . . . . . 143 C6
Butts The
 Aynho OX17 . . . . .35 D7
 Long Compton CV36 . . .27 F6
 Merton OX25 . . . . . . .95 D8
 Standlake OX29 . . . . 137 D3
Butts Way OX49 . . . . 167 C1
Buxton Ave RG4 . . . . 258 F4
Buxton Cl OX26 . . . . .65 A2
Buzzard Rise 16
 OX11 . . . . 218 C7
Buzzards Cl OX17 . . . . .9 D5
Byfield Rd OX7 . . . . . . .5 F7
Byeway The OX16 . . . .16 F7
Byres The HP17 . . . . 130 F6
Byron Cl OX14 . . . . . 179 C5
Byron Rd OX16 . . . . . .16 A3
Byron Way OX26 . . . .65 C3

C

Cadel's Row 6 SN7 . . 172 F3
Cadogan Pk OX20 . . . .91 B6
Cadogan Pl RG4 . . . . 259 B3
Cadwell La OX44, OX49 184 E4
Caernarvon Way OX16 . .15 F6
Caesars Gate NN13 . . 24 A6
Calais Dene 2 OX18 . . 135 A3
Calais La OX29 . . . . . 136 E6
Calamint Cl OX11 . . . 218 B8
Calcot Cl OX3 . . . . . . 124 E1
Calcroft La
 Clanfield OX18 . . . . . 133 C2
 Langford GL7 . . . . . . 132 E3
CALDECOTT 179 E6
Caldecott Chase OX14 179 E5
Caldecott Cl OX14 . . . 179 D6
Caldecott Prim Sch
 OX14 . . . . 179 D5
Caldecott Rd
 Abingdon-on-Thames
  OX14 . . . . 179 D6
 Abingdon-on-Thames
  OX14 . . . . 179 E6
Calder Cl OX16 . . . . . .16 F7
Calder Way OX11 . . . 201 B2
Caldicott Cl OX10 . . . 203 B6
Caldwell Rd 3 OX16 . . .16 F4
Calender Pl 2 OX2 . . 122 D8
Caleta Cl RG4 . . . . . . 259 D2
Callow Dr OX15 . . . . . .21 E3
CALTHORPE 16 D3
Calthorpe Rd OX16 . . 16 C5
Calthorpe St OX16 . . . 16 C5
Calves Cl OX5 . . . . . 108 D8
Calvin Thomas Way
 Wallingford OX10 . . . 203 A!
 Wallingford OX10 . . . 221 A7
 Wallingford OX10 . . . 221 A8
Cambridge Terr OX1 . . 261 B1
Cam Cl OX11 . . . . . . 200 F1
Camden Cl GL56 . . . . .26 F5
Camel Cross OX12 . . . 214 C5
Camellias The OX16 . . .9 B1
Cameron Ave OX14 . . 160 C1
Cameron Ct 10 OX16 . . 16 D5
Campbell Cl OX26 . . . .65 E2
Campbell Rd OX4 . . . 142 A5
Campbells Cl OX20 . . 91 C6
CAMP CORNER 145 F4
Campden Cl OX28 . . . 103 E1
Camp Ind Est OX9 . . 146 B4
Campiohall Dr OX11 . . 219 B7
Campion Cl
 Carterton OX18 . . . . 115 E1
 12 Sandford-on-Thames
  OX4 . . . . 142 F1
Campion Pl OX26 . . . . 65 D4
Campion Rd OX14 . . . 180 B8
Campion Way OX28 . . 104 D2
Camp La OX17 . . . . .2 D4
Camp Rd
 Upper Heyford OX25 . . 63 A8
 Upper Heyford OX25 . . 63 B8
 Upper Heyford OX25 . . 63 C8
CAMPSFIELD 91 E3
Canada Cl OX16 . . . . .16 D7
Canada La SN7 . . . . 172 E4
Canal Cl OX5 . . . . 77 C1
Canal Ct OX12 . . . . . 214 C7
Canal Ho 4 OX12 . . . 214 D5
Canal La Bodicote OX15 . .16 F1
 Bodicote OX15 . . . . . 17 A1
Canal Rd OX5 . . . . . . 92 C4
Canal St Banbury OX16 . . 16 D5
 Oxford OX2 . . . . 261 A3
Canal Way
 East Challow OX12 . . 214 A5
 Enslow OX5 . . . . 77 C1
Canal Wharf OX25 . . . .48 F6
Canal Yd OX5 . . . . . . .92 C4
Candytuft Way OX11 . . 200 A1
Candytuft Wy OX11 . . 218 A8
Candy Way OX13 . . . . 159 B6
CANE END 251 F4
Cane La OX12 . . . . . . 214 D8
Canning Cres OX14 . . 141 E5
Cannons Field OX3 . . 123 F6
Canon Hills Gdns SN6 . 209 C6
Canons Dr GL7 . . . . . 150 E3
Canterbury Cl OX16 . . 17 A7
Canterbury Rd OX2 . . 123 B4
Capel Cl OX2 . . . . . . 123 B8
Capri Sq OX10 . . . . . 203 B4
Caps La OX10 . . . . . . 221 B2
Captains Mill OX28 . . 104 B2
Caraway Fields OX27 . . 65 D7
Cardiff Mews RG1 . . . 258 F1
Cardiff Rd RG1 . . . . . 258 F1
Cardigan St
 Oxford OX2 . . . . 261 A3
 Oxford OX2 . . . . 261 A4
Cardinal Cl Oxford OX4 142 B3
 Reading RG4 . . . . . . 259 B2
Cardwell Cres OX3 . . 124 B2
Carew Cl RG31 . . . . . 257 B4
Carey Cl OX2 . . . . . . 108 F1
Cariad Ct RG8 . . . . . 249 B7
Caribou Cl RG6 . . . . . 260 E1
Carisbrooke Cl RG4 . . 259 C6
Carlesgill Pl RG9 . . . 254 E7
Carling Rd RG4 . . . . . 252 E6
Carlisle Dr 10 OX16 . . 65 D1
Carlisle Rd RG31 . . . . 257 E3
Carlton Cl OX12 . . . . 196 C1
Carlton Rd
 Cutteslowe OX2 . . . . 109 B1
 Reading RG4 . . . . . . 258 E5
Carole's Way OX4 . . . 142 A3

Caroline Ct OX20 . . . .91 B6
Caroline St OX4 . . . . 123 E1
Carpenter Cl OX4 . . . 142 C2
Carpenters Sq 2
 OX28 . . . . 104 A1
Carr Ave OX18 . . . . . 115 C2
Carrdus Sch The OX17 . .17 C8
Carriage Cres 3
 OX18 . . . . 118 A7
Carrick Rd OX28 . . . . 103 B2
Carse Cl OX14 . . . . . 160 B3
Carswell Circ OX25 . . 63 C8
Carswell Com Primary Sch
 OX14 . . . . 179 E7
Carswell Ct 2 OX14 . . 179 E7
Carswell La SN7 . . . . 154 A1
CARSWELL MARSH. . . 154 A3
Carter Cl OX3 . . . . . . 124 F2
Carter Cres
 Faringdon SN7 . . . . . 172 E1
 Woodstock OX20 . . . .91 D5
Carter Dr OX15 . . . . . .21 E2
Carters Cl OX18 . . . . 115 D2
Carters La HP18 . . . . 129 B7
CARTERTON 115 C4
Carterton Com Coll
 OX18 . . . . 115 D3
Carterton Ind Est
 OX18 . . . . 115 E1
Carterton L Ctr OX18 . .115 F4
Carterton Mobile
 OX18 . . . . 133 D8
Carterton Park Cvn Site
 OX18 . . . . 133 D8
Carterton Prim Sch
 OX18 . . . . 115 E3
Carterton Rd OX18. . . 116 B3
Cartmel OX26 . . . . . . 80 C8
Cartmel Mws OX26 . . 80 C8
Cartwright Gdns OX7 . . 35 D7
Carwithen Cl HP17. . . 130 F7
Cascade Cnr OX13 . . . 156 D1
Cascade Rd OX15. . . . 30 A8
CASSINGTON 107 C2
Cassington Rd
 Bladon OX20 . . . . . . 107 B8
 Eynsham OX29 . . . . . 121 A8
 Yarnton OX5 . . . . . . 108 B4
Casson La OX29 . . . . 117 C8
Castell Pl OX29 . . . . . 120 D7
Castle Cl Benson OX10 . 203 F4
 Bicester OX27 . . . . . . .65 F7
Castle Cres SN7 . . . . 193 E8
Castle Fields OX27. . . . 50 B4
Castle La OX10 . . . . . 221 D8
Castle L Ctr The OX10 . 221 D8
Castle Mews OX1 . . . 261 A2
Castle Mill OX1 . . . . 123 A2
Castle Mill Ho OX1 . . 123 A3
Castle Mws OX18 . . . 116 A4
Castle Piece OX12 . . . 194 F2
Castle Quay Sh Ctr
 OX16 . . . . 16 D6
Castle Rd
 Shirburn OX49 . . . . . 186 D4
 Wootton OX20 . . . . . . .75 F5
Castle Sq OX10 . . . . 203 F4
Castle St Banbury OX16 . 16 C6
 Deddington OX15 . . . . .33 F4
 Marsh Gibbon OX27 . . .67 F3
 Oxford OX1 . . . . 261 B2
 Steventon OX13 . . . . 198 F3
 Wallingford OX10 . . . 221 D8
Castle Wlk OX11 . . . . 200 E2
Caswell La OX18 . . . . 116 F6
Catharine Cl OX14 . . . 160 F3
Catherine Cl SN6 . . . 209 C6
Catherine St OX4 . . . 142 A7
Catkins Cl SN7 . . . . . 172 E2
Cat La Ewelme OX10 . . 204 F4
 Stadhampton OX44. . . 163 D1
Catmore Cl OX12 . . . 214 D8
Catmore Rd RG20. . . . 234 F1
Catsham La OX7 . . . . . 72 C5
Catsham Mill Cl OX5. . . 77 C6
Catslip RG9 . . . . 224 F2
Cat St OX12 . . . . 216 D6
Catterick Rd OX26 . . . .65 B1
Catte St OX1 . . . . . . 261 C2
Cattle Mkt OX7 . . . . . .42 E3
Catwell Cl OX4 . . . . . 142 B6
Caudwell Cl
 Drayton OX14 . . . . . 179 B1
 Grove OX12 . . . . 196 E1
CAULCOTT. 63 B5
Causeway Banbury OX16 . 16 F6
 Bicester OX26 . . . . . . .65 E1
 Bletchingdon OX5 . . . 93 A8
Causeway Cl OX29 . . . 129 D1
Causeway The
 11 Banbury OX16 . . . . .16 E6
 East Hanney OX12 . . . 197 A6
 Reading RG4 . . . . . . 259 D1
 Steventon OX13 . . . . 198 F4
 Woodstock OX20 . . . . 91 A6
Causmans Way RG31 . 257 C2
Cavalier Rd OX4 . . . . 130 A1
Cavell Rd OX4 . . . . . 142 A5
Cavendish Caravan Pk 11
 OX11 . . . . 219 A8
Cavendish Dr OX3 . . . 123 E5
Cavendish Pl OX27 . . . 52 D1
Cavendish Rd
 Oxford OX2 . . . . 123 B8
 Reading RG4 . . . . . . 259 C6
Cavendish Wlk OX9 . . 130 B1
CAVERSFIELD. 65 C7
CAVERSHAM 259 D4
CAVERSHAM
 HEIGHTS 258 F3
Caversham Hill RG4 . . 259 B4

CAVERSHAM PARK . . 259 C5
Caversham Park Dr
 RG4 . . . . 259 C5
Caversham Park Prim Sch
 RG4 . . . . 259 D6
Caversham Park Rd
 RG4 . . . . 259 E6
Caversham Prim Sch
 RG4 . . . . 259 A3
Caversham Rd RG1 . . 259 A1
Caversham Wharf
 RG1 . . . . 259 A1
Cave St OX4 . . . . 123 F1
Cawley Rd OX7 . . . . . .23 B5
Cawsam Gdns RG4 . . 259 C4
Cawse St OX16 . . . . . .16 F3
Caxton Cl RG30 . . . . 258 C1
Caxton Ct RG9. . . . . . 244 E1
Cecil Aldin Dr RG31. . 257 C4
Cecil Sharpe Cl OX3 . 124 C2
Cedar RG9 . . . . 244 D2
Cedar Cl OX16 . . . . . . 16 D2
Cedar Cres OX9 . . . . 147 D8
Cedar Ct OX4 . . . . . . 142 C5
Cedar Dr Bicester OX26 . .65 F3
 Pangbourne RG8 . . . 256 C4
 Witney OX28 . . . . . . 104 D2
Cedar Rd
 Carterton OX18 . . . . 115 F5
 Faringdon SN7 . . . . . 172 E3
 Oxford OX2 . . . . 140 D7
Cedars The
 Benson OX10 . . . . . . 204 A5
 Reading RG31 . . . . . 257 D2
Cedar Villa OX16 . . . . .16 B6
Cedar Wood Cres RG4 259 B4
Celandine Cl 8 OX26 . . 65 C4
Celandine Pl 8 OX4 . . 142 F1
Celsea Pl OX10 . . . . . 221 A1
Cemetery Rd
 Abingdon-on-Thames
  OX14 . . . . 179 D7
 Bicester OX26 . . . . . . .65 E1
Centaury Pl OX4 . . . . 143 A2
Centenary Bsns Pk
 RG9 . . . . 244 F1
Centenary Way OX29 . 117 C2
Central Dr Didcot OX11 200 F1
 Didcot OX11 . . . . . . 201 A1
Centremead OX2 . . . 141 A8
Centre Rise OX33. . . . 143 D6
Centre St OX16 . . . . . .16 E7
Century Cl SN7 . . . . 173 A3
Century Row OX2. . . . 123 B7
Cessna Cl OX7 . . . . . .68 C3
CHACOMBE. 10 F4
Chacombe CE VA Prim
 Acad OX17 . . . . .10 F4
Chacombe Cres OX16. . .9 D3
Chacombe Rd
 Middleton Cheney OX17 . 10 F4
 Upper Wardington OX17. 10 E8
Chadelworth Wy OX13 156 F1
CHADLINGTON. 57 F1
Chadlington CE Prim Sch
 OX7 . . . . .57 C1
Chadlington Rd
 Chadlington OX7 . . . . .57 F1
 Oxford OX1 . . . . 123 C1
 Spelsbury OX7 . . . . . .72 F8
Chadwich Ave OX13 . . 199 C2
Chadwick Pl OX26. . . . 80 F6
Chaffinch Rd OX26. . . . 66 A1
Chaffinch Way OX15. . . 17 A1
Chaffinch Wlk OX4 . . 142 F1
Chaffinch Wy OX15 . . .16 F1
Chailey Gdns OX11 . . 219 B1
Chain Alley OX1 . . . . 261 A2
Chainhill OX12 . . . . . 233 A7
Choinhill Rd OX12 . . . 214 F2
Chalcraft Cl RG9 . . . . 254 C8
Chalcroft Cl OX29. . . . 118 A5
Chalfont Rd OX2. . . . . 123 B5
CHALFORD 167 B6
Chalford Cl OX7 . . . . . .42 F3
Chalford Ct OX7 . . . . . 43 A3
Chalford Rd OX9 . . . . 167 A4
CHALGROVE 184 E6
Chalgrove Com Prim Sch
 OX44 . . . . 184 D6
Chalgrove Rd OX9 . . . 130 A1
Chalgrove Way RG4 . . 259 B6
Chalker Way
 Banbury OX16 . . . . . . 17 A4
 Banbury OX16 . . . . . . 17 A6
Chalk Farm Rd HP14 . . 188 D5
Chalk Hill
 Aston Tirrold OX11 . . 237 F8
 Hunt's Green RG9 . . . 254 C6
CHALKHOUSE
 GREEN 253 A1
Chalkhouse Green La
 Caversham RG4 . . . . . 259 C8
 Sonning Common RG4 . 253 A1
Chalkhouse Green Rd
 RG4 . . . . 252 E2
Chalkpit La OX39 . . . 168 D5
Challenor Cl OX14 . . . 179 E4
Challow Rd OX12 . . . . 214 B5
Chalmore Gdns OX10 . 221 D6
Chalvey Cl 3 OX26 . . . 65 D1
Chalvey Rd OX26 . . . . 65 D1
Chamberlain Cl 3
 OX18 . . . . 115 D3
Chamberlaine Ct OX16 . 16 D6
Chamberlain Pl OX5. . . .92 C1
Chambers Ct SN7. . . . 173 A2
Chambrai Cl OX14 . . . 200 F8
Chamomile Pl OX16 . . . .9 A2
Chamomile Way 9
 OX11 . . . . 218 B7

Champion Rd RG4 . . . 259 C1
Champion Way OX4 . . 142 B3
Champs Chapel Mus★
 OX12 . . . . 216 C6
Champs Cl OX14 . . . . 160 C2
Chancellor Ct OX4. . . . 142 D4
Chancel Way
 Lechlade-on-Thames
  GL7 . . . . 150 C4
 Marcham OX13 . . . . . 178 C7
Chandler Cl OX18. . . . 134 F4
Chandler Mews OX18 . 115 E1
Chandlers Cl
 Abingdon-on-Thames
  OX14 . . . . 160 C1
 Wantage OX12 . . . . . 214 E4
Chandlings Manor Sch
 OX1 . . . . 160 B7
Chandos Cl OX16 . . . .16 E5
Chantenay Cl OX27 . . . 65 D6
Chapel Cl
 Blackthorn OX25 . . . . .82 A3
 Deddington OX15 . . . . .34 E4
 Leafield OX29 . . . . . . .86 E3
 South Stoke RG8 . . . . 239 C3
 Wantage OX12 . . . . . 214 E4
Chapel Dr OX25 . . . . . 81 C3
Chapel End
 Great Rollright OX7. . . . 29 A4
 Swerford OX7 . . . . . . .30 F3
Chapel Furlong OX11 . 218 C3
Chapel Hill
 Brize Norton OX18 . . 116 B4
 Swerford OX7 . . . . . . .30 F3
 Swerford OX7 . . . . . . .31 A3
 Watchfield SN6 . . . . . 191 C1
 Wootton OX20 . . . . . . .75 F4
Chapel La
 Adderbury OX17 . . . . .23 A4
 Balscote OX15 . . . . . . 14 C8
 Benson OX10 . . . . . . 203 F4
 Berrick Salome OX10 . . 204 B7
 Bledlow Ridge HP14 . . 169 E3
 Blewbury OX11 . . . . . 237 A8
 Bodicote OX15 . . . . . . .22 E8
 Chalgrove OX44 . . . . 184 D6
 Charney Bassett OX12 . 175 F2
 Cropredy OX17 . . . . . . .4 F2
 Enstone OX7 . . . . 58 F5
 Fernham SN7 . . . . . . 193 A4
 Great Bourton OX17 . . . 9 D5
 Kingham OX7 . . . . 55 A5
 Little Tew OX7 . . . . . . 45 B5
 Milton OX15 . . . . .22 C3
 Nettlebed RG9 . . . . . 224 E2
 North Leigh OX29 . . . 105 B7
 Northmoor OX29 . . . 138 C2
 Oxford OX4 . . . . 142 B2
 Poffley End OX29 . . . 104 B5
 Ratley OX15 . . . . .2 A3
 Shipton-under-Wychwood
  OX7 . . . . .85 D7
 Shotteswell OX17 . . . . .8 C7
 Standlake OX29 . . . . 137 D3
 Sutton Courtenay OX14 200 A8
 Turweston NN13 . . . . .24 B7
 Uffington SN7 . . . . . 211 C7
Chapel Lane OX13 . . . 36 C8
Chapel Mews 6 OX26 . .65 E1
Chapel & Pope's Tower★
 OX29 . . . . 138 B8
Chapel Rd
 Ashbury SN6 . . . . . . 228 A7
 Brookend OX7 . . . . . . .72 C8
 Chadlington OX7 . . . . .57 C1
 South Leigh OX29 . . . 119 B6
 Stanford in the Vale
  SN7 . . . . 194 FR
Chapel Row
 Chadlington OX7 . . . . .72 C8
 Cropredy OX17 . . . . . . .4 F2
 Little Compton GL56 . . .26 F1
Chapel Sq
 Deddington OX15 . . . . .33 F4
 East Hendred OX12 . . 216 D6
Chapel St Bicester OX26 .65 E1
 Bledington OX7 . . . . . .54 D2
 Bloxham OX15 . . . . . . 21 E4
 Hook Norton OX15 . . . .30 B7
 Oxford OX4 . . . . 141 F8
 Warmington OX17 . . . . .3 A4
 Watlington OX49 . . . . 186 B2
Chapel Way
 Childrey OX12 . . . . . 213 C4
 Oxford OX2 . . . . 122 D1
Chapelwick Cl SN6 . . 209 B6
Chapman Cres SN7 . . 172 F2
Chapmans La Brill HP18 .97 F2
Chapmans Piece
 OX18 . . . . 100 E5
Charbridge La OX26 . . 66 C2
Charbridge Way OX26 . 66 C2
CHARLBURY 73 C3
Charlbury Mus★ OX7. . 73 B4
Charlbury Prim Sch
 OX7 . . . . .73 C4
Charlbury Rd
 Charlbury OX7 . . . . . . .57 C7
 Charlbury OX7 . . . . . . .73 A7
 Charlbury OX7 . . . . . . .73 C1
 Chipping Norton OX7 . . 42 F1
 Enstone OX7 . . . . 58 F4
 Finstock OX7 . . . . .88 D7
 Finstock OX7 . . . . 88 D8
 Hailey OX29 . . . . 103 F2

Charlbury Rd continued
 Middletown OX29 . . . 104 A7
 Oxford OX2 . . . . 123 C5
 Shrivenham SN6 . . . . 209 B6
 Spelsbury OX7 . . . . . . .72 F8
Charlbury Sta OX7. . . . 73 A3
Charles Cl OX9 . . . . . 130 A1
Charles Dr OX9 . . . . . 130 A1
Charles Evans Way
 RG4 . . . . 259 D2
Charles Ho RG9 . . . . 244 E3
Charles Rd
 Carterton OX18 . . . . 133 D8
 Cholsey OX10 . . . . . . 239 A8
Charles Shouler Way
 OX25 . . . . .80 C7
Charles St OX4 . . . . . 141 F6
Charlotte Ave
 Bicester OX27 . . . . . . .65 D6
 Caversfield OX27 . . . . .65 D7
Charlotte Cl
 Reading RG4 . . . . . . 258 F4
 Shrivenham SN6 . . . . 209 B6
Charlotte Mws RG9 . . 254 E8
CHARLTON 214 F5
Charlton Ct OX12 . . . 215 A5
Charlton Gdns OX12 . . 214 F5
CHARLTON-ON-
 OTMOOR. 95 A4
Charlton-on-Otmoor CE
 Prim Sch OX5. . . . . .95 A4
Charlton Pk OX12 . . . 214 F5
Charlton Prim Sch
 OX12 . . . . .214 F5
Charlton Rd Aynho OX17 35 C7
 Croughton NN13 . . . . . 36 B8
 Wantage OX12 . . . . . 214 F5
Charlton Village Rd
 OX12 . . . . 214 F5
Charney Ave OX14 . . . 160 C2
CHARNEY BASSETT . . 176 A2
Charney Rd OX13 . . . 176 B6
Charter Ho 1 OX12 . . 214 E4
Charter The 8 OX14. . 179 F7
Charterville Ct OX29 . . 102 E2
Charter Way OX10 . . . 221 C7
Chartwell Dr OX7 . . . . 73 C4
Charvil La RG4 . . . . . 260 F3
Chase Barn OX27 . . . . 37 B3
CHASTLETON 40 D7
Chastleton Ho★ GL56. . 40 D7
Chastleton Rd GL56. . . 40 D7
Chatham Cl OX25 . . . . 63 B8
Chatham Rd OX1 . . . . 141 D5
Chatsworth Cl RG4 . . 259 C6
Chatsworth Dr OX16. . 16 E3
Chatterpie La OX29. . . 89 F5
Chaucer Bus Pk OX26. .66 A2
Chaucer Cl
 Bicester OX26 . . . . . . 65 C4
 Reading RG4 . . . . . . 259 A5
Chaucer Ct OX10 . . . 204 F4
Chaucer's La OX20. . . 91 A6
Chaundy Rd OX5 . . . . 77 C5
Chaunterell Way
 OX14 . . . . 179 D6
CHAWLEY 140 A6
Chawley La OX2 . . . . 140 A6
Chawley Rd OX2. . . . . 140 A5
Chazey Cl RG4 . . . . . 258 C7
CHAZEY HEATH 258 C7
 RG4 . . . . 258 D7
Chazey Heath RG4. . . 252 C5
Chazey Rd RG4 . . . . . 258 D3
Cheapside OX18 . . . . 134 E3
Chearsley Rd HP18 . . 129 E7
Cheatle Cres OX18. . . 100 E4
Cheatle Ct OX18 . . . . 100 E4
CHECKENDON 241 C5
Checkendon CE Prim Sch
 RG8 . . . . 241 C5
Checker Wlk OX14. . . 179 F7
Chedworth Dr OX28 . . 117 E8
Cheers Farm OX14. . . 179 C5
Chelford Way RG4 . . . 258 F4
Chelmscote Row OX17 . .10 F8
Chelsea Cl RG30 . . . . 257 F1
Cheltenham Rd OX18 . 100 E4
Chenderit Sch OX17. . . 11 A1
Cheney Cl OX3 . . . . . 124 A1
Cheney Gdns OX17 . . . 10 F1
Cheney La OX3 . . . . . 124 A1
Cheney Rd OX16 . . . . .16 F8
Cheney Sch OX3 . . . . 124 B1
Cheneys Piece OX10 . . 203 F5
Cheney Student Village
 OX3 . . . . 124 A1
Chepstow Dr OX26. . . .65 B1
Chepstow Gdns OX16. . .15 C5
Chepstow Rd RG31 . . 257 D2
Chequers Cl OX33 . . . 125 D7
Chequers End OX11. . 217 E8
Chequers La OX12 . . . 194 F2
Chequers Pl
 Cholsey OX10 . . . . . . 220 F2
 Oxford OX3 . . . . 124 C1
Cherbury Gn OX12 . . . 214 D8
Cheriton Pl RG4 . . . . 252 F5
Cherry Cl
 Kidlington OX5. . . . . 108 C7
 Reading RG4 . . . . . . 259 D1
 Sandford-on-Thames
  OX4 . . . . 142 F1
 Stratton Audley OX27 . . 52 D1
 Warborough OX10. . . 203 B6
Cherry Croft OX12. . . 215 B6
Cherry La OX27 . . . . . 65 D6
Cherry Orch
 Great Coxwell SN7 . . 192 C8

Cherry Orch *continued*
Highworth SN6 . . . . 190 A6
Cherry Rd OX16 . . . . . . 16 A7
Cherrys Cl OX15 . . . . . . 21 D3
Cherry St OX6 . . . . 52 D1
Cherry Tree Ave 6
OX4 . . . . 124 C5
Cherry Tree Cl
Grove OX12 . . . . 214 E8
Kingston Bagpuize
OX13 . . . . 176 D8
Stoke Row RG9 . . . . . . 242 A5
Cherry Tree Ct
Harwell OX11 . . . . . . 217 E7
Oxford OX2 . . . . 140 D7
Woodgreen OX28 . . . . 104 E1
Cherry Tree Dr OX13 . . 159 C2
Cherry Tree Mws
OX28 . . . . 104 E1
Cherry Tree Rd
Chinnor OX39 . . . . . . 168 C6
10 Didcot OX11 . . . . . 200 B1
Cherry Tree Way
3 Carterton OX18 . . . 115 E4
12 Carterton OX18 . . . 115 E5
Witney OX28 . . . . 104 E1
Cherry Wlk OX26 . . . . . 80 E6
Chervil Gr OX27 . . . . . . 65 D7
Cherwell Ave OX5 . . . . 109 A8
Cherwell Bank OX25 . . . 62 A6
Cherwell Bsns Ctr OX5 . 92 C2
Cherwell Cl
Abingdon-on-Thames
OX14 . . . . 160 B1
7 Bicester OX26 . . . . . 65 D1
Didcot OX11 . . . . 200 F4
Wallingford OX10 . . . . 221 D7
Cherwell Coll (Greyfriars)
OX1 . . . . 261 B2
Cherwell Coll Oxford
OX1 . . . . 261 B2
Cherwell Ct OX5 . . . . . . 92 D1
Cherwell Dr
6 Banbury OX16 . . . . . 16 D6
Headington OX3 . . . . . 124 A5
Marston OX3 . . . . 123 F5
Cherwell Lodge OX2 . . 123 C8
Cherwell Rd
Berinsfield OX10 . . . . . 182 C6
Reading RG4 . . . . 259 A6
Cherwell Sch The
OX2 . . . . 123 C6
Cherwell St
Banbury OX16 . . . . 16 D5
Oxford OX4 . . . . 123 F1
Cherwood Cl OX27 . . . . 66 A7
Cherwood House Cotts
OX27 . . . . 66 A7
Cheshire Dr OX25 . . . . . 63 C8
Cheshire Rd OX9 . . . . . 148 B2
Chester Rd 12 OX26 . . . 65 E1
Reading RG4 . . . . 259 A2
Chester St Oxford OX4 . 141 F7
CHESTERTON 79 F7
Chesterton CE Prim Sch
OX26 . . . . 79 F8
Chester Way OX16 . . . . 15 F6
Chestlion La OX18 . . . . 133 E1
Chestnut Ave
Faringdon SN7 . . . . . . 172 E3
Oxford OX3 . . . . 124 D4
Radley OX14 . . . . 160 E4
Reading RG4 . . . . 259 E4
Thame OX9 . . . . 147 D8
Chestnut Cl
Brize Norton OX18 . . . . 116 C3
17 Carterton OX18 . . . 115 E5
Carterton OX18 . . . . . 115 E5
Chesterton OX26 . . . . . 80 A7
Launton OX26 . . . . 66 D1
Middle Assendon RG9 . . 243 F8
Witney OX28 . . . . 104 B2
Chestnut Cotts RG8 . . . 249 A6
Chestnut Ct OX4 . . . . . 142 C3
Chestnut Dr
Abingdon-on-Thames
OX14 . . . . 179 B3
Ascott-under-Wychwood
OX7 . . . . 71 B2
Didcot OX11 . . . . 218 B8
Chestnut End OX26 . . . 65 E4
Chestnut Gdns SN6 . . . 209 B7
Chestnut Gr RG8 . . . . . 257 D5
Chestnut Pl OX49 . . . . 186 B1
Chestnut Rd
Mollington OX17 . . . . . . 4 A3
Oxford OX2 . . . . 140 D7
Chestnuts The
Abingdon-on-Thames
OX14 . . . . 160 C1
Deddington OX15 . . . . . 34 E4
Kirtlington OX5 . . . . . . 78 A4
Lower Shiplake RG9 . . . 255 A3
Wantage OX12 . . . . . . 214 F5
Chestnut Tree Cl
OX13 . . . . 159 C1
Chestnut Vale OX17 . . . . 4 A3
Chestnut View OX18 . . 133 C5
CHETWODE 53 E8
Chetwode Banbury OX16 16 A8
Banbury OX17 . . . . 17 C6
Chetwode Grange Rd
MK18 . . . . 53 D7
Chetwynd Mead 1
OX18 . . . . 135 A3
Chetwyn Mead OX18 . . 134 F3
Cheviot Way OX16 . . . . . 8 F1
Cheyne La OX18 . . . . . 134 E3
Cheyney Wlk OX18 . . . . . 1 C6
Chibnall Cl OX44 . . . . . 184 D6
Chichester Cl OX26 . . . . 65 E2

Chichester Pl OX18 . . 116 C3
Chichester Wlk 8
OX16 . . . . 9 A1
Chiers Dr OX14 . . . . . . 179 C1
Chilbridge Rd OX29 . . . 120 C7
CHILDREY 213 C4
Childrey Way
Abingdon-on-Thames
OX14 . . . . 160 B2
East Challow OX12 . . . 213 F4
Chilford Barns
Churchill OX7 . . . . 55 E5
Churchill OX7 . . . . 55 E5
Chilgrove Dr OX25 . . . . . 49 E1
Chillbrook OX11 . . . . . . 217 E6
Chillingworth Cres
OX3 . . . . 142 E8
Chillingworth Ct OX3 . 142 E8
CHILSON 71 F3
Chilson Hill
Ascott-under-Wychwood
OX7 . . . . 71 F2
Chilson OX7 . . . . 72 A2
Chilswell La
Boars Hill OX1 . . . . . . 140 F3
Sunningwell OX1 . . . . . 141 A2
Chilswell Rd OX1 . . . . . 141 C7
Chilswell Valley Nature
Reserve★ OX1 . . . . . 141 A4
Chiltern App OX26 . . . . 65 E3
Chiltern Bank RG9 . . . . 252 E7
Chiltern Bsns Ctr OX4 142 E4
Chiltern Cl
Benson OX10 . . . . 203 F5
Benson OX10 . . . . 203 F5
Berinsfield OX10 . . . . . 182 D5
Chalgrove OX44 . . . . . 184 E6
Chalgrove OX44 . . . . . 184 E6
Henley-on-Thames RG9 . 254 D8
Chiltern Cres OX10 . . . 221 B8
Chiltern Ct RG4 . . . . . . 259 B6
Chiltern Dr HP14 . . . . . 188 F4
Chiltern Gdns
Watlington OX49 . . . . . 186 C1
Woodcote RG8 . . . . . . 241 A1
Chiltern Gr OX9 . . . . . . 148 A7
Chiltern Hts RG4 . . . . . 259 C4
Chiltern Nursery &
Training Coll RG4 . . . 259 B3
Chiltern Rd
Reading RG4 . . . . 259 C4
Rotherfield Peppard
RG9 . . . . 252 E7
Chiltern Ridge OX49 . . 186 C4
Chilterns End Cl RG9 . 254 C8
Chilterns The OX1 . . . . 261 B2
Chiltern View
Chinnor OX39 . . . . 168 C5
Little Milton OX44 . . . . 163 F6
Purley on Thames RG8 . 257 D5
Tetsworth OX9 . . . . . . 166 B8
Tetsworth OX9 . . . . . . 166 B8
Chiltern Wlk RG8 . . . . . 256 D5
CHILTON 235 E8
Chilton Cl OX14 . . . . . . 160 B1
Chilton Cty Prim Sch
OX11 . . . . 235 C8
Chilton Field Way
OX11 . . . . 217 C1
Chilton Field Wy
OX11 . . . . 235 C8
Chilton Rd
Chilton OX11 . . . . 217 F2
Long Crendon HP18 . . . 129 C7
Upton OX11 . . . . 218 B2
Chilworth Ho Sch
OX33 . . . . 145 C6
Chilworth Rd OX44 . . . 145 D3
CHIMNEY 155 B6
CHIMNEY-END 86 E4
Chimney Meadow National
Nature Reserve★
OX18 . . . . 155 A5
Chinalls Cl MK18 . . . . . 39 D6
China Piece OX10 . . . . . 203 E5
Chinnock Brook OX11 . 200 F3
CHINNOR 168 D7
Chinnor Hill OX39 . . . . 168 E4
Chinnor Hill Nature
Reserve★ OX39 . . . . 168 F5
Chinnor & Princes
Risborough Rly★
OX39 . . . . 168 E7
Chinnor Rd
Aston Rowant OX9 . . . . 167 D2
Bledlow OX39 . . . . 149 F1
Bledlow Ridge HP14 . . . 169 C2
Chinnor OX39 . . . . 168 A4
Chinnor OX39 . . . . 168 F4
Thame OX9 . . . . 148 C5
Towersey OX9 . . . . . . 148 E5
Chinnor Sta★ OX39 . . . 168 D5
Chipmunk Rd OX10 . . . 204 D3
Chipperfield Park Rd
OX15 . . . . 21 F6
CHIPPING NORTON 42 F2
Chipping Norton L Ctr
OX7 . . . . 42 F2
Chipping Norton Mus★
OX7 . . . . 42 F2
Chipping Norton Rd
Chadlington OX7 . . . . . 57 A3
Churchill OX7 . . . . 55 E5
Great Rollright OX7 . . . 29 F4
Hook Norton OX15 . . . . 29 F4
Hook Norton OX15 . . . . 30 A5
Hook Norton OX15 . . . . 30 A5
Little Tew OX7 . . . . 44 D8
Little Tew OX7 . . . . 45 B6
Chipping Norton Sch
OX7 . . . . 42 F2

Chipping Norton War
Memorial Com Hospl
OX7 . . . . 42 F3
CHIPPING WARDEN 5 E6
Chipping Warden Prim
Acad OX17 . . . . 5 F7
CHISELHAMPTON 163 A2
Chiselhampton Hill
OX44 . . . . 162 F5
Choicehill Rd OX7 . . . . 42 E6
Cholesbury Grange
OX3 . . . . 124 A4
CHOLSEY 221 A1
Cholsey Cl OX4 . . . . . . 142 C4
Cholsey Prim Sch
OX10 . . . . 220 F2
Cholsey Sta OX10 . . . . 220 E1
Cholsey & Wallingford
Rly★ OX10 . . . . 220 F3
Cholswell Ct OX13 . . . . 159 C3
Cholswell Rd OX13 . . . . 159 C2
Chorefields OX5 . . . . . . 92 D1
Choswell Spring OX4 . . 142 E1
Chowns Cl OX9 . . . . . . 148 A7
Chris Muir Pl OX11 . . . . 200 B2
Christ Church Cath★
OX1 . . . . 261 C1
Christ Church Cath Sch
OX1 . . . . 261 B1
Christ Church Coll
OX1 . . . . 261 B2
Christchurch Ct OX16 . . 16 D6
Christ Church Old Bldgs
OX1 . . . . 261 A2
Christ Church Picture
Gall★ OX1 . . . . 261 C2
Christchurch Way
OX14 . . . . 200 A7
CHRISTMAS
COMMON 207 B7
Christmas La OX9 . . . . . 147 C8
Christopher Rawlins CE
Prim Sch OX17 . . . . . 23 A4
Church Ave
Henley-on-Thames
RG9 . . . . 244 E2
Kings Sutton OX17 . . . . 23 F5
Church Cl
Adderbury OX17 . . . . . 23 A3
Ascott-under-Wychwood
OX7 . . . . 71 C2
4 Bampton OX18 . . . . 134 E3
Benson OX10 . . . . 203 F4
Black Bourton OX18 . . . 133 F5
Charlbury OX7 . . . . 73 B3
Cuddesdon OX44 . . . . . 144 C3
East Hagbourne OX11 . . 218 F5
Farmoor OX2 . . . . 121 C2
Fringford OX27 . . . . . . 52 D7
Great Bourton OX17 . . . 9 D8
Islip OX5 . . . . 93 F1
Longcot SN7 . . . . 192 C2
Merton OX25 . . . . 95 B8
Rotherfield Greys RG9 . 243 D1
South Hinksey OX1 . . . . 141 B5
Stanton St John OX33 . . 125 D7
Wardington OX17 . . . . . 5 E1
Weston-on-the-Green
OX25 . . . . 78 F2
Weston-on-the-Green
OX25 . . . . 79 A1
Church Cotts OX44 . . . . 161 E3
Church Cowley Rd
OX4 . . . . 142 B5
Church Cowley St James
CE Prim Sch 5 OX4 . 142 C4
CHURCH END
Bletchingdon 93 B8
Ducklington 118 C4
Long Crendon 129 D7
South Leigh 119 D6
Swerford 30 E3
Church End
Bletchingdon OX5 . . . . 78 B1
Bletchingdon OX5 . . . . 93 C8
Blewbury OX11 . . . . . . 219 A1
Croughton NN13 . . . . . 36 D8
Drayton St Leonard
OX10 . . . . 183 B6
Great Rollright OX7 . . . 29 F3
South Leigh OX29 . . . . 119 C6
Standlake OX29 . . . . . 137 C6
Waterstock OX33 . . . . . 145 D8
CHURCH ENSTONE 58 F7
Church Farm Ct OX29 . 137 D4
Churchfield RG9 . . . . . . 223 D3
Churchfield La OX18 . . 203 E4
Churchfields OX29 . . . . . 89 C7
Church Furlong OX15 . . 20 C8
Church Gn
Long Crendon HP18 . . . 129 D7
Stanford in the Vale
SN7 . . . . 194 E8
Witney OX28 . . . . 118 B7
CHURCH
HANBOROUGH 106 D6
Church Hill
Chilton OX11 . . . . 235 D8
Forest Hill OX33 . . . . . 125 D4
Great Haseley OX44 . . . 164 E8
Little Milton OX44 . . . . 163 F6
Stonor RG9 . . . . 225 D8
Tackley OX5 . . . . 77 B5
Tiddington OX33 . . . . . 145 B6
Warmington OX17 . . . . . 3 A2
Churchhill Pl OX5 . . . . . 108 B7
Church Hill Rd OX4 . . . 142 B4
CHURCHILL 55 E5
Churchill Cl
Didcot OX11 . . . . 200 C1
Woodstock OX20 . . . . . 91 B6

Churchill Cres
Sonning Common RG4 . . 253 A6
Thame OX9 . . . . 148 B8
Churchill Dr OX3 . . . . . 124 C1
Churchill Gate OX20 . . . 91 C5
Churchill Hospl OX3 . . 142 C8
Churchill Pl
Chipping Norton OX7 . . 42 F2
Wolvercote OX2 . . . . . 122 F8
Churchill Rd
Bicester OX26 . . . . 65 F3
Chipping Norton OX7 . . 42 D1
Churchill OX7 . . . . 55 F6
Didcot OX11 . . . . 200 C1
Kidlington OX5 . . . . . . 108 E8
Kingham OX7 . . . . 55 A5
Sarsden OX7 . . . . 56 B8
Churchill & Sarsden
Heritage Ctr★ OX7 . . 55 D6
Churchill Way OX29 . . 106 B8
Church Iris Cl OX25 . . . 81 E4
Church La
Adderbury OX17 . . . . . 23 A3
Ashbury SN6 . . . . 228 A7
Aston OX18 . . . . 135 E4
Aston Rowant OX9 . . . . 167 D3
Banbury OX16 . . . . 16 D6
Barford St John OX15 . . 33 A7
Barford St Michael OX15 32 F7
Bicester OX26 . . . . 65 E1
Bishopstone SN6 . . . . . 227 C4
Bledington OX7 . . . . . . 54 D2
Bledlow HP27 . . . . 169 E8
Brightwell-cum-Sotwell
OX10 . . . . 202 E3
Burford OX18 . . . . 100 E5
Cassington OX29 . . . . . 107 C2
Chacombe OX17 . . . . . 10 E4
Chalgrove OX44 . . . . . 184 D6
Charlbury OX7 . . . . 73 B3
Charlton-on-Otmoor OX5 95 A4
Chinnor OX39 . . . . 168 D6
Claydon OX17 . . . . 1 D1
Coleshill SN6 . . . . 191 B8
Croughton NN13 . . . . . 36 D8
Drayton OX14 . . . . 179 C1
Drayton St Leonard
OX10 . . . . 183 B5
Dry Sandford OX13 . . . 158 F5
Epwell OX15 . . . . 13 A5
Ewelme RG9 . . . . 206 B1
Fawley RG9 . . . . 226 C2
Fernham SN7 . . . . 193 A4
Fringford OX27 . . . . . . 52 D7
Fulbrook OX18 . . . . . . 100 F6
Hailey OX29 . . . . 104 A6
Hampton Poyle OX5 . . . 93 A4
Hanwell OX17 . . . . 8 F4
Harwell OX11 . . . . 217 E7
Hornton OX15 . . . . 7 C6
Horton-cum-Studley
OX33 . . . . 112 A5
Ipsden OX10 . . . . 240 C8
Islip OX5 . . . . 93 F1
Kirtlington OX5 . . . . . . 78 A4
Langford GL7 . . . . 132 D1
Kidlington OX5 . . . . . . 92 F2
Kingham OX7 . . . . 55 A4
Marcham OX13 . . . . . . 178 C6
Marsh Gibbon OX27 . . . 67 F3
Ratley OX15 . . . . 2 A3
Reading RG4 . . . . 259 A2
Shellingford SN7 . . . . . 193 F8
Shipton-under-Wychwood
OX7 . . . . 85 D8
Somerton OX25 . . . . . . 48 F6
Stokenchurch HP14 . . . 188 D5
Stonesfield OX8 . . . . . . 89 C7
Stratton Audley OX27 . . 52 D1
Sutton Courtenay OX14 180 A1
Upton OX11 . . . . 218 C2
Wantage OX12 . . . . . . 214 D4
Wargrave RG10 . . . . . . 255 C2
Watlington OX49 . . . . . 186 B2
West Hanney OX12 . . . 196 E6
Wootton OX20 . . . . 75 F4
Wroxton OX15 . . . . 15 B8
Church Terr
Bicester OX26 . . . . 65 E1
Hatford SN7 . . . . 174 D2
Church View
Ardley OX27 . . . . 50 C3
Ascott-under-Wychwood
OX7 . . . . 71 C2
Bampton OX18 . . . . . . 134 E3
Banbury OX16 . . . . 16 B4
Berinsfield OX10 . . . . . 182 C5
Brackley NN13 . . . . 24 A7
Carterton OX18 . . . . . 115 E2
Charlton-on-Otmoor OX5 95 A5
Freeland OX29 . . . . . . 106 A6
Grove OX12 . . . . 196 E1
Highworth SN6 . . . . . . 190 A6
Radley OX14 . . . . 160 E3
Stoke Row RG9 . . . . . . 241 F5
6 Wantage OX12 . . . . 214 D5
Church View Cotts
SN7 . . . . 192 C2
Church View Rd OX28 . 117 F7
Churchward OX11 . . . . 200 E4
Churchward Cl OX12 . . 196 D2
Churchway RG20 . . . . . 235 B1
Church Way
Oxford OX2 . . . . 122 D1
Oxford OX4 . . . . 141 F4
Sparsholt OX12 . . . . . . 212 E4
CHURCH WESTCOTE . . . 68 D6
Church Wlk
Ambrosden OX25 . . . . . 81 C3
Banbury OX16 . . . . 16 C5
Bishopstone SN6 . . . . . 227 C4

Church Wlk *continued*
Combe OX29 . . . . 90 A4
Faringdon SN7 . . . . . . 173 A4
Oxford OX2 . . . . 123 B4
Shipton-under-Wychwood
OX7 . . . . 70 D1
Shrivenham SN6 . . . . . 209 C7
Upper Heyford OX25 . . . 62 F8
Churh La Cropredy OX17 . 4 A3
Mollington OX17 . . . . . . 4 A3
Churn Est
Blewbury OX11 . . . . . . 236 E6
Upton OX11 . . . . 236 C7
Churnet Cl OX11 . . . . . 201 B2
Churn Rd OX11 . . . . . . 236 B1
Cinnamenta Rd OX3 . . 142 E8
Cinnamon Cl OX44 . . . 184 C7
Circourt Rd OX12 . . . . . 195 F3
Circular Rd OX25 . . . . . 80 C5
Circular Rd West OX26 . 80 C5
Circus St OX4 . . . . 141 E8
City of Oxford Coll
(Blackbird Leys Campus)
OX4 . . . . 142 E2
City of Oxford Coll (Oxford
Campus) OX1 . . . . . . 261 A1
City Rd
Bledlow Ridge HP14 . . . 189 D6
Waterend HP14 . . . . . . 189 D5
CITY THE 189 D6
Clacks La
Crowmarsh Gifford
OX10 . . . . 204 E1
Crowmarsh Gifford
OX10 . . . . 222 C8
Clairmore Gdns RG31 . 257 C5
CLANFIELD 152 E8
Clanfield CE Prim Sch
OX18 . . . . 152 E8
Clanfield Cres RG31 . . . 257 C2
Clanfield Rd OX18 . . . . 134 E2
Clapcot Way OX10 . . . . 221 C8
CLARE 165 E2
Clarence Pl OX11 . . . . . 218 E7
Clarence Rd RG9 . . . . . 244 D2
Clarendon Cl OX14 . . . 180 B8
Clarendon Dr OX9 . . . . 130 A1
Clarendon Rise RG31 . . 257 B4
Clare Pl OX29 . . . . 117 D7
Clare Terr OX18 . . . . . . 115 D1
Claridge Cl OX16 . . . . . 209 B7
Claridge Gdns OX17 . . . 9 D7
Clarkes Ct OX16 . . . . . . 16 C6
Clarks La CV36 . . . . 28 A5
Clarks Row OX1 . . . . . . 261 B1
Clarkston Rd OX18 . . . . 115 D1
CLATTERCOTE 4 D7
Clay Bank OX15 . . . . . . 30 A7
Clay Cl RG31 . . . . 257 B1
CLAYDON 1 D1
Claydon Cl 4 RG4 . . . . 259 A2
Claydon La OX17 . . . . . . 1 A4
Claydon Rd
Appletree NN11 . . . . . . 5 C8
Claydon NN11 . . . . 1 C1
Claydon OX17 . . . . 1 A1
Claydon OX17 . . . . 4 B8
Cropredy OX17 . . . . . . 4 F3
Cropredy OX17 . . . . . . 4 F4
Clayfields SN6 . . . . 209 A3
Clay Hill Cl OX7 . . . . . . 58 E6
Clay La OX10 . . . . 204 C2
Claymond Rd OX3 . . . . 124 F4
Claypit OX12 . . . . 214 A5
Claypit La SN7 . . . . 211 A7
Claypits Cl OX16 . . . . . . 16 A4
Claypits La SN6 . . . . . . 209 C7
Clays Cl OX3 . . . . 124 A5
Clear Water Pl OX2 . . . 123 B5
Clearway House Ind Est
OX16 . . . . 17 A6
Cleavers OX39 . . . . 168 B6
Cleavers Sq 8 OX4 . . . 142 E1
Cleave The OX11 . . . . . 217 E7
CLEEVE 249 D7
Cleeve Ct RG8 . . . . 249 B7
Cleeve Down RG8 . . . . 249 D7
Cleeve Park Cotts
RG8 . . . . 249 D8
Cleeve Rd RG8 . . . . 249 B7
Cleeves Ave OX7 . . . . . 42 F4
Cleeves Cnr OX7 . . . . . 42 F5
Clematis Pl OX4 . . . . . . 142 F2
Clements Cl OX12 . . . . 214 F6
Clements Green OX11 . 219 F5
Clements Mead RG31 . 257 B1
Clements Rd
Chalgrove OX44 . . . . . 184 E6
Henley-on-Thames RG9 . 244 C3
Clements Wy SN7 . . . . 173 A2
Cl End OX13 . . . . 199 B8
Clerkenwell Cotts
HP17 . . . . 130 F5
Clevedon Ct 3 OX5 . . . 108 F4
Clevedon Rd RG31 . . . . 257 E3
Cleveland Cl OX5 . . . . . 109 A7
Cleveland Dr OX4 . . . . . 142 C5
Clevelands OX14 . . . . . 160 A1
CLEVELEY 59 C4
Cleveley Rd OX7 . . . . . . 58 F5
Clevemede RG8 . . . . . . 249 C7
Cleycourt Rd SN6 . . . . 209 A6
Clifden Rd HP18 . . . . . 127 C5
Clifford Pl OX2 . . . . 122 D8
Clifford Terr OX20 . . . . . 75 F4
CLIFTON 34 E4

Clifton Cl OX26 . . . . **66** A2
Clifton Dr
Abingdon-on-Thames
OX14 . . . . **179** F8
Bloxham OX15 . . . . **21** C4
CLIFTON HAMPDEN . **181** C4
Clifton Hampden CE Prim
Sch OX14 . . . . **181** D4
Clifton Hamton Rd
Chiselhampton OX44 . . . **162** F2
Chiselhampton OX44 . . . **163** A2
Clifton Park Rd RG4 . . **259** A3
Clifton Rd OX15 . . . . . **34** C4
Clifton Rise RG10 . . . . **255** E1
Clinton Cl OX4 . . . . **141** F3
Clive Rd OX4 . . . . **142** C5
Clock Ct OX25 . . . . **48** B3
Clock Ho The [2] OX18 **115** E2
Clock Tower Ct SN7 . . **172** E2
Cloisters The
Ewelme OX10 . . . . **204** F3
[3] Oxford OX1 . . . . . **141** C7
Reading RG4 . . . . **259** A3
[1] Wantage OX12 . . . . **214** D4
Clonmel Cl RG4 . . . . . . **259** D2
Closes The OX5 . . . . **92** E1
Close The
Ardington OX12 . . . . . . **215** E5
Aston Tirrold OX11 . . . . **237** F8
Benson OX10 . . . . **203** F5
Chipping Warden OX17 . . . **5** F6
Epwell OX15 . . . . **13** A5
Great Bourton OX17 . . . . . **9** D7
Henley-on-Thames RG9 . **244** D1
Henley-on-Thames RG9 . **254** D8
Lechlade-on-Thames
GL7 . . . . **150** C5
Salford OX7 . . . . **42** A5
Stanton Harcourt OX29 . **138** A8
Stoke Lyne OX27 . . . . . . **51** B5
Woodcote RG8 . . . . **250** F8
Clover Cl Oxford OX2 . . **140** B6
Wantage OX12 . . . . **215** A6
Clover Fields OX11 . . . **218** C7
Clover La [3] OX29 . . . **117** B8
Clover Mead OX26 . . . . .**65** E5
Clover Pl
Eynsham OX29 . . . . . . **120** D7
Oxford OX4 . . . . **142** F2
Clump La OX15 . . . . **8** A5
Coach House Ct RG8 . . **256** E5
Coach House Mews
Bicester OX26 . . . . **80** F8
[4] Reading RG4 . . . . **259** C2
Coach La SN7 . . . . **173** A4
Coalport Way
[7] Reading RG30 . . . . **257** E1
Reading RG30 . . . . **257** E1
Coates Cl OX12 . . . . . . **215** A5
Coates La
Cookley Green OX49 . . . **206** C2
Ewelme RG9 . . . . **206** C2
Cobbetts Cl OX29 . . . . **120** F8
Cobden Cres OX1 . . . . **141** C7
Cobden Ctr The OX11 . **200** E4
Cochrane Rd OX10 . . . **204** D1
Cockcroft Rd OX11 . . . **218** E7
Cockpit Cl OX10 . . . . . . **91** B6
Cockshoot Cl OX29 . . . . **89** C7
Cockslease La RG9 . . . **226** B6
Cockwell La SN7 . . . . . **192** D6
Coffin Cl SN6 . . . . **190** A6
COGGES **118** C8
Cogges Hill Rd OX28 . . **118** D7
Cogges La OX29 . . . . . **119** C1
Cogges Manor Farm Mus★
OX28 . . . . **118** A8
Coghill Cl OX5 . . . . **93** A8
Coker Cl OX26 . . . .**65** E1
Cokethorpe Sch OX29 **117** E1
Colborne Rd OX11 . . . **218** D8
COLD HARBOUR
Oxford **141** D5
Woodcote **250** C4
Cold Harbour RG8 . . . **250** C4
Coldharbour Cl RG9 . . **254** C8
Coldharbour Rd OX12 . **234** A7
Coldicutt St RG4 . . . . . **259** C1
Cole Cl OX11 . . . . **200** F3
Colegrave Rd OX15 . . . .**21** E5
Colegrove Down OX2 . **140** A6
Coleman Cl OX15 . . . . . **21** C4
Colemans Hill OX3 . . . **124** E3
Coleridge Cl
[1] Bicester OX26 . . . . .**65** C4
Oxford OX4 . . . . **142** D6
Coleridge Dr OX14 . . . **179** D5
Colerne Rd OX18 . . . . . **115** E3
Colesbourne Rd OX15 . **21** D3
COLESHILL **191** A8
Coleshill Dr SN7 . . . . . **172** E2
Coles La OX44 . . . . **184** C7
Collcutt Cl OX33 . . . . . **143** C7
College Cl Holton OX33 **126** C1
Radley OX14 . . . . **160** E3
Thame OX9 . . . . **129** E1
College Cotts OX25 . . . .**95** C8
College Ct OX7 . . . . **33** B4
College Farm
Benson OX10 . . . . **203** F4
Chadlington OX7 . . . . . . **57** B1
College Farm Cotts
OX13 . . . . **177** D4
College Farm La SN6 . **228** A6
College Fields OX17 . . . **35** C7

College Flats OX4 . . . . **142** B2
College La
Long Compton CV36 . . . **28** A4
Oxford OX4 . . . . **142** B2
College Pl OX29 . . . . . **117** B7
College Sq OX13 . . . . . **156** B3
College The
Marsh Gibbon OX27 . . . . .**67** F3
Swinbrook OX18 . . . . . **101** F3
College Way OX33 . . . **143** B6
Collets Cotts OX44 . . . **145** C2
Collett OX11 . . . . **200** E4
Collett Dr
Bampton OX18 . . . . . . **135** A4
Wolvercote OX2 . . . . . **122** D8
Collett Rd OX16 . . . . . . **16** F5
Colletts Way OX29 . . . **117** B8
Collett Way OX12 . . . . **196** D1
Colley Cl HP18 . . . . **98** A1
Colley Wood OX1 . . . . **141** D2
Collice St OX5 . . . . **109** F8
Collier Cres [9] OX28 . **104** A1
Colliers La RG9 . . . . . . **252** F8
Collier's La
Faringdon SN7 . . . . . . **173** A4
Radnage HP14 . . . . . . **189** A7
Collingbourn Rd
OX12 . . . . **194** F2
Collington Way OX13 . **156** F1
Collingwood Ave
OX11 . . . . **218** D8
Collingwood Cl OX14 . **159** F1
Collins Dr OX15 . . . .**21** E3
Collins End RG8 . . . . . **251** B2
Collinsmith Dr OX12 . . **196** E1
Collinsons Row OX7 . . . **73** B3
Collins St OX4 . . . . **141** F8
Collinwood Cl OX3 . . . **124** F3
Collinwood Rd OX3 . . . **124** F3
Collyer Rd HP14 . . . . . **188** E4
Colmore La RG9 . . . . . **252** E8
Colne Cl
[4] Bicester OX26 . . . . .**65** D1
Grove OX12 . . . . **196** D1
Colne Dr
Berinsfield OX10 . . . . . **182** D6
Didcot OX11 . . . . **201** A3
Coln Rd OX11 . . . . **217** B3
Colonnade The RG31 . **257** C2
Colony Rd
Sibford Gower OX15 . . . **18** E6
Sibford Gower OX15 . . . **18** E7
Sibford Gower OX15 . . . **19** A8
COLONY THE **18** F7
Colony The OX15 . . . . . **18** F7
Colterne Cl OX3 . . . . . **124** A5
Coltman Ave HP18 . . . **129** C6
Colton Rd SN6 . . . . . . **209** A6
Coltsfoot Leyes OX26 . **65** D4
Coltsfoot Sq [5] OX4 . **142** F1
Columbia Way OX12 . . **214** C8
Columbine Gdns OX4 . **143** A1
Colvile Cl OX18 . . . . . . **134** F4
Colville Wlk OX16 . . . . . **16** E7
Colwell Dr
Abingdon-on-Thames
OX14 . . . . **179** C8
Abingdon-on-Thames
OX14 . . . . **179** D7
Oxford OX3 . . . . **125** A4
Witney OX28 . . . . **117** F6
Colwell Rd OX10 . . . . . **182** C5
Colyton Way RG8 . . . . **257** D5
COMBE **90** A5
Combe CE Prim Sch
OX29 . . . .**90** A4
Combe Gate OX29 . . . . .**90** A4
Combe Mill★ OX29 . . . .**90** B3
Combe Rd Oxford OX2 . **123** A2
Stonesfield OX8 . . . . **89** D7
Combes La SN7 . . . . . . **173** A4
Combe Sta OX29 . . . . . . **90** B3
Combewell OX44 . . . . . **143** C2
Comfrey Rd OX4 . . . . . **142** F3
Comice Way [3] OX13 . **199** C3
COMMON
BEAUCHAMP **210** D3
Common Cl
North Leigh OX29 . . . . **105** B6
Shrivenham SN6 . . . . . **209** C7
Common Farm La
SN6 . . . . **190** C6
Common La
Binfield Heath RG9 . . . **254** A3
Chipping Norton OX7 . . . **42** C2
Common Leys Farm
Campus/Abingdon and
Witney Coll OX29 . . . **104** C8
Common Rd
Beckley OX3 . . . . **110** F2
North Leigh OX29 . . . . **105** B6
Common The
Ewelme OX10 . . . . **204** F3
Stokenchurch HP14 . . . **188** E5
Stoke Row RG9 . . . . . . **242** B4
Compass Cl [4] OX4 . . **142** C4
Comper Foundation Stage
School OX4 . . . . **142** A7
Complins Cl OX2 . . . . . **123** A6
Compton Cl OX11 . . . . **200** F1
Compton Ct CV36 . . . . . **27** C7
Compton Dr OX14 . . . . **160** B2
Compton Rd
Banbury OX16 . . . . **16** D6
Shrivenham SN6 . . . . . **209** F7
Shrivenham SN6 . . . . . **210** A6
Compton Terr [1]
OX10 . . . . **221** C7
Compton Way
Eynsham OX29 . . . . . . **120** C8
Witney OX28 . . . . **104** C1

Concord Ave **142** B2
Banbury OX16 . . . . **16** D6
Banbury OX16 . . . . **16** D6
Banbury OX16 . . . . **16** D7
Condor Cl RG31 . . . . . . **257** C3
Conduit Hill Rise OX9 . **147** E7
Conduit House (North
Hinksey)★ OX2 . . . . . **140** F7
Conduit Rd OX14 . . . . . **179** E7
Coneygar Fields OX7 . . .**47** F1
Conifer Cl OX2 . . . . **140** C8
Conifer Dr
Bicester OX26 . . . . **65** E5
Reading RG31 . . . . **257** B2
Conifer Rise OX16 . . . . . .**9** B1
Conigre OX39 . . . . **168** B6
Conisboro Ave RG4 . . . **258** E5
Conisboro Way RG4 . . **258** E5
Coniston Ave OX3 . . . . **124** A4
Coniston Dr RG30 . . . . **257** F2
Connaught Ho RG9 . . . **244** E3
Connolly Dr
Carterton OX18 . . . . . . **115** D4
Carterton OX18 . . . . . . **115** D4
Constable Pl OX18 . . . . **135** A3
Constables Croft OX25 . **96** E7
Constantine Cl SN6 . . . **209** A6
Constitution Hill OX10 **221** E4
Convent The OX7 . . . . . **68** D6
Conway Dr OX16 . . . . . . **15** F5
Conway Rd OX13 . . . . . **159** D2
Conyger Cl OX5 . . . . **93** E1
Congyrea La GL56 . . . . . **40** D6
Congyree Terr OX7 . . . . **42** F3
Cookham Gr OX14 . . . . **201** B5
Cook La OX10 . . . . **221** E1
COOKLEY GREEN **206** D1
Cook Row OX7 . . . . **71** C2
Cooks Hill OX15 . . . .**14** B5
Cooks La OX7 . . . .**41** F5
Coolidge Cl [1] OX3 . . **124** D1
Coombe Cotts RG8 . . . **248** F6
Coombe End RG8 . . . . . **250** C3
Coombe Hill Cres OX9 **147** E8
Coombe Pk Rd RG9 . . . **256** C8
Coombe Rd RG20 . . . . **247** A3
Coombes Cl OX7 . . . . . . **85** D8
Coombe The RG8 . . . . . **248** F6
Cooper Cl
Chipping Norton OX7 . . . **42** F3
Upper Heyford OX25 . . . **63** C7
Cooper Mews [5]
OX28 . . . . **118** A8
Cooper Pl OX3 . . . . **124** F3
Cooper Rd RG9 . . . . . . **244** D3
Cooper Sch The OX26 . . **65** F4
Coopers Cl OX33 . . . . . **143** F8
Coopers Court Rd
HP14 . . . . **188** D5
Coopers Gate OX16 . . . **16** C7
Coopers Gn OX26 . . . . . .**65** F5
Coopers La
Abingdon-on-Thames
OX14 . . . . **179** E6
Wantage OX12 . . . . . . **214** F5
Coopers Piece OX10 . . **221** C8
Coopers Pightle RG4 . **252** D3
Cop Cl HP18 . . . . **129** D7
Copcot Cl OX33 . . . . . . **143** D6
Cope Cl OX2 . . . . **140** D8
Copenhagen Dr OX14 . **159** D1
Cope Rd OX16 . . . . **16** C6
Copperage Rd
Chilton OX12 . . . . **234** A2
Farnborough OX12 . . . **233** D1
West Ilsley OX12 . . . . . **233** F1
West Ilsley RG20 . . . . . **235** A2
West Ilsley RG20 . . . . . **235** B1
Copperfield Cl OX12 . . **214** D6
Copperfields RG4 . . . . **258** F3
Coppice Cl OX16 . . . . . . **16** E4
Coppice La OX12 . . . . . **213** D6
Coppice Piece OX10 . . **203** F5
Coppice The
Stokenchurch HP14 . . . **188** E5
Witney OX28 . . . . **104** B3
Coppice Wy OX26 . . . . . **66** E2
Coppock Cl OX3 . . . . . . **124** D2
Coppock Gdns OX18 . . **115** D3
Copse Ave RG4 . . . . . . **259** E3
Copse Cl RG31 . . . . **257** D3
Copse End RG4 . . . . . . **259** D3
Copse La OX3 . . . . **124** A5
Copse Mead RG5 . . . . **260** F1
Copse The
Abingdon-on-Thames
OX14 . . . . **160** C1
Wargrave RG10 . . . . . . **255** E3
Copson La OX44 . . . . . **163** C2
Copthorne Rd OX5 . . . . **108** E7
Corallian Dr [8] SN7 . . **172** E1
Coral Springs Way
OX29 . . . . **117** D6
Corbett Cl OX25 . . . .**63** B8
Corbett Rd OX18 . . . . . **115** C1
Corbetts Wy OX9 . . . . . **147** F7
Cordrey Gn OX4 . . . . . . **141** F4
Corfe Mews RG4 . . . . . **259** E4
Coriander Way [6]
OX4 . . . . **142** F1
Cormorant Cl [10] OX11 **218** B7
Corn Avill Cl OX14 . . . . **160** C2
Corn Bar OX28 . . . . . . **117** F8
Corncrake Way OX26 . . **66** A1
Corndell Gdns [4]
OX28 . . . . **118** A8
Corneville Rd OX14 . . . **179** B2
Cornfield Ct OX18 . . . . **117** E7
Cornfields OX3 . . . . . . **138** C5
Cornflower Cl OX11 . . . **200** B1
Cornflower Dr OX10 . . **221** A2

Cornflower Wy OX25. . . .**81** D3
Corn Hide [4] OX29. . . . .**90** B1
Cornhill La OX12. . . . . . **213** E5
Cornish Rd OX7 . . . . **42** D1
Cornmarket
[1] Faringdon SN7 . . . **172** F4
Thame OX9 . . . . **147** F8
Cornmarket St OX1 . . . **261** B2
Corn St OX28 . . . . **118** A8
Cornwall Cl RG31 . . . . **257** B4
Cornwall Cl OX4 . . . . . **142** A5
Cornwallis Cl OX4 . . . . **142** A5
Cornwallis Rd OX4 . . . **142** A5
CORNWELL **41** C3
Cornwell OX7 . . . . **41** C3
Coromandel OX14 . . . . **179** D4
Coronation Cotts
OX18 . . . . **152** E8
Coronation La OX17 . . . .**8** D7
Corpus Christi Coll
OX1 . . . . **261** C2
Corunna Cres OX4 . . . . **142** E6
COSCOTE **218** D5
Cosford Gdns OX26 . . . .**66** A4
Cosin Cl OX4 . . . . **142** A8
Cossicle Mead OX11 . . **219** B1
Costar Cl OX4 . . . . **142** D3
COTE **136** A2
Cote La OX7 . . . . **73** B8
Cote Rd Aston OX18 . . . **135** E3
Aston OX18 . . . . **135** F3
Cote OX18 . . . . **136** A3
COTHILL **158** E3
Cotman Cl OX14 . . . . . **179** E5
Cotmore Cl OX9 . . . . . . **148** B7
Cotmore Field OX9 . . . **148** B7
Cotmore Gdns OX9 . . . **148** B7
Cotmore Pk OX9 . . . . . **148** C7
Cot's Gn OX5 . . . . **92** D1
Cotshill Gdns OX7 . . . . .**42** F3
Cotswold Cl
Minster Lovell OX29 . . **102** E2
Sibford Ferris OX15 . . . . **19** B7
Cotswold Cnr OX7 . . . . . **29** A3
Cotswold Cres
Chipping Norton OX7 . . . **42** E1
Marston OX3 . . . . **123** F5
Cotswold Crescent Bglws
OX7 . . . .**42** E1
Cotswold Dene OX29 . **137** A5
Cotswold Mdw OX28 . . **117** D7
Cotswold Pk [3] OX11 . **200** C2
Cotswold Rd OX2 . . . . . **140** B6
Cotswold Terr OX7 . . . . .**42** E1
Cotswold View OX7 . . . . **73** B4
Cotswold Way
Carterton OX18 . . . . . . **115** D4
Cotswold Wildlife Park &
Gardens★ OX18 . . . . **114** C5
Cottage Rd SN7 . . . . . . **194** D3
Cottages The
Burford OX18 . . . . **114** A5
Long Crendon HP18 . . . **129** C6
Cottesford Rd NN13 . . . . **38** A8
Cottesmore La OX10 . . **204** D5
Cottesmore Rd OX4 . . . **142** A3
COTTISFORD **37** F3
Cotton Cl OX12 . . . . . . **194** D1
Cottongrass Rd
Didcot OX11 . . . . **200** A1
Didcot OX11 . . . . **218** A8
Cotts Field HP17 . . . . . **130** E6
Cotwold Bsns Pk
OX28 . . . . **103** B1
Couching St OX49 . . . . **186** B1
Coulings Cl OX12 . . . . **216** D7
Council Cotts RG4 . . . . **252** B5
Council Hos
Binfield Heath RG9 . . . **254** B2
Bloxham OX15 . . . . **21** D3
Spelsbury OX7 . . . .**72** F8
Council Hos The
Barford St Michael
OX15 . . . .**32** F5
Charlbury OX7 . . . . **73** B3
Hanwell OX17 . . . .**8** E3
Nettlebed RG9 . . . . **224** E2
Council Houses The
OX17 . . . .**10** F8
County Rd NN13 . . . . . . **24** A6
County Trad Est OX4 . . **142** F4
County View OX15 . . . . . **34** D4
Coupland Rd OX13 . . . . **159** A6
Court Cl Kidlington OX5 **108** D8
Shipton-under-Wychwood
OX7 . . . .**85** D7
Court Close Rd OX9 . . . **148** E7
Court Dr OX10 . . . . **203** B5
Courtenay Cl OX14 . . . **200** A7
Courtenay Dr RG4 . . . . **259** B7
Courtenay Rd OX12 . . . **214** E5
Court Farm Barns OX5 . **78** B6
Court Farm Rd OX4 . . . **141** F3
Courtfield Rd OX33 . . . **125** D7
Court Gdns RG8 . . . . . . **249** C4
Court Hill Rd
Letcombe Bassett
OX12 . . . . **232** C7
Letcombe Regis OX12 . . **214** A1
Courtiers Gn OX14 . . . . **181** D4
Courtington La OX15 . . . **21** D5
Courtland Rd OX4 . . . . **142** A4
Courtlands RG4 . . . . . . **258** E3

Courtlands Hill RG8 . . **256** C4
Courtlands Rd OX7 . . . . **85** D8
Court Place Gdns OX4 **141** F3
Court Rd OX12 . . . . **214** A2
Courts Gdns OX28 . . . . **118** D8
Court The OX14 . . . . . . **159** E1
Courtyard The
Aston OX18 . . . . **135** D3
Banbury OX17 . . . . **17** D5
Crawley OX29 . . . . **103** D5
Milton OX15 . . . . **22** C3
Tadmarton OX15 . . . . . . **21** A6
Covent Cl OX14 . . . . . . **160** B3
Cover Dr OX5 . . . . **16** D1
Coverley Rd OX3 . . . . . **142** D7
Covert Cl OX27 . . . .**49** F7
Covert The OX20 . . . . . . **91** C5
Cowderoy Pl SN7 . . . . . **194** E7
Cowells Rd OX20 . . . . . . **91** C5
Cow La
Denchworth OX12,
SN7 . . . . **195** E4
Didcot OX11 . . . . **200** F2
Grove OX12 . . . . **196** B5
Harwell OX11 . . . . **217** F8
Kennington OX1 . . . . . **141** E1
Longworth OX13 . . . . . **156** C3
Marcham OX13 . . . . . . **178** D3
Moulsford OX10 . . . . . **238** F3
Reading RG1 . . . . **258** E1
Steeple Aston OX25 . . . .**62** B8
Sutton Courtenay OX11 **199** F2
Swerford OX15 . . . . **30** B4
Swerford OX7 . . . . **30** B2
Cowleaze OX39 . . . . . . **168** B6
Cowleaze Cl SN6 . . . . . **209** B6
Cowleaze Cnr OX18 . . . **134** C2
COWLEY **142** E5
Cowley Bsns Ctr OX4 . **142** F3
Cowley Junc OX4 . . . . . **142** E4
Cowley Pl OX4 . . . . **141** E8
Cowley Rd Oxford OX4 **142** A7
Oxford OX4 . . . . **142** B2
Cowper Cl [2] OX26 . . . **65** C4
Cowslip Gate [2] OX11 **218** B7
Cowslip Rd OX12 . . . . . **215** A6
Coxfield Cl HP14 . . . . . **188** F5
Cox La
Chipping Norton OX7 . . . **42** B2
Stanton St John OX33 . . **125** D7
COXLEASE **226** A5
Coxmoor Cl OX7 . . . . . . **54** F4
Cox's Alley OX3 . . . . . . **124** E3
Cox's Ct SN7 . . . . **194** E7
Cox's Ground OX2 . . . . **123** A5
Coxs La
Crowmarsh Gifford
OX10 . . . . **222** A6
Enstone OX7 . . . . **58** F4
Stoke Row RG9 . . . . . . **242** A5
Coxs Rd SN6 . . . . **209** B6
Cox Way OX4 . . . . **159** F4
Coxwell Gdns SN7 . . . . **172** F3
Coxwell Hall Mews
SN7 . . . . **172** F1
Coxwell Lodge Dr
SN7 . . . . **172** E1
Coxwell Rd SN7 . . . . . . **172** E1
Coxwell St SN7 . . . . . . **172** F3
Cozens Cl HP18 . . . . . . **129** B7
Cozens Gr
Shrivenham SN3 . . . . . **208** F5
Shrivenham SN6 . . . . . **209** A5
Cozens La OX7 . . . .**54** F4
Crabhill La OX12 . . . . . **214** C8
Crab Tree Cl OX15 . . . . . **21** E6
Crabtree Cnr OX10 . . . . **240** D7
Crabtree La OX14 . . . . **179** B2
Crabtree Pl OX14 . . . . . **180** B7
Crabtree Rd
Haddenham HP17 . . . . **130** F5
Oxford OX14 . . . . **140** D8
Crafts End OX11 . . . . . **235** E8
Crafts Mill Terr OX7 . . . . **42** D2
Cranberry Ave OX27 . . . **65** D6
Cranberry Rd OX28 . . . **104** E1
Cranbourne Gdns
RG30 . . . . **258** A2
Cranbrook Ct OX28 . . . **118** A6
Cranbrook Dr OX1 . . . . **160** E7
Crane Furlong SN6 . . . **190** A7
Cranesbill Dr OX26 . . . . **65** D5
Cranesbill Way [7]
OX4 . . . . **142** E1
Cranfield Uni at
Shrivenham SN6 . . . **209** E8
Cranford House Sch
OX10 . . . . **238** F5
Cranham St OX2 . . . . . **261** A4
Cranham Terr OX2 . . . . **261** A4
Cranleigh Cl OX16 . . . . . **16** A4
Cranley Rd OX3 . . . . . . **124** F4
Cranmer Cl RG31 . . . . **257** B3
Cranmer Rd OX4 . . . . . **142** E6
Cranston Ct [1] OX4 . . **142** B3
Cranwell Ave OX18 . . . **115** F2
Cranwell Rd GL54 . . . . . **68** B3
Craster Ct OX16 . . . . . . **16** D3
Cratlands Cl OX44 . . . . **163** C2
Craufurd Rd OX4 . . . . . **142** E6
Craven Comm SN7 . . . . **211** D7
Craven Way OX11 . . . . **218** E2
Crawborough OX7 . . . . . **73** C4
Crawborough Terr OX7 **73** C4
Crawborough Villas
OX7 . . . . **73** C4
CRAWLEY **103** E4
Crawley Mill Ind Est
OX29 . . . . **103** D4
Crawley Rd
Witney OX28 . . . . **103** F3

Crawley Rd *continued*
Witney OX28 . . . . **104** A2
Crawshay Dr RG4 . . . . **259** B7
Cray Ct OX11 . . . . **200** F4
Craysleaze RG4 . . . . . . **252** D3
CRAY'S POND **250** D6
Crays Pond Cl RG8 . . . **250** D6
CRAZIES HILL **255** F6
Crazies Hill RG10 . . . . **255** E6
Crazies Hill CE Prim Sch
RG10 . . . . **255** F6
CR Bates Ind Est HP14 **188** E5
Creampot Cl OX17 . . . . . .**5** A2
Creampot Cres OX17 . . . .**4** F2
Creampot La OX17 . . . . . **4** F2
Crecy Hill Nature
Reserve★ OX5 . . . . **77** C7
Crecy View Pl OX5 . . . . . **77** C6
Crecy Wlk OX20 . . . . **91** C5
Cremyll Rd RG1 . . . . . . **258** F1
Crendon Ct [3] RG4 . . **259** A2
Crendon Rd HP18 . . . . **128** D3
Crescent Cl OX4 . . . . . **142** D6
Crescent Rd
Oxford OX4 . . . . **142** D6
Reading RG31 . . . . **257** D1
Crescent The
Adderbury OX17 . . . . . . **23** A5
Bicester OX26 . . . . **65** D3
Carterton OX18 . . . . . . **133** C8
East Hagbourne OX11.. **218** F6
Long Wittenham OX14 . **201** D8
Lower Shiplake RG9 . . **255** B4
Oxford OX2 . . . . **123** A3
Sandford-on-Thames
OX4 . . . . **161** C8
Steeple Aston OX25 . . . .**62** B4
Witney OX29 . . . . **104** C2
Crescent Way OX13 . . . **220** F1
Cress Hill Pl OX3 . . . . . **124** F4
Cresswell Cl OX5 . . . . . **108** C5
Crest The
Bledlow Ridge HP14 . . **189** F8
Reading RG4 . . . . **259** C5
Cricket Ground HP14 . **188** D5
Cricket Rd
Bodicote. OX15 . . . . **16** D1
Oxford OX4 . . . . **142** B6
Cricklade Rd SN6 . . . . **190** A5
Crick Rd OX2 . . . . **123** C4
Cripley Pl OX2 . . . . **123** A1
Cripley Rd OX2 . . . . . . **123** A1
Crispin Cl RG4 . . . . **258** C5
Crispin Pl
Harwell OX11 . . . . **217** C3
Wallingford OX10 . . . . **221** D7
Crisp Rd RG9 . . . . **244** C3
Crista Pl OX18 . . . . **115** C5
Croasdell Cl OX14 . . . . **179** E4
CROCKER END RG9 . . . **225** A2
Crocker End
Nettlebed RG9 . . . . **224** F3
Nettlebed RG9 . . . . **224** F2
Crockmore La
Fawley RG9 . . . . **226** C1
Henley-on-Thames RG9. **244** C8
Crockwell Cl OX26 . . . . .**65** E2
Crockwell St CV36 . . . . . **27** F7
Croft Ave OX5 . . . . **108** F8
Croft Cl Marston OX3 . . **123** F4
Merton OX25 . . . . **95** C3
Thame OX9 . . . . **148** A7
Croft Cotts OX14 . . . . . **181** C5
Croft Ctyd HP17 . . . . . **130** F5
Croft Dr Milton OX13 . . **199** C4
Pangbourne RG9 . . . . . **256** B4
Croft End OX12 . . . . . . **214** A2
Crofters Ct [13] OX28 . **118** A6
Crofters Mews [6]
OX28 . . . . **118** A8
Croft La Adderbury OX17 . **23** A4
Brighthampton OX29 . . **137** B2
Hook Norton OX15 . . . . . **29** F6
Croft Mdw SN7 . . . . . . **194** F7
Croft Rd Goring RG8 . . . **249** C5
Marston OX3 . . . . **123** F4
Thame OX9 . . . . **148** A7
Wallingford OX10 . . . . **221** C7
Croft's La OX15 . . . . **30** A6
Crofts The OX28 . . . . . **118** A7
Croft Terr [16] OX10 . . **221** D7
Croft The
Aston Tirrold OX11 . . . . **219** F1
Didcot OX11 . . . . **218** B8
East Hagbourne OX11.. **218** F5
Haddenham HP17 . . . . **130** F5
Harwell OX11 . . . . **217** E8
Marsh Baldon OX44 . . . **162** A4
Nuneham Courtenay
OX44 . . . . **162** A4
Oxford OX3 . . . . **124** C3
Oxford OX3 . . . . **124** C3
West Hanney OX12 . . . **196** F7
Croft Villas [2] OX10. . **221** C7
Croft Way RG8 . . . . **250** F8
Cromer Cl RG31 . . . . . . **257** C1
Cromwell Ave OX9 . . . . **130** A1
Cromwell Cl
Chalgrove OX44 . . . . . **184** E6
Chalgrove OX44 . . . . . **184** E6
Faringdon SN7 . . . . . . **173** A3
Henley-on-Thames RG9. **254** E8
Marston OX3 . . . . **123** F4
Cromwell Ct OX16 . . . . . **16** B7
Cromwell Dr OX11 . . . . **219** A7
Cromwell Pk OX7 . . . . . .**42** F4
Cromwell Rd
Banbury OX16 . . . . **16** A6
Henley-on-Thames RG9. **254** E8
Reading RG4 . . . . **259** B2
Cromwells OX10 . . . . . **221** F7

Cromwell St OX1 . . . . . 261 B1
Cromwell Way OX5 . . . . 109 A7
Cronshaw Cl OX11. . . . . 200 E2
Crookdale Beck OX11. 201 A3
Crook's Terr OX12 . . . . 214 D5
Croom Cotts OX11 . . . . 217 A4
CROPREDY 4 E2
Cropredy CE Prim Sch
    OX17. . . . . 4 F1
Cropredy La OX17 . . . . . . 4 F1
Cropredy Lawn Rd OX17 .4 D4
Cross Ave OX10. . . . . . . 204 D2
Cross Cl OX10 . . . . 204 E2
Cross Hands Hill OX7 . .41 A5
Cross Hill Rd OX17. . . . .22 F4
Crossing La Claydon OX17 1 D1
    Claydon OX17. . . . . .4 C8
Cross Keys Rd RG8 . . . 239 C4
Crosslands OX27 . . . . . . .52 D6
Crosslands Dr OX14. . . 159 E1
Cross Leys OX7. . . . . . . .42 E2
Cross Rd OX10. . . . . 220 F2
Cross's La OX7 . . . . .56 E1
Cross St OX4 . . . . 141 F8
Cross The OX29 . . . . .89 C7
Cross Tree La GL7 . . . . 132 B5
Crossville Cres OX11. . 200 D2
Crossway OX7. . . . . .60 F8
Crossways The OX27. . . .50 C4
Crotch Cres OX3. . . . . . 124 A4
Crouch Hill Rd OX16. . . .16 A4
Crouch St OX16. . . . . . . .16 C5
CROUGHTON 36 D7
Croughton All Saints CE
    Prim Sch NN13. . . . . . .36 D8
Croughton American
    Elementary Sch NN13 .36 E6
Croughton Rd
    Aynho OX17. . . . . .35 D7
    Aynho OX17. . . . . .35 F7
    Croughton NN13 . . . . . .36 A7
Crowberry Rd OX4. . . . 142 F2
Crowcastle La OX5 . . . . .77 F6
CROWELL. 168 B4
CROWELL HILL. 168 D2
Crowell Rd
    Chinnor OX39. . . . . . . 168 B5
    Crowell OX39 . . . . 168 A4
    Oxford OX4 . . . . 142 C4
Crow La
    Great Bourton OX17. . . . .9 D7
    Wootton OX20. . . . . . . .75 C7
CROWMARSH
    GIFFORD. 221 F7
Crowmarsh Gifford CE
    Prim Sch OX10. . . . . . 221 F7
Crowmarsh Hill OX10 . 222 B6
Crown Cl OX12 . . . . 214 C7
Crown Fields OX11 . . . . 217 E8
Crown La Benson OX10 203 F4
    Dorchester OX10. . . . . 182 D1
    South Moreton OX11. . . 220 A5
Crownmarsh Rd OX27 . .64 F6
Crown Mdw OX12 . . . . . 197 C2
Crown Mews 3 OX14. 179 E7
Crown Rd
    Kidlington OX5. . . . . . . 108 D8
    Wheatley OX33 . . . . . . 144 B8
Crown Sq Benson OX10 204 A4
    Wheatley OX33 . . . . . . 144 B8
Crown St OX4 . . . . 141 F8
Crown Wlk OX26 . . . . . . .65 E1
Crows Foot RG8 . . . . . . 247 A6
CROWSLEY 253 C4
Crowsley Pk RG9 . . . . . 253 F5
Crowsley Rd RG9 . . . . . 255 A3
Crowsley Way RG4 . . . 252 E5
Croxford Gdns OX5. . . 108 E6
Croxton Sq OX26 . . . . . .65 A2
Crozier Cl OX2 . . . . 140 D8
Crumps Butts OX26 . . . .65 E2
Crundel Rise OX28. . . . 103 F1
Crutch Furlong OX10 . 182 C6
Cuckamus La OX29 . . . 105 B6
Cuckoo Cl OX27 . . . . . . .65 F6
CUDDESDON. 144 B3
Cuddesdon Cl OX18. . . 250 F8
Cuddesdon Rd
    Chiselhampton OX44. . . 162 F5
    Chiselhampton OX44. . . 163 A5
    Horspath OX33 . . . . . . 143 C6
    Horspath OX33 . . . . . . 143 C5
Cuddesdon Way OX4 . 142 F2
Cuddesdon Rd OX44 . 163 A6
Cues La SN6. . . . . 227 C4
CULHAM. 180 B2
Culham Cl OX14 . . . . . . 160 A1
Culham No 1 Site
    OX14 . . . . 181 A3
Culham Rd OX14. . . . . . 180 A5
Culham Science Ctr
    OX14 . . . . 181 A3
Culham Science Ctr
    OX14 . . . . .B4 0
Culham Sta OX14. . . . . 180 F3
Cullen Pl OX11 . . . . 218 E8
Cullerne Cl OX14 . . . . . 160 A3
Cullerns The SN6. . . . . 190 A6
Cullum Ho OX33. . . . . . 144 C8
Cullum Rd OX33 . . . . . . 144 C8
Culworth Rd OX17. . . . . .5 F6
Cumberford OX15 . . . . .21 D3
Cumberford Cl OX15. . .21 C3
Cumberford Hill OX15 .21 D4
Cumberland Rd OX4. . 142 B7
Cumberlege Cl OX3. . . 123 E7
Cummings Cl OX3. . . . . 123 E7
CUMNOR. 139 D5
Cumnor CE Prim Sch
    OX2. . . . . 139 E5
CUMNOR HILL 140 C7

Cumnor Hill OX2. . . . . . 140 B7
Cumnor Rd
    Cumnor OX2. . . . . 139 C8
    Wootton OX2. . . . . 159 A8
Cumnor Rise Rd OX2 . 140 C8
Cunliffe Cl OX2. . . . . . . 123 C6
Cunningham Dr OX15 . . .21 C4
Cup & Saucer OX17. . . . .4 F2
CURBRIDGE 117 C6
Curbridge Bsns Pk
    OX28 . . . . 103 B1
Curbridge Pk Rd OX29 103 B1
Curbridge Rd
    Ducklington OX29 . . . . 118 A4
    Witney OX28. . . . . 117 E7
Curie Ave OX14 . . . . . . 217 B3
Cursus The GL7. . . . . . 150 C5
Curtis Ave OX14 . . . . . . 180 B7
Curtis Cl SN6. . . . . 191 D1
Curtis Rd Kidlington OX5 .92 E1
    Shrivenham SN6 . . . . . 209 B6
Curtiss Cl Bicester OX26 66 A5
    Grove OX12. . . . . 214 B8
Curtyn Cl OX14 . . . . . . 179 D8
Curzon Gate OX HP14 188 E5
Cuthwine Pl GL7. . . . . . 150 C5
CUTTESLOWE. 109 B2
Cutteslowe Prim Sch
    OX2 . . . . 109 C1
Cuttle Brook Gdns
    OX9. . . . . 129 E1
Cuttle Brook Nature
    Reserve★ OX9 . . . . . 147 E8
CUXHAM 185 D3
Cuxham Rd
    Watlington OX49. . . . . 185 E3
    Watlington OX49. . . . . 186 A2
    Watlington OX49. . . . . 186 B1
Cwmcarn RG4. . . . . 258 F6
Cygnet Cl OX9. . . . . 166 B8
Cygnet Ct OX14. . . . . . 179 E6
Cypress Gdns OX26. . . .65 F5
Cyprus Terr OX2. . . . . . 122 F8

D

Dacey Dr OX25 . . . . .63 B8
Dacre Ave RG4 . . . . 259 E4
Daedas View OX15. . . . .33 E5
Daedings The OX15. . . . .33 E4
Dagdale Dr OX11 . . . . . 200 F3
Daimler Ave OX16 . . . . .15 F8
Dairy Ct OX7. . . . . .73 A4
Dairyground The OX15. 14 A5
Dairy Mdw OX13. . . . . . 177 C5
Dairy Sand OX5. . . . . . . .92 F8
Daisy Bank
    Abingdon-on-Thames
    OX14. . . . . 160 B1
    Abingdon-on-Thames
    OX14. . . . . 180 B8
    Brookend OX7 . . . . .72 A8
Daisy Hill OX25. . . . . . . .47 D5
Daisy La OX12 . . . . 215 A6
Dakota Dr Grove OX12. 214 C8
    Townsend OX12 . . . . . 194 C1
Dale Cl Brackley NN13 . .24 A7
    Oxford OX4 . . . . 141 B8
    Oxford OX4 . . . . 261 A1
Dale Pl OX5 . . . . .92 E1
Dale The OX3. . . . . 125 A4
Dale Way OX25 . . . . .63 C7
Dale Wlk OX29 . . . . 118 A5
Dalton Ave OX11. . . . . . 217 A2
Dalton Cl OX13 . . . . 199 C2
Damer Gdns RG9 . . . . . 254 E8
Damson Dr OX11 . . . . . 200 B1
Damson Trees SN6 . . . 209 A6
Dancers Hill OX7 . . . . . .73 C3
Dandridge Cl OX12 . . . 197 C7
Danesmoor OX16. . . . . .16 B8
Danes Rd OX26 . . . . .65 C2
Daniel Shepherd Ave
    OX11. . . . . 200 B2
Dan Read Parade
    OX11. . . . . 200 B2
Danvers Cl OX15. . . . . . .15 C2
Danvers Rd
    Broughton OX15 . . . . . .15 C2
    Oxford OX4 . . . . 142 A3
Darby Cl OX15. . . . . .21 E3
Darcey Lode OX11 . . . . 201 B2
Dards Rd OX25 . . . . .49 C1
Darell Rd RG4 . . . . 258 F3
Darent Pl OX11. . . . . . . 201 A2
Dark La
    Great Coxwell SN7 . . . 192 C8
    Reading RG31 . . . . 257 B2
    Sunningwell OX13. . . . 159 E5
    Wargrave RG10. . . . . . 255 D2
    Witney OX28. . . . . 104 A1
    Wroxton OX15 . . . . .15 A7
Darlington Link OX1. . . 261 C4
Darnell Wlk OX26. . . . . .65 E4
Darrell Way OX14. . . . . 159 F1
Dart Dr OX11. . . . . 200 E3
Dart Rd OX13. . . . . 159 C2
Dashwood Ave OX5. . . 108 B5
Dashwood Banbury
    Academy OX16. . . . . . .16 F6
Dashwood Ct
    Aston Rowant OX49 . . . 167 D3
    2 Banbury OX15. . . . . .16 D5
Dashwood Mews OX7. . .77 F4
Dashwood Prim Sch 19
    OX16. . . . . .16 D5
Dashwood Rd
    Banbury OX16. . . . . . . .16 D5
    Oxford OX4 . . . . 142 A3
Dashwood Rise OX25 . .47 D6

Dashwood Terr 1
    OX16. . . . . .16 C5
Dasset Rd OX17 . . . . .3 E8
Datchet Gn OX10 . . . . . 202 F2
Daubeny Rd OX14 . . . . 141 F6
Daubigny Mead OX18. 116 C4
Davenant Ct OX2 . . . . . 109 A1
Davenant Rd OX2. . . . . 123 A8
Davenport Cl OX7 . . . . . .29 A3
Davenport Pl OX49 . . . 186 B1
Davenport Rd OX28. . . 103 F1
Daventry Rd
    Banbury OX16. . . . . .9 F1
    Banbury OX16. . . . . . . .16 F7
    Chacombe OX16 . . . . . .10 A3
David Nicholls Cl OX4. 142 B2
David Walter Cl OX2. . 109 B1
Davies Rd OX16. . . . . . . .15 E6
Davis Cl
    Carterton OX18. . . . . . 115 E2
    Stonesfield OX29. . . . . .89 D8
Davis Gdns OX27 . . . . . .65 F7
Dawls Cl OX7. . . . . .73 A4
Dawson St 1 OX4 . . . 141 E8
Daylesford 54 D8
Daylesford Rd OX7 . . . . .55 A5
Days Ground SN6. . . . . 209 C7
Day's La OX10 . . . . 204 F2
Deacon Field RG8 . . . . 239 C3
Deacon Way
    Banbury OX16. . . . . . . .16 B5
    Reading RG30 . . . . 258 A2
Deadman's La
    Goring Heath RG8. . . . . 251 C4
    Goring Heath RG8. . . . . 251 C5
DEAN. 57 E1
Dean Butler Cl OX12. . 214 C5
Dean Cl OX16. . . . . .16 E8
DEAN COURT 140 B8
Dean Court Rd OX2. . . 140 B7
Deanes Cl OX13 . . . . . . 198 F4
Deanfield Ave RG9. . . 244 D5
Deanfield Rd
    Henley-on-Thames
    RG9. . . . . 244 D1
    Oxford OX2 . . . . 122 B1
Deans Ct OX26 . . . . .65 F1
Deans Farm RG4 . . . . . 259 D1
Dean Wood Cl RG8 . . . 240 E1
Dearlove Cl OX14 . . . . 159 E2
Dearne Pl OX11. . . . . . . 201 A2
Deaufort Cl OX5. . . . . . .92 E1
DEDDINGTON. 33 E4
Deddington Castle
    Earthworks★ OX15 . . . 34 A4
Deddington CE Prim Sch
    OX15 . . . . .33 F5
Deddington Hill OX15. .33 F6
Deddington Rd
    Great Tew OX7 . . . . .31 E1
    Great Tew OX7 . . . . .31 E2
    Great Tew OX7 . . . . .45 D8
Dee Cl OX26. . . . . .65 D1
Deene Cl OX17 . . . . .23 B4
Deerhurst Cl GL56 . . . . .26 F1
Deer Park Rd OX28. . . 117 D7
Deers Cl OX15 . . . . .22 E8
Deers Farm
    Bodicote OX15. . . . . . . .22 E7
    Bodicote OX15. . . . . . . .22 E7
Deer's La RG8 . . . . 241 C2
Deer Wlk OX4 . . . . 142 F1
Defence Academy of the
    United Kingdom
    SN6. . . . . 209 E7
Defiant Cl OX26 . . . . . . .66 A3
De Havilland Rd GL56 .88 B5
De Havilland Way
    OX29 . . . . 117 C8
Delafield Cl HP14. . . . . 188 F4
Delamare Way OX2. . . 140 B7
Delapre Dr OX16. . . . . . .16 F7
De La Warr Dr OX17 . . .8 E2
De La Warr End OX17. . .8 E2
Delbush Ave OX3 . . . . . 125 B4
Delfin Way OX7. . . . . . . .48 B8
Dell Rd RG31 . . . . 257 C2
Dells Common HP14. . 189 C1
Dell The HP14. . . . . 188 F3
Dellwood Pk RG4. . . . . 258 F4
Delly Cl OX29. . . . . 104 A7
DELLY END. 104 A8
Delly End OX29. . . . . . . 104 A7
Delly Hill OX29 . . . . 104 A6
Delta Dr OX44. . . . . 143 C1
Demesne Furze OX4 . . 124 C1
De Montfort Rd RG1. . 259 A1
Denbeigh Pl RG1 . . . . . 258 F1
Denbigh Cl OX16 . . . . . .15 F4
Denbigh Rd OX9. . . . . . 130 A1
Denby Way RG30 . . . . . 257 F2
Denchfield Rd OX16. . . .16 D2
DENCHWORTH. 196 A4
Denchworth Rd
    Charney Bassett OX12 . 175 F2
    Charney Bassett OX12 . 176 A2
    Charney Bassett OX13 . 176 A1
    Grove OX12. . . . . 196 D2
    Shellingford OX12. . . . 194 A8
    Wantage OX12 . . . . 214 C6
Dene Cl RG4. . . . . 260 A5
Denefield Gdns RG31. 258 B3
Denefield Sch RG31. . 257 B3
Dene Hollow OX11. . . . 235 E8
Dene Rd Oxford OX3. . . 142 D8
    Oxford OX4 . . . . 142 D8
Dene Rise OX28 . . . . . . 104 A1
Denman's La OX2. . . . . 139 C5
Denmark St OX4. . . . . . 141 E8
Denny Gdns OX4 . . . . . 142 C2
Dent Cl OX25 . . . . .81 C3

DENTON. 144 B1
Denton Cl
    Abingdon-on-Thames
    OX14. . . . . 180 B8
    Oxford OX4 . . . . 142 A5
Denton Hill OX44. . . . . 144 B2
Denton La OX44 . . . . . . 143 F1
Dents Cl OX3. . . . . 124 A5
Derby Rd RG4. . . . . 259 B3
Derwent Ave
    Didcot OX11 . . . . 201 A1
    Oxford OX3 . . . . 124 A4
Derwent Cl OX13 . . . . . 159 C2
Derwent Rd OX26. . . . . .65 B3
Desborough Cres OX44 142 A3
Desmesne Furze OX4 . 124 C1
Des Roches Sq OX28. . 118 B7
Devereux Pl OX4 . . . . . 142 A3
Devil's Hill RG9. . . . . . . 253 D6
De Vitre Pl OX12. . . . . . 214 D8
Devon Cl OX10 . . . . 204 D3
Devon Dr RG4 . . . . 259 E4
Devon Pl OX18 . . . . 115 F2
Devonshire Gdns
    RG31. . . . . 257 B3
Devon Way
    Banbury OX16. . . . . . . .15 F8
    Banbury OX16. . . . . . . .16 A8
Dexter Cl OX16 . . . . .16 D4
Dexter Gdns
    Kingston Bagpuize
    OX13. . . . . 156 F1
    Kingston Bagpuize
    OX13. . . . . 157 A1
Diamond Ct OX2. . . . . . 123 B6
Diamond Dr
    Didcot OX11 . . . . 218 B7
    Didcot OX11 . . . . 218 B8
Diamond Pl OX2. . . . . . 123 B6
Diamond Wy OX11. . . . 235 C8
Dibdare Furlong OX5. .77 C6
Dibleys OX11 . . . . 237 A8
Dickens Cl
    Bicester OX26 . . . . .65 C3
    Reading RG4 . . . . 259 D2
Dickenson Ct OX7. . . . . .42 F3
Dickenson Rd OX15. . . .21 E3
Dickredge The OX25. . .62 B8
DIDCOT 200 D3
Didcot Com Hospl
    OX11 . . . . 218 C8
Didcot Girls' Sch
    OX11 . . . . 200 D1
Didcot L Ctr OX11 . . . . 218 F7
Didcot Parkway Sta
    OX11 . . . . 200 F2
Didcot Pk OX11. . . . . . . 200 E4
Didcot Railway Ctr (Mus)★
    OX11 . . . . 200 F2
Didcot Rd
    Blewbury OX11 . . . . . . 219 B3
    Brightwell-cum-Sotwell
    OX10. . . . . 202 D3
    Didcot OX11 . . . . 218 A4
    Didcot OX11 . . . . 218 A8
    Long Wittenham OX14 . 201 D8
Didcot Wave L Pool
    OX11 . . . . 218 E7
Dido Rd OX11 . . . . 217 A1
Digberry La RG9. . . . . . 224 C5
Digging La OX13. . . . . . 157 F5
DIGGS. 130 F5
Dillon Cl OX15. . . . . .22 E8
Dimbles Gate OX39. . . 168 C7
Dirac Pl OX11 . . . . 219 A8
Distons La OX7 . . . . .42 E3
Ditchedge La
    Sibford Gower OX15. . . .12 E2
    Sibford Gower OX15. . . .18 D7
Ditchend Cotts OX44. 164 A5
Ditchley Rd OX7. . . . . . .73 E5
Dittander Cl OX26 . . . . .65 F4
Divinity Rd Oxford OX4 124 B1
    Witney OX29. . . . . 103 B1
    Witney OX29. . . . . 117 B7
Dixey Cres OX18. . . . . . 135 A4
Dixon's Row OX12. . . . 214 E8
Dixs La OX11 . . . . 220 A5
Dobson's La
    Fawley RG9 . . . . 226 C1
    Fawley RG9. . . . . 244 C8
Doctors Spinney NN13 .25 B4
Dodgson Rd OX4 . . . . . 142 C4
Dodson Ct OX14 . . . . . . 179 F8
Doe Lea OX11. . . . . 200 F3
Dog Cl OX17. . . . . .22 F3
Dogkennel La OX7. . . . 193 F7
Dog Kennel La OX7. . . .85 C7
Dog La Childrey OX12 . 213 C3
    Rotherfield Peppard
    RG9. . . . . 242 D1
    Rotherfield Peppard
    RG9. . . . . 253 B8
DOGMORE END 241 D4
Dogmore End La RG9. 241 D4
Doily Cl OX15. . . . . .30 A7
Dollicott HP17. . . . . 130 F6
Dolphin La OX18. . . . . . 100 F6
Dominie Pl OX29 . . . . . 117 B7
Donaldson Cl OX16 . . . .16 A6
Don Boscoe Cl 3
    OX4. . . . . 142 D6
Doncaster Cl 4 OX26. 65 C1
Don Cl OX11. . . . . 201 A3
Donegal Cl RG4 . . . . . . 259 C3
Donkin Hill RG4 . . . . . . 259 C3
Donnington Bridge Rd
    OX4. . . . . 141 F6
Donnington Cl OX28 . . 117 D7
Donnington Lodge
    OX4. . . . . 141 F6

Donnington Pl OX12 . . 214 D6
Don Stuart Pl OX4 . . . . 142 B7
Dora Carr Cl OX3 . . . . . 124 A5
Dora Gr OX49. . . . . 186 A2
Dorcas Rd OX16 . . . . . . .17 A6
DORCHESTER 182 C1
Dorchester Abbey Mus★
    OX10 . . . . 182 D1
Dorchester Cl OX3. . . . 124 F1
Dorchester Cres OX14 160 A1
Dorchester Ct
    4 Kidlington OX5. . . . 108 F8
    Oxford OX2 . . . . 123 B6
Dorchester Gr OX16 . . .15 F4
Dorchester Pl OX9. . . . 147 F8
Dorchester Rd OX10 . . 182 F4
Dorchester St Birinus CE
    Sch OX10 . . . . 182 D1
Dor Cl OX13 . . . . 135 A3
Doris Field Cl OX3. . . . 124 A3
Dormer Rd OX9 . . . . . . 148 B6
Dormers The SN6 . . . . 190 B6
Dorn Cl OX7 . . . . .60 F8
Dornford La
    Tackley OX20. . . . . .76 D8
    Wootton OX20. . . . . . . .76 D4
Dorn View OX20. . . . . . .76 A4
Dorothy Hodgkin Rd
    OX1. . . . . 261 C3
DORTON. 98 F1
Douglas Downes Cl
    OX3. . . . . 124 E2
Douglas Dr OX12 . . . . . 214 B8
Douglas Rd RG4 . . . . . 259 D2
Dovecot Cl OX15. . . . . . .21 A2
Dovecote Cl
    Haddenham HP17. . . . . 130 F6
    Milcombe OX15. . . . . . .21 A2
Dovecote La OX25 . . . . .48 F6
Dovecote Mws 8
    OX11. . . . . 200 B1
Dovecote Pl OX29 . . . . 117 C5
Dove Ct
    3 Bicester OX26 . . . . . .65 C1
    Carterton OX18. . . . . . 115 E4
Dovedale Cl RG4 . . . . . 258 F3
Dove Gn OX26 . . . . .65 B3
Dovehouse Cl OX29 . . 120 F8
Dove House Cl OX2 . . . 122 F8
Dove House La OX44. . 144 C3
Dove La RG9 . . . . 252 D8
Doveleat OX39. . . . . . . 168 D7
Dover Ave OX16 . . . . . . .15 F6
D'Overbroecks Coll (The
    Swan Sch) OX2 . . . . . 123 B5
D'Overbroeck's Oxford
    OX2 . . . . 261 A4
D'Overbroeck's Oxford
    (Sixth Form) 1 OX2. 123 B8
Dover Cl OX2 . . . . 140 C7
Dovetrees OX18 . . . . . . 115 E3
Dowding Cl OX14 . . . . . .65 B3
Dowell Ct 13 SN7. . . . 172 F3
DOWN END 30 B7
Downhill La OX29. . . . . 104 B4
DOWNINGTON 150 B3
Downlands SN7 . . . . . . 192 D2
Downs Cl OX11 . . . . 217 E6
Downside
    Chilton OX11. . . . . 217 C1
    Chilton OX11. . . . . 235 C8
    West End OX10. . . . . . . 220 F1
    West End OX10. . . . . . . 221 A1
Downside End OX3 . . . 125 A3
Downside Rd OX3 . . . . 125 A3
Downsmead SN8 . . . . . 245 D1
Downs Rd
    Aldworth RG20 . . . . . . 247 A4
    Curbridge OX29. . . . . . 117 B7
    Didcot OX11 . . . . 218 D7
    Standlake OX29. . . . . . 137 B6
    Witney OX29. . . . . 103 B1
    Witney OX29. . . . . 117 B7
Downs The OX29 . . . . . 137 C5
Downs View
    Aston Tirrold OX11 . . . 237 F8
    Highworth SN6 . . . . . . 190 A6
Downsview Rd
    Grove OX12. . . . . 214 A8
    Wantage OX12 . . . . 214 B7
Downs Way
    Chilton OX11. . . . . 217 C1
    Reading RG31 . . . . 257 C2
Downsway Prim Sch
    RG31. . . . . 257 C3
Dow St OX25 . . . . .63 C8
Doyley Rd Oxford OX2 141 A8
    Wallingford OX10. . . . . 203 C1
Dragonhill Rd SN7. . . . 211 B2
Dragon Sch OX2. . . . . . 123 C4
Drake Ave OX14 . . . . . . 218 D8
Drake La OX28. . . . . 104 D1
Drakes Dr HP18. . . . . . 129 E5
Drakes Farm HP18. . . . 129 E5
DRAYCOTT 145 F8
DRAYCOTT OX9. . . . . . 127 F1
Draycott Rd OX9. . . . . . 145 F8
Draycott Rd
    Kingston Bagpuize
    OX13. . . . . 156 D1
    Longworth OX13. . . . . 156 D1
Draymans Croft 10
    OX26. . . . . .65 E2
Drayman's Wlk 7
    OX4. . . . . 142 C4
Dray's La RG9 . . . . 253 A8
DRAYTON
    Abingdon-on-Thames . 179 A1
    Banbury. 15 D8

Drayton Com Prim Sch
    OX14 . . . . 179 B2
Drayton East Way
    Drayton OX14 . . . . 199 D8
    Sutton Courtenay OX13 199 E8
Drayton Mill OX13 . . . . 199 D7
Drayton Rd
    Abingdon-on-Thames
    OX14. . . . . 179 D5
    Banbury OX15. . . . . . . .15 C8
    Berinsfield OX10. . . . . . 182 E3
    Dorchester OX10. . . . . 182 D2
    Drayton OX14 . . . . 179 D1
    Milton OX13. . . . . 199 D7
    Sutton Courtenay OX14 199 F8
DRAYTON ST
    LEONARD 183 A5
Dresden Way RG30 . . . 257 F1
Drew Cl OX13 . . . . 176 C8
Drewett Cc OX2. . . . . . 122 E8
Drewitts Cnr OX11. . . . 217 E7
Drift Acre OX15. . . . . . . .20 D7
Drift Ctr OX4 . . . . 142 F4
Drift La Hornton OX15. . . .7 F1
    Wroxton OX15 . . . . .15 A8
Drinkwater Cl OX25. . . .97 C7
Drivers La OX15. . . . . . . .27 A1
Drive The Enstone OX7. .58 F6
    Kidlington OX5. . . . . . . .92 B2
Drove Acre Rd OX4 . . . 142 A7
Drovers Cres OX9. . . . . 129 D1
Drovers La RG9. . . . . . . 226 C8
Droveside OX10. . . . . . 220 F1
Drove Way OX12. . . . . . 212 B4
Drove Wy OX11. . . . . . . 235 B8
Dr Radcliffe's CE Sch
    OX25 . . . . .48 B1
Dr South's CE (Voluntary
    Aided) Prim Sch OX5. .93 E1
Druce Way OX4. . . . . . . 142 F3
Druids Wlk
    Chinnor OX39. . . . . . . 168 C6
    Didcot OX11 . . . . 200 E2
Dryden Ave
    Bicester OX26 . . . . .65 B3
    Woodfield OX26 . . . . . . .65 B4
Dry La OX29 . . . . 102 D3
Drylands Rd OX29 . . . . 102 E2
DRY SANDFORD 158 F5
Dry Sandford Prim Sch
    OX13 . . . . 158 F6
Drysdale Cl OX14 . . . . . 160 E2
Duchess Cl RG8 . . . . . . 256 D7
Duck End La OX29 . . . . 120 C1
Duck La
    Ludgershall HP18. . . . . .98 C8
    Ludgershall HP18. . . . . .98 D8
DUCKLINGTON. 118 A4
Ducklington CE Prim Sch
    OX29 . . . . 118 B3
Ducklington La OX28. 117 F7
Duck Sq OX39 . . . . 168 C6
Dudcote Field 13
    OX11. . . . . 200 C2
Dudgeon Dr 4 OX4. . 142 B2
Dudley Cl RG31. . . . . . . 257 F1
Dudley Ct OX2. . . . . 123 B7
Dudley Gdns OX4. . . . . 123 F1
Dudley La RG9. . . . . 226 F7
Dudley Mews RG31. . . 257 F1
Dudwell OX11 . . . . 200 E3
Duffield Cl OX14. . . . . . 160 B2
Duffield Pl OX13. . . . . . 178 C7
Duffield Rd RG5 . . . . . . 260 F1
Duke of York Ave
    OX14 . . . . 199 D3
Dukes Cl HP18. . . . . 128 C2
Dukes Meadow Dr
    Banbury OX16. . . . . .8 F2
    Hanwell Fields OX16. . . . .9 B2
Dukes Rd OX5 . . . . 108 F8
Duke St Banbury OX16. .16 E6
    Henley-on-Thames RG9. 244 E2
    Oxford OX2 . . . . 122 F1
Dulas Cl OX11. . . . . 200 F2
Dumas Cl OX26. . . . . . . .65 C2
Dumbarton Way RG4 . 259 E5
Dunbar Dr OX9 . . . . 130 A1
Duncan Cl OX20 . . . . . . 120 D8
Duncan Gdns RG8 . . . 257 C4
Dundas Cl OX14 . . . . . . 180 B8
Dunkins Cl OX26. . . . . . .65 C2
Dunlin Ct Banbury OX16. .16 E3
    4 Banbury OX16. . . . . . .65 F1
Dunluce Gdns RG8. . . 256 C5
Dunmore Prim Sch
    OX14 . . . . .159 F1
Dunmore Rd OX14. . . . 159 E2
Dunnock Cl OX26. . . . . .66 A1
Dunnock End 12 OX11 200 C2
Dunnock Rd OX11. . . . . .16 F1
Dunnock Way
    Sandford-on-Thames
    OX4. . . . . 142 F1
    Wargrave RG10. . . . . . 255 C3
Dunsden Cl OX11 . . . . . 200 D1
DUNSDEN GN RG4 . . . 259 F7
DUNSDEN GREEN . . . 259 F7
Dunsden Green RG4. . 260 A8
Dunsden Way RG9. . . . 260 A8
Dunsomer Hill
    North Moreton OX11. . . 219 F6
    North Moreton OX11. . . 220 A7
Dunstan Ave OX7 . . . . . .42 E2
Dunstead La OX13. . . . 122 B6
Dunster Cl RG4 . . . . . . 259 C6
DUNS TEW 47 D6

Duns Tew Rd
Duns Tew OX7 . . . . 47 C2
Hempton OX7 . . . . 33 A3
Dunthrop Rd OX7. . . . . . 44 A4
Durant Way RG31. . . . . 257 D3
Durham La
Cassington OX29 . . . . . 107 C1
Cassington OX29. . . . . 121 C8
Durham Mews 5 OX16 . .9 A1
Durnells 14 OX11. . . . . 200 C2
DUXFORD 155 D4
Duxford Cl
Bicester OX26. . . . . 66 B4
Carterton OX18. . . . . . 115 E3
Dyers Hill OX7. . . . . . . .73 B4
Dyer Straits OX11. . . . . 234 F8
Dyggel The SN7 . . . . . . 194 D7
Dynham Pl OX3. . . . . . . 124 D1
Dysons Wood RG4. . . . . 258 E8
Dysonswood La RG4 . . . 258 E8

E

Eady Rd OX25. . . . . .63 B8
Eagle Dr GL54 . . . . .68 B3
Eagle Ind Est OX28 . . . 118 A8
Eagle La SN6 . . . . 191 C1
Eagles SN7 . . . . 172 F3
Eagles Close Almshouses
7 . . . . 214 D4
Eagle Sq SN7. . . . . 192 E7
Earlsfield Cl RG4 . . . . . 259 E4
Earls La OX15 . . . . .33 F4
Earl St OX2. . . . . 122 F1
Earlstoke Cl OX16 . . . . . .16 E8
Early Rd OX28 . . . . 104 D2
EASINGTON Banbury . . 16 C3
Chalgrove 185 C7
Easington Gdns OX16. . 16 C4
Easington Rd OX16 . . . . 16 C4
Eason Dr OX14 . . . . 160 C1
EAST ADDERBURY 23 B3
East Allcourt GL7 . . . . . 150 C4
East Ave OX4. . . . . 142 A8
Eastbrook Cl OX6. . . . . . .97 E7
Eastbury Ct 2 OX12 . . . 214 D5
EAST CHALLOW. 214 A5
Eastchurch OX4 . . . . . . 141 F3
East Cl OX16. . . . . .16 F7
EASTEND 57 D1
EAST END Adderbury . .23 B4
Hook Norton 30 B7
Swerford 30 F3
East End OX29. . . . . 90 D4
Brookend OX7 . . . . 72 C8
Chadlington OX7 . . . . . 57 D1
Chalsey OX10 . . . . 221 A2
Combe OX29 . . . . 90 D3
Hook Norton OX15 . . . . 30 B7
Easterfield OX12. . . . . . 196 E1
Eastern Ave
Milton OX4. . . . . 199 F4
Oxford OX4 . . . . 142 B3
Eastern By Pass OX9. . 148 C7
Eastern By-Pass Rd
Oxford OX3, OX4. . . . . 142 E5
Oxford OX4 . . . . 142 A3
Eastern Ho OX4 . . . . . . 142 B3
Eastern Terr OX15. . . . . .22 E8
East Field OX3 . . . . 142 E7
Eastfield Ct 2 SN7 . . . 172 F4
Eastfield La
Whitchurch-on-Thames
RG8. . . . . 256 D7
Woodcote RG8. . . . . . . 250 E6
Eastfield Pl OX4 . . . . . . 142 F6
Eastfield Rd OX8, OX28 104 B3
Eastfields OX11. . . . . . 237 A8
Eastgate OX15. . . . . 7 C7
EAST GINGE 216 B2
EAST HAGBOURNE . . . 218 F6
EAST HANNEY 197 B6
East Hawthorn Rd
OX25. . . . . 81 D4
EAST HENDRED. 216 E7
Eastleach Down Farm La
OX18. . . . . 113 A4
EASTLEACH MARTIN . 131 B7
EASTLEACH
TURVILLE 131 A8
EAST LOCKINGE. 215 D3
Eastmanton La OX12.. 212 F3
Eastons OX11. . . . . 240 C8
East Oxford Prim Sch
OX4 . . . . 141 F8
East Paddocks OX14. . 199 D7
East Point Bsns Pk
OX4 . . . . 142 C3
Eastrop Highworth SN6. 190 B5
Highworth SN6 . . . . . . 190 D6
Eastrop Inf Sch SN6. . . 190 A5
East St Helen St OX14. 179 F6
East St Banbury OX16 . . .16 E7
Bicester OX26. . . . . 65 D3
Bodicote OX15. . . . . . . 22 E8
Didcot OX11. . . . . 219 A8
Fritwell OX27. . . . . 36 B1
Fritwell OX27. . . . . .49 F7
Fritwell OX27. . . . . 50 A8
Long Compton CV36 . . .27 F6
Oxford OX2 . . . . 123 A1
Oxford OX2 . . . . 141 A8
Thame OX9 . . . . 148 A8
East View
Blackthorn OX25. . . . . .82 A3
Kirtlington OX5. . . . . . . .77 F3
East View Cl RG10. . . . 255 E2

East View Rd RG10. . . . 255 E2
Eastview Terr SN6. . . . 190 A6
East Vw OX5. . . . . 78 A3
East Way OX14 . . . . 199 B8
Eastway Mobile Home Pk
OX14. . . . . 199 B8
Eastwood Rd
Stokenchurch HP14. . . 188 D3
Witney OX29 . . . . 103 C1
EATON 139 B3
Eaton Cl SN7 . . . . 172 E2
Eaton Ct OX2 . . . . 123 C8
EATON HASTINGS. . . . 171 E7
Eaton Rd
Appleton OX13 . . . . . . 158 A8
Eaton OX13. . . . . 139 B2
Ebbes La OX12 . . . . 197 B7
Ebbsworth La SN6. . . . 209 A6
Eccles Cl RG4 . . . . 259 C2
Eckersley Sch of English
The OX1. . . . . 261 A2
Edencroft SN6. . . . . . . 190 B7
Eden Croft OX14. . . . . . 160 A2
Eden Ct OX11. . . . . 201 A1
Eden Dr OX3 . . . . 124 B4
Edenhall Cl RG31 . . . . . 257 D3
Eden Rd OX3 . . . . 124 A4
Eden Way OX26. . . . . . . .65 B2
Edgar Milward Cl
RG30. . . . . 258 A1
Edgcote Way OX16 . . . . .9 D3
Edgcott Rd OX27 . . . . . . .67 F2
Edgecombe Rd OX3 . . . 124 F4
Edgecote La OX17 . . . . . .5 E2
Edgehill OX9 . . . . 129 F2
Edge Hill La OX17. . . . . .2 A5
Edgeway Rd OX3 . . . . . 123 F3
Edgeworth Dr OX18. . . 115 C2
Edinburgh Cl OX16 . . . . .15 E7
Edinburgh Dr
Didcot OX11 . . . . 200 F1
Kidlington OX5. . . . . . 109 A8
Edinburgh Way OX16. . .15 E6
Edington Pl OX12. . . . . 196 D1
Edington Rd OX28 . . . . 117 D8
Edington Sq OX28 . . . . 117 D8
Edith Ct OX1 . . . . 141 D1
Edith Moorhouse Prim Sch
OX18. . . . . 115 D2
Edith Rd OX1. . . . . 141 C7
Edmonds Ct OX11 . . . . 218 D8
Edmund Halley Rd
OX4. . . . . 142 B1
Edmund Rd OX4 . . . . . . 142 C5
Edmunds Dr OX26 . . . . .80 F6
Edmunds Rd OX16 . . . . .15 F5
Edon Bsns Pk OX33. . . 145 A6
Edsell Cres OX9 . . . . . . 147 F6
Edward Abraham Rd
OX1. . . . . 261 C3
Edward Feild Prim Sch
OX5 . . . . .108 F7
Edward Rd OX1. . . . . . . 141 E2
Edward St
Abingdon-on-Thames
OX14. . . . . 179 D7
Banbury OX16 . . . . .16 F6
Edward Stone Rise
OX7. . . . . 42 D1
Edward Strauss Pk
OX13. . . . . 177 A8
Edward Street Bsns Ctr
OX16 . . . . .16 F6
Edwin Ct OX2. . . . . 122 F1
Edwin Rd OX11. . . . . . . 218 D7
EF International Language
Sch OX3 . . . . 124 A2
Egerton Cl
Brackley NN13. . . . . . . 24 A7
Brackley NN13. . . . . . . 24 A7
Egerton Rd Oxford OX4 142 A4
Wallingford OX10 . . . . 221 C7
Eglin St OX25. . . . . 63 A8
Egrove Cl OX1. . . . . 141 E4
Eider Way 15 OX11. . . 218 C7
Eighth Ave OX3. . . . . . 142 F8
Eighth St OX11 . . . . . . 217 B3
Elamhurst Way OX18 . 115 D5
Elbourne OX11 . . . . 218 C8
Elderberry Cl OX12 . . . 196 F7
Elder Cl Didcot OX11. . 218 C6
Reading RG31 . . . . 257 C1
Elderdene OX39 . . . . . . 168 D8
Elderfield Cres OX11.. 235 D8
Elderfield Rd
Bicester OX27. . . . . .65 F7
Bicester OX27. . . . . 66 A7
Elder Way
Sandford-on-Thames
OX4. . . . . 142 F1
Wantage OX12 . . . . . . 215 B6
Eldridge Cl OX14 . . . . . 159 F2
Eleanor Cl OX4 . . . . 142 B4
Electric Ave OX2. . . . . . 141 A8
Eleventh St OX11 . . . . 217 B2
Eliot Cl RG4 . . . . 259 A4
Elizabeth Ave OX14. . . 160 C2
Elizabeth Cl RG9. . . . . . 254 A8
Elizabeth Dr OX12 . . . . 214 D6
Elizabeth Jennings Way
OX2. . . . . 123 A6
Elizabeth Pl OX3. . . . . 124 B5
Elizabeth Rd
Henley-on-Thames
RG9. . . . . 254 B8
Mongewell OX10 . . . . . 221 E5
Stokenchurch HP14. . . 188 F4
Elizabeth Rise OX16 . . .16 B4

Ellesmere Cl RG4. . . . . 259 B3
Ellesmere Rd OX4 . . . . 142 A4
Elliots Way RG4 . . . . . . 259 B2
Elliott Cres OX26 . . . . . .80 F6
Ellis La OX7 . . . . .42 E1
Ellison Dr OX15. . . . . . . .8 F1
Ell's La OX15 . . . . 21 C7
Elmbank Ct OX29 . . . . . 117 C6
Elm Bridge Mead
OX10. . . . . 203 E5
Elm Bridge Rdbt
OX10. . . . . 203 D4
Elm Cl
Ambrosden OX25 . . . . . 81 C4
Bicester OX26. . . . . 65 E4
Carterton OX18. . . . . . 115 F4
Chinnor OX39. . . . . . . 168 C5
Tetsworth OX9. . . . . . 166 B8
Wheatley OX33 . . . . . . 144 C7
Witney OX28 . . . . 117 E8
Elm Cres OX7 . . . . .73 C4
Elmcroft RG8. . . . . 249 C5
Elm Ct
Henley-on-Thames
RG9. . . . . 254 D7
Sonning Common RG4. . 252 F4
Elm Dr Chinnor OX39. . 168 C5
Garsington OX44. . . . . 143 D2
Elm Farm Cl OX12 . . . . 214 D7
Elm Gr
Brize Norton OX18 . . . 116 C5
Brize Norton OX18 . . . 116 C5
Kidlington OX5. . . . . . 108 F6
Milton-under-Wychwood
OX7. . . . . 70 B1
Elmhurst Rd RG8 . . . . . 249 C7
Elmhurst Way OX18. . . 115 E5
Elmhurst Wlk RG8. . . . 249 C7
Elm La OX25. . . . . 81 C4
Elmleigh Ct RG4. . . . . . 259 C3
Elm Pk OX11 . . . . 200 B1
Elm Pl OX29 . . . . 120 C8
Elm Rd Faringdon SN7 . 172 E3
North Moreton OX11. . 220 A8
Tokers Green RG4. . . . . 258 D7
Wantage OX12 . . . . . . 214 F6
Elmscote Rd OX16 . . . . 16 D2
Elms Dr OX3. . . . . 124 A5
Elms Farm Bsns Pk
OX12. . . . . 214 E7
Elmsfield Farm Ind Est
OX7. . . . . 42 D3
Elmside SN7 . . . . 193 A5
Elms Par OX2. . . . . 122 D1
Elms Rd
Cassington OX29 . . . . . 107 C2
Oxford OX2 . . . . 122 D1
Thame OX9 . . . . 147 F8
Elms The
Highworth SN6 . . . . . . 190 A5
Langford GL7. . . . . 132 D1
Wantage OX12 . . . . . . 215 B6
Elmstone Dr RG31. . . . 257 C1
Elms Way RG9. . . . . 224 D3
Elmthorpe Rd OX2. . . . 122 E8
Elm Tree Cl
Blackthorn OX25. . . . . .82 A4
Oxford OX4 . . . . 142 B3
Elm Tree Farm OX25. . .82 A4
Elm Trees HP18. . . . . . 129 B7
Elm Tree Wlk OX13 . . . 159 C1
ELSFIELD 110 C1
Elsfield Rd OX3. . . . . . . 123 F6
Elsfield Way OX2 . . . . . 109 B1
Elsley Rd RG31 . . . . 257 E3
Elstow Ave RG4. . . . . . . 259 C6
Elstree Cl RG31. . . . . . . 257 D2
Elswith Cl OX12. . . . . . 214 D8
Eltham Ave RG4 . . . . . . 259 E5
Elton Cl OX3. . . . . 125 B4
Elton Cres OX33 . . . . . . 144 C7
Elton Field OX9. . . . . . . 148 A6
Elton Rd OX16. . . . . .16 E2
Elvendon La RG8 . . . . . 250 C7
Elvendon Rd RG8. . . . . 249 D7
Elwes Cl OX14 . . . . 180 B8
Elwes Rd OX13 . . . . . . 178 D6
Ely Cl
Abingdon-on-Thames
OX14. . . . . 179 C6
Carterton OX18. . . . . . 115 E3
Elyham RG8. . . . . 257 B5
Emden Ho OX3 . . . . 124 D4
Emma La RG10 . . . . 255 E2
Emmanuel Christian Sch
OX4 . . . . 142 B2
Emmens Cl RG8 . . . . . . 241 D3
Emmens La RG8 . . . . . . 241 E2
EMMER GREEN 259 B6
Emmer Green Ct RG4. 259 C5
Emmer Green Prim Sch
RG4. . . . . 259 B6
Emmer Green Rd
Binfield Heath RG4. . . 253 F1
Binfield Heath RG9. . . 254 A2
EMMINGTON 149 A1
Emmington View
OX39. . . . . 168 C7
Emperor Gdns OX4 . . . 142 E1
Empire Dr OX18 . . . . . . 115 C5
Empire Rd OX4. . . . . . . 142 E1
Empson Cres 3 OX28. 104 A2
Empstead Ct RG9. . . . . 244 D2
Endeavour Acad OX3 . 125 A3
Eney Cl OX14 . . . . 160 C2
Englands La OX10 . . . . 158 A8
Englefield Cl SN7. . . . . 194 D7
English La RG9 . . . . 223 E1
ENSLOW 77 C1
ENSTONE 58 F6

Enstone Airfield Complex
(Ind Est) OX7. . . . . 59 D8
Enstone Prim Sch OX7. .58 F7
Enstone Rd
Charlbury OX7. . . . . 73 B4
Great Tew OX7 . . . . 45 C7
Little Tew OX7 . . . . 44 E4
Little Tew OX7 . . . . 45 A5
Little Tew OX7 . . . . 45 B3
Middle Barton OX7 . . . . 60 E8
EP Collier Prim Sch 11
RG1. . . . . 259 A1
EPS Ind Est OX17. . . . . . .5 E8
Epsom Wy OX26. . . . . . . 65 C1
EPWELL 13 B6
Epwell Rd Epwell OX15. 13 A4
Shutford OX15. . . . . . . 13 C6
Equine Way OX39. . . . . 168 B7
Erica Cl Banbury OX16 . . .9 A1
Oxford OX4 . . . . 142 F3
Eric Ave RG4 . . . . 259 A6
Eridge Road OX26. . . . . 65 A2
Erlestoke Ave OX14. . . 201 B5
Ermin St SN8. . . . . 245 E1
Ermont Way
Banbury OX16 . . . . .16 F8
Banbury OX16 . . . . 17 A7
Ernest Rd OX11. . . . . . . 218 E8
Ernicote Cl OX25 . . . . . .81 E4
Esingdon Dr OX9 . . . . . 148 A6
Essex Rd OX9. . . . . 148 B7
Essex St OX4 . . . . 142 A7
Essex Way RG4 . . . . 253 A3
Ester Carling La RG9. . 252 D8
Estover Way OX39 . . . . 168 B6
Ethelhelm Cl OX14. . . . 160 C3
Ethelred Ct OX3 . . . . . . 124 C4
Eton Cl OX28 . . . . 118 D7
Europa Sch UK OX14. . 180 C4
Euston Way OX12. . . . . 214 A8
Evans Cl OX29 . . . . 120 E8
Evans Ct OX5. . . . . 108 F8
Evans La OX5. . . . . 108 F8
Evans Rd OX29 . . . . 120 E8
Evans Wy OX7. . . . . .42 E1
Evelin Rd OX14 . . . . . . 159 E1
Evelyn Cl OX2 . . . . 140 B8
Evenley Rd
Mixbury NN13. . . . . . . 24 C1
Mixbury NN13. . . . . . . 24 D1
Evenlode Cl OX16. . . . . .16 B7
Evenlode Cl
6 Bicester OX26. . . . . . 65 D1
Charlbury OX7. . . . . 73 B4
Grove OX12. . . . . 196 D1
North Leigh OX29 . . . . 105 B6
Evenlode Cres OX5 . . . . 92 A2
Evenlode Ct OX28. . . . . 118 B8
Evenlode Dr
Berinsfield OX10 . . . . . 182 C6
Didcot OX11 . . . . 200 F1
Long Hanborough OX29 . 90 A1
Evenlode Ho OX26. . . . . 65 D2
Evenlode La
Chastleton GL56 . . . . . 40 D7
Fawler OX29 . . . . .88 F6
Evenlode Pk OX14 . . . . 160 B1
Evenlode Twr OX14 . . . 142 E2
Everard Cl 2 OX3 . . . . 124 D1
Eversley Ct OX7. . . . . . . .57 B1
Eversley La OX7 . . . . 55 E5
Evesham Rd RG4 . . . . . 259 B5
Ewart Cl OX26 . . . . 65 D3
EWELME 204 F4
Ewelme CE Prim Sch
OX10 . . . . .204 F3
Ewelme Watercress Beds
Nature Reserve★
OX10 . . . . 204 D4
Ewert Pl OX2 . . . . 123 B6
Ewin Cl OX3. . . . . 123 F5
Ewin Ct OX3. . . . . 123 F5
Exbourne Rd OX14. . . . 179 D7
Exchange La OX15. . . . . .21 C7
Exe Cl OX11 . . . . 200 F1
Exeter Coll OX1 . . . . . . 261 B2
Exeter Ct Didcot OX11. 219 B8
5 Kidlington OX5. . . . 108 F8
Exeter Dr 8 OX26 . . . . 65 C1
Exeter Rd OX5. . . . . .92 C1
EXLADE ST RG8. . . . . . 241 B1
EXLADE STREET 251 B8
Eynsford Cl RG4 . . . . . . 259 E5
EYNSHAM 120 E7
Eynsham Com Prim Sch
OX29 . . . . 120 F8
Eynsham Ct OX29. . . . . 105 C5
Eynsham Pk OX29 . . . . 105 D5
Eynsham Rd
Cassington OX29. . . . . 107 C2
Eynsham OX29. . . . . . . 106 A3
Farmoor OX2. . . . . 121 C1
Oxford OX2 . . . . 140 B8
Sutton OX29 . . . . 120 A2
Eyot Pl OX4 . . . . 141 E7
Eyres La OX10 . . . . 204 D4
Eyres La OX10 . . . . 204 E5
Eyston Way OX14 . . . . . 179 C7

F

Faber Cl OX4 . . . . 142 C2
Fairacres OX14 . . . . 179 C7
Fairacres Rd
Didcot OX11 . . . . 218 E8
Oxford OX4 . . . . 141 F6
Fairacres Shopping & Trad
Est OX14. . . . . 179 C6
Fairchild HP17 . . . . 130 E7

Fair Cl OX26. . . . . .65 F4
Fairfax Ave OX3 . . . . . . 123 E4
Fairfax Cl Banbury OX16. 16 A5
Reading RG4 . . . . 259 B3
Fairfax Ctr OX5. . . . . . . 108 F6
Fairfax Gate OX33 . . . . 144 C8
Fairfax Rd
Chalgrove OX44. . . . . . 184 D5
Kidlington OX5. . . . . . 108 F6
Oxford OX4 . . . . 142 E6
Fairfield Cholsey OX10. 220 F1
Standlake OX29. . . . . . 136 F8
Fairfield Cl OX12 . . . . . 214 D8
Fairfield Dr OX28 . . . . . 117 F7
Fairfield Pl
Abingdon-on-Thames
OX14. . . . . 179 F8
7 Carterton OX18 . . . 115 F5
Carterton OX18. . . . . . 115 F5
Fairfield Rd RG8. . . . . . 249 D7
Fairford Rd
Lechlade-on-Thames
GL7. . . . . 150 B4
Reading RG31 . . . . 257 C2
Fairford Way OX26 . . . . 66 A4
Fairhaven Rd OX27 . . . . .65 F7
Fairlawn End OX2 . . . . . 122 F8
Fairlawn Flats OX2 . . . 122 F8
Fairlawn Wharf OX14 . 179 F6
Fairleigh Dickinson Uni
(Wroxton Coll) OX15 . .15 B8
Fairlie Rd OX4. . . . . 142 B3
Fair Mile Cholsey OX10. 221 B2
Henley-on-Thames RG9. 254 C4
Fairmile Ct RG9 . . . . . . 244 D3
Fair Mile The OX10 . . . 238 E4
Fairspear Rd OX29 . . . . .86 D4
Fairthorne Way SN6 . . 209 B6
Fair View OX3 . . . . 142 D7
Fairview Rd OX16. . . . . . 16 D4
Fairview Trad Est RG9. 254 F8
Fairways 160 F2
Fairway The OX16 . . . . . 16 A6
Fakenham St 6 OX26 . . 65 C1
Falcon Cl Banbury OX26. 16 A4
Carterton OX18. . . . . . 115 C3
Oxford OX4 . . . . 142 B3
Falcon Dr 18 OX11 . . . 218 C7
Falcon Mead OX26. . . . . 81 A8
Falcon Villas OX7 . . . . . 73 C5
Falkland Cl OX18 . . . . . 100 F4
Falkland Ho 4 OX18. . . 115 E2
Falkland Rd RG4. . . . . . 259 B2
Falkner's Cl OX17. . . . . . 23 A4
Fallowfield Cl RG4. . . . 259 B4
Fallow Field Cl OX13 . . 199 B8
Fallowfield Cres OX28. 104 D1
Fallowfields OX26 . . . . . .65 F2
Fallowfields Ct 3 OX26 65 F2
Fallow Way OX16. . . . . . .16 E2
Falstaff Cl OX29 . . . . . . 120 E8
Fane Cl OX26. . . . . 65 D3
Fane Ho OX10 . . . . 182 D6
Fane Ho 2 OX26 . . . . . . .65 E2
Fane Rd OX3 . . . . 123 E5
Fanshawe Pl OX4 . . . . . 142 E5
Fanshawe Rd OX9 . . . . 148 B8
Faraday Ave OX11 . . . . 217 B2
Faraday Rd OX12 . . . . . 214 A8
Faraday St OX11. . . . . . 201 B3
Farbury End OX7 . . . . . . .29 B3
FARINGDON 172 E3
Faringdon Com Coll
SN7. . . . . 172 E1
Faringdon Inf Sch
SN7. . . . . 172 E4
Faringdon Jun Sch
SN7. . . . . .172 F4
Faringdon L Ctr SN7. . .172 F1
Faringdon Park Ret Pk
SN7. . . . . 173 A2
Faringdon Rd
Abingdon-on-Thames
OX13. . . . . 159 A2
Abingdon-on-Thames
OX14. . . . . 179 D8
Cumnor OX2 . . . . 139 E2
Gozzard's Ford OX13. . 158 C2
Gozzard's Ford OX13. . 158 F2
Kingston Bagpuize
OX13. . . . . 156 F1
Kingston Bagpuize
OX13. . . . . 176 A8
Lechlade-on-Thames
GL7. . . . . 150 E3
Pit Down RG17 . . . . . . 230 C2
Shrivenham SN6 . . . . . 209 C7
Shrivenham SN6 . . . . . 209 D8
Stanford in the Vale
SN7. . . . . 194 D6
Stanford in the Vale
SN7. . . . . 194 D7
Watchfield SN6 . . . . . . 191 E1
West Challow OX12. . . 213 E6
Faringdon Road SN7. . 192 C6
Farleigh Mews RG4. . . 259 E5
Farleigh Rd
Shrivenham SN6 . . . . . 209 A6
Shrivenham SN6 . . . . . 209 A6
Farley Cl OX29 . . . . .89 C8
Farley La OX29 . . . . .89 D8
Farman Cres GL54 . . . . .68 A4
Farm Cl Aston OX18 . . . 135 E2
Chalgrove OX44. . . . . . 184 D5
Ickford HP18. . . . . 127 F3
Kidlington OX5. . . . . . . .92 F2
Purley on Thames RG8. 257 C5
Sandford-on-Thames
OX4. . . . . 142 F1

Farm Cl continued
Sonning Common RG4. . 252 E5
Farm Close La OX33 . . 144 B8
Farm Close Rd OX33 . . 144 B8
Farm Ct SN6 . . . . 227 D4
Farm End Grove OX12 . 214 D8
Woodstock OX20. . . . . . 91 A7
Farmer Pl OX3 . . . . 123 F4
Farmers Cl OX28 . . . . . 104 B2
Farmers Ct OX18 . . . . . 152 E8
Farmfield Rd
Banbury OX16 . . . . 16 D3
Calthorpe OX16. . . . . . 16 D3
Farmhouse Cl OX29. . . 138 A8
Farmhouse Mdw
OX28 . . . . 117 E7
Farmhouse Mews
OX49. . . . . 186 B2
Farmiloe Cl RG8. . . . . . 257 C4
Farmington Dr OX28. . 117 E8
Farm La Crawley OX29. 103 D5
New Yatt OX28 . . . . . . 104 F1
Warmington OX17. . . . . .2 F3
Farm Mill La OX28 . . . . 118 B7
FARMOOR 121 C3
Farmoor Ct OX2. . . . . . 121 C2
Farm Piece SN7 . . . . . . 194 D7
Farm Pl OX39. . . . . 149 E1
Farm Rd
Abingdon-on-Thames
OX14. . . . . 159 F2
Brackley NN13. . . . . . . 24 A6
Churchill OX7. . . . . 55 C8
Goring RG8 . . . . 249 C6
Henley-on-Thames RG9. 254 F8
Farmstead Cl OX12 . . . 196 D1
Farm Way OX16 . . . . . . .16 F3
FARNBOROUGH 3 F8
Farnborough Hall★
OX17. . . . . 3 E7
Farnborough Rd OX17. . .3 C6
Farndon Rd OX2. . . . . . 123 B4
Farnham Ct 6 OX5 . . . 108 F8
Farnham Dr RG4. . . . . . 259 E4
Farriers Cl OX27 . . . . . . 52 C6
Farriers Mead OX25 . . . 80 A4
Farriers Mews OX14 . . 180 A7
Farriers Rd OX7 . . . . . . .60 E8
Farthings The OX13. . . 178 C7
Faulder Ave OX18. . . . . 115 D3
Faulkener Rd OX15 . . . . 21 C4
Fawkner Way SN7 . . . . 194 D7
FAWLER Finstock. 88 E7
Uffington 211 F5
Fawler La OX7. . . . . 88 D7
Fawler Rd
Charlbury OX7. . . . . 73 C2
Fawler OX29 . . . . .88 F7
Stonesfield OX29. . . . . .89 A7
Uffington OX12, SN7. . 211 E6
FAWLEY 226 D2
FAWLEY BOTTOM 226 B2
Fawley Bottom La
RG9. . . . . 226 B1
Fawley Court Mus★
RG9 . . . . 244 F5
FAWLEY GREEN 226 D2
Featherbed La
Bishopstone SN6. . . . . 227 A1
East Hendred OX12. . . 216 F8
Milton Hill OX13 . . . . . 199 A1
Mixbury NN13. . . . . . . 38 D5
Shrivenham SN6 . . . . . 209 D1
Featherbow La OX15. . . .2 B3
Feathers Yd 2 OX10 . . 221 D7
Feilden Cl OX29 . . . . . . 118 B4
Feilden Gr OX3 . . . . 124 A3
Felix Rd OX11. . . . . 200 B2
Fells Cl HP18. . . . . 129 D6
Feltwell Cl OX18. . . . . . 115 E3
FENCOTT 95 D5
Fencott Rd OX5. . . . . . . 95 A4
Fenlock Ct OX29. . . . . . .90 F1
Fenlock Rd OX29 . . . . . . .90 F1
Fennel St OX27 . . . . 65 D7
Fennel Way OX14 . . . . . 180 C6
Fenny Compton Rd
OX17. . . . . 1 D1
Fen Violet Dr OX11. . . . 200 B1
Fenway
Steeple Aston OX25 . . . 48 A1
Steeple Aston OX7 . . . . .47 F1
Ferguson Pl OX14 . . . . 180 C8
Fergusson Rd OX16. . . . .16 E7
Fermi Ave OX11 . . . . . . 217 A1
Fernbrook Rd RG4. . . . . 258 F5
Fern Cl OX12 . . . . 214 C7
Ferndale Cl
Reading RG31 . . . . 257 E3
Stokenchurch HP14. . . 188 E4
Ferndale Rd OX16 . . . . . .15 F7
Ferndale St SN7 . . . . . . 173 A4
Ferne Cl RG8 . . . . 249 C7
Fern Glen RG31. . . . . . . 257 C1
Ferngrove 9 SN7 . . . . . 172 F3
FERNHAM 193 A4
Fernham Gate SN7 . . . 172 E1
Fernham Rd
Faringdon SN7. . . . . . . 172 E1
Little Coxwell SN7. . . . 192 E8
Longcot SN7 . . . . 192 D2
Shellingford SN7. . . . . 193 D6
Fernhill Cl
Kidlington OX5. . . . . . 108 D8
Milcombe OX15. . . . . . 21 A2
Tiddington OX9 . . . . . . 146 A6
Fernhill Rd OX5. . . . . . . 108 A8
Fern Hill Rd OX4. . . . . . 142 C5
Fern La OX18. . . . . 115 F5

Ferny Pl OX14 . . . . 160 E3
Ferrers Way 4 GL7 . . 150 E3
Ferriston OX16 . . . . .9 A1
Ferry Ct OX14 . . . . 179 F6
Ferry Hinksey Rd OX2. 123 A1
Ferry La Goring RG8 . 249 B6
  Moulsford OX10 . . . . . 239 A4
  South Stoke OX13, RG8 239 B4
  Wargrave RG10. . . . . . 255 C2
Ferry Mills OX2. . . . . . 141 A8
Ferry Pool Rd OX2. . . 123 C6
Ferry Rd Marston OX3 . 123 F3
  South Stoke RG8. . . . . 239 B4
Ferry Sports Ctr OX26 123 B8
Ferry Way OX14 . . . . . 239 B8
Ferry Wlk OX14 . . . . . 179 F6
Fetti Pl OX12 . . . . 214 F6
Fettiplace Cl OX13. . . 158 A7
Fettiplace Rd
  Marcham OX13 . . . . . . 178 D6
  Oxford OX3 . . . . 124 E5
  Witney OX28 . . . . 117 E8
FEWCOTT 50 C5
Fewcott Gn OX27 . . . . . 50 C4
Fewcott Rd OX27. . . . . .49 F7
Fewcott View OX27. . . .49 F7
FIDDLERS HILL. 85 D6
Fiddlers Hill OX7. . . . . .85 E6
Fidler's Orchard OX11 217 E2
Fidlers Wlk RG10 . . . . 255 E2
FIELD ASSARTS 102 F8
Field Ave OX4 . . . . . . 142 F2
Field Cl Ickford HP18 . 128 A3
  Kidlington OX5. . . . . . 108 F8
  Kingston Bagpuize
    OX13. . . . . 156 D1
  Stonesfield OX29. . . . . 89 C8
  Yarnton OX5 . . . . 108 B6
Field Ct OX25. . . . . 47 C5
Fielden Cl OX10 . . . . . 204 D2
Field End
  Long Crendon HP18 . . 129 F5
  Wargrave RG10. . . . . . 255 F2
Fielden Rd OX10. . . . . 204 D2
Fieldfare Cl OX26. . . . . .65 F1
Fieldfare Rd
  8 Oxford OX4 . . . . . 142 G1
  9 Oxford OX4 . . . . . 142 E1
  Sandford-on-Thames
    OX4. . . . . 161 E8
Field Farm Bsns Ctr
  OX6 . . . . .67 A5
Field Gdns
  East Challow OX12 . . . 213 F5
  Steventon OX13. . . . . 199 A5
Field Ho OX2 . . . . 140 C8
Field House Dr OX2. . 123 A8
Field La OX44 . . . . . . 144 B3
Fieldmere Cl OX28. . . 117 F8
Field Rd Kingham OX7. . 54 F3
  Murcott OX5 . . . . 96 A5
Fieldside
  Abingdon-on-Thames
    OX14. . . . . 159 C1
  East Hagbourne OX11.. 219 A5
  Long Wittenham OX14. 201 C8
  Long Wittenham OX14. 201 D8
  Upton OX11. . . . . . . 218 C2
Fieldside Lawson La
  OX11. . . . . 235 E8
Field St OX29. . . . . 65 E2
Field The OX13 . . . . . 158 F6
Field View
  Bodicote. OX15 . . . . . . 16 F1
  Reading RG4 . . . . . . 259 B3
Field View La OX5 . . . 92 A8
Fiennes Rd
  Banbury OX16 . . . . . . 16 A5
  Oxford OX4 . . . . 142 A3
FIFIELD 69 C2
Fifield Barns OX10. . . 204 C5
Fifield Farm Barns
  OX10. . . . . 204 C5
Fifteenth St OX11 . . . 217 A2
Fifth Ave NN13 . . . . . . .36 E7
Fifth St NN13 . . . . .36 E7
Fifth Street E NN13 . . . 36 E7
FILCHAMPSTEAD . . . 139 C8
FILKINS 132 C5
Filkins Rd GL7. . . . . . 132 C2
Finch Cl OX3 . . . . 124 C1
Finchdale Cl OX18. . . 115 D3
Finches La SN8. . . . . . 245 E1
Finches The SN8 . . . . 245 C2
Finchley La OX26. . . . . 65 D1
Finham Brook OX11 . . 200 F3
Finlay Dr
  Henley-on-Thames
    RG9. . . . . 244 E2
  Henley-on-Thames RG9. 244 E3
Finlay Ho RG9 . . . . . . 244 E3
FINMERE 39 D6
Finmere CE Prim Sch
  MK18. . . . . 39 D6
Finmere Rd
  Fulwell MK18. . . . . . . .25 F1
  Westbury NN13. . . . . 25 D3
Finmore Cl 3 OX14. . 179 E8
Finmore Rd OX2. . . . 140 D8
Finsbury Pl OX7 . . . . . .42 E3
FINSTOCK 88 C5
Finstock CE Prim Sch
  OX7. . . . . .88 C5
Finstock Sta OX7 . . . . 88 D7
Fir Cl OX10 . . . . 240 D7
Fircroft Banbury OX16 . 16 A4
  Bicester OX26. . . . . . . .65 F5
Fircroft OX31 RG31 . . 257 C1
Firebrass Hill
  Ewelme OX10 . . . . . . 204 F5

Firebrass Hill continued
  Ewelme OX10 . . . . . . 205 A5
Firefly Cl OX7 . . . . 68 C3
Fir La OX25. . . . . .48 B1
Firs Cl OX7 . . . . 54 D2
Firs Mdw
  1 Oxford OX4 . . . . . 142 F1
  Sandford-on-Thames
    OX4. . . . . 161 E8
First Ave Didcot OX11.. 200 D2
  Oxford OX3 . . . . 142 F8
Firs The Oxford OX2 . . 123 B8
  Townsend OX12 . . . . 194 E1
  Wroxton OX15. . . . . . . 15 A8
First St Croughton NN13 .36 F6
  Harwell OX11 . . . . . . 217 C2
First Turn OX2. . . . . . 122 F8
Fir Tree Ave OX10 . . . 221 B8
Firtree Cl OX16. . . . . . . 8 F1
Fir Tree Cl OX13. . . . . 156 E1
Fir Tree Cotts RG20. . 235 A2
Fir Tree Jun Sch
  OX10 . . . . 221 B8
Fir Tree Paddock
  RG20 . . . . 235 A2
Fisher Cl Banbury OX16 . 16 F8
  Drayton OX14 . . . . . . 179 A1
Fishermans Wharf
  OX14. . . . . 179 F4
Fisher Row OX1 . . . . . 261 A2
Fishers Cl OX29. . . . . 104 A6
Fishers Cottages 6
  RG4. . . . . 259 C6
Fishers Cotts RG4 . . . 259 C6
Fishers Ct RG4 . . . . . 259 C6
Fisher's La OX7. . . . . . .73 B3
Fish Ponds OX9 . . . . . 129 E1
Fitzcount Way OX10 . . 203 D1
Fitzharry's Rd OX14. . 179 F8
Fitzharrys Sch OX14. . 159 F1
Fitzherbert Cl OX4. . . 141 F4
Fitzwaryn Pl OX12 . . . 214 C6
Fitzwaryn Sch OX12 . 214 C6
Five Acre OX31 . . . . . 257 B1
Fiveacres OX5. . . . . . . .95 E4
Five Acres Prim Sch
  OX25 . . . . 81 D4
Five Mile Dr OX2 . . . . 109 A1
Fiveways Cl SN8. . . . . 245 E1
Flambards 1 RG4 . . . 259 C2
Flanders Cl OX26 . . . . .80 F8
Flatford Pl OX5. . . . . . 92 C2
Flavian Cl OX26. . . . . . 79 F7
Flavius Gate NN13 . . . 24 A7
Flax Cres 14 OX18 . . 115 E5
Flaxfield Rd OX4. . . . 142 F2
Fleet Way OX11. . . . . 219 A8
Fleetwood Way OX9 . 129 F2
Fleming Cl
  Bicester OX26. . . . . . . 65 C4
  Middle Barton OX7. . . .60 F8
Flemings Rd OX20. . . . 91 C6
Flemming Ave OX44 . 184 C7
Fletcher Cl
  Faringdon SN7. . . . . . 173 A3
  Steventon OX13. . . . . 198 E4
  Yarnton OX5 . . . . 108 B5
Fletcher Rd OX4. . . . . 142 E6
Flexney Pl OX3 . . . . . 124 D1
Flexneys Paddock
  OX29 . . . . 138 A8
Flight Hill OX7. . . . . . .46 B7
Flint Cl RG9 . . . . 254 A7
Flint Hollow OX39 . . . 168 B6
Flint St HP17. . . . . . . 130 F5
Floral Cl OX12. . . . . . 214 E8
Florence Cl OX5. . . . . 108 F8
FLORENCE PARK. . . . 142 B5
Florence Park Rd OX4 142 B5
Florey Pl OX18 . . . . . 135 E3
Florey's Cl OX29. . . . . 104 A6
Flowe Dr OX12 . . . . . 215 B6
Flowercrofts RG4. . . . 254 A7
Flower's Hill RG8. . . . 256 C4
Floyd's Row OX1 . . . . 261 B1
Fludger Cl OX10. . . . . 221 C7
Fluellen Pl OX26. . . . . 65 D5
Fluk Dr OX15. . . . . 33 E5
Fogwell Rd OX2 . . . . . 122 B1
Foliat Cl OX12. . . . . . 214 E5
Foliat Dr OX12. . . . . . 214 E5
Folland Cl OX7 . . . . . . 42 F4
Follets Cl OX5 . . . . . . 108 B5
Folly Bridge OX1. . . . 261 B1
Folly Bridge Ct OX1. . 261 B1
Folly Cl OX16 . . . . . . 16 D6
Folly Cres
  Highworth SN6 . . . . . 190 A4
  Watchfield SN6. . . . . 191 E1
Folly Ct OX15. . . . . . . 19 C7
Folly Dr SN6. . . . . . . 190 A7
Folly Gn RG8 . . . . . . 250 E8
Folly Orchard Rd RG8. 240 E1
Folly View Cres SN7 . 172 E2
Folly View Rd SN7. . . 172 F2
Folly Way SN6. . . . . . 190 A7
Fontwell Rd OX26 . . . 65 E1
Ford Cres OX16. . . . . . 16 A2
Ford La
  Drayton St Leonard
    OX10. . . . . 183 B6
  East Hendred OX12... 216 D6
  Frilford OX13. . . . . . 178 A7
Ford's Cft OX9. . . . . . 148 A6
Fords Cl
  Bledlow Ridge HP14. . 189 F8
  Horspath OX33. . . . . 143 C6
FORDWELLS. 102 D8
Forest Cl
  Launton OX26. . . . . . . 66 D2

Forest Cl continued
  Milton-under-Wychwood
    OX7. . . . . 70 B1
Foresters
  Beacon's Bottom
    HP14. . . . . 189 C5
  Chinnor OX39 . . . . . . 168 B6
Foresters Tower OX4 . 124 E1
Foresters Way 5 OX5 . 92 E1
Forest Gr OX18 . . . . . 100 E3
FOREST HILL. 125 F4
Forest Hill RG30 . . . . 257 F2
Forest Rd Charlbury OX7 73 A4
  Oxford OX3 . . . . 124 F3
Forest Row OX10 . . . . 222 D3
Forestry Hos OX49. . . 207 A7
Forest Side OX11 . . . . 141 D2
Forge Cl Benson OX10. 203 F4
  Horton-cum-Studley
    OX33. . . . . 112 A5
  Marsh Gibbon OX27 . . .67 F3
  Merton OX25. . . . . . . 95 D8
  Reading RG4 . . . . . . 259 C2
Forge La OX17. . . . . 3 E8
Forge Pl OX27. . . . . . . .49 F7
Forgeway OX16. . . . . . 9 A1
Forrest Cl
  Shrivenham SN6. . . . . 209 A6
  Shrivenham SN6 . . . . 209 A6
Forster La OX2 . . . . . 139 E4
Forsters La OX12 . . . . 231 E6
Forsythia Cl OX26. . . . .65 E5
Forsythia Wlk OX16. . . 9 B1
Fortescue Dr OX26 . . . 80 A7
Forties The OX44 . . . . 145 A2
Fortnam Cl OX3 . . . . . 124 A3
Forty Cross OX11 . . . . 237 A8
Forty Gn HP27 . . . . . . 149 F3
FORTY GREEN 149 F3
Forty The
  Bishopstone SN6. . . . 227 D5
  Cholsey OX10 . . . . . . 220 F2
FOSCOT 69 D8
Foscote Rise OX16. . . . 16 E4
Fosseway Ct
  Lechlade-on-Thames
    GL7. . . . . 150 C5
  Lechlade-on-Thames
    GL7. . . . . 150 C5
Fosse Way The OX18. . 116 C3
Foster Rd OX14 . . . . . 159 F3
Fosters La RG9 . . . . . 254 B1
Fothergill Pl OX9 . . . . 147 F8
Foudry Cl OX11 . . . . . 201 A2
Foundation Sq OX25. . .80 E6
Foundry St OX16 . . . . . 16 C6
Fountain Ct OX14. . . . 179 F8
Fourteenth St OX11. . 217 B3
Fourth Ave NN13 . . . . . 36 E6
Fourth Ave (East) OX3 142 F8
Fourth St
  Croughton NN13 . . . . .36 E6
  Harwell OX11 . . . . . . 217 B3
Fowler Cl 4 OX18 . . . 134 F4
Fowler Rd OX16 . . . . . .16 E7
Fowlers Ct OX7. . . . . . 43 A3
Fowlers Farm Rd
  HP14. . . . . 188 E4
Fowlers Rd OX7 . . . . . 43 A3
Foxborough Rd OX14. 160 E2
Foxburrow Cl OX29 . . 120 A1
Foxburrow La OX29 . . 103 F4
Foxbury Ct OX29. . . . 138 A8
Foxbury La 2 OX16. . 115 E5
Fox Cl Bampton OX18 . 134 F3
  Chipping Norton OX7 . . 42 F2
  Garsington OX44. . . . 143 D2
  Hailey OX29. . . . . . . 104 A4
Foxcombe Ct OX14 . . 179 C8
Foxcombe Dr OX1 . . . 159 B8
FOXCOMBE HILL. . . . 159 F8
Foxcombe La OX1 . . . 141 A1
Foxcombe Rd
  Boars Hill OX1. . . . . . 140 F1
  Sunningwell OX1. . . . 141 A2
Fox Cover OX39 . . . . . 168 C6
Foxcover View SN7 . . 211 D7
Fox Cres OX5. . . . . . . 141 E5
Foxcroft Dr OX18 . . . 115 D1
Foxden Way OX17 . . . . 9 D7
Foxdown Cl OX5. . . . . .92 E1
Foxfield OX7. . . . . .42 F2
Foxfield Ct OX7. . . . . . 42 F2
Fox Furlong OX4 . . . . 142 A1
Foxglove Cl
  Bicester OX26. . . . . . . 55 A4
  6 Oxford OX4 . . . . . 142 E1
Foxglove La OX11 . . . 218 D4
Foxglove Rd OX5 . . . . 108 B8
Foxglove Wy OX11. . . 218 B8
Foxhall Manor Pk
  OX11. . . . . 200 D2
Foxhall Rd OX11. . . . . 200 D1
Fox Heath Gdns RG4. 251 E5
Fox Hill Tackley OX20 . . 76 F7
  Tackley OX5. . . . . 77 A7
Foxhill Cl RG4 . . . . . . 260 A5
Foxhill La RG4. . . . . . 259 E6
Foxholes Nature Reserve*
  . . . . 69 C5
Fox La Bicester OX26. . . 65 D1
  Middle Barton OX7 . . . 60 E8
  Souldern OX27 . . . . . . 35 E3
  Wantage OX12 . . . . . 214 C6
  Wootton OX1. . . . . . 159 D7
Foxtail Cres OX16. . . . 16 F2
Foxton Cl OX11 . . . . . 200 B2
Foxtowns Gn OX15 . . 21 B4
Foxwell Dr OX3. . . . . 124 C5
Foxwood OX18 . . . . . 135 E3

Foxwood Cl
  Aston OX18 . . . . 135 E3
  Banbury OX16 . . . . . . 16 D5
Foxwood La OX18 . . . 114 C6
Framlands OX12 . . . . 214 B5
Framlingham Dr RG4 . 259 E5
Frampton Cl RG5 . . . . 260 E1
Frances Rd OX7. . . . . . .60 F8
Francis Brown Way
  OX44. . . . . 184 E6
Francis Little Dr OX14 179 D6
Frank Cook Ct OX5 . . . 92 F1
Franklin Cl
  Chalgrove OX44. . . . . 184 D6
  Kidlington OX5. . . . . . 92 F1
Franklin Furrows SN7 194 D7
Franklin Gdns OX11... 201 A3
Franklin Rd OX3 . . . . 124 B3
Franklyn Cl OX14 . . . . 159 F2
Franks La OX13. . . . . . 198 F4
Frank Wise Sch OX16...16 B5
Fraser Ave RG4. . . . . 259 C6
Fraser Cl OX16 . . . . . . .16 B6
Fraser Gdns OX10 . . . 221 C6
Frax Cl OX13 . . . . 156 F1
Frederick Rd OX4. . . . 142 D4
Freeborn Cl OX5. . . . . .92 F2
Freehold St OX25. . . . . 62 D8
FREELAND 106 A7
Freeland CE Prim Sch
  OX29 . . . . 106 A7
Freeland Rd OX29 . . . 106 A7
Freelands Cotts OX33. 125 D7
Freelands Rd OX4 . . . 141 F5
Freeman Rd OX11 . . . 200 C1
Freemans Cl SN7 . . . . 211 C3
Frenchay Rd OX2 . . . . 123 A5
French Cl OX28. . . . . 117 F7
French Gdns OX10 . . . 221 F7
French Laurence Way
  OX44. . . . . 184 D6
Frensham Cl OX16. . . . . 9 A1
Frethern Cl OX18 . . . . 100 E4
Frethern Ct OX18 . . . . 100 E4
Frewin Cl OX1 . . . . . . 261 B2
Friars Cl SN6 . . . . 209 A6
Friar's Ct
  Clanfield OX18. . . . . . 152 E6
  Clanfield OX18. . . . . . 152 F6
Friars' Entry OX1 . . . . 261 B2
Friars Furlong HP18 . . 129 F7
Friars Hill Wroxton OX15. .8 A2
  Wroxton OX16. . . . . . . 7 F2
Friars Mws OX14 . . . . 179 B1
Friars Wharf
  Oxford OX1 . . . . 141 C8
  Oxford OX1 . . . . 261 B1
Friday Ct Thame OX9 . 129 F1
  Thame OX9 . . . . 129 F1
Friday La OX33 . . . . . 144 B8
Friday St RG9 . . . . . . 244 E2
Friends Cl OX29 . . . . . 89 C7
Friend Way OX26 . . . . 80 F6
Frieze Way OX5 . . . . . 108 F4
Frieze Wy OX5. . . . . . 108 F5
FRILFORD 178 A7
Frilford Rd OX13. . . . . 178 C6
Frilsham St OX14 . . . . 200 A7
Frimley Yard OX11. . . 219 F1
FRINGFORD 52 D6
Fringford CE Prim Sch
  OX27. . . . . 52 C6
Fringford Rd OX27. . . . .65 F7
Friswell Rd OX16 . . . . 16 A3
Frith The OX11. . . . . . 201 B2
Fritillary Ave OX39. . . 168 C5
Fritillary Mews OX39. . 118 C3
FRITWELL 49 E7
Fritwell CE Prim Sch
  OX27. . . . . 49 F7
Fritwell Rd Ardley OX27. 50 B4
  Somerton OX25. . . . . . 48 F6
  Somerton OX25. . . . . . 49 A6
Frog Al OX11 . . . . 218 E3
Frog La Bloxham OX15. . 21 D4
  Milton-under-Wychwood
    OX7. . . . . 70 B1
Frogmore La
  Long Crendon HP18 . . 129 C5
  Stanford in the Vale
    SN7. . . . . 194 E8
FROGS' ISLAND 202 C2
Frome Rd OX11 . . . . . 217 C1
Frost Ct OX25 . . . . .63 B8
Frouds Cl OX12 . . . . . 213 C4
Fruitlands OX29 . . . . 120 D8
Frys Hill OX4 . . . . 142 E1
Fry's Mdw SN7 . . . . . 174 E1
Fuchsia Wlk OX16 . . . . 9 B1
FULBROOK 100 F7
Fulbrook Hill OX18 . . . 100 F6
Fullbrook Cres RG31. . 257 D3
Fuller Cl SN6. . . . . . . 209 B7
Fullers Field OX44 . . . 145 C2
Fullers Rd OX11 . . . . . 219 E1
Fuller Wy OX13 . . . . . 198 F5
Fullwell Cl OX14 . . . . 159 E1
Fulmar Cl OX26. . . . . . .66 B4
Fulmar Pl OX12. . . . . 196 D1
FULWELL Enstone. 58 F3
  Westbury. 25 A2
Fulwell Rd
  Finmere MK18. . . . . . 39 C7
  Finmere MK18. . . . . . 39 C7
  Fulwell NN13 . . . . . . 25 B2
  Westbury NN13. . . . . 25 A2
Furlong Cl OX4 . . . . . 142 D3
Furlong Cres OX5. . . . .92 F8

Furlong Row OX18. . . 152 E6
Furlongs Drayton OX13 199 B8
  Drayton OX13 . . . . . . 179 B1
Furlongs The OX9 . . . 147 C6
Furlong The OX29 . . . 137 B6
Furrow Corner OX11. . 200 B2
Furrow Cres 1 OX29 . 117 B8
Furrows End OX13. . . 199 B8
FYFIELD
  Kingston Bagpuize. . . 157 C2
  Lechlade-on-Thames. . 131 B4
Fyfield Cl OX12 . . . . . 214 F4
Fyfield Rd OX2 . . . . . 123 C4
Fynn Ct OX25. . . . . . . .63 B8

G

Gadge Cl OX9 . . . . . . 129 E1
GAGINGWELL. 59 F7
GAINFIELD. 174 F3
Gainfield SN7. . . . . . . 174 F4
Gainsborough Cres
  4 Henley-on-Thames
    RG9. . . . . 244 C1
  Henley-on-Thames RG9. 254 C8
Gainsborough Gn
  OX14. . . . . 179 E5
Gainsborough Hill
  RG9. . . . . 254 C8
Gainsborough Rd RG9 254 D8
Gaisford Rd OX4. . . . . 142 C4
Gales Ct GL7 . . . . 150 C4
Galingale Cl OX26. . . . .65 E4
Gall Cl OX14. . . . . 180 C8
Galley Field OX14 . . . 180 B8
Gallosbrook Wy OX25. .78 F1
GALLOWSTREE
  COMMON. 252 C5
Gallowstree Rd RG9 . 252 E7
Galpin Cl OX4 . . . . . . 142 A7
Galsworthy Dr RG4 . . 259 C5
Gangsdown Hill RG9. 223 E4
Gap The OX13 . . . . . . 178 D6
Gap Way RG8. . . . . . . 250 E8
Garage Yd OX7 . . . . . . 70 A5
GARDEN CITY 108 C5
Garden City OX9 . . . . 148 B7
Garden Cl Banbury OX16 16 C7
  Didcot OX11 . . . . . . 218 C7
Gardeners Cl OX26. . . . 80 F8
Gardeners Copse RG4 253 B2
Gardenia Wy OX16. . . 115 E5
Gardens Cl HP14. . . . 188 F4
Gardens The
  Langford GL7. . . . . . 132 D2
  South Stoke RG8. . . . 239 C3
Garde Rd RG4 . . . . . . 260 E3
Gardiner Cl
  Abingdon-on-Thames
    OX14. . . . . 180 C8
  Wheatley OX33. . . . . 144 B8
Gardiner St OX3. . . . . 124 D2
Gardner Way OX15 . . . 23 A6
GARFORD 177 D5
Garford Cl OX14 . . . . 160 B2
Garford Rd OX2 . . . . . 123 C5
Garner Cl OX18 . . . . . 115 C5
Garners Field OX17. . . . 9 C7
Garnes La OX18 . . . . . 100 F6
Garrett Pl OX18 . . . . . 116 A4
GARSINGTON 143 E1
Garsington CE Prim Sch
  OX44. . . . . 143 E2
Garsington Rd OX4 . . 142 E4
Garsons La
  Checkendon OX10. . . 241 B6
  Ipsden OX10 . . . . . . 240 E6
Garston Cl OX12. . . . . 214 E5
Garston Ct OX18 . . . . 116 B5
Garston La OX12 . . . . 214 E5
Garth Rd OX11. . . . . . 200 E1
Garth The Oxford OX2 . 140 D8
  Yarnton OX5 . . . . 108 B6
Garton End
  Cray's Pond RG8 . . . . 250 D6
  Whitchurch Hill RG8 . 250 E3
Gary O'Donnell Dr
  OX11. . . . . 200 B2
Gas Alley OX9 . . . . . . 148 A8
Gascoigne Way OX15. . 21 C7
Gaskells End RG4. . . . 258 D8
Gas La OX7. . . . . 85 D8
Gassons Mead OX18 . 133 C5
Gassons Rd GL7 . . . . 150 C5
Gassons The GL7. . . . 132 B5
Gassons Way GL7. . . . 150 C4
Gate Fernham SN7 . . . 172 E1
Gatehampton Rd RG8. 249 C5
Gateley OX33 . . . . . . 143 D6
Gateway Prim Sch
  OX18. . . . . 115 E2
Gathorne Rd OX3. . . . 124 D2
Gatteridge St OX16 . . . 16 D5
Gauntlets Cl OX15 . . . 21 E5
Gaveston Gdns OX15... 33 E4
Gaveston Rd OX11. . . 217 E7
Gavray Dr Bicester OX26 66 B1
  Bicester OX26. . . . . . . 81 B8
GAWCOMBE 68 C2
Gaydon Cl OX18 . . . . 115 E3
Gaydon Wlk 2 OX26.. 66 A4
Gayhurst Cl RG4. . . . 259 D6
Gealer Gr SN6. . . . . . 209 C6
Gelt Burn OX11. . . . . 201 B2
Geminus Rd OX26 . . . . 80 A7
Gentian Cl OX26. . . . . .65 D5
Gentian Mews OX11... 218 D4
Gentian Rd OX4 . . . . . 142 E1
Geoffrey Barbour Rd
  OX14. . . . . 179 F8

Geoffreyson Rd RG4 .. 258 E5
Geoffrey Tuttle Dr
  OX10. . . . . 204 C2
George And Dragon Cl
  OX27. . . . . .49 F7
George Moore Cl OX4 142 A6
George Morland Ho 8
  OX14. . . . . 179 F6
George Parish Rd OX16 15 E7
George Rd HP14. . . . . 188 E5
George St Banbury OX16 16 D5
  Bicester OX26. . . . . . . 65 D3
  Oxford OX1 . . . . 261 B2
  Reading RG1, RG4 . . 259 B1
George Street Mews
  OX1. . . . . 261 A2
Gerard Pl OX4. . . . . . 142 A5
Germander Way OX26 . 65 D5
Gessey Cl 2 OX29. . . . 90 A1
Gibbs Cres OX2. . . . . 261 A1
Gibbs Rd OX16 . . . . . . 16 E7
Gibraltar Hill OX5. . . . 77 A1
GIBRALTER 77 B1
Gibson Cl OX14. . . . . 160 A3
Gibson Dr OX25 . . . . . .63 C7
Gibson La HP17. . . . . 130 F5
Gidley Way OX33 . . . . 143 D7
Giernalls Rd OX29 . . . 104 A6
Giffard Way HP18. . . . 129 C7
Gifford Cl RG4. . . . . . 259 E5
Giles Cl OX4. . . . . 142 B2
Giles Ctr OX18. . . . . . 115 E2
Giles Pl OX18. . . . . . . 135 A4
Giles Rd OX4 . . . . 142 C2
Gilkes Yd OX16. . . . . . .16 B5
Gillett Cl OX16. . . . . . .16 B5
Gillett Rd OX16. . . . . . 16 B5
Gillians Way OX4 . . . . 142 B6
Gilligans Way SN7 . . . 173 A3
Gillotts Cl RG9. . . . . . 254 B8
Gillott's Hill RG9. . . . 254 C7
Gillott's La RG9. . . . . 254 C7
Gillott's Sch RG9 . . . 254 B7
Gilmore Ct SN6. . . . . 190 A5
Ginge Brook OX14 . . . 199 F8
Ginge Cl OX14. . . . . . 160 B2
Ginge Rd OX12 . . . . . 216 B5
Gipsy La
  Great Coxwell SN7 . . . 192 C8
  Grove OX12. . . . . . . 214 F8
  Oxford OX3 . . . . 124 B1
  Reading RG4 . . . . . . 259 E1
Girdlestone Cl OX3 . . 124 D1
Girdlestone Rd OX3. . 124 D1
Glades The OX26 . . . . 66 D2
Glade The RG31 . . . . 257 C4
Gladstone Cl OX3. . . . 124 E3
Gladstone Rd OX3 . . . 124 E3
Glamis Pl OX16. . . . . . .15 F6
Glanville Gdns OX16... 16 B6
Glanville Rd OX4 . . . . 142 B7
Glean Cotts OX28. . . . 104 D1
Glebe Cl
  Ambrosden OX25 . . . . 81 D4
  Moulsford OX10 . . . . 238 F5
  Shrivenham SN6. . . . . 209 C6
Glebe Cotts
  Postcombe OX9. . . . . 166 F4
  South Stoke RG8. . . . 239 C3
Glebe Ct
  Carterton OX18. . . . . 115 F3
  Duns Tew OX25. . . . . . 47 D5
Glebe Dr NN13 . . . . . . 24 A7
Glebe Farm Bsns Pk
  OX15. . . . . .7 E7
Glebe Field OX15. . . . 16 D1
Glebe Gdns
  Grove OX12. . . . . . . 196 E1
  Sonning RG4 . . . . . . 260 E3
Glebe House Dr MK18. .25 E3
Glebe La RG4. . . . . . . 260 E3
Glebelands
  Bampton OX18 . . . . . 134 E4
  Oxford OX3 . . . . 142 D7
Glebe Pl SN6. . . . . . . 190 A6
Glebe Rd Cumnor OX2 . 139 C5
  Didcot OX11 . . . . . . 218 E7
  East Challow OX12 . . 214 A5
  Purley on Thames RG8. 257 B5
  Stanford in the Vale
    SN7. . . . . 194 D7
Glebe Ride RG8. . . . . 249 B6
Glebe St OX4 . . . . 123 F1
Glebe The
  Aldworth RG8 . . . . . . 247 F3
  Aynho OX17. . . . . 35 D7
  Culham OX14. . . . . . 180 B3
  Cumnor OX2. . . . . . . 139 E5
  Highmoor Cross RG9 . 242 E5
  Hook Norton OX15 . . . 30 B8
  Lewknor OX49 . . . . . 187 B8
  Standlake OX29. . . . . 137 C4
  West Challow OX12... 213 D5
  Wheatley OX33. . . . . 144 B8
Glen Cl OX27 . . . . 52 D1
Glenham Rd OX9 . . . . 148 B8
Glenmore Bsns Ctr
  OX29. . . . . 103 C1
Glenmore Rd OX18 . . 115 D4
Glenrhondda RG4 . . . 258 F6
Glen Wy OX26 . . . . . . 66 A2
Gliffard Ho 5 RG4. . . 259 C1
Glimbers Gr
  Chinnor OX39 . . . . . . 168 C5
  Chinnor OX39 . . . . . . 168 C5
Glissand Way OX18 . . 114 C6
Glory Farm Prim Sch
  OX26. . . . . .66 A4

Gloucester OX28. . . . . . . 104 B1
Gloucester Court Mews
  OX28. . . . . 104 B1
Gloucester Gn OX1 . . 261 B2
Gloucester La OX1. . . 261 A2
Gloucester Mews 4
  SN7. . . . . 172 F4
Gloucester Pl OX12 . . 214 C8
Gloucester St
  Faringdon SN7. . . . . . . 172 F4
  Oxford OX1 . . . . 261 B2
Glover Mews OX20. . . . . .91 B6
Glovers Cl
  Chipping Norton OX7 . . . 42 E2
  Woodstock OX20. . . . . . 91 C6
Glovers La OX11. . . . . . . .10 F1
Glovers Wlk OX28 . . . 118 D8
Glyme Cl
  Abingdon-on-Thames
    OX14. . . . . 160 B1
  Woodstock OX20. . . . . . 91 B7
Glyme Dr OX10 . . . . . 182 D6
Glyme Way OX29 . . . . 106 B8
GLYMPTON 75 D8
Glympton Rd OX20. . . . .75 E6
Glyn Ave OX11. . . . . . 218 D8
Glyncastle RG4 . . . . . 258 F5
Glyndebourne Gdns
  OX16. . . . . .9 A1
Glyn Rd OX10. . . . . . . 203 D1
Glynswood OX39. . . . . 168 C6
Gobles Ct OX26. . . . . . . .65 F1
Goddards La OX7. . . . . .42 E3
Godfrey Cl
  6 Abingdon-on-Thames
    OX14. . . . . 179 E6
  Oxford OX3 . . . . 124 C1
Godfrey Rd OX7. . . . . . .68 B4
Godfreys Cl Brill HP18. . .98 B1
  Grove OX12 . . . . 196 F1
GODINGTON 53 E3
Godstow Cl RG5 . . . . . 260 E1
Godstow Rd
  Wolvercote OX2 . . . . . . 122 D8
  Wolvercote OX2 . . . . . . 122 D8
Godwin Row OX18. . . . 116 A5
Godwyn Cl OX14. . . . . 179 E8
Goffe Cl OX9 . . . . 148 A8
Goffs Hill RG8. . . . . . . 250 D4
Goff St OX2 . . . . 122 D8
Goggs The OX49. . . . . 186 A1
Golafre Rd OX14. . . . . 179 E5
Golby Rd OX15 . . . . .21 E3
Goldbury Cotts OX12. . 216 B4
Goldcrest Gdns 20
  OX11. . . . . 218 C6
Goldcrest Way
  Bicester OX26. . . . . .80 F7
  Bicester OX26. . . . . .81 A8
GOLDEN BALLS 182 A8
Golden Cross OX1 . . . 261 B2
Golden Hills OX39 . . . 168 D6
Golden La Salford OX7. . .41 F5
  Salford OX7. . . . . 42 A5
Golden Rd OX4 . . . . . . 142 A7
Golden Villa Cl OX16. . . 16 A6
Golders Cl HP18. . . . . 127 F3
Goldfinch Cl OX26. . . . . .65 F1
Goldfinch La OX10. . . . 221 A2
Goldings Rd OX5. . . . . . .30 A8
Goldman Dr OX25 . . . . . .63 B8
Goldsmith Cl
  3 Bicester OX26. . . . . . 65 C4
  Wantage OX12 . . . . 215 A5
Goldsmith's La OX10. . 221 D7
Goldsmith's Terr 7
  OX10. . . . . 221 D7
Gold St OX44 . . . . 163 F6
Goldstone Ct
  Barton-on-the-Heath
    CV36. . . . . 27 A5
  Long Compton CV36 . . . . 27 F5
Gooch OX11. . . . . 200 E4
Gooch Dr OX11. . . . . . 200 E4
Goodall Cl OX9 . . . . . . 244 D1
Goodenough Dr OX12. 215 A6
Goodey Cl OX4 . . . . . . 142 C3
Goodlake Ave
  East Challow OX12. . . . 214 A5
  2 Wantage OX12 . . . . 172 F3
Goodliffe Gdns RG31. . 257 C4
Goodrich Cl RG4. . . . . 259 E5
Goodrington Cl OX16. . .16 B6
Goodsons Ind Mews
  OX9 . . . . .147 F8
Goodson Wlk OX3 . . . 123 F3
Goodwood Cl OX26. . . . 65 C1
Goor La SN8. . . . . 245 C4
Gooseacre OX14. . . . . 160 E2
Goosecroft La RG8 . . . 257 B5
Goose Gn OX15. . . . . . . 33 F3
Goose Green Cl OX2. . 122 E8
Goose La OX15 . . . . 22 D8
Goose Wlk OX15. . . . . . 21 D4
GOOSEY 195 B4
GOOSEY GREEN. 195 B4
Goosey La SN7 . . . . . . 195 A4
Gordon Cl OX3 . . . . . . 123 F5
Gordon Dr OX14 . . . . . 160 C1
Gordon Pl RG30 . . . . . 258 C1
Gordon Rd OX25. . . . . . 63 C8
Gordon St OX1 . . . . . . 141 D6
Gordon Way OX28 . . . 118 A7
Gordon Woodward Way
  OX1. . . . . 141 D5
GORING 249 D6
Goring CE Prim Sch
  RG8 . . . . 249 C7

GORING HEATH 251 A3
Goring Lodge 7 OX1 . 141 C7
Goring Rd RG8 . . . . . . 250 E8
Goring & Streatley Sta
  RG8 . . . . 249 C6
Gorselands RG4 . . . . . 259 A6
Gorse Leas OX3 . . . . . 124 B5
Gorton Playne OX7 . . . . 70 D1
Gorwell OX49. . . . . . . 186 B2
Gosbrook Ho 4 RG4. . 259 C1
Gosbrook Rd RG4. . . . 259 B2
GOSFORD 108 F7
Gosford Cl OX5. . . . . . 108 F6
Gosford Hill Ct OX5. . 108 F7
Gosford Hill Sch OX5. 108 F7
Goslyn Cl 3 OX3 . . . . 124 D1
Gossway Fields OX5 . . 78 A3
Gott Cl OX27 . . . . 66 A6
Gough Cl OX29 . . . . . . 105 A6
Goulde La RG8 . . . . . . 248 B4
Goulders Cotts OX10. . 255 F7
Gouldland Gdns OX3. . 124 B5
Goulds Gr OX10 . . . . . 204 F1
Goulds Grove OX10 . . 205 A2
Goulds Villas OX16 . . . 16 A5
Gower Rd OX12. . . . . . 214 A8
GOZZARD'S FORD. . . 158 E2
Graces Ct 4 OX7 . . . . 73 C4
Grafton Ho OX29 . . . . 168 D7
Grafton Lodge 17 OX16 16 D5
Grafton Orch OX39 . . . 168 D7
Grafton Rd OX26. . . . . 65 A2
Grahame Ave RG8 . . . 256 D5
Grahame Cl OX11. . . . 237 A8
Graham Rd OX23 . . . . 65 D3
Grainge Cl NN13. . . . . 25 A5
Grammar School Hill
  OX7 . . . . .73 B3
Gramp's Hill OX12 . . . 231 E6
Granage La OX13 . . . . 156 F1
Granary Cl OX28. . . . . 103 A1
Granary Way OX29 . . . 138 A8
Grandison Ho RG9. . . . 244 E3
GRANDPONT. 141 D7
Grandpont Pl OX1 . . . 261 B1
Grandy Cres OX13 . . . 199 C2
Grange Ave RG9 . . . . . 253 A8
Grange Beck OX11. . . 201 A3
Grange Cl Goring RG8 . 249 B6
  Highworth SN6. . . . . . 190 A5
Grange Court Bsns Pk
  OX14 . . . . 180 C7
Grange Ct OX2 . . . . . . 140 B8
Grange Farm Rd HP14 189 B7
Grange La
  3 Carterton OX18 . . . 115 E5
  Sibford Ferris OX15 . . . 19 D7
Grange Mews OX26 . . . .66 E2
Grange Mill Ct OX29 . . 120 D7
Grange Pk OX25 . . . . . 48 A1
Grange Rd
  Banbury OX16 . . . . 16 D2
  Henley-on-Thames RG9. . 244 E1
  Oxford OX4 . . . . 142 B2
Grangers Pl OX28. . . . 104 B1
Grange Sch The OX16. . 16 D3
Grange The
  Hook Norton OX15 . . . . 30 C8
  Kingham OX7. . . . . .54 F4
  Reading RG4 . . . . 258 D6
Grantham Ho OX2 . . . 261 A4
Grants Mews 2 OX4. . 141 F8
Granville Ct OX3 . . . . . 124 A1
Granville Way OX26. . . .66 B2
Grasmere Ave RG30 . . 257 F2
Grass Hill RG4. . . . . . . 258 E3
Grassland Cl OX29 . . . 117 B8
Grates The OX4. . . . . . 142 C4
Gravel Cl OX10 . . . . . . 203 F4
Gravel Hill
  Henley-on-Thames
    RG9. . . . . 244 D2
  Reading RG4 . . . . 258 F6
  Sonning Common RG9. . 252 F6
Gravel Hill Cres RG9. . 252 F6
Gravel La Drayton OX14 179 B1
  Warborough OX10. . . . . 203 B7
Gravel Pits OX5. . . . . . 108 B6
Gravel Pits La OX5. . . . 108 B6
Gravel Rd RG4, RG9 . . 253 F1
Gravel Wlk
  Drayton St Leonard
    OX10. . . . . 183 B5
  Faringdon SN7. . . . . . . 172 F3
Graveney Dr RG4. . . . . 258 E3
Graven Hill Rd
  Bicester OX26. . . . . . . .80 F6
  Bicester OX26. . . . . . . .81 A7
Gravenhill Rd N OX26. .80 F7
Gravenhill Road N
  OX26. . . . . .81 A7
Gravett Cl RG9 . . . . . . 254 C8
Grayling Ct 9 RG1. . . 259 A1
Grays Cl OX44 . . . . . . 184 C7
Grays Rd OX3 . . . . 124 B2
GREAT BARRINGTON . 99 C8
GREAT BOURTON 9 D8
Great Clarendon St
  OX2. . . . . 261 A3
Great Close Rd OX5. . 108 C5
GREAT COXWELL . . . 192 C7
Great Coxwell Barn★
  SN7. . . . . 172 B1
Great Coxwell Rd SN7 192 C8
GREAT HALCOMBE . . 183 E6
GREAT HASELEY 164 E8
Great Mead
  Didcot OX11 . . . . 219 A6
  Oxford OX1 . . . . 261 A3
GREAT MILTON 145 B2

Great Milton CE Prim Sch
  OX44 . . . . 145 C3
Great Oaks RG8 . . . . . 250 D4
GREAT RISSINGTON . . 83 A7
GREAT ROLLRIGHT. 29 B3
Great Rollright CE Prim
  Sch OX7. . . . . 29 B3
GREAT TEW. 45 D7
Great Tew County Prim
  Sch OX7. . . . . 45 D7
Great Western Dr
  OX11. . . . . 200 E2
Great Wolford Rd GL56 26 C7
Grebe Cl OX14. . . . . . . 179 F5
Grebe Rd Banbury OX16. .16 E3
  Bicester OX26. . . . . 65 F1
Grebe Sq GL54 . . . . . . .68 B4
Greenacres OX14. . . . . 179 B2
Greenacres Ct OX12. . 214 C4
Greenacres La OX18. . 135 D3
Green Bit La The HP18. 98 C8
Green Cl Benson OX10. 204 A5
  Bicester OX26. . . . . 65 F2
  Didcot OX11 . . . . 218 F6
  Steventon OX13. . . . . . 198 F5
  Steventon OX13. . . . . . 199 A5
  Wallingford OX10 . . . . 221 C7
Green Cnr OX28 . . . . . 104 C2
GREENEND 72 A7
Green End Rd HP14. . . 189 E5
Greene's Tutorial Coll
  OX1 . . . . 261 B2
Green Farm OX17. . . . . 23 A4
GREENFIELD 207 A4
  Britwell Salome OX49. . 206 E3
Greenfield OX49. . . . . 207 A6
Greenfield Cres
  Stonesfield OX29. . . . . . 89 D7
  Wallingford OX10 . . . . 221 B8
Greenfield Rd OX29. . . 89 D7
Greenfields OX25. . . . . 96 D7
Greenfinch Cl OX4 . . . 142 F1
Greenfinch Rd OX11. . 200 B2
Green Furlong OX10. . 182 C5
Greengates 5 SN7 . . . 172 F3
Green Ground OX33 . . 127 A2
Greenheart Way OX13 156 E1
Green Hill
  Adderbury OX15 . . . . . . 23 A6
  Oxford OX4 . . . . 143 A2
Greenhill Ct OX16 . . . . 16 D4
Greenhills Pk OX15 . . . 21 E5
Green Hitchings OX44 145 C2
Greenings Mead
  HP18. . . . . 129 D7
Green La Ascott CV36. . 18 C2
  Banbury OX16. . . . . 16 D4
  Bledlow Ridge HP14 . . 189 D5
  Chadlington OX7 . . . . . . 57 B4
  Chesterton OX26. . . . . . 79 F7
  Ewelme OX10 . . . . 204 D4
  Henley-on-Thames RG9. 254 D8
  Little Tew OX7 . . . . 44 D5
  Little Tew OX7 . . . . 44 E3
  Little Tew OX7 . . . . 44 F2
  Little Tew OX7 . . . . 45 A5
  Longworth OX13 . . . . . 156 C2
  Milton-under-Wychwood
    OX7. . . . . 70 B1
  North Leigh OX29 . . . . 105 A7
  Oxford OX2 . . . . 140 A8
  Pangbourne RG8 . . . . . 256 C5
  Sonning Common RG4. . 252 F5
  South Newington OX15. .31 F7
  Stokenchurch HP14. . . 188 C5
  Sunningwell OX13 . . . . 160 A6
  Swalcliffe OX15. . . . . . 14 A1
  Uffington SN7 . . . . 211 C7
  Upper Arncott UX25. . . .96 E7
  Warborough OX10. . . . 202 F8
  Warborough OX10. . . . 203 B7
  Woodcote RG8. . . . . . . 250 F7
  Wootton OX13. . . . . . . 159 A5
Greenlands OX5. . . . . . .70 A1
Green Lane Flats
  OX10. . . . . 202 E3
Greenleas Ave RG4 . . . 259 B7
Greenmere OX10 . . . . 202 E3
Greenmore RG8 . . . . . 250 F8
Green Mws OX29 . . . . 102 D2
Green N The OX10 . . . 203 C8
Green Pl OX1. . . . . 141 D6
Green Rd Didcot OX11 . 218 F7
  Harwell OX11 . . . . 217 F7
  Kidlington OX5. . . . . . . 108 E8
  Oxford OX3 . . . . 124 F3
  Shillingford OX10 . . . . 203 B4
Green Ridges OX3 . . . 125 A4
Greens Garth OX15. . . . 21 F5
Greens Keep HP17. . . . 130 F6
Green's Rd OX29 . . . . 120 E8
Green St OX4. . . . . 142 A7
Green S The OX10 . . . 203 C8
Greenswrd The OX17. . 5 E1
Green Templeton Coll
  OX2 . . . . 261 A4
GREEN THE Ludgershall. 98 C8
  North Aston. 48 A6
Green The
  Adderbury OX17 . . . . . . 23 A4
  Alvescot OX18. . . . . . . 133 C5
  Ascott-under-Wychwood
    OX7. . . . . 71 C2
  Aston Rowant OX49 . . . 167 D3
  Barford St Michael OX15 32 E6
  Baydon SN8. . . . . 245 E1
  Bladon OX20. . . . . 91 B2
  Bledington OX7 . . . . . . 54 C2
  Bletchingdon OX5. . . . . 93 A8

Green The continued
  Cassington OX29. . . . . 107 C2
  Chalgrove OX44. . . . . . 184 D6
  Charlbury OX7. . . . . 73 C4
  Charney Bassett OX12 . 176 A2
  Chesterton OX26. . . . . . 79 F7
  Chilton OX11 . . . . 235 E8
  Chipping Norton OX7 . . 42 E2
  Clanfield OX18. . . . . . . 152 E8
  Cropredy OX17 . . . . 4 F2
  Cuddesdon OX44. . . . . 144 B2
  Cuddesdon OX44. . . . . 144 B2
  Culham OX14. . . . . 180 A3
  Drayton OX14 . . . . 179 B1
  East Hanney OX12 . . . . 197 B7
  Fawler OX7. . . . . 88 E6
  Fernham SN7. . . . . 193 A4
  Fifield OX7. . . . . 69 C2
  Freeland OX29 . . . . . . 106 B5
  Fringford OX27 . . . . 52 C6
  Garsington OX44. . . . . 143 E1
  Great Bourton OX17 . . . . 9 D8
  Great Milton OX44 . . . 145 B2
  Great Rollright OX7. . . . 29 A3
  Great Tew OX7 . . . . 45 D7
  Hethe OX27. . . . . 52 A7
  Highworth SN6. . . . . . 190 A5
  Hook Norton OX15 . . . . 30 B7
  Hornton OX15. . . . . .7 C6
  Horspath OX33 . . . . . . 143 C5
  Horton-cum-Studley
    OX33. . . . . 112 A5
  Kingham OX7. . . . . 55 A5
  Kingston Blount OX39. . 167 F4
  Launton OX26. . . . . 66 E2
  Leafield OX29 . . . . .86 F3
  Little Barrington OX18 . . 99 B6
  Longcot SN7 . . . . 192 C2
  Lyford OX12. . . . . 176 C1
  Marcham OX13. . . . . . . 178 D6
  Marsh Baldon OX44 . . . 162 A3
  Middle Assendon RG9. . 243 F8
  Milcombe OX15. . . . . . . 20 F2
  Nettlebed RG9. . . . . . . 224 E2
  North Aston OX25. . . . . 48 B6
  North Aston OX25. . . . . 48 B7
  North Leigh OX29 . . . . . 89 D2
  Shenington OX15. . . . . . .6 E2
  Shrivenham SN6 . . . . . 209 A6
  Shutford OX15. . . . . . . 14 B5
  Standlake OX29. . . . . . 137 D3
  Stanton Harcourt OX29 138 A8
  Steventon OX13. . . . . . 199 A5
  Stoke Lyne OX27. . . . . . 51 B5
  Sutton Courtenay OX14 180 A1
  Swalcliffe OX15. . . . . . . 19 F8
  Tackley OX5. . . . . 77 B5
  Townsend OX12 . . . . . 194 E2
  Turweston NN13. . . . . . 24 C8
  Uffington SN7 . . . . 211 D7
  Upper Heyford OX25. . . 62 F8
  Warmington OX17. . . . . . 3 A4
  West Hanney OX12 . . . 196 E5
Green Trees RG9 . . . . . 252 F7
Greenway
  Haddenham HP17. . . . 130 F5
  Lower Heyford OX25. . . 63 A4
  Thame OX9 . . . . 129 F1
Greenway La 3 OX29. . 90 A1
Greenways RG8 . . . . . 256 D5
Greenway The OX12 . . 216 B6
Greenwich La OX29. . . .87 B3
Greenwood Ave OX39. 168 C6
Greenwood Cl RG4 . . . 252 E5
Greenwood Dr OX26. . . 65 B3
Greenwood Gr OX3. . . 178 D7
Greenwood Mdw
  OX39. . . . . 168 D6
Greenwood Wy OX11 . 218 B8
Gregory Est OX49. . . . 185 C3
Gregory Pl OX29. . . . . 117 C7
Grenoble Rd
  Oxford OX4 . . . . 143 A1
  Sandford-on-Thames
    OX4. . . . . 142 D1
Grenville Way OX9. . . 130 B1
Gresham Way RG30. . . 258 A2
Gresham Way Ind Est
  RG30 . . . . 258 A2
Greville Rd OX17 . . . . . .8 E1
Greygoose La GL56. . . . 41 B6
Greyhound La OX9. . . . 129 F1
Greyhound Mws OX12 214 A1
Greyhound Wlk OX9 . . 147 F8
Grey La OX28. . . . . 104 D1
Greys Cl OX16 . . . . 15 F6
Greys Court★ RG9. . . . 243 C3
GREYS GN RG9 . . . . . 243 C2
GREYS GREEN 243 C2
Greys Hill RG9. . . . . . . 244 D1
Greys Rd RG9 . . . . 254 C8
Greystoke Rd RG4 . . . 259 C4
Greystones Ct
  Alvescot OX18. . . . . . . 133 C5
  Kidlington OX5. . . . . 92 D1
Griffin Cl OX17 . . . . 23 A5
Griffin Rd OX9 . . . . . . 148 C8
Griffith Rd OX16. . . . . . .9 C1
Griffiths Cl OX29. . . . . 138 C3
Griffiths Gdns OX27. . . 66 A7
Grimmer Way RG8. . . . 250 F8
GRIMSBURY 16 F5
Grimsbury Dr OX16. . . .16 F7
Grimsbury Gn OX16. . . 16 E8
Grimsbury Green OX16. 16 E8
Grimsbury Sq OX16. . . .16 F7
Grindon La OX10 . . . . 205 B1
Grosvenor Pl OX12 . . . 214 B5

Grosvenor Rd
  7 Banbury OX16 . . . . . 16 D5
  Oxford OX2 . . . . 140 E6
  Reading RG4 . . . . 259 C4
GROVE 196 F1
Grove Bsns Pak OX12 . 214 A8
Grove CE Prim Sch
  OX12 . . . . 196 E2
Grove Cotts
  Brightwell-cum-Sotwell
    OX10. . . . . 202 D2
  Little Coxwell SN7. . . . 192 E7
  Reading RG4 . . . . 259 A5
Grove Ct
  Deddington OX15 . . . . . 33 F4
  Oxford OX4 . . . . 142 A5
Grove Farm The OX14 199 C1
Grove Hill
  Highworth SN6 . . . . . . 190 A7
  Reading RG4 . . . . 259 A4
  Woodstock OX20. . . . . . 91 A6
Grove La
  Ewelme OX10, OX49. . . 205 A6
  Spelsbury OX7. . . . . 72 E8
Grovelands
  Kidlington OX5. . . . . 92 D1
  Kidlington OX5. . . . . . . 108 D8
  Witney OX28 . . . . 104 B3
Grovelands Ctr OX12. . 196 D1
Grovelands Rd OX3 . . 125 A2
Grove Mews RG4 . . . . 259 B5
Grove Park Dr
  Ardington OX12. . . . . . 215 C3
  Grove OX12. . . . . 197 B1
Grove Pk Dr OX12 . . . 194 F3
Grove Rd Bladon OX20. .91 C3
  Henley-on-Thames RG9. 244 E1
  Harwell OX11 . . . . 217 D8
  Reading RG4 . . . . 259 B6
  Sonning Common RG4. . 252 F5
  South Stoke RG8. . . . . 239 E2
  Wantage OX12 . . . . . . 214 E6
Groves Ind Est OX7 . . . .70 B1
Grove St Banbury OX16. . 16 D5
  Oxford OX2 . . . . 123 B7
  Wantage OX12 . . . . . . 214 D5
Grove Terr OX11. . . . . 218 D4
Grove The
  Abingdon-on-Thames
    OX14. . . . . 160 B2
  Bourton SN6 . . . . 209 A3
  Deddington OX15 . . . . . 33 F4
  Great Milton OX44 . . . 145 C1
Grundy Cl OX14. . . . . . 180 B8
Grundy Cres OX1 . . . . 141 E1
Grunsell Cl OX3 . . . . . 124 C5
Guardian Ct 3 OX16. . . 16 E6
Guelder Rd OX4 . . . . . 142 D1
Guelder Rose 19 OX11 218 C7
Guernsey Way 2 OX16. . 8 F1
Guild Cl OX28 . . . . 117 E6
Guildenford OX18 . . . . 100 E5
Guildford Ct 7 OX5. . . 108 F8
Guild Ho The 2 OX12. 214 E4
Gulley Row OX25. . . . . . 95 D8
Gullicote La OX17 . . . . . 8 E3
Gulliver's Cl OX15 . . . . . 8 B4
Gurden Pl OX3 . . . . . . 124 F4
Gurl Cl OX3 . . . . 124 E4
Gurney Cl RG4. . . . . . . 258 D5
Gurney Dr RG4 . . . . . . 258 D5
Gwilym Ct 5 OX10. . . 221 C2
Gwyneth Rd OX4 . . . . 142 A2

H

Habitat Way OX10 . . . 221 B7
Hackers La OX7 . . . . . . .55 E4
Hack La CV36. . . . . .27 E8
HADDENHAM 130 E6
Haddenham Bsns Pk
  HP17. . . . . .130 F7
Haddenham & Thame
  Parkway Sta HP17. . . 130 E6
Hadden Hill
  Brightwell-cum-Sotwell
    OX11. . . . . 202 A2
  Didcot OX11 . . . . 201 D1
Haddon Pl OX18. . . . . 115 F3
Hadland Rd OX14. . . . 180 C8
Hadleigh Rise RG4. . . . 259 E5
Hadow Rd OX3 . . . . . . 124 A4
Hadrian Cl SN6. . . . . . 209 A6
Hadrian's Gate NN13. . . 24 A7
Hafod OX12 . . . . 214 D5
Hagbourne CE Prim Sch
  OX11 . . . . 218 F5
Hagbourne Cl RG8. . . . 250 F8
Hagbourne Rd
  Didcot OX11 . . . . 219 A8
  East Hagbourne OX11. . 219 D2
HAILEY Wallingford . . 240 E8
  Witney 104 A6
Hailey Ave OX7. . . . . . . .42 E1
Hailey CE Prim Sch
  OX29 . . . . 104 A6
Hailey Cres OX7. . . . . . .42 E1
Hailey Croft OX39. . . . 168 B6
Hailey Rd
  Chipping Norton OX7 . . . 42 D1
  Witney OX8, OX29. . . . 104 B3
Hailles Gdns 1 OX26. . .65 C4
Haines Ct OX13. . . . . . 178 D7
Haldane Rd
  Oxford OX1 . . . . 261 B4
  Oxford OX4 . . . . 142 A2
  Reading RG4 . . . . 258 E5
Hale Rd OX10. . . . . . . 203 F3
Halestrap Way OX17. . . 23 F5

Hale The OX26. . . . . . . .79 F7
Halfpenny La OX10 . . 238 E5
Halifax Green HP17. . . 130 E6
Halifax Rd Bicester OX26 66 A3
  Mongewell OX10. . . . . 221 E5
Halifax Way OX29. . . . 138 B7
Hall Cl Banbury OX16 . . .15 E4
  North Aston OX25. . . . . 48 B6
  Pyrton OX49. . . . . 186 A3
Hallett Cl OX12. . . . . . 214 C4
Hall Farm Paddocks
  OX29 . . . . 107 F8
Halliday Hill OX3 . . . . 124 B5
Halliday La OX2 . . . . . 140 D8
Halls Cl Drayton OX14. . 179 C1
  Oxford OX2 . . . . 140 B7
Halls La OX12 . . . . 197 B7
Hallsmead Ct 8 RG1 . 259 A1
Halse Water OX11 . . . . 201 A2
Halton Rd OX18. . . . . . 115 F2
Hambidge La
  Lechlade-on-Thames
    GL7. . . . . 150 B6
  Lechlade-on-Thames
    GL7. . . . . 150 C5
Hambleden Dr OX10 . . 221 B8
Hamble Dr OX14. . . . . 160 B1
Hamble Rd OX11 . . . . 201 A1
Hambleside OX26. . . . . .65 B2
Ham Corner OX11 . . . . 217 D8
Hamcroft OX12. . . . . . 214 C5
Hamels La
  Boars Hill OX1. . . . . . . 140 F1
  Boars Hill OX1. . . . . . . 160 A8
Hamel The OX1. . . . . . 261 A2
Hamel Wlk OX1. . . . . . 261 A2
Hamfield OX12 . . . . . . 214 C4
Hamilton Ave RG9 . . . 244 E1
Hamilton Cl
  Banbury OX16 . . . . 16 E7
  Bicester OX26. . . . . 65 E3
Hamilton Dr OX12 . . . 214 A5
Hamilton Pl RG9. . . . . 241 D5
Hamilton Rd
  Oxford OX2 . . . . 123 B7
  Thame OX9 . . . . 130 A1
  Wargrave RG10. . . . . . 255 E2
Ham La OX18 . . . . 135 E1
Hamlet The RG4 . . . . . 252 B5
Hamlyn Cl OX12 . . . . . 214 A2
Hammer La
  Dorchester OX10. . . . . 182 F2
  Warborough OX10. . . . 183 A1
Hammett Pl OX18. . . . 115 D1
Hammond's End RG8 . 241 B4
Hampden Ave OX9. . . . 147 F7
Hampden Cl
  Banbury OX16. . . . . . . .15 F5
  Bicester OX26. . . . . 66 A3
  Chalgrove OX44. . . . . . 184 D6
  Faringdon SN7. . . . . . . 173 A3
Hampden Dr OX5. . . . . 108 F6
Hampden Rd
  Oxford OX4 . . . . 142 C4
  Reading RG4 . . . . 259 B2
  Wantage OX12 . . . . . . 214 E5
Hampden Sq
  Upper Heyford OX25. . . 49 D1
  Upper Heyford OX25. . . 63 D8
Hampdens Way OX49. 186 C3
Hampden Way OX10 . . 204 F4
Hampdon Villas OX27. . .67 F7
Hampstead Hill RG9. . 260 C8
Hampton Dr OX17 . . . . .23 F6
HAMPTON GAY 92 D5
Hampton Gay Village St
HAMPTON POYLE. 93 B4
Ham Rd OX12. . . . . . . 214 C4
Hamstyles OX49. . . . . 205 E7
Hana Cl OX17. . . . . 0 F2
Hanborough Bsns Pk
  OX29. . . . . .90 B1
Hanborough Cl OX29 . 120 E8
Hanborough Manor CE Sch
  OX29. . . . . .90 C1
Hanborough Rd OX29. 120 E8
Hanborough Sta OX29. .90 F1
Handley Dr HP17 . . . . 130 E7
Handlo Pl OX3. . . . . . . 124 F4
Handwik Hill OX16. . . . . .9 D3
Hangar La OX12 . . . . . 214 B8
Hanney Rd
  Kingston Bagpuize
    OX13. . . . . 176 D7
  Steventon OX13. . . . . . 198 C6
  Steventon OX13. . . . . . 198 F5
Hannis Rd OX7 . . . . 42 D1
Hanover Cl OX7 . . . . . . 73 C3
Hanover Ct
  Didcot OX11 . . . . 218 E4
  Reading RG4 . . . . 259 C6
  9 Wallingford OX10. . . 221 C7
Hanover Gdns
  Bicester OX26. . . . . 65 E1
  Wargrave RG10. . . . . . 255 F3
Hans Ave OX12 . . . . . . 214 E5
Hanson Dr OX2 . . . . . . 122 C1
Hanson Rd OX14. . . . . 159 F3
HANWELL 8 F4
Hanwell Ct OX17 . . . . . . 8 F4
HANWELL FIELDS 9 B1
Hanwell Fields Com Sch
  OX16 . . . . 9 B1
Hanwood Cl RG5 . . . . 260 C1
Harberton Mead
  Marston OX3. . . . . 123 F3
  Oxford OX3 . . . . 124 A3
Harbord Rd OX2. . . . . 109 B2
Harborne Rd OX5. . . . . 77 C5
Harcourt Arboretum★
  OX44 . . . . 161 E1

Harcourt Cl RG9 244 C1
Harcourt Gn OX12 214 F6
HARCOURT HILL 140 E6
Harcourt Hill OX2 140 E6
Harcourt Ho 5 OX26 65 E2
Harcourt Rd OX12 214 E5
Harcourt Terr OX3 124 B2
Harcourt Way
Abingdon-on-Thames OX14 159 F1
Wantage OX12 214 E5
Hardcastle Dr
Kingston Bagpuize OX13 156 F1
Kingston Bagpuize OX13 157 A1
Harding Cl SN7 173 A3
Hardingham Cl OX18 115 D5
Harding Rd OX14 179 D8
Hardings OX44 184 D6
Hardings Cl OX4 142 B3
Hardings Strings OX11 218 E7
Harding Vale OX13 198 E5
Harding Wy OX13 178 C7
Hardwell Cl OX12 196 D1
HARDWICK Banbury 9 A1
Stoke Lyne 51 D8
Witney 118 F1
Hardwick
Reading RG8 257 B8
Reading RG8 257 D7
Hardwick Ave OX5 108 E7
Hardwick Bsns Pk OX16 9 E2
Hardwick Hill OX16 9 D3
Hardwick Pk OX16 8 F1
Hardwick Prim Sch OX16 16 A8
Hardwick Rd
Hethe OX27 52 A7
Mapledurham RG8 257 B8
Whitchurch-on-Thames RG8 256 D7
Hardy Cl RG4 259 C2
Harebell Rd
Didcot OX11 200 B1
Oxford OX4 142 F2
Harebell Way OX26 65 D4
Harecourt
Wantage OX12 214 F4
Wantage OX12 214 F4
Harefields OX2 109 B1
HARESFIELD 190 B8
Hare Warren Ct RG4 259 B4
Harewood Rd OX16 16 E2
Haricot Vale Rd OX27 65 D7
Harlech Ave RG4 259 D6
Harlech Cl OX16 15 F5
Harlequin Pl OX18 115 D5
Harlequin Way OX16 9 B1
Harley Rd Oxford OX2 122 F1
Reading RG4 259 B2
Harlington Ave OX12 196 E1
Harlow Way OX3 123 F7
Harmans Way OX49 186 A1
Harmon Cl OX27 66 A6
Harolde Cl OX3 124 D4
Harold Hicks Pl OX4 141 F6
Harolds Cl OX29 87 A3
Harold White Cl OX3 124 F2
Harper Cl OX25 96 D7
Harpes Rd OX2 123 B8
HARPSDEN 254 D6
HARPSDEN BOTTOM 254 B6
Harpsden Rd RG9 254 E8
Harpsden Way RG9 254 E7
Harpsden Woods RG9 254 F5
Harpsichord Pl OX4 123 F1
Harrier Dr OX11 200 C2
Harrier Pk OX11 200 D3
Harriers Gd Com Prim Sch OX16 16 C4
Harriers View OX16 16 C4
Harrier Way OX26 66 A4
Harris Cl OX16 15 E6
Harris Gdns GL54 68 B4
Harris Manchester Coll OX1 261 C3
Harrison Pl OX9 129 F1
Harrison's La OX20 91 A6
Harris Rd OX25 63 C7
Harris's La OX13 156 C2
Harrisville OX25 62 B8
Harroell
Long Crendon HP18 129 D5
Long Crendon HP18 129 D6
Harrogate Rd RG4 258 E4
Harrowby Ct OX16 16 D2
Harrowby Rd OX16 16 D2
Harrow Hill CV36 27 F8
Harrow Rd OX4 142 F3
Hart Ave SN7 172 F3
Hart Cl
Abingdon-on-Thames OX14 180 C8
Banbury OX16 9 C1
Upper Rissington GL54 68 B3
Hartley Cl OX10 203 B6
Hartleys Barns OX7 85 D7
Hart Moor Cl HP14 188 E4
Hart Pl OX26 66 A4
Harts Cl OX5 108 D8
Hartshill Cl OX15 21 D3
Hartslock Bridleway
Whitchurch Hill RG8 250 B1
Whitchurch-on-Thames RG8 256 B8
Hartslock Ct RG8 256 B6
Hartslock View RG8 249 E2
Hartslock Way RG31 257 C2
Hart St
Henley-on-Thames RG9 244 E2
Oxford OX2 261 A3
11 Wallingford OX10 221 D7
Hart-Synnot Ho OX2 261 A4
Hart Vw OX15 7 D6
Hart Wlk OX25 63 D8
Harvest Bank OX18 115 E5
Harvest Cres OX18 115 F5
Harvest Gr OX28 104 E2
Harvest Pl RG10 255 E1
Harvest Way OX28 104 E2
Harveys Nurseries Pk Cvn Site RG4 259 C4
HARWELL 217 F7
Harwell Cl OX14 160 A1
Harwell Int Bsns Ctr OX11 217 A1
Harwell Prim Sch OX11 217 D7
Harwell Rd OX14 199 F6
Harwell Science & Innovation Campus OX11 217 C2
Harwood Rd OX11 218 F5
Haseley Rd
Little Milton OX44 163 F6
Little Milton OX44 164 A6
Haseley Trading Est OX44 145 C1
Haslemere Gdns OX2 109 A2
Haslemere Tramway Est OX16 16 E5
Haslemere Way OX16 16 E5
Hasthorpe Rd OX10 221 E5
Hastings Cl OX16 15 F6
Hastings Dr OX18 115 F2
Hastings Hill OX7 55 E5
Hastings Rd OX16 15 F7
Hastoe Grange OX3 124 A4
Hatch Cl OX5 77 F4
Hatch End OX5 77 F4
Hatch End Ind Est OX25 48 B2
Hatchet Hill SN4 227 A2
Hatch Gate La RG10 255 F7
Hatching La OX29 87 A4
Hatch Way OX5 77 F4
Hatfield Pits La OX29 104 C8
HATFORD 174 D4
Hathaways OX33 144 B8
Hatwell Row OX18 115 E2
Havelock Rd OX4 142 C5
Haven Cl OX10 202 D8
Haven The HP14 188 C4
Haven Vale OX12 214 E5
Havers Ave OX14 199 D2
Havill Cres OX15 21 E3
Hawke La OX15 21 D4
Hawker Sq GL54 68 B4
Hawkes Cl OX3 125 A4
Hawkes La
Sibford Gower OX15 13 C1
Sibford Gower OX15 19 C8
Hawkey Rd OX12 215 A6
Hawkins Ho 5 OX18 115 E2
Hawkins St 1 OX4 141 F7
Hawkins Way OX13 159 B6
Hawksbeard Wy OX13 156 D1
Hawksmead OX26 81 A8
Hawksmoor Rd OX2 109 B1
Hawkswell Gdns OX2 123 C7
Hawkswell Ho OX2 123 C7
Hawksworth OX11 200 D4
Hawksworth Cl OX12 196 D1
Hawksworth Pl OX10 220 E1
HAWKWELL 68 D6
Haw La Aldworth RG8 247 E1
Bledlow Ridge HP14 189 F8
Hawlings Row OX4 143 A1
Hawthorn Ave
Oxford OX3 124 D3
Thame OX9 147 E8
Hawthorn Cl
Chinnor OX39 168 B6
Garsington OX44 143 D2
Oxford OX2 140 D8
Wallingford OX10 221 C7
Hawthorn Cres OX12 214 E8
Hawthorn Dr OX18 114 C7
Hawthorne Ave OX13 159 C2
Hawthorne Dr RG9 242 A1
Hawthorne Rd RG4 259 E4
Hawthornes RG31 257 B3
Hawthorn Gdns OX11 217 F7
Hawthorn Gr OX18 115 D1
Hawthorn Hill
South Newington OX15 31 E6
Wigginton OX15 31 E5
Hawthorn Pl OX11 200 B1
Hawthorn Rd
Eynsham OX29 120 E8
Faringdon SN7 172 E3
Hawthorns The
Banbury OX16 16 D3
Sutton Courtenay OX14 180 C1
Hawthorn Way
Kidlington OX5 108 E7
Sonning RG4 260 E3
Hawthorn Wlk 2 OX26 65 F4
Hayday Cl OX5 108 C5
Haydens La RG9 224 A3
Haydon Rd OX11 200 E1
Hayes Ave OX13 176 D8
Hayes Cl OX3 123 F3
Hayes The OX1 261 B2
Hayfield Rd OX2 123 B5
Hayford Ho 5 OX18 115 F5
Hay La 2 OX29 117 B8
Haynes Cl SN7 172 E3
Haynes Rd OX3 123 E5
Hayward Bridge Rd
Brookhampton OX10 183 C8
Stadhampton OX44 163 C1
Hayward Dr OX18 115 D1
Hayward Rd OX2 109 B2
Haywards Cl
Henley-on-Thames RG9 244 C1
Wantage OX12 214 E5
Haywards Rd OX14 199 B7
Hayway La
Bampton OX18 134 E1
Bampton OX18 135 A1
Scotland End OX15 29 F8
Hazel Ave OX9 147 E8
Hazel Cl
Abingdon-on-Thames OX14 159 E1
East Challow OX12 214 A5
Witney OX28 104 E2
Hazel Cres OX5 108 F6
Hazeldene GL7 150 D5
Hazeldene Cl
Eynsham OX29 120 F7
North Leigh OX29 105 B6
Hazeldene Gdns OX16 16 D3
Hazel End OX44 143 D2
Hazel Gdns
Didcot OX11 218 B8
Sonning Common RG4 252 F5
Hazel Gr Bicester OX26 65 F4
Stoke Row RG9 242 B2
Wallingford OX10 221 C7
Hazells La Filkins GL7 132 B5
Shrivenham SN6 209 C6
Hazelmoor La RG4 252 D4
Hazelnut Path OX14 160 E7
Hazel Rd Oxford OX2 122 C1
Purley on Thames RG8 257 C4
Hazelrig Dr OX9 148 A8
Hazelton Cl OX9 147 E8
Hazel Wlk OX5 108 F6
Hazelwood Cl RG31 257 C1
HEADINGTON 124 C4
HEADINGTON HILL 124 A2
Headington Prep Sch 1 OX3 124 C2
HEADINGTON QUARRY 124 E2
Headington Rd
Oxford OX3 124 A2
Oxford OX4 123 F1
Headington Rdbt OX3 124 F3
Headington Sch OX3 124 B2
Headley Ho OX3 124 A4
Headley Way OX3 124 B3
Healey Cl OX14 179 E6
Hean Cl OX14 160 B2
Hearns La RG4 252 C5
Hearthway OX16 9 B1
Heath Cl Milcombe OX15 20 F2
Oxford OX3 142 D8
Heathcote Ave OX16 16 E2
Heathcote Pl OX14 160 C1
Heath Ct OX15 30 B7
Heath Dr RG9 254 A1
Heather Cl
Carterton OX18 115 E4
Sonning Common RG4 253 A5
Heather Pl OX3 123 F4
Heather Rd
Bicester OX26 65 E5
Milton OX14 199 D6
Heath Farm La OX29 105 A6
Heathfield Ave RG9 254 B2
Heathfield Cl RG9 254 B2
HEATHFIELD VILLAGE 93 E6
Heath La OX20 91 B1
Heath The OX7 70 A2
Heatley Rd Oxford OX4 142 B1
Sandford-on-Thames OX4 161 B8
Heatley Way OX2 122 C1
Heaton Rd OX26 65 A1
Hedge End OX20 91 C6
Hedge Hill Rd OX12 213 F5
Hedgehog La OX28 103 F1
Hedgemead Ave OX14 160 C2
Hedgerley OX39 168 B6
Hedges Cl OX3 124 E3
Hedges The OX15 14 B8
Heet Rd OX27 82 E5
Heigham Ct SN7 194 D7
Heights The OX2 140 C8
Helen Rd OX2 122 F1
Hellebourine Cl OX4 142 F1
Helwys Pl OX5 92 D2
Hemdean Hill RG4 259 A3
Hemdean House Sch RG4 259 A3
Hemdean Rd RG4 259 A3
Hemdean Rise RG4 259 A3
Hemingway Dr OX26 65 C2
Hemplands
Great Rollright OX7 29 A3
Poffley End OX29 104 C6
HEMPTON 33 B4
Hempton Rd
Barford St Michael OX15 32 F5
Deddington OX15 33 E4
Hempton OX7 33 A1
HEMPTON WAINHILL 188 F6
Henderson Ho OX10 221 B7
Hendon Pl OX26 66 A4
Hendred Ho OX4 142 B6
Hendreds CE Prim Sch The OX12 216 D6
Hendred St OX4 142 B6
Hendred Way OX14 160 B1
Henfield View OX10 203 B8
Henge Cl OX17 22 E3
Henge Ct OX9 129 D1
Hengest Gate OX11 217 E7
Hengrove Cl OX3 124 D5
Henley Ave OX4 142 A5
Henley Coll The (Deanfield Bldgs) RG9 244 D1
Henley Coll The (Rotherfield Bldgs) RG9 244 C1
Henley Dr SN6 190 A7
Henley Gdns 9 OX26 65 E2
Henley L Ctr RG9 254 B7
HENLEY-ON-THAMES 244 B1
Henley-on-Thames Sta RG9 244 E1
Henley Rd
Berinsfield OX10 182 A7
Brightwell-cum-Sotwell OX11 202 F7
Dorchester OX10 182 D1
Nuneham Courtenay OX44 181 F8
Play Hatch RG4 260 A5
Reading RG4 259 D3
Sandford-on-Thames OX4 161 B8
Shillingford OX10 203 A6
Shillingford, Bridge End OX10 202 F7
Shiplake RG9 254 E1
Shiplake RG9 260 C8
Shiplake RG9 260 D8
Henleys La OX14 179 B1
Henley St OX4 141 F7
Henley Trinity Sch RG9 244 D1
Hennef Way OX16 16 E8
Henor Mill Cl OX14 160 B2
Henrietta Rd OX9 130 A1
Henry Blyth Gdns OX9 147 F7
Henry Box Cl OX28 118 A7
Henry Box Sch The OX28 118 A7
Henry Gepp Cl OX17 23 B4
Henry Rd OX2 122 F1
Henry Taunt Cl OX3 124 E5
HENSINGTON 91 D7
Hensington Cl OX20 91 C6
Hensington Rd OX20 91 B6
Hensington Wlk OX20 91 C6
HENTON 149 E2
HENWOOD 140 A1
Henwood OX2 139 F3
Henwood Cotts OX1 139 F1
Henwood Dr OX1 140 A1
Herald Gdns OX13 156 D1
Herald Way 3 OX26 66 A4
Herbert Cl OX4 142 B7
Herb Farm The★ RG4 253 A4
Hercules Cl
Upper Rissington GL54 68 B3
8 Upper Rissington OX7 68 B3
Hereford Cl OX26 80 C8
Hereford Way 1 OX16 8 F1
Heritage Cl
Hook Norton OX15 30 B8
Wallingford OX10 221 D6
Heritage La OX7 71 B2
Herman Cl
Abingdon-on-Thames OX14 180 B8
East Hanney OX12 197 C7
Hermitage Rd OX14 179 E6
Hermon Rd OX16 8 E1
Hernes Cl OX2 123 B8
Hernes Cres OX2 123 B8
Hernes Oak OX39 168 D8
Hernes Rd OX2 123 B8
Heron Cl OX18 115 C3
Heron Ct
Abingdon-on-Thames OX14 179 F4
Bicester OX26 66 B1
Heron Dr Bicester OX26 66 B1
Witney OX28 103 F1
Heron Island RG4 259 C1
Heron La OX11 200 C2
Heron Rd OX10 204 D3
Heron Shaw RG8 249 C7
Herons Pl OX2 123 B8
Herons Wlk OX14 159 F1
Heron Way OX16 16 A4
Herringcote OX10 182 D2
Herschel Cres OX4 142 C3
Herschel Ct OX4 142 C3
Herschel St OX11 201 B3
Hertford Cl
Bicester OX26 65 F3
Reading RG4 259 D6
Hertford Coll OX1 261 C2
Hertford Ct 8 OX5 108 F8
Hertford St OX4 142 A7
HETHE 52 A8
Hethe Rd
Cottisford NN13 38 A3
Hardwick OX27 51 D8
Hewett Ave RG4 258 D4
Hewett Cl RG4 258 D4
Hewetts Cl OX29 87 A3
Hewett Wood OX10 239 C4
Hewgate Ct RG9 244 E1
Hexham Rd OX25 80 C8
Hey Croft OX29 120 E7
Heydock Rd OX26 80 C8
Heydons Terr OX17 3 E8
Heyford Cl OX29 137 C5
Heyford Hill La OX4 141 F2
Heyford Hill Rdbt OX4 141 F2
Heyford Ho 7 OX16 16 E6
Heyford Leys OX25 63 C8
Heyford Mead 2 OX5 92 D1
Heyford Park Free Sch OX25 63 D8
Heyford Pk OX25 63 C8
Heyford Rd
Kirtlington OX5 78 A5
Middleton Stoney OX25 64 A4
Middleton Stoney OX5 63 F5
Somerton OX25 48 F5
Somerton OX25 48 F6
Steeple Aston OX25 62 B7
Heyford Sta OX25 62 C6
HEYTHROP 44 A4
Heythrop Pk
Church Enstone OX7 58 E8
Enstone OX7 44 C1
Hibiscus Way OX18 115 E5
Hicks Cl
Chalgrove OX44 184 E6
9 Faringdon SN7 172 E1
Hailey OX29 104 A6
Shrivenham SN6 209 A7
Hidden Brook OX13 178 A7
Hid's Copse Rd OX2 140 B7
Higgs Cl OX11 219 A6
High Acres OX16 16 E4
Higham Way OX16 16 E5
Highbank Cl OX3 124 A4
Highbridge Cl RG4 259 E5
Highclere Gdns
Banbury OX16 15 E6
Wantage OX12 214 D6
Highcliffe Cl RG5 260 F1
HIGH COGGES 118 F6
High Cogges OX29 118 F7
High Cross Way OX3 124 E5
Highdown Ave RG4 259 A6
Highdown Hill Rd RG4 259 A6
Highdown Sch & Sixth Form Ctr RG4 259 A5
HIGHFIELD 65 C3
Highfield HP18 129 C7
Highfield Ave OX3 124 C1
Highfield Cl OX9 147 C8
Highfield Pk RG10 255 F3
Highfield Rd
Reading RG31 257 C4
Wargrave RG10 255 F4
High Furlong
Banbury OX16 16 B8
Banbury OX16 16 B8
High House Cl OX18 152 E8
High Land Cl HP18 98 A1
Highlands Banbury OX16 9 A1
Hardwick OX16 9 B1
Lower Tadmarton OX15 21 A6
Highlands La RG9 254 A8
High Mdw
Reading RG4 258 D3
Sibford Gower OX15 13 A1
HIGHMOOR 242 D7
HIGHMOOR CROSS 242 E5
Highmoor Rd RG4 258 F3
High Rd
Brightwell-cum-Sotwell OX10 202 E3
Brightwell-cum-Sotwell OX10 203 A2
High Road Cotts OX10 202 D3
High St
Abingdon-on-Thames OX14 179 F7
Adderbury OX17 23 A4
Ardington OX12 215 E5
Ascott-under-Wychwood OX7 71 C2
Ashbury SN6 228 A7
Aston OX18 135 D3
Bampton OX18 134 F3
Banbury OX16 16 D6
Barford St Michael OX15 32 F5
Beckley OX3 111 A3
Benson OX10 203 F4
Bishopstone SN6 227 D4
Bloxham OX15 21 E5
Bodicote OX15 22 D8
Burford OX18 100 E5
Chalgrove OX44 184 C7
Chalgrove OX44 184 D6
Charlton-on-Otmoor OX5 95 A4
Childrey OX12 213 C4
Chinnor OX39 168 D7
Chipping Norton OX7 42 E3
Clifton Hampden OX14 181 C3
Cropredy OX17 4 F2
Croughton NN13 36 C8
Cuddesdon OX44 144 B2
Culham OX14 180 B3
Cumnor OX2 139 D5
Deddington OX15 33 F4
Didcot OX11 218 F8
Dorchester OX10 182 D1
Drayton OX13 199 B8
Drayton OX14 179 B1
Drayton St Leonard OX10 183 B5
East Hendred OX12 216 E6
Ewelme OX10 204 E4
Ewelme OX10 204 F3
Ewelme OX10 204 F4
Eynsham OX29 120 E7
Fernham SN7 193 A4
Fifield OX7 69 B2
Finstock OX7 88 B5
Goring RG8 249 A6
Great Rollright OX7 29 A3
Haddenham HP17 130 F6
Harwell OX11 217 E7
Highworth SN6 190 A5
High St *continued*
Hinton Waldrist SN7 155 F2
Hook Norton OX15 30 B7
Islip OX5 93 F1
Kidlington OX5 92 E1
Kingston Blount OX9 167 F3
Lechlade-on-Thames GL7 150 C4
Lewknor OX49 187 B8
Little Milton OX44 163 F6
Long Crendon HP18 129 D6
Long Wittenham OX14 201 D8
Longworth OX13 156 B3
Ludgershall HP18 98 B8
Lyneham OX7 70 D5
Middleton Cheney OX17 17 F8
Milton OX14 199 D5
Milton-under-Wychwood OX7 70 A1
Nettlebed RG9 224 D2
North Moreton OX11 220 A7
Oxford OX1 261 C2
Pangbourne RG8 256 C5
Ramsden OX7 87 F4
Ramsden OX7 88 A3
Ratley OX15 2 A3
Shipton-under-Wychwood OX18 85 D8
Shrivenham SN6 209 C6
Shutford OX15 14 A5
Sonning RG4 260 D4
Souldern OX27 35 E3
South Moreton OX11 219 F5
South Newington OX15 31 F7
Standlake OX29 137 D3
Stanford in the Vale SN7 194 E7
Steventon OX13 199 A4
Stonesfield OX29 89 C7
Streatley RG8 249 C6
Sutton Courtenay OX14 200 A8
Tetsworth OX9 166 B8
Thame OX9 129 E1
Tiddington OX9 146 F1
Uffington SN7 211 D7
Upper Heyford OX25 48 F1
Upton OX11 218 C2
Wallingford OX10 221 D7
Wargrave RG10 255 D2
Watchfield SN6 191 D1
Watlington OX49 186 B2
Wheatley OX33 144 B8
Whitchurch-on-Thames RG8 256 C7
Witney OX28 118 B8
Woodstock OX20 91 B6
Hightown Gdns OX16 16 D3
Hightown Leyes OX16 16 D3
Hightown Rd OX16 16 D4
High View OX12 214 A4
High View Ct OX14 179 D1
HIGHWORTH 190 B6
Highworth Pl OX28 118 A7
Highworth Rd
Faringdon SN7 172 E2
Shrivenham SN6 209 A7
Highworth Warneford Sch SN6 190 A4
Highworth Way RG31 257 B2
Hikers Way HP18 129 F4
Hillary Dr OX11 218 E7
Hillary Way OX33 144 C7
HILL BOTTOM 250 E3
Hill Bottom RG8 250 D3
Hill Bottom Cl RG8 250 E3
Hill Cl Charlbury OX7 73 C3
Chipping Norton OX7 42 E1
East Challow OX12 213 F4
East Challow OX12 214 A4
Hillcraft Rd OX33 125 D7
Hill Cres OX7 88 C5
Hillcrest La RG9 252 F7
Hillcrest Pk Sch OX7 43 D3
Hill Ct OX18 115 D4
Hill Farm Ct OX39 168 D6
Hill Farm La OX25 47 D6
Hill Farm Rd HP14 188 A6
Hill Field OX15 19 B7
Hill Gdns RG8 249 A6
Hill Ho OX25 62 A8
Hilliard Ho OX14 179 E5
Hilliat Fields OX14 179 B1
Hilliers Cl OX14 200 A8
Hill Lands RG10 255 D2
Hill Lawn Ct OX7 42 E3
Hill Mead OX11 217 D8
Hill Piece OX11 235 E7
Hill Prim Sch The RG4 259 C5
Hill Rd Chinnor OX39 168 D5
Lewknor OX49 187 C6
Watchfield SN6 191 D1
Watlington OX49 206 E8
Hill Rise
Great Rollright OX7 29 A3
Horspath OX33 143 D6
Woodstock OX20 91 A8
Hillsale Piece 7 OX4 142 B2
Hillsborough Cl 3 OX4 142 B3
Hillsborough Rd OX4 142 B4
Hillside Harwell OX11 217 B3
Little Wittenham OX14 202 B6
Oxford OX2 140 B6
Whitchurch-on-Thames RG8 256 D8
Hillside Cl Banbury OX16 16 E3
Upper Arncott OX25 96 E7

Hillside Cotts OX14 . . 202 A6
Hillside Rd OX7. . . . . . . .46 E1
Hillside View OX39 . . 168 B5
Hill The Aynho OX17 . . . . 35 C7
  Bourton SN6 . . . . 209 A3
  Burford OX18 . . . . 99 F1
  Burford OX18 . . . . 100 E4
  Garsington OX44. . . . . . 143 E1
  Shilton OX18 . . . . 115 B5
  Souldern OX27 . . . . .35 F3
Hilltop HP18. . . . . 129 D5
Hilltop Ct OX4 . . . . 142 B8
Hilltop Gdns OX5 . . . . . . 93 F1
Hill Top La OX39 . . . . . 168 F4
Hilltop Rd RG4 . . . . . . 258 D5
Hill Top Rd OX4 . . . . . . 142 B8
Hill View
  Carterton OX18. . . . . . 115 D4
  Kingston Lisle OX12 . . . 212 B4
  Oxford OX3 . . . . 125 A4
  Uffington SN7 . . . . . . 211 C7
Hillview OX31. . . . . 257 B2
Hillview Cres OX16 . . . . 16 A7
Hill View La OX1. . . . . 159 A8
Hill View Prim Sch
  OX16 . . . . .16 A7
Hillview Rd
  Abingdon-on-Thames
  OX14. . . . . 159 F2
  Oxford OX2 . . . . 123 A1
Hillwerke OX39. . . . . . 168 C6
Hillyard Barns OX14 . . 200 A8
Hilton Rd OX16. . . . . . . .16 B6
Hinksey Bsns Ctr OX2. 122 D1
Hinksey Hill OX1. . . . 141 B3
Hinksey Hill Interchange
  OX1. . . . . 141 C3
Hinksey Pool (Outdoor)
  OX26 . . . . 141 C6
Hinshelwood Rd OX1 . 261 C3
Hinton Crossing HP27 149 E4
HINTON PARVA 227 A3
Hinton Rd
  Hinton Waldrist SN7 . . 155 F2
  Longworth OX13 . . . . . 156 B3
Hinton Springs SN4. . . 227 B3
HINTON WALDRIST. . . 155 F3
Hirstwood RG30 . . . . . 257 C1
Hiskins OX12 . . . . 214 B5
Hitching Ct OX14 . . . . 179 C7
Hitchman Dr OX7. . . . . .42 E2
Hitchmans Mws OX7. . .42 E2
Hithercroft
  Cholsey OX10, OX11. . . 220 D5
  Wallingford OX10 . . . . 221 A6
  Wallingford OX10 . . . . 221 B7
  West End OX10. . . . . . 220 E1
Hithercroft Ct OX10. . . 221 B6
Hithercroft Ind Est
  OX10. . . . . 221 B7
Hive Mews 🖪 OX14. . . 179 F6
Hixet Wood OX7. . . . . . .73 B3
Hobart Wy OX7. . . . . . . 33 D4
Hobbs Cl OX14 . . . . . . 180 B8
Hobbs End RG9. . . . . . 254 B8
Hobbshill SN7. . . . . . . 193 A4
Hobbs Rd SN7. . . . . . . 173 A2
Hobby Cl OX4 . . . . 142 F1
Hobby Gn OX14. . . . . . 159 E2
Hobbyhorse La OX14. . 200 B7
Hobby Rd OX15. . . . . . . 17 A1
Hobson Rd OX2. . . . . . 123 B7
Hocker Bench
  Bishopstone SN6. . . . . 227 C4
  Bishopstone SN6. . . . . 227 B4
Hocket The RG9 . . . . . 244 D3
Hockmore St OX4 . . . . 142 C4
Hode Garth OX9 . . . . . 148 B6
Hodge Ct OX1 . . . . . . 141 C7
Hodges Cl
  🖪 Banbury OX16 . . . . . .16 F3
  Stokenchurch HP14. . . 188 F4
Hodgkin Way OX1. . . . 201 B3
Hodgson Cl OX27. . . . . .49 F7
Hofmann Mws RG9. . . 254 F8
Hogarth Pl OX14. . . . . 179 E5
Hogg End Bloxham OX15 .21 E4
  Chipping Warden OX17. . .5 F6
Holborn Hill
  Letcombe Basset
  OX12. . . . . 213 C1
  Letcombe Bassett OX12 231 D7
Holcombe La OX10 . . . 183 D6
Holcombe Pl
  Brookhampton OX10. . . 183 C8
  Stadhampton OX44. . . . 163 C1
Holford Rd OX16. . . . . 117 F7
Holkam Cl RG30. . . . . 257 F1
Holland Cl OX39 . . . . . 168 D7
Holland Pl OX3. . . . . . 142 E8
Holland Rd OX14 . . . . 160 A2
Hollandridge La
  Christmas Common
  OX49. . . . . 207 A7
  Stonor OX49, RG9. . . . 207 A8
Holland Rise OX17. . . . .23 F4
Hollandtide La
  Berrick Salome OX10 . . 204 D7
  Chalgrove OX10. . . . . . 184 D2
Holley Cres OX3 . . . . . 124 E3
Holliers Cl
  Sydenham OX39 . . . . . 167 D8
  Thame OX9 . . . . 147 F8
Holliers Cres OX7. . . . . .60 F8
Hollies Ct The 🖪 OX16. 16 D5
Hollington HP18. . . . . 129 B7
Hollis Cl OX28. . . . . . . 118 D7

Holloway Hill OX15 . . . . 12 A2
Holloway La
  Minster Lovell OX29 . . . 102 D2
  Northend RG9 . . . . 207 F5
  Winderton OX15 . . . . . . 12 A1
Holloway Rd
  Wheatley OX33 . . . . . . 144 B8
  Witney OX28 . . . . 118 A8
Holloway Rd The SN7. 192 B8
Holloway The
  Harwell OX11 . . . . 217 E6
  Mollington OX17 . . . . . . .4 A3
Hollow Furlong OX29 . 107 C2
Hollow Rd OX15 . . . . . .20 F7
Hollow Rd The
  Faringdon SN7. . . . . . . 172 B1
  Great Coxwell SN7 . . . 192 B8
HOLLOWS THE 28 A4
Hollow Way Aynho OX17 35 C7
  Carterton OX18. . . . . . 115 B5
  Childrey OX12 . . . . . . 213 C3
  Chilton OX11 . . . . 235 F5
  Oxford OX3, OX4. . . . . 142 D6
  Upton OX11. . . . . 218 C1
Hollybush Rd
  Carterton OX18. . . . . . 115 D2
  Hook Norton OX15 . . . . 30 B8
Hollybush Row OX1. . . 261 A2
Holly Cl Bicester OX26 . . 65 F5
  Highmoor Cross RG9 . . 242 E5
  Kidlington OX5. . . . . . 108 E7
Holly Ct OX4. . . . . 142 E3
Hollyhocks OX11 . . . . 217 B7
Holly La
  Abingdon-on-Thames
  OX14. . . . . 179 B2
  Didcot OX11 . . . . 218 B8
  Wroxton OX15. . . . . . . .8 B1
Holmemoor Dr RG4. . . 260 C2
Holme Park Farm La
  RG4. . . . . 260 C2
Holmes Pk OX3. . . . . . 124 A3
Holmes Rd 🖪 SN7. . . . 172 D1
Holmlea Rd RG8. . . . . 249 C5
Holm Sq OX26. . . . . . . .65 E5
Holm Way OX26 . . . . . . .65 F5
Holt Cl OX26. . . . . 65 A1
HOLTON. 126 C2
Holt The
  Abingdon-on-Thames
  OX14. . . . . 179 F8
  Mollington OX17 . . . . . . .3 F3
  Mollington OX17 . . . . . . .4 A3
  Purley on Thames RG8 . 257 D4
Holt Weer Cl OX2. . . . 109 B1
HOLWELL. 114 A7
Holyoake Rd OX3 . . . . 124 D3
Holyrood Cl RG4. . . . . 259 D6
Holy Trinity Rc Sch
  OX7 . . . . .42 F3
Holywell Bsns Ctr
  OX2 . . . . 141 A8
Holywell Cl OX14 . . . . 160 C2
Holywell Fordla OX1. . 123 E2
Holyw Ellford La OX1. 261 C3
Holywell Music Room★
  OX1. . . . . 261 C3
Holywell St OX1. . . . . 261 C3
Home Cl
  Carterton OX18. . . . . . 115 D2
  Epwell OX15 . . . . 13 A6
  Kidlington OX5. . . . . . . 92 E1
  Shabbington HP18. . . . 128 D3
  Wheatley OX33 . . . . . 126 B2
  Wolvercote OX2 . . . . . 122 D8
  Wootton OX13. . . . . . 159 B7
Home Croft RG31. . . . 257 B1
Home Farm
  Ardington OX12. . . . . . 215 D5
  Crowmarsh Gifford
  OX10. . . . . 221 F7
Home Farm Barns
  OX18. . . . . 133 B6
Home Farm Cl
  Ambrosden OX25 . . . . . 81 C3
  Bladon OX20 . . . . 91 B3
  Chesterton OX26. . . . . .79 F8
  Chesterton OX26. . . . . . 80 A8
  East Hendred OX12. . . . 216 D7
  Shipton-under-Wychwood
  OX7 . . . . .85 D7
Home Farm Cotts
  Leafield OX29 . . . . . . 102 F8
  Rousham OX25 . . . . 62 A4
Home Farm Ct OX17. . .23 B4
Home Farm Dr OX15. . . .6 D8
Homefarm La OX25. . . .48 B3
Home Farm Mews
  OX12. . . . . 196 A4
Homefield Cl HP14 . . . 188 E4
Homelands Way RG9 . 244 D1
Homeleaze Rd SN6 . . . 209 E8
Home Pk OX18 . . . . . . 133 D8
Homestall Cl OX2. . . . 122 B1
Homestead Cres OX25 . 63 A8
Homestead Rd OX16. . .16 E2
Homestead The
  Binfield Heath RG9 . . . 254 B1
  Bladon OX20 . . . . 91 C3
  Kidlington OX5. . . . . . 108 D8
  Thame OX9 . . . . 129 E1
Hone Ct OX7 . . . . .73 B3
Honesty Way OX25. . . . 81 D3
Honeybottom La OX13 159 B5
Honeyham Cl OX18 . . . 116 C3
Honey La OX10 . . . . . . 220 F1
Honey Meadow Cl
  RG4. . . . . 259 D2
Honeysuckle Cl OX26 . . .65 F5
Honeysuckle Gr OX4. . 143 A2
Honeysuckle Way
  OX11. . . . . 218 C8

Honeysuckle Wy OX25 . 81 D3
Honor Cl OX5. . . . . . . 108 F8
HOOK END. 251 E7
Hookend La RG8. . . . . 251 D8
Hook End La RG8. . . . 249 B1
HOOK NORTON 30 A8
Hook Norton Brewery★
  OX15 . . . . .29 F7
Hook Norton Brewery Mus
  & Visitor Centre★
  OX15 . . . . .29 F7
Hook Norton CE Prim Sch
  OX15 . . . . .30 B8
Hook Norton Rd
  Great Rollright OX7. . . . 29 B4
  Great Rollright OX7. . . . 29 E1
  Over Norton Common
  OX7. . . . . .43 C7
  Sibford Ferris OX15 . . . 19 B7
  Swerford OX7 . . . . .30 F3
Hooks Cl GL7. . . . . . . 132 E1
Hoopswell OX11. . . . . 217 D8
Hopcraft Cl OX25 . . . . .96 E7
Hopcraft La OX15. . . . . 33 F4
Hopcroft Ave OX25 . . . . 80 E6
Hope Cl OX16 . . . . 16 A6
Hope Way OX2 . . . . . . 122 C1
Hop Gdns RG9. . . . . . 244 D2
Hopkins Ct 🖪 OX4. . . . 142 D6
Hopkins Way OX11 . . . 218 B7
Hopton Rd OX9 . . . . . . 130 A1
Hordern Cl HP17 . . . . 130 F6
HORLEY 8 B4
Horleydr OX16. . . . . .9 D3
Horley Path Rd
  Horley OX15 . . . . .8 B3
  Wroxton OX15. . . . . . . .8 B1
Hornbeam Cl
  Banbury OX16 . . . . . . 16 B5
  Purley on Thames RG8 . 257 C5
Hornbeam Dr OX4. . . . 143 A2
Hornbeam Rd OX26. . . . .65 F5
Horne OX27 . . . . 66 A7
Horne La OX29 . . . . . . 117 D7
Horn Hill OX15 . . . . . . .32 F6
Horn Hill Rd OX17 . . . . . 9 A2
Horn La Chastleton GL56 40 A4
  East Hendred OX12. . . . 216 D5
Hornsby Fields OX11. . 218 B8
Hornsea Cl RG30 . . . . 257 E1
Horns La OX29. . . . . . . 90 A3
Horns Way OX29. . . . . 137 C3
HORNTON 7 C7
Hornton Dr OX16 . . . . . .9 D3
Hornton Hollow OX15. .21 D4
Hornton La Horley OX15 . .8 A5
  Hornton OX17 . . . . .7 F6
Hornton Prim Sch OX15 .7 C6
Horsa Cl OX12. . . . . . 214 C8
Horsa La OX11. . . . . . 235 C8
Horse Close Cotts
  OX44. . . . . 164 D8
Horse Cl The RG4. . . . 259 C4
Horsecroft SN7. . . . . . 194 E7
Horsecroft Way RG31. 257 B4
Horse Fair
  Banbury OX16 . . . . . . 16 C6
  Chipping Norton OX7 . . 42 E3
  Deddington OX15 . . . . . 33 F4
Horse Leys RG9. . . . . . 254 A7
Horseman Cl OX3. . . . 124 A5
Horsemere La OX29 . . 107 D2
Horsepath Park Cvn Site
  OX33. . . . . 143 D6
Horsepond Rd RG4 . . . 252 B5
Horseshoe La
  Brookend OX7. . . . . . . 72 B8
  Wootton OX20. . . . . . . .75 F4
Horse Shoe La OX7 . . . 72 B8
Horseshoe Pk RG8. . . 256 D5
Horseshoe Rd
  Bledlow Ridge HP14 . . 189 C8
  Pangbourne RG8. . . . . 256 D5
Horseshoes Cl OX13 . . 158 A7
Horseshoes La OX10. . 203 F4
Horseshoes Pl OX9 . . . 148 A7
Horsham Cl OX16. . . . . .8 F1
HORSLEYS GREEN . . . 189 C3
Horsleys Green Rd
  HP14. . . . . 189 C3
HORSPATH 143 D6
Horspath Athletics &
  Sports Gd OX4 . . . . . 143 A6
Horspath CE Prim Sch
  OX33. . . . . 143 C7
Horspath Driftway
  OX3 . . . . 142 E7
Horspath Rd OX4 . . . . 142 E6
Horspath Rd Ind Est
  OX4 . . . . .142 F6
Horton Ave OX9 . . . . . 148 A7
Horton Cl OX9 . . . . . . 148 A7
HORTON-CUM-
  STUDLEY 112 A6
Horton General Hospl
  OX16 . . . . 16 D4
Horton La OX15 . . . . . . 21 A2
Horton Rd OX33 . . . . . 111 C1
Horton View OX16. . . . 16 C3
Horwood Cl OX3. . . . . 124 C3
Hosker Cl OX3. . . . . . 125 A3
Hotspur Cl HP17 . . . . 130 E6
Hound Cl OX14 . . . . . 160 C2
Howard Ave OX12 . . . 196 E1
Howard Cornish Rd
  OX13. . . . . 178 D7
Howard Rd
  Banbury OX16. . . . . . . .16 F6
  Upper Heyford OX25. . . 63 C8
Howard St OX4 . . . . . 142 A6

Howberry La RG9. . . . 223 E3
Howbery Bsns Pk
  OX10. . . . . 203 F1
Howbery Farm OX10. . 221 F7
Howbery Pk
  Crowmarsh Gifford
  OX10. . . . . 221 F8
  Wallingford OX10 . . . . 203 F1
Howden Gn OX13. . . . 199 A5
Howe Cl OX33 . . . . . . 144 A8
Howe Hill OX49. . . . . . 206 D8
Howell Cl 🖪 OX2. . . . 122 F8
Howe Rd OX49 . . . . . . 206 C8
Howes La Bicester OX26 . 65 B3
  Chipping Norton OX7 . . .42 F1
Howgate Dr RG8. . . . . 249 C7
Howland Rd OX9 . . . . 148 B7
Howland Road Bsns Pk
  OX9 . . . . 148 C6
Hoyle Cl OX28 . . . . . . 104 A3
Hubble Cl OX3. . . . . . 124 E5
Huckleberry Cl RG8. . . 257 C4
Hudleston Ave OX10 . . 204 C2
Hudson Cl OX15 . . . . . .33 F4
Hudson St
  Bicester OX26. . . . . . . 65 D3
  Deddington OX15 . . . . . .33 F4
Huggett Cl 🖪 OX18. . . 115 D3
Hugh Allen Cres OX3 . 123 F3
Hugh Carson Cl RG4. . 252 F5
Hughes Cl OX7 . . . . . . 73 C2
Hughes Cres SN7. . . . 192 C3
Hughes Ho OX4 . . . . . 141 F8
Hugh Price Ho OX4 . . 142 B7
Hull La OX26 . . . . .80 F6
Humber Cl
  Didcot OX11 . . . . 201 A1
  Wantage OX12 . . . . . 214 E5
Humber St OX15. . . . . .21 E4
Humber Wlk OX16. . . . .15 F8
Humfrey Rd OX3. . . . . 124 F4
Humphries Cl OX18. . . 115 E3
Humphries Gn OX12 . . 214 E3
Hunder Ct OX1 . . . . . . 141 D2
Hundley Way OX7 . . . . 73 C4
Hundred Acres Cl
  OX3 . . . . 142 E7
HUNGERFORD
  GREEN. 247 F4
Hungerford Rd OX13. . 217 B8
Hunsdon Rd OX4 . . . . 142 A4
Hunt Cl OX26. . . . . . . .65 E2
Hunt Ct HP14. . . . . . . 188 F4
Hunter Ave OX12 . . . . 197 C7
Hunter Cl
  Abingdon-on-Thames
  OX14. . . . . 160 B3
  Oxford OX4 . . . . 142 E6
  Upper Rissington GL54 . . 68 B3
Huntercombe RG9. . . . 223 F4
HUNTERCOMBE END . . 224 B4
Huntercombe End La
  RG9. . . . . 224 B4
Huntercombe Pl RG9 . 224 A5
Hunter Combe Pl RG9 224 A5
Hunters Chase RG4. . . 258 F5
Hunters Cl OX12 . . . . 196 C1
Hunters Field SN7 . . . 194 E7
Hunters Piece SN6 . . . 209 A2
Hunters Point OX39. . . 168 C6
Huntingdon Rd OX26 . . 80 C8
Hunt Rd OX9 . . . . 148 B7
Hunts Cl OX18. . . . . . 100 E4
Hunt's Cl OX8 . . . . 89 C7
Hunts Rd OX18. . . . . . 100 E4
HUNT'S GREEN. 254 B6
Hurdeswell
  Long Hanborough OX29 . 90 A1
  🖪 Long Hanborough
  OX29. . . . . 106 A8
Hurricane Cl OX29. . . . 117 C7
Hurst Cl OX10 . . . . . . 221 C6
Hurst La Freeland OX29 106 A7
  Oxford OX2 . . . . 140 B6
Hurst Rise Rd OX2. . . . 140 C8
Hurst St OX4 . . . . 141 F7
Huscarle Way RG31. . . 257 C4
Hutchcombe Farm Cl
  OX2. . . . . 140 C7
Hutchcomb Rd OX2. . . 140 C8
Huts The SN7. . . . . . . 174 F8
Huxley Cl Bicester OX26. 65 C3
  Wootton OX13. . . . . . 159 B6
Hyacinth Wlk OX4 . . . 161 E8
Hyde Copse OX13. . . . 178 D7
Hyde Gr OX15 . . . . . . 21 C3
Hyde Mdw View 🖪
  OX28. . . . . 104 A3
Hyde Pl
  Abingdon-on-Thames
  OX14. . . . . 179 D5
  Oxford OX2 . . . . 123 A7
Hyde Rd OX12 . . . . . . 196 A5
Hydes The RG31. . . . . 257 C4
Hyde The OX14 . . . . . 179 D5
Hydrangea Wlk OX16 . . .9 B1
Hyetts Gdns GL7. . . . . 132 B6
Hythe Bridge St OX1. . 261 A2

Ian Mikardo Way RG4. 259 D2
Ibstone Ave RG4. . . . 259 E5
Ibstone Rd HP14. . . . 188 C3
Icehouse La RG9. . . . 244 C7
ICKFORD 128 A3
Ickford Rd
  Shabbington HP18. . . . 128 D2
  Tiddington OX9 . . . . . 127 F1
  Tiddington OX9. . . . . . 145 F8
  Worminghall HP18 . . . 127 E6

Ickford Sch HP18. . . . 128 A3
Ickleton Rd OX12. . . . 214 B4
Icknield Cl
  Chinnor OX39 . . . . . . 168 A4
  Didcot OX11 . . . . 200 C1
Icknield Com Coll
  OX49 . . . . 186 B2
Icknield Cotts RG8. . . 249 A6
Icknield Pl OX5 . . . . . 108 E7
Icknield Line The (Chinnor
  & Princess Risborough
  Rly)★ OX39 . . . . . . 168 E7
Icknield Pl RG8. . . . . 249 D8
Icknield Rd
  Goring OX10 . . . . . . 239 F2
  Goring RG8 . . . . 249 D8
Icknield Way SN6. . . . 227 C4
Icknield Way (Bridleway)
  Wantage OX12 . . . . . 214 F4
  Wantage OX12 . . . . . 215 A4
Icomb Rd OX7. . . . . . . 54 A3
Idbury Cl OX28 . . . . . 117 D7
Idbury Rd OX7. . . . . . . 69 A3
IDSTONE 227 F5
Idstone Hill SN6. . . . . 228 A4
Idstone Rd SN6. . . . . 228 A6
IFFLEY 141 F4
Iffley Mdw Nature
  Reserve★ OX4 . . . . . 141 E5
Iffley Mead Sch OX4 . .141 F5
Iffley Rd OX4 . . . . 141 F7
Iffley Turn OX4 . . . . . 142 A5
Ilchester Mews RG4 . . 259 E6
Ilex Cl RG4 . . . . 252 F4
Ilges La OX10. . . . . . . 221 A2
Ilkley Rd RG4. . . . . . . 258 E3
Illingworth Ave RG4 . . 259 E6
ILMER 149 F8
Ilmer La HP27. . . . . . 149 F8
Ilsley Cl RG4. . . . . . . 252 F5
Ilsley Rd OX3. . . . . . . 124 E4
Imperial Ct RG9 . . . . . 244 E1
Imray Pl OX10 . . . . . . 221 B7
Independent Bsns Pk
  HP14. . . . . 188 C5
Industrial Est 🖪 OX28. 104 B1
Ingham La OX49. . . . . 186 B1
Ingleby Paddocks OX5. 77 D1
Ingle Cl OX3. . . . . . . 124 B4
INGLESHAM 150 B1
Inglewood Cl RG4 . . . 252 F6
Ingrebourne Way
  Didcot OX11 . . . . 200 F3
  Didcot OX11 . . . . 201 A3
Inkerman Cl OX14 . . . 159 D1
Innovation Dr OX14. . . 199 E4
Innsworth Rd OX18 . . . 115 E3
Inott Furze OX3. . . . . . 142 D7
Insall Rd OX7. . . . . . . .42 E4
Inst of Virology &
  Experimental
  Microbiology OX1. . . 261 C3
IPSDEN 240 C7
Ireton Cl OX44. . . . . . 184 D6
Ireton Ct OX9. . . . . . . 129 F1
Iris La OX29 . . . . 89 C7
Iron Down Hill OX15,
  OX7. . . . . 32 C3
Irons Ct OX7. . . . . .60 F8
Ironside Dr SN6 . . . . . 191 D1
Ironstone Hollow OX15 30 C8
Ironstone La
  Balscote OX15. . . . . . . 14 E8
  Wroxton OX16. . . . . . . .7 F1
Ironstones OX16. . . . . 16 A8
Isabelle Spencer Way
  OX29. . . . . 117 C7
Isambard OX14 . . . . . 218 F8
Ishree Cotts RG9 . . . . 242 A5
Isis Ave OX26. . . . . . . .65 B2
Isis Bsns Ctr OX4 . . . .142 F6
Isis Cl
  Abingdon-on-Thames
  OX14. . . . . 160 B1
  Chilton OX11 . . . . 235 D4
  Long Hanborough OX29 106 B8
  South Hinksey OX1. . . 141 E5
Isis Ct RG1 . . . . 259 B1
ISLIP 109 F8
Islip Rd
  Bletchingdon OX5. . . . . 93 A7
  Oxford OX2 . . . . 123 B8
Islip Sta OX5 . . . . .93 F1
Itchen Cl OX11 . . . . . 201 A3
Ivatt Wlk OX16. . . . . . .16 E8
Ivies The OX12. . . . . . 214 D4
Ivybank RG31. . . . . . . 257 C1
Ivy Cl Didcot OX11 . . . 218 B8
  Oxford OX4 . . . . 142 D5
Ivydene Rd RG30 . . . . 258 C1
Ivy La Mollington OX17. . .4 A3
  Oxford OX3 . . . . 124 C4
  Shutford OX15. . . . . . . 14 B5
Izzard Rd OX25 . . . . . . .63 B8

Jackdaw La OX4. . . . 141 E7
Jackdaw Rd OX11. . . 200 D5
Jackies La OX33. . . . 144 C7
Jackman Cl OX14. . . . 180 A7
Jacksmeadow SN7 . . 211 D7
Jackson Cl OX18. . . . 115 C8
Jackson Cole Ho OX1. 261 A2
Jackson Dr OX1. . . . . 141 D2
Jackson Rd
  Bledington OX7. . . . . . 54 D2
  Cutteslowe OX2. . . . . 109 B1

Jacksons La
  Mapledurham RG4 . . . 258 C5
  Reading RG4 . . . . . . 258 B5
Jack Straw's La OX3 . . 124 A3
Jacobs Cl OX28. . . . . 104 B1
Jacobsyd OX7. . . . . . . .60 F8
James Cl OX25 . . . . . . 63 C8
James Ct OX18 . . . . . 152 E8
James St OX4 . . . . . . 141 F8
James Wolfe Rd OX4 . 142 C7
Janaway OX4. . . . . . . 142 A1
Janaway Ct 🖪 OX18 . . 115 D2
Jane Morbey Rd
  Thame OX9 . . . . 147 F7
  Thame OX9 . . . . 148 A7
Jane Seaman Ct OX4 . 143 A1
Japonica Cl OX26. . . . .65 F5
Japonica Wlk OX16. . . .9 B1
Jarn Way OX1. . . . . . . 140 D1
Jarvis Circle OX17. . . . .8 E1
Jarvis' La OX26. . . . . . .66 B2
Jasmine Cl OX4. . . . . 142 F3
Jasmine Pl OX26 . . . . .65 F5
Jasmine Way 🔟 OX18 115 E5
Jasmine Wlk OX16. . . . .9 B1
Jasper La OX18. . . . . 115 D5
Javelin Way OX10 . . . 204 D3
Jay Cl OX26 . . . . 81 A8
Jaynes Cl OX16. . . . . . 16 D2
Jefferson Cl RG4 . . . . 259 C7
Jeffersons Piece OX7. . 73 C4
Jefferson Way OX3 . . . 148 A7
Jeff's Terr OX7. . . . . . .73 B4
Jemmetts Cl OX10. . . . 182 D1
Jenkinson Rd OX17. . . . .8 E2
Jenkins Way OX13. . . . 176 C8
Jennings La OX11 . . . 217 E7
Jenyns Ct OX14. . . . . 179 C6
JERICHO 261 A3
Jericho St OX2 . . . . . 261 A4
Jerome Way OX5 . . . . .92 B6
Jersey Dr 🖪 OX16. . . . .9 A1
Jersey Rd OX4. . . . . . 142 A3
Jervis Cl OX7. . . . . . . .60 F8
Jespers Hill SN7. . . . . 173 A3
Jesses La HP18. . . . . 129 C6
Jessops Cl
  Marston OX3 . . . . 123 E5
  Oxford OX3 . . . . 124 A5
Jesus Coll OX1 . . . . . 261 B2
Jethro Tull Gdns
  OX10. . . . . 221 E7
Jetty The OX17. . . . . . . .5 E1
Jeune Hall 🖪 OX4 . . . 141 F8
Jeune St OX4 . . . . . . 141 F8
Joan Lawrence Pl
  OX3. . . . . 124 E1
Jobs La
  Bradwell Grove OX18 . . 114 C8
  Burford OX18 . . . . . . 100 C1
John Allen Ctr OX4. . . 142 C5
John Allen Way OX4 . . 142 C5
John Blandy VC Prim Sch
  OX13 . . . . 156 E1
John Buchan Rd OX3 . 124 B5
John Fulkes Ave
  Thame OX9 . . . . 147 F7
  🔟 Thame OX9. . . . . . 148 A7
John Garne Way OX3 . 124 A2
John Hampden Prim Sch
  OX9 . . . . 148 A7
John Henry Newman Acad
  The OX4 . . . . 142 B2
John Jones Cl OX14 . . 159 F1
John Kallie Ho OX4. . . 142 B6
John Lopes Rd OX29 . . 120 E7
John Mason Rd OX14 . 180 A8
John Mason Sch OX14 179 E8
John Morris Rd OX14 . 179 E5
John Parker Cl OX4. . . 141 F3
John Piers La OX1. . . . 141 C5
John Radcliffe Cl OX3 . 124 C4
John Radcliffe Hospl
  OX3 . . . . 124 C4
John Smith Dr OX4. . . 142 D4
John Snow Pl OX3. . . . 124 E3
Johnson Cl OX44. . . . . 143 D2
Johnstone Pl 🔟 OX10. 221 D7
Johnstones Way OX7. . .42 E2
Jones Cres 🖪 SN7. . . . 172 D1
Jones Way HP14. . . . . 189 D2
Jones Wy OX17. . . . . . .8 E1
Jordan Cl Didcot OX11. 201 A2
  Reading RG4 . . . . . . 259 C5
Jordan Hill OX2 . . . . . 109 A2
Jordan Hill Rd OX2. . . 109 A2
Jordans Cl OX7. . . . . . .88 A3
Jordon Hill Bsns Pk
  OX2 . . . . 109 A2
Josey Cl RG4. . . . . . . 252 F6
Joslin Cres 🔟 OX11. . . 200 C2
Jourdain Rd OX4. . . . . 142 F3
Jowett Wlk OX1. . . . . 261 C3
Joyce Green RG9. . . . 224 E1
Joyces Rd SN7. . . . . . 194 D8
Joyce Way
  Steventon OX13. . . . . 198 D5
  Steventon OX13. . . . . 199 A5
Jubilee Ave OX14. . . . 199 D4
Jubilee Cl OX25 . . . . . .62 A8
Jubilee Cotts OX12. . . 215 E5
Jubilee Ct OX16 . . . . . 16 D5
Jubilee Gdns
  Thame OX9 . . . . 147 D8
  Wantage OX12 . . . . . 214 B5
Jubilee La OX7 . . . . . . .85 A8
Jubilee Rd HP14. . . . . 188 F3

Jubilee Terr OX1 . . . . . 261 B1
Jubilee Way
Didcot OX11 . . . . 219 A8
Witney OX28 . . . . 104 E1
Jubliee Wy OX26 . . . . . 66 A2
Judds Cl OX28 . . . . 118 D8
Judges Cl OX5 . . . . 108 D8
Judges Rd RG9 . . . . 241 E4
Jugglers Cl OX16 . . . . . 16 E8
Junction Rd
Banbury OX16 . . . . 16 E6
Churchill OX7. . . . . 55 E4
Oxford OX4 . . . . 142 D6
Juniper Cl OX16 . . . . . . 9 B1
Juniper Ct
4 Abingdon-on-Thames
OX14 . . . . 179 D7
4 Banbury OX16 . . . . 16 D5
Juniper Dr OX4 . . . . . . 142 B8
Juniper Gdns OX26 . . . . 65 E5
JUNIPER HILL. 37 D6
Juniper Rd RG31 . . . . . 257 D2
Juniper Way OX11 . . . . 200 B1
Juxon St OX2. . . . . 261 A4

K

Kames Cl OX4 . . . . 142 B5
Karenza HP14 . . . . 188 E5
Kassam Stad (Oxford Utd
FC) OX4. . . . . 142 D1
Katchside OX14. . . . . . . 199 F6
Katherine's Wlk GL7 . . 150 D4
Kaye Ct OX7 . . . . 73 C4
Kearsey Ct OX7. . . . . . . 73 C4
Keats Cl **4** OX26 . . . . . 65 C4
Keats Dr OX11 . . . . 218 B8
Keats Rd OX16. . . . . 16 A4
Keble Cl GL7 . . . . 150 D5
Keble Coll OX1 . . . . . . 261 B4
Keble Rd Bicester OX26 . . 65 F3
Oxford OX1 . . . . 261 B4
Kedge Rd RG4. . . . . . . 252 E5
Kedleston Rise OX16. . . . 16 E2
Keel Dr Townsend OX12 194 F2
Townsend OX12 . . . . . . 194 F2
Keele Cl OX25 . . . . 63 B8
Keene Cl OX4 . . . . 161 B8
Keens Cl OX7. . . . . 58 F5
Keens La OX39 . . . . . . 168 D6
Keepers Cl OX16. . . . . . 16 D1
Keeys Cl OX27. . . . . 50 C4
Kelburne Rd OX4 . . . . . 142 B4
Kelham Hall Dr OX33 . 144 B7
Kellogg Coll (Norham
Manor) OX2. . . . . 123 C4
Kelly's Rd OX33. . . . . . 143 F8
KELMSCOTT 151 D3
Kelmscott Cl RG4. . . . . 258 F3
Kelmscott Manor★
GL7. . . . . 151 E2
Kelmscott Rd
Kelmscott GL7. . . . . . . 151 B3
Lechlade-on-Thames
GL7. . . . . 150 F3
Kelso Mews RG4. . . . . 259 E6
Kelso Rd OX26. . . . . 80 C8
Kelvedon Way RG4 . . . 258 F3
Kempson Cres OX4 . . . 142 A2
Kemps Rd OX17 . . . . . . 23 A5
Kempster Cl OX14 . . . . 180 B8
Kempton Cl OX26. . . . . . 65 B1
Ken Bellringer Wy
OX11. . . . . 200 B2
KENCOT 132 F5
Kendal Ave RG4 . . . . . 259 E5
Kendall Cres OX2. . . . . 109 B1
Kendal Piece OX7 . . . . . 73 C4
Kenhill Rd OX15. . . . . . . 6 E2
Kenilworth Cl OX4 . . . . 142 B4
Kenilworth Mws OX4 . . 142 A7
Kenilworth Rd OX4 . . . 142 A7
Kenilworth Way OX16. . . 15 F5
Kenley Ave OX18 . . . . . 115 E3
Kennedy Cl OX4 . . . . . 142 E7
Kennedy Cres OX10. . . . 220 F1
Kennedy Dr RG8. . . . . . 256 E5
Kennedy Ho OX16 . . . . . 16 B6
Kennedy Rd OX26. . . . . . 65 B1
Kennel Cottages NN13. . 38 A3
Kennel La OX13. . . . . . 199 A5
Kennels La OX7. . . . . . . 42 B2
Kennet Cl
Berinsfield OX10. . . . . . 182 C4
Bicester OX26 . . . . 65 D1
Grove OX12 . . . . 196 D1
Kennet Rd
Abingdon-on-Thames
OX14 . . . . 160 B1
Harwell OX11 . . . . 217 C1
Kennett Pl **3** OX11 . . . 219 A8
Kennett Rd OX3 . . . . . . 124 D2
Kennetts Hos OX15 . . . . 21 D4
KENNINGTON. 160 E7
Kennington Rd
Kennington OX1 . . . . . . 141 E2
Kennington OX1, OX14 . . 160 E5
Radley OX14 . . . . 160 E5
Kennington Rdbt OX1. . 141 D3
Kennylands Rd RG4. . . 253 A3
Kensington Cl
Abingdon-on-Thames
OX14 . . . . 179 E4
Kings Sutton OX17 . . . . 23 F6
Kent Cl
Abingdon-on-Thames
OX14 . . . . 180 B8
Bicester OX26. . . . . 65 D1
Kent Mws OX12. . . . . . 214 D4
Kentons La RG10. . . . . 255 D8

Kenton's La RG10. . . . . 255 D7
Kents Bank OX29 . . . . 106 C8
Kentwood Cl
Cholsey OX10 . . . . 220 F1
Reading RG30 . . . . 257 E1
Kentwood Hill RG31 . . 257 E1
Kenville Rd OX1 . . . . . 141 D2
Kernham Dr RG31 . . . . 257 C4
Kerry Cl **2** OX16. . . . . . . 9 A1
Kersington Cres OX4 . 142 D3
Kerwood Cl OX20. . . . . . 91 C7
Keston Cl RG4. . . . . . . 259 C2
Kestrel Cl OX18. . . . . . 115 D3
Kestrel Cres
Oxford OX4 . . . . 142 D2
Witney OX28. . . . . 103 F1
Kestrel Pl OX49. . . . . . 186 A2
Kestrels The OX12 . . . . 196 D2
Kestrel Way OX26 . . . . . 81 A7
Kestrel Wy OX11. . . . . . 200 B2
Ketchmere Cl HP18 . . . 129 C6
Kethero OX7 . . . . 85 D7
Kew Win OX1. . . . . 201 A2
Keydale Rd OX33 . . . . . 143 F8
Keyser Rd OX15 . . . . 22 E8
Keyte's Cl OX17. . . . . . . 23 B4
Kibble Cl OX11 . . . . . . 219 A8
KIDDINGTON. 60 B2
Kiddington Dr
Kiddington OX20 . . . . . . 59 F1
Spelsbury OX7. . . . . 74 D7
Kiddington Rd
Middle Barton OX7 . . . . 60 E5
Middle Barton OX7 . . . . 60 B6
Over Kiddington OX20. . . 60 A1
KIDLINGTON 108 D7
Kidlington & Gosford
Sports Ctr OX5. . . . . . 108 F7
Kidlington Rd OX5. . . . . 93 D1
KIDMORE END 252 D3
Kidmore End CE Prim Sch
RG4. . . . . 252 D3
Kidmore End Rd RG4 . 259 B7
Kidmore La RG4. . . . . . 252 E4
Kidmore Rd RG4. . . . . . 258 F5
Kilbale Cres OX16 . . . . . 16 D4
Kildare Gdns OX4 . . . . 259 C3
Kilkenny La OX18. . . . . 115 E6
Kiln Ave OX39 . . . . . . 168 D5
Kiln Cl Aston OX18. . . . 135 D3
Sandford-on-Thames
OX4. . . . . 161 C8
Stanford in the Vale
SN7. . . . . 174 E1
Kiln Cres OX11 . . . . . . 235 C8
Kiln La Drayton OX14 . . 179 B1
Garsington OX44. . . . . . 143 C2
Shiplake Row RG9. . . . . 254 C2
Wheatley OX33. . . . . . 144 A8
Kiln Rd RG4 . . . . 259 D8
Kiln Terr SN7. . . . . 173 B3
Kimbells La HP18 . . . . 128 D2
Kimber Cl OX33 . . . . . 144 B8
Kimberley Villas **12**
OX16. . . . . 16 D5
Kimber Rd OX14. . . . . . 179 C7
Kimbers Cl OX12 . . . . . 196 A4
Kimmeridge Rd OX2. . . 140 A5
Kimmeridge Way **3**
SN7. . . . . 172 E1
Kinecroft OX10 . . . . . . 221 D7
Kineton Rd OX1 . . . . . 141 C7
King Alfred Dr OX1 . . . 200 F1
King Alfred's Acad (Centre
Site) OX12 . . . . 214 D4
King Alfred's Acad (East
Site) OX12 . . . . 214 F4
King Alfred's Sch (West
Site) OX12 . . . . 214 B4
King Cl OX44 . . . . 184 E6
King Edward St OX1 . . 261 C2
Kingerlee Rd OX17 . . . . . 8 E1
Kingfisher Cl OX14 . . . 179 F5
Kingfisher Dr
Banbury OX16 . . . . 16 E3
Didcot OX11 . . . . 200 C2
Witney OX28. . . . . 118 A6
Kingfisher Gn OX4. . . . 142 F1
Kingfishers OX12 . . . . . 214 E8
Kingfisher Sch OX14. . . 180 B8
Kingfisher Way OX26 . . 81 A8
KINGHAM. 55 A4
Kingham Dr OX18. . . . . 115 D2
Kingham Hill OX7. . . . . . 55 B8
Kingham Hill Sch OX7. . . 41 B1
Kingham Prim Sch OX7 . 55 A5
Kingham Rd OX7 . . . . . . 55 E5
Kingham Sta OX7. . . . . . 54 F2
King Henry Ave OX10 . . 221 A8
King James Way RG9 . . 254 C8
Kings Acre RG10. . . . . 255 F2
Kings Ave Bicester OX26 65 D1
Highworth SN6 . . . . 190 A5
Marcham OX13 . . . . . . 178 D7
Kings Cl Ashbury SN6 . . 228 A7
Benson OX10. . . . . 203 F5
Henley-on-Thames RG9. . 244 D2
Letcombe Regis OX12. . . 214 A2
Worminghall HP18 . . . . 127 D5
King's Cl OX9. . . . . 147 F8
Kingsclere Rd OX26 . . . . 65 D2
Kings Common Cl
RG9 . . . . 254 B1
Kings Copse Pk OX44 . 143 C1
King's Cross Rd OX2. . . 123 B7
Kings Ct OX18 . . . . 115 E3
KING'S END 65 D1
King's End OX26. . . . . . . 65 D1
Kingsey Rd Thame OX9 148 B8
Towersey OX9 . . . . 130 D1

Kings Farm Cl SN7. . . 192 C3
Kings Farm La RG9 . . . 253 E6
Kingsfield Cres OX28 . 104 C1
Kingsgate OX4 . . . . . . 142 D4
King's Head Ct OX7. . . . . 42 E3
King's Head La OX5 . . . . 93 F1
Kingsholm OX11 . . . . . 218 F5
Kingside OX12. . . . . . . 194 F2
Kingsland Rd OX16 . . . . 16 E7
Kingsley Rd **5** OX26 . . 65 C4
Kingsmead GL7. . . . . . 150 C5
Kings Meadow Ind Est
OX2 . . . . 140 F8
Kings Meadow Prim Sch
OX26 . . . . 65 B3
King's Mill La OX3. . . . 123 F2
Kings Mws RG8. . . . . . 249 C6
King's Orch OX10 . . . . 202 E3
King's Oxford (St Josephs)
5 OX4. . . . . 142 D6
King's Oxford (St
Michaels) OX1 . . . . . 261 B2
Kings Rd Bloxham OX15 . . 21 D7
Henley-on-Thames RG9. . 244 E2
King's Rd Banbury OX16. .16 B6
Henley-on-Thames RG9. . 244 D2
Reading RG4 . . . . 259 C2
Kings Row HP14 . . . . . 188 E5
King's Sch The OX29 . . 104 D3
Kings Stile OX17. . . . . . 10 F1
KINGS SUTTON 23 F6
Kings Sutton Rd OX17 . .17 E4
Kings Sutton Sta OX17. . 23 E5
King St
Abingdon-on-Thames
OX14 . . . . 179 D4
2 Faringdon SN7. . . . 172 D1
Oxford OX1 . . . . 123 B3
Oxford OX1 . . . . 261 A4
KINGSTON
BAGPUIZE 156 E2
Kingston Bagpuize
House★ 176 E8
KINGSTON BLOUNT . . 167 F3
Kingston Blount Rd
HP14 . . . . 188 B7
Kingston Bsns Pk
OX13. . . . . 176 F8
Kingston Business Pk
OX13. . . . . 177 A8
Kingston Cl OX14. . . . . 179 F8
Kingston Cl OX2. . . . . . 261 A4
Kingston Dr OX26. . . . . . 65 B1
KINGSTONE
WINSLOW 228 B8
Kingston Hill
Chinnor OX49 . . . . 167 F2
Stokenchurch OX39. . . . 188 B8
Kingston Hts OX29. . . . 105 B7
KINGSTON LISLE 212 A4
Kingston Lisle Bsns Ctr
OX12 . . . . 212 B4
Kingston Rd
Frilford OX13. . . . . 177 D7
Oxford OX2 . . . . 123 B4
KINGSTON STERT 167 D7
Kingsway Banbury OX16. .16 E5
Reading RG4 . . . . 259 E6
Kingsway Cotts OX16 . 135 D2
Kingsway Dr OX5 . . . . 109 A8
Kings Wlk
Henley-on-Thames
RG9 . . . . 244 D2
Wantage OX12 . . . . . . 214 D5
Kingswood La
Ludgershall HP18 . . . . . 98 F6
Swinbrook OX18 . . . . . 85 D1
Swinbrook OX18 . . . . . 101 C8
Swinbrook OX18 . . . . . 101 E7
King Wlk OX11 . . . . . . 200 E2
Kinson Rd RG30 . . . . . 258 A1
Kipling Cl OX26. . . . . . . 65 C4
Kirby Cl
Middle Barton OX7 . . . . 60 F8
South Moreton OX11. . . 219 F5
Kirby Pl OX14 . . . . 142 D5
Kirk Cl Cutteslowe OX2. . 109 A1
Kennington OX1 . . . . . . 160 E8
Reading RG31 . . . . 257 D3
Kirkfell Cl RG31. . . . . . 257 C2
Kirkham Cl RG4 . . . . . 259 E6
Kirlington Rd OX26 . . . . 78 E8
KIRTLINGTON. 77 F4
Kirtlington CE Prim Sch
OX5 . . . . 78 A4
Kirtlington Quarry Nature
Reserve★ OX5 . . . . . . 77 C4
Kirtlington Rd
Chesterton OX26. . . . . . 79 A8
Lower Heyford OX25. . . . 62 F4
Upper Heyford OX25. . . . 63 A7
KITEBROOK. 26 D3
Kitebrook End Rd GL56 26 C3
Kitebrook House Sch
GL56. . . . . 26 C3
Kit La RG8. . . . . 241 D6
Knapp Cl OX14 . . . . . . 179 D8
Knappe Cl RG9 . . . . . . 254 C8
Knaptons Croft OX25 . . 62 D6
KNIGHTON 210 E3
Knighton Cl RG4. . . . . . 259 A3
Knighton Hill SN6 . . . . 210 E1
Knighton Way OX26 . . . 65 B1
Knightsbridge La
OX49. . . . . 186 B5
Knights Gn OX12 . . . . . 194 F2
Knights Ho OX1 . . . . . . 124 F2
Knights Rd OX4. . . . . . 142 E2

Knights Way RG4 . . . . 259 B5
Knoll Cl OX12. . . . . . . 231 E7
Knolles Dr SN7. . . . . . . 194 D7
Knolles Rd OX4. . . . . . 142 C5
Knoll The RG31. . . . . . 257 B2
Knollys Cl OX14. . . . . . 160 A3
Knott Oaks OX29 . . . . . 89 F5
Knowlands SN6. . . . . . 190 A7
Knowle Cl RG4 . . . . . . 258 D4
KNOWLE END 2 A5
Knowle La OX25 . . . . . . 79 B1
Knowsley Rd RG31. . . . 257 C3
Krebs Gdns OX4 . . . . . 142 A4
Kybald St OX1 . . . . . . 261 C2
Kyetts Cnr OX17 . . . . . . 4 F2
Kynaston Rd
Didcot OX11 . . . . 218 F8
12 Didcot OX11. . . . . . 219 A8
Kysbie Cl OX14 . . . . . 159 F3

L

Laburnum Ave OX13 . . 159 C1
Laburnum Cl
Ambrosden OX25 . . . . . 81 C3
Carterton OX18. . . . . . 115 F4
Laburnum Cres OX5 . . 108 E6
Laburnum Gr
Banbury OX16. . . . . 16 D2
Didcot OX11 . . . . 218 F8
Laburnum Rd OX2 . . . 140 D7
Lacemakers
Chinnor OX39 . . . . 168 C6
Long Crendon HP18 . . . 129 C7
Lacey Cres OX44. . . . . 184 E6
Lacey Dr OX9. . . . . 148 B7
Lackmore Gdns RG8. . . 250 F8
Ladburn La
Bradwell Grove OX18 . . 114 F7
Shilton OX18 . . . . 115 A6
Ladder Hill OX33 . . . . . 144 A7
Ladenham Rd OX4. . . . 142 E3
Ladies Wlk RG9. . . . . . 224 A8
Ladman Villas SN7. . . . 173 E7
Ladycroft Pk OX11. . . . 219 A1
Lady Gr OX11, OX11 . . 201 B4
Ladygrove Cl OX14 . . . 179 D6
Ladygrove Paddock
OX14 . . . . 179 D6
Ladygrove Park Prim Sch
OX11. . . . . 200 F2
Lady Jane Ct RG4. . . . . 259 B3
Lady Margaret Hall
OX2 . . . . 123 D4
Lady Pl OX14 . . . . 200 A8
Ladywell Cl OX29 . . . . 105 C6
Lady Wlk SN7 . . . . 211 C7
Laggots Cl SN7 . . . . . . 155 F2
Lains Ct OX12 . . . . 214 D7
Lakefield Rd OX4. . . . . 142 B1
Lake Rd
East Hagbourne OX11. . 218 E6
Shrivenham SN6 . . . . . 209 D7
Lake Sch of English The
OX1 . . . . 261 A2
Lakeside
Cutteslowe OX2. . . . . . 108 C3
Witney OX28. . . . . 118 A6
Lakeside Ind Est OX29 137 F7
Lakeside Rd OX39 . . . . 168 D5
Lakesmere Cl OX5. . . . . 92 C2
Lake St OX1 . . . . 141 D6
Lake View NN13. . . . . . . 38 A3
Lakeview Dr OX26 . . . . . 80 D8
Lake Wlk OX17 . . . . 23 B4
Lamarsh Rd OX4. . . . . 122 E1
Lambe Ave OX14 . . . . 199 C3
Lambert Wlk OX9 . . . . 129 F1
Lamb La OX20. . . . . 91 B2
Lamble Wlk OX12. . . . 197 C7
Lamborough Hill
OX13. . . . . 159 B6
Lambourne Cres OX26 . 65 F1
Lambourne Rd RG4. . . 252 E5
Lambourne Way OX17 . 23 A4
Lambrick Way OX14 . . 179 E4
Lambourn Rd OX4 . . . 142 A3
Lambridge La RG9. . . . 244 D3
Lambridge Wood Rd
RG9 . . . . 244 B4
Lambs Cl OX5 . . . . 92 E2
Lamb's Cres OX16 . . . . 16 E4
Lambs La OX20. . . . . . . 75 F4
Lambton Cl OX4 . . . . . 142 E7
Lambwath Stream
OX11. . . . . 200 F2
Lammas Cl OX14 . . . . 159 F1
Lammas Land OX13. . . 199 B8
Lamorna Cres RG31. . . 257 C1
Lampitts Gn OX15 . . . . 15 A8
Lancaster Ave OX10 . . 204 D3
Lancaster Cl OX26 . . . . 66 A4
Lancaster Dr
Stanton Harcourt
OX29. . . . . 138 A7
Upper Rissington GL54. . 68 B4
Lancaster Pl OX18 . . . . 115 E1
Lanchester Dr OX16 . . . 15 F4
Lancott La OX29 . . . . . 137 B4
Lancut Rd OX28 . . . . . 103 E1
Landells OX18 . . . . . . 134 E4
Lander Cl OX26 . . . . . . 79 F7
Landscape Cl OX25 . . . 79 A5
Landscape Rd OX25. . . 79 A5
Landseer Wlk OX14. . . 179 E5
Lane Cl Horley OX15 . . 8 B4
Lane The Horley OX15 . . 8 B4
Kidlington OX5. . . . . . . 108 D8
Lane End OX10 . . . . . . 222 A7
Lane Ness OX10 . . . . . 203 E5
Lanes End OX26 . . . . . . 66 C2
Langton Bsns Ctr OX26 66 A2

Lanes The OX18 . . . . . 134 F1
Lane The Ashbury SN6 . 228 A7
Lane The GL56 . . . . 40 D7
Chilton OX11 . . . . 235 E8
Cuddesdon OX44. . . . . 144 B2
Fritwell OX27. . . . . 49 F7
Great Tew OX7 . . . . 45 C7
Great Tew OX7 . . . . 45 C7
Hempton OX15 . . . . 33 B4
Hinton Parva SN4 . . . . 227 A4
Lower Heyford OX25. . . . 62 D6
Uffington SN7 . . . . . . 211 C7
Woolstone SN7 . . . . . . 211 A5
Langdale Ct OX28 . . . . 118 B8
Langdale Gate OX28 . . 118 B8
Langdale Rd
Thame OX9 . . . . 130 B1
Thame OX9 . . . . 148 A8
LANGFORD 132 C2
Langford Bsns Pk The
OX5 . . . . 92 B2
Langford Cl RG4. . . . . 259 C5
Langford Gdns OX26. . . 65 C2
Langford La
Bicester OX25 . . . . 80 C4
Bicester OX25 . . . . 80 E3
Kidlington OX5. . . . . . . 92 A2
Wendlebury OX25. . . . . 80 D5
Langford Locks
Kidlington OX5. . . . . . . 92 C2
Kidlington OX5. . . . . . . 92 C2
Langford Village CP Sch
OX26 . . . . 81 A8
Langford Way
Freeland OX29 . . . . 106 A8
1 Long Hanborough
OX29 . . . . 90 A1
Langhams Way RG10 . . 255 E2
LANGLEY 86 C4
Langley Cl OX3 . . . . . . 124 D2
Langley La OX18. . . . . 152 D5
Langley Rd
Abingdon-on-Thames
OX14. . . . . 159 F2
Chalgrove OX44. . . . . . 184 C6
Langleys La OX29. . . . . 137 C1
Langston Cl OX7. . . . . . 55 E5
Langston Priory
Workshops OX7. . . . . . 54 F2
Langton Ave OX26 . . . . 81 A4
Langtree Sch RG8 . . . 250 F8
Lanham Way OX4. . . . . 142 B2
Lansdown Cl OX16. . . . . 16 B3
Lansdowne Rd OX3 . . . 159 A6
Lansdown Rd SN7 . . . . 173 A3
Lapsley Dr OX16. . . . . . . 9 C2
Lapwing Cl OX26 . . . . . 81 A8
Lapwing La
Cholsey OX10 . . . . 221 A1
Watchfield SN6 . . . . . . 191 D2
Larch Cl Bicester OX26. . 65 E4
Kingston Bagpuize
OX13. . . . . 156 E1
Oxford OX2 . . . . 140 D8
Larch Ct RG4 . . . . 259 B3
Larch Dr Didcot OX11. . . 218 C7
Larch End OX44 . . . . . 143 D2
Larches The
Carterton OX18. . . . . . 115 C2
Oxford OX3 . . . . 125 A3
Larch La OX26 . . . . . . 104 D1
Lardon Cotts RG8. . . . . 249 A6
Larissa Cl RG31. . . . . . 257 E1
Larkdown OX12. . . . . . 214 F4
Larkfield Cholsey OX10. . 220 F1
Cholsey OX10 . . . . 221 A1
Larkfields OX3 . . . . . . 124 E2
Lark Hill
Ardington OX12. . . . . . 215 A2
Oxford OX2 . . . . 123 A6
Lark Hill Dr OX18 . . . . 116 A4
Larkhill Pl OX14 . . . . . 159 D1
Larkhill Rd OX14. . . . . 179 D8
Larkins La OX3 . . . . . . 124 D4
Larkmead Sch OX14 . . 179 C8
Lark Rise Ct NN13 . . . . 37 F3
Larkrise Prim Sch
OX14 . . . . 142 A6
Larksfield Cl OX18 . . . 133 C8
Larkspur Gr OX26 . . . . 104 E1
Larkspur Sq OX26 . . . . 65 E4
Larkswood Cl RG31. . . 257 D3
Larsen Cl OX25 . . . . . . 63 D8
LASHBROOK 255 B4
Lashbrook Mead RG9 . 255 B4
Lashbrook Rd RG9 . . . 255 B4
Lashford La OX13 . . . . 158 F7
Lashlake Rd OX9 . . . . . 129 F1
Latcham Ct OX7 . . . . . . 43 A3
Latchford La OX44 . . . 164 F7
Lathbury Rd OX2 . . . . 123 B5
Lathbur Dr SN6. . . . . . 191 F1
Latimer Grange
Oxford OX3 . . . . 124 C2
Oxford OX3 . . . . 124 C2
Latimer Rd
Carterton OX18. . . . . . 115 E2
Oxford OX3 . . . . 124 C2
Latton Cl OX13 . . . . . . 156 D1
Laud's Cl RG9 . . . . 244 C1
Launceston Ave RG4. . 259 E6
Laundry Cotts GL56. . . . 40 C7
Laundry Dr SN6. . . . . . 191 F1
Sandford St Martin OX7. 46 C1
Sandford St Martin OX7. 46 B2

Jub–Len 275

Launton CE Prim Sch
OX26 . . . . 66 D2
Launton Rd
Bicester OX26. . . . . 66 A3
Stratton Audley OX27. . . 66 D8
Launton Road Ret Pk
. . . . 66 B3
Laureate Gdns **2**
RG9 . . . . 244 D1
Laurel Cl Banbury OX16 . 16 D1
Carterton OX18. . . . . . 115 D3
Chalgrove OX44. . . . . . 184 D7
Laurel Cres OX12 . . . . 214 E8
Laurel Ct OX4 . . . . 142 A8
Laurel Dr Hornton OX15. . 6 E1
Kingston Bagpuize
OX13. . . . . 156 E1
Laurel Farm Cl OX3. . . 124 C4
Laurels The
Fringford OX27 . . . . 52 C6
Great Coxwell SN7 . . . 192 C8
Pangbourne RG8. . . . . 256 D5
Sonning RG5 . . . . 260 E1
Stadhampton OX44 . . . 163 C2
Tetsworth OX9. . . . . . . 166 B8
Laurence Allison Mews
RG4 . . . . 258 C2
Lavender Cl OX16. . . . . . 9 B1
Lavender Pl
Bampton OX18 . . . . . . 134 F3
Carterton OX18. . . . . . 115 C2
Lavender Rd OX25 . . . . 81 D4
Lavender Sq OX18 . . . . 134 F3
Lavender View
Witney OX28. . . . . 104 D2
Witney OX28. . . . . 104 E2
Lawns The HP18. . . . . . 98 B1
Lawn Upton Cl **5** OX4 142 B2
Lawrence Ave SN6. . . . 209 B7
Lawrence Cl
Banbury OX16. . . . . 9 D2
Childrey OX12 . . . . 213 C4
Lawrence Fields OX25 . 62 B8
Lawrence La OX18. . . . 100 E5
Lawrence Leys OX15. . . 21 E5
Lawrence Rd OX4 . . . . 142 C5
Lawrence Way OX26 . . . 65 C2
Lawson Dr RG4. . . . . . 258 C5
Lawson Rd RG9. . . . . . 254 F7
Lawton Ave OX18 . . . . 115 C2
Laxton Way OX16. . . . . . 8 F1
Lay Ave OX10. . . . . . . 182 C6
Laytom Rise RG31 . . . 257 C3
Leabrook Cl OX16 . . . . . 16 D2
Leach Rd
Berinsfield OX10. . . . . . 182 D5
Bicester OX26. . . . . 65 C2
Leadent Dr OX12 . . . . 213 C3
Leadholm Cl OX17 . . . . 23 F5
LEAFIELD. 86 E3
Leafield CE Prim Sch
OX29 . . . . 86 F3
Leafield Rd
Crawley OX29 . . . . 103 C5
Oxford OX4 . . . . 142 C6
Ramsden Heath OX7. . . 87 E4
Shipton-under-Wychwood OX7,
OX29. . . . . 86 B5
Leafield Tech Ctr OX29 .86 C3
Lea Gr OX11 . . . . 200 F2
Lea La HP18 . . . . 129 F4
Leamington Dr SN7. . . 172 E2
Leander Way OX1 . . . . 141 E4
Lea Rd RG4. . . . . 252 F5
Leas La OX13 . . . . 178 D7
Leaver Rd RG9 . . . . . . 244 C1
Lechlade Ct GL7. . . . . . 150 E3
LECHLADE-ON-
THAMES 150 D3
Lechlade Rd
Burford OX18 . . . . 100 F3
Buscot SN7 . . . . 171 C7
Faringdon SN7. . . . . . . 172 C5
Highworth SN6 . . . . . . 190 A7
Highworth SN6 . . . . . . 190 A8
Langford GL7. . . . . 132 A2
Lechlade-on-Thames
GL7. . . . . 151 A7
Lechlade-on-Thames GL7,
SN7. . . . . 150 B2
Upper Inglesham SN6. . 170 A6
Leckford Pl OX2 . . . . . 261 A4
Leckford Rd OX2 . . . . 261 A4
Ledbury Cl RG30. . . . . 258 C1
Ledgers Cl OX14 . . . . . 142 C2
LEDWELL. 46 C5
Ledwell Rd
Great Tew OX7 . . . . 45 E6
Sandford St Martin OX7. 46 A5
Sandford St Martin OX7. 46 B2
Lee Ave OX14. . . . . . . 180 B8
Lee Cl Charlbury OX7. . . 73 C3
Kidlington OX5. . . . . . . 92 D2
Lee Ct OX9 . . . . 147 F8
Lee Rd HP27. . . . . 169 F6
Lees Hts OX7 . . . . 73 C3
Lees The SN7 . . . . 172 F3
Le Hall Pl OX17. . . . . . . 22 F1
Leicester Cl RG9. . . . . 244 D3
Leiden Rd OX3 . . . . . . 142 E4
Leigh Cl OX29 . . . . . . 105 B5
Leigh Croft OX13 . . . . 159 A7
Leigh Gr OX16. . . . . 16 C5
Lely Ct OX4. . . . . 179 E5
Lemongrass Rd OX27 . . 65 D7
Lennox Gdns OX16. . . . 16 A4

Lenthal OX5 .... 93 A7
Lenthall Rd
Abingdon-on-Thames OX14 .... 179 F8
Oxford OX4 .... 141 F3
Lenton Rd OX16 .... 16 D2
Leoline Jenkins Ho OX4 .... 142 B7
Leon Cl OX4 .... 141 F8
Leopold St OX4 .... 142 A7
Lerwick Croft OX26 .... 66 A4
Leslie Harvey Cl OX29. 117 C8
Lesparre Cl OX14 .... 179 B2
Lester Cl OX17 .... 23 A6
Lester Way OX10 .... 221 B7
Letchmere Cl OX5 .... 77 C6
Letcombe Ave OX14 .. 179 F8
LETCOMBE BASSETT. 231 F7
Letcombe Ct OX12 .... 214 E4
Letcombe Hill OX12 ... 214 A4
Letcombe Rd OX12 ... 214 B3
LETCOMBE REGIS 214 B2
Letcombe Wlk OX12 .. 196 D1
Level The OX15 .... 6 E2
Levenot Cl OX16 .... 16 F6
Leveret Pl OX28 .... 103 F1
Leverkus Ho OX39 .... 168 C6
Leverton Gdns OX12 .. 214 C5
Levery Cl OX14 .... 180 C8
LEW 117 B1
Lewell Ave OX3 .... 123 F4
Lewendon Hill RG8 ... 248 E4
Lewin Cl 1 OX4 .... 142 C4
Lewington Cl OX44 ... 164 D8
Lewis Cl OX3 .... 125 A2
Lewisfield Way OX20 .. 91 D6
Lewis Rd OX7 .... 42 D2
LEWKNOR 187 B8
Lewknor CE Prim Sch OX49 .... 187 B8
Lewknor Cl OX49 .... 187 A7
Leyburne Gdns OX39 .. 168 C7
Leyesland Ct OX16 .... 16 D3
Leyes The OX15 .... 33 F4
Leys App OX7 .... 42 E2
Leys Cl OX15 .... 15 A8
Leys Field OX25 .... 81 E4
Leys Ho OX16 .... 16 C6
Leyshon Rd OX33 .... 144 C7
Leys Pl OX4 .... 142 A7
Leys Rd OX2 .... 139 C5
LEYS THE 118 A7
Leys The
Adderbury OX17 .... 22 F3
Chipping Norton OX7 ... 42 D2
Lyneham OX7 .... 70 E5
Salford OX7 .... 41 F5
Leys View GL7 .... 132 E1
Leys Villas OX28 .... 118 A7
Ley The OX20 .... 91 C6
Liberator Cl OX29 .... 138 A7
Liberator La OX12 .... 214 C8
Liberty Cl OX28 .... 117 E8
Library Ave OX11 .... 217 B2
Liddell Rd OX4 .... 142 C4
Liddiard Cl
Kennington OX1 .... 160 E8
Wantage OX12 .... 214 D6
Liddiard's Row 7 SN7 172 F3
Liddon Rd OX44 .... 184 D6
Lido Rd OX11 .... 234 F8
Lidsey Rd OX16 .... 16 A5
LIDSTONE 58 B6
Lidstone Rd OX7 .... 58 D5
Lilac Cl RG8 .... 257 C5
Lilac Way 4 OX18 .... 115 E4
Lily Cl OX26 .... 65 D5
Limbeck Way OX29 .... 89 D8
Limborough Rd OX12 . 214 D5
Lime Ave Banbury OX16 . 16 E4
Stoke Row RG9 .... 242 A1
Lime Cres OX26 .... 65 F5
Lime Ct 3 RG9 .... 254 E8
Lime Gr Chinnor OX39 .. 168 D6
Kingston Bagpuize OX13 .... 156 D1
Milton under Wychwood OX7 .... 85 A8
Lime Kiln OX12 .... 214 C6
Lime Kiln Rd OX5 .... 77 C5
Lime Rd OX2 .... 140 D7
Limes The
Crowmarsh Gifford OX10 .... 221 F7
Dorchester OX10 .... 182 D2
Minster Lovell OX29 ... 102 E2
Stratton Audley OX27 ... 52 D1
Limestone La 7 SN7 . 172 E1
Limes Way HP18 .... 128 D2
Limetree Cl OX12 .... 196 D1
Lime Tree Cl OX18 .... 115 D3
Lime Tree Rd RG8 .... 249 B6
Limetrees OX11 .... 217 E1
Lime Walk OX11 .... 200 B1
Lime Wlk Oxford OX3 .. 124 C2
Witney OX28 .... 104 E1
Limmings La OX9 .... 148 A6
Linacre Cl OX11 .... 219 B8
Linacre Coll OX1 .... 261 C3
Linacre Ct OX3 .... 124 F2
Lince La OX5 .... 77 E2
Linch Farm OX2 .... 122 B6
Linch Hill Fishery★ OX29 .... 138 B5
Lincoln Cl Banbury OX16 .16 B6
Bicester OX26 .... 66 A4
Standlake OX29 .... 137 D4
Upper Rissington GL54 .. 68 B4
Lincoln Coll OX1 .... 261 B2
Lincoln Gdns OX11 ... 219 B8
Lincoln Grove OX20 .... 91 B3
Lincoln Pk NN13 .... 24 A5
Lincoln Pl OX9 .... 147 F8
Lincoln Rd OX1 .... 141 D5
Lincombe La OX1 .... 159 E7
Lincraft Cl OX5 .... 108 E7
Linden Cotts RG8 .... 250 E2
Linden Cres OX12 .... 196 F1
Linden Ct OX3 .... 124 D3
Linden Gate OX11 .... 217 E7
Linden Gdns OX18 .... 115 D6
Linden Rd OX26 .... 65 F2
Lindh Rd OX25 .... 63 C8
Lindsay Dr OX14 .... 160 B2
Lingfield Rd OX26 .... 65 B1
Lingwell Cl OX39 .... 168 C5
Linkside Ave OX2 .... 108 F2
Links Rd OX1 .... 160 E8
Link The Banbury OX16 .. 16 A6
Marston OX3 .... 123 E4
Oxford OX3 .... 124 F3
Linkwood Rd OX29 ... 103 C1
Linnet Cl
Clifton Hampden OX14 .... 182 B4
Oxford OX4 .... 142 D2
Linnet Gr 11 OX11 .... 218 B6
Linnet Rd OX15 .... 16 F1
Linton Rd OX2 .... 123 C5
Lion Brewery The OX1 .... 261 A2
Lion Cl OX13 .... 178 C6
Lion Mdw RG9 .... 224 D2
Lipscombe Pl OX18 ... 115 D4
Lisa Head Ave OX11 ... 200 B2
Lister Cl RG8 .... 257 C5
Litchfield Cl OX7 .... 58 F5
Little Acreage OX3 .... 123 F6
Little Baldon Farm Cotts OX44 .... 162 B1
LITTLE BARRINGTON ... 99 B6
LITTLE BLENHEIM 108 A5
Little Blenheim OX5 .. 108 B5
LITTLE BOURTON 9 D5
Little Bowden La RG8. 256 A4
Little Brewery St OX4. 123 F1
Little Bridge Rd OX15 .. 21 D4
Littlebrook Mdw OX7 .. 70 D1
Little Bury OX4 .... 143 A2
LITTLE CHESTERTON ... 79 F5
LITTLE CLANFIELD 152 B7
Little Clarendon St
Oxford OX1 .... 123 C3
Oxford OX1 .... 261 B3
LITTLE COMPTON 27 A1
Little Compton La GL56 40 E8
Little Compton Rd GL56 .... 27 A3
LITTLE COXWELL 192 E7
Little Croft Rd RG8 ... 249 C5
Little Ct OX12 .... 214 D7
LITTLE FARINGDON 150 F8
Little Field OX4 .... 142 D3
Littlegate St OX1 .... 261 B1
Little Glebe RG4 .... 260 E3
Little Gn OX15 .... 21 D4
Little Ground OX15 .... 22 C3
LITTLE HASELEY 164 D6
Littlehay Rd OX4 .... 142 B5
LITTLE HEATH 250 C6
Little Henley Field RG9 .... 254 A7
Little Hinton La SN4 .. 227 A3
Little Hitchen OX10 ... 221 F7
Little Howe Cl OX14 .. 160 E3
LITTLE ICKFORD 128 B3
Little Ickford HP18 .... 128 A3
Littlejohn's La RG30 .... 258 C1
Little La Aynho OX17 .... 35 C7
Bledington OX7 .... 54 D2
Brightwell-cum-Sotwell OX11 .... 202 D3
Cholsey OX10 .... 220 F2
Eynsham OX29 .... 120 F8
Horley OX15 .... 8 B4
Milton OX14 .... 199 C5
Wantage OX12 .... 214 D4
Little Langlands OX11 .... 218 F7
Little Lees OX7 .... 73 C3
LITTLE LONDON 160 D8
Little London GL7 .... 150 B4
Little London La OX13 176 C8
Little Martins OX11 ... 202 D3
LITTLE MILTON 164 A6
Little Milton CE Prim Sch OX44 .... 163 F6
LITTLE MINSTER 102 E3
Littlemoor Field OX39 168 C5
LITTLEMORE 142 C1
Littlemore Rd OX4 .... 142 C4
Littlemore Rdbt OX4 .. 142 B3
Little Owl Dr 8 OX15 ... 16 F1
Little Paddock OX27 ... 52 C7
LITTLE ROLLRIGHT 28 A1
Littlestead Cl RG4 .... 259 E5
LITTLESTEAD GREEN. 259 E7
LITTLE TEW 45 A5
Little Tew Rd
Church Enstone OX7 .... 58 F8
Enstone OX20 .... 59 A7
Enstone OX7 .... 44 F1
LITTLE TINGEWICK 39 E6
LITTLE WITTENHAM .. 202 B7
Little Wittenham Rd
Little Wittenham OX14 .... 202 A7
Long Wittenham OX14 . 201 F8
Little Wood HP14 .... 188 E5
Little Woodcote Cl RG4 .... 258 D4
LITTLEWORTH Benson. 203 E4
Littleworth
Faringdon 173 E7
Wheatley 143 F7
Littleworth Bsns Ctr OX33 .... 143 F7
Littleworth Hill OX12 . 214 C5
Littleworth Ind Est OX33 .... 143 F7
Littleworth Pk OX33 .. 143 F8
Littleworth Rd
Benson OX10 .... 203 F4
Wheatley OX33 .... 144 A8
Livingstone Cl OX5 ... 108 B7
Lobelia Rd OX4 .... 142 F2
Lock Approach RG8 .. 249 B6
Lock Cres OX5 .... 108 E6
Lock Ct OX18 .... 116 A4
Lock Dr 4 OX16 .... 16 F4
Lockheart Cres OX4 .. 142 D4
Lockheed Cl OX16 .... 16 C8
Lockinge Cl OX11 .... 218 E7
Locks La OX12 .... 214 C4
Lockstile Mead RG8 .. 249 C6
Lockstile Way RG8 ... 249 C6
Lockway OX14 .... 199 A8
Locombe Hill GL7 .... 131 B8
Lodden Ave OX10 .... 182 C5
Loddon Cl
Abingdon-on-Thames OX14 .... 160 B1
2 Bicester OX26 .... 65 D1
Loddon Dr Didcot OX11 201 B1
Wargrave RG10 .... 255 B1
Loder Rd OX11 .... 217 E7
Lodersfield GL7 .... 150 C4
Lodge Cl Banbury OX16 . 16 D4
Bicester OX26 .... 65 E5
Marston OX3 .... 123 F7
Lodge Hill OX14 .... 160 B4
Lodge Hill Intc OX14 .. 160 B5
Lodge Rd OX29 .... 90 F1
Lodge Terr OX7 .... 42 F3
Logic La OX1 .... 261 C2
Lombard St
5 Abingdon-on-Thames OX14 .... 179 F7
Eynsham OX29 .... 120 E7
Lombard Way OX16 .... 17 A7
Lomond Ave RG4 .... 259 E5
London Ct OX3 .... 124 C2
London La OX7 .... 71 C2
London Oxford Airport OX5 .... 92 A4
London Pl OX4 .... 123 F1
London Rd
Aston Rowant OX49 .. 167 C1
Aston Tirrold OX11 ... 237 E7
Bicester OX26 .... 80 F8
Blewbury OX11 .... 236 E8
Chastleton GL56 .... 40 F8
Chipping Norton OX7 .. 43 B3
Milton Common OX9 .. 146 B3
Moreton-in-Marsh GL56 . 26 B4
Oxford OX3 .... 124 D3
Oxford OX4 .... 124 F3
Postcombe OX9 .... 166 F4
Salford GL56 .... 41 B7
Sonning RG6 .... 260 C1
Tiddington OX9, OX44 . 145 E5
West Hagbourne OX11 . 218 A4
Wheatley OX33 .... 126 A1
Wheatley OX33 .... 144 D7
London St SN7 .... 173 B4
London Wlk OX7 .... 43 A3
London Yd 1 OX16 .... 16 C6
Long Alley Almshouses 10 OX14 .... 179 F6
Long Barn OX14 .... 200 A8
Long Barrow OX17 .... 5 F7
Longbridge RG9 .... 256 D3
Long Cl Oxford OX2 .... 122 B1
Oxford OX3 .... 142 E8
LONG COMPTON 27 F6
LONGCOT 192 C2
Longcot & Fernham CE Prim Sch SN7 .... 192 C2
Longcot Rd
Fernham SN7 .... 192 F4
Fernham SN7 .... 193 A4
Longcot SN7 .... 192 B1
Shrivenham SN6 .... 209 D6
LONG CRENDON 129 B6
Long Crendon Courthouse★ HP18 .... 129 D7
Long Crendon Ind Est HP18 .... 129 E5
Long Crendon Rd HP18 .... 128 D3
Long Crendon Sch HP18 .... 129 C7
Long Dean RG9 .... 254 A7
Longdon Cres 2 OX16 . 16 F3
Longelandes Cl OX16 .. 16 A8
Longelandes Way OX16 16 B8
Longfellow Cl 1 OX26 . 65 C3
Longfellow Dr OX14 .. 179 C5
Longfellow Rd OX16 .... 16 B4
Longfield OX7 .... 47 C5
Longfields Bicester OX26 65 F2
Marcham OX13 .... 178 D7
Longfields Ct OX26 .... 65 F2
Longfields Prim Sch OX26 .... 65 F2
Long Ford Cl OX1 .... 141 C7
Longford Pk Rd
Bodicote OX15 .... 16 F1
Bodicote OX15 .... 16 F1
Bodicote OX15 .... 22 F8
Longford Way OX11 .. 200 F2
Long Furlong HP17 ... 130 F6
Long Furlong Prim Sch OX14 .... 160 A3
Long Furlong Rd OX13 .... 159 D4
Long Ground OX4 .... 142 E1
LONG HANBOROUGH .. 90 B1
Longhurst Cl RG4 .... 259 C3
Long La Oxford OX4 ... 142 C3
Reading RG31 .... 257 B3
Reading RG8 .... 257 A2
Longlands Rd
Bicester OX26 .... 66 B4
Oxford OX4 .... 142 E3
Long Lane Prim Sch RG31 .... 257 B3
Longleat Cl OX16 .... 16 E2
Longleat Dr RG31 .... 257 B3
Long Mdw RG8 .... 249 B5
Longmead OX14 .... 159 E1
Longore
Stonesfield OX29 .... 89 C8
Stonesfield OX29 .... 89 D8
Long Place OX29 .... 106 A8
Long Toll RG8 .... 251 A5
Long Tow OX13 .... 159 D2
Longwall OX4 .... 142 B3
Long Wall HP17 .... 130 F5
Long Wall Cl OX17 .... 23 B4
Longwall St OX1 .... 261 C2
LONG WITTENHAM .. 201 D8
Long Wittenham CE Prim Sch OX14 .... 201 D8
Long Wittenham Rd
Didcot OX11 .... 201 F3
North Moreton OX11 .. 219 F8
LONGWORTH 156 C3
Longworth Cl OX16 .... 16 E7
Longworth Prim Sch OX13 .... 156 C3
Longworth Rd
Charney Bassett OX12 .... 176 A3
Longworth OX13 .... 156 E3
Oxford OX2 .... 261 A4
Lonsdale Ct OX7 .... 29 A3
Lonsdale Rd OX2 .... 123 B7
Loom La 6 OX28 .... 104 A1
Loop Rd GL54 .... 83 A8
Lord Cl OX18 .... 115 D3
Lord Fielding Cl OX16 .... 9 F1
Lord Grandison Way OX16 .... 9 C2
Lords La OX26 .... 65 D5
Lords Piece Rd OX7 ... 42 D1
Lord William's Sch OX9 .... 147 D8
Lord Williams's Sch Lower Sch OX9 .... 148 B8
Lormay Pl NN13 .... 25 A4
Lostock Pl OX11 .... 200 F2
Lovage Vw OX27 .... 65 D7
Lovatt Cl OX18 .... 115 D5
Lovegrove Ave OX12 .. 214 A5
Lovegrove's La RG8 ... 241 C4
Love La OX49 .... 186 B2
Lovelace Cl OX14 .... 160 A3
Lovelace Dr OX5 .... 109 A8
Lovelace Green OX11. 201 B3
Lovelace Rd OX2 .... 109 A1
Lovelace Sq OX2 .... 109 A1
Lovell Cl
Ducklington OX29 .... 118 B4
Henley-on-Thames RG9. 254 C8
Minster Lovell OX29 ... 102 E2
Lovell Way HP17 .... 130 E6
Loverock Rd RG30 .... 258 D1
Lowell Pl OX28 .... 118 A8
Lower Armour Rd RG31 .... 257 D1
LOWER ARNCOTT 81 C1
LOWER ASSENDON .. 244 A6
LOWER BASILDON ... 249 E2
Lower Blackberry La OX4 .... 162 A8
Lower Black Berry La OX44 .... 143 A2
Lower Boddington Rd OX17 .... 4 E7
LOWER BOURTON 208 F3
LOWER CAVERSHAM . 259 D1
Lower Cherwell St OX16 .... 16 D5
Lower Church St HP14 .... 188 E5
Lower Cl OX15 .... 22 E8
Lower Comm SN7 .... 211 D8
Lower Cres OX29 .... 102 E3
Lower Elmstone Dr RG31 .... 257 C1
LOWER END Alvescot . 133 C5
Leafield 87 A4
Long Crendon 129 B7
Lower End
Alvescot OX18 .... 133 C4
Great Milton OX44 .... 145 B3
Leafield OX29 .... 86 F3
Leafield OX29 .... 87 A3
Piddington OX25 .... 97 E8
Ramsden OX7 .... 88 A2
Salford OX7 .... 41 F4
Shutford OX15 .... 14 B5
Lower End Cotts CV47 ... 2 F8
Lower Farm Barns OX27 .... 65 A8
Lower Farm Cl HP18 .. 128 D3
Lower Farm La
Mollington OX17 .... 3 F3
Sandford-on-Thames OX4 .... 161 B6
Lower Greensands 6 SN7 .... 172 E1
Lower Hades Rd OX5 ... 77 B6
Lower Ham Yard OX11 .... 219 F1
Lower Henley Rd RG4. 259 D3
LOWER HEYFORD 62 D6
Lower Heyford Rd
Lower Heyford OX25 .... 62 F6
Lower Heyford OX25 .... 63 B5
LOWER HIGHMOOR .. 242 F6
Lower High St OX18 .. 100 E5
Lower Icknield Way OX39 .... 168 D8
LOWER ODINGTON 54 A8
LOWER RADLEY 161 A3
Lower Radley Cvn Pk OX14 .... 160 F2
Lower Rd
Blackthorn OX25 .... 82 A4
Chilton OX11 .... 235 D8
Chinnor OX39 .... 168 C7
Freeland OX29 .... 106 E7
Garsington OX44 .... 143 C1
Garsington OX44 .... 162 D7
Long Hanborough OX29 .. 90 F1
Postcombe OX9 .... 166 F4
Southend OX44 .... 162 F6
LOWER SHIPLAKE 255 A3
Lower St
Barford St Michael OX15 .... 32 E6
Islip OX5 .... 93 F1
LOWER TADMARTON .. 20 F7
LOWER WAINHILL 168 E7
Lower Wharf OX10 .... 221 D7
Lower Whitley Rd OX2 .... 139 C8
Lower Wlk OX44 .... 161 F1
LOWER WOLVERCOTE 122 D7
Lowes Cl
Lower Shiplake RG9 ... 255 B4
Stokenchurch HP14 .... 188 C5
Lowfield Ct RG4 .... 259 C5
Lowfield Gn RG4 .... 259 E4
Lowfield Rd RG4 .... 259 D5
Loyd Cl OX14 .... 160 A3
Loyd Rd OX11 .... 218 D6
Lucas Pl OX4 .... 141 F5
Lucca Dr OX14 .... 179 D4
Lucerne Ave OX26 .... 65 D4
Lucerne Dr OX44 .... 163 C2
Lucerne Rd OX2 .... 123 C8
Lucey Cl RG31 .... 257 B3
Luckett Cl OX18 .... 135 F3
Lucky La OX16 .... 16 C5
Ludbridge Cl OX12 .... 216 D7
Ludford Gdns OX15 .... 21 D3
LUDGERSHALL 98 D8
Ludgershall Rd
Brill HP18 .... 98 B4
Brill HP18 .... 98 E4
Piddington OX25 .... 97 E7
Ludlow Dr Banbury OX16 15 F8
Thame OX9 .... 148 A8
Ludlow Rd
Bicester OX26 .... 65 B1
Bicester OX26 .... 65 B2
Ludsden Gr OX9 .... 148 A8
Luker Ave RG9 .... 244 D3
Lumberd Rd OX14 .... 160 B2
Lummas Mead OX39 .. 168 C5
Lune Cl OX11 .... 201 A1
Lupin La 4 OX18 .... 115 E5
Lupton Rd Thame OX9 . 148 A6
Wallingford OX10 .... 221 B7
Luscombe Cl RG4 .... 259 D2
Luther Ct OX1 .... 261 B1
Luther St OX1 .... 261 B1
Lutyens Ct OX7 .... 68 B4
Lych Gate La OX44 .... 145 B2
Lycroft Cl RG8 .... 249 C7
Lydalls Cl OX11 .... 200 D1
Lydalls Rd OX11 .... 200 E1
Lydes The OX10 .... 183 D6
Lydia Cl OX3 .... 124 F4
Lydsee Gate OX12 .... 214 B5
Lyefield Ct RG4 .... 259 B6
Lye Valley OX3 .... 142 D7
Lye Valley Nature Reserve★ OX3 .... 142 D8
LYFORD 176 C1
Lyford Cl OX14 .... 179 B2
Lyford Way OX14 .... 160 B2
Lymbrook Cl OX29 .... 119 C5
Lyme Gr RG31 .... 257 D1
Lymington Gate RG4 .. 258 E5
Lynams Sch OX2 .... 123 A7
Lynch The OX12 .... 216 D5
Lynch Way OX11 .... 236 A8
Lyndene Rd OX11 .... 200 D3
Lyndhurst Rd
Goring RG8 .... 249 C6
Reading RG30 .... 258 A1
Lyndworth Cl OX3 .... 124 E4
Lyndworth Mews OX3. 124 E3
LYNEHAM 70 E5
Lyneham Cl
Carterton OX18 .... 115 E3
Witney OX28 .... 103 E1
Lyneham Ct
Charlton OX12 .... 214 F4
Wantage OX12 .... 214 F4
Lyneham Rd
Bicester OX26 .... 66 B3
Kingham OX7 .... 55 C1
Milton-under-Wychwood OX7 .... 70 B3
Milton-under-Wychwood OX7 .... 70 C8
Lyne Rd Kidlington OX5 .. 92 C1
Kidlington OX5 .... 92 D1
Lynges Cl OX14 .... 160 B2
Lynmouth Ct RG1 .... 259 B1
Lynmouth Rd
Didcot OX11 .... 218 E8
Reading RG1 .... 259 A1
Lynn Cl OX3 .... 123 F4
Lynt Farm Cotts SN6 .. 170 B6
Lynt Farm La SN6 .... 170 B5
Lynton Ct 10 RG1 .... 259 A1
Lynton La OX29 .... 107 D2
Lynt Rd SN6 .... 170 A5
Lyon Cl
Abingdon-on-Thames OX14 .... 160 A1
Didcot OX11 .... 201 A3
Lysander Cl 5 OX26 ... 66 A4
Lysander Cres SN6 ... 191 C1
Lytham End RG31 .... 257 B3
Lytton Rd OX4 .... 142 B5

M

Mabel Prichard Sch
Oxford OX4 .... 142 C2
Oxford OX4 .... 142 E2
Maberley Cl OX14 .... 179 C6
Mably Gr OX12 .... 214 D6
Mably Way OX12 .... 214 D7
Macaulay Cl 4 OX26 ... 65 C3
Macdonald Cl OX11 .... 200 D1
Macdonald La OX29 .. 117 C7
Mackenzie Ave OX14 .. 199 D3
Mackenzie Cl 3 OX26 . 65 C3
Mackley Cl OX15 .... 33 E4
MACKNEY 220 D8
Mackney La OX10 .... 202 E1
Maclean Dr OX13 .... 176 C8
Macray Rd OX29 .... 118 B4
Maddle Rd RG17 .... 229 C1
Madley Brook and Springfield Sch OX28 .... 104 D2
Madley Brook La OX28 .... 104 E2
Madley Way OX28 .... 104 E2
Mafeking Row OX49 .. 186 E4
Magdalen Cl OX26 .... 65 F3
Magdalen Coll OX1 ... 123 E1
Magdalen Coll Sch OX4 .... 141 E8
Magdalen Ct OX11 .... 219 B8
Magdalene Quarry Nature Reserve★ OX3 .... 124 E3
Magdalen Pl
2 Carterton OX18 .... 115 D2
3 Carterton OX18 .... 115 D2
Magdalen Rd OX4 .... 141 F7
Magdalen St E OX1 ... 261 B3
Magdalen St OX1 .... 261 B2
Magnette Cl 9 OX14 .. 179 F7
Magnolia Cl OX5 .... 108 E7
Magnolias The
Banbury OX16 .... 9 B1
2 Bicester OX26 .... 65 F5
Magnolia Way 1 OX18 .... 115 E4
Magpie Alley OX7 .... 85 D8
Magpie La OX1 .... 261 C2
Maguire Cl OX12 .... 214 C8
Maharajah's Well★ RG9 .... 241 F5
Maidcroft Rd OX4 .... 142 C5
Maiden Erlegh Chiltern Edge Sch RG4 .... 252 E4
Maiden Rd OX16 .... 16 D1
Maiden's Cl SN6 .... 191 D1
MAIDENSGROVE 225 C5
Maidley Cl OX28 .... 104 C2
Main Ave OX4 .... 161 C8
Main Pk OX18 .... 133 D8
Main Rd Alvescot OX18. 133 B6
Appleford OX14 .... 200 F7
Boarstall HP18 .... 97 B2
Broughton OX15 .... 15 C1
Curbridge OX29 .... 117 C6
East Hagbourne OX11 .. 218 E5
East Hagbourne OX11 .. 219 A5
Fawler OX7 .... 88 E7
Fyfield OX13 .... 157 B2
Fyfield OX13 .... 157 C2
Glympton OX20 .... 75 A8
Kiddington OX20 .... 59 F1
Long Hanborough OX29 . 90 D1
Middleton Cheney OX17 .. 17 F8
Middleton Cheney OX17 .. 17 F8
Milcombe OX15 .... 20 F2
Milcombe OX15 .... 21 A2
Over Kiddington OX20 .. 60 A1
Stanton Harcourt OX29. 138 B8
Swalcliffe OX15 .... 19 E8
Swalcliffe OX15 .... 20 A8
Tadmarton OX15 .... 20 C8
Main St Adlestrop GL56. 40 C3
Barton Hartshorn MK18 . 39 D1
Bledington OX7 .... 54 D2
Charney Bassett OX12 . 175 F2
Checkendon RG9 .... 241 F5
Chesterton OX25 .... 80 A4
Chetwode MK18 .... 53 E8
Chilton OX11 .... 235 D8
Clanfield OX18 .... 152 E7
Claydon OX17 .... 1 D1
Claydon OX17 .... 4 D8
Duns Tew OX25 .... 47 D5
East Hanney OX12 .... 197 B6
Farnborough OX17 .... 3 E8
Finmere MK18 .... 39 D6
Forest Hill OX33 .... 125 E4

Main St *continued*
Fringford OX27 52 C6
Great Bourton OX17 9 D8
Grove OX12 214 E8
Hanwell OX17 8 F4
Hethe OX6 52 A8
Letcombe Regis OX12 214 A2
Long Compton CV36 27 F6
Mixbury NN13 38 D8
Mollington OX17 4 A3
North Newington OX15 15 B4
Oddington OX5 94 C2
Over Norton OX7 42 F5
Poundon OX27 67 F7
Shalstone MK18 25 E6
Sibford Ferris OX15 19 B7
Sibford Gower OX15 18 F8
Sibford Gower OX15 19 A8
Tadmarton OX15 20 B8
Turweston NN13 24 C8
Westbury NN13 25 A4
West Hagbourne OX11 218 C4
West Hanney OX12 196 E6
West Ilsley RG20 235 A2
Weston-on-the-Green OX25 79 F3
Wroxton OX15 15 A8
Maisonettes The RG8 249 D8
Majors Rd SN6 191 D2
Makins Rd RG9 254 B8
Malet Cl HP14 188 F5
Malford Rd OX3 124 F4
Mallard Cl OX4 142 D2
Mallard Dr
Didcot OX11 200 B1
Witney OX28 118 A6
Mallards Way
Bicester OX26 66 A1
Bicester OX26 80 F8
Mallard Way OX12 196 D1
Mallins La SN7 192 D3
Mallinson Ct OX2 123 A1
Mallory Ave RG4 259 D6
Mallow Cl OX13 156 D1
Mall The SN6 209 E7
Maltfield Rd OX3 124 B5
Malthouse SN6 228 A7
Malthouse Cl SN6 228 B7
Malthouse La
Bodicote OX15 22 D8
Brighthampton OX29 137 A3
Dorchester OX10 182 D1
Long Compton CV36 27 F6
Shutford OX15 14 B5
Malthouse Paddock SN7 174 E8
Malthouses SN6 228 B7
Malthouse Wlk 4 OX16 16 D6
Maltings Ct OX15 21 D4
Maltings The
2 Carterton OX18 115 F5
West Ilsley RG20 235 B1
Maltsters OX29 89 C7
Malvern Cl
Banbury OX16 16 D2
2 Didcot OX11 200 C2
Malyns Cl OX39 168 C7
Malyns Way RG31 257 B4
Managua Cl RG4 259 E2
Manchester Terr 2 OX26 65 F2
Mandarin Pl OX12 196 D1
Mandeville Cl OX14 160 A2
Mandhill Cl OX12 214 E8
Mandlebrote Dr OX4 142 B1
Manning Cl OX15 21 E2
Mannings Cl OX15 19 B7
Manor Ave GL7 150 E3
Manor Barns Bsns Pk OX7 88 C6
Manor Cl
Appleford OX14 200 F8
Aston OX18 135 E2
Cassington OX29 107 C2
Chilton OX11 217 E1
Drayton OX14 179 B1
Enstone OX7 58 F5
Great Bourton OX17 9 D8
Lewknor OX49 187 A8
Shrivenham SN6 209 B7
West Hagbourne OX11 218 C4
Manor Cotts OX29 138 B7
Manor Court Yd OX33 127 B2
Manor Cres
Didcot OX11 200 D1
Standlake OX29 137 D3
Stanford in the Vale SN7 194 E7
Manor Ct
Abingdon-on-Thames OX14 179 E6
Banbury OX16 16 E7
Carterton OX18 115 D2
Chadlington OX7 57 C1
Wootton OX20 75 F4
Manor Dr OX33 143 C6
Manor Farm OX14 180 A2
Manor Farm Barns OX5 95 A4
Manor Farm Cl
Kingham OX7 54 F5
Merton OX25 95 D8
Tiddington OX9 145 F6
Manor Farm Cotts
Garford OX13 177 D5
Wendlebury OX25 80 A3
Manor Farm La
Balscote OX15 14 D8
Balscote OX16 7 C1
Chesterton OX26 80 A7
Didcot OX11 218 E5
Manor Farm La *continued*
Tidmarsh RG8 256 C2
Manor Farm Rd
Barton Hartshorn MK18 39 D3
Barton Hartshorn MK18 39 E2
Dorchester OX10 182 D1
Horspath OX33 143 C6
Manor Farm Wy OX39 149 E2
Manor Fields OX12 214 A2
Manor Gdns GL7 150 C4
Manor Gn
Harwell OX11 217 E7
Stanford in the Vale SN7 194 E7
Manor Gr OX1 160 E7
Manor Ho★ OX5 108 B4
Manor Hospl Oxford The, (Nuffield Health) OX3 124 C3
Manor La
Clanfield OX18 152 E8
Shrivenham SN6 209 B6
West Hendred OX12 216 B5
Manor Orch OX15 8 B4
Manor Pk Banbury OX16 16 E8
Claydon OX17 1 D1
Oxford OX3 124 C3
Manor Pl OX1 123 E2
Manor Prep Sch The OX13 159 C1
Manor Rd
Adderbury OX17 22 E3
Banbury OX16 16 F8
Bladon OX20 91 B2
Brize Norton OX18 116 B4
Carterton OX18 115 D5
Chinnor OX9 149 A6
Didcot OX11 200 D1
Ducklington OX29 118 A4
Fringford OX27 52 D7
Goring RG8 249 B5
Great Bourton OX17 9 D8
Henley-on-Thames RG9 254 D8
Oxford OX1 123 E2
Oxford OX1 261 C3
Sandford St Martin OX7 46 C1
South Hinksey OX1 141 B5
Towersey OX9 148 F7
Wantage OX12 232 C5
Whitchurch-on-Thames RG8 256 C7
Witney OX28 118 C7
Woodstock OX20 91 A7
Wootton OX13 159 A7
Manor Sch OX11 200 D1
Manorsfield Rd OX26 65 E2
Manor View
Bampton OX18 134 E4
Bucknell OX27 64 F8
Manor Way OX5 92 F2
Manor Wood Gate RG9 255 A4
Manor Yd OX27 52 D7
Mansell Cl OX29 106 D6
Mansell Pl OX18 115 D1
Mansfield Coll OX1 261 C3
Mansfield Gdns OX11 219 B8
Mansfield Rd OX1 261 C3
Mansmoor Rd OX5 94 F7
Manston Cl OX26 66 B3
Manzel Rd OX27 66 A6
Manzil Way OX4 142 A8
Maple Ave OX5 108 F7
Maple Cl Bodicote OX15 16 E1
Oxford OX2 140 D8
Sonning Common RG4 253 A4
Maple Cotts SN7 172 E3
Maple Ct Goring RG8 249 B6
Kidlington OX5 108 F7
Mapledene RG4 258 E3
MAPLEDURHAM 257 E6
Mapledurham Dr RG8 257 C5
Mapledurham Ho★ RG4 257 E6
Mapledurham View RG31 257 D2
Mapledurham Watermill★ RG4 257 D6
Maple Furlong OX10 203 E5
Maple Gdns OX13 199 D6
Maple Gr RG5 260 E1
Maple Ho RG4 259 C3
Maple Rd Bicester OX26 65 F2
Didcot OX11 200 B1
Faringdon SN7 172 E3
Thame OX9 147 D8
Maples The
Carterton OX18 115 D1
Grove OX12 196 D2
Maple Way OX7 71 B2
Maplewell OX29 89 C7
Maplewell Ho OX29 89 D7
MARCHAM 178 D6
Marcham CE Prim Sch OX13 178 D6
Marcham Rd
Abingdon-on-Thames OX14 179 C6
Drayton OX14 179 A6
Marcham OX13 178 F6
March Rd OX17 3 D3
Marchwood Ave RG4 259 C8
Marcourt Rd HP14 188 F3
Mardy RG4 258 E5
Margaret Cl
Banbury OX16 16 A5
Bicester OX26 65 D4
Margaret Rd
Adderbury OX17 23 B5
Oxford OX3 124 E2
Maria Cres OX12 214 E5
Marie Cl OX27 67 F7
Marigold Cl 12 OX4 142 F1
Marigold Cres OX11 200 A1
Marigold Wlk 1 OX26 65 E5
Marina Way OX14 179 F4
Marines Dr SN7 172 F2
Mariot Ct 8 OX10 221 D7
Marjoram Cl OX4 143 A2
Marjoram Way OX11 218 B7
Market End Ct OX26 65 D3
Market End Way OX26 65 D3
Market Pl
4 Abingdon-on-Thames OX14 179 F7
Banbury OX16 16 D6
Chipping Norton OX7 42 E2
Chipping Norton OX7 42 E3
Deddington OX15 33 F4
Didcot OX11 200 F1
Faringdon SN7 172 F4
Henley-on-Thames RG9 244 D2
Lechlade-on-Thames GL7 150 C4
3 Wallingford OX10 221 D7
Wantage OX12 214 D4
Woodstock OX20 91 A6
Market Sq
Bampton OX18 134 E3
Bicester OX26 65 F1
Lower Heyford OX25 62 D6
Witney OX28 118 B8
Market St
Charlbury OX7 73 B4
Chipping Norton OX7 42 E3
Oxford OX1 261 B2
Woodstock OX20 91 B6
Markhams Ct OX5 95 A4
Mark Rd OX3 124 E2
Markus Ave OX9 147 F6
Marlborough Ave OX5 92 D2
Marlborough Cl
Carterton OX18 115 E1
Eynsham OX29 120 E8
Faringdon SN7 172 F3
Kidlington OX5 92 D2
Kings Sutton OX17 23 F6
1 Oxford OX4 142 B2
Marlborough Cres
Long Hanborough OX29 106 B8
Woodstock OX20 91 A7
Marlborough Ct OX2 122 F1
Marlborough Dr OX29 107 C1
Marlborough Gdns SN7 172 F2
Marlborough Ho 18 OX16 16 D5
Marlborough La
Stanford in the Vale SN7 194 E7
Witney OX28 118 A8
Marlborough Pl
2 Banbury OX16 16 D5
Charlbury OX7 73 B3
Eynsham OX29 120 E8
Faringdon SN7 172 E2
Marlborough Rd
Banbury OX16 16 D5
Chipping Norton OX7 42 F4
Oxford OX1 141 C7
Marlborough St SN7 172 F3
Marlborough Terr OX29 90 A4
Marley Cl OX2 140 A8
Marley Ind Est OX16 16 D8
Marley La OX44 184 C7
Marley Way OX16 16 D7
Marlie Gdns OX13 177 A8
Marling Cl RG31 257 C2
Marlow Cl OX10 221 B8
Marlow Ct RG4 259 D3
Marlowe Cl OX16 15 F6
Marlow Rd
Henley-on-Thames RG9 244 E3
Stokenchurch HP14 188 F3
Marmyon Ho RG9 244 E3
Marns Hey OX12 214 C5
Marriott Cl
Cutteslowe OX2 109 B1
Wootton OX20 76 A4
Marriotts Cl OX28 118 B8
Marriott's Cl
Haddenham HP17 130 F6
11 Witney OX28 104 A1
Marriotts La HP17 130 F6
Marriotts Way HP17 130 F6
Marsack St RG4 259 C2
Marshall Cl
Chipping Norton OX7 42 E1
Purley on Thames RG8 257 D4
Witney OX29 117 C7
Marshall Cres OX7 46 E1
Marshall Rd
9 Banbury OX16 16 E6
Oxford OX4 142 D6
MARSH BALDON 162 B3
Marsh Baldon CE Prim Sch OX44 162 A4
Marsh Cl OX5 108 C5
Marsh Ct OX14 179 F8
Marsh End OX9 147 B1
Marsh Furlong OX18 135 E3
MARSH GIBBON 67 F3
Marsh Gibbon CE Sch OX27 67 F3
Marsh Gibbon Rd
Blackthorn OX25 82 D3
Blackthorn OX27 82 B6
Piddington OX25 97 E8
Marsh La
Clanfield OX18 152 F8
Clanfield OX18 153 A8
Clanfield OX18, SN7 153 B7
Crowmarsh Gifford OX10 222 A8
East Challow OX12 213 F7
Fyfield OX13 157 B4
Marston OX3 124 A5
Wallingford OX10 222 A8
Witney OX28 104 B1
Marshland Sq RG4 259 B5
Marsh Pl RG8 256 D5
Marsh Rd
Ambrosden OX25 81 C3
Oxford OX4 142 C6
Shabbington HP18 128 D3
Marsh Way
Carterton OX18 115 F3
Uffington SN7 210 F6
Woolstone SN7 211 A5
MARSTON 123 E6
Marston Cl OX16 9 D3
Marston Ferry Ct OX2 123 C6
Marston Ferry Rd OX2 123 D6
Marston Rd
Marston OX3, OX4 123 F3
Thame OX9 130 A1
Thenford OX17 11 E1
Marston St OX4 141 F8
Marten Gate OX16 16 E3
Marten Pl RG31 257 C3
Martens Cl SN6 209 A6
Martens Lake OX13 156 C2
Martens Rd SN6 209 B6
Martin Cl Bicester OX26 80 F8
Oxford OX29 140 C8
Martin Cooper Cl RG4 259 D3
Martin Ct OX2 123 B7
Martins La
Dorchester OX10 182 D2
Standlake OX29 137 C4
Martin Way OX12 214 B8
Martyns Way OX10 204 F4
Mary Box Cres OX29 117 C7
Mary Ellis Way
Witney OX29 117 B7
Witney OX29 117 B8
Maryfield OX12 214 E4
Marygreen OX12 214 D8
Marylands Gn OX44 162 D2
Marymead
Cholsey OX10 220 F2
Cholsey OX10 220 F2
Mary Price Cl OX3 124 A3
Mary Shunn Way OX12 214 F4
Mary Towerton Sch The HP14 189 D3
Mary Whipple Ct OX12 214 C4
Mascall Ave OX3 142 E7
Mascord Cl OX16 16 A5
Mascord Rd OX16 16 A5
Masefield Cres OX14 179 C5
Masefield Rd OX16 16 A4
Masey Cl 4 OX3 124 D1
Mason Cl OX18 115 E4
Masons Ct OX12 215 E6
Masons Gr OX29 105 A7
Masons Rd OX3 124 E1
Massey Rd
7 Thame OX9 147 A7
Townsend OX12 194 F3
Mathematical Inst Univ of Oxford OX1 261 A4
Mather Rd OX3 124 F4
Mathews Way OX13 159 B6
Matilda Way OX14 180 C1
Matlock Rd RG4 258 E4
Matson Dr RG9 244 F2
Matthew Arnold Sch OX2 140 C7
Mattock Cl OX3 124 D2
Mattocks Wlk OX44 161 F1
Mattock Way OX14 160 B3
Maud Cl OX26 65 C4
Maud Hale Cotts 11 OX14 179 F6
Maud Ho OX12 214 F5
Maule Cl OX15 21 E2
Maunde Cl OX26 79 F7
Maunds The OX15 33 F4
Mavor Cl OX20 91 A7
Mawkes Cl SN7 194 D7
Mawle Ct 1 OX16 16 D5
Mawles La OX7 85 D8
Maxwell Ave OX11 217 B3
Maycroft 4 OX26 65 F4
Mayfair Rd OX4 142 B4
Mayfield Ave OX12 196 F1
Mayfield Cl
Carterton OX18 115 D1
Chalgrove OX44 184 D6
Mayfield Dr RG4 259 D3
Mayfield Rd
Banbury OX16 16 D2
Farmoor OX2 121 B2
Oxford OX2 123 B7
Mayott's Rd 1 OX14 179 E7
Mays Cl OX27 49 F7
MAYS GREEN 254 B5
May Tree Cl OX26 65 E3
Maytree Wlk RG4 259 E4
Mayweed Rd 9 OX15 16 F1
McCabe Pl OX3 124 A3
McCrae's Wlk RG10 255 D2
Mcculloch Mdws OX10 221 F7
Mcguire Rd
Upper Heyford OX25 49 C1
Upper Heyford OX25 63 C8
McKay Trad Est OX26 80 F8
McKee Sq OX10 204 D2
McKeever Pl 5 OX16 16 E6
Mclaren Way OX11 201 B3
McMullan Cl OX10 221 C8
Mdw La OX13 199 F3
Mead Cl RG4 259 D2
Meaden Hill OX3 124 B5
Mead La Eynsham OX29 120 F8
Eynsham OX29 121 A7
Longcot SN7 192 D2
Longcot SN7 192 D2
Lower Basildon RG8 249 F1
Witney OX28 104 B1
Meadow Bank SN7 172 F3
Meadowbank Cl
Ascott-under-Wychwood OX7 71 B2
Long Crendon HP18 129 C7
Meadow Cl
Farmoor OX2 121 B3
Goring RG8 249 C6
Grove OX12 196 E1
Moulsford OX10 238 F4
Shipton-under-Wychwood OX7 70 D1
Meadow Ct OX12 214 A7
Meadow End OX18 100 E6
Meadow La
Crowmarsh Gifford OX10 222 A6
Didcot OX11 200 A3
Fulbrook OX18 100 F6
Long Crendon HP18 129 E4
Oxford OX4 141 E7
Oxford OX4 141 F5
Pangbourne RG8 256 D5
Shipton-under-Wychwood OX7 70 D1
6 Witney OX28 104 A1
Meadow Pl OX7 55 D5
Meadow Prospect OX2 122 D8
Meadow Rd
Chinnor OX39 168 D6
Henley-on-Thames RG9 244 E1
Reading RG1 258 F1
Watchfield SN6 191 E2
Meadowside
Abingdon-on-Thames OX14 179 E6
Reading RG31 257 B1
Meadowside Ct 1 OX14 179 E6
Meadowside Rd RG8 256 D5
Meadows The
Bletchingdon OX5 93 A8
Lower Bourton SN6 208 F3
Watlington OX49 186 B2
Meadowsweet Way
Hardwick OX16 9 A2
Oxford OX4 124 B6
Meadow View
Adderbury OX17 23 A4
Banbury OX16 16 E4
Kidlington OX5 92 E2
3 Lechlade-on-Thames GL7 150 D5
Long Crendon HP18 129 E4
Oxford OX2 123 C8
Wendlebury OX25 79 F3
Witney OX28 118 C8
Meadow View Rd OX1 160 F8
Meadow Way
Carterton OX18 115 F5
Didcot OX11 218 C7
Faringdon SN7 172 F2
Kingham OX7 54 F3
Lower Caversham RG4 259 D2
Thame OX9 129 F1
Yarnton OX5 108 C5
Meadow Wlk OX20 91 C6
Mead Platt HP14 188 D5
Mead Rd
Barford St Michael OX15 32 F7
Yarnton OX5 108 C4
Meads Cl OX14 179 B2
Meadsfarm La OX16 16 E8
Meadside OX10 202 E8
Meads The OX12 196 E7
Mead The OX17 3 F3
Mead Way OX5 92 E2
Mead Wlk OX11 200 E2
Meashill Way OX11 234 F8
Medcroft Rd OX5 77 B6
Medhurst Way 3 OX4 142 B2
Medill Cl RG8 240 E1
Medina Cl OX11 201 B1
Medina Gdns OX26 65 B2
Medlar Rd SN6 209 C7
Medlicott Dr OX14 179 C6
Medlock Gr OX11 200 F3
Medway OX12 197 B6
Medway Cl OX13 159 C3
Medway Gr 5 OX11 219 A8
Medway Rd OX13 159 C3
Meer The OX10 204 A5
Melbourne Cl OX16 16 E3
Melrose Ct OX16 8 F1
Melton Dr OX11 200 E1
Melville Cl OX26 65 B2
Membury Way OX12 214 D8
Memorial Ave RG9 254 E2
Mendip Hts 6 OX11 200 C2
Menmarsh Rd
Horton-cum-Studley OX33 112 D1
Menmarsh Rd *continued*
Worminghall HP18 127 A8
Worminghall HP18 127 E6
Worminghall OX33 126 F8
Menpes Rd RG31 257 C4
Mercer Gdns 10 SN7 172 F3
Mercian Rd OX9 129 D1
Mercury Cl
Bampton OX18 134 F3
2 Bampton OX18 135 A3
Mercury Ct OX18 134 F3
Mercury Rd OX4 143 A2
Meredith Cl OX26 65 C3
Mere Dyke Rd OX13 198 F5
Mere La MK18 39 E6
Mereland Rd OX11 218 E7
Mere Rd Finmere MK18 39 D6
Wolvercote OX2 122 F8
Merewood Ave OX3 125 A4
Merganser Dr OX26 81 B8
Meriden Ct OX10 221 C7
Merlin Cl Benson OX10 204 D2
Bodicote OX15 16 E1
Carterton OX18 115 D3
Upper Rissington GL54 68 B3
Merlin Rd
Abingdon-on-Thames OX13 159 B2
Oxford OX4 142 E2
Merlin Way OX26 81 B8
Merritt Rd OX11 200 C1
Merrivale's La OX15 21 E4
Merrivale Sq OX2 123 A4
Merrymouth Rd OX7 69 A2
Mersey Way OX11 201 A3
Merthyr Vale RG4 259 A6
MERTON 95 D8
Merton Cl Didcot OX11 219 B8
Eynsham OX29 120 D7
Merton Coll OX1 261 C2
Merton Ct
Eynsham OX29 120 D7
Oxford OX2 123 A4
Merton Rd OX25 81 C3
Merton St Banbury OX16 16 E6
Oxford OX1 261 C2
Merton Way OX5 108 B5
Merton Wlk OX26 65 F3
Metcalfe Cl
Abingdon-on-Thames OX14 179 E4
Drayton OX15 15 D8
Meteor Cl Bicester OX26 66 A3
Upper Rissington GL54 68 B3
Meteor Row OX12 214 C8
Mewburn Rd OX16 16 B5
Mews The Baydon SN8 245 B5
Highworth SN6 190 A6
Sonning RG4 260 D4
Warborough OX10 203 B5
Watchfield SN6 191 D1
Meyseys Cl OX3 142 E7
Mezereon Spur OX11 218 B8
Michaelis Rd OX9 129 E1
Michaelmas Cl OX17 10 F1
Michaels Chase RG4 259 C3
Michael's St OX1 123 C1
Micklands Prim Sch RG4 259 D4
Micklands Rd RG4 259 E4
Mickle Way OX33 125 E4
Middi Haines Ct SN6 190 A6
MIDDLE ASSENDON 243 F7
MIDDLE ASTON 48 B3
Middle Aston La OX25 48 A4
Middle Aston Rd OX25 48 A6
MIDDLE BARTON 60 F7
Middle Barton Rd OX25 47 D5
Middle Barton Sch OX7 61 A8
Middle Farm Cl OX39 168 C5
Middle Furlong OX11 201 B2
Middle Gd OX33 144 F7
Middle Hill OX15 30 B7
Middle La Balscote OX15 14 C8
Shotteswell OX17 8 D8
Middle Orch OX7 54 D2
Middle Rd Burford OX18 99 B6
Stanton St John OX33 125 D7
Middle Row
Chipping Norton OX7 42 E3
Great Rollright OX7 29 A3
Middle Springs RG8 249 C8
Middle St OX5 93 F1
MIDDLETON CHENEY 11 A1
Middleton Cheney Com Prim Sch OX17 17 F8
Middleton Cheney Rd OX16 17 C6
Middleton Cl OX16 17 A7
Middleton Pk
Middleton Stoney OX25 63 E3
Middleton Stoney OX25 63 E5
Middleton Stoney OX25 63 F3
Middleton Stoney OX25 63 F4
Middleton Stoney OX25 64 A4
Middleton Stoney OX25 64 B3
Middleton Rd
Banbury OX16 16 F7
Bucknell OX27 64 F8
Chacombe OX17 10 E4
MIDDLETON STONEY 64 B3
Middleton Stoney Rd
Ardley OX27 50 B1
Bicester OX26 65 C1
Middleton Stoney OX27 64 B7
MIDDLETOWN 104 A6
Middle Way
Chinnor OX39 168 B6

Middle Way continued
Islip OX5 ....93 F1
Oxford OX2 ....123 B7
Middleway Bottom
OX12 ....213 C2
Midget Cl OX14....179 D5
Midsummer Mdw RG4 258 F6
Midway OX17........11 A1
Midwinter Ave OX14..199 C3
MILCOMBE 21 B2
Miles Dr
Brize Norton OX18 ..116 A4
Carterton OX18.......115 F4
Grove OX12.........214 E8
Miles East OX11....218 B8
Milestone Ave RG10..260 F6
Milestone Cl HP14...188 E5
Milestone La OX25....79 A3
Milestone Rd OX18 ..115 D1
Milestone View Ct
RG4............259 E4
Mileway Gdns OX3..124 C1
Milford La
Wootton OX20........75 F4
Wootton OX20........76 A4
Milford Pl OX20.....76 A4
Milking La OX28, OX29. 104 A3
Millais Cl OX2 ......140 D7
Millar Cl Benson OX10 . 203 F5
Benson OX10.......203 F5
Mill Arts Ctr★ OX16...16 D6
Millaway La SN7....195 C5
Millbank OX2........141 A8
Millbank Wy OX8....198 F4
Millbrook Cl
Blewbury OX11 ......219 A1
Wallingford OX10 ...221 C7
Millbrook Sch OX12 ..196 D1
Millbrook Sq OX12...196 E1
Millbuck Ind Est OX28 118 B6
Millbuck Ind Est OX28 118 B6
Mill Cl Chadlington OX7.. 57 A1
Charlton-on-Otmoor OX5 95 A5
Deddington OX15 .....33 E4
Middle Assendon RG9.. 243 F8
Milldown Ave RG8....249 C7
Milldown Rd RG8....249 C7
MILLEND 57 A2
Mill End Chadlington OX7 56 E3
Chadlington OX7......57 A1
Kidlington OX5.......93 A1
Miller Ho OX16 ......16 A6
Miller Pl OX13.......199 A5
Miller Rd Banbury OX16.. 16 A6
Wheatley OX33.......144 C7
Miller's Acre ■ OX2.. 109 B1
Millers Cl
Chalgrove OX44......184 C7
Goring RG8.........249 B7
North Leigh OX29 ....105 B6
Millers Ct RG4.......259 C1
Millers La Hornton OX15 ..7 C7
Stoke Row OX15......2 C1
Millers Mews OX28...104 B1
Millers Turn OX39 ...168 B6
Millers Wy OX15.....10 F1
Millets Farm Cotts
OX13............177 D5
Millet Way OX28.....103 A1
Millfield Ave OX27....67 F3
Millfield Cl OX27 ....67 F3
Milford Rd RG1......258 F1
Mill Gn Bampton OX18 . 134 E2
Reading RG4........259 C1
Mill Green ■ RG4....259 C1
Mill Green OX18 ....134 E2
Millham The OX12...216 B6
Millinton Rd OX10...221 C8
Mill La Adderbury OX17.. 23 A3
Alvescot OX18.......133 C6
Benson OX10........203 F4
Black Bourton OX18 ..133 F5
Brackley NN13.......24 A6
Cassington OX29 .....106 F2
Cassington OX29 .....107 C2
Chalgrove OX44......184 C6
Charlton-on-Otmoor OX5 95 A5
Chinnor OX39 ....168 B7
Chipping Warden OX17...5 F6
Clanfield OX18.......152 D8
Croughton NN13......36 C7
Drayton OX15 ....15 D8
East Challow OX12 ..213 E7
East Hendred OX12....216 D6
Fringford OX27 ......53 A5
Great Bourton OX17....9 F7
Great Haseley OX44 ..164 D8
Grove OX12.........214 E2
Haddenham OX9 .....130 B3
Henley-on-Thames RG9. 254 F8
Horton-cum-Studley
OX33............112 A6
Islip OX5...........109 E8
Kidmore End RG4 ....252 C1
Kings Sutton OX17 ....23 F4
Kirtlington OX5.......77 F4
Lechlade-on-Thames
GL7............150 F4
Lechlade-on-Thames
GL7............151 A3
Lower Heyford OX6....62 D6
Lower Shiplake RG9 ..255 A2
Marston OX3........123 E8
Marston OX3........123 F7
Middle Barton OX7....60 F8
Milton OX14.........141 F4
Oxford OX4.........141 F4
Path Hill RG4........251 F1

Mill La continued
Reading RG4.........257 F7
Sandford St Martin OX7. 46 B1
Sandford St Martin OX7.. 60 A8
Shenington OX15......6 E2
South Moreton OX11...219 F5
South Moreton OX11...220 A5
Spelsbury OX7.......72 E2
Stadhampton OX44...163 D2
Stokenchurch HP14....188 C5
Stratton Audley OX27.. 52 D3
Sutton Courtenay OX14 199 F7
Sutton Courtenay OX14 200 A7
Tidmarsh RG9.......256 D2
Upper Arncott OX25...96 E7
Upper Heyford OX25....48 F1
Wallingford OX10 ....221 D7
Westbury NN13.......25 A4
West Hendred OX12...216 C6
Weston-on-the-Green
OX25...........79 A2
Wigginton OX15 .....31 C6
Wigginton OX15 .....31 C7
Wootton OX20........75 F4
Mill Lane Com Prim Sch
OX39............168 B7
Mill Mdw OX29......118 C3
Millmoor Cres OX29 ..120 E8
Mill Orch OX12 ......197 A6
Mill Paddock
■ Abingdon-on-Thames
OX14...........179 F6
Letcombe Regis OX12.. 214 A2
Mill Rd
Abingdon-on-Thames
OX14...........179 C5
Chipping Norton OX7...42 C2
Goring RG8.........249 C7
Lower Shiplake RG9 ..255 B3
Marcham OX13.......178 D5
Nettlebed RG9.......224 E3
Reading RG4........259 C1
Shabbington HP18....128 E1
Stokenchurch HP14....188 C5
Stratton Audley OX6....52 E1
Wolvercote OX2......122 D8
Mill St Mews OX29...120 E7
Mills La OX15 ....15 A8
Mill St Eynsham OX29.. 120 E8
Islip OX5...........109 E8
Kidlington OX5.......92 F1
Oxford OX2.........123 A1
Stanton St John OX33.. 112 B1
Stanton St John OX33.. 125 E8
Stanton St John OX33.. 126 A8
Steventon OX13......198 F3
Wantage OX12.......214 D5
Witney OX28........104 A1
Mill Stream OX10....203 F4
Millstream Ct OX2...122 D8
Millview OX7........42 E2
Mill View OX49 .....185 D3
Millway Cl OX2......122 D8
Millway Furlong HP17 130 E6
Millway La OX13.....157 E6
Millwood End OX29...90 A1
Millwood Farm Barns
OX29...........90 A1
Millwood Vale OX29...90 A1
Millwright Cl ■ OX16.. 16 B6
Milne Cl OX16 ......16 C4
Milne Pl OX3 ....124 B5
MILTON Banbury......22 C3
Didcot.............199 C5
Milton Bsns & Tech Ctr
OX13............199 A2
Milton CE Prim Sch
OX14............199 C2
Milton Cl
■ Bicester OX26.......65 C3
Henley-on-Thames RG9. 244 D2
MILTON COMMON ...146 B3
Milton Cres OX33 ....125 F4
Milton Gate OX13....199 D3
Miltongated Rd OX15...33 F6
Milton Gated Rd OX17.. 22 C2
Milton Heights ■
OX13............199 C2
MILTON HILL........199 B2
Milton Hill
Milton Heights OX13...199 B3
Milton Hill OX13 .....199 B3
Rowstock OX13.......217 B8
Milton Intc OX14......199 C3
Milton La OX13......199 A5
Milton Manor Dr OX44 163 F6
Milton Manor House★
OX14............199 C5
Milton Park Est OX14 . 199 E4
Milton Pk OX13......199 C4
Milton Rd Didcot OX11. 200 B3
Drayton OX13.......199 D8
Drayton OX14.......179 D1
Milton OX17........22 C2
Oxford OX4.........142 B6
Shipton-under-Wychwood
OX7............70 C1
Stadhampton OX44...163 C2
Sutton Courtenay OX14 199 F6
Milton St OX16 ......16 C5
MILTON-UNDER-
WYCHWOOD 70 C1
Milton Village St OX15. 22 C3
Milvery Way OX4.....142 B3
Minchery Farm Cotts
OX4............142 C1
Minchery Rd OX4.....142 C1
Minchins Cl OX14....180 C8

Minnow La OX18 .....99 B6
Minns Bsns Pk OX2...122 D1
Minns Rd OX12 ......196 F1
Minster Ind Pk OX29...103 B1
MINSTER LOVELL 102 F2
Minster Lovell Hall &
Dovecote★ OX29....103 A3
Minster Rd
Brize Norton OX18 ...116 B5
Oxford OX4.........142 A8
Minster Riding OX29.. 102 F4
Minton Cl OX29......257 F1
Mint The ■ OX10....221 D7
Minty Cl OX29.......115 C1
Mirfield Rd OX28 ....117 E8
Mistletoe Gn OX4....142 E1
Mistletoe Mews OX11. 218 B8
Mitchell Cl Thame OX9. 147 E8
Wootton OX13.......159 A7
Mitchellway OX13 ...199 C2
Mitchell Way OX13 ..199 C2
Mitford Cotts OX18...99 E1
MIXBURY 24 D1
Mixbury Rd NN13.....24 B2
Moat Cl OX18.......116 B3
Moat La OX27.......67 F2
Moat's Cres OX9.....148 A8
Moat The OX7.......54 F5
Mobbs La OX15......30 B7
Moberly Cl OX4......141 F8
Model Cotts OX18 ...133 F4
Modern Art Oxford★
OX1............261 B2
Mogridge Dr OX4....142 A2
Moir Ct OX12........214 D5
Mold Cres OX16 .....16 A6
Mole Pl OX4.........143 A1
Moley Gdns OX12....214 E4
MOLLINGTON 4 A3
Mollington La
Shotteswell OX17 .....3 D2
Shotteswell OX17 .....8 D8
Warmington OX17.....3 B4
Mollington Rd
Claydon OX17 ....1 D1
Claydon OX17 ....4 D8
Shotteswell OX17 .....8 D8
Molyneux Dr OX15....22 E8
Molyns Ho RG9.......244 E3
Monahan Way OX18 ..116 A5
Monarchs Ct OX10....203 F4
Monard Terr ■ OX4 ..141 F7
Mondays Field OX10...203 E5
MONGEWELL 221 E4
Monique Ct ■ OX16...9 A1
Monkley Ct ■ RG4 ..259 C1
Monks Cl
Carterton OX18......115 D5
Dorchester OX10.....182 E1
Oxford OX4.........142 D2
West Hanney OX12 ..196 E6
Monks Lode OX11 ...200 F3
Monks Mead OX10...202 E2
Monks Wlk
Lechlade-on-Thames
GL7............150 E3
Marcham OX13.......178 D5
Monmouth St ■ RG1. 259 A1
Monmouth Rd OX1 ..141 D5
Monnhan Way OX18.. 115 F4
Mons Way OX14......159 D1
Montabaur Rd NN13 ..24 A7
Montague St RG4.....259 C2
Montagu Rd OX2 ....140 D8
Montfort Gate RG4...259 E4
Montgomery Rd OX27..66 A7
Montpelier Dr RG4 ..259 D5
Montrose Way OX9...148 A8
Monument Ind Pk
OX44...........184 F7
Monument Rd
Chalgrove OX44......184 E6
Chalgrove OX44......184 E6
Monument St OX16 ..16 C5
Moody Rd OX3.......123 F3
Moonraker La OX18.. 134 F3
Moor Ave OX28......104 A1
Moorbank OX4 ......142 E2
Moorbrook OX11 ....200 D4
Moor Cl OX39 ....168 C5
Moorend La
Thame OX9.........129 F1
Thame OX9.........130 A2
Moorfield Cl OX16....16 E6
Moorgate GL7.......150 B4
Moorhen Wlk OX4...142 E1
Moor La
South Newington OX15..31 F7
Southrop GL7........131 B2
Moorland Cl OX28...103 F1
Moorland Rd OX28...117 F8
Moorlands The
Benson OX10........204 A4
Kidlington OX5.......92 E2
Moor Pond Cl OX26...65 F2
Moors Cl OX29 ......118 A5
Moors Dr The OX17...17 F8
MOORS THE 118 A5
Moors The
Kidlington OX5.......92 D2
Pangbourne RG8.....256 D5
Morecambe Ave RG4. 258 E5
Moreland Rd OX11...218 B7
Morello Cl OX27......65 D6
MORETON Appleton...157 A7
Thame...........147 D5
Moreton Ave OX10...221 B7
Moreton La
Moreton OX29........157 A8
Newbridge OX29.....156 F7
Northmoor OX29.....138 B1

Moreton La continued
Thame OX9..........147 E8
Moreton Rd
Aston Tirrold OX11 ...219 F2
Moreton OX9........147 C6
Oxford OX2.........123 B6
Morgan Cl OX16......15 F8
Morgan Vale OX14...159 E2
Morlais RG4.........259 A5
Morland Cl OX33 ....144 B8
Morland Rd OX13....178 D6
Morlands OX12......197 B7
Morrell Ave OX4.....142 A8
Morrell Cl OX5 ......108 D8
Morrell Cres OX4....142 A2
Morrells Cl OX11 ....200 D1
Morrell Way OX26 ...81 C6
Morris Cl OX7 ....42 E1
Morris Cres OX4.....142 B6
Morris Dr Banbury OX16. 15 D7
Kingston Bagpuize
OX13............157 A1
Morris Ho OX4 ......142 C4
Morse Rd OX11......218 D6
Mortimer Dr OX3 ....123 F4
Mortimer Rd OX4....141 F3
Morton Ave OX5 .....108 E7
Morton Cl
Abingdon-on-Thames
OX14............180 C8
Kidlington OX5.......108 E8
Morton King Cl HP18. 128 D3
Mortree Ct SN6......209 B6
Moses Winter Way
OX10............221 B7
Mosquito La OX10 ...204 D2
Moss Cl RG4.........259 C5
Mott Cl OX29........117 C7
Motte The OX14 .....179 F7
MOULSFORD 238 F4
Moulsford Prep Sch
OX10............239 A6
Mountfield RG8......249 C7
Mountfield Rd OX28...117 F7
Mount Owen Rd OX18. 135 A3
Mount Pl Oxford OX2.. 123 A2
Oxford OX2.........261 A3
Mount Pleasant
Bishopstone SN6.....227 D4
Kidlington OX5.......92 C2
Lechlade-on-Thames
GL7............150 C4
Shipton-under-Wychwood
OX7............85 E7
Wardington OX17 .....5 E1
Mount Pleasant Cotts
OX12............216 D6
MOUNT SKIPPETT....88 A4
Mount St OX2 ....123 A2
Mount The
Reading RG4........258 F3
Tetsworth OX9.......166 B8
Tetsworth OX9.......166 B8
Mount View RG9....244 D2
Mount View Ct RG9...244 D2
Mousey La OX10.....221 D7
Mowbray Dr RG30....258 A1
Mowbray Fields Nature
Reserve★ OX11 ....218 E6
Mowbray Rd OX11...218 E6
Mowforth Cl RG8....240 E1
Mudstone Pike ■
SN7............172 F1
Mulberries The OX12. 197 A6
Mulberry Cl OX2.....123 A8
Mulberry Dr
Bicester OX26.......65 E5
Wheatley OX33......144 B8
Mulcaster Ave OX5...108 F8
Mullard Way OX14...179 E7
Mullein Rd OX26.....65 E5
Mullens Terr RG4....258 D6
Mumbery Hill RG10...255 E1
MURCOTT 95 F4
Murcott Rd
Horton-cum-Studley
OX5............96 C3
Upper Arncott OX25...96 D6
Murdoch Cl OX18....100 E3
Murdoch Pl OX2.....122 C1
Murdoch Cl OX15.....33 E4
Murdock Rd OX26....66 A2
Murray Ct OX2.......123 C4
Murren Croft OX10...221 E7
Murren The OX10....221 D6
Murreys La OX15.....32 E6
Museum of the History of
Science★ OX12 ....261 B2
Museum Rd
Oxford OX1.........123 C2
Oxford OX1.........261 B3
Musgrave Rd OX39 ..168 D7
Mus of Oxford★ OX1. 261 B2
Musson Cl ■ OX14...179 E6
Mustard La RG4......260 E2
Muswell Hill HP18....97 E3
Myrtle Cl
Long Hanborough OX29. 90 B1
Reading RG31.......257 C3

N

Nalder Gn OX12 .....214 A5
Naldertown OX12....214 C5
Napier Ct OX14......180 B7
Napier Rd OX4.......142 D5
Nappins Cl HP18......129 D5
Narrow Hill OX28....104 B2
Naseby Cl OX9.......130 B1
Nash Cl OX4.........142 D4
Nash Dr OX14.......179 C6
Nash La OX29.......106 A7
Nash Rd OX25........63 B8
National Herb Ctr The★
OX17............3 A3
Navigation Way OX2.. 123 A5
Nbury Hill OX15......14 B5
Neals La RG9........242 A2
NEAT ENSTONE 58 F5
Neave Mews ■ OX14. 179 F6
Needlemakers HP18 ..129 D7
Neill Pl OX4.........142 B1
NEITHROP 16 A6
Neithrop Ave OX16....16 B7
Neithrop Cl OX16.....16 B7
Nell Hill SN6........227 D4
Nelson Cl OX10......221 C8
Nelson Rd RG4.......259 C2
Nelson St Oxford OX2.. 261 A3
Thame OX9.........147 F8
Nene Gr OX11.......201 B2
Nene Rd OX13.......159 C2
Netheravon Cl OX18..115 E2
Nether Cl NN13.......24 A7
NETHERCOTE 17 B7
Nethercote La OX49...167 A1
Nethercote Mdw CV36..27 F7
Nethercote Rd
Banbury OX17.......17 D8
Tackley OX5........77 C6
NETHERCOTT 77 D6
Nether Durnford Cl
OX3............142 F7
NETHERTON 157 B3
Netherton La OX13 ..157 C3
Netherton Rd OX13...157 E6
NETHER WESTCOTE..68 F5
Netherwoods Rd OX3. 124 F2
NETHER WORTON....32 C1
Netherworton Rd
Barford St Michael
OX15...........32 E5
Barford St Michael OX7 . 32 E3
Netley Cl RG4.......259 E6
Netting St OX15 .....30 A7
NETTLEBED 224 D2
Nettlebed Com Sch
RG9............224 D2
Nettlebed Mead OX4. 142 E1
Nettleton Dr OX25....163 C7
Network Oxford Trade Pk
OX4............142 C2
Neunkirchen Way OX26 81 A7
Neville Way SN7.....194 E7
Nevis Rd RG31......257 D1
Newalls Rise RG10...255 E2
Newbarn Cl OX9.....148 A2
Newberry La OX10...203 B1
Newbery Cl RG31....257 D1
New Bldgs
Uffington SN7.......211 D8
Whitchurch Hill RG8 ..250 D2
Newbold Cl OX16.....16 E4
NEW BOTLEY 122 E1
NEWBRIDGE 156 E8
New Bridge St OX14.. 104 B1
Newbury Hill View
OX10............183 C8
Newbury Rd
East Hendred OX12...216 E5
Rowstock OX11......217 B6
Newbury St OX12 ....214 D4
Newcastle Dr ■ OX26. 65 D1
New Close Farm Rd
OX39...........149 C3
New Close La OX28 ..117 F5
New Coll OX1 ....261 C2
New College La OX1 . 261 C2
New College Sch OX1. 261 C2
New College Sq OX25...48 F1
Newcombe Cl OX15....21 A1
Newcombe Cl OX2....123 A7
New Cross Rd OX3...124 E3
Newells Cl OX44.....163 C1
Newells La RG4......258 C3
Newell's La
Mapledurham RG4 ...258 B6
Tokers Green RG4....258 B7
Newfield Rd RG4....252 F6
New Foscote Private Hospl
The OX16 ....16 D4
Newgate Rd OX5.....95 E5
NEW HEADINGTON ..124 C1
New High St OX3....124 C2
New Hill RG8........257 C5
NEW HINKSEY 141 D6
New Hinksey CE Prim Sch
OX1............141 C6
New Hope Terr ■
RG1............259 A1
New House Yd OX7 ...42 A5
NEWINGTON 183 E6
Newington Rd OX44 ..163 C1
New Inn Hall St ■ OX1. 261 B2
New Inn Rd OX3 ....111 A2
NEWLAND 118 D8
Newland
■ Witney OX28 .....104 C1
Witney OX28........104 C1
Newland Cl OX29....120 E7
Newland Mill OX28...104 C1
Newland Rd OX16....16 D5
Newland Rd OX16....16 D5
Newlands Ave
Didcot OX11........218 E7
Reading RG4........259 B3
Newlands Cl OX20...196 C1
Newlands La RG9....242 B5
Newlands St OX20...120 E8
Newlands Wy OX10...239 B8
Newlin Cl OX4.......141 F3

New Look Mobile Home Pk
OX18...........115 E1
Newman Ct Oxford OX4 123 C1
Witney OX29.......103 C1
Newman Rd OX4 ....142 B3
Newmans Cl OX11....218 C3
NEW MARSTON 123 F4
New Marston Prim Sch
OX3............124 A5
Newmill La OX28....103 F2
New Mill Mews ■
OX28...........104 A1
Newnham Gn OX10...221 F7
Newnham Hill RG9 ..242 B5
NEWNHAM MURREN. 221 E6
NEW OSNEY 261 A2
New Pl OX17........4 F2
New Pond La OX5 ....95 A5
Newport Rd RG1.....259 A1
Newport Cl OX5 .....108 D7
Newport Terr ■ OX26. 65 F2
New Rd Adderbury OX17. 22 F2
Bampton OX18......134 F4
Banbury OX16.......16 C5
Beckley OX3........111 B2
Bledington OX7......54 D2
Bletchingdon OX5 ....93 B8
Charney Bassett OX12. 175 F2
Childrey OX12.......213 B6
East Hagbourne OX11.. 219 A6
Glympton OX20......75 D8
Great Tew OX7......45 D7
Hailey OX29........104 A6
Kingham OX7........54 F4
Long Hanborough OX29. 90 B1
Lower Shiplake RG9 ..255 A3
Marcham OX13......178 C6
Milcombe OX15......21 A1
Oxford OX1.........261 B2
Radley OX14........160 E2
Ratley OX15.........2 A4
Shiplake Row RG9....254 B2
Shotteswell OX17 ....8 C8
Shrivenham SN6.....209 E3
Stokenchurch HP14...188 F4
Sutton OX29........120 A1
Wallingford OX10.....221 D7
Warborough OX10....203 B6
Watlington OX49.....186 B2
Woodstock OX20.....91 B6
New Row
Ambrosden OX25 ....81 C3
Bucknell OX27.......64 F8
Newscut La OX17.....4 F2
New St
Abingdon-on-Thames
OX14...........179 F7
Bicester OX26.......65 E3
Chipping Norton OX7...42 E3
Deddington OX15 ....33 F3
Henley-on-Thames RG9. 244 E3
Newtec Pl OX4 ......141 F7
Newton Ave RG4 ....259 D5
Newton Cl
■ Bicester OX26 .....65 D1
Chinnor OX39 ......168 C5
Didcot OX11........201 A3
NEWTON PURCELL....39 B2
Newton Rd OX1 .....141 C7
Newton Way OX10...204 A5
NEWTOWN
Henley-on-Thames ...254 F8
Wallingford 221 E1
Newtown
Chastleton GL56......40 F8
Ipsden OX10........240 C3
Little Compton CV36...26 F1
New Town GL56......40 F8
New Town Cotts SN6 . 227 D4
Newtown Gdns RG9 ..254 E8
New Town La SN6....227 D4
Newtown Rd RG9....254 E8
NEW YATT 104 E7
New Yatt Bsns Ctr
OX29...........104 F7
New Yatt La OX29 ...104 D7
New Yatt Rd OX29...104 E5
New Yatt Rd OX28,
OX29...........104 E4
Niagara Rd RG9......254 E8
Nias Ave SN7........172 D1
Nicholas Ave OX3....123 F4
Nicholas Rd RG9.....254 B8
Nichol Ct ■ SN7.....172 F3
Nicholson Rd OX3....123 F3
Nickling Pl OX17......8 E2
Nickling Rd OX17 ....8 E2
Nicolls Cl OX10......221 B1
Nigel Ct NN13.......24 A5
Nightingale Ave OX4.. 142 F1
Nightingale La SN3...208 A5
Nightingale Pl OX26...81 A8
Nightingale Wy ■
OX11...........200 C2
Nimrod Bsns Pk OX28 103 D1
Nine Acres Cl OX7....73 B4
Nine Acres La OX7....73 B4
Nineteenth St
East Hendred OX11...216 D4
Harwell OX11.......217 A1
Ninety Cut Hill OX18. 102 A4
Ninth Ave (North) OX3,
OX4............142 F1
Ninth St OX11.......217 B2
Nire Rd RG4........259 C2
Nixon Rd OX4.......141 F5
Nizewell Head OX25...62 B8
Noble Rd RG9.......254 F8
Nobles Cl Grove OX12 . 196 D1

Nobles Cl *continued*
Oxford OX2 . . . . **140** A8
NOKE **110** C7
Nolay Cl OX10 . . . . . . **204** E4
Norah Way OX4 . . . . **124** B5
Noral Cl OX16 . . . .**9** D2
Noral Way OX4 . . . .**9** D2
Nor Brook Cl OX14. . . **160** C2
Norcot Rd RG30 . . . . . **258** A1
Norfolk Cl OX14. . . . . **160** E2
Norfolk St OX1 . . . . . . **261** B1
Norham End OX2 . . . . **123** C4
Norham Gdns OX2. . . **261** B4
NORHAM MANOR . . . **261** C4
Norham Mws OX2 . . . **123** D4
Norham Rd OX2 . . . . **123** C4
Norman Ave
Abingdon-on-Thames
OX14. . . . . **160** A1
Henley-on-Thames RG9. **244** E1
Normandy Cres OX4 . . **142** E5
Norman Pl RG1. . . . . . **259** B1
Norman Rd RG4 . . . . . **259** C4
Norman Smith Rd [10]
OX4. . . . . **142** F1
Normanstead RG9 . . . **244** D1
Norman Way OX10. . . **221** C7
Norreys Ave OX1 . . . . **141** D6
Norreys Cl OX11 . . . . . **218** D7
Norreys Dr OX26. . . . . .**79** F7
Norreys Rd
Cumnor OX2 . . . . **139** F5
Didcot OX11 . . . . **218** D8
Norridge Way OX29. . . **106** C8
Norries Dr OX10 . . . . . **203** D1
Norris Cl
Abingdon-on-Thames
OX14. . . . . **160** B2
Adderbury OX17 . . . . . .**22** F2
Norris Rd OX25. . . . . . .**96** E8
Norseman Rd OX12. . . **214** C8
Northampton Rd
Oxford OX1 . . . . **141** D5
Weston-on-the-Green
OX25. . . . .**79** A4
Weston-on-the-Green
OX25. . . . .**79** B1
Weston-on-the-Green
OX25. . . . .**94** B8
NORTH ASTON **48** B6
North Aston Rd OX25 . . .**47** D6
North Ave OX14 . . . . . **160** A2
North Bar Pl OX16 . . . . .**16** C6
North Bar St OX16 . . . . .**16** C6
Northbourne CE Prim Sch
OX11 . . . . **218** E7
Northbourne Ct OX11 . **218** E8
Northbourne Prim Sch
OX11 . . . . **218** D7
NORTHBROOK **62** E1
Northbrook Ho [1]
OX4. . . . . **142** E2
Northbrook Rd RG4. . . **259** D6
North Bush Furlong
OX11. . . . . **201** B1
North Cl OX9 . . . . **145** F7
Northcot La OX16. . . . . .**16** B7
NORTHCOURT **160** A1
Northcourt La OX14. . . **160** A1
Northcourt Mews
OX14. . . . . **159** F1
Northcourt Rd OX14 . . **159** F1
Northcourt Wlk OX14 . **180** A4
North Croft OX11 . . . . **218** F5
North Culham Est
OX14 . . . . **181** A5
Northdown OX13 . . . . **156** D1
Harwell OX11 . . . . **217** C7
North Dr Grove OX12 . . **196** E2
Swerford Heath OX7. . . .**31** B3
Swerford Heath OX7. . . .**31** C3
Swerford Heath OX7. . . .**31** C2
North Drive OX7. . . . . . .**31** E2
NORTHEND **207** E6
Northend Rd RG9 . . . . **207** F5
Northern Bypass Rd
OX29 . . . . **107** F2
Northern By-Pass Rd
Cutteslowe OX3. . . . . . **108** E1
Oxford OX3 . . . . **124** C5
Northern House Sch
OX2 . . . . **123** B7
Northern Perimeter Rd
OX14. . . . . **179** E4
Northfield Ave RG9 . . . **255** A4
Northfield Cl OX4. . . . . **142** C2
Northfield Cotts OX2 . **122** A8
Northfield Ct RG9 . . . . **244** D3
Northfield End RG9. . . **244** D1
Northfield Farm La
OX28. . . . . **104** D1
Northfield Rd
Abingdon-on-Thames
OX14. . . . . **160** A3
Lower Shiplake RG9 . . . **255** B4
Oxford OX3 . . . . **124** E4
Reading RG1. . . . . **259** A4
Woodgreen OX28 . . . . **104** D1
Northfield Row [1]
OX28. . . . . **104** D1
Northfield Sch OX4. . . **142** D1
Northfield Sq OX28 . . . **104** D1
Northford Cl SN6. . . . . **209** C8
Northford Hill SN6. . . . **209** D8
Northford Ind Est SN6 **209** C8
North Gn Kirtlington OX5 .**77** F4
West Hanney OX12 . . . . **196** F7
North Hill HP18. . . . .**98** A1
North Hinksey CE Prim
Sch OX2 . . . . **140** E8
North Hinksey La OX2 **140** E8

NORTH HINKSEY
VILLAGE **140** E8
North Hinksey Village
OX2. . . . . **140** F7
North Kidlington Prim
Sch
[4] Kidlington OX5. . . . .**92** D1
[3] Kidlington OX5. . . . .**92** E1
North La OX25. . . . .**79** A2
NORTH LEIGH **105** B7
North Leigh Bsns Pk
OX29 . . . . **105** C2
North Leigh
CE(Controlled) Sch
OX29 . . . . **105** B6
Northleigh La OX29 . . **104** D8
North Leigh La OX29. . .**88** D1
North Leigh Roman Villa∗
OX29 . . . .**89** D3
North Lodge OX2 . . . . **122** D1
North Manor OX44. . . **143** E2
North Manor Estate The
OX44 . . . . **143** D2
Northmead La
Charney Bassett OX12 . **195** F7
Denchworth OX12. . . . **196** A7
North Mill Rd HP27 . . . **149** F5
NORTHMOOR **138** C2
Northmoor Pk OX29 . . **138** C2
Northmoor Pl OX2 . . . **123** C5
Northmoor Rd OX2 . . **123** C5
NORTH MORETON. . . **220** A7
Northolt Rd OX18. . . . **115** E3
North Oxfordshire Acad
OX16 . . . .**15** E8
North Parade Ave
OX2. . . . . **123** C4
North Pl OX3 . . . . **124** D3
North Quay OX14 . . . . **179** F4
North Rd Didcot OX11. . **200** D2
Moulsford OX10 . . . . . **238** F4
North Side
Steeple Aston OX25 . . . .**48** A1
Steeple Aston OX25 . . . .**62** E8
North St Aston OX18. . . **135** E3
Banbury OX16 . . . .**16** E7
Bicester OX26 . . . .**65** E2
Fritwell OX27. . . . .**49** E7
Islip OX5 . . . .**93** F1
Marcham OX13 . . . . . . **178** C6
Middle Barton OX7 . . . . .**60** F8
Oxford OX2 . . . . **123** A1
Reading RG4 . . . . **259** B2
Thame OX9 . . . . **129** F1
Watchfield SN6 . . . . . . **191** D1
NORTH STOKE **221** D1
Northumberland Ct [4]
OX16 . . . .**16** E6
Northview Prim Sch
SN6. . . . . **190** A7
North Way
Cutteslowe OX2. . . . . . **109** A1
Oxford OX3 . . . . **124** E4
Steventon OX13 . . . . . **198** F4
NORTH WESTON **146** F8
Northwood Cres OX18 **115** E4
Northwood Rd OX29 . . **103** C1
Norton Cl OX3. . . . . . . **124** D2
Norton Ct OX12. . . . . . **214** A2
Norton Green Ct OX7 . . .**42** E2
Norton Pk OX7 . . . .**42** F4
Norton Terr OX2. . . . . **102** D8
Norton Way OX18. . . . **115** F3
Norwood Ave OX13 . . **156** E1
Nosworthy Way OX10. **221** E5
Notley Rd OX4 . . . . **259** B4
Nottingham Fee OX11 **236** F8
Nottwood La RG9 . . . . **242** A5
Nourse Cl OX3. . . . . . . **110** B5
Nowell Rd OX4 . . . . . . **142** A3
Nuffield Cl
Bicester OX26. . . . .**65** F3
[9] Didcot OX11. . . . . **219** A8
Nuffield Coll OX1. . . . . **261** A2
Nuffield Dr OX16 . . . . . .**16** A8
Nuffield Health The Manor
Hospl Oxford OX3 . . **124** C3
Nuffield Hill OX9 . . . . . **223** F4
Nuffield Ind Est OX4 . . **142** C2
Nuffield La OX10 . . . . . **203** B7
Nuffield Orthopaedic Ctr
OX3 . . . . **124** F1
Nuffield Place∗ RG6 . . **223** F4
Nuffield Rd OX3 . . . . . **124** F1
Nuffield Trade Pk
OX14 . . . . **179** C7
Nuffield Way OX14 . . . **179** C7
NUNEHAM
COURTENAY **161** E3
Nuneham Pk
Clifton Hampden
OX44. . . . . **181** C7
Nuneham Courtenay
OX44. . . . . **161** D1
Nuneham Sq OX14. . . **179** F8
NUNEY GREEN **251** E3
NUNEY GREEN **251** E3
Nunhide La RG8 . . . . . **256** F1
Nunnery Cl OX4 . . . . . **142** D2
Nunney Brook OX11 . . **200** F3
Nun's Acre RG8 . . . . . **249** B7
Nurseries Rd OX5. . . . **108** D8
Nursery Cl
Chinnor OX39 . . . . **168** C7
Lower Shiplake RG9 . . . **255** A4
Oxford OX2 . . . . **122** D1
Oxford OX3 . . . . **124** F3
Nursery Dr OX16. . . . . . .**16** D1
Nursery End SN7 . . . . **194** D7

Nursery Gdns RG8 . . . **257** B5
Nursery La OX16. . . . . . .**16** C7
Nursery Rd OX29 . . . . **105** C7
Nursery The OX14 . . . **200** A8
Nursery View SN7 . . . . **173** B3
Nuthatch Cl [1] OX4 . . **142** E1
Nut Hatch Cotts RG8. . **241** D3
Nuthatch Way OX26 . . . .**65** F1
Nyatt Rd OX14. . . . . . . **180** C8
Nye Bevan Cl OX4 . . . . **142** A8

O

Oak Ave OX14 . . . . **160** E6
Oak Cl OX26. . . . .**65** F4
Oak Cotts OX10 . . . . . **239** D6
Oakdale Ct [3] OX10. . **221** C7
Oakdale La OX28 . . . . **104** E3
Oakdale Rd OX28 . . . . **104** D3
Oakdale Wlk [1] OX4 . **124** C5
Oakdene RG8. . . . . **250** E6
Oakdene Cl RG8 . . . . . **250** E3
Oak Dr Kidlington OX5. . . .**92** F1
Shipton-under-Wychwood
OX7. . . . .**70** C1
Shipton under Wychwood
OX7. . . . .**85** C8
Oakend Lea OX11. . . . **219** C8
Oak End Way OX39 . . . **168** D6
Oakes La OX4 . . . . **121** C2
Oakesmere OX13 . . . . **158** B6
Oakey Cl OX18. . . . . . . **133** C5
Oak Farm Cl
Milcombe OX15. . . . .**20** F2
Tetsworth OX9. . . . . . . **166** B7
Oak Farm Dr OX15. . . . . .**20** F2
Oakfield Ind Est OX29. **120** D6
Oakfield Pl
Witney OX28 . . . . **118** B7
Witney OX28 . . . . **118** B7
Oakfield Rd OX18. . . . . **115** D1
Oakford Ct RG9. . . . . . **254** C8
Oak Gr RG4. . . . . **259** B5
Oakhall Ct HP18 . . . . . **127** F8
Oakham Cl RG31. . . . . **257** D2
Oakham Rd
Little Compton GL56 . . . .**27** B1
Little Compton GL56 . . . .**27** C2
Oak Hall La OX11. . . . . . .**21** C2
Oak La Ambrosden OX25. .**81** D4
Stanford in the Vale
SN7. . . . . **194** F6
Oakland Cl OX29. . . . . **105** F2
Oakland Rd OX16 . . . . . .**16** D2
Oaklands OX2 . . . . **121** B3
OAKLEY **168** B5
Oakley Ct OX10 . . . . . . **222** F5
Oakley Ho OX13 . . . . . **158** C2
Oakley La OX39. . . . . . **168** B6
Oakley Pk OX13 . . . . . **158** C2
Oakley Rd
Chinnor OX39 . . . . **168** C6
Horton-cum-Studley
OX33. . . . . **112** C5
Reading RG4 . . . . **258** F4
Worminghall HP18 . . . . **127** E6
Oakmead OX24 . . . . . . **104** D2
Oak Rd SN6 . . . . **191** C1
Oakridge OX25 . . . .**48** B3
Oaks Caravan Pk
OX13 . . . . **177** B8
Oaks Meade OX18 . . . **115** F4
Oaksmere OX18 . . . . . **158** A6
Oaks Rd RG9 . . . . **255** A4
Oak St GL7. . . . . **150** C4
Oaks The OX18 . . . .**63** C5
Oakthorpe Pl OX2 . . . . **123** B6
Oakthorpe Rd OX2. . . . **123** B6
Oak Tree Cl OX29 . . . . **105** C6
Oak Tree Copse RG8. . **257** E3
Oak Tree Rd RG31 . . . . **257** E2
Oak Tree Wlk RG8 . . . . **257** D5
Oak View OX18 . . . . . . **114** C7
Oakwood Place OX29. **117** B4
Oakwood Wy OX2 . . . . **140** A5
Oasis Pk OX29 . . . . **120** D6
Oasis Rd OX29. . . . . . . **120** D6
Oat Cl RG9 . . . . **254** A7
Oathurst Est OX18 . . . **134** F3
Oatland Rd OX11 . . . . . **218** E8
Oatlands Cl OX10 . . . . **203** B7
Oatlands Rd OX2 . . . . . **122** F1
Observatory Cl OX10. . **204** A4
Observatory St OX2. . . **261** A4
Ochre Cl OX33. . . . . . . **144** B8
Ock Dr OX10. . . . . **182** D5
Ockham Ct OX2 . . . . . **123** C4
Ockley Brook OX11 . . . **201** A2
Ock Mdw SN7 . . . . **194** F7
Ock Meadow Nature
Reserve∗ OX14 . . . . **179** B5
Ock Mews [5] OX14 . . **179** E7
Ock Mill Cl OX14 . . . . . **179** D6
Ock St
Abingdon-on-Thames
OX14. . . . . **179** D6
Abingdon-on-Thames
OX14. . . . . **179** E7
O'Connors Rd OX29 . . **102** E2
Octavian Way NN13. . . . .**24** A7
Oday Hill OX14 . . . . . . **179** F5
ODDINGTON **94** E2
Oddley La HP27. . . . . . **169** D8
Odiham Ave RG4 . . . . . **259** E5
Odiham Cl OX18. . . . . . **115** F3
Odstone Hill
Ashbury SN6 . . . . **228** D7
Compton Beauchamp
SN6. . . . . **210** C1
Ody Cl OX12. . . . . **214** A5

Offa Pl OX9. . . . . **129** D1
Offas Cl OX10. . . . . **204** A5
Offlands Cl OX10 . . . . . **238** F6
Offutt Dr OX25. . . . .**63** C8
Ogbourne Cl OX12. . . . **214** B5
OISE Oxford OX1 . . . . . **261** B2
Olaf Schmid Mews
OX11. . . . . **200** B2
Old Abingdon Rd
Kennington OX1 . . . . . **141** D4
Oxford OX1 . . . . **141** D6
Old Arncott Rd OX26. . . .**81** C3
Old Bakery The OX1 . . **261** A2
Old Barn Cl
Benson OX10 . . . . **204** A4
Reading RG4 . . . . **259** A6
Old Barn Ground OX3. **142** F7
Old Bath Rd
Sonning RG4 . . . . **260** D1
Sonning RG4 . . . . **260** E2
Old Bix Rd Bix RG9 . . . . **243** F7
Swan Wood RG9 . . . . . **242** D7
Old Blackalls Dr OX10. **221** A3
Old Bldgs [13] OX10 . . **221** D7
OLD BOARS HILL **159** D8
Old Boars Hill
Boars Hill OX1. . . . . . . **140** D1
Wootton OX1. . . . . **159** C8
Old Botley [5] OX2 . . . **122** D1
Old Bourne OX11 . . . . . **200** F3
Old Brewery La RG9 . . **244** E2
Old Bridge Rd OX15. . . . .**21** E4
Old Bryars Cl HP18 . . . **128** C3
Old Burford Rd OX7 . . . . .**54** D1
Old Camp Rd RG9 . . . . **224** E2
Old Canal View OX12 . **214** C6
Old Chapel Cl OX5. . . . . .**92** E1
Old Coach Rd OX13 . . . **157** F2
Old Coachyard The [1]
OX28. . . . . **104** B1
Old Copse Gdns RG4. . **252** F6
Old Council Hos The
Horley OX15 . . . .**8** B4
South Newington OX15. . .**31** F7
Old Creamery OX9. . . . **147** E8
Old Croft Cl OX39 . . . . **167** F4
Old Dairy The [3]
OX28. . . . . **118** D8
Old Dashwood Hill
HP14. . . . . **189** F2
Old Didcot Rd OX11. . . **202** C2
Oldean Cl RG31. . . . . . **257** D1
Old Farm Cl
Abingdon-on-Thames
OX14. . . . . **180** C8
Worminghall HP18. . . . **127** D5
Old Farm Cres RG31. . . **257** C2
Old Field OX44 . . . . **164** A7
Old Forge Cl OX7 . . . .**54** D2
Old Forge Dr OX7 . . . .**29** A3
Old Forge The RG8 . . . . **249** A6
Old Forge Yard OX15 . . . .**19** F8
Old George Yd OX18. . . **100** E5
Old Glebe OX15. . . . .**20** C8
Old Gn The OX33 . . . . . **112** A5
Old Greyfriars St OX1 . **261** B1
Old Greys La RG9. . . . . **244** D1
Old Grimsbury Rd OX16 .**16** E7
Old Henley Rd
Nuffield. OX10. . . . . . . **222** F8
Nuffield OX10 . . . . **223** A7
Old High St OX3 . . . . . . **124** D3
Old Hill
Little Compton CV36 . . . .**27** F2
Little Rollright CV36 . . . . .**28** A3
Long Compton CV36 . . . .**28** A4
Old Hill La
Little Compton CV36 . . . .**27** F2
Little Rollright CV36 . . . . .**28** A2
Old Icknield Way
OX10. . . . . **222** D7
Old Johns Cl OX7. . . . . . .**60** F8
Old Kiln Rd OX29. . . . . **120** B8
Old Kiln The RG9 . . . . . **224** E2
Old London Rd
Benson OX10 . . . . **204** A4
Benson OX10 . . . . **204** E1
Chipping Norton OX7 . . . .**56** C7
Tiddington OX9 . . . . . . **145** F4
Wheatley OX33 . . . . . . **144** D8
Old Luxters Farm
Brewery∗ RG9 . . . . . **226** F7
Old Manor Ct
Horley OX15 . . . .**8** B4
Letcombe Regis OX12. . **214** A2
Old Man's La OX12. . . . **197** B4
Old Marston Rd
Marston OX3 . . . . **123** F4
Oxford OX3 . . . . **124** A4
Old Mill Cl OX12 . . . . . **196** E1
Old Mill The
Pangbourne RG8. . . . . **256** D6
[6] Wantage OX12 . . . . **214** D4
Old Milton Rd
Milton OX11. . . . . **200** A4
Milton OX13. . . . . **199** F4
Old Moor OX14 . . . . . . **199** D5
Old Moor Cl OX10 . . . . **221** C2
Old Nursery La OX11. . **202** C2
Old Nursery View
OX1. . . . . **141** D3
Old Orchard OX39 . . . . **149** E2
Old Parr Cl OX16. . . . . . .**16** D5
Old Parr Rd OX16 . . . . . .**16** D4
Old Place Yd OX26. . . . . .**65** E1
Old Plough Wlk OX15 . . . .**33** A4
Old Pound The OX13. . **159** B6
Old Railway Cl GL7 . . . **150** D5
Old Rd
East Hendred OX12. . . . **216** E6

Old Rd *continued*
Great Tew OX7 . . . .**45** D7
Littleworth OX33. . . . . **143** E8
Oxford OX3 . . . . **124** B1
Oxford OX3 . . . . **124** E1
Ratley OX15. . . . .**2** A4
Old Rd The RG9 . . . . . . **225** C8
Old Reading Rd
Crowmarsh Gifford
OX10. . . . . **221** F5
Newnham Murren OX10 **221** F6
Old Rectory OX25. . . . . . .**48** F1
Old Rectory Ct OX25 . . . .**80** A4
Old Rectory Mews
OX28. . . . . **118** A7
Old Sawmill Pl OX39. . **168** D6
Old Sawmills Rd SN7 . . **172** F2
Old Sch La OX27. . . . .**49** F7
Old School Cl OX7. . . . . . .**65** F7
Old School End OX15. . . .**30** A7
Old School Green
RG9. . . . . **224** D2
Old School Ho The OX7 . .**70** B2
Old School La OX12. . . **213** F5
Old School Pl
Banbury OX16 . . . .**16** E6
Watlington OX49. . . . . **186** B1
Old School The OX4 . . **142** C6
Old Skimmingdish La
OX26. . . . .**66** A5
Old Stables The OX3. . **124** C4
Old Stables Yd OX12. . **214** A1
Old Station Way OX29 **120** D6
Old Station Yd [6]
OX14. . . . . **179** F7
Old Timber Yard
OX10. . . . . **239** A8
OLD TOWN **24** A7
Old Town NN13. . . . .**24** A7
Old Union OX9. . . . . . . **129** C1
Old Vicarage La SN3. . **208** A3
Old Wallingford Way
OX14. . . . . **200** B8
Old Warehouse Flats The
OX28. . . . . **104** C1
OLD WARREN **246** E6
Old Well Ct RG4 . . . . . . **260** D4
Oldwell Rd OX4 . . . . . . **124** C5
Old Wharf Rd SN7 . . . . **210** C8
Old Windmill Way
HP18. . . . . **129** C7
Old Witney Rd OX29. . . **120** D8
OLD WOODSTOCK **91** A7
Oliver Rd OX4 . . . . **142** E5
Olley Cres OX29 . . . . . . **117** C8
Olson Cotts HP14. . . . . **188** F4
Olympic Ave OX14 . . . **199** E4
Omega Pk OX11 . . . . . . **200** E3
One End La OX10 . . . . . **203** F4
Onley Ct [8] OX1 . . . . . **141** C7
Onslow Dr OX9 . . . . . . **130** B1
Onslow Gdns RG4 . . . . **259** C3
Oracle Parkway RG5. . **260** A1
Orange Cl SN6. . . . . . . **190** A6
Oratory Dr The
Woodcote RG8. . . . . . . **241** B1
Woodcote RG8. . . . . . . **251** A8
Oratory Prep Sch The
RG8 . . . . **250** D4
Oratory Sch The RG8 . . **251** A8
Orchard Ave RG4 . . . . . **252** F5
Orchard Cl
Abingdon-on-Thames
OX14. . . . . **160** A1
Banbury OX16 . . . .**16** B6
Buckland SN7 . . . . **174** E8
Carterton OX18. . . . . . **115** D8
Carterton OX18. . . . . . **133** D8
Cassington OX29. . . . . **107** C2
Chalgrove OX44. . . . . . **184** D7
Charney Bassett OX12 . **175** F2
Combe OX29 . . . .**90** A4
Didcot OX11 . . . . **200** E1
East Hanney OX12 . . . . **197** B6
East Hendred OX12. . . . **216** D7
Eynsham OX29 . . . . . . **120** F7
Henley-on-Thames RG9. **244** E1
[4] Henley-on-Thames
RG9. . . . . **254** E8
Lechlade-on-Thames
GL7. . . . . **150** C4
Salford OX7 . . . .**41** F4
Salford OX7 . . . .**42** A5
Shiplake RG9. . . . . **254** E2
Thame OX9 . . . . **148** A8
Upper Arncott OX25 . . . .**96** D6
Upton OX11. . . . . **218** C2
Wallingford OX10 . . . . . **221** D6
Warborough OX10. . . . **203** B7
Wheatley OX33 . . . . . . **144** D2
Orchard Coombe RG8 **250** D3
Orchard Cotts OX7. . . . . .**57** B1
Orchard Ct OX4 . . . . . . **142** B4
Orchard Ctr The OX11. **200** F1
Orchard Field RG4. . . . **252** C5
Orchard Field La OX20. .**91** D3
Orchard Fields Com Sch
OX16 . . . .**15** F6
Orchard Furlong
OX12. . . . . **213** C4
Orchard Gdns OX12. . . **213** D5
Orchard Gr
Bloxham OX15 . . . .**21** D3
Reading RG4 . . . . **259** E4
Orchard Ground OX7 . . . .**69** C2
Orchard Haven OX10. . **202** D8
Orchard Hill OX4 . . . . . **172** E3
Orchard La
Bicester OX27. . . . .**65** F6
Boars Hill OX1. . . . . . . **140** C1

Orchard La *continued*
East Hendred OX12. . . . **216** D6
Upper Heyford OX25 . . . .**62** F8
Orchard Meadow Prim Sch
OX4 . . . . **142** D2
Orchard Piece OX17 . . . . .**4** A3
Orchard Pl
Upper Heyford OX25. . . .**62** F8
Westbury NN13. . . . .**25** A4
Orchard Rd Ardley OX27 .**50** B4
Buckland SN7 . . . . **174** E8
Hook Norton OX15 . . . . .**30** B8
Oxford OX4 . . . . **140** A8
Orchard Rise
Burford OX18 . . . . **100** E4
Chesterton OX26. . . . . . .**79** F8
Orchard Row OX18 . . . **100** F6
Orchard Sq OX27 . . . .**65** F6
Orchard The
Appleton OX13 . . . . . . **158** A8
Ascott-under-Wychwood
OX7. . . . .**71** B1
Brighthampton OX29. . . **137** A4
East Challow OX12 . . . . **214** A5
Horton-cum-Studley
OX33. . . . . **112** C6
Merton OX25 . . . .**95** D8
Orchard View OX17 . . . . .**4** F2
Orchard Way
Banbury OX16 . . . .**16** B6
Bicester OX26 . . . .**65** C3
Chinnor OX39. . . . . . . **168** C6
Harwell OX11 . . . . **217** D7
Kidlington OX5. . . . . . . **108** F8
[4] Kidlington OX5. . . . **109** A8
Kingham OX7. . . . .**54** F4
Marcham OX13 . . . . . . **178** C6
Middle Barton OX7 . . . . .**46** E1
Oxford OX4 . . . . **142** C3
Wantage OX12 . . . . . . **214** E4
Witney OX28 . . . . **118** A8
Orchard Wlk OX49. . . . **186** C2
Orchid Cl OX26 . . . .**65** E5
Orchid Mews OX11 . . . **218** B8
Orchids The
Chilton OX11 . . . . **235** D7
Lower Basildon RG8 . . . **249** D2
Orchid Way OX18. . . . . **115** E4
Ordnance Rd OX11 . . . **200** D2
Oregano Ct OX11 . . . . **218** B7
Oregon Ave RG31 . . . . **257** D3
Oriel Coll OX1 . . . . **261** C2
Oriel Ct OX11. . . . . **219** B8
Oriel Sq OX1. . . . . **261** C2
Oriel St OX1 . . . . **261** C2
Oriel Way OX26. . . . .**65** F3
Orkney Pl OX28. . . . . . . **117** F8
Ormond Rd
Thame OX9 . . . . **130** A1
Wantage OX12 . . . . . . **214** E4
Orpine Cl OX26. . . . .**65** D5
Orpwood Way OX14 . . **179** C6
Orwell Cl RG4 . . . . **258** F4
Orwell Dr OX11. . . . . . . **201** A1
Osberton Rd OX2 . . . . . **123** A7
Osborne Cl
Bicester OX26 . . . .**65** C3
Kidlington OX5. . . . . . . **108** D7
Wolvercote OX2 . . . . . **122** F8
Osiers The OX10 . . . . . **183** B5
Osler Rd OX3 . . . . **124** C3
OSNEY **123** A1
Osney Cl OX15. . . . .**30** B7
Osney La Oxford OX1 . . **123** A1
Oxford OX1 . . . . **261** A2
Osney Mead OX2 . . . . . **141** A8
Osney Mead Ind Est
OX2 . . . . **141** A8
Osney Mews OX2. . . . . **123** A1
Osprey Cl OX4. . . . .**81** B8
Osprey Pl OX11. . . . . . . **200** C2
Osterley Dr RG4 . . . . . . **259** E6
Osterley Gr OX29. . . . . . .**16** B4
Oswestry Rd OX1 . . . . . **141** D5
Otmoor La Beckley OX3 **111** A4
Charlton-on-Otmoor OX5 .**95** A4
Otmoor View OX25 . . . . .**95** C8
Otters Reach OX1. . . . . **141** E1
Ottery Way OX11 . . . . . **201** A2
Our Lady of Lourdes
Catholic Prim Sch [1]
OX28 . . . . **117** E7
Our Lady's Abingdon Jun
& Sen Sch OX14 . . . . **180** A4
Our Lady's RC Prim Sch
OX4 . . . . **142** D5
Ouse Cl OX11. . . . . **200** F3
Ouseley Cl OX3 . . . . . . **123** F4
Outham Rd OX16 . . . .**9** D3
Outram Rd OX4 . . . . . . **142** B5
Oval The Bicester OX26 . .**65** D3
Didcot OX11 . . . . **200** C2
Oxford OX4 . . . . **142** A3
Overbrooke Gdns OX4 **143** A2
Overbury [1] OX18. . . . **115** E5
Overdale Cl OX4 . . . . . . **124** E4
Overdown Rd RG31. . . . **257** D3
OVER KIDDINGTON **60** A1
Overlanders End RG31 **257** E3
Overmead OX4 . . . . **179** E4
Overmead Gn OX4 . . . . **142** E2
OVER NORTON **42** E5
Over Norton Rd OX7. . . . .**42** F4
Overstrand Cl OX26. . . . .**66** A4
OVERTHORPE **17** D6
Overthorpe Rd
Banbury OX16 . . . .**17** A6
Overthorpe OX17 . . . . . .**17** C7

Overton Dr
Reading RG4 . . . . **259** D3
Thame OX9 . . . . **130** B1
OVER WORTON **46** D7
OVERY OX10. . . . . **202** E8
Owen Pl OX18 . . . . . **115** D4
Owens Way OX4. . . . . **142** C6
Ower Dr OX25 . . . . **49** C1
Owlington Cl OX2. . . . **122** C1
Ox Cl OX14 . . . . **180** A8
Oxen Piece OX44 . . . . **145** C2
Oxeye Ct OX4. . . . . . . **161** E8
OXFORD **261** C1
Oxford Airport OX5. . . **92** A4
**Oxford Brookes Univ
(Gipsy La Campus)**
OX3 . . . . **124** B2
**Oxford Brookes Univ
(Harcourt Hill Campus)**
OX2 . . . . **140** D6
**Oxford Brookes Univ
(Headington Hill Campus
)** OX3 . . . . **124** A2
**Oxford Brookes Univ
(Marston Road Site)**
OX3 . . . . **124** A3
**Oxford Brookes Univ
(Wheatley Campus)**
OX33 . . . . **144** C8
Oxford Bsns Ctr The
OX1 . . . . **261** A1
Oxford Bsns Park N
OX4 . . . . **142** D5
Oxford Bsns Park S
OX4 . . . . **142** D4
Oxford Bsns Pk OX2 . . **109** A2
Oxford Bus Mus★ OX29 **90** E1
Oxford Castle Unlocked★
OX1 . . . . **261** A2
**Oxford & Cherwell Valley
Coll** OX14 . . . . **16** B5
Oxford Cl
Kingston Bagpuize
OX13. . . . . **156** F1
Kirtlington OX5 . . . . . **77** F4
Oxford Cres
Didcot OX11 . . . . **200** C1
Didcot OX11 . . . . **218** C8
Oxford Ct OX25. . . . . . **79** A2
Oxford Down OX39 . . **168** B7
Oxford English Acad 4
OX5 . . . . **92** E1
Oxford English Ctr The 4
OX2 . . . . **123** C4
Oxford High Sch (Jun Sch)
1 OX2. . . . . **123** C4
**Oxford High Sch (Senior
Sch)** OX2 . . . . **123** C6
Oxford Hill
2 Witney OX28 . . . . . **104** D1
Witney OX28 . . . . . . **118** D8
Witney OX28, OX29. . . **118** D8
**Oxford House Sch of
English** OX33. . . . . . . **144** B8
Oxford Ice Rink★ OX1 **261** A1
Oxford Int Coll of Beauty
2 OX28 . . . . **104** B1
Oxford La OX12 . . . . . **196** E2
Oxford Media & Bsns Sch
OX1 . . . . **261** B2
Oxford Montessori Schools
OX3 . . . . **110** D2
Oxford Motor Pk OX5. . **92** B2
Oxford Parkway OX2 . **109** A4
Oxford Playhouse★
OX1 . . . . **261** B3
Oxford Rd
Abingdon-on-Thames OX1,
OX13, OX14 . . . . **160** B5
Abingdon-on-Thames
OX13. . . . . **160** B6
Abingdon-on-Thames
OX14. . . . . **160** A2
Adderbury OX15 . . . . . **23** A6
Adderbury OX17 . . . . . **23** A3
Benson OX10. . . . . . . **203** E4
Bicester OX25, OX26. . . **80** D8
Bicester OX26 . . . . **80** B6
Bletchingdon OX5. . . . . **93** A7
Bodicote OX15. . . . . . . **16** D3
Burford OX18 . . . . . . **100** E4
Burford OX18 . . . . . . **101** C2
Clifton Hampden OX14,
OX44. . . . . **181** E6
Cumnor OX2 . . . . **139** F5
Cutteslowe OX2. . . . . **109** A3
Dorchester OX10. . . . **182** D2
Dorchester OX10. . . . **182** E2
Duns Tew OX25 . . . . . . **47** F5
Enstone OX7 . . . . **58** F5
Enstone OX7 . . . . **59** A4
Eynsham OX29 . . . . . **120** F7
Eynsham OX29 . . . . . **121** A4
Farmoor OX2, OX29 . . **121** A4
Frilford OX13. . . . . . . **178** A2
Garford OX13 . . . . . . **177** E3
Garsington OX44. . . . **143** C2
Grove OX12. . . . . **197** A3
Hampton Poyle OX5 . . . **93** B3
Horspath OX33 . . . . . **143** B6
Kidlington OX5. . . . . . **108** F7
Kingston Bagpuize
OX13. . . . . **156** F1
Kingston Bagpuize
OX13. . . . . **157** A1
Kirtlington OX5 . . . . . . **77** F3
Long Compton CV36 . . . **27** F5

Oxford Rd continued
Long Compton CV36 . . . . **28** B4
Marston OX3 . . . . **123** F5
Middleton Stoney OX25. . **64** A3
Oxford OX4 . . . . **142** B3
Oxford OX4 . . . . **142** C5
Reading RG8, RG30,
RG31. . . . . **257** D4
Southcoombe OX7 . . . . . **43** E2
South Leigh OX29 . . . . **105** B1
South Leigh OX29 . . . . **119** A8
Steeple Barton OX25 . . . **61** E4
Stokenchurch HP14. . . **188** C5
Thame OX9 . . . . **129** A1
Thame OX9 . . . . **147** D8
Tiddington OX9 . . . . . . **145** E6
Weston-on-the-Green
OX25. . . . . **79** F4
Woodcote RG8. . . . . . **240** E1
Woodstock OX20. . . . . . **91** B6
Woodstock OX20. . . . . . **91** C5
Oxford Retail Pk OX4 . **142** E4
Oxford Sch of English
OX1 . . . . **261** B2
Oxford Science Pk The
OX4 . . . . **142** C1
Oxfordshire Mus The★
OX20 . . . . **91** A6
Oxford Spires Acad
OX4 . . . . **142** B7
Oxford Spires Bsns Pk
OX5 . . . . **92** B3
Oxford Sq SN6. . . . . . **191** C1
Oxford St Reading RG4. **259** A2
Woodstock OX20. . . . . . **91** B6
Oxford Sta OX2. . . . . . **123** A1
Oxford Study Ctr OX2. **109** A1
Oxford Tutorial Coll
OX1 . . . . **261** C2
Oxford Union The★
OX1 . . . . **261** B2
Oxford University Mus of
Natural History The★
OX1 . . . . **261** B3
Oxford University Press
OX2 . . . . **261** A3
Oxford Way OX44. . . . **184** B7
Oxhey Hill OX17 . . . . . . **4** D3
Oxhey Rise OX15 . . . . . **31** B7
Oxlease OX28. . . . . . . **118** C8
Oxlip Leyes OX26 . . . . . **65** D4
Oxon Pl SN6. . . . . **227** D4
Oxpens Rd OX1 . . . . . **261** A1
Ozone L Pk OX4 . . . . . **142** D1

P

Packers La SN7. . . . . . **211** C7
Packhorse La OX13 . . . **178** D6
Pack La OX7. . . . . **61** B7
Pack & Prime La RG9 . **244** C2
Paddick Cl RG4. . . . . . **260** E3
Paddock Cl
Benson OX10. . . . . . . **204** A4
Chalgrove OX44. . . . . **184** D7
Wantage OX12 . . . . . **214** F6
Paddock Farm La OX15 **22** D8
Paddock Mews
Kingston Bagpuize
OX13. . . . . **156** D1
Kingston Bagpuize
OX13. . . . . **156** D1
Paddock Rd
Ardley OX27 . . . . **50** B4
Reading RG4 . . . . **259** D1
Wallingford OX10 . . . . **221** D7
Paddocks The
Aston OX18 . . . . **135** E2
Bampton OX18 . . . . . **134** C1
Chinnor OX39 . . . . . . **168** D8
Deddington OX15 . . . . . **33** E4
East Hanney OX12 . . . **197** B6
Enstone OX7 . . . . **58** F4
Mollington OX17 . . . . . . **3** F3
Souldern OX27 . . . . . . **35** E3
Yarnton OX5 . . . . **108** B5
Paddock The
Chilton OX11 . . . . **235** D8
Highworth SN6 . . . . . **190** A5
Kennington OX1 . . . . . **160** F7
Kingston Bagpuize
OX13. . . . . **156** D1
Somerton OX25. . . . . . . **48** F5
Paddox Cl OX2 . . . . . . **123** A8
Paddox The OX2. . . . . **123** A8
Padley Cl OX7 . . . . **43** A4
Page Furlong OX10. . . **182** D2
Page's Bottom RG9. . . **224** F5
Pages La OX15 . . . . **7** C6
Pages Orch RG4 . . . . . **252** E5
Paget Rd OX14 . . . . . . **142** E6
Pagisters Rd OX14. . . **160** C2
Paines Hill OX25. . . . . . **62** B8
Painswick Cl OX28. . . **103** E1
Painters Cl OX15 . . . . . . **21** D4
Pain Way OX10 . . . . . . **183** B3
Palladian Ct OX4 . . . . **142** B6
Palmer Ave OX25 . . . . . **96** F8
Palmer Cl OX11. . . . . . **218** B8
Palmer Pl OX14. . . . . . **179** E5
Palmer Rd
Faringdon SN7. . . . . . **173** A2
Oxford OX3 . . . . **124** E1
Palmers OX12 . . . . **214** F5
Pampas Cl OX18. . . . . **115** E1
PANGBOURNE **256** C6
Pangbourne Coll RG8 **256** A4
Pangbourne Hill RG8 . **256** C5
Pangbourne Lodge Dr
RG8 . . . . **256** C5

Pangbourne Mews
RG8 . . . . **256** D6
Pangbourne Pl RG8. . . **256** D6
Pangbourne Prim Sch
RG8 . . . . **256** E5
Pangbourne St RG30. . **258** B1
Pangbourne Sta RG8 . **256** C6
Panshill OX5 . . . . **96** D2
Paper Mill Cotts OX18 . **99** D6
Paper Mill La OX11 . . . **220** A5
Papist Way OX10 . . . . **239** B8
Parade The
Kidlington OX5. . . . . . **108** F6
Oxford OX3 . . . . **124** D3
Paradise OX17. . . . . **23** F5
Paradise La OX15. . . . . **21** A2
Paradise Mews RG9 . . **244** D2
Paradise Rd RG9 . . . . **244** C1
Paradise Sq OX1 . . . . . **261** A1
Paradise St OX1 . . . . . **261** A2
Paradise Terr OX7 . . . . **42** D1
Park 34 OX11. . . . . **200** E3
Park Ave
Highworth SN6 . . . . . **190** A5
Kidlington OX5. . . . . . . **92** D2
Shrivenham SN6 . . . . **209** D7
Park Cl Avon Dassett CV47 **2** F8
Banbury OX16 . . . . **16** C6
Bladon OX20 . . . . **91** B3
Cutteslowe OX2. . . . . **109** B2
Didcot OX11 . . . . **218** D8
Hanwell OX17 . . . . **8** F4
Hook Norton OX15 . . . . **30** B6
Kirtlington OX5 . . . . . . **77** F5
Middleton Stoney OX25. . **64** A4
North Leigh OX29 . . . . **105** C6
Sonning Common RG4. **253** A6
Yarnton OX5 . . . . **108** B4
PARK CORNER **224** C6
Park Cres OX14. . . . . . **179** E7
Park Ct
Long Compton CV36 . . . **27** F4
Thame OX9 . . . . **148** A8
Park Dr OX13. . . . . **199** E4
Park End Bladon OX20 . . **91** B2
Bodicote OX15. . . . . . . **16** E1
Croughton NN13 . . . . . **36** D8
Park End Cl OX15. . . . . . **16** E1
Park End Ct OX15. . . . . **16** E1
Park End Pl OX1. . . . . . **261** A2
Park End St OX1. . . . . **261** A2
Park End Works NN13 . **36** D7
Parker Cl OX18 . . . . . . **116** A5
Parker Rd OX1 . . . . . . **141** B5
Parkers Cir OX7 . . . . . . **43** A3
Parkers Cl SN7 . . . . . . **173** A3
Parkers Hill OX9. . . . . **166** B8
Parker St OX4 . . . . . . **141** F6
Park Farm Bsns Ctr
OX25 . . . . **63** E5
Park Farm Cl OX25 . . . . **81** C3
Park Farm Cotts OX25 . **63** E5
Park Farm Pl OX29 . . . **137** F2
Park Hill
Hook Norton OX15 . . . . **30** B7
Wheatley OX33 . . . . . **126** B1
Parkhill Dr RG31. . . . . **257** D2
Park La Appleton OX13 . **158** A7
Ardington OX12. . . . . **215** D3
Bladon OX20 . . . . **91** B2
Checkendon RG4 . . . . **251** E6
Kingston Blount OX39. . **167** F3
Long Hanborough OX29 . **90** D1
North Newington OX15. . **15** C4
Stanford in the Vale
SN7. . . . . **195** B6
Stokenchurch HP14. . . **188** E6
Stonor RG9 . . . . **225** D6
Swalcliffe OX15. . . . . . . **19** E7
Woodstock OX20. . . . . . **91** B6
Parkland Pl OX26. . . . . . **80** F8
Parklands
Appleton OX13 . . . . . **158** C7
Banbury OX16 . . . . **16** B7
Farmoor OX2. . . . . . . **121** E2
Freeland OX29 . . . . . . **105** F7
Oxford OX3 . . . . **124** E1
Park Rd
Abingdon-on-Thames
OX14. . . . . **179** E7
Banbury OX16 . . . . **16** B6
Chipping Norton OX7 . . **42** F4
Combe OX29 . . . . **90** B5
Didcot OX11 . . . . **218** D6
Didcot OX11 . . . . **218** D8
Ducklington OX29 . . . . **118** A4
Faringdon SN7. . . . . . **172** F2
Henley-on-Thames RG9. **244** E1
Hook Norton OX15 . . . . **30** B7
Kiddington OX20 . . . . . **59** F1
Kiddington OX20 . . . . . **60** A2
North Leigh OX29 . . . . **105** B6
Witney OX28 . . . . **103** F1
Park Rise OX25 . . . . **81** C3
Parkside
Checkendon RG8 . . . . **241** D3
Cuddesdon OX44. . . . **144** C3
Henley-on-Thames RG9. **244** C2
North Leigh OX29 . . . . **105** C6
Park Side
Marcham OX13 . . . . . **178** C6
Woodstock OX20. . . . . . **91** A6
Parkside Ind Est OX28 **118** B6
Park Sports Ctr The
OX33 . . . . **126** B1
Park Sq OX14. . . . . . . **199** D4
Parks Rd OX1 . . . . **261** B3
Park St Bladon OX20 . . . **91** B2
Charlbury OX7 . . . . **73** B3
Thame OX9 . . . . **148** A7
Woodstock OX20. . . . . . **91** A6

Park Terr
East Challow OX12 . . . **214** A5
Thame OX9 . . . . **148** A7
Park The Cumnor OX2. . **139** E4
East Challow OX12 . . . **214** A5
Harwell OX11 . . . . **217** E6
PARK TOWN **123** D4
Park Town OX2. . . . . . **123** C4
Park View
Crowmarsh Gifford
OX10. . . . . **222** A6
Sydenham OX39 . . . . **148** F1
Wantage OX12 . . . . . **214** E5
Park View La OX18 . . . **115** E5
Park View Rd OX28 . . . **104** D1
Park Wall La RG8. . . . . **249** D1
Park Way OX3. . . . . . . **123** C4
Parkway OX4 . . . . **142** D4
Parkway Dr RG4. . . . . **260** E3
Park Wlk RG8 . . . . **257** D5
Parliament Rd OX9 . . . **129** F1
Parma Ho OX2 . . . . . . **123** B7
Parrs Rd HP14. . . . . . . **188** E4
Parry Cl OX3 . . . . **123** F3
Parsley Pl Banbury OX16 . **8** F2
Hardwick OX16. . . . . . . **9** A7
Parsonage Cl OX12 . . . **215** A6
Parsonage Ct SN6. . . . **190** A6
PARSONAGE GREEN. . **247** E4
Parson Piece OX16. . . . **16** B2
Parsons Dr OX20 . . . . . **91** C5
Parson's La OX10. . . . . **204** F3
Parsons Mead OX14 . . **159** E2
Parsons Pl OX4. . . . . . **142** A8
Parsons St OX17. . . . . . **23** A4
Parson's St OX16 . . . . . **16** D6
Partridge Chase OX26. . **81** A8
Partridge Cl
Didcot OX11 . . . . **200** B2
Sutton Courtenay OX13 **199** E6
4 Wantage OX12. . . . **214** E4
Partridge Ct OX17 . . . . **22** F3
Partridge La OX13 . . . **157** A1
Partridge Pl OX5 . . . . . **92** C1
Partridge Wlk OX4. . . . **143** A1
Pascali Pl OX16. . . . . . . **9** A1
Passey Cres OX10 . . . . **204** A4
Patching Cl OX29. . . . . . **87** F7
Patch Ridings OX29. . . . **88** B6
Patemore La
Pishill Bank RG9 . . . . **207** B1
Watlington OX49, RG9 . **206** E2
Paternoster La OX10. . **220** F1
Pathfinder View OX11 **235** C8
PATH HILL. **251** A1
Path Hill Reading RG8. . **257** A8
Whitchurch Hill RG8 . . . **250** F1
Patrick Haugh Rd OX25 **96** F7
Patrick Rd RG4 . . . . . . **259** B2
Patricks Orch SN7 . . . **211** D7
Patrick Steptoe Cl
OX29 . . . . **117** C8
Pattison Pl OX4. . . . . . **142** A3
Pauling Rd OX3. . . . . . **124** E1
Pauls Way OX49 . . . . . **186** B2
Paxmans Pl OX16. . . . . **16** C4
Payne Place 3 OX29 . **106** A8
Paynes End OX27. . . . . **65** F4
PEACHCROFT. **160** C2
Peachcroft Rd OX14 . . **160** B2
Peacock Ho 6 OX12. . **214** D4
Peacock Mews OX11. . **200** B2
Peacock Rd OX3. . . . . **123** F3
Peake Dr OX16 . . . . **16** F3
Peaks La OX29. . . . . **89** C7
Pearce Ct OX29. . . . . . **147** F8
Pearce Dr
Chipping Norton OX7 . . **42** E2
Faringdon SN7. . . . . . **172** D1
Pearces Mdw RG9 . . . **224** D3
Pearce Way OX4. . . . . **148** B7
Pearman Pl RG4. . . . . **252** E5
Pearson Rd RG4 . . . . . **260** D3
Pear Tree Cl OX7 . . . . . . **70** B1
Pear Tree Cotts RG9. . **243** D1
Pear Tree Farm Ind Units
OX27 . . . . **67** E2
Peartree Interchange
OX2. . . . . **108** E2
Pear Tree Wlk
15 Carterton OX18 . . . **115** E5
Carterton OX18. . . . . **115** E5
Peascroft HP18. . . . . . **129** D6
Pease Pl OX11. . . . . . . **218** F8
Peat Moors OX3. . . . . . **142** D8
Pebble Ct OX18. . . . . . **101** D5
Pebble Hill OX44 . . . . . **162** B4
Pebble La NN13 . . . . . . **24** A7
Peeble Dr OX11 . . . . . . **219** A8
**Peeble Hill Mobile Home
Pk** OX14 . . . . **160** E6
Peel Cl
Ducklington OX29 . . . . **118** B4
Reading RG4 . . . . **259** D2
Peel Pl Carterton OX18. **115** E2
Oxford OX1 . . . . **141** D5
Peep-O-Day La OX14 . **179** F3
Pegasus Cl OX11 . . . . **217** E1
Pegasus Ct 5 OX1. . . **141** C7
Pegasus Rd
Oxford OX4 . . . . **142** F2
Oxford OX4 . . . . **142** F3
Pegasus Sch OX4. . . . **142** F2
Pegasus Way HP17 . . . **130** E7
Pegasus Wy HP17 . . . . **130** D6
Peggs Farm Rd
Great Haseley OX44. . . **164** F7
Great Haseley OX44. . . **165** A6
Pegswell La OX44 . . . . **145** B2
Pelham Rd OX9. . . . . . **130** B1

Pelican Ct OX29 . . . . . **120** E8
Pembroke Coll OX1. . . **261** B1
Pembroke Ct 3 OX4. . **141** F8
Pembroke Ho 6 RG4. **259** C1
Pembroke La OX14 . . . **199** D5
Pembroke St
Oxford OX1 . . . . **261** B1
Reading RG4 . . . . **259** C3
Oxford OX4 . . . . **123** C1
Pembroke Way OX26 . . **65** F3
Pemscott Cl OX18 . . . . **133** C5
Pendennis Ave RG4. . . **259** C6
Pendles Paddock
HP14. . . . . **188** F2
Pendon Mus★ OX14 . . **201** C8
Penfield OX7 . . . . **42** E5
Penfold Ct OX3. . . . . . **124** B5
Penhill Ind Pk OX16 . . . **9** B1
Penhurst Gdns OX7 . . . **42** E3
Pen La OX13, OX14. . . **159** F5
Penley Cl OX39 . . . . . . **168** B6
Penlon Pl OX14. . . . . . **180** A7
Penn Cl
Abingdon-on-Thames
OX14. . . . . **160** C2
Reading RG4 . . . . **259** A6
Pennington Pl OX9 . . . **130** B1
Penn The OX7. . . . . **42** E5
Penny Cl SN6. . . . . **209** B7
Pennycress Rd OX4 . . . **143** A2
Pennyfarthing Pl OX1. **261** B2
Pennyhooks La SN6 . . **209** B8
Penny Piece RG4 . . . . **249** C7
Pennyroyal RG8 . . . . . **250** F5
Pennyroyal Pl OX11. . . **200** A1
Pennywell Dr OX2 . . . **140** B8
Penpont Water OX11 . **201** A2
Penrhyn Cl OX16. . . . . . **15** E7
Penrose Cl OX16. . . . . . **16** A5
Penrose Dr OX16 . . . . . **16** A6
Penrose Gdns OX26. . . **79** F7
Pensclose OX28 . . . . . **104** C1
Pensfield OX10. . . . . . **203** E4
Penstones Ct SN7 . . . **194** E7
Pentagon The OX14. . . **180** B7
Pen Way OX16. . . . . **9** B1
Peppard CE Prim Sch
RG9 . . . . **253** A8
PEPPARD COMMON. . . **252** F8
Peppard Hill RG9 . . . . **252** F8
Peppard La RG9 . . . . . **254** E7
Peppard Rd RG4. . . . . **253** D3
Pepper Alley
8 Banbury OX16 . . . . . **16** D6
Deddington OX15 . . . . . **34** E4
Peppercorn Ave OX3 . **142** E8
Perch Rise OX12. . . . . **214** B6
Percy St OX4 . . . . **141** F6
Peregrine Rd OX4 . . . . **142** D2
Peregrine Way
Bicester OX26 . . . . **81** A8
Grove OX12. . . . . **196** D1
Periam Cl RG9. . . . . . . **254** C8
Pitt Rivers Mus★ OX1 **261** B3
Perimeter Rd
Culham OX14. . . . . . . **180** D4
Harwell OX11 . . . . **217** C1
Periwinkle Pl 3 OX4. . **142** F2
Perkins OX1 . . . . **141** D2
Perkins Cl OX15 . . . . **7** C7
Perpetual Park Dr
RG9 . . . . **254** F8
Perrinsfield GL7. . . . . . **150** D6
Perrin St OX3 . . . . **124** C2
Perrott Cl OX29. . . . . . **105** A7
Perrys Rd SN7. . . . . . . **194** D8
Perseverance Hill
RG9 . . . . **254** A5
Peterley Rd OX4 . . . . . **142** F6
Peter's Way OX4 . . . . . **142** C3
Pether Rd OX3 . . . . . . **124** E1
Pethers Piece OX18. . . **100** D5
Petre Pl OX5 . . . . **92** F1
Pettiwell OX44 . . . . . . **162** D8
Petypher Gdns OX13. . **156** F1
Pevensey Ave RG4. . . . **259** E5
Pheasant Wlk OX4 . . . **142** A1
Phelps Pl OX4 . . . . **123** F1
Phelps The OX5 . . . . . **108** D8
Philcote St OX15 . . . . . . **33** F4
Phillimore Rd RG4. . . . **259** C8
Phillips Dr OX7 . . . . **43** A4
Phipps Rd OX4 . . . . . . **142** D4
Phoebe Ct OX2. . . . . . **123** A5
Pickenfield OX9 . . . . . **148** B7
Pickering Row OX12. . **214** E5
Pickets La
Cholsey OX10 . . . . . . **239** D8
North Stoke OX10 . . . **221** D1
Pickett Ave OX3. . . . . **142** E7
Pickett Piece
Stonesfield OX29. . . . . **89** D8
Stonesfield OX29. . . . . **89** D8
Pickett's Cl OX10 . . . . **203** F5
Picklers Hill OX14 . . . **160** A2
Picton Way RG4 . . . . . **259** B4
PIDDINGTON. **97** E7
**PIDDINGTON COW
LEYS.** **82** D3
Piddington Rd
Blackthorn OX27 . . . . . **82** F8
Ludgershall HP18 . . . . . **98** A8
Marsh Gibbon OX27. . . . **67** F1
Piddington OX25. . . . . . **97** F8
Piece Cl OX27 . . . . **67** F3
Pieces The OX18 . . . . **134** C1
Pierce's Hill RG31 . . . . **257** C1
Piers Row OX15 . . . . . . **33** E4
Pigeon Farm Rd HP14 **188** E5

Pigeonhouse La OX5. . . **95** F3
Pigeon House La
OX29. . . . . **106** C6
Piggott's Rd 1 RG4 . . **259** C1
Piggy La OX26. . . . . **65** E1
Pightles The OX10. . . . **204** D5
Pike Reach OX12 . . . . **214** C6
Pikeshaw Way RG31. . **257** C2
Pike Terr OX1 . . . . **261** B1
Pilcher Ct OX4 . . . . . . **123** F1
Pilgrims Cl SN6 . . . . . **191** F2
Pilgrim's Way The
OX11 . . . . **237** A8
Pill La GL56 . . . . **26** F1
Pillwort La OX11. . . . . **218** B8
Pilmore Mdw OX39 . . . **168** B7
Pilots Pl HP17 . . . . **130** E6
Pimpernel Cl OX4 . . . . **143** A2
Pinchester Cl GL56 . . . . **27** A1
Pinchgate La OX5 . . . . . **93** D7
Pine Cl Bicester OX26. . . **65** F5
Garsington OX44. . . . **143** C2
Oxford OX4 . . . . **142** F3
Pinecroft OX18 . . . . . . **115** D2
Pine Rise Oxford OX2. . **140** B7
Witney OX28. . . . . . . **104** D2
Pines The SN7. . . . . . . **172** E3
Pinetree Ct RG4 . . . . . **259** A5
Pinewood Ct 1 OX18. **115** E2
Pinewood Dr RG4 . . . . **258** E5
Pinewood Sch SN6 . . . **209** A2
Pine Woods Rd OX13 . **156** B1
Pinfold Cl OX15. . . . . . . **30** B8
Pingle Dr OX26. . . . . . . **80** E8
Pinhill Rd OX16. . . . . . . **16** B7
Pink Hill La OX29 . . . . **120** E6
Pinners Way HP18 . . . **129** D7
Pinnocks Way OX2 . . . **140** B8
Pinsley Rd OX29 . . . . . **106** B8
Pioneer Rd
Bicester OX26. . . . . **81** B6
Faringdon SN7. . . . . . **172** F2
Pioneer Way OX26. . . . . **80** C8
Pipe Line OX16 . . . . **16** D7
Pipers Croft OX16 . . . . **16** A4
Piper St OX4 . . . . **124** D2
Pipit Cl OX4 . . . . **142** E1
Pipits Croft OX26. . . . . **81** A8
Pipkin Way OX4 . . . . . **142** A6
Pipley Furlong OX4. . . **142** B2
PISHILL. **225** D8
PISHILL BANK. **207** B1
Pishill Bank
Nettlebed RG9. . . . . . **225**
Pishill Bank RG9 . . . . **207** B1
PISHILL BOTTOM. . . . **207** A1
Pitch The HP14. . . . . . **189** D3
Pitmaston Cl OX16. . . . . **8** F1
Pitreavie Ave OX18 . . . **115** E4
Pits La OX29. . . . . **104** C7
Pitters Piece HP18. . . . **129** B7
Pittick Cl
2 Freeland OX29. . . . **106** A8
4 Long Hanborough
OX29 . . . . **90** A1
Pittsbarn La OX7 . . . . . **68** F5
Pitts Barn La OX7. . . . . **68** F5
Pitts La Earley RG4 . . . **260** D4
Sandford St Martin OX7 . **46** B3
Sandford St Martin OX7 . **46** B3
Pitts Rd OX3. . . . . **124** E3
Pixey Cl OX5 . . . . **108** B5
Pixey Pl OX2 . . . . **122** F8
Pixton Cl OX11 . . . . . . **218** D8
Pk Corner
Nettlebed RG9. . . . . . **224** C7
Nettlebed RG9. . . . . . **224** C7
Pk End Pl OX1 . . . . **261** A2
Pk Nobles La OX2 . . . . **140** A4
Pk Vale OX15 . . . . **16** D4
Plain Rd The OX15. . . . . **14** B5
Plain The OX4. . . . . . . **141** E8
Plane Tree Way OX30. . **91** C6
Plantation Ave OX13. . **178** D7
Plantation Rd
Chilton OX11 . . . . **234** F8
Oxford OX2. . . . . **261** A4
Plantation The OX17. . . . **4** F1
Plater Dr OX2 . . . . **123** A4
PLATT THE. **163** A7
Playfield Rd OX1. . . . . **160** E7
Playford Ct OX9 . . . . . **147** F8
PLAY HATCH. **259** F5
Playhatch Rd RG4 . . . . **260** B5
Playing Cl The OX7. . . . **73** B4
Playing Field Rd NN13 . **25** A4
Pleck La OX39. . . . . . . **167** F4
Plot Rd OX15 . . . . **14** B6
Plough Cl
Warborough OX10. . . . **203** B6
4 Witney OX29. . . . . **117** B8
Wolvercote OX2 . . . . . **122** F8
Plough Cnr OX39 . . . . **148** F1
Plough La
Drayton OX13 . . . . . . **199** B8
Drayton OX14. . . . . . **179** B1
Shiplake RG9. . . . . . . **254** E1
Ploughley Cl
Ardley OX27 . . . . **50** C4
Kidlington OX5. . . . . . **108** D8
Ploughley Rd
Ambrosden OX25 . . . . . **81** C5
Ambrosden OX25 . . . . . **81** D3
Lower Arncott OX25 . . . **81** D1
Upper Arncott OX25 . . . **96** B8
Plover Cl OX28 . . . . . . **103** F1
Plover Dr OX4 . . . . **142** E1
Plover End 9 OX11. . . **200** B1
Plowden Pk OX49. . . . . **167** F3
Plowden Way RG9 . . . . **254** E1

Plumbe Ct OX12 ... 214 D6
Plumdon La OX25 ... 33 E2
Plum La OX7 ... 85 D7
Plumpton Rd OX26 ... 80 C8
Pluto Rd OX11 ... 234 F8
Plym Dr OX11 ... 201 A2
Pochard Pl 5 OX4 ... 142 F1
Pocock La OX10 ... 221 E1
Pococks Cl OX18 ... 134 F3
POFFLEY END ... 104 C6
Poffley End OX29 ... 104 B5
Pointer Pl OX13 ... 178 D6
Point Pl Witney OX28 .. 103 F2
2 Witney OX28 ... 104 A2
Polecat End La
Forest Hill OX33 ... 125 F4
Forest Hill OX33 ... 126 B5
Pollard Pl OX18 ... 134 F4
Pollocks La OX10 ... 221 E1
Polstead Rd OX2 ... 123 B4
Polsted Rd RG31 ... 257 D1
Pond Cl Oxford OX3 ... 125 A3
West Ilsley OX12 ... 233 E1
Pond End Rd RG4 ... 253 A6
Pond Hill OX8 ... 89 C7
Pond La RG4 ... 258 A6
Ponds La OX3 ... 123 F6
Pontefract Rd OX26 ... 80 C8
Pony Rd OX4 ... 142 F6
Pool Cl GL56 ... 26 F1
Pool Close Cotts GL56 .. 26 F1
Poole Cl OX13 ... 176 C8
Pooles La OX7 ... 73 B3
Poolside Cl OX16 ... 16 B5
Popes Acre HP17 ... 130 F5
Pope's Piece OX28 ... 103 F1
Poplar Cl Banbury OX16 .. 16 E2
Garsington OX44 ... 143 C2
Kidlington OX5 ... 108 F7
Poplar Farm Cl OX7 ... 70 A1
Poplar Farm Rd OX44 . 184 D7
Poplar Rd OX2 ... 122 C1
Poplars Pk OX14 ... 201 C8
Poplars Rd OX17 ... 10 F4
Poplars The
Didcot OX11 ... 218 B7
Launton OX26 ... 66 D1
Poplar Way
Ickford HP18 ... 127 F4
Ickford HP18 ... 128 A4
Popplestone Cl SN7 .. 194 D7
Poppy Cl Bicester OX25 . 81 D4
Southmoor OX13 ... 156 F1
Yarnton OX5 ... 108 B7
Poppy Field Way OX17 . 11 A1
Poppylands OX26 ... 65 D4
Poppy Rd OX12 ... 215 A6
Poppy Terr OX18 ... 115 F5
Portal Dr OX25 ... 63 C8
Portal Drive N OX25 ... 63 C8
Portal Drive S OX25 ... 63 C7
Portcullis Dr OX10 ... 221 D6
Port Hill RG9 ... 224 B2
Port Hill Rd OX10 ... 203 F5
Portland Pl OX7 ... 42 F3
Portland Rd
Milcombe OX15 ... 21 A2
Oxford OX2 ... 123 B7
Portman Rd RG30 ... 258 C1
Portmeirion Gdns
RG30 ... 257 F1
Portobello Cl OX27 ... 65 D6
Portway Aynho OX17 ... 35 D7
Banbury OX16 ... 16 A8
Croughton NN13 ... 36 E7
Didcot OX11 ... 218 C7
Faringdon SN7 ... 172 F3
Wantage OX12 ... 214 D4
Port Way Caulcott OX25 .. 62 F3
Caulcott OX5 ... 63 A1
Crowmarsh Gifford
OX10 ... 221 F4
Ipsden OX10 ... 240 A8
Kirtlington OX5 ... 77 F8
Kirtlington OX5 ... 78 A7
Lower Heyford OX25 ... 62 F6
Mongewell OX10 ... 221 F5
Wantage OX12 ... 215 A5
Portway Cl OX12 ... 216 D7
Portway Cres NN13 ... 36 E7
Portway Dr NN13 ... 36 D7
Portway Gdns OX17 ... 35 D7
Portway Mews OX12 .. 214 D4
Portway Rd OX27 ... 36 E3
PORTWAYS ... 207 B8
POSTCOMBE ... 166 F5
Post Office La
Letcombe Regis OX12 .. 214 A1
5 Wantage OX12 ... 214 D4
Potash Cl HP17 ... 130 F5
Potash Mead OX10 ... 203 F5
Potenger Way OX14 .. 179 D6
Pot Kiln La
Nettlebed RG9 ... 224 E3
Woodcote RG8 ... 250 E7
Potteries La
Chilton OX11 ... 217 C1
Chilton OX11 ... 235 C8
POTTER'S HILL ... 86 C2
Potters La
Ewelme OX10 ... 204 F1
Ewelme OX10 ... 205 A1
Ewelme OX10 ... 223 A8
Pottery Fields RG9 ... 224 E2
Pottery Piece OX4 ... 142 E1
Pottery Rd RG30 ... 257 F1
Pottle Cl OX2 ... 122 B1
Pott's Cl Faringdon SN7 172 E3
Great Milton OX44 ... 145 B3
Poulter Rd OX17 ... 8 E1
Poulton Pl OX4 ... 142 F3
Pound Bank OX7 ... 46 B3
Pound Cl
Ducklington OX29 ... 118 B4
Kirtlington OX5 ... 77 F4
Shrivenham SN6 ... 209 A7
Yarnton OX5 ... 108 B5
Pound Cotts RG8 ... 249 A6
Pound Croft OX12 ... 214 D8
Pound Ct OX15 ... 33 F4
Pound Field Cl OX3 ... 124 E5
Pound Field Rd OX18 . 135 F3
Pound Hill
Charlbury OX7 ... 73 A4
Poundon OX27 ... 67 D7
Pound La
Cassington OX29 ... 107 C2
Cholsey OX10 ... 220 F2
Clanfield OX18 ... 133 E1
Murcott OX5 ... 95 F5
Sibford Gower OX15 ... 13 A2
Sonning RG4 ... 260 E2
Stanton St John OX33 .. 125 D8
Upton OX11 ... 218 C2
POUNDON ... 67 E7
Poundon Rd OX26 ... 67 C6
Pound Piece SN6 ... 228 A7
Pounds Farm Rd
RG17 ... 246 E3
Pound The
Bloxham OX15 ... 21 E5
Cholsey OX10 ... 220 F2
Fernham SN7 ... 193 A4
North Newington OX15 .. 15 B4
Wantage OX12 ... 215 A5
Pound Way 7 OX4 ... 142 C4
Poveys Pl SN6 ... 227 D4
Powell Cl OX33 ... 125 F4
Powley Pl RG31 ... 257 D3
Powys Gr OX16 ... 15 F7
Preachers La OX1 ... 261 B1
Preece Ct OX18 ... 115 E1
Prentice Ct GL54 ... 68 B3
Prescote Manor Farm Bsns
Pk OX17 ... 5 B3
Prescott Ave OX16 ... 15 F6
Prescott Cl OX16 ... 16 A6
Press Way 3 OX2 ... 122 D8
Prestidge Pl OX5 ... 108 F8
Preston Bissett Rd
MK18 ... 53 F6
PRESTON
CROWMARSH ... 203 F2
Preston Rd OX14 ... 179 E4
Prestwich Pl OX2 ... 122 F1
Prestwick Burn OX11 . 200 F3
Prew Bunglows
Great Rollright OX7 ... 29 A3
Great Rollright OX7 ... 29 A3
Prew Cotts OX7 ... 29 A3
Price Cl OX26 ... 65 F3
Price Way OX18 ... 115 C5
Prichard Rd OX3 ... 124 A3
Priest Cl RG9 ... 224 D3
Priest End OX9 ... 129 E1
Priest Hill
Nettlebed RG9 ... 224 D4
Reading RG4 ... 259 A3
Priest Hill La OX29 ... 103 F5
Priest's Moor La OX10 182 F1
Primrose Cl
Purley on Thames
RG8 ... 257 C5
Witney OX28 ... 104 E1
Primrose Dr OX26 ... 65 E4
Primrose La OX18 ... 134 E2
Primrose Pl 20 OX4 ... 142 F1
Primsdown Ind Est
OX7 ... 42 C3
Prince Christian Victor
Berkshire Memorial
Homes OX12 ... 214 D2
Prince Dr SN6 ... 209 B7
Prince Gr OX14 ... 160 A3
Princes Ride OX20 ... 91 C6
Princess Gdns OX12 .. 214 C8
Princes St OX4 ... 141 F8
Princethorpe Dr OX16 .. 16 F7
Prince William Dr
RG31 ... 257 C1
Printers Rd 2 RG30 .. 258 F1
Prior Cres OX13 ... 198 F5
Prior Dr OX14 ... 179 B1
Prior Mill La 1 OX28 . 104 B1
Prior Pl OX12 ... 194 F2
Prior's Forge OX2 ... 109 B1
Priors La SN7 ... 155 F3
Priors Wlk GL7 ... 150 E3
Priory Ave RG4 ... 259 A2
Priory Bank Cotts
OX44 ... 145 C2
Priory Cl Bicester OX26 .. 65 F1
Horton-cum-Studley
OX33 ... 112 B5
Priory Copse RG9 ... 252 F6
Priory Cotts★ OX13 .. 198 F3
Priory Ct
1 Bicester OX26 ... 65 E1
Cutteslowe OX2 ... 109 B1
Reading RG4 ... 259 A2
Priory Farm Cotts OX27 67 E2
Priory Gn
Highworth SN6 ... 190 A6
Highworth SN6 ... 190 B6
Priory La
Ascott-under-Wychwood
OX7 ... 71 D2
Bicester OX26 ... 65 E1
Burford OX18 ... 100 E5
Lyneham OX7 ... 70 D5
Marcham OX13 ... 178 D6
Priory Mead SN7 ... 192 D2
Priory Mews 14 OX10 . 221 D7
Priory Orch OX12 ... 214 C5
Priory Rd Bicester OX26 . 65 F1
8 Chipping Norton OX7 . 43 A3
Lyneham OX7 ... 70 D5
Oxford OX4 ... 142 C2
Wantage OX12 ... 214 D4
Priory Vale Rd OX16 ... 16 F7
Pritchard Cl OX10 ... 182 C6
Proctor Way
Faringdon SN7 ... 173 A2
Upper Rissington OX7 ... 68 C3
Project Timescape★
OX14 ... 202 A6
Promenade Rd RG4 ... 259 A2
Prospect Cl OX29 ... 89 C7
Prospect Pk
Horspath OX33 ... 143 C7
Horspath OX33 ... 143 C7
Prospect Pl OX49 ... 186 B2
Prospect Rd
Banbury OX16 ... 16 D5
Upton OX11 ... 218 C2
Prospect St RG4 ... 259 B2
Prosser Way OX14 ... 159 E2
Provost Cl GL54 ... 68 B3
Prue Cl OX16 ... 15 E2
Prunus Cl OX4 ... 142 F3
Pryor Cl RG31 ... 257 B4
Puck La OX28 ... 104 B1
Puddleduck La SN7 ... 192 B8
Pudlicote La
Chilson OX7 ... 71 E6
Shorthampton OX7 ... 72 B5
Pudsey Cl OX14 ... 179 E4
Pugsden La OX13 ... 199 A4
Pulford Way OX13 ... 199 C2
Pulker Cl OX4 ... 142 C4
Pullens Field OX3 ... 124 A2
Pullens La OX3 ... 124 A2
Pulling Cl SN7 ... 172 F3
Pulpit Hill
Childrey OX12 ... 213 A4
Sparsholt OX12 ... 212 F4
Puma Cl OX10 ... 204 D2
Pumbro OX29 ... 89 C7
Purcell Rd OX3 ... 123 F3
Purchas Rd OX11 ... 200 C4
Purfield Dr RG10 ... 255 E2
Purland Cl OX4 ... 142 C6
Purley CE Inf Sch RG8 257 C5
Purley La RG8 ... 257 C5
Purley Magna RG31 ... 257 C4
PURLEY ON THAMES . 257 B6
Purley Rise RG8 ... 257 A5
Purley Village RG8 ... 257 C5
Purley Way RG8 ... 256 E5
Purrants La OX29 ... 86 E1
Purser Cres OX9 ... 147 F6
Purslane OX14 ... 180 B8
Purslane Dr OX26 ... 65 D4
Purslane Rd OX26 ... 65 D5
PUSEY ... 175 B6
Pusey La OX1 ... 261 B3
Pusey St OX1 ... 261 B3
Putman Cl OX9 ... 148 B8
Putman Pl RG9 ... 244 E1
Pye St SN7 ... 173 A3
Pykes Cl OX14 ... 160 B3
Pym Wlk OX9 ... 129 F1
PYRTON ... 186 B4
Pyrton La OX49 ... 186 A2
Pytenry Cl OX14 ... 160 B3
Pytts La OX18 ... 100 E5

Q

Quadrangle The
Bicester OX26 ... 65 E1
Wolvercote OX2 ... 122 F8
Woodstock OX20 ... 91 C7
Quadrant The OX14 ... 180 B7
Quaker La OX10 ... 203 B8
Quakers Ct 10 OX14 ... 179 F7
Quantock Ave RG4 ... 259 D5
Quantock View
7 Didcot OX11 ... 200 C2
7 Didcot OX11 ... 200 C2
Quarhill Cl OX7 ... 42 E5
Quarrington Pl OX49 . 186 B1
Quarry Cl Bloxham OX15 21 C4
Enstone OX7 ... 59 A5
Long Crendon HP18 ... 129 C7
Quarry End OX5 ... 108 B8
Quarry Ground
Fifield OX7 ... 69 B2
Idbury OX7 ... 69 A5
Quarry High St OX3 ... 124 E3
Quarry Hollow OX3 ... 124 E2
Quarry La Charlbury OX7 73 C4
Lower Shiplake RG9 ... 255 A4
Quarry Rd
Chadlington OX7 ... 57 B2
Hornton OX15 ... 7 A8
Oxford OX3 ... 124 E2
Sunningwell OX13 ... 159 F7
Witney OX28 ... 104 A2
Quarry School Pl OX3 . 124 E2
Quarry The
Bayworth OX13 ... 159 F7
East End OX29 ... 89 D2
Quartermain Cl OX4 .. 142 A6
Quartermain Rd OX44 . 184 C7
Quarterman Way
OX29 ... 120 C8
Quebec Rd RG9 ... 254 E8
Queen Annes Gate
RG4 ... 259 C3
Queen Anne's Sch
RG4 ... 259 B3
Queen Cl RG9 ... 244 E1
Queen Eleanor Ct
OX29 ... 106 B8
Queen Elizabeth Cl 8
OX11 ... 219 A8
Queen Elizabeth Ho
OX1 ... 261 B3
Queen Emma's Dyke
OX28 ... 117 F8
Queen Emma's Prim Sch
OX28 ... 117 F7
Queenford Farm OX10 182 E2
Queen Gdns OX11 ... 217 E8
Queen St Mews RG9 .. 244 E1
Queens Ave
Bicester OX26 ... 65 E2
Highworth SN6 ... 190 A6
Kidlington OX5 ... 109 A8
Queen's Ave OX10 ... 203 B1
Queensborough Dr
RG4 ... 258 E5
Queens Cl
Carterton OX18 ... 115 E1
Dorchester OX10 ... 182 D1
Oxford OX2 ... 140 B8
Thame OX9 ... 129 F2
Watchfield SN6 ... 191 D2
Queen's Cl OX29 ... 120 E7
Queen's Coll The OX1. 261 C2
Queens Cres
Clanfield OX18 ... 152 E8
Drayton OX15 ... 15 D8
Queen's Cres SN6 ... 209 B7
Queens Ct Bicester OX26 65 E2
Clanfield OX18 ... 152 E8
Goring RG8 ... 249 C6
Queens La
Eynsham OX29 ... 120 E7
Oxford OX1 ... 261 C2
Queens Rd
Cholsey OX10 ... 220 F1
Cholsey OX10 ... 221 A1
Queen's Rd
Banbury OX16 ... 16 B6
Carterton OX18 ... 115 E1
Reading RG4 ... 259 C1
Thame OX9 ... 148 B8
Queens Row OX12 ... 194 F2
Queens St OX15 ... 21 D4
Queen St
Abingdon-on-Thames
OX14 ... 179 F7
Bampton OX18 ... 134 F3
Dorchester OX10 ... 182 D1
Eynsham OX29 ... 120 E7
Henley-on-Thames RG9. 244 E1
Hook Norton OX15 ... 30 B7
Middleton Cheney OX17 .. 17 F8
Oxford OX1 ... 261 B2
Reading RG4 ... 259 A3
Queensway
Banbury OX16 ... 16 B4
Didcot OX11 ... 218 E7
Reading RG4 ... 259 D6
Queens Way OX11 ... 219 F8
Queensway Sch OX16 .. 16 A4
Quercus Ct OX2 ... 123 B6
Quick Row 2 OX18 ... 134 F4
Quickset Cl OX7 ... 72 F8
Quintan Ave OX25 ... 81 D4

R

Race Farm Cotts
OX13 ... 176 E8
Race Farm La OX13 ... 176 F8
RACK END ... 137 E3
Rack End OX29 ... 137 E3
Rackham Pl OX2 ... 123 A6
Radband Nook OX18 .. 135 A4
Radbone Hill OX7 ... 42 F6
Radcliffe Camera Liby
OX1 ... 261 C2
Radcliffe Rd OX4 ... 141 F5
Radcliffe Science Liby
OX1 ... 261 B3
Radcliffe Sq OX1 ... 261 C2
RADCOT ... 152 F4
Radcot Cl RG5 ... 260 E1
Radcot Rd
Clanfield OX18 ... 152 B6
Faringdon SN7 ... 172 F6
Kelmscott OX18 ... 151 F7
RADFORD ... 59 F5
Radford Cl OX4 ... 141 F3
Radish Cl OX27 ... 65 D7
RADLEY ... 160 E3
Radley CE Prim Sch
OX14 ... 160 E3
Radley Coll OX14 ... 160 D4
Radley Ct OX14 ... 160 B1
Radley Ho OX2 ... 123 C6
Radley Rd
Abingdon-on-Thames
OX14 ... 160 C1
Radley OX14 ... 160 D2
Radley Road Ind Est
OX14 ... 160 B1
Radley Sta OX14 ... 160 F2
RADNAGE ... 189 D8
Radnage CE Prim Sch
HP14 ... 189 D6
Radnage Common Rd
HP14 ... 189 D5
Radnage La HP14 ... 169 C2
Radnor Cl RG9 ... 244 E2
Radnor Rd OX10 ... 221 B8
Radway Rd CV47 ... 2 A8
Rae Cres OX12 ... 215 A5
RAF Benson OX10 ... 204 C2
RAF Benson Com Prim Sch
OX10 ... 204 D2
Raf Croughton Rd
NN13 ... 36 F7
Raghouse La OX27 ... 49 F5
Raglan Gdns RG4 ... 259 C4
Ragley Mews RG4 ... 259 D6
Ragnall's La OX33 ... 111 F7
Rahere Rd OX4 ... 142 C4
Railway Cotts SN7 ... 195 A2
Railway La OX4 ... 142 B2
Railways Cotts RG8 ... 249 C6
Railway Terr GL7 ... 150 D5
Railway View RG8 ... 256 D6
Rainbow Way OX14 ... 160 B3
Raincliffe Cl OX17 ... 35 C7
Raleigh Cres OX28 ... 117 D7
Raleigh Park Rd OX2 . 140 E7
Ramillies Cl OX20 ... 91 C7
Rampion Cl OX4 ... 143 A2
RAMSDEN ... 88 A3
RAMSDEN HEATH ... 87 F4
Ramsey Rd OX3 ... 124 E3
Ramsons Cres 4
OX11 ... 218 B7
Ramsons Way OX14 ... 180 C8
Randolph Ave OX20 ... 91 D6
Randolph Rd RG1 ... 259 A1
Randolph St 7 OX4 ... 141 F8
Range Rd
Witney OX28, OX29 ... 117 C8
Witney OX29 ... 117 C8
Rannal Dr OX39 ... 168 C6
Rasen Rd 9 OX26 ... 65 D1
Rastel Ho 2 OX16 ... 16 E6
Ratcliffe Ct OX10 ... 221 B1
RATLEY ... 2 A4
Rattlecombe Rd OX15 ... 6 D2
Rau Ct OX27 ... 66 A7
Raven Cl OX25 ... 63 C8
Ravencroft OX26 ... 81 A7
Raven Rd Didcot OX11 . 200 B2
Stokenchurch HP14 ... 188 F4
Ravensbourne Dr RG5 260 E1
Ravenscroft Rd RG9 .. 244 D2
Ravensmead
Banbury OX16 ... 16 A4
Chinnor OX39 ... 168 D6
Raven Way SN6 ... 209 B7
Rawdon Way SN7 ... 173 A2
Rawlings Gr OX14 ... 179 D8
Rawlins Cl OX17 ... 23 A5
Rawlinson Cl
Chadlington OX7 ... 57 B1
Radley OX14 ... 160 E3
Rawlinson Rd OX2 ... 123 B5
Rawlins Rise RG31 ... 257 D3
Rawson Cl OX2 ... 108 F1
Rawthey Ave OX11 ... 200 F4
Ray Ct OX11 ... 201 A2
Rayford La OX7 ... 61 A8
Raymond Rd OX26 ... 65 C4
Raymund Rd OX3 ... 123 F5
Raynham Cl OX18 ... 115 E4
Ray Rd OX26 ... 65 D1
Rayson Ho OX3 ... 124 B4
Rayson La OX29 ... 117 C7
Ray View OX5 ... 94 F4
Ray Vw OX25 ... 81 E4
Reade Ave OX14 ... 180 B8
Reade Cl OX7 ... 70 B1
Reade's La RG4 ... 252 D4
READING ... 259 A4
Reading Blue Coat Sch
RG4 ... 260 C3
Reading Ct 2 OX26 ... 65 E3
Reading Rd
Aldworth RG8 ... 248 A2
Cholsey OX10 ... 239 A7
Goring RG8 ... 249 E6
Harwell OX11 ... 217 D6
Henley-on-Thames RG9. 254 F8
Lower Basildon RG8 ... 249 D2
Lower Shiplake RG9 ... 255 A4
Pangbourne RG8 ... 256 D5
Purley-on-Thames RG8. 257 B5
Reading RG31 ... 257 C4
Shiplake RG9 ... 254 F2
Streatley RG8 ... 249 A6
Upton OX11 ... 218 B3
Wallingford OX10 ... 221 C4
Wallingford OX10 ... 221 D6
Wantage OX12 ... 215 B5
West Hendred OX12 ... 216 B7
Whitchurch Hill RG8 ... 251 C2
Woodcote RG8 ... 240 F1
Reading Ret Pk RG30 . 258 B1
Read Pl OX26 ... 80 F6
Recreation Ground
SN6 ... 209 B7
Recreation Rd
Wargrave RG10 ... 255 E2
Woodstock OX20 ... 91 C6
Rectory Cl
Marsh Gibbon OX27 ... 67 F3
Upper Hayford OX25 ... 49 A8
Warmington OX17 ... 3 A4
Wendlebury OX25 ... 80 A4
Rectory Cres OX7 ... 60 E8
Rectory Ct OX49 ... 187 B8
Rectory Farm Cl OX12 196 F7
Rectory Gdns OX15 ... 15 D8
Rectory Hill RG9 ... 206 A1
Rectory La
Aston Tirrold OX11 ... 237 F8
Bix RG9 ... 243 D7
Fringford OX27 ... 52 C6
Kingston Bagpuize OX13 176 F8
Letcombe Bassett OX12 231 E7
Longworth OX13 ... 156 B3
Middleton Cheney OX17 .. 10 F1
Rectory La *continued*
South Weston OX9 ... 166 E1
Woodstock OX20 ... 91 A6
Rectory Lane Trad Est
OX13 ... 176 F7
Rectory Mdw OX39 ... 168 D7
Rectory Rd
Great Haseley OX44 ... 145 C1
Great Haseley OX44 ... 164 D8
Great Haseley OX44 ... 164 E8
Hook Norton OX15 ... 30 B8
Oxford OX4 ... 141 F8
Reading RG4 ... 259 A2
Streatley RG8 ... 248 C7
Red Arrows Cl 19 OX7 .. 68 B3
Redberry Cl RG4 ... 259 D5
Red Bridge Hollow
OX1 ... 141 C4
Redcar Rd 11 OX26 ... 65 D1
Red Copse La OX1 ... 141 A2
Red Cross Rd RG8 ... 249 C6
Rede Cl OX3 ... 124 E1
Red Hill RG9 ... 254 A5
Red House Dr RG4 ... 253 A5
Red House Rd OX15 ... 22 E8
Red Kite Cl OX13 ... 199 E6
Red Kite Rd OX39 ... 168 C5
Red Kite Wy OX11 ... 200 C2
Red La Chinnor OX39 ... 168 F3
Chinnor Hill OX39 ... 169 A3
Ewelme OX49, RG9 ... 206 D2
Woodcote RG8 ... 240 C3
Woodcote RG8 ... 241 A1
Redland Rd OX3 ... 124 B5
Redlands Cl SN6 ... 190 A4
Redlands Row GL56 ... 27 A1
Red Lion Dr HP14 ... 188 D5
Red Lion Mews SN6 .. 190 A6
Red Lion Sq OX1 ... 261 B2
Red Lion St
Cropredy OX17 ... 4 F2
Kings Sutton OX17 ... 23 F5
Redmayes OX18 ... 135 E2
Redmoor Cl OX4 ... 142 C2
Redmoor Ct OX26 ... 65 C3
Red Oak La NN13 ... 25 A4
Red Poll Cl OX16 ... 16 A8
Redwing Cl OX26 ... 66 A1
Redwing End 13 OX11. 218 B6
Redwood Cl
Kingston Bagpuize
OX13 ... 156 E1
Oxford OX4 ... 143 A2
Redwood Way RG31 .. 257 D3
Reed Cl OX28 ... 104 E2
Reedmace Cl OX4 ... 143 A2
Reedmace Rd
Bicester OX26 ... 65 E4
Bodicote OX16 ... 16 E1
Reeds Cl OX12 ... 214 C5
Reed St OX11 ... 218 B8
Reema Hos The SN6 .. 190 B1
Rees Ct OX16 ... 16 A2
Regal Cl 11 OX14 ... 179 F7
Regal Ct 2 OX26 ... 65 F1
Regal La OX29 ... 90 E1
Regal Way SN7 ... 172 F3
Regency Hts RG4 ... 258 E4
Regent Ct OX7 ... 42 E3
Regent Dr OX29 ... 90 E1
Regent Gdns OX11 ... 219 B8
Regent Mews SN7 ... 172 F4
Regent Oxford OX2 ... 123 C5
Regents Park Coll
OX1 ... 261 B3
Regents Riverside 7
RG1 ... 259 A1
Regent St OX4 ... 141 F8
Regis Pl OX12 ... 214 A2
Reid Cl OX16 ... 16 B6
Reid Pl OX25 ... 63 B7
Reliance Way
Long Hanborough OX29 . 90 E1
Oxford OX4 ... 142 B7
REMENHAM ... 244 F3
Remenham La RG9 ... 244 F3
Remenham Row RG9 . 244 F2
Remus Gate NN13 ... 24 A6
Remy Pl OX4 ... 141 F5
Renault Ho OX4 ... 141 F6
Renown Ct 2 OX29 ... 90 E1
Rest Harrow 2 OX4 .. 142 F2
Restharrow Mead OX26 65 C4
Retford Cl RG5 ... 260 F1
Retreat Gdns OX10 ... 221 E7
Retreat La HP14 ... 169 D2
Revell Cl OX10 ... 221 C7
Rewley Abbey Ct OX1. 261 A2
Rewley Rd OX1 ... 261 A2
Reynard Ct 3 OX26 ... 65 E2
Reynolds Cl OX7 ... 70 D1
Reynolds Ct OX7 ... 73 D3
Reynolds Way
Abingdon-on-Thames
OX14 ... 179 E5
East Challow OX12 ... 213 F5
Rhigos RG4 ... 258 F6
Rhine Cl RG4 ... 259 D2
Rhino Row OX18 ... 114 C6
Ribston Cl Banbury OX16 .. 8 F2
Banbury OX17 ... 8 F1
Ribstone Pl OX16 ... 8 F1
Richard Gray Ct OX1 .. 261 A2
Richard Jones Rd
OX29 ... 103 C2
Richard Nevill Ct 2
RG4 ... 259 C2
Richards La OX2 ... 123 A7

Richardson Ct OX4 ... 123 F1
Richards Way OX3 ... 124 F2
Richens Dr OX18 ... 115 C2
Richfield Ave RG1 ... 258 F1
Richman Gdns OX16 ...15 F8
Richmere Rd OX11 .. 218 F7
Richmond Rd
  Bicester OX26 .... 65 B1
  Oxford OX1 .... 261 A3
  Reading RG4 .... 258 E4
Richmond St OX17 ....23 F5
Rickyard Cl OX1 .... 261 A3
Rickyard The
  Ardington OX12 .... 215 D5
  Chalgrove OX44 ...... 184 C6
  Fulbrook OX18 .... 100 F6
  Shutford OX15 .... 14 A5
Riddell Pl OX2 ...... 109 A1
Riders Way OX39 .... 168 C6
Ride The
  Appleton OX13 .... 158 B5
  Nuneham Courtenay
    OX44 .... 161 F1
Ridge Cl OX16 ...... 16 D4
Ridgefield Rd OX4 .. 142 A4
Ridge Hall Cl RG4 .. 258 E3
Ridgemont Cl OX2 .. 123 A4
Ridgemount Cl RG31.. 257 B2
Ridge The
  Lower Basildon RG8 .. 249 F1
  Tackley RG5 .... 77 C6
Ridgeway RG10 ...... 255 C2
Ridge Way HP18 ..... 129 F5
Ridgeway CE Prim Sch
  The OX12 .... 213 B3
Ridgeway Cl
  East Hendred OX12.. 216 E7
  Nuffield RG9 .... 223 D3
Ridgeway Ct OX12 .. 214 D7
Ridgeway Rd
  Didcot OX11 .... 218 F7
  Oxford OX3 .... 124 F3
Ridgeway The
  Ashbury SN6 .... 228 F8
  Bloxham OX15 .... 21 E4
  Chilton OX12 .... 234 C7
  Nettlebed RG9 ...... 224 D2
  Reading RG4 .... 259 B3
  Uffington SN7 .... 211 B1
  Wantage OX12 ...... 232 D5
  Woolstone SN6 ...... 229 A8
Riding La OX29 ...... 103 C7
Ridings Bglws OX29 ..86 E3
Ridings Cl OX29 ..... 89 C8
Ridings The
  Banbury OX16 ......16 F7
  Kidlington OX5 ...... 92 C1
  Kingston Bagpuize
    OX13 .... 176 C8
  Leafield OX29 .... 86 E2
  Oxford OX3 .... 142 F8
  Reading RG4 .... 259 C8
  Reading RG8 .... 257 B1
  Stonesfield OX29.... 89 C8
Ridley Rd OX4 ...... 142 E6
Riely Cl OX29 .... 90 C1
Riley Cl OX14 .... 179 D6
Riley Dr OX16 .... 15 F8
Riley Ho OX4 .... 142 C4
Rimes Cl OX13 ...... 156 F1
Rimmer Cl OX3 ..... 123 F5
Ring The OX17 ......10 E4
Ringwood Rd
  Oxford OX3 .... 125 A3
  Reading RG30 ...... 258 A1
Ripley Ave OX29 .... 102 E2
Riplcy Rd RG30 ..... 258 A1
Ripon Cl OX26 ...... 80 C8
Ripon Coll OX44 .... 144 B3
Rippington Ct
  Drayton OX14 ...... 179 B2
  Drayton OX14 ...... 179 B2
Rippington Dr OX3 ... 123 F4
Rise The
  Adderbury OX17 ...... 23 A4
  Islip OX5 ....93 F1
  Kingston Blount OX39.. 167 F4
  Reading RG4 .... 259 B4
Rising Hill OX25 ......48 E1
RISINGHURST 125 A3
Rissington Cl RG31 .. 257 B2
Rissington Dr OX28.. 117 E8
Rissington Sch The
  GL54 ....68 B4
Rivacres RG8 .... 250 E3
River Cl OX14 .... 179 E5
River Gdns RG8 ..... 257 D5
River La RG8 .... 249 B5
Rivermead L Complex
  RG1 .... 258 F2
Rivermead Rd OX4 .. 141 F3
River Rd RG4 .... 258 D3
River & Rowing Mus★
  RG9 .... 244 F1
Riverside OX16 ......16 E5
Riverside Ct
  Oxford OX1 .... 141 C7
  2 Reading RG4 .... 259 A2
Riverside Gdns
  OX28 .... 104 B1
Riverside Pk
  Reading RG30 ...... 258 B2
  Wallingford OX10 ... 221 E8
Riverside Pk & Pools
  OX10 .... 221 E8
Riverside Rd OX2 .. 123 B4
River View
  Kennington OX1 .... 141 E1

River View *continued*
  Sandford-on-Thames
    OX4 .... 161 A7
  Shillingford OX10 ... 203 B4
Riverview Rd RG8 ... 256 C5
River View Terr OX14.. 179 E6
Rivington Glebe GL56.. 27 A1
Rivy Cl OX14 .... 180 C8
Roach Bank OX12.... 214 B6
Road Eight OX11..... 217 A1
Road Eighteen OX11.. 217 B1
Road Eleven OX11 ... 217 A1
Road Fifteen OX11... 217 A1
Road Five OX11...... 217 A1
Road Four OX11..... 217 B1
Road Nine OX11..... 217 A1
Road One OX11...... 217 A1
Roadside Cotts SN7.. 171 E6
Road Six OX11....... 217 B1
Road Thirteen OX11 .. 217 B1
Road Twelve OX11... 217 A1
Road Two OX11..... 217 A1
Robert Palmer Cotts The
  RG4 .... 260 D3
Robert Piggott CE Inf Sch
  RG10 .... 255 E1
Robert Piggott CE Jun Sch
  RG10 .... 255 D1
Robert Robinson Ave
  OX4 .... 142 C1
Roberts Cl OX3 ..... 125 A4
Roberts Dr OX26..... 81 A7
Robert Sparrow Gdns
  OX10 .... 222 A6
Robey Ave 10 SN7 ... 172 C1
Robin Cl OX14 .... 179 D8
Robin Gibb Rd
  Thame OX9 .... 147 F6
  Thame OX9 .... 148 A6
Robin Hill OX29...... 90 A4
Robin Pl OX4 .... 142 E1
Robins Cl
  Barford St Michael
    OX15 ....32 F6
  Great Rollright OX7.... 29 B3
Robins Ct SN7 .... 173 A2
Robinson Cl
  Blewbury OX11 ...... 237 A8
  Carterton OX18..... 115 D3
  Oxford OX1 .... 261 C3
Robinson Rd OX1.... 159 A7
Robins Platt OX39 ... 168 B6
Robins Way OX26.... 81 A7
Robinswood OX16 ... 16 A4
Robins Wy OX15...... 16 F1
Robin Wy OX11...... 200 C2
Robsart Pl OX2 ..... 139 E4
Rochester Ave RG5... 260 E1
Rochester Pl OX7.... 73 C3
Rochester Way OX17 .. 23 B5
Rochford Gdns OX26.. 66 A4
Rockbourne Gdns
  RG30 .... 258 A1
Rock Cl
  Barford St Michael
    OX15 ....32 F6
  Carterton OX18..... 115 D3
Rock Edge OX3 ..... 124 D2
Rock Edge Nature
  Reserve★ OX3 .... 124 D1
Rockery The OX11.... 217 C1
Rock Farm La OX4.... 161 B8
Rockfort Ind Est OX10 221 B7
Rock Hill OX7 ....42 F3
Rockhill Farm Ct OX7.. 42 F3
Rockley Cotts OX2.... 139 E1
Rock Rd OX18 ...... 115 D3
Rock The
  Barford St Michael
    OX15 ....32 F6
  Barford St Michael OX15.. 32 F6
Rocky Banks OX18.... 115 F6
Rocky La
  Shepherd's Green
    RG9 .... 243 B4
  Stoke Row RG9 .... 242 B4
Roding Way OX11.... 201 A2
Rodney Pl OX13 ..... 156 C3
Rodway Rd RG30 .... 257 F1
Roebuck Ct OX11.... 219 A8
Roebuck Rise RG31.. 257 D5
Roentgen Ave OX11... 217 A2
Rofford La OX44..... 164 B3
Roger Bacon La OX1.. 261 B1
Roger Dudman Way OX1,
  OX2 .... 123 A2
Rogers St OX2....... 123 B7
ROKE 204 B7
Rokeby Dr RG4...... 258 D8
ROKEMARSH 204 A6
Rolfe Pl OX3 .... 124 A3
Rollright Rd CV36....29 B6
Rollright Stones★ OX7 28 B2
Rolls Ct OX2........ 214 D5
Roman Cl Kirtlington OX5 77 F3
  Kirtlington OX5 ...... 78 A3
Roman Fields OX11... 235 B8
Roman Pl Didcot OX11.. 200 D2
  Tackley OX5........ 77 C6
Roman Rd
  Berinsfield OX10..... 182 C6
  Berinsfield OX10..... 182 C7
  Wheatley OX33..... 144 C7
Roman Way
  Beckley OX3 .... 111 B3
  Bicester OX26 ...... 65 E2
  Brackley NN13...... 24 A7
  Lechlade-on-Thames
    GL7 .... 150 D5
  Oxford OX4 .... 142 F5
  Shrivenham SN6.... 209 A7

Roman Way *continued*
  Thame OX9 .... 147 D8
  Wantage OX12 ...... 214 C6
Roman Wlk SN6 ..... 191 E2
Romany Cl RG30..... 258 A1
Romany La RG30 .... 258 A1
Romney Rd OX16 .... 8 F1
Romsey Rd RG30 .... 258 A1
Romulus Way NN13... 24 A6
Rookery
  Abingdon-on-Thames
    OX13............. 159 B1
  Shippon OX13 ...... 159 B1
Rookery Cl OX15......22 E8
Rookery Ct
  Didcot OX11 .... 200 B2
  7 Didcot OX11...... 200 C2
Rookery Ho OX44.... 143 E1
Rookery The 1 OX5 .. 92 D1
Rookery Way OX26 ... 65 D3
Rooks End OX12 ..... 194 F2
Rooks La OX9 .... 147 F8
Roosevelt Dr OX3 .... 124 B1
Roosevelt Rd OX29 .. 106 B8
Roper Rd OX25 ...... 63 C8
Rope Way OX15 ......30 B6
Rope Wlk 5 OX16 .... 16 D4
Rosamund Dr OX20... 91 A7
Rosamund Rd OX2.... 122 E8
Rose Ave OX14 ..... 159 F3
Rosebank OX15........21 E5
Rosebay Cres OX11.. 218 A4
Rosebay Gdns 2 OX4.. 124 C5
Rosebery Rd OX4 .... 258 D7
Rose Cl Bucknell OX27 .. 64 F7
  Carterton OX18..... 115 D2
Rose Cnr OX9 .... 89 C7
Rose Cott OX17.........8 F4
Rose & Crown Ct OX2.. 89 C7
Rosedale Ave OX16.....9 A4
Rose Gdns OX4...... 140 C8
ROSE HILL 142 A4
Rose Hill OX4 ...... 142 B4
Rosehill Ho RG4 .... 259 C7
Rosehill Pk RG4 .... 259 C7
Rose Hill Prim Sch
  OX4 .... 142 A3
Rose La OX1........ 261 C2
Rosemary Cres 1
  RG4 .... 253 A4
Rosemary Ct OX4.... 141 F7
Rosemary Gdns OX27.. 65 D6
Rosemary La OX13... 134 C3
Rosemead RG10 ..... 255 D2
Rosemead Ave RG31.. 257 B3
Rose Pl OX1......... 261 B1
Roses La OX7........41 F5
Rose Terr OX12...... 196 A4
Rose Way OX15......16 F1
Rosina Wlk OX16 ......9 A1
Rosmary Dr OX16.......9 A1
Ross Ct OX11 .... 144 F1
Rossendale Rd RG4... 259 D3
Ross Rd 3 RG1...... 259 A1
Rotary Way OX16 ......9 B2
Rotha Field Rd OX2... 109 A1
ROTHERFIELD
  GREYS............ 243 D1
ROTHERFIELD
  PEPPARD......... 253 A8
Rotherfield Rd
  Cholsey RG8 .... 221 B1
  Henley-on-Thames
    RG9 .... 254 E7
Rotherfield Way RG4.. 259 B4
Rother Garth OX11 ... 201 A3
Rother Rd OX16 ....8 F1
Rothwell Gdns RG5... 260 F1
Rothwells Cl OX10... 221 A2
Rothwell Wlk RG4 ... 259 D2
Rotten Row OX10.... 182 D1
Round Close Rd
  Adderbury OX17 ....22 F3
  Hook Norton OX15 ... 30 A7
Roundham Cl OX5.... 92 D1
Roundhead Dr OX9... 129 F2
Roundhill Ct HP17 ... 130 E8
Roundhills Mead SN6.. 190 B7
Roundhouse La
  Lechlade-on-Thames
    GL7 .... 150 B3
  Stonor RG9 .... 226 D5
Roundtown OX17 .....35 C7
Roundway The OX3... 124 F3
Rouses La GL7....... 132 B5
ROUSHAM..........62 B4
Rousham Park House &
  Gdn★ OX25 .... 62 B5
Rousham Rd
  Tackley OX25........62 A8
  Tackley OX5........ 77 C7
Routh Rd OX3 ...... 124 F4
Routs Gn HP14 ..... 169 D2
ROUT'S GREEN..... 169 D2
Roves Farm★ SN6.... 208 B6
Roves La SN6....... 208 B7
Rowallan Cl RG4 .... 259 D6
Rowan Cl
  Carterton OX18..... 115 D3
  11 Didcot OX11..... 200 D3
  Kidlington OX5...... 108 F8
  Sonning Common RG4.. 252 F4
Rowan Dr OX28..... 104 E2
Rowan Gr OX4...... 143 A1
Rowan Rd OX26 .....65 E3
Rowans The OX10 ... 220 E1
Rowborough La SN3.. 208 A4
Rowel Dr OX5.......92 B1
Rowell Way OX7......42 F3
Row La RG4 .... 259 E7

Rowland Cl
  Benson OX10........ 204 D3
  Wallingford OX10 ... 203 C1
  Wolvercote OX2 .... 122 D8
Rowland Hill Ct OX1 .. 261 A2
Rowland Rd OX10 ... 221 A1
Rowlands Ho OX3 ... 125 A3
Rowles Cl OX1...... 141 E1
Rowles Paddock
  RG20 .... 235 A2
Rowney Pl OX4 ..... 142 A4
ROWSTOCK 217 B7
Row The
  Bletchingdon OX5 ... 93 A8
  Glympton OX20 ...... 75 D8
  Hinton Waldrist SN7 ... 155 F2
  Lechlade-on-Thames
    GL7 .... 150 F7
  Lyneham OX7........ 70 D5
  Mollington OX17 ....3 F3
  Stanton Harcourt OX29. 138 A8
Roxburgh Dr OX11... 200 D3
Royal Berkshire Ct
  OX11 .... 218 F7
Royal Mans RG9 .... 244 E1
Royston Dr OX26 .....65 B1
Ruck Keene Cl OX26 .. 65 C2
Ruddy La OX29 ...... 74 C1
Rufus Isaacs Rd RG4.. 259 B2
Rugge Furlong OX11.. 201 B1
Rumbolds Cl OX10... 203 F5
Rumpenny OX39 .... 168 C7
Rumsey's La OX11... 237 A8
Rupert Cl
  Chalgrove OX44...... 184 D6
  Henley-on-Thames RG9. 244 E3
Rupert Ho Sch RG9 .. 244 E2
Rupert Rd
  Chalgrove OX44..... 184 D6
  Oxford OX4 .... 142 E6
Rupert's La RG9 .... 244 E3
Rupert Way OX9..... 130 A1
RUSCOTE 16 A7
Ruscote Arc OX16 ....16 B8
Ruscote Ave OX16 ....16 B8
Ruscote Sq OX16 .....16 B7
Rushall Rd OX9 ..... 130 A1
Rushbeds Wood Nature
  Reserve★ HP18 .... 98 D4
Rush Common Sch
  OX14 .... 160 B1
Rushland Field OX39.. 168 E8
Rushmead Copse
  OX14 .... 160 C2
Rushmore La
  Woodcote RG8....... 240 E2
  Woodcote RG8...... 241 A3
Rushway OX10....... 221 F7
Rushy Furrow La
  Chalgrove OX44...... 184 E6
  Chalgrove OX49..... 185 A5
Ruskin Ave OX14 ... 179 E5
Ruskin Cl
  Cumnor Hill OX2 ..... 140 D6
  Didcot OX11 .... 219 A8
Ruskin Coll Oxford OX1 261 A3
  Oxford OX4 .... 124 C4
Ruskin Rd OX16 ..... 16 C3
Ruskin Wlk OX26 .....65 F3
Russ Ave SN7....... 173 A3
Russell Craggs La
  OX12 .... 214 F4
Russell Ct OX2 ..... 123 B4
Russell Jackson Cl
  OX10 .... 182 C6
Russell Rd RG4 ..... 258 D7
Russell St Bloxham OX15.21 E3
  Oxford OX2 .... 123 C2
RUSSELL'S WATER .. 224 F8
Russell Way OX7 .....43 A4
Russet Ave GL7...... 150 E3
Russet Ct RG4 ..... 252 E5
Russet Dr 2 OX13 ... 199 C3
Russet Glade RG4 ... 259 C7
Russet Rd OX27 ...... 50 C4
Russett Ave OX18.... 115 F5
Russley Gn SN8...... 245 D1
Rutherford Ave OX11. 217 B3
Rutherford Cl OX14... 160 A1
Rutherford Pl OX11... 218 D7
Rutherford Rd OX12 .. 215 B6
Rutherway OX2...... 123 A3
Rutten La OX5....... 108 A6
Rutters Cl OX5...... 108 D8
Ruttle Cl OX10...... 221 B1
Rycote La OX9 ...... 146 C5
Rydal Ave RG30..... 257 F2
Ryder Cl
  Summertown OX2.... 123 A6
  Yarnton OX5 .... 108 B6
Rydes Cl OX15........22 E8
Rydes The OX15 ......22 E8
Rye Cl OX16 ....8 F1
Ryecote Chapel★
  OX9 .... 146 D6
Rye Cres OX28....... 103 A1
Ryecroft Cl
  Sonning RG5....... 260 E1
  Wargrave RG10..... 255 E2
Rye Gdns OX14 ..... 199 F6
Rye Grass OX26 ......91 C6
Rye St Antony Sch
  OX3 .... 124 B3
Rylands OX3........ 123 F5
Rymans Cres
  East Hagbourne OX11.. 218 F5
  East Hagbourne OX11.. 219 A6
Rymans Ct OX11..... 200 E1
Rymers La OX4...... 142 B5
Rymill Rd OX16...... 16 A2

S

Sackler Liby OX1.... 261 B3
Sackville Ct OX17....8 E4
Sacred Heart Cath Prim
  Sch RG9 .... 244 D1
Sadlers Cl SN7 ..... 172 E2
Sadlers Croft OX44 .. 143 E1
Sadlers Ct OX14 .... 160 B3
Sadlers The RG31.... 257 B1
Sadler Wlk OX1...... 261 A1
Saffrey Mws HP17 ... 130 E6
Saffron Cl OX26 ..... 65 C5
Saffron Cres OX18... 115 E4
Saffron Ct OX14 .... 180 B8
Sage Cl OX16..........8 F1
Sage Dr 8 OX11..... 218 B7
Sage Rd RG31 ...... 257 C3
Sage St OX27....... 65 D7
Sage Wlk 4 OX4 .... 142 F1
Said Business Sch
  OX1 .... 261 A2
St Alban's Ct 5 OX10.. 221 D7
St Aldate's OX1...... 261 B1
St Aloysius' RC Prim Sch
  OX2 .... 123 B4
St Amand Dr OX14.. 179 E6
St Amand's RC Prim Sch
  OX12 .... 216 E5
St Andrews CE Prim Sch
  Chinnor OX39 ...... 168 C7
  Oxford OX3 .... 123 F3
St Andrews Cl OX14 .. 160 C2
St Andrews Ct OX9 .. 147 F8
St Andrews Ho OX39.. 168 C6
St Andrew's La OX3... 124 D4
St Andrews Rd OX11. 218 F8
St Andrew's Rd
  Chinnor OX39 ...... 168 C5
  Henley-on-Thames
    RG9 .... 254 D8
St Anne's Cl
  Bicester OX26....... 65 F4
  Henley-on-Thames
    RG9 .... 244 D1
St Anne's Coll OX2 .. 261 B4
St Annes Ct OX11 ... 219 B7
St Annes Mws OX12.. 214 D4
St Anne's Rd
  Banbury OX16 ...... 16 D3
  Oxford OX3 .... 124 D2
  Reading RG4 ...... 259 A2
St Anthony's Coll OX2.. 261 A4
St Antony's Coll OX49.. 185 A5
St Anwayrd OX3 .... 125 A3
St Barnabas Prim Sch
  OX2 .... 261 A3
St Barnabas Rd RG4.. 259 A6
St Barnabas St OX2.. 261 A3
St Benets Way RG4 .. 259 C6
St Bernard's Rd OX2.. 261 A4
St Birinus Ct GL7.... 150 C5
St Birinus Sch OX11.. 218 F7
St Catherine's Coll
  OX1 .... 123 E2
St Catherines Ho OX4.. 123 E1
St Christophers CE Prim
  Sch OX4 .... 142 C6
St Christopher's CE Sch
  GL7 .... 132 C1
St Christopher's Pl
  OX4 .... 142 C6
St Clare's Coll (Main
  Campus) OX2 ...... 123 B6
St Clement's St OX4 .. 123 F1
St Cristopher Cotts 4
  SN7 .... 172 F3
St Cross Bldg OX1 .. 261 C3
St Cross Coll OX1 ... 261 B3
St Cross Coll (Annexe)
  OX1 .... 261 C3
St Cross Rd OX1 .... 261 C3
St David's Cl RG4.... 258 F5
St David's St NN13.... 24 A8
St Denys Cl SN7 .... 194 E7
St Ebba'S Cl OX4 ... 124 E1
St Ebbe's CE Prim Sch
  OX1 .... 141 C7
St Ebbe's St OX1 .... 261 B2
St Edburg's CE Prim Sch
  OX26 .... 80 C8
St Edburg's Cl OX26 . 65 C2
St Edith's Way OX26.. 65 C2
St Edmund Hall OX1.. 261 C2
St Edmund's La 4
  OX14 .... 179 F6
St Edmund's RC Prim Sch
  OX14 .... 180 A8
St Edward's Ave
  Oxford OX2 .... 123 A7
  Summertown OX2.... 123 A6
St Edwards Ct OX2 .. 123 B6
St Edward's Sch
  Oxford OX2 .... 123 B7
  Oxford OX2 .... 123 B7
St Francis CE Prim Sch
  OX4 .... 142 A4
St Francis Cl OX3.... 142 E7
St Francis Rd HP14 .. 189 D3
St Frideswides Ct
  OX11 .... 218 E8
St Gabriels 10 OX12.. 214 D4
St Georges Cl OX10.. 220 F1
St George's Cl OX10 . 220 F1
St George's Cres OX16 16 C4

St Georges Gate OX1 . 261 A2
St Georges Gn OX10 . 203 C1
St George's Pl OX1 .. 261 B2
St Georges Rd OX10 . 221 C8
St George's Rd
  Buckland SN7 ...... 154 D1
  Buckland SN7 ...... 174 F8
St Giles OX5............ 93 A8
St Giles' OX1........ 261 B3
St Giles Cl OX25 ..... 80 A4
St Gregory the Great
  (Voluntary Aided) RC
  Secondary Sch OX4. 142 A6
St Helens Ave OX10.. 203 F3
St Helens Cres OX10.. 204 A3
St Helen's Ct OX14... 179 F6
St Helen's Mews 5
  .... 179 F6
St Helen's Mill 12
  OX14 .... 179 F6
St Helen's Pas OX1 .. 261 C2
St Helens Rd OX10 .. 203 F4
St Helen's Wharf OX14 179 F6
St Hildas Cl OX11 ... 219 B7
St Hilda's Cl OX26 .....65 F4
St Hilda's Coll OX4 .. 141 E6
St Hughs
  Banbury OX16 ...... 16 C3
  Stokenchurch HP14... 188 F4
St Hugh's Cl OX7.....65 F4
St Hugh's Coll OX2 .. 123 B6
St Hughs Pl HP14.... 188 F4
St Hughs Rise OX11.. 219 B7
St Hugh's Sch SN7 ... 174 B8
St Ives La OX29 .... 214 E8
St Ives Rd OX12..... 214 E8
St James OX12 ...... 214 D6
St James CE Sch
  OX12 .... 197 A4
St James Cl RG8.... 256 C6
St James Ct OX29.... 89 C7
St James Ct OX14 ... 160 E3
St James Terr OX14.. 160 E2
St James View OX12.. 197 B6
St James Wy OX12... 196 F7
St John Fisher Catholic
  Prim Sch OX4 ..... 142 D3
St Johns Cl OX13 ... 157 C2
St John's Cl OX11.... 219 A8
St John's Coll OX1 .. 261 B3
St John's Ct
  3 Banbury OX16 .... 16 D5
  Grove OX12........ 196 E1
St Johns Dr
  Carterton OX18..... 115 E3
  Kidlington OX5....... 92 F1
St John's Gn 16 OX10. 221 D7
St John's Ho 2 OX16. 16 C5
St Johns La
  Shillingford OX10 ... 203 B6
  Whiteoak Green OX29..87 F1
St John's Prim Sch
  OX10 .... 221 C7
St Johns Priory Sch
  3 Banbury OX16 .... 16 C5
  13 Banbury OX16 ... 16 E6
St Johns RC Prim Sch
  OX16 ....16 E3
St Johns Rd
  Grove OX12........ 196 E1
  Tackley OX5........ 77 C6
  Wallingford OX10 ... 221 C7
St John's Rd
  Abingdon-on-Thames
    OX14 .... 180 A3
  Banbury OX16 ...... 16 C5
  Reading RG4 ...... 259 C2
St John's Row OX14 . 201 C8
St John's St
  Bicester OX26....... 65 E2
  Lechlade-on-Thames
    GL7 .... 150 D4
St John St OX1 ..... 261 B3
St John's Terr 7
  OX10 .... 221 C7
St John's Way OX15 .. 33 B4
St John the Evangelist CE
  Prim Sch OX4 .....115 F4
St Josephs Cl OX2... 135 D2
St Joseph's RC Prim Sch
  Banbury OX16 ......15 F6
  Carterton OX18..... 115 D2
  Oxford OX3 .... 124 A4
  Thame OX9 .... 147 E8
St Katherine's Rd RG9 254 D2
St Kenelm's CE Sch
  OX29 .... 102 E2
St Kenelms Cl OX29... 102 E2
St Laurence CE Prim Sch
  OX10 .... 203 B7
St Lawrence CE Prim Sch
  GL7 .... 150 D3
St Lawrence Cl OX10.. 203 B8
St Lawrence Ho OX10. 203 B8
St Lawrence Rd
  Lechlade-on-Thames
    GL7 .... 150 D4
  South Hinksey OX1.. 141 E4
St Leonards CE Prim Sch
  OX16 ....16 F6
St Leonards Cl OX49.. 186 B2
St Leonard's Cl OX16. 16 F6
St Leonard's Ct OX7... 54 D2
St Leonard's Ct OX11. 221 D6
St Leonards La OX10. 221 D7
St Leonard's Rd OX3. 124 D3
St Leonard's Sq 10
  OX10 .... 221 D6
St Lucians La OX10 .. 221 D6
St Lukes Ct RG4 .... 259 B4

St Luke's Rd OX4 142 D5
St Lukes Way RG4 259 B5
St Margaret Rd RG9 254 F4
St Margaret's Rd OX2 123 B4
St Mark's Rd RG9 254 D8
St Martins RC Prim Sch RG4 259 E6
St Martin's Rd OX4 142 A3
St Martins St OX10 221 D7
St Mary's 9 OX12 214 D4
St Mary & St John CE Prim Sch OX4 141 E6
St Mary's Ave RG8 257 D5
St Mary's CE (Aided) Prim Sch OX16 16 C6
St Mary's CE Inf Sch OX28 118 B7
St Mary's CE Prim Sch OX7 42 E2
St Marys Cl OX44 184 D6
St Mary's Cl
2 Banbury OX16 16 C6
1 Bicester OX26 65 D1
Henley-on-Thames RG9 254 A8
Kidlington OX5 92 E2
Oxford OX4 142 B2
Wheatley OX33 144 B8
St Mary's Ct
Bampton OX18 134 E2
Witney OX28 118 A7
St Mary's Gn OX14 159 F1
St Mary's Ho OX33 144 B8
St Mary's La OX7 30 E3
St Marys Mead OX28 118 B7
St Mary's RC Prim Sch OX26 65 E2
St Marys Rd
Adderbury OX17 22 F2
East Hendred OX12 216 E5
St Mary's Rd
East Hendred OX12 216 E6
Oxford OX4 141 F7
St Mary's Sch RG9 254 E8
St Marys St OX10 221 D7
St Marys Way OX12 214 C5
St Marys Wlk OX25 48 C6
St Mary's Wlk OX27 50 C3
St Michaels OX12 214 D4
St Michaels Ave SN6 190 A5
St Michael's Ave OX14 179 E7
St Michael's CE Prim Sch
Marston OX3 123 F2
Steventon OX13 198 F4
St Michaels Cl
Fringford OX27 52 D6
Shipton-under-Wychwood OX7 85 D8
St Michael's La OX5 107 F8
St Michael's St OX1 261 B2
St Michaels Way OX13 198 F4
St Nicholas CE Inf Sch OX10 221 C8
St Nicholas CE Prim Sch OX12 213 F4
St Nicholas' Gn OX14 159 F1
St Nicholas Pk (Cvn Pk) OX3 123 F7
St Nicholas Pl OX12 214 A5
St Nicholas Prim Sch OX3 123 F5
St Nicholas Rd
Oxford OX4 142 C2
Tackley OX5 77 C6
Wallingford OX10 221 C8
St Nicolas CE Prim Sch OX14 179 F8
St Omer Rd OX4 142 C5
St Paul's Cres OX2 140 D8
St Peter's Ave RG4 258 E3
St Peter's CE Inf Sch OX18 133 C5
St Peter's CE Prim Sch OX29 107 C2
St Peters Cl
South Newington OX15 31 F7
Stoke Lyne OX27 51 B5
Wootton OX13 159 B6
St Peter's Cl OX29 107 D2
St Peter's Coll OX1 261 B2
St Peter's Cres OX26 65 F4
St Peter's Gate NN13 24 A7
St Peter's Hill RG4 258 F3
St Peters Pl 4 OX10 221 D7
St Peters Rd
Abingdon-on-Thames OX14 160 C1
Didcot OX11 218 E8
St Peter's Rd
Brackley NN13 24 A8
Wolvercote OX2 122 F8
St Peter's St OX10 221 D7
St Philip & St James' CE VA Prim Sch OX2 123 A4
St Rualds Cl 15 OX10 221 D7
St Rumbolds Rd OX10 221 D7
St Stephens Cl 5 RG4 259 A2
St Swithun's CE Prim Sch OX1 160 E8
St Swithuns Rd OX1 160 E8
St Thomas More RC Prim Sch 1 OX5 108 E7
St Thomass Cl SN7 155 F2
St Thomas St
Deddington OX15 33 F3
Oxford OX1 261 A2
St Vernon Wy OX16 8 F2
Salegate La OX4 142 D5
Salesian Gdns OX4 142 D6
Salesian Ho 1 OX4 142 D6
SALFORD 41 F5
Salford Rd OX3 123 E4
Salisbury Cres OX2 123 B8
Salisbury Wlk 1 OX26 65 C1
Sallow Cl 1 OX26 65 F5
Salmon Cl OX15 21 F6
Salop Cl SN6 209 B6
Salter Cl OX1 141 C7
Salters La
Little Compton CV36 26 E2
Ludgershall HP18 98 C8
Salt La OX9 166 E2
Salt Way Banbury OX16 15 F3
Saltway
Banbury OX16 16 A3
Saltway La OX15 12 A4
Saltway Nature Reserve★ OX7 74 B3
Salvia Cl OX16 15 F7
Samian Way OX10 202 D8
Samor Way OX11 218 D8
Samphire Cl 1 OX11 218 B7
Samphire Rd OX4 142 F2
Samuelson Ct 16 OX16 16 D5
Sandcroft Rd RG4 258 E6
Sandell Cl OX16 16 B5
Sanderling Cl OX26 81 A8
Sanderling Wlk OX16 16 E3
Sanders Rd OX4 142 C1
Sandfield Rd OX3 124 B3
Sandfine Rd OX15 15 B2
Sandford Cl
Abingdon-on-Thames OX14 160 B2
Woodcote RG8 250 F8
Sandford Dr RG5 260 F1
Sandford Gn OX16 15 F7
Sandford La OX1 160 F7
Sandford Mount OX7 73 C3
SANDFORD-ON-THAMES 161 B7
Sandford Park OX7 73 C3
Sandford Rd OX4 142 A1
Sandford Rise OX7 73 C3
SANDFORD ST MARTIN 46 C2
Sandford St Martin Rd OX7 46 C1
Sandgate Ave RG30 257 F2
Sandhill SN6 209 A7
Sandhill Rd OX5 108 A8
SANDHILLS 125 B4
Sandhills Com Prim Sch OX3 125 B4
Sand La OX3 111 A2
Sandleigh Rd OX13 159 A7
Sandpiper Cl OX26 81 A8
Sandpiper Walk OX11 200 B1
Sandpit Hill
Finmere MK18 39 D6
Finmere MK18 39 F6
Sandpit La
Farley Hill RG4 253 E1
Reading RG4 259 F8
Sandpits Dr OX18 116 A4
Sandringham Rd
Didcot OX11 219 B8
Kings Sutton OX17 23 F5
Sands Cl OX2 139 E5
Sands Hill SN7 172 F2
Sands La OX15 31 F7
Sands Rd
South Moreton OX11 219 F6
South Moreton OX11 220 A6
Sands The
Benson OX10 204 C6
Milton-under-Wychwood OX7 70 B1
Sands Way OX10 203 F5
Sand View SN7 172 F2
Sandwood Rd OX26 65 B1
Sandycroft Cl OX5 108 B7
Sandy La
Boars Hill OX1 140 C2
Cholsey OX10 220 E1
Hatford SN7 174 C4
Kingston Bagpuize OX13 156 E1
Long Crendon HP18 129 B6
Oxford OX4 142 E3
Shrivenham SN6 209 B6
Tiddington OX9 145 F5
Upper Rissington GL54 68 A4
Yarnton OX5 108 C7
Sandy Lane Ct GL54 68 A4
Sandy Lane Est OX9 145 F7
Sandy Lane W OX4 142 D3
Sansbury Dr OX16 15 E2
Sansoms Ct OX20 91 D6
Sarajac Ave OX12 213 F4
SARSDEN 55 F3
Sarsden Cl OX7 57 B1
SARSDEN HALT 55 D6
Sarsden Rd OX7 55 F4
Sarum Cl OX18 115 F3
Satin La OX15 33 F3
SATWELL 242 E4
Satwell
Busgrove Wood RG9 242 A3
Satwell RG9 242 F3
Satwell Cl RG9 243 A3
Saunders Cl OX49 186 B2
Saunders Ct RG8 257 B5
Saunders Rd OX4 142 B6
Saunders Wood Copse HP14 188 F4
Savile Rd Oxford OX1 123 D2
Oxford OX1 261 C3
Savile Way OX12 196 D1
Saw Cl OX44 184 C7
Sawpit Rd OX4 142 E3
Sawpits La GL56 40 A1
Saxel Cl OX18 135 E3
Saxifrage Sq 4 OX4 142 E1
Saxon Cl OX10 221 C7
Saxon Ct
Benson OX10 203 F4
Bicester OX26 65 F1
Oxford OX3 124 C3
Saxon Orch SN6 191 D2
Saxon Pl
Pangbourne RG8 256 D6
Wantage OX12 214 B5
Saxons Cl GL7 132 B5
Saxons Heath OX14 201 D7
Saxon Sq OX9 129 D1
Saxons Way OX11 219 A7
Saxon Way Oxford OX3 124 B4
Witney OX28 118 A7
Saxton Rd OX14 179 E5
Sayer Milward Terr 20 OX10 221 D7
Sayers Orch OX11 200 D1
Saywell Cres OX29 120 D8
Scafell Cl RG31 257 B2
Scampton Cl OX26 66 B3
Scantlebury Way OX12 215 A5
Scarsbrook Cres OX7 43 A4
Schilling St OX25 63 A8
Sch La Banbury OX16 16 C6
Tiddington OX9 146 A6
Sch of Geography & the Environment OX1 261 C3
Schofield Ave OX28 104 A3
Schofield Gdns OX28 104 A3
Schofields Way OX15 21 E5
Scholar Cl SN6 191 F2
Scholar Pl OX2 140 C7
Scholars Acre OX18 115 D4
Scholars Cl RG4 258 F2
Scholar's Mews OX2 123 B6
Scholars Rise HP14 188 E4
Schongau Cl OX14 179 D4
School Cl Ickford HP18 128 A3
Long Compton CV36 27 F5
Longworth OX13 156 C3
Steventon OX13 198 F4
Westbury NN13 25 A4
School Cotts RG9 243 C2
School Ct OX2 261 A3
School End Aynho OX17 35 C7
Chetwode MK18 53 D8
Schooler's La GL56 40 C3
Schoolfields RG9 254 E1
School Hill
Minster Lovell OX29 102 F3
Mollington OX17 3 F3
Wargrave RG10 255 D1
School La
Appleford OX14 200 F8
Aston Rowant OX9 167 E3
Black Bourton OX18 133 F5
Chilson OX7 71 F3
Coleshill SN6 191 B8
Cropredy OX17 4 F1
East Garston RG17 246 F2
Great Bourton OX17 9 D7
Great Bourton OX17 9 F8
Grove OX12 196 E1
Harwell OX11 217 E7
Henley-on-Thames RG9 244 D1
Kingston Bagpuize OX13 156 F1
Middleton Stoney OX25 64 A4
Milton OX14 199 D5
4 Milton Heights OX14 199 C3
Minster Lovell OX29 102 E3
North Newington OX15 15 C4
Reading RG4 259 A2
Reading RG4 259 B6
Shabbington HP18 128 D3
Stadhampton OX44 163 C2
Stoke Lyne OX27 51 B5
Stoke Row RG9 241 F4
Upper Heyford OX6 62 F8
Wargrave RG10 255 D2
Warmington OX17 2 F4
Warmington OX17 3 A4
Wigginton OX15 31 B6
Wigginton OX15 31 B7
School of St Helen & St Katherine OX14 179 D8
School Paddock OX27 64 F8
School Pl OX1 141 D6
School Rd
Ardington OX12 215 D5
Finstock OX7 88 C5
Kidlington OX5 92 E1
West Hanney OX12 196 F6
School Row OX16 16 F6
School View OX16 16 F6
School Yd OX44 163 C2
Schuster Cl OX10 239 B8
Science Oxford★ OX4 123 F1
SCOTLAND END 30 A7
Scotland End OX15 30 A7
Scotsgrove Cotts OX9 130 A4
Scotsgrove Hill
Thame OX9 129 F3
Thame OX9 130 A3
Scots Pine Way OX11 218 B7
Scott Cl Bicester OX26 65 C3
Kidlington OX5 108 D8
Reading RG4 259 A5
Scott Rd OX2 123 B8
Scotts Cnr NN13 25 A4
Scotts La OX27 67 E2
Scours La
Reading RG30 258 B1
Reading RG30 258 B2
Scrutton Cl OX3 124 E3
Seacourt Rd OX2 122 C1
Sealham Rd OX29 118 B4
Second Ave OX11 200 D2
Second St
Croughton NN13 36 E6
Harwell OX11 217 C3
Sedgefield
Bicester OX26 65 B1
Bicester OX26 80 B8
Sedgefield Cl RG4 252 F6
Sedgemoor Dr OX9 130 A1
Sedgesmith Way OX12 214 F4
Sedge Way 8 OX18 115 F5
Sedgewell Rd RG4 252 F6
Seed Gr RG31 257 E3
Seelscheid Way OX26 81 A7
Seesen Way OX12 214 E4
Sefton Pl OX15 22 E7
Sefton Rd OX3 124 E3
Segrave Cl RG10 260 E2
Segsbury Ct OX12 214 B5
Segsbury Rd OX12 214 B5
Selborne Gdns RG30 258 A1
Sellwood Dr OX18 115 E3
Sellwood Rd OX14 159 F1
Selwyn Cres OX14 160 E2
Send Rd RG4 259 C1
Sentinel St OX12 194 C1
Sermon Cl OX3 124 F2
Setler Ho 1 OX16 16 E6
Setts The SN7 172 E2
Seven Acres
Long Crendon HP18 129 B7
Thame OX9 148 A8
Seven Barrows RG17 230 B2
Sevenfields SN6 190 A7
SEVENHAMPTON 190 B2
Seven Sisters Wy OX2 140 A5
Seventeenth St OX11 217 A2
Seventh Ave (North) OX3 142 F8
Severalls Cl OX10 203 D1
Severalls Cotts OX10 203 B3
Severn Cl OX26 65 B3
Severn Cres 2 OX11 219 A8
Severn Rd
Abingdon-on-Thames OX13 159 D2
Harwell OX11 217 B1
Sewell Cl OX14 160 C1
Sewells La OX39 167 E8
Seymour Ct 2 OX9 148 A7
Seymour Pk Rd OX39 168 D6
SHABBINGTON 128 D3
Shabbington Rd
Ickford HP18 128 A4
Long Crendon HP18 129 A4
Shabbington HP18 128 F4
Worminghall HP18 127 F5
Shackleton Cl 4 OX26 66 A4
Shades The OX16 16 C5
Shadwell Rd OX10 182 C5
Shaftesbury Rd OX3 124 E5
Shakenoak OX29 105 C6
Shakespeare Cl RG4 259 D5
Shakespeare Dr OX26 65 C3
Shakespeare Rd OX29 120 D8
SHALSTONE 25 E6
Shannon Cl OX12 196 F1
Shannon Rd
Bicester OX26 65 B2
1 Didcot OX11 219 A8
Sharland Cl OX12 214 E8
Sharman Beer Ct OX9 147 E8
Sharpes Cotts OX26 66 E2
Shaw Cl OX26 65 C3
Shaws Copse OX14 160 F2
Sheards La SN7 194 E7
Shearings The OX15 30 A7
Shearwater Dr OX26 81 B8
Sheen Cl OX27 65 F6
Sheepdrove RG17 246 B8
Sheep St Bicester OX26 65 E2
Burford OX18 100 E5
Charlbury OX7 73 B3
Highworth SN6 190 A5
Sheepstead Rd
Marcham OX13 158 D1
Marcham OX13 178 C8
Sheepwash La OX13 199 A4
Sheepway Ct OX4 142 A4
Sheepways La RG4 258 B8
Sheep Wlk
Reading RG4 259 B4
Sharmans Pit OX27 36 F1
Tusmore Park OX27 37 A1
Sheerstock HP17 130 E5
Sheffield Cl RG9 256 C5
Sheldonian Theatre★ OX1 261 C2
Sheldon Rd HP18 128 A3
Sheldon Rise RG4 259 A4
Sheldons Piece OX49 186 A2
Sheldon Way OX4 142 C3
Shelford Pl OX3 124 D1
Shelley Cl
Abingdon-on-Thames OX14 160 A1
Banbury OX16 16 A3
Oxford OX3 124 F2
Shelley Rd OX4 142 B6
SHELLINGFORD 193 F7
Shellingford CE Voluntary Aided Prim Sch SN7 193 F7
Shellingford Cross Roads SN7 174 B1
Shellingford Rd OX18 115 F3
SHENINGTON 6 E2
Shenington CE Prim Sch OX15 6 F2
Shenington Kart Club★ OX15 6 C2
Shenington Rd
Epwell OX15 13 C7
Shenington Rd *continued*
Shenington OX15 6 A3
Shenington OX15 6 B1
Shepard Way OX7 42 F3
Shepherd Gdns OX14 179 C6
Shepherds Cl
Grove OX12 196 D2
Sibford Gower OX15 19 B8
Weston-on-the-Green OX25 79 A2
Shepherds Gn RG9 243 A3
SHEPHERD'S GREEN 243 A3
Shepherds Hill
Sandford-on-Thames OX4 142 F1
Sonning RG6 260 C1
Steeple Aston OX25 48 A1
Shepherds House La RG6 260 A1
Shepherds La RG4 258 D6
Shepherds Wlk
Woodley RG6 260 C1
Wroxton OX15 15 B8
Sher Afzal Cl OX4 142 C5
Sherard Rd OX1 261 C4
Sheraton Dr RG31 257 B1
Sherborne St GL7 150 C4
Sherbourne Rd OX28 117 D8
Shergold Rd 6 OX18 134 F4
Sheridan Ave RG4 258 F4
Sheriff's Dr OX2 122 F8
Sherrington Rd OX12 261 C4
Sherwood Ave OX14 180 A7
Sherwood Cl OX26 66 D2
Sherwood Gdns RG9 254 C8
Sherwood Pl
Barton OX3 124 E4
Purley on Thames RG8 257 B4
Sherwood Rd
Didcot OX11 200 D1
Didcot OX11 218 D8
Sherwood Rise RG8 257 B5
SHIFFORD 136 E1
Shifford La OX29 137 C2
Shilbrook Manor OX18 133 F4
Shillbrook Ave OX18 115 D5
Shilldeane Dr OX18 115 D4
SHILLINGFORD 203 B6
Shillingford Ct OX10 203 A6
Shillingford Rd OX10 203 C3
Shilson La OX7 73 B3
SHILTON 115 B5
Shilton Rd
Burford OX18 100 F3
Burford OX18 101 A1
Carterton OX18 115 D4
Shingleton Way 1 OX18 134 F4
Shinmoor Cl OX11 201 B2
SHIPLAKE 254 F2
Shiplake Bottom RG9 252 F6
Shiplake CE Prim Sch RG9 254 E2
Shiplake Coll RG9 254 F1
SHIPLAKE ROW 254 C2
Shiplake Sta RG9 255 B4
SHIPPON 159 C1
Ship St OX1 261 B2
Shipston Rd CV36 27 E7
Shipton Cl RG31 257 C2
SHIPTON-ON-CHERWELL 92 B6
Shipton Rd
Ascott-under-Wychwood OX7 71 B1
Fulbrook OX18 100 F7
Fulbrook OX18 101 A8
Fulbrook OX7 85 C2
Shipton-under-Wychwood OX7 70 B1
Woodstock OX20 91 D6
Shipton Sta OX7 70 E2
SHIPTON UNDER WYCHWOOD 85 E8
SHIRBURN 186 D4
Shirburn Rd
Lewknor OX49 187 A7
Shirburn OX49 186 F6
Watlington OX49 186 C2
Shirburn St OX49 186 C2
Shire Lake Cl OX1 261 B1
Shires Bsns Pk The NN13 24 A6
Shires Rd NN13 24 A6
Shirley Pl OX2 261 A4
Shirvilles Hill RG8 250 E7
Shoe La
East Hagbourne OX11 218 F5
Oxford OX1 261 B2
Shooters Hill RG8 249 F1
Shooter's Hill RG8 256 C6
SHORES GREEN 118 F8
Short Dro SN4 227 A4
Shorte Cl OX3 142 E7
Short Furlong OX11 201 B2
SHORTHAMPTON 72 B5
Shortlands Hill OX10 238 D4
Short St
Pangbourne RG8 256 D5
1 Reading RG4 259 B2
Watchfield SN6 191 D1
Short The RG8 257 D5
Shotover OX3 125 A2
Shotover Corner SN7 211 C6
Shotover Ctry Pk★ OX3 143 B8
Shotover Est
Risinghurst OX33 125 F2
Wheatley OX33 126 A2
Shotover Kilns OX3 124 F1
Shotover Trad Est OX3 124 F1
SHOTTESWELL 8 D7
Shrewsbury Pl OX18 134 E3
Shrieves Cl OX14 160 B2
Shrimpton Cl HP18 129 B6
SHRIVENHAM 209 B7
Shrivenham CE Prim (Controlled) Sch SN6 209 B7
Shrivenham Hundred SN6 191 D2
Shrivenham Hundred Bsns Pk SN6 191 D2
Shrivenham Rd
Highworth SN6 190 B3
Longcot SN7 192 C1
Longcot SN7 192 C2
Lower Bourton SN3 208 C3
Shrubbery The GL7 150 C4
Shute Ave SN6 209 D8
SHUTFORD 14 B6
Shutford Rd
Balscote OX15 14 C8
Balscote OX16 7 C2
Epwell OX15 13 D6
North Newington OX15 15 B4
Tadmarton OX15 20 E8
Shuttleworth Cl OX10 221 E5
Siareys Cl OX39 168 C6
SIBFORD FERRIS 19 A7
SIBFORD GOWER 19 A8
Sibford Gower Endowed Prim Sch OX15 19 A8
Sibford Rd Epwell OX15 13 A5
Hook Norton OX15 19 B3
Hook Norton OX15 30 B8
Shutford OX15 13 E3
Sibford Sch OX15 19 B7
Sibthorp Rd OX1 261 C3
Sideleigh Rd OX15 22 E8
Sidings Ind Est The NN13 24 A8
Sidings Rd OX7 55 E5
Sidings The
Hook Norton OX15 30 C7
Wallingford OX10 221 C7
Sidney Smith Pl OX29 117 C8
Sidney St OX4 141 F7
SIGNET 100 C1
Signet End OX18 100 E3
Signet Hill OX18 100 B3
SIGNET HILL OX18 100 B2
Silibaravi Dr OX26 81 A7
Silkdale Cl OX4 142 D5
Silver Birches OX33 125 E7
Silverdale Rd RG10 255 E1
Silver La OX12 213 D6
Silver Mead HP18 127 D5
Silver Rd OX4 142 A7
Silver St Bourton SN6 209 A2
Chacombe OX17 10 E4
Fernham SN7 193 A4
Tetsworth OX9 166 B8
Wroxton OX15 8 B1
Wroxton OX15 15 B8
Silver Street N OX17 10 E4
Silverthorne Dr RG4 258 E6
Silverweed Rd OX15 16 F1
Simmns Cl OX33 125 D7
Simmonds Wlk OX12 214 D6
Simmons Rd RG9 244 D3
Simmons Way OX9 129 F1
Simms La OX7 43 A4
Simon Ho OX3 124 D3
Simons Cl RG31 257 C4
Simon's Cl OX33 144 A8
Simons La OX7 85 D7
Simon's Way MK18 25 E7
Simpson Dr OX25 63 C8
Simpsons Way OX1 160 E8
Sinclair Ave OX16 16 A7
Sinclair Dr OX16 16 A7
Singers Cl RG9 254 E8
Singers La RG9 244 E1
Singletree OX4 142 B4
Sinnels Field OX7 85 E8
Sinnet Ct OX4 142 A8
Sinodum Cl OX14 201 D7
Sinodun Rd
Didcot OX11 218 F7
Wallingford OX10 203 C1
Sinodun Row OX14 200 F7
Sinodun View OX10 203 B8
Sint Niklaas Cl OX14 179 D4
Sir Bevys Cl OX2 122 B1
Sir Chetwode Cl
Didcot OX11 218 B8
Didcot OX11 218 B8
Sires Hill
Long Wittenham OX11, OX14 201 E5
North Moreton OX11 202 C4
Sir Frank Williams Ave OX11 200 B2
Sir Georges La OX17 23 A4
Sir Henry Jake Cl OX16 9 C2
Sir James Martin Way OX44 184 E7
Sir Mortimer's Terr OX14 199 D6
Sir William Dunn Sch of Pathology OX1 261 C4
Siskin Rd Bicester OX26 66 A1
Upper Rissington GL54 68 A5
Six Acres OX10 203 B7
Sixpenny La OX44 184 E6
Sixteenth St OX11 217 B3

Sixth St Croughton NN13..**36** E7
Harwell OX11......**217** B3
Skarries View RG4...**258** D8
Skelton Ct OX4......**123** F1
Skerritt Way RG8...**257** D4
Skilton Rd RG31.....**257** C3
Skimmingdish La
Bicester OX26.........**66** B5
Bicester OX27.........**65** F6
Skinner Rd OX26......**66** D2
Skinners La SN7......**173** A4
Skipper Cl OX39...**168** C5
Skippett La OX7......**88** A4
Skippon Way OX9...**129** F2
Skittle Alley OX17.....**35** C7
Skittle Gn HP27.....**149** F3
Skylark Fields OX14..**180** C1
Skylark Pl OX4......**142** D2
Skylark Rd OX15......**16** C6
Skylarks Cres GL54...**68** B3
Skylark Way OX28...**103** F1
Slade Cl OX3.......**124** C1
SLADE END......**202** F1
Slade End OX10.....**202** F2
Slade End Rdbt OX10..**203** A2
Slade Farm Cotts OX5 ..**63** B1
Slade Hill NN13......**24** C1
Slade Rd Cholsey OX10..**221** A2
Didcot OX11.........**200** C1
Stokenchurch HP14....**188** E4
Slade The Charlbury OX7 **73** C4
Oxford OX3.........**142** E8
Oxford OX4.........**142** D8
Slate Cres OX29......**89** D7
Slatters Ct OX29......**90** A1
Slave Hill HP17.......**130** F5
Slaymaker Cl OX3.....**124** F2
Slingsby Cl GL54......**68** B3
Sloane Cl RG8.......**249** C6
Slopes The RG4......**259** D2
Small Ho OX15.......**19** C7
Smith Barry Cir GL54...**68** B4
Smith Barry Cres GL54..**68** B4
Smith Barry Rd GL54....**68** B4
Smith Cl RG4.......**252** F5
Smith Ct OX10.......**221** B7
Smith's Cl OX18......**135** E2
Smiths Cl 5 OX11....**200** D1
Smiths Cvn Site OX15...**21** F3
Smiths Farm La OX11..**200** D1
Smith's Hill OX12.....**231** F5
Smiths Rickyard OX12 **216** D7
Smiths Wharf 3
OX12..........**214** D5
Snakehill La
Hempton OX15.......**33** B4
Hempton OX15.......**33** B6
Snipe Rd GL54.......**68** A4
Snowberry Cl OX15....**13** D5
Snowdon Mede OX3..**124** A4
Snowdrop Dr OX11....**218** C7
Snowshill Dr OX28....**117** D8
Snows La OX33......**125** D8
Snowswick La
Buscot SN6........**171** A1
Buscot SN6........**170** E5
Snuff La OX17........**8** C8
Snuggs La OX12......**197** B7
Soane End RG4......**259** A7
Soden Pl
Kingston Bagpuize
OX13...........**156** D1
Kingston Bagpuize
OX13...........**156** D1
Soden Rd
Upper Heyford OX25....**49** D1
Upper Heyford OX25....**63** D8
Sollershott OX2......**108** F2
Solters Cl HP18.......**98** C8
SOMERTON......**48** F6
Somerton Rd OX27....**49** C7
Ardley OX27........**50** B4
North Aston OX25......**48** A6
North Aston OX25......**48** B7
Upper Heyford OX25....**48** F1
Somerville OX11......**219** B8
Somerville Coll OX2....**261** A3
Somerville Ct OX17....**23** D3
Somerville Dr OX26....**65** F4
Somerville Pl OX18....**100** E3
Songers Cl OX2......**140** B8
Songthrush Rd
Bodicote OX15.......**16** F1
Bodicote OX15.......**17** A1
SONNING.......**260** E4
Sonning CE Prim Sch
RG4...........**260** D2
SONNING COMMON ..**252** E5
**Sonning Common Prim
Sch** RG4........**252** F5
Sonning Common Rd
Binfield Heath RG4 ....**253** E3
Binfield Heath RG9 ....**254** A3
SONNING EYE.....**260** C5
Sonning Gate RG10 ...**260** E2
Sonning La RG4......**260** D2
Sonning Mdws RG4....**260** C1
Soot La OX17........**3** A4
Sopwith Rd GL54.....**68** A5
Sorrel Cres 7 OX11..**218** B7
Sorrel Mead OX26....**65** E5
Sorrel Rd
Bicester OX25.......**81** D4
Oxford OX4.........**143** A2
Sorrel Way OX18....**115** E4
Sotwell St OX10.....**202** F2
SOULDERN......**35** E4

Southampton St
Faringdon SN7......**172** F3
3 Faringdon SN7......**172** F4
Southam Rd
Banbury OX16........**9** C4
Banbury OX17........**9** D4
Farnborough OX17......**3** F7
Mollington OX17.......**4** A3
South Ave
Abingdon-on-Thames
OX14...........**159** F2
Henley-on-Thames RG9..**254** E8
Kidlington OX5......**108** F6
South Bank
South Stoke RG8......**239** C3
Turweston NN13......**24** C7
South Bank Cottages
OX10...........**239** C3
South Bar St OX16.....**16** C5
South Bridge Row
OX1...........**261** B1
Southby OX18......**134** F4
Southby Cl
Appleton OX13......**158** A8
Cholsey OX10......**221** B1
South Cl OX5.......**108** F5
SOUTHCOOMBE.....**43** D3
Southcroft OX3......**123** F6
Southdale Rd OX2....**123** B8
Southdown Ct SN7....**194** F7
Southdown Rd RG4....**259** B5
South Dr Great Tew OX7 **31** D2
Harwell OX11.......**217** C3
Sonning RG4.......**260** C1
SOUTHEND Garsington..**162** E8
Henley-on-Thames....**226** C8
Southend OX44......**162** E8
South End
Great Rollright OX7.....**29** A3
Haddenham HP17......**130** F5
Southend Comm RG9 **226** C8
Southend Cotts OX5...**78** A3
Southern Ave OX26....**66** A5
Southern By-Pass Rd
Kennington OX1......**141** D4
Oxford OX2........**140** E4
Southerndene Cl
RG31...........**257** C2
Southern Rd OX9....**147** E8
Southfield Dr OX14..**199** F7
Southfield Jun Sch
SN6...........**190** A5
Southfield La OX27....**49** F7
Southfield Pk OX4....**142** B8
Southfield Rd
Eynsham OX29......**120** D6
Oxford OX4.........**142** A8
South Gate Ct GL54...**68** A3
South Gn OX5.......**108** F5
South Hills HP18......**98** A1
SOUTH HINKSEY....**141** C5
Southill Bsns Pk OX7 ...**88** B8
Southlands OX18....**135** E2
SOUTH LAWN......**85** F2
South Lawn
Shipton under Wychwood
OX18............**85** F3
Witney OX28........**117** F7
South Leigh CE Sch
OX29...........**119** A7
South Lodge The 2
OX26...........**65** E1
Southmead Ind Pk
OX11...........**200** D4
South Mere OX18....**116** C3
SOUTHMOOR.....**156** D1
Southmoor Gdns
OX13...........**156** E1
Southmoor Pl
Oxford OX2........**123** B4
Oxford OX2........**261** A4
Southmoor Rd OX2....**123** A4
Southmoor Way OX14 **199** F5
South Moreton Sch
OX11...........**219** F5
SOUTH NEWINGTON ..**31** E7
South Newington Rd
Barford St Michael
OX15...........**32** A8
Barford St Michael OX15 **32** D6
Bloxham OX15.......**21** B1
South Par OX2......**123** B7
South Park Ave OX11 **218** D7
South Park Ct 5 OX4 **141** F8
South Parks Rd OX1..**261** C3
South Quay OX14....**179** F4
Southridge Farm Rd
RG8...........**228** D1
SOUTHROP Hook Norton **.30** B6
Lechlade-on-Thames...**131** A3
Southrop CE Prim Sch
GL7...........**131** A4
Southrop Rd
Eastleach Martin GL7...**131** A7
Hook Norton OX15.....**30** B6
South Row OX11.....**235** D7
South Side OX25......**62** A8
South St Banbury OX16..**16** E7
Blewbury OX11......**237** A8
Caulcott OX25.......**63** B5
Letcombe Regis OX12..**214** A1
Middle Barton OX7.....**60** F8
Oxford OX2........**141** A8
Reading RG4.......**259** B2
Watchfield SN6......**191** D1
SOUTH STOKE.....**239** C4
South Stoke Prim Sch
RG8...........**239** B4
South Stoke Rd
South Stoke OX10.....**239** F4

Southampton St continued
Woodcote RG8.......**240** B2
South View
Great Bourton OX17.....**9** D7
Tiddington OX9......**145** F7
4 Wallingford OX10....**221** C7
South View Ave RG4..**259** C2
South View Pk RG4....**259** C2
Southwell Rd OX26....**80** C8
SOUTH WESTON....**166** E1
Southwold 3 OX26....**65** F4
Southwold La OX26....**65** E6
Southwold Prim Sch 7
OX26...........**65** E1
Southwood Rd OX29..**103** C5
Sovereign Cl OX11....**219** A8
Sovereign Pl OX10....**221** C7
Spa Cl SN6........**190** B7
Span Green La HP18....**97** E1
Span Hill RG4......**260** B7
Spans The HP18......**97** E1
Spareacre La OX29...**120** E8
Sparrows Wy GL54....**68** B3
Sparrow Way OX4....**142** F1
Sparsey Pl OX2......**109** B1
Spears The OX5.....**108** B6
Speedwell Croft 2
OX26...........**65** E5
Speedwell St OX1....**261** B1
SPELSBURY.......**72** F8
Spelsbury Rd OX7.....**73** A6
Spencer Ave OX15...**108** B5
Spencer Cl Goring RG8..**249** D7
Woodstock OX20......**91** D7
Spencer Ct OX4.....**142** B4
Spencer Ct 14 OX16...**16** D5
Spencers Ct SN7.....**194** D7
Spendlove Ctr The OX7 **73** B4
Spenlove Cl OX14....**159** F2
Spenser Cl OX26......**65** C3
Spey Rd OX13.......**159** C3
Speyside 3 OX18....**115** D5
Spiceball Country Pk★
OX16...........**16** D6
Spiceball Park Rd
OX16...........**16** D6
Spiceball Park Sp Ctr
OX16...........**16** D6
Spicers La OX29.....**104** C6
Spiers La OX27.......**67** F2
Spinage Cl SN7......**173** A3
Spindleberry Cl OX4..**142** E2
Spindlers OX5.......**92** F2
Spindleside 1 OX26...**65** F4
Spinney Bank OX17....**23** F5
Spinney Cl RG4......**259** B7
Spinney Dr OX16......**16** F3
Spinney Field OX4....**142** E1
Spinneys Cl OX14....**160** F3
Spinneys The OX7.....**58** F5
Spinney The
Abingdon-on-Thames
OX14...........**159** D1
East Hendred OX12....**216** D6
Launton OX26.......**66** D2
Lechlade-on-Thames
GL7...........**150** C4
Spitfire Cl
Benson OX10.......**204** B2
Bicester OX26.......**66** A3
Spitfire Dr OX29.....**117** B7
Spitfire Pl 20 OX7....**68** B3
Spooner Cl OX3.....**124** E3
SPRIG'S ALLEY.....**168** F1
Sprigs Holly OX39....**168** F1
Sprigs Holly La HP14..**189** B8
Spring Cl OX28......**118** A7
Spring Copse OX1...**141** C3
Springdale 6 OX10...**221** C7
Spring Farm Ct OX7....**47** D5
Spring Farm Mews
RG8...........**239** C1
Springfield OX17......**8** C7
Springfield Ave OX16..**16** C3
Springfield Cl OX49...**186** C1
Springfield Dr OX14..**179** E8
Springfield End RG8...**249** C8
Springfield Gdns
OX39...........**168** C7
Springfield Hollow
HP14...........**188** E5
Springfield Mews RG4 **259** B4
Springfield Oval
Witney OX28.......**103** F1
Witney OX28.......**103** F2
Springfield Pk OX28..**103** F1
Springfield Rd
Bicester OX27.......**65** F7
Kidlington OX5......**108** F8
Oxford OX2........**140** C8
Stokenchurch HP14....**188** F4
Wantage OX12......**214** F4
Springfields OX25.....**81** D3
Springfield Sch OX28 **104** D2
Springfield Wy OX14..**199** E6
Spring Gdns
Abingdon-on-Thames
OX14...........**179** D7
Banbury OX16.......**16** B6
East Hanney OX12....**197** C7
Lechlade-on-Thames
GL7...........**150** C4
Spring Hill OX13....**176** C8
Springhill Rd RG8....**249** C8
Spring Hill Rd OX5...**107** F8
Spring La
Aston Tirrold OX11....**237** D8
Cholsey OX10......**239** C1
Cropredy OX17.......**4** F1

Spring La continued
15 Didcot OX11......**200** C2
Great Bourton OX17.....**9** D5
Horspath OX33......**143** C7
Idbury OX7.........**69** B4
Oxford OX3........**124** F2
Oxford OX4........**142** D2
Playhatch RG4......**260** B5
Watlington OX49....**186** C1
Spring Meadows Bsns Ctr
RG10...........**255** F5
Spring Path OX9.....**147** E8
Spring Pl OX7.......**42** E2
Spring Rd OX14.....**179** D7
Spring St OX7.......**42** E3
Springs The
Chalgrove OX44.....**184** E6
Witney OX28.......**118** A7
Spring Terr 2 OX14..**179** D7
Springwell Hill
Bletchingdon OX5......**78** A1
Bletchingdon OX5......**93** A8
Springwell Ho 6 OX16..**16** D5
Spring Wlk RG10....**255** D1
Springwood La RG9..**253** A7
Spruce Dr OX26......**65** F5
Spruce Gdns OX4....**161** E8
Spruce Rd OX5.....**108** E7
Spurrett Gdns 3
OX18...........**115** D2
Spur The RG10......**255** D5
Square Firs OX29.....**90** A5
SQUARE THE......**59** A6
Square The
3 Abingdon-on-Thames
OX14...........**179** F7
Aston OX18........**135** E3
Aynho OX17.........**35** C7
Brightwell-cum-Sotwell
OX10...........**202** D2
Churchill OX7........**55** E5
Ducklington OX29....**118** B4
Enstone OX7........**58** C2
Epwell OX15........**13** A5
Eynsham OX29......**120** E7
Great Tew OX7.......**45** D7
Kings Sutton OX17.....**23** F5
Long Crendon HP18...**129** C6
Longworth OX13....**156** B3
Milton-under-Wychwood
OX7...........**70** B1
Oxford OX2........**122** D1
2 Oxford OX4.......**142** C4
Pangbourne RG8....**256** D6
Swalcliffe OX15......**19** F8
Squires Cl OX18......**116** C3
Squires Ho 5 OX12...**214** D5
Squires Rd SN6......**191** D1
Squire's Wlk OX10...**221** D6
Squirrel Gdns OX28...**103** F1
Squitchey La OX2.....**123** A8
Stable Cl Finmere MK18.**39** C7
Oxford OX1........**261** A2
Stable Cotts GL56......**40** C2
Stableford La OX26....**79** E8
Stable Rd OX26......**65** E3
Stables The GL7......**150** D5
Staddlestone Rd RG31 **257** C2
STADHAMPTON....**163** D2
Stadhampton Prim Sch
OX44...........**163** C2
Stadhampton Rd
Drayton St Leonard
OX10...........**183** B6
Drayton St Leonard
OX10...........**183** B7
Great Milton OX44....**145** B1
Little Milton OX44....**163** F5
Little Milton OX44....**163** F5
Stadium Way RG30...**258** B1
Stadium Ind Est RG30 **258** B1
Staffordshire Dr RG30..**257** F1
Staggs Rd 5 OX9....**148** A7
Stag Row HP18.....**128** C2
Stainer Pl OX3......**123** F4
Stainfield Rd OX3....**124** B5
Stainswick La
Shrivenham SN6.....**209** C4
Shrivenham SN6.....**209** D3
Stallard Cl SN8......**172** E1
Stallpits La
Shrivenham SN6.....**208** F7
Shrivenham SN6.....**209** A7
Stallpits Rd SN6.....**209** A7
Stanbridge Cl OX16....**16** A5
Standhill La OX44....**164** E5
STANDLAKE......**137** D4
Standlake CE Prim Sch
OX29...........**137** D2
Standlake Rd
4 Ducklington OX28 ..**118** B4
Ducklington OX29....**118** C2
Hardwick OX29......**118** E2
Northmoor OX29....**138** A2
Standon Ct OX3.....**124** C2
Stanford Dr OX14....**179** F8
**STANFORD IN THE
VALE**..........**194** E7
Stanford in the Vale CE
Prim Sch SN7.....**194** E7
Stanford Rd
Buckland SN7......**174** F6
Faringdon SN7......**173** D2
Stanier Pl OX16......**16** E7
Staniland Ct OX14.....**179** F5
Stanley Cl Oxford OX2 **140** D8
Yarnton OX5........**108** B7
Stanley Rd OX4......**141** F7
Stanmore Cres OX18..**115** E4
Stansfeld Pl OX3.....**124** E1
Stansfield Cl OX3....**124** F1

Stanton Cl OX28....**117** E8
Stanton Cotts OX33..**125** D7
**STANTON
HARCOURT**....**138** A8
**Stanton Harcourt CE Prim
Sch** OX29......**138** B8
Stanton Harcourt Ind Est
OX29...........**138** A7
Stanton Harcourt Rd
Eynsham OX29......**120** D8
South Leigh OX29....**119** D5
Witney OX28.......**118** C8
Witney OX28.......**118** D7
Stanton Rd
Forest Hill OX33.....**125** E4
Oxford OX2........**140** E6
STANTON ST JOHN...**125** E7
Stanton St John Rd
HP18...........**112** F5
Stanville Rd OX2....**140** B7
Stanway Cl OX28....**103** D1
Stanwell Cl OX17.....**11** A1
Stanwell Dr OX17.....**11** A1
Stanwell La OX17......**9** D1
Stanwell Lea OX17....**11** A2
Stapleton Rd OX3....**124** C2
Star Cl OX29......**120** D8
Stares Ct OX7.......**42** E1
Starina Croft
14 Banbury OX16.......**9** A1
14 Banbury OX16.......**9** A1
Star La SN6.......**191** C1
Starnham Rd OX29...**118** A4
Star Rd RG4......**259** C2
Starveall Rd RG8.....**247** D6
Starwort Path 4 OX4 **142** F2
Station App
Bicester OX26........**65** F1
Kidlington OX5......**108** F7
Station Approach OX16 **16** E5
Station Field Ind Est
OX5...........**92** C2
Station La OX28....**118** B6
Station Rd Ardley OX27 **50** C3
Ascott-under-Wychwood
OX7...........**71** B2
Ashbury SN6.......**228** A7
Aynho OX17.........**35** B6
Bampton OX18......**134** E6
Baulking SN7.......**193** F1
Blackthorn OX25......**82** A4
Bletchingdon OX5......**93** A8
Brize Norton OX18....**116** C3
Chinnor OX39......**168** C6
Chipping Norton OX7...**42** D2
Cholsey OX10......**220** F1
Clifton Hampden OX14..**181** A3
Cropredy OX17.......**4** F1
Culham OX14.......**180** F3
East Hanney OX12....**197** B5
Enslow OX5.........**77** B1
Eynsham OX29......**120** E7
Faringdon SN7......**172** F3
Goring RG8........**249** C6
Grove OX12........**214** E8
Haddenham HP17....**130** E5
Henley-on-Thames RG9 **244** E1
Highworth SN6......**190** A6
Hook Norton OX15.....**19** F1
Hook Norton OX15.....**30** C8
Kingham OX7........**54** F3
Kirtlington OX5......**77** F3
Langford GL7......**132** D2
Launton OX26.......**66** E3
Launton OX26.......**67** A4
Lechlade-on-Thames
GL7...........**150** D5
Lower Heyford OX25....**62** D6
Marsh Gibbon OX27....**67** F3
Milcombe OX15......**20** E1
Pangbourne RG8....**256** C6
Pangbourne RG9....**256** C6
Shipton-under-Wychwood
OX7...........**70** E1
Shrivenham SN6.....**209** B5
South Leigh OX29....**119** C5
Uffington SN7......**211** E8
Upton OX11........**218** C2
Wallingford OX10....**221** C8
Wargrave RG10.....**255** C1
Wheatley OX33......**144** B8
Station Road Ind Est
OX11...........**200** F1
Station Yard Ind Est
Adderbury OX17......**23** B2
Chipping Norton OX7...**42** D2
Station Yd
Steventon OX13.....**199** A4
Thame OX9........**148** A7
Tiddington OX9......**145** F7
Staunton Rd OX3....**124** B3
Staverton Rd OX2....**123** B5
Steady's La OX29....**138** B7
STEEPLE ASTON....**62** A7
Steeple Barton OX7....**61** D7
Steeple Cl OX15......**21** E4
Steepness Hill
Barford St Michael
OX15...........**32** F4
Barford St Michael OX7..**32** F4
Hempton OX7.......**33** A4
Steep Rise OX3.....**124** C5
Stenter La OX28....**104** A1
Stenter Mews 5
OX28...........**104** A1
Stenter Rise 4 OX28 **104** A1
Stenter Sq OX28....**104** A1
Stenton Cl OX14....**179** E5
Stephen Ct OX3.....**124** C3

**Stephen Freeman Com
Prim Sch** OX11...**200** C2
Stephen Rd OX3....**124** C3
Stephens Cl GL7.....**150** B4
Stephens Field OX10.**221** E8
Stephenson Ho OX1..**261** B1
Stephenson Rd OX2..**214** A8
Steppingstone La SN6 **209** A4
Stepp La SN7......**173** A2
Steptoe Cl OX12....**196** D2
Sterling Cl
Bicester OX26........**66** A3
Kidlington OX5.......**92** E1
Kidlington OX5......**108** E8
Sterling Rd OX5....**108** E8
Sterling Road App OX5 **.92** E1
Sterling Way RG30..**258** B1
Stert Rd OX39......**167** G4
Stert St OX14......**179** F7
Stevens Cl OX2.....**123** B4
Stevens La RG9.....**252** B8
Stevenson Cl
Bicester OX26........**65** C3
East Hanney OX12....**197** C2
Stevenson Dr OX4...**179** D8
Stevens Way SN7....**172** D2
STEVENTON......**198** E4
Steventon Rd
Drayton OX14......**199** B7
East Hanney OX12,
OX13...........**197** E7
Stewart St OX1.....**141** C6
Stickley Ct SN7.....**173** A2
Stile Rd OX3.......**124** D3
Stileway Rd
Chilton OX11......**234** F8
East Hendred OX12...**216** F3
Stimpsons Cl OX2....**122** B1
Stirling Cl
Carterton OX18.....**115** C3
Reading RG4.......**259** D6
Wantage OX12......**214** E5
Stirling Ct OX16......**15** F6
Stirlings Rd 4 OX12 **214** D4
STITCHENS GREEN..**248** F3
Stockey End OX14...**160** C2
Stockfields Pl HP14...**188** D5
Stockham Pk OX12...**214** C5
Stockham Prim Sch
OX12...........**214** C5
Stockham Way OX12..**214** C5
Stocking La OX15......**6** D2
Stockleys Rd OX3....**124** A5
Stockmore St OX4...**141** F8
Stock Rd OX9......**148** B7
Stocks Gn OX18.....**115** E4
Stocks La
Carterton OX18.....**115** E4
Steventon OX13....**198** F4
Stocks Mws 5 OX18..**115** E4
Stocks The OX7......**57** B1
Stocks Tree Cl OX5...**108** B5
Stocks Wlk 2 OX18..**115** E4
Stockton Rd OX26....**65** B1
Stockwell La OX33...**127** D1
STOKE LYNE......**51** B5
Stoke Lyne Rd OX27...**52** D1
STOKENCHURCH...**188** E5
Stokenchurch Prim Sch
HP14...........**188** E5
Stoke Pl OX3......**124** C4
STOKE ROW......**241** F4
Stoke Row CE Sch
RG9...........**241** F4
Stoke Row Rd
Rotherfield Peppard
RG9...........**252** E8
Sonning Common RG9..**242** C2
Stoke Row RG9.....**242** A4
Stokes View RG8....**256** C5
STOKE TALMAGE...**165** F3
Stoke Talmage Rd
OX9...........**166** B6
Stonebridge Cl OX28..**104** C2
Stonebridge Rd OX13 **198** F5
Stoneburge Cres OX26..**65** E3
Stonebury Cl OX12...**214** E5
Stonechat Rd OX15...**16** F1
Stone Cl OX2......**122** B1
Stonecrop Leyes 3
OX26...........**65** E5
Stone Ct
11 Banbury OX16.....**16** D5
Great Rollright OX7....**29** A3
Stonefield Cl SN6....**209** C6
Stonefield Dr SN6....**190** A4
Stonegables OX28...**118** A6
Stoneham Pk RG8....**257** B2
Stonehill OX14......**179** D3
Stone Hill OX15......**21** D4
Stonehill La
Abingdon-on-Thames
OX14...........**179** D3
Kingston Bagpuize
OX13...........**176** D8
Stonehill Wlk OX14...**179** D4
Stonehouse RG8....**249** E2
Stone House Cl OX13 **156** E1
Stoneleigh Cl OX7.....**57** B1
Stoneleigh Dr OX18..**115** D5
Stone Mdw OX2.....**123** A5
Stone Quarry La OX4..**142** A4
STONESFIELD......**89** D7
Stonesfield OX11....**219** A7
Stonesfield La OX7....**73** C2
Stonesfield Prim Sch
OX29...........**89** C7
Stonesfield Rd
Combe OX29........**90** A5
Stonesfield OX29.....**74** F1

Stonesfield Rd continued
Stonesfield OX29. . . . . . 89 E6
Wootton OX20. . . . . . . 75 B2
Stonesfield Riding
Spelsbury OX7. . . . . . . 89 C8
Stonesfield OX29. . . . . . 89 C8
Stone St Oxford OX4. . 142 A8
Reading RG30 . . . . 258 B1
Stoney La
Little Haseley OX44. . . . 164 F5
Stoke Talmage OX9 . . . . 165 C2
Stoke Talmage OX9,
OX49. . . . . 185 E8
Stonhouse Cres OX14. 160 E2
STONOR 225 F6
Stonor Cl OX11. . . . . . . 200 E1
Stonor Gn OX49 . . . . . . 186 B1
Stonor Ho★ RG9 . . . . . 226 A7
Stonor Pl OX3 . . . . 124 B2
Stopford Pl OX7. . . . . . .42 E1
Storksbill La OX13. . . . 156 F1
Stort Cl OX11 . . . . 200 F3
Stour Cl OX11 . . . . 201 A1
Stoutsfield Cl OX5. . . . 108 A5
Stow Ave OX28 . . . . . . 117 D8
Stowford Ct OX3 . . . . . 124 F5
Stowford Rd OX3 . . . . . 124 F4
Stowhill OX12 . . . . 213 C3
Stowood Cl OX3. . . . . . 124 E4
Stow Rd Bledington OX7. 54 C2
Fifield OX7. . . . . 69 B2
Strachay Cl RG8 . . . . . . 256 C3
Strafford Way OX9. . . . 148 A8
Straight Mile Rd OX33 111 F3
Straight Mile The
Shipton-on-Cherwell
OX5. . . . . 92 A5
Woodstock OX20. . . . . . .91 F5
Strainges Cl OX29 . . . . 118 B4
Stranks Cl SN6 . . . . . . 190 A4
Stratfield Rd
Kidlington OX5. . . . . . . 108 E6
Oxford OX2 . . . . 123 B6
Stratford Dr OX29 . . . . 120 D8
Stratford La OX20 . . . . .76 B2
Stratford Rd
Chipping Norton OX7 . . . 43 A7
Drayton OX15. . . . . 15 E8
Shenington OX15. . . . . . .6 F6
Stratford Row OX29 . . 142 D2
Stratford St OX4. . . . . 141 F7
Stratford Way OX5. . . . 80 C8
Stratford Wlk 2 OX18 115 E3
Stratford Wy 7 OX26 . . 65 C1
Strathmore Cl OX18 . . . 115 D5
STRATTON AUDLEY 52 D1
Stratton Audley Manor
OX27 . . . . 52 D1
Stratton Audley Rd
Chetwode MK18. . . . . . 53 C7
Fringford OX27 . . . . 52 D5
Poundon OX27. . . . . . . 53 D1
Poundon OX27. . . . . . . 67 E8
Stoke Lyne OX27. . . . . . 51 B5
Stratton Way OX14 . . . 179 F7
Strawberry Hill OX15 . . .21 E5
Strawberry Path OX4 . 142 F2
Strawberry Terr OX15. . .21 E5
Stream Rd OX11. . . . . . 218 C2
Streamway Cl OX11. . . 218 D8
STREATLEY 249 A7
Streatley CE Prim Sch
RG8. . . . . 248 F6
Streatley Hill RG8 . . . . 248 F6
Streatley Lodge 6
OX1. . . . . 141 C7
Street The
Crowmarsh Gifford
OX10. . . . . 221 F7
Ewelme OX10. . . . . . . 204 E4
Ipsden OX10. . . . . 240 C7
Moulsford OX10. . . . . . 239 A4
Moulsford OX10. . . . . . 239 A6
North Stoke OX10. . . . . 221 D1
South Stoke RG8. . . . . . 239 B3
Stoke Lyne OX27. . . . . . 51 B5
Tidmarsh RG8 . . . . 256 D2
Stroud Cl OX16. . . . . . . .16 E8
Strrling Cl OX17. . . . . . .23 F6
Stuart Cl RG4. . . . . 259 B5
Stuart's La RG9. . . . . . 244 D1
Stuart Way OX9 . . . . . 130 A1
Stubble Cl OX2. . . . . . . 140 A8
Stubbs Ave OX3 . . . . . . 142 E7
Stuchfield Cl OX25. . . . .79 F4
Studdridge Ct HP14. . . 188 C4
Stud Farm Cl OX17 . . . . .5 E1
STUDLEY GREEN 189 E3
Studley Rd OX5. . . . . . . .96 F1
Sturges Cl OX3 . . . . . . 124 D5
Sturt Cl OX7. . . . . 73 C2
Sturt Rd OX7 . . . . 73 C3
Sturt Wood OX29 . . . . . 89 D2
Styles Cl OX27. . . . . . . .67 E2
Styles The OX11. . . . . . 217 D7
Sudbury Ct SN7 . . . . . . 173 A4
Sudbury La OX13. . . . . 156 C3
Suffolk Ct OX17. . . . . . .67 F3
Suffolk Ho OX10. . . . . . 204 E4
Suffolk Way OX14 . . . . 179 D6
Sugarswell Bsns Pk
OX15 . . . . .6 C4
Sugarswell La OX15. . . . .6 B6
Sugworth Cres OX14. . . 160 E6
Sugworth La OX14. . . . 160 D6
SULHAM. 256 D2
Sulham Hill
Sulham RG8. . . . . 257 A1
Sulham RG9. . . . . 256 E3
Sulham La RG8 . . . . . . 256 E3
Summerfield OX1 . . . . . 141 D6

Summerfield Rd OX2 . . 123 B7
Summerfield Rise
RG8. . . . . 249 D7
Summer Fields OX14 . . 160 B3
Summer Fields Sch
OX2 . . . . 123 B7
Summerhill Rd OX2. . . . 123 B7
Summer Ley
Barford St Michael
OX15. . . . . .32 F6
Hempton OX15 . . . . 33 A6
Summers Cl
Adderbury OX17 . . . . . . 23 A5
Kingston Bagpuize OX13 156 F1
Summerside SN7 . . . . . 174 F8
Summerside Rd SN7. . . 174 E8
Summerton Pl OX7 . . . . .42 F3
Summertown 123 C7
Summertown OX2 . . . . 123 C7
Summertown Ct OX2 . . 123 A7
Summertown Ho OX2. . 123 A7
Summit House Cl RG8 . 250 F7
Sunderland Ave OX2. . . 109 A1
Sunderland Cl OX29 . . . 89 C7
Sunderland Dr OX26. . . 66 A4
Sundew Cl OX4. . . . . . . 143 A2
Sungold Pl OX18. . . . . . 115 D5
SUNNINGWELL. 159 E6
Sunningwell CE Prim Sch
OX13 . . . . 159 E6
Sunningwell Rd
Oxford OX1 . . . . 141 D6
Sunningwell OX13. . . . . 159 E4
Sunny Bank OX7. . . . . . 29 A3
SUNNYMEAD 123 B8
Sunnymeade Ct 2
OX2 . . . . 109 B1
Sunny Rise OX33 . . . . . 143 D6
Sunnyside
Benson OX10. . . . . 203 F5
Oxford OX4 . . . . 142 D6
Wheatley OX33 . . . . . . 144 C8
Sunrise Hill OX11. . . . . 236 B1
Sun Rising Hill OX15. . . . .6 C8
Supergas Ind Est
OX28 . . . . 103 B1
Surley Row RG4 . . . . . . 259 A5
Sussex Dr
4 Banbury OX16 . . . . . . .8 F1
Banbury OX16 . . . . .15 F8
Sutherland Beck OX11 200 F3
SUTTON 120 B1
Sutton Cl OX14 . . . . . . 179 F7
SUTTON
COURTENAY 200 B8
Sutton Courtenay CE Prim
Sch OX14 . . . . 199 F6
Sutton Courtenay La
OX14. . . . . 199 F5
Sutton Dr OX15. . . . . . . 21 D3
SUTTON GREEN 120 B2
Sutton La OX29 . . . . . . 120 B1
Sutton Rd Milton OX14. 199 E6
Oxford OX3 . . . . 124 B5
SUTTON WICK 179 C2
Sutton Wick La OX14 . . 179 C2
Suzan Cres OX12 . . . . . 214 E5
Swailbrook Dr OX7. . . . 55 A4
Swain Ct OX28. . . . . . . 118 A6
SWALCLIFFE. 19 F8
Swalcliffe Barn★ OX15 .19 F8
Swalcliffe Lea OX15 . . . .14 B1
Swalcliffe Park Sch Trust
OX15 . . . . .19 F8
Swalcliffe Rd OX15 . . . . 20 B8
Swale Dr OX11. . . . . . . 201 A2
Swallow Cl
Bicester OX26. . . . . 81 A8
11 Oxford OX4 . . . . 142 F1
Swallow Mews 8
OX11. . . . . 200 C2
Swan Cl Blackthorn OX25 82 A3
Grove OX12. . . . . 196 D1
Lechlade-on-Thames
GL7. . . . . 150 C4
Middleton Cheney OX17 .17 F8
Swan Close Rd OX16. . . 16 D5
Swan Ct Oxford OX1 . . . 261 A2
7 Witney OX28 . . . . . . 118 A8
Swan Gdns OX9 . . . . . . 166 B8
Swanhall La OX29 . . . . 104 B5
Swan La Burford OX18 . . 100 E5
Faringdon SN7. . . . . . . 172 F4
Great Bourton OX17 . . . . .9 D8
Long Hanborough OX29 . 90 B1
Swanlands Ho OX29 . . . 120 E7
Swan Lane OX18 . . . . . 100 E5
Swan Mews 10 OX11. . . 200 C2
Swann Wlk Thame OX9 147 F8
Thame OX9 . . . . 147 F8
Swansea Rd RG1 . . . . . 259 A1
Swansea Terr RG31. . . . 257 D1
Swansfield
Bicester OX26. . . . . 81 A7
Lechlade-on-Thames
GL7. . . . . 150 D6
Swan St Eynsham OX29 120 E7
Oxford OX2 . . . . 123 A1
Swanston Field RG8. . . 256 D7
Swarbourne Cl OX11. . . 200 F2
Sweeps La OX18. . . . . . 100 E5
Sweet Briar OX13. . . . . 178 C6
Sweet Green Cl OX3 . . . 125 B4
Sweetmans Rd OX2 . . . 140 F2
Swere The OX15. . . . . . . 33 E5
SWERFORD. 30 E3
SWERFORD HEATH. 31 C4
Swerford Heath Hill
OX15. . . . . .30 F5
Swerford Rd OX15. . . . . 30 B5
Swift Cl Bicester OX26. . 65 C3

Swift Cl continued
13 Oxford OX4 . . . . 142 F1
Oxford OX4 . . . . 143 A1
Swift Ct OX28 . . . . 103 F1
Swift Dr OX15. . . . . .17 A1
Swift Way OX10 . . . . . . 204 D3
Swinbourne Rd OX4 . . . 142 B2
SWINBROOK 101 E5
Swinbrook Cl RG31. . . . 257 D3
Swinbrook Ct OX28 . . . 118 B7
Swinbrook Rd OX7 . . . . .85 E6
Swinburne Rd
Abingdon-on-Thames
OX14. . . . . 180 A8
Oxford OX4 . . . . 141 F6
Swindon Rd SN6. . . . . . 190 A5
Swindon St SN6 . . . . . . 190 A5
SWINFORD 121 B5
Swinford Mus★ GL7. . . 132 B5
Swingburn Pl OX18 . . . 118 A8
Swin La OX18. . . . . 101 E5
Swinnerton Ho RG9. . . 244 E1
Swinstead Ct OX44 . . . 184 D6
Swiss Farm RG9. . . . . . 244 D4
Sworford La OX33 . . . . 144 F5
Sycamore Cl
Abingdon-on-Thames
OX13. . . . . 159 C1
6 Carterton OX18. . . . 115 D3
Long Hanborough OX29 . 90 B1
Sibford Gower OX15. . . . 19 A8
Watlington OX49. . . . . . 186 A2
Witney OX28 . . . . 104 C2
Sycamore Cres OX14 . . 160 E7
Sycamore Ct RG8. . . . . 256 C6
Sycamore Dr
Banbury OX16 . . . . .16 D2
Carterton OX18. . . . . . . 115 D3
Thame OX9 . . . . 147 D8
Sycamore Gdns OX26. . .65 F4
Sycamore Pl OX18 . . . . 114 D7
Sycamore Rd
Ambrosden OX25 . . . . . 81 C4
Launton OX26. . . . . 66 D2
Oxford OX2 . . . . 140 D7
Sycamores The OX3 . . . 124 E4
Sycamore Terr OX15. . . 21 D4
Sycamore Wlk OX12 . . . 196 D1
Sycamore Wy
Didcot OX11. . . . . 218 C7
17 Didcot OX11. . . . . . 218 C7
SYDENHAM 167 D8
Sydenham Cl OX17 . . . . .23 B4
Sydenham Gr
Sydenham OX39. . . . . . 167 E8
Sydenham OX39. . . . . . 167 E8
Sydenham Rd
Sydenham OX39. . . . . . 167 D8
Sydenham OX9 . . . . . . 167 E8
Sylvester Cl OX18. . . . . 100 E5
Symeon Pl RG4. . . . . . . 258 F3
Sympson Cl 5 OX14 . . . 179 E6
Synderford Cl OX11. . . 201 A2
Syringa Wlk OX16 . . . . . .9 B1
Sywell Rd SN6. . . . . . . 209 A6

T

TACKLEY 77 C5
Tackley CE Prim Sch
OX5 . . . . .77 C6
Tackley Pl OX2. . . . . . . 123 B4
Tackley Rd OX25. . . . . . .62 B2
Tackley Sta OX5. . . . . . . 77 C6
Tacks La HP17. . . . . 130 F6
TADMARTON 20 C8
Tadmarton Park OX15 . 21 A6
Tadmarton Rd
Bloxham OX15. . . . . 21 B5
Lower Tadmarton OX15. . .20 F6
TADPOLE. 154 C5
Taggs Gate OX3 . . . . . . 124 F5
Tait Dr OX25. . . . . 63 B7
Talbot Cl Banbury OX16 .15 F8
Harwell OX11 . . . . 217 D7
Reading RG4 . . . . 259 D2
Talbot Fields OX18 . . . . 135 A3
Talbot Rd OX2. . . . . 109 A2
Talbot Way RG31. . . . . 257 C3
Talisman Bsns Ctr The
OX26 . . . . .80 F8
Talisman Rd OX26. . . . . .80 F8
Tamar Cres OX16. . . . . . .65 B3
Tamarisk Cres OX18 . . . 115 F5
Tamarisk Gdns 7 OX26 65 E5
Tamar Way OX11 . . . . . 201 A2
Tamesis Pl RG4. . . . . . . 259 B1
Tamina Cl OX18. . . . . . . 115 D5
Tancred Gr OX26. . . . . . .80 F6
Tangmere Ave OX18. . . 115 E4
Tangmere OX26. . . . . . . .66 B4
Tanners Cl OX16. . . . . . . .10 F1
Tanners Ct OX7. . . . . . . .73 B3
Tanners La
Adderbury OX17 . . . . . . .22 F3
Burford OX18 . . . . 100 D4
Eynsham OX29 . . . . 120 F7
Tokers Green RG4. . . . . 258 F8
Tannery Cl OX18. . . . . . 100 E5
Tannery Gdns OX18. . . 134 E4
Tannery Yd OX18 . . . . . 100 F5
Tansy Way OX18 . . . . . . 115 E5
Taphouse Ave OX28 . . . 104 B2
Tarragon Dr OX4 . . . . . 142 F1
Tarragon Terr OX27 . . . .65 D7
Tarrant Ave OX28. . . . . 104 D2
Tar Rd
High Cogges OX29 . . . . 118 F4
Rushy Common OX29. . . 119 A3
Tarret Burn OX11. . . . . 200 F2

TASTON 58 B1
Taston Rd OX7 . . . . .73 A8
Tatham Rd OX14 . . . . . 159 F1
Tatlings Rd OX13 . . . . . 198 F5
Tattersalls OX2. . . . . . . 123 B8
Taunton Rd
3 Bicester OX26 . . . . . 65 C1
Bicester OX26. . . . . 80 C8
Taverner Pl OX3. . . . . . 123 F4
Tavistock Ave OX11. . . 218 D7
Tavy Cl OX11 . . . . 200 F3
Tawney St OX4 . . . . . . 142 A8
Tayberry Cl OX27 . . . . . .65 D6
Tay Gdns OX26 . . . . 65 C3
Taylor Cl OX26 . . . . .65 E4
Taylor Inst Main Liby
OX1. . . . . 261 B3
Taylors Cl OX20 . . . . 91 C5
TAYNTON. 100 A8
Tays Gateway OX15. . . . .33 F4
Tchure The
Charlton-on-Otmoor
OX5. . . . . 95 A4
Deddington OX15. . . . . . 33 F4
Teal Cl Banbury OX16 . . .16 E3
Didcot OX11. . . . . 218 C7
Grove OX12. . . . . 196 D1
Sandford-on-Thames
OX4. . . . . 142 F1
Teale Cl OX25 . . . . .96 E7
Teasel Bank
Harwell OX11. . . . . 217 F7
Harwell OX11. . . . . 217 F7
Teasel Way OX18 . . . . . 115 F5
Technology Dr OX5. . . . .92 B2
Teescroft OX11. . . . . . . 201 A3
Telford Cres RG5. . . . . . 260 F1
Telford Rd OX26. . . . . . .66 B3
Telford Road Ind Est
OX26. . . . . .66 B3
Templar Ho OX4. . . . . . 142 C5
Templar Rd OX2. . . . . . 109 B1
Templars Cl OX33 . . . . 144 A8
Templars Square Sh Ctr 5
OX4 . . . . 142 C4
Temple Cl OX15 . . . . . . .21 C5
Temple Cloisters 2
OX4 . . . . 142 D6
TEMPLE COWLEY 142 C5
Temple Cowley Pool &
Fitness Ctr OX4 . . . . 142 C6
Temple Ho RG6. . . . . . . 244 E3
Temple Mill La OX15. . . .18 F5
Temple Mill Rd OX15 . . 19 A8
Temple Mws OX4. . . . . 142 C6
Temple Rd OX4. . . . . . . 142 C6
Temple St Brill HP18 . . . .98 B1
Oxford OX4 . . . . 141 E8
Templeton Ho RG9 . . . . 254 F7
Ten Acre Caravan Pk
OX4. . . . . 161 C8
Tenby Ave RG4. . . . . . . 259 D5
Ten Cottages CV47 . . . . .1 B8
Tenlands OX17 . . . . .17 E8
Tennis The OX29 . . . . . 107 D2
Tennyson Cl OX16 . . . . . .16 A3
Tennyson Dr OX14. . . . . 179 C5
Tennyson Mws RG9. . . 255 A4
Tenpenny OX10. . . . . . . 202 D8
Tenth St OX11. . . . . 217 B3
Tern Wlk OX4 . . . . 142 E1
Terrace The OX7 . . . . . . 70 A1
Terrett Ave OX3 . . . . . . 125 B4
Terrington Cl OX14. . . . 160 A2
Territorial Wy OX2 . . . . 142 F7
Tessa Rd RG1 . . . . 258 F1
Tetbury Dr OX28. . . . . . 103 D1
TETSWORTH 166 A8
Tetsworth Prim Sch
OX9 . . . . 166 B8
Tewer The OX8. . . . . 89 C7
Tew La Glympton OX20. . 60 D1
Wootton OX20. . . . . . . .75 F6
Tew Rd OX7 . . . . 59 A5
TF Smith Bldgs OX28 . . 118 C8
Thackley End OX2. . . . . 123 B5
THAME. 148 C7
Thame Com Hospl
OX9 . . . . 148 A8
Thame La
Clifton Hampden
OX14. . . . . 181 B5
Clifton Hampden OX44. . 181 B6
Thame L Ctr OX9 . . . . . 147 D8
Thame Park Rd OX9 . . . 147 F4
Thame Pk Bsns Ctr
OX9 . . . . 148 A7
Thame Pk Rd 1 OX9 . . . 148 A7
Thame Rd
Blackthorn OX25. . . . . . 82 A3
Chinnor OX39. . . . . 168 B8
Great Haseley OX44 . . . 164 E8
Great Haseley OX44. . . . 164 F7
Great Milton OX33 . . . . 145 E3
Great Milton OX44 . . . . 145 C2
Haddenham HP17. . . . . 130 D5
Haddenham HP17. . . . . 130 F2
Haddenham HP17. . . . . 130 F6
Little Milton OX44. . . . . 163 F7
Long Crendon HP18 . . . 129 D5
Long Crendon HP18,
OX9. . . . . 129 D3
Long Crendon OX9 . . . . 129 D3
Piddington OX25, HP18. . 97 D6
Stadhampton OX44. . . . 163 C1
Sydenham OX39 . . . . . . 148 F1
Tetsworth OX9. . . . . . . 166 E6
Thame OX9 . . . . 147 E2
Tiddington OX33. . . . . . 145 A6
Tiddington OX9. . . . . . . 146 A2
Towersey OX9. . . . . 148 E7

Thame Rd continued
Warborough OX10. . . . . 183 D1
Warborough OX10. . . . . 203 B8
Thames Ave
Bicester OX26. . . . . 65 B3
Pangbourne RG8 . . . . . 256 D6
Reading RG1 . . . . 259 A1
Thames Bank RG8 . . . . 249 B7
Thames Ct
Abingdon-on-Thames
OX14. . . . . 180 A7
4 Didcot OX11. . . . . . 219 A8
Eynsham OX29 . . . . 120 E7
Goring RG8 . . . . 249 B6
Oxford OX1 . . . . 261 B1
Thames Dr RG10. . . . . . 260 F7
Thames Gdns OX7. . . . . .73 B4
Thames Ho RG9 . . . . . . 244 E3
Thameside RG9 . . . . . . 244 E2
Thameside Court
Residential Pk OX29 138 E3
Thameside OX29. . . . . . 138 E5
Thameside Prim Sch
Abingdon-on-Thames
OX14. . . . . 179 D5
Reading RG4 . . . . 259 B2
Thameside Reach
OX10. . . . . 239 A4
Thames International 8
OX28 . . . . 118 A8
Thames Mead OX10 . . . 221 E7
Thames Pk OX10 . . . . . . 221 E7
Thames Rd Goring RG8 . 249 B6
Harwell OX11. . . . . 217 A3
Thames Reach RG8. . . . 257 D5
Thames Side
6 Reading RG1 . . . . . 259 A1
12 Reading RG1 . . . . . 259 A1
Thames Side Prom
RG4. . . . . 259 A2
Thames St
Abingdon-on-Thames
OX14. . . . . 179 F6
Charlbury OX7. . . . . 73 B4
Eynsham OX29 . . . . 120 E7
Lechlade-on-Thames
GL7. . . . . 150 C3
Oxford OX1 . . . . 261 B1
Sonning RG4. . . . . 260 D4
Wallingford OX10 . . . . . 221 D7
Thames Valley Bsns Pk
RG6. . . . . 260 C4
Thames Valley Park Dr
RG6. . . . . 260 B3
Thames Valley Pk Dr
Reading RG4 . . . . 260 A1
Reading RG6 . . . . 259 F1
Thames View
Abingdon-on-Thames
OX14. . . . . 180 A7
Cholsey OX10 . . . . 221 C1
Cholsey OX10 . . . . 239 C8
Thames View Bsns Ctr
OX14. . . . . 180 A7
Thames View Ind Pk
OX14. . . . . 180 A7
Thames View Rd OX4. . . 141 F3
Thatchers Cl OX15. . . . . .13 A5
The Acorns OX18 . . . . . 115 D1
The Bicester Sch
OX26. . . . . .65 D2
The Boundary Bsns Pk
OX44. . . . . 143 F3
The Cherwell Sch South
Site OX2. . . . . 123 C6
The Croft OX13 . . . . 178 D6
The Fairway OX16 . . . . . .16 A4
The Heights Prim Sch
RG4. . . . . 259 B2
The La OX26. . . . . .80 A7
The Limes OX16 . . . . . . .16 C4
Thelwell Ho OX4. . . . . . 142 B7
The Marlborough CE Sch
OX20. . . . . .91 B6
The Mulberry Bush Sch
OX29. . . . . 137 C2
Thenford Rd
Middleton Cheney
OX17. . . . . .11 D1
Thorpe Mandeville OX17 .11 F5
Thenfordway OX16 . . . . .9 D3
Theobald Dr RG31. . . . . 257 D4
The Orch OX16 . . . . .16 C6
The Oxford Acad OX4 . . 142 C2
The Paddocks OX13 . . . 178 D6
The Ridgeway OX1 . . . . 140 D1
The Rissington Sch
(Great Rissington Site)
GL54. . . . . .83 A7
The Ruskin Sch of Art
Oxford OX1 . . . . 261 C2
Oxford OX1 . . . . 141 F8
The Shades OX16. . . . . . .16 C5
Thesiger Rd OX14 . . . . . 179 F8
Thetford Mews RG4 . . . 259 D6
The Village Cl OX25. . . . .96 D6
Third Acre Rise OX2. . . . 140 B8
Third St NN13 . . . . .36 E6
Thirlmere Ave RG30 . . . 257 F1
Thirsk Rd
7 Bicester OX26 . . . . . 65 C1
Bicester OX26. . . . . 80 C8
Thirteenth St OX11. . . . 217 A2
Thistlecroft Cl OX14. . . 160 B2
Thistledown RG31. . . . . 257 C1
Thistle Down Cl OX4. . . 161 E8
Thistle Dr OX4. . . . . 143 A2
Thomas Higgs La 1
SN7. . . . . 172 D1
Thomas Mews OX4 . . . . 123 F1
Thomas Pl OX18. . . . . . 116 A4

Sto-Tit 285

Thomas Reade Prim Sch
OX14 . . . . 180 B8
Thompson Dr OX27. . . . .65 F7
Thomson Ave OX11. . . . 217 B3
Thomson Terr OX4 . . . . 142 A2
Thornbury Rd OX29. . . . 120 D7
Thornbury Rise OX16 . . .15 F5
Thorncliffe Rd OX2 . . . . 123 B6
Thorne Cl
Henley-on-Thames
RG9. . . . . 254 B7
Kidlington OX5. . . . . 92 C1
Thorney Leys OX28 . . . . 117 E6
Thorney Leys Bsns Pk
OX28. . . . . 117 F6
Thornfield RG9 . . . . 242 A4
Thornhill OX17 . . . . .10 F1
Thornhill Cl
7 Carterton OX18. . . . 115 F5
Wantage OX12. . . . . . . 214 D5
Thornhill Wlk OX14. . . . 159 E1
Thorningdown OX11. . . 235 D8
Thorpe OX16. . . . . .16 F6
Thorpe Dr OX16. . . . . . . .16 F6
Thorpe La OX16. . . . . . . .16 F6
Thorpe Mead OX16 . . . . .16 F6
Thorpe Rd
Chacombe OX17 . . . . . . 11 B4
Middleton Cheney OX17. . 17 D8
Overthorpe OX17 . . . . . .17 D8
Upper Wardington OX17. . 11 B7
Williamscot OX17. . . . . .10 D8
Thorpes Field OX18. . . . 133 C5
Thorpe St OX11. . . . . . . 219 E1
Thorpe Way OX16. . . . . . .16 F5
Thorpe Way Ind Est
OX16. . . . . .16 F5
Three Corners Rd
OX4. . . . . 143 A2
Three Fields Rd OX3 . . . 142 E8
Three Gables La RG8 . . 249 A7
Three Michaels Yd
OX18. . . . . 115 D1
Three Pigeons Cl 3
OX12. . . . . 214 E4
Three Poplar Mobile Home
Pk OX14. . . . . 201 C7
Threshers Ct 3 OX18. . 115 F5
Thrift Pl OX4 . . . . 142 F2
THRUPP Faringdon 153 A2
Thrupp La OX14 . . . . . . 160 D1
Thrupp Turn
Faringdon OX18 . . . . . . 153 B2
Faringdon SN7. . . . . . . 172 F8
Faringdon SN7. . . . . . . 172 F8
Radcot SN7 . . . . 152 F1
Thurne View OX11. . . . . 201 A1
Thurston Cl 4 OX14 . . . 179 E6
Thyme Cl
11 Hardwick OX16 . . . . .9 A1
3 Sonning Common
RG4. . . . . 253 A4
Thyme Gdns OX11 . . . . 218 B8
Tibbs Rd HP17. . . . . 130 E6
Tichborne OX9 . . . . 148 A8
Ticknell La 3 OX7. . . . . 73 C4
Ticknell Piece Rd OX7 . . 73 C4
TIDDINGTON 145 F7
Tidford Cotts GL7. . . . . 150 C3
TIDMARSH 256 C2
Tidmarsh Ct RG9 . . . . . 256 C2
Tidmarsh La
Oxford OX2 . . . . 123 C1
Oxford OX1 . . . . 261 A2
Tidmarsh RG8 . . . . 256 B2
Tidmarsh Rd RG8. . . . . 256 C4
Tidmarsh St RG30 . . . . 258 B1
Tidmore La RG8 . . . . . . 240 F1
Tidworth Row OX18 . . . 152 E8
Tigel Mews RG30 . . . . . 257 E1
Tiger Moth Pl OX29. . . . 117 B7
Tighe Cl OX12. . . . . 214 C6
Tilbury Cl RG4. . . . . 259 C3
Tilbury La OX2 . . . . 122 C1
Tilebarn Cl RG9 . . . . . . 244 C1
Tilebarn La
Henley-on-Thames
RG9. . . . . 244 B1
Henley-on-Thames RG9. 254 B8
Tilehouse Cl OX3 . . . . . 124 C3
TILEHURST 257 E1
Tilehurst Sta RG31 . . . . 257 E3
Tilgarsley Rd OX29 . . . . 120 D8
Tilling Cl RG31 . . . . 257 B2
Tilsley Pk OX14. . . . . . . 159 E3
Tilsley Rd OX7. . . . . .42 D1
Timbers La RG9 . . . . . . 223 D2
Timbers The OX26. . . . . .66 E1
Timber Way OX39 . . . . . 168 C6
Timber Yard Cotts OX7 . 74 C8
Timms Rd OX16. . . . . . . .16 D2
Timms The SN7. . . . . . . 194 D3
Timothy Way 5 OX4. . . 142 F2
Timsbury Ct OX13 . . . . 199 A4
Timsbury Ct OX13. . . . . 199 A4
Tingewick Bypass
MK18. . . . . .39 B5
Tinkerbush La OX12 . . . 214 D6
Tinkers La Bicester OX26 65 E2
Mollington OX17. . . . . . . 3 F3
Tirrold Way OX12. . . . . . 214 F5
Titchener Cl OX26 . . . . . .65 D4
Tite La OX15. . . . . 30 B7
Tithe Ct OX16. . . . . 16 A5
Tithe La OX15 . . . . 34 D5
Tithings The OX15. . . . . . .19 F8
Titup Hall Dr OX3. . . . . 124 E1

Tiverton Cl RG5 . . . . . . 260 E1
Toast La RG9 . . . . 255 B4
TOKERS GREEN 258 D8
Tokers Green La
  Tokers Green RG4. . . . 252 D1
  Tokers Green RG4. . . . 258 D7
Tolgate Seat 11 OX26 . . . 65 E2
Tollbrook Cnr OX5. . . . . . 78 D1
Tollbrook Corner OX5 . . 93 C8
Tollgate Ho 4 OX26 . . . . 65 E2
Tollgate Rd OX14 . . . . . 180 B3
Tollington Ct SN7 . . . . . 172 E1
Tolsey Mus★ OX18 . . . . 100 E5
Tom Brown's School Mus★
  SN7. . . . . 211 C7
Tomgaughan Way
  OX11. . . . . 218 B6
Tomkin's Almshouses 4
  OX14. . . . . 179 E7
Tompkins La OX27 . . . . . 67 E2
Tony Humphries Rd
  OX16. . . . . 15 E7
Tooleys Boatyard★
  OX16. . . . . 16 D6
TOOT BALDON 162 B6
Toot Hill Butts OX3 . . . 124 F3
Top La OX20 . . . . 75 F3
Toppless La OX29 . . . . . . 88 E5
Top Station Rd NN13. . . 24 A8
Top Station Road Ind Est
  NN13 . . . . 24 A8
Torpy Cl OX13 . . . . 199 C2
Torridge Dr OX11. . . . . . 201 A2
Tothill OX7 . . . . 70 D1
TOUCHBRIDGE 97 E1
Tower Cl
  Abingdon-on-Thames
  OX14. . . . . 179 D6
  Marcham OX13 . . . . . 178 D6
  Reading RG4 . . . . 259 C8
Tower Cres OX1 . . . . . . 261 B2
Tower Ct
  Carterton OX18. . . . . 115 E2
  Witney OX28 . . . . 103 F1
Tower Est OX44 . . . . . . 185 E2
Tower Gdns 4 OX11. . . 200 C2
Tower Hill OX18 . . . . . . 117 F8
Tower Hill Bsns Pk
  OX27 . . . . 67 D7
Tower Hill Com Prim Sch
  OX28 . . . . 104 A1
Tower Pk OX10 . . . . 182 D6
Tower Rd OX10 . . . . 182 D6
TOWERSEY 148 E7
Towersey Dr OX9. . . . . . 148 B7
Towersey Rd OX9. . . . . . 148 B8
Tower View SN7. . . . . . . 172 F2
Towing Path The OX2. 122 E4
Town Cl Finmere MK18. . 39 D6
  Sutton Courtenay OX14 200 A7
TOWNEND 215 F5
TOWN END 189 C8
Townend Cl NN13 . . . . . . 36 D8
Town End Rd
  Bledlow Ridge HP14 . . 189 C8
  Faringdon SN7. . . . . . 172 F2
Town Farm Cl
  Lewknor OX49. . . . . . 187 B8
  Thame OX9 . . . . 147 D8
Town Furlong
  Appleton OX13 . . . . . 158 A8
  Bodicote OX15. . . . . . . 22 D8
Town Furze OX3 . . . . . . 142 D7
Town Gn The OX5 . . . . . 92 F1
Town Hill OX15 . . . . 2 A3
Townlands Memorial
  Hospl RG9 . . . . 244 D2
Town Pond La OX13 . . . 176 D8
TOWNSEND Grove . . . 196 D2
  Wantage 214 A4
  Wheatley. 127 D2
Townsend
  Abingdon-on-Thames
  OX14. . . . . 179 F5
  Banbury OX16. . . . . . . 16 B6
  Barford St Michael OX15 .32 F5
  Harwell OX11 . . . . . . 217 E8
  Harwell, Chilton OX11.. 217 D1
  Marsh Gibbon OX27 . . . 67 E2
  Townsend OX12 . . . . . 194 D2
Towns End OX29 . . . . . 104 A6
TOWN'S END 67 D2
Townsend Cottages
  OX10 . . . . 239 C3
Townsend La
  Marsh Gibbon OX27 . . . 67 E2
  Middleton Cheney OX17 . .11 F6
Townsend Rd
  Aldworth RG8 . . . . . . 247 E3
  Shrivenham SN6 . . . . 209 A6
  Streatley RG8 . . . . . . 249 A7
  Witney OX29 . . . . 117 C7
Townsend Sq OX4 . . . . 141 F6
Towns Field
  Banbury OX16. . . . . 8 E1
  Banbury OX16. . . . . . . 15 E8
Townside HP17 . . . . . . 130 F5
Town The OX15. . . . . 31 F7
Town Well End OX27. . . 49 E7
Toy La OX7 . . . . 42 C2
Toynbee Cl OX2 . . . . . . 140 D8
Trafford Rd
  Oxford OX3 . . . . 124 E3
  Reading RG1 . . . . 258 E1
Traitors Ford La
  Ascott OX15. . . . . 18 D4
  Sibford Ferris CV36. . . 18 C6
Trajan Rd SN6. . . . . 209 A6

Tram Hill HP18 . . . . 98 B2
Tramway Ind Est The
  OX16. . . . . 16 E5
Tramway Rd OX16 . . . . . 16 E5
Transport Way
  Oxford OX4 . . . . 142 F4
  Oxford OX4 . . . . 143 A4
Treadwells SN7 . . . . . . 194 E7
Treble House Terr
  OX11. . . . . 237 A8
Tredegar Rd RG4 . . . . . 259 A6
Tree Close Bay OX4. . . 142 A4
Treeground Pl OX5. . . . 108 E8
Tree La OX4. . . . . 142 A4
Trefoil Dr OX26. . . . . 65 C4
Trefoil Pl OX4 . . . . 143 A2
Trefoil Way OX4 . . . . . . 115 F5
Treforgan RG4 . . . . 258 F5
Trelawney Dr RG31 . . . 257 B1
Trenchard Ave OX14. . . 199 C3
Trenchard Circ OX25 . . 49 D1
Trenchard Cl
  12 Upper Rissington
  OX7 . . . . 68 B3
  Wallingford OX10 . . . . 221 C7
Trenchard La OX27 . . . . 65 F6
TRENCH GREEN 258 A8
  Trench Green RG4. . . . 258 A8
Trendell Pl OX14 . . . . . 159 E1
Trent Cres OX26. . . . . . . 65 B3
Trenthams Cl RG8 . . . . 257 B5
Trent Rd OX11. . . . . 201 A2
Treverne Ctyd OX39 . . 168 D6
Trevor Pl OX4 . . . . 142 B5
Trident Bsns Pk OX11. 200 C4
Triggs Mead OX10 . . . . 203 E5
Trill Mill Ct OX1 . . . . . . 261 B1
Trinder Rd OX12. . . . . . 214 E4
Trinder Way OX18 . . . . 115 D4
Tring Rd RG31. . . . . 257 C2
Trinity Cl
  Abingdon-on-Thames
  OX14. . . . . 160 B2
  Banbury OX16. . . . . . . 15 E7
  Bicester OX26. . . . . . . 65 F3
Trinity Coll OX1 . . . . . . 261 B3
Trinity Ct 7 OX7 . . . . . . 43 A3
Trinity Rd
  9 Chipping Norton
  OX7 . . . . 43 A3
  Oxford OX3 . . . . 124 F2
Trinity Sq 10 OX7 . . . . . 43 A3
Trinity St OX1 . . . . 261 B1
Trinity Way OX17 . . . . . 23 D3
Tristram Rd OX29. . . . . 118 B4
Troika Cl 4 OX16. . . . . . . 9 A1
Trots La OX7 . . . . 85 D7
Trout Hollow HP27 . . . 169 E8
Troy Cl OX3 . . . . 142 E7
Troy La OX5 . . . . 77 F3
Truelocks Way OX12. . 214 F6
Truemper Gr OX27. . . . . 65 F7
Trust Cnr RG9. . . . . 254 E8
Tubb Cl OX26. . . . . 65 C2
Tubbs Cl OX12. . . . . 214 D8
Tubbs Yd OX26. . . . . 80 A7
TUBNEY 157 F2
Tucker Rd OX4 . . . . 142 E3
Tuckers La SN4. . . . . . . 227 A3
Tuckers Rd SN7 . . . . . . 173 A3
Tuckmill Mdws Nature
  Reserve★ SN6 . . . . . 209 B8
Tucks La OX13. . . . . 156 B4
Tudor Cl Banbury OX16 . 16 D2
  Oxford OX4. . . . . 141 F4
  8 Wallingford OX10. . 221 C7
  19 Wallingford OX10.. 221 C7
Tudor Ct OX2 . . . . 140 A8
Tudor Hall Sch OX16. . . 22 A8
Tudor Wlk OX11. . . . . . . 217 D7
Tuer The OX7 . . . . 57 A2
Tullis Cl OX14 . . . . 199 F7
Tulwick Cl OX12. . . . . . 214 D7
Tulwick La OX12. . . . . . 197 A2
Tumbledown OX2 . . . . 139 D6
Tumbler Way OX18 . . . 115 D5
Tumbling Bay Ct OX2. 123 A1
Tumim Ct OX10. . . . . . . 221 B7
Tuns La RG9. . . . . 244 E2
Turberville Cl OX14 . . . 179 E6
Turley La OX29 . . . . 104 A8
Turl St OX1. . . . . 261 B2
Turnagain La OX14 . . . 179 F6
Turn Again La OX1. . . . 261 B1
Turnberry Cl OX26. . . . . 66 B4
Turner Cl OX4 . . . . 142 D6
Turner Ct OX5. . . . . 108 F7
Turner Dr OX2. . . . . 140 D7
Turner Rd OX14 . . . . . . 179 D5
Turners Cl OX14 . . . . . . 160 F2
Turners Gn OX49 . . . . . 205 D7
Turner's Green La
  Britwell Salome OX49. . 205 D8
  Cuxham OX49 . . . . . . 185 C2
Turnfields HP18 . . . . . . 128 A3
Turnpike Rd
  Bicester OX27. . . . . . . 66 A6
  Highworth SN6 . . . . . 190 A6
  Oxford OX2 . . . . 140 B6
Turnstone Gn OX26. . . . 81 A8
Turret Ho OX3 . . . . 124 C3
Turrills Row OX20 . . . . . 91 C5
TURVILLE PARK 207 F3
TURWESTON 24 C8
Turweston Manor
  NN13. . . . . 24 C8
Turweston Rd NN13 . . . . 24 B3
Tuscan Cl RG30. . . . . . . 257 E1
Tweed Cres OX26. . . . . . 65 B3
Tweed Dr OX11. . . . . 200 F4
Twelve Acre Dr OX14 . 160 C3

Twentieth St OX12. . . . 216 F2
Twin Oaks RG4 . . . . . . 259 B6
Two Rivers Ind Est
  OX28 . . . . 118 B6
Two Tree Hill RG9 . . . . 254 B8
TWYFORD 23 B5
Twyford Ave OX17 . . . . 23 A6
Twyford Gdns OX17. . . . 23 A6
Twyford Gr OX17 . . . . . . 23 A6
Twyford Mill Ind Est
  OX17. . . . . .23 A2
Twyford Rd
  Adderbury OX17. . . . . 23 C7
  Poundon OX27. . . . . . . 67 F7
Twynhams Rd OX5. . . . . 77 C6
Tyburn Glen OX11 . . . . 200 F2
Ty-Craig OX26. . . . . 65 F2
Tyler Cl RG4. . . . . 258 E5
Tylorstown RG4 . . . . . . 258 F5
Tymawr
  Caversham RG4. . . . . 258 F5
  Reading RG4. . . . . . . 258 F5
Tyndale Cl OX18 . . . . . . 115 E2
Tyndale Pl OX33. . . . . . 144 C8
Tyndale Rd OX4 . . . . . . 141 E8
Tyne Ave OX11 . . . . 200 F2
Tyne Hill Epwell OX15. . .12 F5
  Sibford Gower OX15. . . 13 B2
  Sibford Gower OX15. . . 19 C8
Tyne Rd OX13 . . . . 159 C2
Tyne Sq 6 OX11. . . . . . 219 A8
Tyrell Cl SN7 . . . . 194 D7
Tyrell Way OX13 . . . . . 156 F1
Tyrrell Rd OX16. . . . . 16 A2
Tyrrells Cl OX11 . . . . . . 217 D6
Tyrrell's Way OX14 . . . 199 E6
Tysoe Rd OX15. . . . . 12 E6
Tyte End OX7. . . . . 29 B3
Tythings The OX17. . . . . 10 F2
Tythrop Way
  Thame OX9 . . . . 129 F2
  Thame OX9 . . . . 130 A1
  Thame OX9 . . . . 148 B8

U

UFFINGTON 211 D7
Uffington Castle★
  SN7. . . . . 211 B1
Uffington CE Prim Sch
  SN7. . . . . 211 C7
Uffington Trad Est
  SN7. . . . . 193 E1
Uffington White Horse★
  SN7. . . . . 211 C2
Ulfgar Rd OX2. . . . . 122 F8
Ullswater Dr RG31. . . . 257 D3
Ulster Cl RG4. . . . . 259 D5
Underhill OX10 . . . . 239 A4
Underhill Cir OX3. . . . . 124 F4
Unicorn Sch The 5
  OX14 . . . . 179 D7
Unicorn St OX15. . . . . . 21 D4
Union Sq OX20 . . . . 75 F4
Union St Banbury OX16 . 16 B6
  Oxford OX4 . . . . 141 F8
  Woodstock OX20. . . . . 91 B6
Union Way OX28. . . . . . 117 F8
Unity Cl RG4. . . . . 259 B6
Unity Ct RG4 . . . . 259 B5
University Coll OX1 . . . 261 C2
Univ of Oxford Department
  of Education OX2 . . . 261 B4
Univ of Oxford Faculty of
  Music OX1 . . . . 261 B1
Univ of Oxford Inst of
  Experimental Psychology
  OX1 . . . . 261 C3
Univ of Oxford (Manor Rd
  Building)** OX1. . . . . 123 E2
Univ of Oxford Science
  Area OX1 . . . . 261 C4
Untons Pl SN7. . . . . 173 A3
Upavon Way OX18 . . . . 115 C3
Upland Park Rd OX2. . . 123 A8
Upland Rise OX17 . . . . . . 9 D5
Uplands Rd RG4. . . . . . 258 E5
UPPER ARNCOTT 96 E7
Upper Barr 3 OX4 . . . . 142 C4
Upper Bolney Rd RG9. 254 D4
Upper Brook Hill OX20 .91 B6
Upper Campsfield Rd
  OX20. . . . . 91 E5
Upper Common SN7 . . . 211 D7
Upper Crale SN7 . . . . . 194 D8
Upper Cres OX29 . . . . . 102 E2
Upper Cross La OX11 . 218 F5
Upper Culham La
  RG10. . . . . 255 E8
Upper End
  Fulbrook OX18. . . . . . 100 F7
  Fulbrook OX18. . . . . . 101 A7
  Salford OX7 . . . . 42 A5
  Shipton-under-Wychwood
  OX7. . . . . 85 D6
Upper Farm Rd OX11. . 235 C8
Upper Field OX39 . . . . 168 C5
Upper Fisher Row
  Oxford OX1 . . . . 123 B1
  Oxford OX1 . . . . 261 A2
Upper Gn SN7 . . . . 194 E8
UPPER HEYFORD 62 E8
Upper Heyford Rd
  Middleton Stoney OX25. .63 F8
  Middleton Stoney OX27. 64 A8
Upper High St OX9 . . . 147 F8
Upper Icknield Way
  Bledlow HP27 . . . . . . 169 E7
  Chinnor HP14 . . . . . . 169 B7
  Chinnor OX39 . . . . . . 168 E6

UPPER INGLESHAM . . 170 B6
Upper Lambourn Rd
  RG17 . . . . 245 F6
UPPER
  MAIDENSGROVE . . 225 A7
Upper Mdw OX4 . . . . . . 124 E1
UPPER MILTON 84 F7
Upper Rd
  Kennington OX1 . . . . 141 D3
  Kennington OX1 . . . . 141 E2
Upper Red Cross Rd
  RG8. . . . . 249 C6
UPPER RISSINGTON . . .68 B4
UPPERTON 185 A1
  Britwell Salome OX49. . 205 C7
UPPER WARDINGTON . .10 F8
UPPER WARGRAVE . . . 255 F7
Upper Warren Ave
  RG4. . . . . 258 D3
Upperway Furlong
  OX11. . . . . 201 B2
Upper Windsor St
  OX16. . . . . 16 D4
Upper Wlk OX44. . . . . . 161 E1
UPPER
  WOLVERCOTE 122 F8
Upper Woodcote Rd
  RG4. . . . . 258 D5
Uppingham Dr RG5. . . 260 F1
Uppingham Gdns RG4 . 259 D6
Upstone Way OX18 . . . 116 A4
Upthorpe Dr OX12 . . . . 214 E6
UPTON Burford 100 C5
  Didcot 218 C2
Upton Cl
  Abingdon-on-Thames
  OX14. . . . . 160 A1
  Banbury OX16. . . . . . . 15 E6
  Henley-on-Thames RG9 . 244 E1
  Oxford OX4 . . . . 142 C2
Upton Ct OX16. . . . . 16 C5
Upton House★ OX15 . . . .6 D8
Upway Rd OX3 . . . . 124 B5
Upwood Dr OX18 . . . . . 115 E4
Urquhart La OX10. . . . . 241 A7
Ushercombe View
  OX15. . . . . 20 B8
Usher Dr OX16. . . . . 8 F1
Usk Way OX11. . . . . 201 B3
UTC Oxfordshire OX11 218 B8
Uxmore Rd RG8 . . . . . . 241 E4

V

Vale Ave OX12. . . . . 196 E1
Vale Cres RG30 . . . . . . 257 E1
Vale & Downland Mus★
  OX12. . . . . 214 D4
Valence Cres OX28 . . . 103 E1
Valentia Cl
  Bletchingdon OX5. . . . 92 F8
  Bletchingdon OX5. . . . 93 A8
Valentia Rd OX3. . . . . . 124 C2
Valentine Cres RG4. . . 259 C4
Vale Rd Harwell OX11. . 217 B3
  Witney OX28 . . . . 117 E8
Valery Rd OX26. . . . . 81 C6
Valetta Way OX10. . . . . 204 D3
Vale View OX12. . . . . . . 214 A5
Valley Cl Brackley NN13. .24 A8
  Goring RG8 . . . . 249 C6
  Reading RG4 . . . . 259 A4
Valley Cotts RG9. . . . . . 243 F8
Valley Cres NN13. . . . . . 24 A8
Valley Rd Banbury OX16. 16 D4
  Brackley NN13. . . . . . . 24 A8
  Finmere MK18. . . . . . . 39 D6
  Henley-on-Thames RG9 . 254 B8
  Horspath OX33 . . . . . . 143 F4
Valley Rise NN13 . . . . . . 24 A8
Valley Road Sch RG9 . 254 C8
Valley View
  Great Bourton OX17 . . . .9 D8
  Lower Heyford OX25. . . 62 E6
Van Alloys Bsns Pk
  RG9 . . . . 242 A4
Vanbrugh Cl OX20 . . . . 91 A7
Van Diemans SN7 . . . . 194 D8
Van-Dieman's La OX4 . 142 C3
Van Dieman's Rd OX9 . 147 F7
Van Diemens Cl OX39. 168 C7
Vane Rd OX9 . . . . 148 B8
Vanner Rd OX28 . . . . . 104 C2
Vantage Bsns Pk OX16 . .21 F8
Varsity Cl GL54 . . . . .68 B3
Vastern Rd RG1 . . . . . . 259 A1
Vauxhall Way OX11 . . . 200 D2
Venables Cl OX2. . . . . . 261 A4
Vendee Drive OX26. . . . 80 B8
Venetia Cl RG4 . . . . . . 259 C7
Venneit Cl OX1 . . . . . . 123 A2
Venners Water OX11. . . 201 A3
Ventfield Cl OX33. . . . . 112 A5
Ventnor Rd RG31 . . . . . 257 D1
Ventura Bsns Pk OX18 .115 F4
Venvell Cl OX7 . . . . 58 F5
Vera Wood Cl OX16. . . . 23 A4
Verbena Way 2 OX4 . . 142 E1
Verinia Cl OX20 . . . . 91 C6
Verlam Gr OX11 . . . . . . 201 B2
Vermont Dr OX20. . . . . . 91 A7
Vernon Ave OX2 . . . . . . 140 E6
Vernon Ho OX7. . . . . 42 E2
Vervain Cl 4 OX26. . . . . 65 C5
Vesey Ct 3 OX18. . . . . 134 F4
Vespasian Wy OX26. . . .79 F7
Vestry Cl OX12 . . . . 196 D2
Vetch Pl OX4 . . . . 142 F2
Vicarage Cl
  Aston OX18 . . . . 135 D2

Vicarage Cl continued
  Chalgrove OX44. . . . . 184 D7
  Grove OX12. . . . . 196 E1
  Oxford OX4 . . . . 142 B2
Vicarage Ct
  5 Banbury OX16 . . . . 16 D5
  Oxford OX1 . . . . 141 D6
Vicarage Flats OX17 . . . . 4 F2
Vicarage Gdns OX17. . . . 4 F2
Vicarage Hill OX12. . . . 214 A4
Vicarage La
  Long Compton CV36 . . .27 F6
  Oxford OX1 . . . . 141 C6
  Piddington OX25 . . . . . 97 E6
  Shrivenham SN6 . . . . 209 C6
  Streatley RG8 . . . . . . 249 A6
Vicarage Rd
  Didcot OX11 . . . . 218 F8
  Henley-on-Thames RG9. 254 E8
  Kidlington OX5. . . . . . 92 F1
  Oxford OX1 . . . . 141 D6
  Steventon OX13. . . . . 198 E4
Vicarage Wood Way
  RG31. . . . . 257 B1
Vicars Row 2 OX12. . . 214 D4
Vickers Rd GL54 . . . . . . .68 B5
Vickers Way OX12 . . . . 214 C8
Vicks Cl OX18 . . . . 100 E5
Victoria Cotts OX18. . . 134 E3
Victoria Ct
  Bicester OX26. . . . . . . 65 F1
  Henley-on-Thames RG9. 244 E1
  Oxford OX1 . . . . 261 B2
  Oxford OX3 . . . . 124 B2
Victoria Gate OX2 . . . . 123 B8
Victoria Gdns OX9. . . . 166 B8
Victoria Mead OX9 . . . 148 A7
Victoria Pl
  12 Banbury OX16 . . . . 16 E6
  Banbury OX16. . . . . . . 16 E6
  Chipping Norton OX7 . . 42 E3
Victoria Rd
  Abingdon-on-Thames
  OX14. . . . . 179 D7
  Bicester OX26. . . . . . . 65 F2
  Oxford OX2 . . . . 123 B8
  Reading RG31 . . . . . . 257 D1
  Reading RG4 . . . . 259 A3
  Wargrave RG10. . . . . 255 E2
Victoria Terr OX15. . . . . 33 F4
Victor St OX1 . . . . 261 A3
Viking Dr OX11 . . . . 219 A7
Viking Terr OX10 . . . . . 204 D3
Villa Cl OX10 . . . . 239 B8
Village Farm Ct OX25 . . 79 A2
Village Rd OX17 . . . . .3 A4
Village St OX10 . . . . . . 239 A4
Villa Rd Chilton OX11 . . 217 C1
  Chilton OX11. . . . . . . 235 C8
Villeboys Cl OX14. . . . . 180 C8
Villiers Ct OX4. . . . . 142 B4
Villiers La OX4 . . . . 142 B4
Villiers Rd OX26. . . . . . . 65 D2
Vine Cotts
  5 Bicester OX26 . . . . 65 E1
  Cuddesdon OX44. . . . 144 B2
Viner Cl OX28 . . . . 104 C2
Vinery The RG10. . . . . . 255 D2
Vines The 2 OX14 . . . . 179 F7
Vine The HP18 . . . . 128 D3
Vineyard OX14 . . . . 179 F7
Vineyard Cl OX16 . . . . . 16 C7
Vintage Pair The 21
  OX7 . . . . 68 C3
Vinters Ho RG31 . . . . . . 257 D1
Vintner Rd 9 OX14. . . . 179 F7
Violet Way OX4 . . . . . . 161 E8
Virgate OX13 . . . . 199 B8
Virginia Gdns HP14. . . 189 F8
Virginia Way OX14. . . . 179 D4
Viscount Ind Est
  Bampton OX18 . . . . . 134 D8
  Brize Norton OX18 . . . 116 D1
Vivienne Ct OX3 . . . . . . 124 D1
Vole Bank OX28 . . . . . . 103 F2
Volunteer Way SN7. . . . 173 A2
Vorda Rd SN6 . . . . 190 A7
Vulcan Vw OX26. . . . . . .66 B4

W

Wadards Ct 4 OX28 . . 118 C2
Wadard's Mdw OX28. . 118 D8
Wadham Cl OX26 . . . . . . 65 F3
Wadham Coll OX1 . . . . 261 C3
Waggon Path OX13 . . . 156 C1
Waggon Pl OX13. . . . . . 156 D1
Wagtail Haven 12
  OX11. . . . . 218 B6
Waine Rush View
  OX28. . . . . 118 B8
Wainhill OX39 . . . . 168 E7
Wainwrights HP18. . . . 129 D6
Waites Cl OX18 . . . . . . 135 E2
WALCOT 72 F4
WALES 23 F5
Wales St OX17. . . . . 23 F5
Waleys Pl 3 RG4. . . . . 259 C2
Walford Rd
  Sibford Ferris OX15 . . 19 B7
  Sibford Ferris OX15 . . 19 B7
Walker Cl
  Woodcote RG8. . . . . . 240 E1
  Woodcote RG8. . . . . . 240 E1
Walker Dr SN7 . . . . 173 A3
Walker La OX13 . . . . . . 176 D8
Walker Rd Banbury OX17. .8 E1
  Upper Heyford OX25. . . 63 C8
Walker's Cl OX18. . . . . . 101 F3

Walkers Dr OX9 . . . . . . 148 B7
Walker's Ht OX7. . . . . . . 88 C5
Walk The Islip OX5 . . . . . 93 F1
  Wootton OX20. . . . . . .75 F4
Wallace Cl OX14. . . . . . 179 E5
Wallbrook Ct OX2 . . . . 122 D1
Walled Gdns OX14. . . . 160 E3
Walled Gdns The OX26. 65 E2
Walled Gdn The RG10 . 255 B2
Waller Ct RG4 . . . . 259 B2
Waller Dr OX16. . . . . 16 A3
WALLINGFORD 221 C6
Wallingford Com Hospl
  OX10 . . . . 221 C6
Wallingford Mus★
  OX10 . . . . 221 D8
Wallingford Rd
  Cholsey OX10 . . . . . . 221 B3
  Crowmarsh Gifford
  OX10. . . . . 221 F2
  Didcot OX11 . . . . 201 B1
  Goring RG8 . . . . 249 C8
  North Moreton OX11. . 202 A1
  South Stoke OX10, RG8 239 C5
  Streatley RG8 . . . . . . 249 A7
  Warborough OX10. . . 203 B5
  Wallingford Sch OX10 221 D8
Wallingford St OX12 . . 214 E4
Wallingford Sta★
  OX10 . . . . 221 B7
Wallin Rd OX17. . . . . . . .22 E2
Walls The SN7. . . . . 194 E7
Wally Cnr OX10. . . . . . . 182 E4
Walmer Rd RG5 . . . . . . 260 F1
Walnut Acre OX10 . . . . 204 E4
Walnut Cl
  Bicester OX26. . . . . . . 65 F5
  Deddington OX15 . . . . 34 E4
  Long Crendon HP18 . . 129 C7
  Sonning Common RG4. 252 E5
  Witney OX28 . . . . 117 F8
  Wootton OX20. . . . . . .75 F4
Walnut Ct
  Faringdon SN7. . . . . . 172 F2
  12 Faringdon SN7. . . . 172 F3
  Stanford in the Vale
  OX12. . . . . 194 E6
Walnut Gdns OX17. . . . . .1 D1
Walnut Gr OX11 . . . . . . 203 B4
Walnut La OX11 . . . . . . 200 B2
Walnut Pl OX11. . . . . . . 217 F7
Walnut Rise OX25 . . . . . 48 F6
Walnut Tree Cl OX39. . 168 D8
Walnut Tree Ct RG8 . . 249 C6
Walnut Trees Hill SN6 228 B7
Walnut Way OX14 . . . . 179 B2
Walpole Cl 7 OX26. . . . . 65 C4
Walsingham Cl OX15 . . 21 C4
Walter Bigg Way
  OX10. . . . . 221 C8
Walterbush Rd OX7. . . . .42 E1
Walter Craft Ct OX7 . . 42 D2
Walter Dyer Dr SN7. . . 172 D1
Walter's Row OX4 . . . . 123 F1
Waltham Ct RG8. . . . . . 249 C8
Waltham Gdns OX16. . . . 17 A6
Walton Ave
  Adderbury OX17 . . . . . 23 B5
  Henley-on-Thames RG9. 254 E8
Walton Cl OX15. . . . . . . .22 E1
Walton Cres OX1 . . . . . 261 A3
Walton La OX1 . . . . 261 B3
WALTON MANOR 261 A4
Walton Manor Ct OX2. 261 A4
Walton St
  Oxford OX1, OX2. . . . . 261 A3
  Oxford OX2 . . . . 261 A4
Walton Well Rd OX2 . . 123 A3
Wanbourne La RG9 . . . 224 D2
Wandhope Way RG31 . 257 C2
Wandle Beck OX11 . . . 200 F3
Wansbeck Dr OX26. . . . .65 B3
Wansbeck Wood
  OX11. . . . . 201 A3
WANTAGE 214 E3
Wantage CE Prim Sch
  OX12 . . . . 214 D3
Wantage Com Hospl
  OX12 . . . . 214 E5
Wantage L Ctr OX12 . . 214 D4
Wantage Rd
  Didcot OX11 . . . . 218 C8
  East Hendred OX12. . . 216 F7
  Farnborough OX12 . . . 233 C1
  Frilford OX13. . . . . . . 177 F5
  Harwell OX11 . . . . . . 217 D6
  Moulsford OX10 . . . . 238 B5
  Rowstock OX11. . . . . 217 A7
  Streatley RG8 . . . . . . 248 F8
  Wallingford OX10 . . . . 203 B1
  Winterdown Bottom
  OX12. . . . . 232 E1
Wapping HP18 . . . . 129 D6
Warbler View OX14. . . . 180 C1
Warbler Wlk OX4 . . . . . 142 E1
WARBOROUGH 203 B8
Warborough Rd
  Letcombe Bassett
  OX12. . . . . 232 A7
  Warborough OX10. . . 203 B6
Warbreck Dr RG31. . . . 257 B3
Warburg Cres OX4. . . . 142 F3
Warburg Nature Reserve★
  RG9 . . . . 225 B5
WARDINGTON 5 E3
Wardington Rd
  Banbury OX16. . . . . . . .9 D3
  Chacombe OX17 . . . . . 10 E5
  Thorpe Mandeville OX17. 11 E6
  Wardington OX17 . . . . . 5 F3

Wardle Ave
Reading RG31 . . . . 257 D1
Reading RG31 . . . . 257 D2
Ward Rd NN13 . . . . 24 A5
Wards Cres OX15 . . . . . . 22 E7
Ward's La OX7 . . . . 88 C5
Wards Rd OX7 . . . . 42 F3
Ware Leys Cl OX27 . . . . . 67 E3
Ware Rd SN7 . . . . 194 C7
WARGRAVE 255 D1
Wargrave Hill RG10 . . . 255 D2
Wargrave Rd
Henley-on-Thames
RG9 . . . . 244 F1
Henley-on-Thames RG9 . 255 B8
Wargrave RG10 . . . . . . 255 C1
Wargrave RG10 . . . . . . 255 D3
Wargrave Sta RG10 . . . 255 C1
WARKWORTH 17 D5
Warkworth Cl OX16 . . . . 15 F8
Warkworth Rd
Middleton Cheney OX17 . 17 E7
Warkworth OX17 . . . . . . 17 D5
Warland Gdns OX5 . . . . 92 D2
Warley Rise RG31 . . . . 257 C2
Warmans Cl OX12 . . . . 214 B5
War Memorial Pl
RG9 . . . . 254 E7
WARMINGTON 3 A4
Warnborough Rd OX2 123 B4
Warneford Hospl OX3,
OX4 . . . . 124 B1
Warneford La OX3,
OX4 . . . . 124 B1
Warneford Rd OX4 . . . 142 A8
Warner Cres OX11 . . . . 218 D7
Warping House Cotts
OX7 . . . . 42 C2
Warps Gr OX44 . . . . . . 164 F1
WARPSGROVE 164 F1
Warpsgrove La
Chalgrove OX44 . . . . . 184 F7
Chalgrove OX44 . . . . . 185 A8
Warren Barn Farm
OX44 . . . . 163 F7
Warren Ct RG4 . . . . . . 258 F2
Warren Hill OX44 . . . . 163 C1
Warren Ho RG4 . . . . . . 258 F2
Warren House Ct RG4 258 F2
Warren Mead OX9 . . . . 148 B6
Warren Rd RG5 . . . . . . 260 D1
Warren Row Rd RG10 . 255 F7
Warren The
Abingdon-on-Thames
OX14 . . . . 180 B8
Hinton Waldrist SN7 . . 156 A2
Reading RG4 . . . . 258 D3
Warren View OX44 . . . . 163 F7
Warriner Sch The OX15 .21 F6
Warwick Cl
Abingdon-on-Thames
OX14 . . . . 180 A8
Carterton OX18 . . . . . 115 C3
Stanford in the Vale
SN7 . . . . 194 E7
Warwick Ct [1] OX26 . . . 66 A4
Warwick Pl HP18 . . . . . 129 D7
Warwick Rd
Banbury OX16 . . . . 16 A7
Banbury OX16 . . . . 16 C6
Hanwell OX16 . . . . 8 E3
Upper Boddington NN11 . .1 F7
Warwick St OX4 . . . . . . 141 F7
Wasbrough Ave OX12 . 214 C6
Washford Glen OX11 . . 201 A4
Washington Rd RG4 . . . 259 B2
Washington Terr OX7 . .60 F8
Wastie's Orch OX29 . . . .90 B1
WATCHFIELD 191 F1
Watchfield Prim Sch
SN6 . . . . 191 D1
Watcombe Manor Ind Est
OX49 . . . . 186 B1
Watcombe Rd OX49 . . . 186 B1
Water Brook Vw OX20 . 91 A7
Watercress Cl
Bodicote OX15 . . . . . . 22 E8
Caversham OX27 . . . . . .65 D7
WATER EATON 109 D5
Water Eaton La OX5 . . . 109 F4
Water Eaton Rd OX2 . . 123 C8
WATEREND 189 C5
Water End Rd
Beacon's Bottom
HP14 . . . . 189 D3
Bledlow Ridge HP14 . . 189 C5
Waterford La OX28 . . . 104 D1
Waterford Rd OX28 . . . 104 D1
Waterfowl Sanctuary &
Children's Farm The ★
OX15 . . . . 20 A1
Watergate Farm La
MK18 . . . . .53 B8
Water La
Adderbury OX17 . . . . . .22 F3
Adderbury OX17 . . . . . .23 A3
Ardley OX27 . . . . 50 C4
Bloxham OX15 . . . . 21 E5
Brackley NN13 . . . . 24 A1
Drayton St Leonard
OX10 . . . . 183 B5
Little Tew OX7 . . . . 45 A6
Steeple Aston OX25 . . . . 62 A8
Witney OX28 . . . . 104 E2
Waterloo Cl OX10 . . . . 239 A7
Waterloo Dr OX16 . . . . .16 E6
Waterloo Rd OX28 . . . . 118 B8
Waterman Pl RG1 . . . . 259 A1
Waterman's Rd RG9 . . 254 F8
Waterman's Way [2]
OX1 . . . . 141 C7

Waterman's Way
RG10 . . . . 255 C1
Watermark Way [1]
OX2 . . . . 122 D8
Watermead OX5 . . . . . 109 A8
Watermeadows The
OX25 . . . . 81 D3
Watermill Way OX3. . . 125 A4
WATERPERRY 127 B1
Waterperry OX33 . . . . . 127 B1
Waterperry Common
OX33 . . . . 127 A3
Waterperry Ct [8] OX16. .16 E6
Waterperry Gdns & Mus of
Rural Life ★ OX33 . . 127 B1
Waterperry Rd
Holton OX33 . . . . 126 E1
Wheatley OX33 . . . . . . 144 D8
Worminghall HP18 . . . . 127 D5
Waterside Cotts RG4. . 260 B4
Waterside Dr RG8 . . . . 257 D5
Waterside Villas OX14 181 F4
Waters La OX17 . . . . . . .11 B1
Waterslade Pens
HP17 . . . . 130 E6
Water St OX25. . . . . . . .48 F6
WATERSTOCK 145 D8
Water Stratford Rd
Finmere MK18 . . . . 25 E1
Finmere MK18 . . . . 39 E8
Watery La
Brackley NN13 . . . . 24 A7
Clifton Hampden OX14 . 181 D4
Hook Norton OX15 . . . . . 30 A7
Sparsholt OX12 . . . . . . 212 F4
Watling La OX10 . . . . . 182 D1
WATLINGTON 186 C2
Watlington Chalk Pit
Nature Reserve ★
OX49 . . . . 186 D1
Watlington Hill ★ OX49 . 207 A8
Watlington Hill ★
OX49 . . . . 206 E8
Watlington Ind Est
OX49 . . . . 186 A2
Watlington Pk
Christmas Common
OX49 . . . . 207 A5
Cookley Green OX49 . . 206 F5
Watlington Prim Sch
OX49 . . . . 186 B2
Watlington Rd
Benson OX10 . . . . 203 F4
Garsington OX44 . . . . . 162 D7
Lewknor OX49 . . . . . . 187 A7
Oxford OX4, OX44 . . . . 143 B2
Shirburn OX49 . . . . . . 186 E6
Watlington St RG9. . . . 224 E2
Watson Cres OX13 . . . . 159 A7
Watts La OX11 . . . . 237 A8
Watts Rd OX16 . . . . .8 F2
Watts Way [1] OX5 . . . . .92 E1
Waveney Cl
Bicester OX26 . . . . 65 B2
Didcot OX11 . . . . 201 A1
Waverley Ave OX5 . . . . 109 A8
Waverley Cl OX17 . . . . . .23 F5
Wavers Ground OX18 . 115 F3
Waxes Cl OX14 . . . . . . 160 C2
Wayfaring Cl OX4. . . . . 161 E8
Wayfarings
Bicester OX26 . . . . 65 E5
Bodicote OX16 . . . . . . .16 F1
Wayland Ave OX12 . . . . 214 A8
Wayland Cres OX11. . . . 217 C1
Wayland Rd OX12 . . . . 196 D1
Waylands SN7 . . . . 211 C7
Wayland's Smithy (Long
Barrow) ★ SN6 . . . . . 228 E7
Waynflete Rd OX3 . . . . 125 A4
Wayside Gdns RG8 . . . . 240 E1
Wayside Ho [4] OX26. . . .65 E3
WEALD 134 D1
Wealden Way RG30. . . 257 E1
Weald Rise RG30 . . . . . 257 F2
Weald St OX18 . . . . 134 E2
Wearn Rd SN7 . . . . 172 E1
Wear Rd OX26 . . . . .65 B2
Weaver Cl HP18 . . . . . . 129 D7
Weaver Croft OX11 . . . . 201 A3
Weavers Branch OX9 . . 129 D1
Weavers Cl OX28 . . . . . 118 A7
Weavers Cotts CV36. . . . .27 F5
Weavers Ct [4] OX18 . . 115 F5
Webb Cl OX16 . . . . .16 E7
Webb Cres OX7. . . . . 42 D2
Webb Dr SN7 . . . . 172 D1
Webbs Cl OX7 . . . . .57 B1
Webb's Cl OX12 . . . . . . 122 D8
Webb's Way OX5 . . . . . .92 F1
Webster Cl OX9 . . . . . . 129 F1
Websters Cl OX29 . . . . 106 A6
Wedgewood Way
RG30 . . . . 257 F1
Wedgwood Rd OX26. . . 66 A3
Weedon Cl OX10 . . . . . 239 A8
Weedon Ct OX10 . . . . . 221 C8
Weeping Cross OX15 . . .22 E8
Weighbridge Row
RG1 . . . . 259 B3
Weir Farm Cl OX25 . . . . 82 A5
Weir La OX25 . . . . 82 A5
Weirs La OX1 . . . . 141 D5
Welch Way [2] OX28 . . 118 A8
Weldon Rd OX3 . . . . . . 123 F3
Weldon Way OX9 . . . . . 148 A8
Welford Gdns OX14. . . 160 E2
Welland Ave OX11 . . . . 201 B2
Welland Cl
Abingdon-on-Thames
OX13 . . . . 159 C2

Welland Cl *continued*
Reading RG31 . . . . 257 C1
Welland Croft OX26. . . .65 B3
Well Bank OX10 . . . . . . .30 B7
Wellborne Rd [5] OX4 . 124 C5
Weller Cl OX10 . . . . . . 204 A8
Wellesbourne Cl OX14 180 B8
Wellesley Cl
Banbury OX16 . . . . 16 E6
Upper Heyford OX25 . . . 63 C8
Wellground
Stokenchurch HP14. . . 187 F1
Stokenchurch HP14. . . 188 B3
Well Hill OX7 . . . . 88 C5
Wellington Ave OX16 . . .16 E6
Wellington Cl OX26 . . . . 66 A3
Wellington Cotts OX7. . .73 B2
Wellington Cres OX29 138 A7
Wellington Pl OX1 . . . . 261 B3
Wellington Rd
Heyford OX25 . . . . 63 C8
Upper Rissington GL54 . . 68 B4
Wellington Sq
Oxford OX1 . . . . 261 B3
Watchfield SN6 . . . . . . 191 D1
Wellington St
Grove OX12 . . . . 214 C8
Oxford OX2 . . . . 261 A3
Thame OX9 . . . . 148 A8
Wellington Way OX7. . . 85 A8
Wellington Wy OX13. . . 176 C8
Well La Curbridge OX29 117 C6
Shenington OX15. . . . . . .6 F2
Stonesfield OX29. . . . . . 89 C7
WELL PLACE 240 F7
Well Place Rd OX10 . . . 240 E7
Wellshead La OX11 . . . 217 E6
Wellsprings OX10. . . . . 202 E2
Well St OX12 . . . . 215 E5
Well View RG9 . . . . 241 F5
Welsh La OX17 . . . . .11 E4
WENDLEBURY 80 A4
Wendlebury Rd
Bicester OX25. . . . . 80 C7
Wendlebury OX25, OX26. 80 B5
Wenlock Cl [5] OX11 . . 200 C2
Wenlock Dr OX26 . . . . . 65 A2
Wenman Cl [10] OX28 . . 104 A1
Wenman Rd
Thame OX9 . . . . 148 A6
Witney OX28 . . . . 117 E8
Wenrisc Dr OX29 . . . . . 102 E2
Wensum Cres OX26. . . . .65 B3
Wensum Dr OX11. . . . . 201 A2
Wentworth Rd
Oxford OX2 . . . . 123 B8
Thame OX9 . . . . 148 A8
Wern The GL7 . . . . 150 B4
Werrell Dr OX1 . . . . . . 159 A7
Wesley Cl
Bicester OX26. . . . . 65 C4
Oxford OX4 . . . . 142 E3
Wesley Dr OX16 . . . . . . .16 B4
Wesley La [6] OX26. . . . .65 C2
Wesley Pl OX17. . . . . . . .10 E4
Wesley Wlk OX28 . . . . . 118 B8
Wessex Cl SN7 . . . . . . 173 A3
Wessex Ind Est OX28. . 118 B6
Wessex Rd
Benson OX10. . . . . . . 204 D2
Didcot OX11 . . . . 218 F8
Wessex Way
Bicester OX26. . . . . . . .65 F1
Grove OX12 . . . . 214 D8
Highworth SN6 . . . . . . 190 B7
Westacott Rd
Bicester OX26. . . . . . . .80 F6
Bicester OX26. . . . . 81 A6
WEST ADDERBURY 22 E6
West Allcourt GL7 . . . . 150 C4
West Ave OX14 . . . . . . 160 A2
West Bar St OX16 . . . . . 16 C5
Westbeech Ct OX16. . . .16 C5
Westbourne Ct OX15. . . 21 E3
Westbrook
Faringdon SN7. . . . . . 172 F3
Grove OX12. . . . . 196 E2
Westbrook Gn OX11 . . 236 F8
Westbrook Rd RG30 . . 258 C1
Westbrook St
Blewbury OX11 . . . . . . 219 A1
Blewbury OX11 . . . . . . 236 F8
WESTBURY 25 B4
Westbury Court Bsns Ctr
OX27 . . . . .67 E3
Westbury Cres OX4 . . . 142 B4
Westbury Ct Bsns Pk
OX27 . . . . .67 E3
Westbury La RG8 . . . . . 257 A6
Westbury Rd NN13. . . . .25 B8
Westbury Terr OX7. . . . . .67 E2
West Castle St OX25 . . . .63 C8
WEST CHALLOW 213 C6
West Chiltern RG8. . . . 250 E8
WESTCOT 212 D3
Westcote Cl OX28 . . . . 117 D7
Westcote Pl OX7 . . . . . . .42 E7
Westcot La OX12 . . . . . 212 D3
WESTCOTT BARTON . . . 60 D8
West Cotts OX27 . . . . . . .52 D1
West Croft OX10. . . . . . 182 C5
West Ct Banbury OX16 . .16 B6
Sonning RG4 . . . . 260 E2
Westdene Cres RG4 . . . 258 E4
West Dr Harwell OX11 . 217 A3
Sonning RG4 . . . . 260 D1
West Edge OX27 . . . . . . .67 E2
WESTEND 57 B1
WEST END Cholsey. . . . 220 F1
Stanton Harcourt 138 C5
West End Aston OX18. . . 135 D2

West End *continued*
Brightwell-cum-Sotwell
OX10. . . . . 202 D2
Carterton OX18. . . . . . 115 A5
Chadlington OX7 . . . . . . 57 B1
Chipping Norton OX7 . . . 42 E2
Cholsey OX10 . . . . 220 E1
Combe OX29 . . . . 89 F4
Combe OX29 . . . . 90 A4
Elms Farm OX29 . . . . . 138 C5
Hornton OX15. . . . . .7 C6
Kingham OX7 . . . . 54 F4
Launton OX26. . . . . 66 D1
Shilton OX18 . . . . 115 A5
Witney OX28 . . . . 104 B2
Witney OX28 . . . . 104 B2
Wootton OX20. . . . . . . .75 F4
West End Cl OX26 . . . . . 66 D1
West End Ind Est
OX28 . . . . 104 B1
West End La
Bishopstone SN6. . . . . 227 C4
Merton OX25. . . . . 95 D8
West End Rd SN6. . . . . 209 B6
Western Ave
[7] Didcot OX11. . . . . . 219 A4
Henley-on-Thames RG9. 254 E8
Milton OX14. . . . . 199 D4
Sonning RG5 . . . . 260 E1
Western By-Pass Rd
Cutteslowe OX2 . . . . . 108 C1
Wytham OX2 . . . . 122 C5
Western Cl RG9 . . . . . . 254 E8
Western Cres OX16. . . . .16 E4
Western Oaks RG31. . . 257 E2
Western Rd
Henley-on-Thames
RG9 . . . . 254 E8
Oxford OX1 . . . . 141 C7
Westfield
Harwell OX11 . . . . 217 D6
Harwell OX11 . . . . 217 D7
Westfield Cl
Benson OX10. . . . . . . 204 A4
Grove OX12. . . . . 214 D7
Oxford OX4 . . . . 142 B6
Westfield Cres RG9 . . . 255 B3
Westfield Farm Mws
OX25 . . . . 48 A1
Westfield Rd
Benson OX10. . . . . . . 203 F5
Benson OX10. . . . . . . 204 A4
Cholsey OX10 . . . . 238 D6
Cholsey OX10 . . . . 238 E8
Long Crendon OX9 . . . 129 A7
Long Wittenham OX14 . 201 D8
Peppershill HP18. . . . . 128 E7
Reading RG4 . . . . 259 B2
Wheatley OX33 . . . . . . 126 A1
Witney OX28 . . . . 104 B2
Westfields OX14 . . . . . . 179 D7
Westfield View OX29 . . .89 F5
Westfield Way OX12. . . 215 A6
Westgate OX7 . . . . 85 D8
Westgate Sh Ctr OX1 . . 261 B2
WEST GINGE 216 A2
West Gr OX2 . . . . 123 B8
WEST HAGBOURNE . . . 218 D4
WESTHALL HILL 100 D6
Westhall Hill OX18. . . . 100 E6
WEST HANNEY 196 F6
West Hawthorn Rd
OX25 . . . . 81 D4
WEST HENDRED 216 C6
West Hill OX12 . . . . . . 214 C4
Westholme Ct OX26 . . . .65 F1
WEST ILSLEY 235 B1
West Ilsley Ho RG20 . . 235 B1
West Ilsley Stables
RG20. . . . . 235 B1
West Kidlington Prim Sch
[2] OX5. . . . . 108 E7
West La Bledlow HP27 . 169 B8
Henley-on-Thames RG9. 244 D2
Westland Cl GL54. . . . . .68 B3
Westland Rd SN7 . . . . . 172 E2
Westlands Ave OX25. . . 79 A2
Westlands Dr OX3 . . . . 124 B5
Westland Way OX20 . . . 91 A7
Westleigh Dr RG4 . . . . 252 F4
WEST LOCKINGE 215 C4
Westminster Cl NN13. . . 24 A7
Westminster Cres
NN13 . . . . 24 A7
Westminster Way
Banbury OX16 . . . . . . .16 F6
Banbury OX16 . . . . 17 A7
Oxford OX2 . . . . 140 E8
Westonbirt Dr RG4 . . . 258 E3
Weston Bldgs OX1 . . . . 261 B2
Weston Bsns Pk OX5. . . .78 F5
Weston Cotts SN7 . . . . 170 D8
Weston Ct CV36 . . . . . . 28 A6
Weston La OX9 . . . . . . 146 F8
Weston Old Bsns Pk
OX25. . . . . 79 A5
WESTON-ON-THE-
GREEN 79 B2
Weston Pk Rd CV36. . . . .27 F4
Weston Rd
Bletchingdon OX5 . . . . .93 A8
Lewknor OX49 . . . . . . 187 A8
Westover St OX25 . . . . . 63 C8
West Oxford Com Prim
Sch [3] OX2. . . . . . . 123 A1
West Oxon Ind Pk
OX18 . . . . 115 F4
West Quay OX14. . . . . . 179 F4
Westridge Ave RG8 . . . 257 C5
WESTRIDGE GN RG8 . . 248 A4
WESTRIDGE GREEN . . 248 B4

Westrop SN6 . . . . 190 A6
Westrup Cl OX3 . . . . . . 123 F7
West St Helen St
OX14 . . . . 179 F6
West St
Banbury OX16 . . . . .16 E7
Bicester OX26 . . . . 65 D3
Chadlington OX7 . . . . . . 57 B1
Childrey OX12 . . . . 213 B3
Chipping Norton OX7 . . . 42 E2
Henley-on-Thames RG9. 244 D2
Kingham OX7 . . . . 54 F5
Oxford OX2 . . . . 123 A1
Shutford OX15. . . . . . . 14 A5
Sparsholt OX12. . . . . . 212 F4
West View Oxford OX4. 142 A4
Somerton OX25. . . . . . . 49 A6
Westwater Way OX11. . 201 B2
Westway RG8 . . . . 249 C8
West Way
Lechlade-on-Thames
GL7. . . . . 150 C5
Oxford OX2 . . . . 122 D1
Oxford OX2 . . . . 140 C8
WESTWELL 99 C1
Westwell Rd OX18 . . . . 100 C4
West Witney Prim Sch
OX28 . . . . 117 E8
Westwood Farm Inf Sch
RG31 . . . . 257 C3
Westwood Farm Jun Sch
RG31 . . . . 257 C3
Westwood Glen RG31. 257 C1
Westwood Rd
Reading RG31 . . . . . . 257 D1
Witney OX29 . . . . 103 C1
Westwood Row RG31. . 257 C2
Wetherby Cl RG4 . . . . . 259 C6
Wetherby Rd OX26. . . . . 65 C1
Weycroft OX11 . . . . . . 201 A3
Weyland Rd OX3. . . . . . 124 E2
Weymann Terr OX4. . . 142 B6
Wey Rd OX10 . . . . 182 D5
W & G Ind Est OX12. . . 213 E6
Whales La OX27 . . . . . . .67 E2
Wharf Cl OX14 . . . . 179 F6
Wharfe La RG9 . . . . . . 244 E2
Wharf La
Lechlade-on-Thames
GL7. . . . . 150 D4
Souldern OX27 . . . . 35 B4
Wharf Rd
Eynsham OX29 . . . . . . 120 F7
Eynsham OX29 . . . . . . 121 A7
Warborough OX10. . . . 203 A6
Wharf The
Pangbourne RG8 . . . . 256 C6
[7] Wantage OX12. . . . 214 D5
Wharton Rd OX3. . . . . . 124 D3
Whatleys Orch SN6 . . . 227 C4
Wheatcroft Cl OX14. . . 160 A2
WHEATFIELD 166 B3
Wheatfield OX39 . . . . . 168 E8
Wheatfield Dr
Witney OX28 . . . . 103 A1
Witney OX29 . . . . 117 B8
Wheatfields OX11 . . . . 218 C7
WHEATLEY 144 A8
Wheatley Bsns Ctr
OX33 . . . . 144 C8
Wheatley CE Prim Sch
OX33 . . . . 144 A8
Wheatley Cl OX16 . . . . . .16 E2
Wheatley Park Sch
OX33 . . . . 126 B2
Wheatley Rd
Cuddesdon OX44 . . . . 144 A5
Cuddesdon OX44. . . . . 144 B4
Forest Hill OX33 . . . . . 125 F4
Garsington OX44 . . . . . 143 E3
Islip OX5 . . . . 109 F8
Islip OX5 . . . . 110 A7
Wheatsheaf Cres
[7] Bampton OX18. . . . 134 F4
Bampton OX18 . . . . . . 135 A4
Wheeler Ave OX20 . . . . 91 C5
Wheeler Ct RG31 . . . . . 257 E1
Wheelers End OX39. . . 168 C6
Wheeler's Rise NN13 . . 36 C8
Wheelwright Ct OX18. 135 D2
Wheelwright Gdns
CV36. . . . . 28 A4
Whichford Rd CV36. . . . .27 A7
Whimbrel Cl OX20. . . . . 66 A1
Whimbrel Way OX16. . .16 E3
Whirlwind Way OX10 . 204 D3
Whistler Way SN7 . . . . 194 D7
Whitaker La [5] OX18. . 134 F4
Whitamore Row RG9 . 254 E8
Whitby Cl RG4. . . . . . . 259 D6
Whitby Gn RG4 . . . . . . 259 D6
Whitcalls La RG9 . . . . . 241 E8
WHITCHURCH HILL . . . 250 E2
WHITCHURCH-ON-
THAMES 256 C7
Whitchurch Prim Sch
RG8 . . . . 256 E7
Whitchurch Rd RG8. . . 256 D6
Whitcliffe Cl OX26. . . . .65 B1
White Barn OX1 . . . . . . 140 C2
Whitecross OX13 . . . . . 159 D4
Whitecross Rd HP17. . . 130 F5
WHITEHALL 241 D3
Whitehall Cl OX29 . . . . 102 D2
Whitehall La RG8. . . . . 241 D3
White Hart OX3. . . . . . 123 F6
White Hart Cl
Benson OX10. . . . . . . 203 F4
Ludgershall HP18 . . . . . 98 B7
White Hart Way OX11. 217 C8
White Hart Wlk [1]
SN7. . . . . 172 F3

White Hill
Henley-on-Thames RG9. 244 F2
Hinton Parva SN4 . . . . 227 A2
Hunt's Green RG8. . . . 254 A5
White Hill La OX1. . . . . 140 A1
Whitehills Gn RG8. . . . 249 C6
Whitehorns Farm Rd
OX12. . . . . 215 A5
Whitehorns Way
OX14. . . . . 179 A1
White Horse SN7 . . . . . 211 D7
White Horse Bsns Pk
SN7. . . . . 194 C7
White Horse Cres
OX12. . . . . 214 C8
White Horse Ho OX12. 214 D7
White Horse Leisure &
Tennis Ctr OX14 . . . . 180 C8
White Horse Mews
OX18. . . . . 100 E4
White Horses Cl OX15 . .22 F8
White Hos MK18. . . . . . 39 D6
White House Cl OX13 . 159 C1
Whitehouse La OX7. . . .42 E3
Whitehouse Rd
North Stoke OX10 . . . . 239 F8
Woodcote RG8. . . . . . 250 F8
White House Rd OX1 . . 141 C7
White La RG9. . . . . 243 F5
Whitelands Farm OX26 .80 B8
Whitelands Way
Bicester OX25 . . . . 80 C7
Bicester OX26 . . . . 80 C8
White Leys Cl OX11 . . . 200 F1
White Lion Wlk [1]
OX16. . . . . 16 D6
Whitelock Rd OX14 . . . 159 F1
White Lodge Cl RG31. 257 B3
WHITEOAK GREEN 87 F1
White Post Rd OX15 . . . .16 E1
White Rd Chilton OX11. 217 D1
East Hendred OX12. . . 216 E7
Oxford OX4 . . . . 142 E6
Whites Forge OX13 . . . 158 A7
White Shoot OX11. . . . 237 A5
Whites La OX14. . . . . . 160 D3
Whites Orch OX11. . . . 219 A1
Whitethorn Way [3]
OX4. . . . . 142 E2
Whiteway OX17. . . . . . . .3 F3
White Way OX5 . . . . . . 108 E8
Whitfield SN7 . . . . 174 E1
Whitfield Gdns OX12. . 197 C7
Whitings La OX29. . . . . 104 B7
Whitley Cl OX12 . . . . . 214 C8
Whitley Cres OX26. . . . . 66 A3
Whitley Dr OX25. . . . . . 63 C8
Whitley La OX29 . . . . . 138 A7
Whitley Rd OX10. . . . . . 221 B7
Whitson Pl OX4. . . . . . 142 A7
Whittall St OX17. . . . . . . 23 F5
Whittington Cres
OX12. . . . . 214 C6
Whittington Pl OX18. . 115 D1
Whittle Cl GL54. . . . . . . .68 B3
Whittle Rd OX9 . . . . . . 148 B8
Whittons Cl OX15. . . . . .30 B8
Whitworth Pl OX2 . . . . 123 A2
Wick Cl
Abingdon-on-Thames
OX14. . . . . 160 C2
Oxford OX3 . . . . 124 E4
Wickets The GL7 . . . . . 132 D1
Wick Farm Pk OX3. . . . 124 E5
Wick Gn OX12 . . . . 196 D2
WICK GREEN 196 E2
Wick Hall OX14 . . . . . . 180 D8
Wicks Cl OX18. . . . . . . 152 E8
Widdowson Cl OX11 . . 201 B3
WIDFORD 101 B4
Widford La
Burford OX18 . . . . 100 F4
Burford OX18 . . . . 101 A3
Widmore La RG4 . . . . . 253 A6
Widnell La OX25. . . . . . . 97 C3
Wigans La
Bledlow Ridge HP14 . . 169 B4
Rout's Green HP14 . . . 169 C3
Wiggins Cl OX15. . . . . . .21 C1
Wiggins Wlk OX49 . . . . 186 B1
WIGGINTON 31 B7
WIGGINTON HEATH . . . 20 B3
Wigginton Rd OX15. . . . 31 D7
Wigmore La RG30 . . . . 258 C3
Wigod Way OX10 . . . . . 203 C1
Wilberforce St OX3. . . 124 D2
Wilcher Cl OX11. . . . . . 218 F6
WILCOTE 88 B3
Wilcote La OX7. . . . . . . .88 B3
Wilcote Rd
North Leigh OX29 . . . . . 89 B1
North Leigh OX29 . . . . 105 B8
Oxford OX3 . . . . 124 F4
Wilcote OX29. . . . . .88 F3
Wilcote Riding OX7. . . . 88 D5
Wilcote View OX29 . . . 105 C6
Wilcox Rd OX7 . . . . .42 F4
Wildbourne OX7 . . . . . . 85 A8
Wilder Ave RG8. . . . . . 256 F6
Wilding Rd OX10 . . . . . 203 C1
Wildmere Cl OX16. . . . . .16 F1
Wildmere Ind Est OX16 .16 F1
Wildmere Rd OX16 . . . . . .9 F1
WILDMOOR 159 F1
Wildmoor Gate OX14 . 159 E1
Wildwood Cl RG6. . . . . 260 D1
Wilkins Cl OX18 . . . . . . 116 A5

Wilkins Ct OX7 . . . . 73 C2
Wilkins Ho OX7 . . . . .42 E1
Wilkinson Pl OX28 . . . . . 103 F1
Wilkins Rd OX4 . . . . 142 E6
Wilkins Way OX12 . . . . . 215 A5
Willes Cl Faringdon SN7 172 F3
  1 Faringdon SN7 . . . . 172 F3
William Bliss Ave OX7 . .42 E2
William Buckland Way
  OX29 . . . . 89 D7
William Cl OX16 . . . . .15 F7
William Fletcher Prim Sch
  OX5 . . . . 108 A5
William Kimber Cres
  OX3 . . . . 124 E3
William Lucy Way
  OX2 . . . . 123 A3
William Morris Cl **5**
  OX4 . . . . 142 D6
William Morris Cty Prim
  Sch OX16 . . . . .15 F7
William Orchard Cl
  OX3 . . . . 124 C4
WILLIAMSCOT 10 C8
Williamscot Hill
  Wardington OX17 . . . . . 10 A5
  Williamscot OX17 . . . . . 10 B6
Williams Hill OX20 . . . . .75 F3
Williams Mews OX28 . . 118 A7
Williamson Way OX4 . . 142 A3
Williams Orch OX10 . . 204 E4
Williams Rd OX25 . . . . . 63 C7
William St OX3 . . . . 123 F3
Willis Ct OX7 . . . . 70 D1
Willoughby Rd OX16 . . . 16 D2
Willowbank OX28 . . . . . 118 A7
Willow Bank Infant & Jun
  Sch RG5 . . . . .260 F1
Willowbrook
  Lower Arncott OX25 . . . 81 E1
  Stanton Harcourt OX29 137 F8
Willow Brook OX14 . . . 179 D7
Willow Cl Cholsey OX10 220 F1
  Garsington OX44 . . . . . 143 D2
  Milton under Wychwood
  OX7 . . . . 85 A8
  Watlington OX49 . . . . . 186 A2
  Yarnton OX5 . . . . 108 B6
Willow Court La OX10 . 238 F5
Willowcroft Com Sch
  OX11 . . . . .218 F8
Willow Dr Bicester OX26 .65 E4
  Carterton OX18 . . . . . . 115 F4
Willow End
  Ambrosden OX25 . . . . . 81 C4
  Didcot OX11 . . . . 218 C7
  Little Compton GL56 . . . 27 A1
Willow Gdns RG31 . . . . 257 B2
Willow La Ickford HP18 128 A4
  Milton OX14 . . . . 199 D5
  Wantage OX12 . . . . . . 214 D3
  Wargrave RG10 . . . . . . 255 C4
Willow Mead OX44 . . . 184 D6
Willow Pike OX14 . . . . 180 C1
Willow Rd
  Ambrosden OX25 . . . . . 81 C4
  Banbury OX16 . . . . 16 D2
  Brackley NN13 . . . . 24 A6
  Chinnor OX39 . . . . 168 C6
  Thame OX9 . . . . 129 F1
Willows Ct RG8 . . . . . . 256 C6
Willows Edge OX29 . . . 120 D8
Willows Gate OX27 . . . . 52 D1
Willowside RG5 . . . . . . 260 F1
Willows Lodge OX27 . . . 52 D1
Willows The
  Grove OX12 . . . . 214 D7
  Highworth SN6 . . . . . . 190 B5
  Oxford OX4 . . . . 124 E4
  Reading RG4 . . . . 259 A2
  Witney OX28 . . . . 104 C1
  Wootton OX1 . . . . 159 A7
Willow Tree Cl OX13 . . 159 C1
Willow Way
  Begbroke OX5 . . . . 92 A1
  Drayton OX14 . . . . 179 B3
  Kennington OX14 . . . . . 160 E2
  Oxford OX4 . . . . 142 E2
Willow Wlk OX12 . . . . . 214 D6
Wills Rd OX11 . . . . 200 C1
Wilmot Cl OX28 . . . . . . 117 F6
Wilmots OX44 . . . . 162 A6
Wilmot Way OX12 . . . . 214 F6
Wilsdon Dr OX5 . . . . . . 92 D1
Wilsham Rd OX14 . . . . 179 F5
Wilson Ave RG9 . . . . . . 254 E8
Wilson Cl OX25 . . . . 63 C8
Wilson Rd OX16 . . . . . . .15 E6
Wilsons Cl OX14 . . . . . 201 C8
Wilson Way OX27 . . . . . .65 F7
Wilwyne Cl RG4 . . . . . . 259 C4
Wimblestraw Rd
  OX10 . . . . 182 C5
Wimborn Cl OX15 . . . . . .33 E4
Wimborne Ave OX16 . . .16 B6
Wimbourne Gdns
  RG30 . . . . 258 A1
Winaway OX11 . . . . 217 C5
Wina Way The OX11 . . 217 D6
Wincanton Rd
  13 Bicester OX26 . . . 65 D1
  Bicester OX26 . . . . 80 C8
Wincey View OX44 . . . . 164 D8

Winchelsea Cl OX16 . . . . .8 F1
Winchester Cl OX16 . . . .16 F7
Winchester Ct **8**
  OX28 . . . . 104 A1
Winchester Rd OX2 . . . 123 B4
Winchester Way OX12 214 C5
Wincroft Rd RG4 . . . . . 258 E5
Windale Ave OX4 . . . . . 142 E1
Windale Community Prim
  Sch OX4 . . . . 142 E1
Windale Ho **2** OX4 . . 142 E2
WINDERTON 12 B6
Winderton Rd OX15 . . . . 12 A3
Windle Gdns OX26 . . . . 65 C2
Windmill Ave OX26 . . . .65 E4
Windmill Cl
  Banbury OX16 . . . . 16 D4
  Chinnor OX39 . . . . 168 B7
  Deddington OX15 . . . . . 33 E4
  North Leigh OX29 . . . . 105 B6
  Towersey OX9 . . . . 148 E7
Windmill Hill
  Great Milton OX33 . . . 144 F1
  Great Milton OX44 . . . 145 A2
  Little Milton OX44 . . . 163 F8
  Little Milton OX44 . . . 164 A8
Windmill Hts OX29. . . . 105 B6
Windmill La
  Bledlow Ridge HP14 . . 189 F8
  Farnborough OX17 . . . . . .3 E8
  Littleworth OX33 . . . . . 143 F7
Windmill Piece OX49 . . 186 A1
Windmill Prim Sch
  OX3 . . . . 124 D2
Windmill Rd
  Haddenham HP17 . . . . 130 F6
  North Leigh OX29 . . . . 105 B6
  Oxford OX3 . . . . 124 D2
  Thame OX9 . . . . 147 F7
  Towersey OX9 . . . . 148 E8
Windmill St
  Brill HP18 . . . . 98 A1
  Deddington OX15 . . . . . 33 E4
Windmill View SN6 . . . 191 C2
Windows Ct OX33 . . . . 144 C7
Windrush OX16 . . . . .16 B8
Windrush Cl
  5 Burford OX26 . . . . 65 D1
  Burford OX18 . . . . 100 E4
  Grove OX12 . . . . 196 D1
  Witney OX28 . . . . 117 E8
Windrush Ct
  Abingdon-on-Thames
  OX14 . . . . 179 C7
  Burford OX18 . . . . 100 E4
Windrush Ind Pk
  OX29 . . . . 103 C1
Windrush L Ctr OX28 . 118 B8
Windrush Mews OX1 . . 201 A3
Windrush Park Rd
  OX29 . . . . 103 C1
Windrush Pl OX29 . . . . 138 B2
Windrush Rd OX10 . . . 182 C4
Windrush Twr OX4 . . . 142 E2
Windrush Valley Rd
  OX28 . . . . 103 E1
Windrush Valley Sch
  OX7 . . . . .71 C2
Windrush Way
  Abingdon-on-Thames
  OX14 . . . . 160 B1
  Standlake OX29 . . . . . 137 C5
Windsor Cl
  5 Bicester OX26 . . . . 65 C1
  Carterton OX18 . . . . . . 115 C2
  Didcot OX11 . . . . 219 A8
  Kings Sutton OX17 . . . . .23 F6
Windsor Cotts OX18 . . 134 E3
Windsor Cres
  East Hagbourne OX11 . . 218 F6
  Marston OX3 . . . . 123 E5
Windsor Dr OX10 . . . . . 221 C7
Windsor St
  Grove OX12 . . . . 214 C8
  Oxford OX3 . . . . 124 D2
Windsor Terr **15** OX6 . 16 D5
Windy Ridge SN7 . . . . 173 A3
Winfield Dr OX29 . . . . . 117 C7
Wingate Cl OX4 . . . . . . 142 E3
Wingfield Cl OX10 . . . . 204 E3
Wingfield Ct OX4 . . . . . 123 F1
Winnyards The OX2. . . 139 E4
Winslet Pl RG30 . . . . . . 258 B1
Winsmore La **2** OX14 . 179 F6
Winston Cl OX5. . . . . . . 108 E7
Winston Dr OX17 . . . . 8 F1
Winston Way RG8 . . . . 257 B5
Winston Wlk OX20. . . . . 91 D7
Winterberry Way RG4 . 258 E6
Winterborne Rd OX14 . 179 D7
Winterbourne Cl **2**
  OX26 . . . . 65 D2
WINTERBROOK 221 C5
Winterbrook OX10. . . . 221 D5
Winterbrook OX10. . . . 221 C5
Winter Gdns Way OX16 . .9 A2
Winter Gdns Wy OX16 . . .8 F2
Winter Gn Cl OX11. . . . 218 C7
Wintergreen Fields
  OX27 . . . . 65 D6
Wintergreen La OX10 . . 221 D5
Winter La OX12 . . . . . . 196 F7
Wintersfield OX10 . . . . 221 F7
Winter's Field OX10 . . . 221 F7
Winters Way OX15 . . . . 21 D4
Wintringham Way
  RG8 . . . . 257 D5

Wirethorn Furlong
  HP17 . . . . 130 E6
Wise Ave OX5 . . . . 92 D1
Wise Cl OX15 . . . . .22 F8
Wise Cres OX27 . . . . . . 52 C6
Wise Ct **3** OX26 . . . . .65 E3
Wisterias The OX16. . . . . .9 B1
Witan Pk Ind Est OX28 118 B6
Witan Way
  Wantage OX12 . . . . . . 214 D6
  Witney OX28 . . . . 118 B8
Witheridge Cross
  OX29 . . . . 104 B5
Withers Cl OX7 . . . . . . .42 E3
Withers Way OX5 . . . . .42 E2
Withington Ct OX14. . . 179 F7
Withington Rd OX26 . . .65 F2
Withycombe Dr OX16 . .15 F6
WITNEY 118 C7
Witney Com Hospl
  OX28 . . . . 118 A8
Witney Com Prim Sch
  OX28 . . . . 104 A3
Witney & District Mus★
  OX28 . . . . 104 B1
Witney Hill OX29 . . . . . 103 E4
Witney La Leafield OX29. .86 F3
  Stonesfield OX29 . . . . . 89 B7
Witney Light OX7 . . . . . 72 C2
Witney Prim Sch
  OX28 . . . . 104 B3
Witneyrd OX29 . . . . . . 137 B6
Witney Rd
  Brize Norton OX18 . . . 116 D5
  Crawley OX29 . . . . 103 F3
  Ducklington OX29 . . . . 118 A5
  Eynsham OX29 . . . . . . 120 D8
  Finstock OX7 . . . . 88 B5
  Kingston Bagpuize OX13 156 F1
  Leafield OX29 . . . . 87 A1
  Long Hanborough OX29 . .89 F1
  Long Hanborough OX29 . 90 A1
  Standlake OX29 . . . . . 137 A4
  Whiteoak Green OX7,
  OX29 . . . . 87 E2
  Witney OX28 . . . . 104 A4
  Witney OX29 . . . . 117 A6
Witney St Burford OX18 100 E5
  Burford OX18 . . . . 100 F4
  Burford OX18 . . . . 101 A3
Wittenham Cl
  Wallingford OX10 . . . . 203 D1
  Woodcote RG8. . . . . . . 250 F8
Wittenham La OX10. . . 202 D8
Wivell Dr OX14 . . . . . . 159 E2
Wixes Piece SN6 . . . . . 228 B7
Woburn Cl
  Cutteslowe OX2. . . . . . 109 B1
  Reading RG4 . . . . 259 A2
Wolage Dr OX12. . . . . . 214 D7
Wolfson Coll OX2. . . . . 123 C5
Wolseley Cl OX16 . . . . . 16 A8
Wolsely Ho OX4 . . . . . . 142 C4
Wolsey Ct OX20 . . . . . . .91 F3
Wolsey Rd
  Cutteslowe OX2. . . . . . 109 B1
  Reading RG4 . . . . 259 A2
WOLVERCOTE 122 E8
Wolvercote Gn OX2. . . 122 F8
Wolvercote Prim Sch
  OX2 . . . . .122 F8
Wolvercote Rdbt OX2. 108 F1
Wood Avens Way **4**
  OX4 . . . . 124 C5
Woodbank
  Kirtlington OX5 . . . . . . .77 F4
  3 Witney OX28 . . . 104 D1
Woodberry Cl RG4. . . . 259 A5
Woodbine Pl OX1. . . . . 261 A2
Woodbridge Cl OX18 . 135 E2
Woodbury Cl RG4. . . . . 252 F5
WOODCOTE 250 F7
Woodcote Prim Sch
  RG8 . . . . 240 F1
Woodcote Rd
  Bicester OX27 . . . . 66 A7
  1 Carterton OX18 . . 115 E3
  Reading RG4 . . . . 258 E4
  South Stoke RG8. . . . . 239 E4
  Woodcote RG8. . . . . . . 240 A3
Woodcote Way
  Abingdon-on-Thames
  OX14 . . . . 179 E4
  Reading RG4 . . . . 258 D5
Wood Cres OX26 . . . . . .80 F6
Woodcroft OX1. . . . . . . 141 E1
WOODEATON 110 B4
Woodeaton Manor Sch
  OX3 . . . . 110 A5
Wood End OX16 . . . . . . .16 E3
Wood Farm Prim Sch
  OX3 . . . . 124 E1
Wood Farm Rd OX3. . . 124 E1
Woodfield Banbury OX16 16 B8
  Cumnor Hill OX2. . . . . 140 B7
Woodfield Cotts RG8 . 249 A6
Woodfield Dr OX7 . . . . . 73 C3
Woodfield Rd OX26 . . . .65 E4
WOODFIELDS 65 C4
Woodford Cl
  Enstone OX7 . . . . .58 F5
  Reading RG4 . . . . 258 E4
Woodford Mill OX28 . . 104 A1
Woodford Way **3**
  OX28 . . . . 118 A8
Woodgate Cl OX12. . . . 196 D1
Wood Gn RG8 . . . . 250 E8

WOODGREEN 104 D2
Woodgreen OX28. . . . . 104 C1
Wood Green MK18. . . . .25 E8
Woodgreen Ave OX16. . 16 A5
Woodgreen Hill **5**
  OX28 . . . . 104 B1
Wood Green Sch
  OX28 . . . . 104 D1
Woodgreen Sq OX39. . 168 C5
Woodhall Dr OX16 . . . . .16 E3
Woodhill Dr OX12 . . . . 214 D8
Woodhill La
  East Challow OX12 . . . 214 A7
  Grove OX12 . . . . 196 A1
Woodhill Lane Cvn Pk
  OX12 . . . . 213 F6
Woodhouse Way OX4. 142 A4
Woodins Way OX1 . . . 261 A2
Wood La Hailey OX29 . . 104 A7
  Kidmore End RG4. . . . . 252 C4
  Kingston Bagpuize
  OX13 . . . . 176 C8
  Leafield OX29 . . . . 87 E1
  North Leigh OX29 . . . . 105 B3
  Sonning Common RG4. 252 F5
  Whiteoak Green OX29 . 103 F8
  Woodcote RG8 . . . . . . 250 D8
Woodland Cl OX26. . . . 66 D1
Woodland Park Cvn Site
  The OX14 . . . . 160 E7
Woodland Rise OX29 . . 89 C7
Woodlands
  Banbury OX16 . . . . 16 B5
  Carterton OX18 . . . . . . 115 F4
  Freeland OX29 . . . . . . 106 A7
  Kidlington OX5 . . . . . . 109 A8
  Standlake OX29 . . . . . 137 D3
Woodlands Brook
  OX12 . . . . 214 F4
Woodlands Cl
  Milton-under-Wychwood
  OX7 . . . . 70 B1
  Oxford OX3 . . . . 124 B3
Woodlands Ct OX28. . . 104 C2
Woodlands Gr RG4 . . . 259 E4
Woodlands Pl OX29. . . 120 E8
Woodlands Rd
  Didcot OX11 . . . . 218 C8
  Lower Shiplake RG9 . . 255 A4
  Oxford OX3 . . . . 124 B3
  Shiplake RG9 . . . . 254 E4
  Sonning Common RG4. 252 F6
  Witney OX28 . . . . 104 C2
Woodlands The OX6. . . .79 F7
Wood Lane Cl RG4. . . . 252 F5
Woodley Cl OX14 . . . . 159 F3
Woodley Gn OX28 . . . . 104 E2
Woodman Ct OX4. . . . . 123 F1
Woodman Villas OX3 . 124 C2
Woodpecker Cl OX26 . . 66 A1
Woodpecker Gn **13**
  OX4 . . . . 142 F1
Woodpecker Wlk
  OX49 . . . . 186 A1
Woodperry Wy OX11 200 B1
Woodperry Rd OX3 . . . 111 B2
Woodpery Hill OX3 . . . 111 D2
Woodpiece Rd OX25. . .96 E7
Woodrow Ct
  5 Carterton OX18 . . 115 E5
  Reading RG4 . . . . 258 F2
WOOTTON UNDERWOOD
  98 . . . . .F3 ROAD
Wrag View SN6. . . . . . . 190 A4
Wren Cl OX33 . . . . 144 B8
Wren Cres
  Bodicote OX15 . . . . . . .16 F1
  Bodicote OX15 . . . . . . .22 F8
Wrenfield Dr RG4. . . . . 258 F5
Wren Rd
  Cutteslowe OX2. . . . . . 109 C1
  Summertown OX2. . . . 123 C8
Wren Way OX26 . . . . . . 66 A1
Wretchwick Way OX26. .81 B8
Wright Cl GL54 . . . . 68 A5
Wright Rd GL54. . . . . . . 68 A5
Wrights La OX29 . . . . . 120 F8
Wrightson Cl OX33 . . . 143 C6
Wroslyn Rd OX29 . . . . 106 A7
Wroslyn Road Ind Est
  OX29 . . . . .105 F2
WROXTON 15 A8
Wroxton CE Prim Sch
  OX15 . . . . .15 A8
Wroxton Ct OX15 . . . . . 15 A8
Wroxton Ho OX15. . . . . 15 B8
Wroxton La OX15 . . . . . .8 B4
Wyatt Cl RG10 . . . . 255 E1
Wyatt Rd **2** OX2. . . . 109 B1
Wychcotes RG4. . . . . . . 258 F3
Wychwood Brewery★ **10**
  OX28 . . . . 118 A8
Wychwood CE Prim Sch
  OX7 . . . . 70 C1
Wychwood Cl
  Benson OX10. . . . . 204 A4
  Carterton OX18. . . . . . 115 D5
  Charlbury OX7 . . . . 73 C4
  Milton-under-Wychwood
  OX7 . . . . 70 A1
  Sonning Common RG4. 252 F5
  Witney OX29. . . . . 117 E8
Wychwood Dr OX7 . . . . 70 A1
Wychwood Gdns OX16. 16 A4
Wychwood La
  Oxford OX3 . . . . 125 A2
  Rissinghurst OX3. . . . . 125 A2

Woolgate Sh Ctr OX28 118 B8
WOOLSTONE 211 B4
Woolstone Rd
  Uffington SN7 . . . . 211 C7
  Woolstone SN7 . . . . . . 211 B5
Wootten Dr OX4 . . . . . 142 A4
WOOTTON
  Abingdon-on-Thames . . 159 A6
  Woodstock. 75 F5
Wootton Bsns Pk OX12 .158 F7
Wootton-by-Woodstock
  CE (Aided) Prim Sch
  OX20 . . . . .75 F4
Wootton Rd
  Abingdon-on-Thames
  OX13. . . . . .159 D4
  Abingdon-on-Thames OX13,
  OX14 . . . . 159 E2
  Abingdon-on-Thames
  OX14. . . . . 179 E8
  Henley-on-Thames RG9. 254 C8
Wootton Road Ind Est
  OX14 . . . . 159 E1
Wootton St Peter's CE
  Prim Sch OX1. . . . . .75 F4
WOOTTON VILLAGE . 159 B7
  OX1. . . . . 159 B7
Wootton Village OX1 . 159 B8
Worcester Coll OX1 . . . 261 A3
Worcester Dr OX11 . . . 219 B8
Worcester Pl
  Kingston Bagpuize
  OX13. . . . . 156 D1
  Oxford OX1 . . . . 261 A3
Worcester Rd
  Chipping Norton OX7 . . 42 A4
  Chipping Norton OX7 . . 42 B2
  Salford OX7. . . . . .41 F4
Worcester Road Ind Est
  OX7 . . . . .42 C3
Worcester St OX1 . . . . 261 A2
Wordsworth Cl
  6 Bicester OX26 . . . 65 C4
  Stanford in the Vale
  SN7. . . . . 194 D8
Wordsworth Rd RG4 . . 259 C2
Wordsworth Rd OX14. 179 D5
Workhouse La OX15. . . 21 D5
Work House Yd OX20 . .75 F4
Worleys La RG10 . . . . . 255 E7
Wormald Rd OX10 . . . . 221 C6
WORMINGHALL 127 E6
Worminghall Rd
  Ickford HP18. . . . . 127 F4
  Townsend OX33 . . . . . 127 B3
WORMLEIGHTON 1 B8
Wormsley Cres HP14 . 188 C4
Wormsley Est
  Northend RG9. . . . . . . 207 F8
  Stokenchurch HP14. . . 187 E2
Wornal Pk HP18. . . . . . 127 C8
WORSHAM 102 B2
Worsham Turn OX29. . 102 B5
Wortham Rd OX11. . . . 200 D2
Worthington Way
  OX12 . . . . 214 D6
WORTON 107 E3
Worton Rd OX7. . . . . . . .46 E1
Wotton End HP18. . . . . 98 C7
Wotton Rd HP18. . . . . . 98 D3
WOTTON UNDERWOOD

Wychwood National
Nature Reserve★
  OX7 . . . . 87 D6
Wychwood Paddocks
  OX7 . . . . .73 B4
Wychwood Sch **3**
  OX2 . . . . 123 C4
Wychwood View
  Charlbury OX7 . . . . 73 D3
  Minster Lovell OX29 . . 102 E2
Wycliffe Hall
  Oxford OX2 . . . . 261 B4
  2 Park Town OX2. . . 123 C4
Wycombe Cl OX4 . . . . 142 A2
Wycombe Rd
  Beacon's Bottom
  HP14. . . . . 189 D3
  Stokenchurch HP14. . . 188 F4
Wycombe Way OX18. . 115 C2
Wye Cl OX26 . . . . .65 B3
Wyfold Cl RG4 . . . . 242 A1
Wyfold La RG4, RG9. . . 252 C8
Wyfold Rd RG4 . . . . . . 252 A6
Wykeham Cres OX4. . . 142 B4
Wykeham Gate HP17 . 130 F5
Wykeham Pk OX9 . . . . 148 A8
Wykeham Rise OX39. . 168 D6
Wykeham Way HP17. . 130 F6
Wykham Gdns OX16 . . .16 B3
Wykham La
  Banbury OX16 . . . . 16 B1
  Broughton OX15 . . . . . 15 E1
Wykham Pl OX16 . . . . . .16 B3
Wylie Cl OX3 . . . . 124 D1
Wynbush Rd OX4 . . . . 142 A3
Wynchway Ho OX15 . . .33 F4
Wyncies The SN6. . . . . 227 B4
Wyndale Cl RG9 . . . . . 244 E1
Wyndham Cres RG5 . . 260 D1
Wyndham Gdns OX10. 221 D6
Wyndham Way OX2. . . 123 A8
Wyndyke Furlong
  OX14 . . . . 179 C8
Wynton Cl **3** OX11 . . 218 B7
Wyre Ct RG31 . . . . 257 C3
Wysdom Way OX18 . . 100 F4
WYTHAM 122 B6
Wytham Cl OX29. . . . . 120 E8
Wytham St OX1. . . . . . 141 D5
Wytham View OX29 . . 120 E8
Wytham Vw OX2. . . . . 122 C1

Y

Yare Cl OX11 . . . . 201 B2
Yarnell's Hill OX2. . . . . 140 D7
Yarnell's Rd OX2 . . . . . 140 E8
YARNTON 108 A6
Yarnton Cl RG4. . . . . . . 259 C6
Yarnton Ct OX5. . . . . . . 108 E8
Yarnton La OX5. . . . . . . 108 D6
Yarnton Rd
  Cassington OX29. . . . . 107 D3
  Kidlington OX5. . . . . . . 108 E8
Yarrow Cl
  6 Didcot OX11. . . . . 218 B7
  Sandford-on-Thames
  OX4. . . . . 142 E1
Yarrow Rd OX16 . . . . . .16 C2
Yatesbury Rd OX18 . . . 115 C4
Yates Meadow SN7. . . 172 D2
Yealm Cl OX11 . . . . . . 200 F4
Yeates Cl OX9 . . . . 129 F1
Yeats Cl OX4 . . . . 142 F1
Yeftly Dr OX4. . . . . 142 A1
Yeld Hall Rd OX14 . . . 160 B2
YELFORD 136 B6
Yellowhammer Pl **11**
  OX11 . . . . 218 B7
Yeoman Cl OX15. . . . . .22 F7
Yeomans Cl NN13 . . . . 24 A4
Yew Cl Bicester OX26 . . .65 E5
  Oxford OX4 . . . . 143 A2
Yew Tree Cl
  Launton OX26 . . . . 66 D2
  Tetsworth OX9. . . . . . . 166 B8
Yew Tree Courtyard
  OX44 . . . . 161 E3
Yew Tree Cres OX11. . 200 C1
Yew Tree Ct RG8 . . . . 249 C6
Yewtree Mews OX14. . 179 F7
Yew Tree Mews OX29. 118 B4
Yew Tree Rise NN13 . . 36 D8
Yew Wlk OX12. . . . . . . 215 D3
Yolsum Cl HP17 . . . . . 130 E6
York Ave OX3 . . . . 124 E1
York Cl OX26 . . . . 66 A3
York Pl OX4 . . . . 142 C5
York Rd Carterton OX18 115 E4
  Henley-on-Thames RG9. 244 D2
  Oxford OX4 . . . . 124 E2
  Reading RG1 . . . . 259 A1
  West Hagbourne OX11. 218 C4
Youens Dr OX9 . . . . . . 148 A7
Youghal Cl SN6. . . . . . 209 B6
Youlbury OX1 . . . . 140 C3
Ypres Way OX14. . . . . 159 D1
Yule Ct **1** OX16 . . . . .16 B6

Z

Zedcor Bsns Pk **3**
  OX28 . . . . 104 B1